ADMINISTRATIVE AND CLINICAL PROCEDURES FOR THE CANADIAN HEALTH PROFESSIONAL

FOURTH EDITION

ADMINISTRATIVE AND CLINICAL PROCEDURES FOR THE CANADIAN HEALTH PROFESSIONAL

FOURTH EDITION

VALERIE D. THOMPSON

CONESTOGA INSTITUTE OF TECHNOLOGY AND ADVANCED LEARNING

Editorial Director: Claudine O'Donnell
Acquisitions Editor: Kimberley Veevers
Marketing Manager: Michelle Bish
Program Manager: John Polanszky
Project Manager: Susan Johnson
Manager of Content Development:
   Suzanne Schaan
Developmental Editor: Rebecca Ryoji
Production Services: iEnergizer Aptara®, Ltd.

Permissions Project Manager: Shruti Jamadagni
Photo Permissions Research: Integra
   Publishing Services
Text Permissions Research: Integra Publishing
   Services
Cover Designer: iEnergizer Aptara®, Ltd.
Cover Image: Goodluz/Shutterstock
**Vice-President, Cross Media and Publishing
Services:** Gary Bennett

Pearson Canada Inc., 26 Prince Andrew Place, Don Mills, Ontario M3C 2T8.

ISBN-13: 978-0-13-399135-2

1   17

Library and Archives Canada Cataloguing in Publication

Thompson, Valerie D., 1948–, author

Administrative and clinical procedures for the Canadian health
professional / Valerie D. Thompson. — 4th edition.
ISBN 978-0-13-399135-2 (paperback)

1. Medical offices–Canada–Management–Textbooks.
2. Medical assistants–Canada.   I. Title.

R728.8.T53 2016   651'.961   C2016-905350-4

 **Pearson**

To Spencer, for his courage and determination. To Dr. Ana Igric and
Dr. Michele Riordon for their extraordinary skills and outstanding care.
Also to the nurses and administrative staff in the intensive care unit at the
Royal Victoria Regional Health Centre in Barrie, Ontario.

Brief Contents

Contents

Preface

The health care system in Canada is close to the hearts of all Canadians. It has undergone tremendous changes in the last decade and continues to face numerous challenges. The very principles of health care as outlined in the Canada Health Act are constantly questioned. Although the principles appear ideal, problems exist and are compounded by the demands of delivering high-quality, comprehensive, cost-effective health care in the twenty-first century. Over the past few years the federal and provincial governments have strategized to improve the accessibility and quality of health care available to Canadians, but wait times for many diagnostic procedures and some surgeries remain long despite measures taken by all levels of government and health care facilities to reduce them. The number of doctors in Canada, particularly family physicians, has increased, but there are still millions of Canadians without a family doctor.

A long-standing challenge with the delivery of primary care is reasonable access (which is supposed to be guaranteed under the Canada Health Act). Primary care is the point at which a person enters the health care system and where the individual should receive or be directed to the care they need, including health education. Typically this point of entry has been a visit to the family doctor—but for many Canadians seeing a family doctor, should they have one, in a timely manner remains difficult.

A team-oriented approach to primary care that uses the skills and knowledge of a variety of clinicians has improved patient access by enabling the patient to directly contact the clinician who can deliver the type of care he or she requires, without seeing a doctor (e.g., a nurse practitioner, podiatrist, mental health counsellor, pharmacist, or a diabetic counsellor). There are also more points of entry to primary care, ranging from tele-help lines to walk-in mental health and health clinics.

Over the past decade a number of primary health care delivery models have been introduced in all jurisdictions across Canada. Each has a somewhat different funding formula and delivers services in a different way. These delivery models have improved patient access to care, but cost effectiveness, impact, pace, and relative success of renewal efforts across jurisdictions is under review. As a result, there continues to be a need for a nationally accepted framework for the delivery of primary care in Canada.

Challenges facing the Canadian health care system include meeting the needs of an aging population, the growing need for comprehensive mental health services, the rising cost of drugs, and adapting to the need to deliver culturally sensitive and appropriate health care to a growing multicultural population.

Increased responsibility has been transferred to administrative professionals in all sectors of health care. Doctors' offices, hospitals, and other health care facilities need skilled and knowledgeable graduates from postsecondary health administration programs who are prepared to meet the challenges offered in this dynamic field. This book will help health professionals in all sectors of health administration meet these challenges. The fourth edition of *Administrative and Clinical Procedures for the Canadian Health Professional* continues to fill the void for a comprehensive and current resource that deals with the complexities of the Canadian health care system, including the unique and diverse entities of provincial/territorial billing and primary care reform.

Administrative and Clinical Procedures for the Canadian Health Professional is designed for use in Canadian postsecondary schools, such as community and private colleges, as well as for health offices, hospitals, and other health care facilities for related in-service programs. It can also be used as a resource by individuals employed in health administration.

ABOUT THE BOOK

This book is divided into five parts. Part I introduces the reader to the concept, roles, and responsibilities of the health professional. It provides an overview of the characteristics, practices, and skills that combine to contribute to the student's success and professional development in health administration.

Part II, *Health in Context*, looks at health and the individual, health and culture, and health in the context of the Canadian health care system. These chapters combine to explain how health affects individuals in a multicultural society as they interface with the Canadian health care system. Chapter 2 discusses how illness can alter the communication and response of patients, their families, and their loved ones in the face of illness. It provides the student with both insight into and strategies for dealing effectively with patients and their families in sickness and in health. It stresses that response to illness is both individual and varied and emphasizes the need for patience, empathy, and understanding. The chapter updates and expands on current health issues, including discussions on leading causes of death, obesity and diabetes, and the movement in Canadian schools to remove unhealthy foods from cafeterias.

Chapter 3 is not intended to replace any courses that students may take on culture and health, but it does provide the student with a cursory knowledge of how culture can affect a person's health beliefs, practices, understanding, and compliance with treatment modalities. Basic strategies for communicating effectively in a multicultural society are discussed. Respect for different beliefs and practices and suggestions for "bridging the gap" between these beliefs and practices and traditional Western approaches to health, illness, diagnosis, and treatment are introduced. The chapter has been further updated with a new section on ageism.

Chapter 4 focuses on the principles and practices of the Canadian health care system. It provides the student with an understanding of the structure and function of health care in Canada. This chapter discusses the increasing role of the consumer in health care and explains the move to a more team-oriented approach to care as a result of primary care reform initiatives, with a focus on the implications of these changes for the health professional. For this edition, recent changes to primary care in several provinces are investigated.

Part III, *Health Care Basics*, provides an overview of the knowledge essential for the Canadian health office professional in all health care settings. Chapter 5 addresses the essential standards and safety in the health care setting. Emphasis is placed on quality assurance, the concept of asepsis, standard precautions, and infection control. This is increasingly important with the current challenges facing health providers, including, for example, the rise in the number and variety of nosocomial infections such as VRE, MRSA, and *C. difficile*. Strategies for preventing injury to patients in various age groups and with disabilities in the health office are also highlighted. The chapter also updates the vaccination protocols for specific provinces.

Chapter 6 is designed to provide students with information about laboratory and diagnostic tests levelled to their need, role function responsibilities, and scope of practice. This includes basic health teaching information and information on the administrative responsibilities related to filling out requisitions and booking tests for patients in both office and hospital settings. The increased use of electronic requisitions is highlighted in this chapter.

Chapter 7 deals with current trends in pharmacology and provides up-to-date information on the most frequently prescribed medications. As well, this chapter discusses the role of the health professional in patient education, handling requests for prescription refills, handling and safely storing drugs in the health office, drugs and the law, and how to effectively communicate with members of the pharmacy team. Tips for recognizing drug-seeking behaviour in patients are included. This edition places more emphasis on electronic prescriptions and how they are initiated and kept secure.

Part IV, *Office Procedures*, examines the basic administrative needs of the health office: communications, scheduling appointments, provincial/territorial billing, and maintenance of medical records. Chapter 8 addresses techniques and strategies to promote effective communication skills, ranging from telephone triage and interacting with patients in person to techniques for effective interprofessional communication. A new section on human relations within the workplace setting rounds out the discussion on effective communication skills. Strategies for the proper use and management of email are also included.

Chapter 9 emphasizes the increasing use of medical software in the computerized office environment, particularly as it pertains to new scheduling procedures, including an expansion of the section on triage.

Chapter 10 summarizes insured services in Canada. This chapter includes recent changes in regulations affecting health care plans and policies across the country. The chapter reflects a national focus, reviewing generic insured physician and hospital services in Canada, the use of billing codes, interprovincial/territorial billing through the reciprocal agreement, and private insurance.

Chapter 11 provides the student with an overview of provincial/territorial health coverage and explains the principles of provincial/territorial billing and billing for primary care organizations. The material presented in this chapter is general in nature, stressing elements that are common across the country; for example, claims review and health card validation.

Chapter 12 discusses the actual process of claims submission and the technologies available to facilitate it, as well as outlining approaches to billing payers other than provincial/territorial health plans.

Chapter 13 focuses on health information management with a focus on electronic medical records and electronic health records. It explains the data entry capabilities of an EMR/EHR system and includes detailed information on the role of the health professional in the conversion process from paper charts to the electronic format. EMR/EHR is updated to include details about how to use them effectively and how the system is evolving.

Part V, *Hospital Procedures*, addresses the needs of graduates from postgraduate programs in health office administration seeking employment in the hospital setting. It focuses on the skills required for employment (primarily as a clinical secretary) within the hospital. Chapters 14 and 15 introduce the student to the hospital setting, discussing a range of topics including the structure and function of hospital departments and hospital charts and documents. Because hospitals are at varying levels of computerization, Part V retains information on processing handwritten orders, including medication orders and working with medication administration records. However, with most facilities moving toward computerized physician order entry, the book also extensively discusses the differences a clinical secretary working in a CPOE environment will encounter.

In many parts of Canada, transcribing doctors' orders (order entry) is a complex responsibility that the clinical secretary still assumes, in particular in facilities with handwritten physicians' orders or facilities that are transitioning to computerized physician order entry. Chapters 16 to 21 explain the order entry process and other responsibilities of the clinical secretary, including orders related to patient entry, IV therapy, nutrition, digestion, respiration, and patient rest and activity. This section of the book reflects the increasing use of a variety of computerized modules in the order entry process. That aside, many hospitals across Canada are still adapting to a computerized environment; even within facilities, some units are more prone to using paper-based charts than others. Therefore, the order entry process as covered in Part V also explains the administrative process for order entry in the manual environment for selected procedures. The overview of vital signs included in the appendix has been removed, but will be available in the Instructor's Manual.

LEARNING FEATURES

The following features of this book aim to help students understand, apply, and retain core concepts and ideas:

- **Learning Objectives.** Each chapter begins with a list of learning objectives related to key concepts contained within the chapter.
- **Illustrations, Figures, and Charts.** Each chapter contains illustrations, figures, and charts to supplement the related text.
- **Key Terms.** Key terms are highlighted in the text and defined in the margins for quick reference. These terms and definitions are also consolidated in a glossary at the end of the book.
- **Tip Boxes.** Short and salient tips are found throughout each chapter that guide students toward excellence in their future health administration roles.
- **Chapter Summaries.** At the end of each chapter, key points from the chapter are summarized.
- **New! What to Watch For.** This new feature appears at the end of relevant chapters and highlights areas within the health care system that are undergoing changes now or are likely to in the near future.
- **Review Questions.** At the end of each chapter, you will find extensive questions designed to review the content of that chapter.
- **Application Exercises.** End-of-chapter application exercises help the student apply skills and knowledge learned in the chapter either through group discussion or independent activities.
- **Websites of Interest.** For further exploration of chapter topics, we have identified pertinent websites at the end of each chapter.

Supplements

These instructor supplements are available for download from a password-protected section of Pearson Canada's online catalogue (http://catalogue.pearsoned.ca). Navigate to your book's catalogue page to view a list of those supplements that are available. Speak to your local Pearson sales representative for details and access.

Instructor's Manual: This manual offers guidance to instructors using the text, including teaching suggestions, solutions to end-of-chapter problems and exercises, and chapter test questions.

PowerPoint Slides: Updated for this edition, these provide a comprehensive selection of slides highlighting key concepts featured in the text to assist instructors delivering the book content.

 Choice Learning: Pearson has partnered with Choice Learning for this new edition. Every student who purchases a new book will have access to a top rated electronic medical record environment. We've also integrated Choice Learning screen captures throughout the text. Choice Learning Inc. has more than seven years' experience implementing electronic medical record classroom solutions within Ontario and private career colleges.

You can augment your existing OHIP billing, medical transcription, office procedures, and privacy curriculum or add a new offering to enhance your Medical Office Administration Program. For more information please visit http://choicelearning.ca.

Learning Solutions Managers: Pearson's Learning Solutions Managers work with faculty and campus course designers to ensure that Pearson technology products, assessment tools, and online course materials are tailored to meet your specific needs. This highly qualified team is dedicated to helping schools take full advantage of a wide range of educational resources by assisting in the integration of a variety of instructional materials and media formats. Your local Pearson Canada sales representative can provide you with more details on this service program.

ACKNOWLEDGMENTS

Publication of a textbook is a collective effort, and this text is no exception. I would like to acknowledge those who have contributed along the way.

I am grateful to Susan D. Milne, BA, MA, Plain Language Consultant, who contributed a section to Chapter 8.

A debt of gratitude is owed to Joanne Polkiewicz, Pharmacist, for her continuing support. Joanne has done a substantive review of Chapter 7 (Pharmacology) for each edition of this text. Her valuable suggestions for improvement and updates are very much appreciated. Thanks also to Janice Hong, MOA, clinical secretary at Women's College Hospital in Toronto and Cambridge Memorial Hospital in Cambridge, Ontario, for her valuable contributions to Chapters 14 to 21.

Thanks to Marnie Fletcher, BA, CCHRA(C), Director of Health Information Services at St. Joseph's Healthcare Hamilton, who contributed significantly to the initial content preparation and organization of Chapter 13. This chapter has been kept current and relevant with the assistance of Gail F. Crook, CHE, CHIM CEO and Registrar, CHIMA. Thank you, Gail, for your expert assistance and guidance.

I am grateful also to Jennifer Purych, published author and educator (former instructor for the Nursing Unit Clerk Program, Vancouver Community College), for taking me on a guided tour of various hospitals in British Columbia, and to Rachel Mann, Maxine Lloyd, and Betty Furtad for updating me on the scope of practice of clinical coordinators in that province. I am also indebted to Heather Geerdink, President of the Medical Office Assistants' Association of British Columbia, for the assistance she provided with respect to medical billing in that province. Linda A. Smith, PID, AED, MEd Instructor, HealthCare Communications Management Department, Vancouver Community College, and Paula Castling, HealthCare Communications Management Professor, Nursing Unit Clerk—thanks for your valuable advice regarding the role and responsibilities of the unit clerk in British Columbia.

I owe a debt of gratitude to the following friends, colleagues, and institutions that have contributed their time, knowledge, and other resources to the development of this book:

- Dawne Barbieri, MA(Ed), BScN, RN, Director of Interprofessional Practice, Research, and Education, Co-Director of the Centre for Education, North York General Hospital

- Elizabeth Barker, RN, BScN, Stratford General Hospital

- Christy Beavis, Clinical Secretary, Grand River Hospital, Kitchener, Ontario

- Jennifer Beavis, Workplace Safety and Insurance Board, Ontario

- Heather Anne Berry, CCHRA(C), BA, HCA(Cert.), Manager, Health Records, South Bruce Grey Health Centre

- Leslie Brown, Manager, Patient Flow, Stratford General Hospital Rachel Brown, MA, MLIS, Senior Advisor, Knowledge Management/Conseillère principale, gestion des connaissances, Canadian Health Services Research Foundation
- Glenn Budgell, Regional Director, Medical Care Plan, Newfoundland and Labrador
- College of Physicians and Surgeons of Ontario
- Lynda Cranston, contributing editor
- Sherry Czekus, Clinical Secretary, Educator, St. Mary's Hospital, Waterloo, Ontario
- Michelle de Moor, BSc.PT, MA, CHE, Operations Director, Vancouver Acute Critical Care, Emergency, Trauma Services, Access and Flow, Regional Director Emergency Program, Vancouver Coastal Health
- Sandra Frisker, Clinical Secretary, St. Mary's Hospital, Kitchener, Ontario
- Betty Furtad, Nursing Unit Clerk, Royal Columbian Hospital, British Columbia
- Penny Giles, RN, BSN, Bedline Manager, Patient Flow-RQBedline, Regina Qu'Apppelle Health Region
- Brenda Hancock, Manager of Medical Affairs and Training, MCP, Department of Health and Community Services, Newfoundland and Labrador
- Huron Perth Enterprise Information Technology Services
- Katherine Kelly, Federal/Provincial/Territorial Relations, PEI Department of Health
- Melissa Kimen, Senior Project Manager, Strategic Priorities Branch, Ministry of Health, Government of Saskatchewan
- Dr. Grace Langford, MD, FRCP, Stratford, Ontario
- Maxine Lloyd, Nursing Unit Clerk, Royal Columbian Hospital, British Columbia
- Gaylene MacDonald, Health Website Project, Corporate Relations and Evaluation, Corporate, PEI Department of Health
- Rachel Mann, Nursing Unit Coordinator, St. Paul's Hospital, British Columbia
- Maureen McCandless, Director, Communications, The Canadian Chiropractic Association
- Dr. Matt McDonale, MD, Stratford Family Health Team
- Dr. Marcie McEwan, General Surgeon, Stratford General Hospital
- Sandra McKenzie, CMS, Medical Office Manager
- Medical Office Assistants' Association of British Columbia
- Ontario Ministry of Health and Long-Term Care
- Doug Pinder, RN, BScN, MBA, Ontario Home Health
- Valerie Pinder, RN, BScN, MEd, Professor, Conestoga College
- Perri Rattelade, Registered Nurse, ICU Royal Victoria Hospital, Barrie ON
- Lynn Strugnell, Director Clinical Programs, Huron Perth Healthcare Alliance–Stratford General Hospital
- Dr. Eric Thomas, MD, Stratford Family Health Team
- Dr. Douglas Thompson, MD, FRCP, Stratford, Ontario
- Jennifer Wamil, Clinical Secretary, St. Mary's Hospital, Kitchener, Ontario
- Nancy White, BScN, Clinical Educator, Maternal/Child, Stratford General Hospital
- Gail Williams, Accreditation Product Development Specialist (Accreditation Canada)

Finally, special thanks goes to the following individuals for their help and support:

- Heather Jeanes, Unit Secretary at North York General Hospital, for her valuable contributions through many emails and phone calls and for sharing her experiences in the box in Chapter 14, "A Day in the Life of a Clinical Secretary."
- Laura Keast and Tony Priam at Choice Learning for their hard work, time, and dedication in resourcing, formatting, and contributing many of the images contained in this book.
- Barb Mines, Clinical Secretary, Medicine, Stratford General Hospital, for sharing her knowledge and experiences with me in the clinical area during several "job shadowing" experiences.
- Sonia Pagliaroli, RN, MHI(c), CPHIMS-CA, Clinical Informatics, North York General Hospital, for facilitating the use of the many screen captures related to the CPOE environment.
- Geoff Spooner, Vice-President of Sales and Marketing, ClickrTime, for his many emails and valuable information provided about self-registration in health care facilities.
- Bonnie Thompson, Clinical Leader, Medicine at Stratford General Hospital, for providing me with clinical time on the medical unit.
- Shandra Weyers, Administrative Assistant to Dr. Thomas, for her contributions in clinical office management and allowing me to share clinical experiences with her.

I would also like to thank several people at Pearson Education Canada for their professional support, including Kimberley Veevers, Executive Acquisitions Editor; Rebecca Ryoji, Developmental Editor; John Polansky, Program Manager; and Susan Johnson, Project Manager.

Valerie Thompson

Part I
Introduction

Part I of this text briefly discusses the history of the roles and responsibilities of individuals working in a variety of health administration positions. Qualities and skills that promote success in this occupation are outlined, along with the importance of professionalism, scope of practice, and interprofessional collaboration. You will learn about the roles and responsibilities of the modern administrative health professional and how your previous work and volunteer experiences can help you.

Chapter 1

The Administrative Health Professional (AHP)

Diego Cervo/Shutterstock

LEARNING OBJECTIVES

On completing this chapter, you will be able to:

1. Discuss the potential workplace settings the AHP may work in, including job titles, roles, and responsibilities.

2. Explain the personal qualities and competencies necessary to be successful for those working in health administration.

3. Apply four ethical principles that are especially relevant to health care settings.

4. Properly apply the five basic steps to ethical decision making.

5. Outline the administrative and clinical responsibilities of the AHP in the medical and dental office setting.

6. Discuss the potential working environments for AHPs, considering job prospects, salaries, and benefits.

7. Demonstrate how to construct an effective résumé and conduct a job search.

8. Discuss the importance of continuing professional development.

The health care profession is dynamic, complex, and challenging. You are entering it during a time of both change and opportunity. A career path in health services administration offers you varied and stimulating job opportunities. The health office includes a wide variety of settings, ranging from a physician's office to dental offices and clinics. The first four parts of this text, although primarily devoted to the medical office, include information on working in a dental office.

L01 WHAT'S IN A NAME?

The term **administrative health professional (AHP)** is used in this book to represent the diverse roles of graduates from health office administration and similar programs. People in this profession work in a wide variety of health care settings and perform a mix of duties that have become increasingly complex. Each health care facility is likely to have its own job title and unique job description—some with more responsibilities than others. A good example is the role of the clinical secretary/unit clerk in hospitals where **computerized physician order entry** has been implemented. The clinical secretary/unit clerk may no longer be responsible for any component of order entry related to medications. Another example is in primary care settings wherein administrative personnel have designated roles as opposed to other settings where the AHP may rotate through various positions in the setting depending on need and circumstance. In such instances, ensuring that you are functioning within your scope of practice is important (as it is in the hospital setting, discussed in Chapter 14). What is common, however, is the knowledge, level of competence, versatility, and degree of professionalism required to perform competently as an AHP in any setting. The role of the administrative health professional is critical in providing efficient, organized health care. Wherever you work, you will be a valued member of a health care team; you will make a significant contribution toward delivering excellent, compassionate, patient-centred health care.

In the occupational setting, a graduate may be assigned a job title such as *medical secretary* or *medical office assistant* or *administrative manager*. In the hospital setting, titles include *nursing unit coordinator*, *nursing unit assistant*, *coordinator*, *communications clerk*, *unit* or *ward clerk*, and *clinical secretary*. In community nursing, the term *nursing coordinator* may be used as the position that often involves arranging a schedule for nurses to visit patients in the community. Dental offices use the titles *dental practice receptionist*, *dental office manager*, *dental treatment coordinator*, and *dental administrative assistant*. Such terms as *clinical secretary* may be used in this book if relevant to the specific occupational setting being discussed.

Client versus Patient

Calling individuals seeking health care either a *patient* or a *client* has been controversial. The concept of calling a patient (someone seeking health care) a client was introduced in the late 1990s, but for the most part the name change never really took hold. The concept was that using the term *client* empowered individuals to become stakeholders in their own health care—to take responsibility for their own health and be active participants in choosing their own treatment options. *Client* typically represents a person who seeks and purchases a service and is, therefore, in control of what that service is and how it is delivered. It was proposed that the term *patient* put the consumer into a position of subservience to some degree—and the provider (presumably a physician) in a position of power to more or less impose health-related decisions upon the person.

In the past, it is true that many health care consumers were, to a large degree, dependent on their physician to diagnose their health problem as well as recommend

administrative health professional (AHP) a graduate from an accredited health office administration program who assumes administrative, communication, and/or clinical responsibilities in a health care setting.

computerized physician order entry (CPOE) an electronic, multifunctional software system used in health care facilities that, among other functions, enables the physician (or other provider) to enter orders directly into the computer.

and implement a plan of care, much of the time with little discussion. Individuals were quite happy to do what the doctor recommended, and they looked to the physician to make these decisions—he or she was in a position of power (actual or perceived) and his or her decisions were usually not questioned.

In recent years, involvement of the individual in every aspect of his or her health care has become the norm. Health care consumers have become more informed about their own health concerns (e.g., by using the internet) and both more proactive and responsible for their own health care decisions. The role of the physician has also shifted from sole decision maker to establishing a collaborative relationship with his or her patients in terms of both diagnosis and treatment. As a result, the term **patient** has evolved and has come to represent an individual who not only seeks health care but who is active in making any related decisions. For example, several years ago a labouring mother whose medical condition indicated that she should have a Caesarian section would likely have been told by the doctor that the baby was in distress, and a section would have been booked. Now, a doctor would likely have a conversation with the mom and dad. He or she would explain what was going on with the baby (perhaps a low heartbeat and decelerations on the fetal monitor), and the doctor might recommend a section, but give the mom the choice of labouring for a limited time to see if things improved (dependent, of course, on the situation).

patient in the past, a person seeking or receiving health care; the term has evolved to represent an individual who is also actively involved in all aspects of his or her care, from diagnosis to treatment, and who assumes responsibility for his or her health.

Administrative Health Professional: The Medical Secretary

The role of the administrative health professional has changed over the years, becoming more responsible and complex (see Figure 1.1). Today, a high level of education and skills are necessary to meet the demands placed on this position. You can see this reflected in the ad illustrated in Figure 1.1.

CENTRAL CLINIC ALBERTA HEALTH SERVICES
Medical Secretary—Primary Care
Start Date: Immediate
Job Number 45323

Multidisciplinary team implements primary health and dental care to the surrounding community. Our services include counselling, harm reduction, advocacy, and community development. We interface with multiple community agencies.

General responsibilities:
You will provide initial and ongoing personal and telephone contact for the professional staff, patients, and visitors. As a member of our primary care health team, you will help facilitate the smooth operation of the clinic's administrative function, perform administrative and selected clinical duties assisting a variety of health providers (intake interviews, blood pressures, urine and blood sugar testing). You will be the frontline person in triaging patients in accordance with clinic protocol and ensuring that scheduling of patients is done in an efficient, patient-oriented manner.

Accountability:
The medical secretary reports to the director of primary care.

Qualifications:
Diploma from a community college health administration program or equivalent, keyboarding speed of 50 wpm or greater, demonstrated computer literacy and the ability to easily adapt to new software, previous experience in health/social services an asset, ability to work well under stress and maintain a calm demeanour, proficient use of proper English in oral and written (also spelling) communication, outstanding communication, conflict management, and interpersonal skills.

Salary Range: $3450–$4350/month plus benefits. May be adjusted depending on education, skills, and experience.

Figure 1.1 An advertisement for an administrative health professional in a physician's office or clinic.

The administrative health professional must have a broad knowledge and skills base. For example, he or she must be computer literate and knowledgeable about provincial/territorial billing and medical office procedures and protocol. He or she must have basic knowledge of pharmacology, laboratory and diagnostic tests, ethics, and human relations. In addition, he or she must have an in-depth command of medical terminology and outstanding communication skills.

Many community colleges and independent business colleges offer health administration programs, which vary from a one-year certificate program to a two- or three-year diploma program. Some programs are accelerated, for example offering a two-year diploma program in a shorter time frame. These programs may offer a combined health office administration/unit clerk program with the opportunity to exit the program after completion of one of the two components. Other colleges offer these programs separately; for example, in most postsecondary institutions in British Columbia, the Nursing Unit Clerk program is a stand-alone opportunity. Some colleges integrate simulated office experiences or co-op or workplace experiences, either throughout the program or at the end.

In the hospital setting, the responsibilities of the **ward clerk** or clinical secretary have also dramatically increased in both scope and volume. Initially, the ward clerk was not allowed to process doctors' orders, take laboratory or diagnostic reports over the telephone, or respond to most physician requests. These tasks were primarily the responsibility of the head nurse. In the past few years, the term *ward clerk* has been replaced in many settings by *clinical secretary*, *clerical associate*, or *communications coordinator* to better reflect the increased responsibilities, notably transcribing physicians' orders. As previously mentioned, responsibilities related to transcribing doctors' orders (also called order entry) have changed in facilities that have computerized physician order entry. In these hospitals, providers enter their orders directly into the computer; this is discussed in Chapter 14. The clinical secretary coordinates almost all written and oral communication and plays key administrative roles. These positions are usually filled by AHP graduates or by long-standing employees who have gained a wealth of knowledge on the job. The duties and responsibilities of the clinical secretary are discussed in more detail in Chapter 14.

ward clerk an individual who manages the administrative and communication needs of a patient-care unit. The title is being replaced with *clinical secretary* or *communications coordinator*.

The Dental Office

Dental administrative assistants are usually graduates of health administration programs or specialty programs for dental administration. Sometimes other members of the dental team (e.g., dental assistants) assume additional administrative responsibilities. However, in most offices operating with a variety of dental health professionals, administrative duties are assumed by a person trained in the administrative field. Conversely, to increase office efficiency some dental offices will cross-train their administrative staff to assume limited chair-side duties, thus multitasking. Additional responsibilities may include sorting, sanitizing, and sterilizing instruments. Some colleges integrate the specific knowledge and skills needed to work in a dental office into an administrative health professional program; others may offer a specialized program in dental administration, such as Vancouver Career College in Kelowna, British Columbia, and the KLC College in Kingston, Ontario.

EMPLOYMENT OPPORTUNITIES

Positions

Administrative health professionals work in a variety of positions with different titles and duties. The following summary outlines some of the more common ones.

Medical Office Assistant

The role of **medical assistant** is more clearly defined in the United States than in Canada. In the United States, the medical assistant primarily assists the physician with clinical tasks but may also handle some administrative responsibilities. This term is often used in British Columbia as well. More closely aligned to the medical assistant in Canada is a recent addition to the health care team of a *physician assistant* whose responsibilities are primarily clinical in nature. In most of Canada, however, the more common term is **medical office assistant** or office manager, and this job description generally includes more administrative than clinical responsibilities. Medical assistants in the United States are trained to take blood specimens, administer injections, give oral medications, administer electrocardiograms and other laboratory tests, and perform other specialized tasks—tasks generally performed by nurses in Canada. Medical assistants also take vital signs, prepare patients for procedures, take health histories, prepare the examination or treatment room, assess patient need when scheduling appointments, and determine when patients need to be seen urgently. Canadian administrative health professionals assume many of these responsibilities in some health care settings.

Integrating some nursing duties into the AHP's job is not new but is becoming more common as the changing face of health care demands multiskilled, versatile, and cost-effective workers. In some offices the AHP assumes expanded duties, such as giving allergy shots and assisting with procedures. The AHP must be trained by the physician or any other qualified health practitioner to carry out these tasks, some of which are legally considered "delegated acts," meaning that the health practitioner involved takes responsibility for the employee's actions.

Administrative Nursing Coordinator

An increasing number of community agencies supply a range of in-home medical services, especially home-based nursing care to patients discharged from hospital with conditions requiring ongoing care and assessment. Community nurses start and maintain intravenous (IV) therapy in the home, apply dressings, and maintain and monitor patients on respirators. These patients may have chest tubes and other complex medical devices. Patients are routinely admitted to the agency's services and discharged when their need for care terminates.

Each agency needs someone in an administrative role, often called a *nursing coordinator*, to coordinate the agency's needs and activities. This person is aware of the caseloads of various nurses, assigns new admissions on the basis of caseload and priority, conveys vital information about patients' medical needs, and keeps track of admissions and discharges. To take on this role, you must be aware of the responsibilities of the various types of nurses within the organization and the related scope of practice for each group (discussed in detail in Chapter 14). You must be able to prioritize information and be familiar with medications, critical lab values, and other components of community care.

Clinic Administrator/Manager

Over the past few years, more **clinics** have appeared; for example, central clinics associated with primary care groups, or those privately owned and operated by independent practitioners such as physiotherapists. At medical clinics, services include a complete range of care from family medicine to day surgery. Clinics such as the Preventous Collaborative Health in Calgary provide a range of preventive health care services (these services are not covered by provincial/territorial plans). A clinic may offer one service or a variety of services by more than one health professional. Managing the administrative needs of a clinic requires excellent organizational skills and the ability to make sound decisions, while working harmoniously with a variety of professionals (and personalities). You must be able to multitask, think quickly, and take responsibility. Specific skills range from triaging and scheduling patients, solving problems, and maintaining a patient-oriented environment while managing the business aspects of the clinic. In addition, you may be responsible for staff scheduling and recruitment. If the clinic is privately operated, you must work toward cost effectiveness while maintaining a high standard of patient care.

Medical Transcriptionist   A medical transcriptionist produces medical reports, correspondence, records, patient-care information, statistics, medical research, and administrative material. In a hospital, transcriptionists are members of a larger team in the medical/health records or the health information management department. The transcriptionist reviews, edits, and formats medical reports and documents that have been either dictated onto a voice recorder or produced by the provider using voice recognition technology. Documents include discharge summaries, referral letters, and reports on health histories, physical examinations, operations, consultations, autopsies, radiology examinations, and obstetrics. Transcriptionists have fast and accurate keyboarding skills; proficient computer skills; excellent language, grammar, and spelling skills; the ability to edit documents; general medical knowledge; sound judgment; and logical problem-solving abilities. A good transcriptionist can spot mistakes in a report and check, when necessary, with the doctor to get the right information. Reports are prepared and stored electronically, with only selected documents printed.

Dental Administrative Assistant   A dental administrative assistant performs many of the same tasks as an administrative health professional; however, the job usually entails more extensive work with insurance forms and billing to various insurance providers. It also requires a sound knowledge of tooth identification systems and tooth anatomy. Dental administrative assistants are also responsible for patient education, accounts payable and receivable, referral systems, and the management and analysis of practice reports. Many scheduling procedures may also differ; it is often necessary to schedule patients for other members of the dental team, such as dental assistants or dental hygienists, as well as for the dentist. In some occupational settings, the dental administrative assistant may be trained to assist the dentist with basic procedures.

Occupational Settings

A wide variety of positions are available for the administrative health professional. The health care field is diverse, and opportunities continue to broaden as the industry restructures and the roles of health care professionals change. Occupational settings range from the fast-paced challenge of the emergency room to the less hectic environment of a specialist's office, and from a busy walk-in clinic with a lot of patient contact to a medical records department with limited public contact. Many positions are also available in sectors of the allied health care and alternative health care fields.

The administrative health professional is considered part of the allied health care field, along with other professions more centred on direct patient care. **Allied health care** includes any duty or function that supports primary health care professionals, such as physicians, in the delivery of health care services. Allied health care professions include physiotherapists, osteopaths, and nurses. Many of these professionals are in independent practice while working collaboratively with other health care professionals. For example, with the current move to community-based care, there has been an increase in the number of independent nursing service organizations. Some sectors of the allied health care industry offer valuable employment opportunities for the AHP.

allied health care any duty or profession that supports primary health care providers, such as physicians, nurse practitioners, or midwives, in delivering health care services.

Information Technologies/EMR Vendors   Electronic medical record (EMR) vendors, such as TELUS or QHR Technologies, are software vendors that are located across Canada. Every office or facility uses medical software. Once purchased and installed, the related software company must train everyone who will be using the software on how to use it. In addition, they must provide the organization with ongoing support. They hire informed individuals for these positions (such as graduates from health administration programs). Each jurisdiction may have other vendors offering such positions, for example, OntarioMD.

Alternative Health Care

Alternative health care, also referred to as **complementary health care**, is considered by most to be the natural approach to treating the causes of illness and disease. Alternative health care includes nontraditional methods and practices such as chiropractic, acupuncture, massage, and aromatherapy. These professions offer the consumer a replacement or an adjunct to traditional health care. Alternative health care professions are growing in number and popularity as Canadians face (and become fed up with) increasingly long waits for medical care. Many allied, alternative, and mainstream health care professionals work independently or in facilities that offer collaborative care to patients as well as a range of health care choices. Alternative and allied health care professionals provide employment opportunities for administrative health professionals with duties and responsibilities similar to those in traditional health care offices. Throughout this book, we focus primarily on physicians' offices and hospitals, the two settings most covered in health administration courses, as it would be impossible to do justice to the whole range of possibilities in a single textbook. But keep in mind that your basic skills and knowledge can take you in many directions.

You might find a job in any of the following workplaces—and even this list is not complete.

Office and Community

- Doctor's office (group or solo practice), generalist or specialist
- Health care agencies
- Regional health authorities
- Ambulatory care or walk-in clinics (also may be called urgent care clinics or centres)
- Primary care group clinic (for rostered patients)
- Dental offices
- Optometry offices
- Community agencies, such as public health
- Victorian Order of Nurses (VON)
- Canadian Red Cross
- Canadian Cancer Society
- CCAC (Community Care Access Centre) or equivalent
- Independent community authorities

Clinics (often connected with hospitals or community-based health services)

- Orthopedics
- Prenatal/postpartum/birthing centres
- Diabetic
- Mental health
- Systemic therapy
- Renal dialysis
- Oncology
- Palliative care
- Laser surgery

Alternative/Allied Health Care Facilities

- Acupuncture
- Reflexology
- Massage therapy
- Aromatherapy
- Chiropractor
- Osteopath

Information Technologies

- QHR Technologies
- TELUS

Hospital Departments

- Admitting/patient registration
- Medical records/information health
- Emergency room
- Laboratory (various departments within the laboratory)
- Maternal/child
- Pediatrics
- Medicine
- Surgery
- Operating room
- Social services
- Radiology

Hospital Departments: Choosing the Right Unit for You   Working in a hospital as a clinical secretary is an exciting vocation offering numerous options (as listed previously). You can choose a unit with a slower pace, or one that is fast moving and exciting. Choosing the unit that suits your abilities is most important. Additionally, selecting an area that meshes with your own preferences is a bonus; for example, palliative care if you are comfortable dealing with individuals suffering from terminal illnesses, or a geriatric unit if you are at home dealing with older people. Keep in mind, though, that once employed by a facility, you may be asked to work on units other than the one you applied for from time to time. Cross-training a clinical secretary, enabling him or her to work in more than one area, is a common practice. Most facilities will post new positions internally first, giving current employees the opportunity to apply.

On a patient-care unit, you will manage almost all aspects of the unit's communication (including organizing admissions, transfers, and discharges), and you may be accountable for the execution of doctor's orders via the unit's computer software system. Two commonly used systems are called Meditech and MedConnect. You will work closely with the nurses, doctors, and other members of the health care team. In addition, you will be a vital link to health care for patients and their loved ones and families. If this interests you, please see a more detailed description of this important vocational choice in Chapter 14.

Other Health care Facilities

- Long-term care facilities (nursing homes)/residential-care facilities
- Seniors' residences/assisted living facilities
- Rehabilitative centres

Other

- Insurance companies
- Community college schools of health sciences or health units
- Provincial or territorial health plan offices
- Health Canada
- Local public health departments
- Industrial health departments
- Medical supply companies
- Private laboratories and diagnostic clinics
- Medical transcription facilities
- Pharmaceutical firms
- Medical software companies
- Veterinary practices
- Canadian Armed Forces

Occupational Settings for the Dental Office Administrator

- General dentist
- Orthodontist
- Pedodontist
- Periodontist
- Prosthodontist
- Oral and maxillofacial surgeon
- Dental hygienist (practising independently)
- Dental distribution or manufacturing company
- Dental department of a hospital
- Dental laboratory
- Public health department
- Dental insurance organizations

L02 ATTRIBUTES AND SKILLS OF THE ADMINISTRATIVE HEALTH PROFESSIONAL

To be a member of any profession demands academic preparation as well as a distinctive set of attributes and skills. A shy person might not suit a marketing position. A person who thrives on artistic creativity and dislikes math (even if good at it) would be poorly suited to a position in accounting. Those who truly succeed in their chosen field usually have a natural affinity for it as well as qualities and skills that enhance their work.

attribute an inborn personal quality or characteristic.

Attributes and skills are not the same thing, though they overlap. A skill is learned. We think of attributes as inherent traits, although certainly some qualities can be developed purposefully. Consider loyalty and honesty. Although you may have a natural propensity for one or the other, you are not born loyal or disloyal, honest or dishonest. These attributes develop as you grow and experience the world around you.

Personal attributes, therefore, are a combination of inborn individual traits and development. Some people just seem to be naturally organized—a desirable trait for anyone working in an office—but organizational ability can be improved through practice; thus, some aspects of organization can be regarded as skills. Skills are more tangible than attributes. You learn to type, you learn health care terminology, you learn how to communicate effectively—although, here again, some people are just naturally effective communicators. Skills may be divided into soft and hard skills. Hard skills are specific and measurable; for example, keyboarding at 50 words per minute. Soft skills are more general; for example, communicating in difficult situations or projecting an image of trust and competency.

Each profession or vocation calls for a certain set of attributes and skills. A good police officer, for example, should have the attributes of courage and the ability to remain calm under stress, and the skills of marksmanship and negotiation.

Because job opportunities for health office professionals vary, a variety of qualities and skills may be suited to different positions. Some, however, are essential for all positions.

Attributes

Professionalism   One of the most important attributes of an administrative health professional is professionalism. The person must recognize his or her career as the important, vital profession it is and one that carries tremendous responsibility. The roots of professionalism lie in the term *profession*. A profession is a grouping of tasks, duties, and responsibilities requiring specialized knowledge and specialized preparation. Some professions, such as nursing, medicine, and law, are formally recognized; others are not. Administering a health office is a profession but currently has no legal boundaries or regulating body. A professional (noun) is an individual who has prepared to work in a profession and, by implication, is one who practises and upholds its standards, rules, and policies. The adjective *professional* describes conduct appropriate to a given profession; more generally, it refers to a courteous, businesslike, respectful attitude, manner, and appearance.

Professional Appearance   Professionalism is conveyed by both appearance and manner. An appropriate professional appearance is imperative for an administrative health professional. You will frequently be the first person that the patient meets. Your appearance will create a lasting impression and may well set the tone for how that person feels about you and your place of employment. If you are negligent in your personal appearance, people may assume that you will be negligent in your work; this impression will reflect badly on both your employer and your occupational setting. Think about how some of the health professionals you have seen dress. You may have seen, for example, nurses wearing shorts and socks with running shoes, jogging suits, or scrubs with less-than-clean sweaters and sporting long, unrestrained hair; dangling earrings; long, painted fingernails; and numerous rings. You may have encountered an administrative assistant in a health office who was dressed conservatively, with a neat lab coat, contained hair, light makeup, and minimal jewellery. Which made a better impression?

There is a time and a place for everything—a fact that seems to be difficult to convey to some health professionals. Many seem to think that the more glamorous they look—or, conversely, the more casual—the more appealing they are. Many students also seem to think that the lessons of decorum they learn become irrelevant after graduation. It cannot be emphasized enough that the health care setting requires professional, appropriate attire.

What is considered professional will vary, within limits, with places of employment. Dress in health care is usually conservative. In the health office or hospital, dress codes may vary from scrubs or uniforms to "dressing casual." Jeans of any description, jogging apparel, shorts, and T-shirts are rarely acceptable. Scrubs are cost effective, convenient to launder, and comfortable. They should be changed daily and kept clean and wrinkle free. If a sweater is worn over scrubs or a uniform, ensure that it is clean, neat, and a neutral colour. Alternatively, a lab coat is also easily laundered and looks crisp and clean. It should be worn only within the health care facility or office. Uniforms/scrubs should be worn only in the facility—most provide change rooms and lockers. This is often an infection-control requirement.

A name tag is always appropriate in the office. Health care facilities usually require that photo ID be worn, for security as well as identification. As in many professions, dress codes in health care are becoming more casual. You need to find the appropriate balance for your work environment—neither too strict and sterile nor too casual. Certain elements, however, transcend setting:

- Neatness
- Cleanliness
- Sensible, discreet use of makeup
- No fragrance (e.g., perfume, aftershave) because of increasing allergies among the public
- Subtle jewellery, if any. Most facilities allow jewellery worn for religious purposes. Body piercings and multiple earrings are discouraged or banned.
- Comfortable, clean shoes

A word about shoes: Shoes must look appropriate, be comfortable, and meet any workplace safety requirements (e.g., no high heels or strappy sandals) and safety standards in such settings as hospitals (which usually require closed-toe shoes). Good foot support is still important if you stand for long periods or do a lot of walking. Choose shoes in neutral colours (e.g., no bright greens or pinks) and materials that can be easily cleaned. Whatever style you choose, keep the shoes clean and in good repair. Keep your laces, if you have them, spotless. Some facilities do not allow employees to wear their work shoes outside.

Many offices and clinics have a dress code, and uniforms are sometimes part of this dress code. Hospitals often prefer the clinical secretary to wear scrubs or appropriate business attire with a clean lab coat over top.

Professional Manner A professional appearance is ineffective unless it is accompanied by a professional manner, behaviour, and attitude. A professional manner is reflected by treating people with respect and kindness; recognizing your professional boundaries and staying within them; and being positive, honest, and trustworthy. Treat each person as unique and important, and even during a brief exchange give him or her your undivided attention. Greet people with a smile and be pleasant. Convey a warm and attentive attitude toward your patients. Address their concerns promptly, follow through with promises, and try to keep a sense of humour while maintaining a caring and friendly environment.

Professionalism also means being proud of yourself and confident in who you are and what you do. Refrain from making personal calls at work or using the workplace telephone. Use the internet at work for work purposes only, and turn your smartphone off when at work (an anticipated emergency is an exception). Adhere to agency rules. It is normally fine to use your cellphone or smartphone on breaks if in a private area. In addition, do not become involved in the personal issues among other members of the health care team. Refrain from taking sides in discussions and issues, work related or otherwise. If there is a serious problem, there will be a proper agency protocol to follow for those affected. Becoming involved will create "sides," bitterness, and even hostilities. This could negatively affect everyone in your workplace. Individuals have been disciplined and even fired for these types of infractions. Preserve workplace relationships if at all possible.

Analytical Thinking   The administrative health professional must be able to grasp and apply concepts and analyze and synthesize facts and information. This ability is partly a matter of natural intelligence, partly the result of consciously developing cognitive skills, and partly the result of a solid knowledge base and familiarity with your job, your roles, and your responsibilities. Good analytical skills are the first step in making good judgments:

- Prioritize and perform multiple tasks, often at the same time.
- Make knowledge-based decisions.
- Solve problems and take action.
- Respond appropriately to emergency situations.

Good Judgment   Good judgment is essential and is required in almost every task or duty that you perform. Good judgment relies not only on a strong knowledge base but also on the ability to weigh consequences and outcomes and make effective decisions. In the health office, you use judgment every time you make an appointment for a patient. You decide how long the appointment should be and how soon the patient needs to see the doctor. You screen the physician's phone calls, deciding which ones to put through to the doctor, which to refer to the nurse, and which to handle yourself.

Triage—assessing patients' need for treatment and the urgency of that need—is an important function in most office or clinic settings. You will sometimes have to decide whether a patient needs to be urgently seen by the physician or sooner than someone else who may be waiting. Judgment is also applied to patients who call the office with health complaints. You must be able to recognize a potential emergency and refer the patient appropriately.

Some decisions will make you unpopular. It can be difficult to face criticism of your decisions. To make sound decisions,

- carefully evaluate and assess facts before making the decision,
- remember that compromise is sometimes necessary, and
- if you are convinced that your decision is the right one, stick to it and accept disapproval with as much equanimity as you can.

triage assessing the seriousness of a patient's presenting problem to determine who needs to have medical help first. For example, someone coming to the emergency department with chest pain would be brought in to see the doctor immediately, whereas someone with a sore throat would be considered a nonurgent case and able to wait.

Approachable Manner and Friendly Personality   An open, approachable manner and friendly personality are among the most important qualities for dealing with the public—all the more so when interacting with people who are anxious or under stress, such as those who are concerned about their own or their relatives' health. You need to speak pleasantly, show empathy and caring, and use diplomacy. Patients should be made to feel that they and their concerns are important. A pleasant, friendly AHP will put patients at ease, create a positive and caring atmosphere, promote trust, and, in many cases, invite a pleasant, friendly response. Patients are more apt to return if you are welcoming. For some providers, this is critical to patient recruitment and retention and the success of their business.

Getting Along with Others   Also called *adaptive interpersonal skills*, the ability to get along with those you work with, manage conflict, and promote a pleasant, accommodating and productive work environment may well be a combination of natural ability and learned skills. A workplace that fosters tolerance and respect for others contributes to an occupational setting that is a pleasure to work in. There is nothing worse from a professional and personal perspective than dreading going to work or dreading having to work with a particular individual. It affects you, those you work with, and the workplace setting in general. There is a higher staff turnover rate in health care facilities that are ruled by tension and stress. Often this is generated by one person. Do not let that person be you. Strategies for effective communication are discussed in more detail in Chapter 8.

Sense of Responsibility   To be successful in the health office setting, you must be accountable for your actions, take responsibility for yourself, and be honest. Patients and employers alike rely and depend on you. You must keep promises, and you must be able to accept and deal with the consequences of your actions. For example, if you are supposed to notify a patient about an abnormal laboratory result, the physician is counting on you to carry through with that action. If you forget, you need to admit your error and take responsibility. Trying to find excuses or blame someone else would be dishonest and unprofessional. Know your limitations and seek help when appropriate. You may sometimes be asked to do something that you do not feel qualified to do. It is far better to say so openly than to do a substandard job or, worse, make a mistake that affects patient care. One graduate commented of her hospital placement: "There is no forgiveness for mistakes in health care, but it is even worse if you do not admit your mistake, correct it, and take steps to ensure that the same mistake does not happen again." When people know they can rely on you, you gain their trust—one of the most valuable things you can establish with employers, peers, and patients.

Flexibility   To be flexible is to have the ability to easily adapt to new or changing requirements. Any given day may start out in a reasonably organized manner, but invariably there will be many days that do not end that way. Patients may not show up for appointments; you may have several patients who need to see the doctor urgently when there are no openings; the physician may be called away to the delivery room or the emergency department, necessitating cancellation of appointments; or a report you expected to have for a patient may be delayed. In the hospital setting, you may get several admissions at the same time, preventing you from tackling your "to do" list. The surgeons may be grumpy and make you bear the brunt of their anger. Being able to reorganize schedules, priorities, and patients and adapt mentally to such changes will reduce your frustration and ultimately help things run more smoothly. Flexibility is also important in terms of being able to assume different responsibilities either in an office (e.g., doing billing or scheduling patients) or a hospital setting (e.g., working in a pre-admit orthopedic clinic and being comfortable if asked to do a shift in the emergency department—with appropriate training, of course).

It is important also to be flexible with respect to your working relationships. You need to be able to work independently and as a member of a team. This involves sharing responsibilities at some times and assuming them at others, changing your way of doing things when a better suggestion comes along, or letting go of something you feel you have ownership of. It may involve changing a procedure rather than clinging rigidly to a policy. Recognize that no rule will fit every person or situation all the time. Flexibility allows for personal and professional growth and opens the door to new opportunities.

Calm Demeanour   The health office, and the patient-care setting in particular, can be hectic and stressful. A high stress level often interferes with a person's ability to remain calm. Yet a calm demeanour in all situations is important. Becoming flustered and anxious can interfere with effective action and communication and may cause you to say or do something you regret. A calm, methodical response is essential in a crisis. For example, suppose you witness a cardiac arrest in a hospital. You must remain calm and focused and remember the steps you are to follow to notify switchboard to announce the code over the hospital public address system. An administrative health professional must be able to control impulsive behaviour, to respond to a variety of situations, and to think clearly and apply knowledge before taking efficient and effective action.

Initiative   Initiative is one of the first qualities an employer looks for. It implies the ability to assess when something needs to be done and to do it; that is, to act without clear guidance. If you have initiative, you can complete tasks independently and seek out new learning opportunities. You go the extra distance to accomplish more than you must.

Tolerance   Tolerance means allowing people to have their own beliefs, opinions, and ways of doing things. It means accepting people for who they are, whether you agree or disagree with their lifestyle, personal decisions, or personal beliefs. Sometimes you need to bite your tongue rather than say something critical. You listen to and support patients, even when you feel tired or fed up.

Empathy   Being empathetic means being able to put yourself in others' shoes and imagine their thoughts and feelings. It gives you an emotional connection that makes the patient feel understood, accepted, and respected regardless of the situation. Do not confuse *empathy* with *sympathy*, the ability to commiserate or share another's feelings. Sympathy is emotional, while empathy involves sensitivity or comprehension.

Ethical Attitude   A person who does not behave ethically has no place in the health profession. Your position is one of trust that demands respect for the patient's rights and beliefs. You must recognize and respect a patient's health care opinions and decisions. *You must be fully aware of confidentiality guidelines* outlined in provincial/ territorial and federal legislation and abide by them. Ethical responsibilities are addressed later in this chapter.

Skills

Although your skill set as an administrative health professional will continually grow, upon graduation you will have established **core competencies**, both cognitive and performance based, in the following areas.

Organizational Skills   As previously noted, being organized can be a natural attribute. However, even the most naturally organized person will have to work to develop organizational skills to manage a busy office or patient-care unit efficiently. To get the necessary things done, you will need to prioritize, establish procedures, and follow through with a well-thought-out, methodical approach. Attention to detail is also important. Remember to ask colleagues for ideas and suggestions and to work together. Good organization applies to every area of your job, from filing, to scheduling appointments, to arranging things in the office. Organization is not something you do before you start: It is an ongoing process you must engage in every day. It pays off, however, in an efficient use of time and saves a great deal of frustration.

Effective Communication   Communication skills are essential in any job involving personal interaction. A person may have the important qualities of empathy and tolerance, but it is communication that conveys these to others. You need to be able to communicate effectively in structured settings with patients, families, significant others, and all members of the health care team. Communication involves both receiving and conveying information accurately and effectively. Communication can be written, oral, or nonverbal (involving facial expressions, gestures, posture, and tone of voice). You need to be proficient at all three.

core competencies the basic or essential skills that one needs to succeed in a particular profession.

Your speech must be clear and articulate. Correct grammar, in both speech and writing, reflects professionalism. If, for example, you say, "her and I" or "it don't," you will sound uneducated and careless. At a deeper level, you must be able to impart and elicit a sense of trust and warmth and listen for the emotional as well as the literal message from patients. You need to be able to control a conversation, when necessary, and to communicate effectively with people from many different cultures. The latter requires the skill and patience to understand the message when the speaker's English is flawed. Knowledge of effective communication skills allows you to assess situations and respond appropriately.

Keyboarding Skills Health office professionals must keyboard accurately and quickly. Many facilities use a minimum typing speed of 55–60 words per minute or higher as a hiring criterion. Most colleges require a minimum speed (perhaps 30 words per minute) as a *prerequisite* for admission to the administrative health professional program, with the expectation that speed will increase by graduation. Computer and medical transcription courses can help increase accuracy and speed. There are also excellent websites for testing and practising your keyboarding skills.

Computer Literacy Competencies in computer literacy are essential for the AHP. Health offices and hospitals are moving steadily toward a paperless system of administration and practice. Computerized environments are constantly being upgraded and improved. You will need a general knowledge of computers and proficiency in word processing programs, accounting software, data management programs, and even presentation software. More importantly, you need to be able to transfer these skills to the customized computer programs that may be used in your workplace. It is important that you be able to embrace new technology and actively work toward staying current. This is especially challenging in physicians' offices and clinics, where software systems are ever-changing or being updated and there is continued improvement in and more comprehensive use of electronic medical and health records. As well, there are hundreds of new billing codes, incentive codes, and blended forms of remuneration that you must be able to manage electronically.

Knowledge of Health care Terminology No one can function competently in the health care environment without knowing the language of medicine and dentistry. Special health care terminology is used daily in health care settings. You need to be able to use medical and dental terms properly, both in speech and writing. This knowledge is applied to almost every aspect of health administration, from transcribing medical dictation documents, to editing voice-dictated documents, to interpreting lab and diagnostic tests, to explaining reports to patients. Understanding medical terminology is also critical in assisting you in responding to or preparing insurance documents and other reports.

Background Knowledge You need an in-depth grasp of anatomy and physiology, pharmacology, and laboratory and diagnostic tests, including designated critical values.

Medical Transcription Straight medical transcription skills are still required in many occupational settings. You must be able to transcribe accurately and to interpret, type, and format various medical reports and documents.

Editing Documents/Voice Recognition Software Voice recognition software such as Dragon is used by many medical practitioners. Even the best software is not perfect—the resulting documents invariably contain mistakes related to the inability of the voice recognition software to accurately record what was said. This is caused by a variety of things ranging from accents to the way the speaker pronounces certain words. Successful use of voice or word recognition software improves with length of use, the amount of "training" the user has, and how well it recognizes the user's voice. Documents produced using such software must be carefully reviewed and mistakes corrected. One missed word can have dire consequences. In one extreme example, a doctor recorded "the baby cried," but the software recorded "the baby died." The mistake was overlooked and the flawed document was sent out, causing serious problems. In addition, these documents must be scanned for correct use of commas, parentheses, apostrophes, and other punctuation.

L03 L04 ETHICS AND THE ADMINISTRATIVE HEALTH PROFESSIONAL

As previously mentioned, ethical behaviour is essential for the AHP. **Ethics** is the study of standards of right and wrong in human behaviour. Ethical perspectives are shaped by culture, ethnicity, religion, upbringing, and social influences. Ethics deal with values and morals. **Values** are the principles, standards, or qualities that a person holds dear. For example, you might value honesty in your friendships or efficiency at work. **Morals** are what a person believes to be right and wrong. For example, you may have a moral belief that one should always keep promises.

Few professions demand a higher **code of ethics** than health care. As a member of a health care team, you have moral obligations to the following:

- Your profession: To uphold excellence in clinical and administrative practice, work within your scope of practice, and have a sense of **duty** to all stakeholders

- The public: To practise in a competent, responsible, and honest manner, maintain public trust, and treat each person with respect; you have a moral obligation to adhere to the rules and laws that govern confidentiality

- Your employer: To be faithful and accountable, and to adhere to the principles and policies of your workplace

- Your colleagues: To recognize their rights and treat them as you would want to be treated

Ethical Principles

Ethical principles provide guidance for moral action and ethical decision making. Ethical principles are applicable to any profession. They provide the foundation from which many professions adopt a code of ethics. The five principles discussed below are widely accepted in the health care profession and should serve as guides for conduct and decision making.

1. *Autonomy.* **Autonomy** recognizes the **right** of a *mentally competent* individual to make independent decisions without coercion, once given the facts. Health professionals may try to influence the patient's decisions, thinking they know what is best. Health professionals have a duty to respect the decisions of informed, autonomous adults. Consider this example: Yoko is dying of cancer and refuses to sign a consent form for chemotherapy. Dr. Berfeltz urges her to do so because he believes that chemotherapy treatments would prolong her life. Yoko believes that the treatments would make her sick and diminish the quality of life she has left. Dr. Berfeltz has a duty to respect Yoko's right to autonomy, and thus to respect her decision. You may not always agree with decisions patients make, but you must respect their right to make them. Although you most certainly will not be in a position to influence a patient's decision regarding such matters, knowledge of decisions that you fundamentally disagree with may weigh heavily on your mind

ethics the philosophical study of standards accepted by society that determine what is right and wrong in human behaviour.

values the beliefs a person holds dear and that guide that person's decisions and behaviour or conduct.

morals what a person believes to be right and wrong pertaining to how to act, treat others, and get along in an organized society.

code of ethics a set of guidelines for ethical conduct.

duty a moral obligation.

autonomy a person's right to self-determination. In health care it refers to a patient's right to make his or her own decisions without coercion—for example, decisions for treatment based on fact and being fully informed of all treatment options.

right a moral, legal, cultural, or traditional claim.

and conscience. In 2015, Canada passed legislation legalizing physician-assisted suicide (euthanasia), the details for which were addressed in 2016 and beyond. Yoko could, when she feels the time is right, seek to have her life ended. This is her right, but many hold that the very act of assisting someone to die contravenes the very essence of a physician's duty to do no harm and preserve life at all costs.

>>> POINTS TO PONDER

If Yoko was a patient in your practice and you knew her fairly well, how would you feel if she chose physician-assisted suicide to end her life?

TIP

Remember that understanding and accepting someone else's ethical stand does not mean you are compromising your own ethical principles.

2. *Veracity.* Veracity, or honesty and truthfulness, is the second universal ethical principle. Not many things are as personal or valued as one's own health, and patients expect honesty from health professionals. Rarely can withholding the truth be justified—even under the guise of sparing the patient bad news. Deceit and dishonesty can rarely be justified at any point in your professional career. Honesty builds trust, which is a critical component of the health professional–patient relationship. This principle includes keeping health information confidential, not disclosing information given to you in confidence by a patient (unless contraindicated by the law), keeping promises, and avoiding conflicts of interest. Honesty is also an essential component for establishing and maintaining good working relationships with your professional peers as well as all members of the health care team. It promotes respect and trust, and contributes to an overall positive work environment. You may not altogether like someone you work with for various reasons, but if you respect and trust them it will make your working relationship easier.

3. *Fidelity.* Also referred to as faithfulness, fidelity refers to meeting the reasonable expectations of others. In health care, it means carrying out obligations and duties to employers, patients, and peers. For example, your employer has the right to expect that you do your job well, honour commitments and contracts, and be respectful of him or her and the organization both at and away from your place of employment. It is important to realize that there may be situations where you feel you have a moral obligation to deviate from the principle of faithfulness because of conflicting moral principles. The situation could involve legal issues as well as moral principles.

4. *Beneficence and Nonmaleficence.* The principle of beneficence requires that we benefit others and act in the person's best interests. The principle holds that we must *do no harm*, remove harm when it is being inflicted, and when possible act to prevent harm from occurring. Nonmaleficence means that we must do no harm and cause no pain or suffering. These are two of the major principles promoting discord and division among health professionals and Canadians at large regarding the legalization of physician-assisted death. If a physician's goal is to preserve life and "do no harm," how can he or she act to help someone end her life?

5. *Justice.* The principle of justice in health care is complicated, encompassing many elements that are legal, moral, and ethical in nature. It concerns fair treatment for all patients and the equitable allocation of available resources (distributive justice). For example, a patient may be denied access to a treatment option because of long waits, or be harmed as a result of an incompetent act on the part of a health care professional.

This principal governs laws addressing patient confidentiality and protects health information. Every jurisdiction has laws overseeing privacy legislation. Under the Personal Information Protection and Electronic Documents Act, you are legally bound to follow legislation protecting the public's health information. The act provides guidelines for the collection, storage, use, and disclosure of all personal information. This legislation will be discussed in Chapter 13.

> ### ⟫⟫ POINTS TO PONDER
>
> If justice considers the fair distribution of treatments and resources, how would you define fairness? Should access to treatment be based on first come, first served? Age? Gender? Socioeconomic status?

Ethical Decision Making

When making ethical decisions, health professionals deal with a wide range of facts, concepts, contexts, principles, and people. Ideally, decision making is organized, includes all affected parties, and considers all the facts and the feelings of people involved. It results in action (or inaction) that brings about the best results for the greatest number of people. Decision making typically follows these five sequential steps:

1. *Identify the problem.* First, determine whether there is a problem. Ethical problems can start off as something small, like an uncomfortable feeling, or they can be significant and easily identified.

2. *Gather information.* Next, gather relevant information from all available resources. Consider who is involved, what principles are involved, and the context of the situation.

3. *Determine the ethical approach.* Examine the possible solutions by using the most reasonable approach. In the process, ask yourself what benefit or harm each course of action will produce for each person involved. Consider the moral rights of those involved. Think about what course of action ensures equal treatment for everyone unless there is a justifiable reason not to do so.

4. *Make a decision.* Explore all practical alternatives before you finalize your decision. Even an action that seems ridiculous might have some valuable ideas hidden in it. You may decide on a blend of alternatives as the best solution.

5. *Take action.* Depending on the situation, you may find it beneficial to analyze the results of your action, and modify your actions if necessary.

Practising your profession in an ethically responsible manner, remaining objective, applying the five universal principles, and making informed decisions are important components of professional and personal success. Rarely will you have to make independent ethical decisions involving a patient; however, you may be asked for input by other members of your health care team when ethical situations arise. If this happens, stay calm, stay focused, and keep an open mind. Careless decisions are made in a hurry; adequate decisions are made with some thought; good decisions are made by applying ethical principles.

L05 DUTIES AND RESPONSIBILITIES

Although the administrative health professional's primary role is administrative, in many offices duties and responsibilities are a blend of clinical and administrative functions. Sometimes there is a fine line between these functions, and sometimes they overlap. In the health office, you may be the providers' main source of support. In the words of one physician: "My staff run the practice. I could not function without them. They keep me organized and the office organized. The patients depend on them too." In a solo dental or medical practice, the office professional may run the office alone, handling clinical as well as administrative responsibilities. In clinics and larger practices, the duties will likely be divided. In some occupational settings, you may have the opportunity to select duties or rotate through different administrative areas, such as reception/booking appointments, filing, communication/telephone, showing patients to examination rooms, or obtaining brief histories. The more common duties and responsibilities are listed subsequently. Specific elements of some of these duties and responsibilities are discussed in appropriate chapters.

Administrative Responsibilities

- Greeting patients
- Managing incoming and outgoing telephone calls
- Managing other forms of communication, such as fax and email
- Scheduling and confirming appointments
- Maintaining the appointment book in an organized and confidential manner
- Reviewing and validating all health cards
- Coordinating consultations, lab procedures, diagnostic tests, and operating room bookings
- Following referral procedures
- Triaging patients
- Entering data
- Reviewing incoming lab results; flagging abnormal results for the physician's attention
- Screening and processing office correspondence
- Initiating and maintaining patient health records in electronic or paper format
- Billing the provincial or territorial system
- Following dental insurance billing procedures
- Keeping oneself informed of all changes in the billing process and maintaining currency
- Maintaining confidentiality
- Maintaining accounting and bookkeeping procedures unique to the office setting (may range from payroll to simple management of petty cash)
- Organizing business trips/meetings for the physician
- Acting as a liaison between the physician and other health care professionals
- Arranging hospital admissions; looking after billing issues related to hospitalized patients

- Managing the physician's schedule (on-call time, time at the ER or walk-in or urgent care clinic, meetings, speaking engagements)
- Speaking with drug reps; arranging meetings with the physician; receiving and signing for pharmacy samples
- Transcribing and editing documents, including those created from voice recognition software
- Preloading charts (includes converting paper-based charts to electronic format and managing electronic medical and health records [EMR and EHR])
- Ordering supplies; maintaining inventory
- Managing capital expenditures
- Maintaining office equipment
- Arranging office cleaning
- Keeping the office/reception area neat and appropriately stocked with reading material
- Setting up examination rooms
- Completing components of insurance and claims forms
- Maintaining office security
- Ensuring the phone message is appropriate and current, or informing the answering service of schedule changes
- Updating the office procedure manual
- Managing staff

Clinical Responsibilities

Administrative health professionals are not trained or expected to perform clinical procedures or any activities within the domain of the nurse or other regulated professionals. Certain activities are regulated and may be performed only by health professionals qualified to do so. Many of these activities are considered controlled acts. For example, prescribing a medication is traditionally within the scope or practice of a physician, nurse practitioner, midwife, or—in some jurisdictions—a pharmacist. Other activities, such as taking vital signs, are not considered controlled acts and may be carried out by anyone trained to do so. Unregulated personnel may perform other procedures in a medical or dental office if the physician or dentist takes responsibility for the personnel's actions (these are known as *delegated acts*).

POINTS TO PONDER

An incident in 2015 involved a health administrator who administered glue to a cut on a toddler's eye while the physician tried to hold the child still—resulting in the child's eye being glued shut. Do you think the health administrator was working within his scope of practice? If asked by the physician to perform this procedure, what would you do?

Administrative health professionals may sometimes carry out the following duties:

- Interviewing patients to complete insurance forms, filling in history forms for new patients, or updating charts
- Escorting the patient into the examination room and taking a brief statement regarding the reason for the visit

- Entering history of the present illness onto the EHR
- Preparing the examination room between patients
- Sanitizing and disinfecting instruments
- Taking weight and vital signs
- Testing urine with a dipstick
- Testing blood sugar
- Preparing infants for well-baby examinations (weighing and measuring length and head circumference)
- Preparing patients for examinations (giving them a gown or having them disrobe appropriately)
- Assisting, as required, with examinations (e.g., being present for a Pap smear or pelvic examination)[1]
- Supporting nervous patients during examinations
- Educating patients
- Explaining tests and procedures to patients or directing them to the appropriate resource
- Ensuring that patients who have had allergy shots remain in the office for approximately 20 minutes in case they develop a serious reaction
- Giving nonurgent, nondiagnostic telephone advice, as directed by the physician

L06 ENTERING THE WORKPLACE

The Workplace Environment

The size, layout, and functionality of health offices differ. Some are designed for a health care team, such as a primary care group, and may include a range of health professionals, usually including several physicians, a nurse practitioner, and perhaps a podiatrist, physiotherapist, and dietician. Other physicians, especially specialists, tend to have smaller offices accommodating one or two doctors. All will have a reception area designed to suit the size of the number of health professionals using the space. Larger offices will likely have several administrative staff members with the tools they need strategically located in the office area (telephones, fax machine, computers). Ideally the office administration area itself will be separate from the waiting/reception area, usually with glass partitions that allow patients to see you and facilitate patient registration. It is important that the area is designed so that telephone conversations and exchanges between staff are not audible in the waiting area.

Even though most physicians' offices and clinics are highly computerized and use EMRs, a large number maintain some paper charts. If present, these charts are usually readily accessible to the administrative staff. Many offices will have basic, relevant, and current information on EMRs, with older information remaining in the patient's paper chart.

If you work in a hospital, you will primarily sit at the nurses' station, with a computer, fax machine, and telephones as your main tools.

Most health offices are open from 9:00 a.m. to 5:00 p.m., but some clinics and offices have evening and weekend hours. A number of physicians only work four-and-a-half

---

[1]Although there is no legal requirement to do so, many physicians request a female staff member to be present during examinations involving vaginal contact. Some patients feel more comfortable with another person present, and having a witness protects both the patient and the physician if accusations of improper conduct arise.

days per week, taking a half day off or using that time to make house calls and catch up on other responsibilities. There is a growing trend for family doctors to divide their time between seeing patients in their office and working in other areas (most of which require special training), such as the ER, a specialty clinic, or doing anesthesia. In such situations two or more doctors may fill in, seeing patients while one is out of the office. Even if a physician is out of the office and no patients are scheduled, their office will likely remain open. During these times you likewise have time to catch up on administrative duties. If you are working for a group of doctors (e.g., in a primary care setting such as a family health team [FHT]), you may be assigned other responsibilities. In group settings where there are multiple administrative staff members, you may be trained to assume a variety of responsibilities requiring you to move from one area to another. One problem that has occurred in such settings concerns staff requiring special accommodation for disabilities—for example, a special computer and desk/work area or a special chair. If rotating within the office is mandatory, such accommodations must be addressed. This would apply to any setting where administrative staff are required to move around.

The dental office usually operates five days a week and does not close for an afternoon. Dental offices and clinics may provide evening or weekend hours.

In a hospital patient-care unit, shifts may be 8 to 12 hours long. Twelve-hour shifts may be from 7:00 a.m. to 7:00 p.m. and 7:00 p.m. to 7:00 a.m. In some hospital departments, however, there is no clinical secretary on overnight duty; there may be a day shift from 7:00 a.m. to 7:00 p.m. and an evening shift from 4 p.m. until midnight, with a three-hour overlap. Most hospital positions require that you work your share of weekends. Departments such as day surgery and outpatient clinics may offer Monday–Friday daytime hours only.

Most health offices close for an hour for lunch. Coffee breaks may be integrated into your working day, especially if you are the only person in the office. In the hospital, the charge nurse, clinical manager, or team leader usually assigns coffee and lunch breaks, which are staggered to ensure that staff are always available. Some facilities start coffee breaks as early as 9:00 a.m. and lunches around 11:30 a.m. Lunch breaks are most often half an hour, and coffee breaks average 20 minutes. Supper breaks in the hospital start at approximately 4:30 p.m. and are finished by 6:00 p.m. (1800 hours—see Figure 1.2—for the 24-hour clock used in most hospitals). Often, your break will depend on how busy you are. Smaller hospitals may not have a cafeteria open during the evening and night shifts, although there may be a coffee bar available.

Job Prospects

Across Canada, employment in the medical environment is expected to grow at least as fast as other occupations over the next several years. Jobs will be created both by growth in health services industries and by retirement. Obviously, some regions offer more job opportunities than do others. Smaller communities can support only so

Dwayne Brown/Brownstock/Alamy Stock Photo

Figure 1.2 The 24-hour clock, used in most hospitals and other health care facilities

regulated profession a field legally restricted to practitioners with a specific professional qualification or provincial or territorial registration.

many individuals in any given occupation. Thus, chances are that not all graduates from programs in smaller communities will find suitable employment locally.

Health office administration is not a **regulated profession**, such as nursing, medicine, or respiratory therapy. There is no legal requirement that an office assistant or clinical secretary have any particular education or qualification. Nevertheless, education and skills are expected in an increasingly responsible job, and graduates of medical/health office administration programs will have the best employment opportunities.

Salaries and Benefits

What salary can you expect as a graduate once you do find a job? Salaries vary; though the pattern is not consistent, experience, location, setting, and the type of job and duties are factors. Typically, hospitals and similar facilities offer somewhat higher wages than do some health offices, but that gap is closing. With increased responsibilities in all sectors of administrative practice, the need for formal education is, in most cases, mandatory; thus, salaries have risen over the past three or four years.

The 2014 statistics state that the average hourly wage for a medical secretary was $24.75, with a corresponding average weekly salary of $875.00. This works out to an average annual salary of approximately $45 000. This may or may not include benefits, depending on what the employer offers. For individuals with more experience, the hourly wage can range between $25.00 and $30.00 per hour.

In the hospital setting, the hourly wage ranges between $23.77 to $28.91, depending on experience and the position held (in some jurisdictions unit clerks have various levels that affect salary—e.g., clerk 1 or clerk 11). The average annual basic salary begins at approximately $31 000 per year. In addition, hourly premiums may apply for evening, night, weekend, or holiday work. In most jurisdictions full-time unit clerks receive benefits as well as vacation time, and employers usually provide remuneration in lieu of benefits to part-time employees. Those employed in hospitals and other large facilities will likely belong to a union. Salaries and other regulations are thus dictated by the collective agreement related to that facility. Remuneration for unit clerks in nursing homes may be less than in hospitals where, for the most part, they belong to a union.

Physicians' offices do not usually offer benefits. However, if the physician works for a primary care reform group, benefits may be included. In some jurisdictions, primary health groups have a chief executive officer and separate board that, among other things, assumes responsibility for hiring administrative staff for their own needs (they may include such services as a central clinic, diabetic counselling, smoking cessation programs, diabetic clinics, and hypertension management) as well as for the physicians involved. Primary care groups typically offer competitive wages plus full benefits and paid holidays. Because wages and the inclusion of paid vacation and benefits vary across the country (among individual practitioners as well as groups and clinics), you should research the current wage and benefit packages offered by facilities in your area. A website listed at the end of this chapter includes a chart reflecting wages for medical secretaries in Canada.

Some industries, such as insurance, hire health office administration graduates to work in their health-related departments and will start a new graduate off at $32 000 to $35 000 a year with full benefits.

L07 L08 PROFESSIONAL GROWTH

Graduation from a health administration program is only the first step in your career. You will continue to grow through workplace experience, continuing education, membership in a professional association, and interaction with colleagues and other health professionals. Current and past employment and volunteer experiences, even if they seem unrelated, also help build general, transferable skills, such as reliability, organizational and communication skills, leadership ability, and teamwork. Workplace experience, if offered by your college program, will also consolidate your skills in a practical setting.

> **TIP**
>
> Check to see whether there is a professional association or an association chapter in the community in which you work. Despite the absence of a provincial/territorial organization, there may be independent chapters of a related association within your community.

Professional Associations

Membership in a professional organization or association has many benefits. Associations support the purpose, mission, and goals of the profession. They help members become involved in the profession; keep them abreast of trends and changes within the field; offer resources, learning materials, and continuing education; and promote cohesiveness and professional pride. Many of these organizations offer student memberships to students in their last year of a college administrative program.

Some professional associations offer a certification program for the membership, achieved by passing an examination or series of examinations. Unlike **licensure**, which is mandatory for regulated professions, certification is usually voluntary. However, the status and tangible proof of meeting standards of practice are assets when seeking employment.

licensure a legal document, obtained after passing written and clinical examinations, that is required for health care practitioners in regulated fields.

Associations may be provincial or territorial, national, or international. Some of the major organizations are profiled subsequently.

The Medical Office Assistants' Association (MOAA) of British Columbia
Founded in 1961, the MOAA of British Columbia is available to individuals working in physicians' offices, hospitals, and other health care facilities who are performing administrative or a blend of administrative and clinical duties. Benefits of membership are similar to those offered by other such organizations. Continuing education is cited as their main objective, with workshops and seminars available through local chapters. As with similar organizations, student membership is available and does offer a number of benefits, including networking within the province and across Canada. The website is provided at the end of this chapter and offers contact information for chapters throughout British Columbia.

The Association of Administrative Assistants
With chapters in Ontario, Alberta, and British Columbia, this organization offers membership to administrative assistants from a variety of professions. The association strives to develop members' skills, knowledge, and professional growth to enhance employment opportunities and establish the value of its certified professional designation of Qualified Administrative Assistant. More information can be obtained from the organization's website, which is listed at the end of this chapter.

International Association of Administrative Professionals (IAAP)
The IAAP is the world's largest association for administrative support staff, with more than 600 chapters and 28 000 members and affiliates worldwide. There are chapters across Canada from St. John's, Newfoundland, to Victoria, British Columbia. Founded in 1942 and headquartered in Kansas City, Missouri, IAAP provides up-to-date research on

office trends, cutting-edge publications, seminars and conferences, and resources to help administrative professionals enhance their skills and become more effective contributors to their employers. The association works to educate employers and the public about the value of administrative professionals and the advantages of an administrative career. Most chapters offer professional development and networking at monthly meetings, seminars, and conferences. IAAP administers two certification programs—the Certified Professional Secretary (CPS) rating and the Certified Administrative Professional (CAP) rating. Detailed information about these designations and how to contact the organization can be obtained from the website listed at the end of this chapter.

Canadian Dental Assistants Association (CDAA)   The CDAA is a voluntary Canadian association for dental administrative assistants. Dental assisting is a health care profession with all of the responsibilities that the title implies. The evolution of the profession is a reflection of the changing nature of dentistry, regulatory structures, new technologies, and Canadian society. In facing this change, the CDAA remains committed to its mission to provide the best possible programs and services to promote the professional growth and recognition of its members.

Membership opportunities for administrative assistants vary across the country. For example, in Ontario any dental business assistant can join the Ontario Dental Assistants Association (ODAA) and take the required coursework to become a CDR (Certified Dental Receptionist) or CDTC (Certified Dental Treatment Coordinator). If you have been approved for a postsecondary health administration program, the ODAA will allow direct writing of the CDR exam instead of having to take the required courses online. Information on contacting the CDAA and the ODAA can be obtained from the websites listed at the end of this chapter. The ODAA website's Links page provides links to the websites of other provincial dental assistant associations.

National Association of Health Unit Coordinators (NAHUC)   The NAHUC is a professional association for health unit coordinators. Its mission is to promote health-unit coordinating as a profession through education and certification. Any individual working as a hospital unit coordinator or unit clerk can apply for membership. Despite the term "National" in the title, the NAHUC claims to be more of an international organization. The NAHUC currently has members in British Columbia, Ontario, and Prince Edward Island. The NAHUC offers certification exams across the United States and Canada. They are in the process of reviewing this textbook for purposes of studying for this exam. More information can be obtained from the organization's website listed at the end of this chapter.

Workplace Experience

Almost any workplace experience is a valuable opportunity for learning, growth, and a contribution to your résumé. Students often underestimate the value of current and past employment experiences. For example, when asked what kind of a part-time job she had, Susan replied, "Nothing much. I work as a supervisor at McDonald's. I know it is not the related experience you are looking for." What Susan did not see was that she had developed a sense of accountability and responsibility as well as leadership and management skills that were transferable to any position. Many recruiters (or interviewers) ask candidates to describe an example of proven leadership. Susan would likely have several. These are transferable skills.

The more closely linked your work experience is to your future career, the more direct the benefits are in terms of specific skills. However, remember that any position will help you develop essential general attributes, such as communication and interpersonal skills and the ability to assume responsibility to handle multiple tasks and to work as a team member. Workplace experience also develops confidence and contributes to your personal development and maturity. Employment experience will make you aware of areas in which you may need to improve. For example, you may find that your organizational skills or your communication skills are lacking. Most employers will ask you about your weaknesses. If you say, "I don't know"—or even worse, "I don't think I have any"—the employer may think you lack insight. Rare is the person who has nothing to improve upon.

You can demonstrate self-awareness, honesty, and the desire for growth by acknowledging the areas in need of improvement in a positive manner. For example, "I have been working to improve my organizational skills and feel that they have improved significantly." Or, "I have sometimes found it difficult to maintain a conversation with a customer, particularly when I am busy, but I have learned some excellent strategies to help me with this." Or, "Computers have always been something that I have shied away from. However, I realize that computer literacy is essential in almost any position, so I have taken several courses, and I am feeling much more comfortable in the computerized environment than I did six months ago. I am looking forward to another course that starts next week," or, "Computer literacy is a huge part of my current college program, and I am doing well."

Experiences obtained during your time at college are also important contributions to your résumé. Involvement in student activities, becoming a peer tutor, assisting with college education days, leadership roles in group activities, excellent attendance, handing in assignments on time, and class participation are all attributes that you can include, if relevant.

Résumés

If you have not already done so, composing a résumé in your first semester is a good idea, especially if you are looking for a part-time job or a volunteer position. It will also give you something to add to as you progress through your program. Keep your résumé in a folder, and add course outlines, assignments you are proud of, and any special student activities or positions you hold, such as peer tutor, class representative on student council, or mentor to a first-year or international student. Update your résumé periodically so that it reflects newly developed skills and attributes.

A résumé must be complete, concise, and properly written. There are several common formats. You may benefit from expert assistance. Student Services in most colleges can provide advice and guidance, as can the websites at the end of this chapter.

Writing a Résumé A résumé is a summary of your current education, work experience, and relevant aspects of your community and personal life. It should be no more than one or two single-sided pages in length. When writing your résumé, use single spacing, 10- or 12-point font (Times New Roman or Arial), and print on 8.5 × 11 white or off-white paper. If you are a new graduate with little relevant experience, make your résumé one page. If you have considerable relevant experience, such as summer jobs, extracurricular leadership, and volunteer experiences, two pages are justified. Remember that résumés containing too much detail crammed into a small space are often discarded because they are untidy looking and difficult to read.

An effective résumé will grab an employer's attention within seconds and motivate him or her to read it all the way through. To achieve this, the résumé should be organized, clear, and concise and should address the skills and knowledge base the employer is looking for. Most employers scan a résumé quickly to determine if the candidate seems to meet the majority of requirements; if so, a more detailed look at the résumé, and perhaps an invitation to an interview, will follow. Remember, the résumé will get you an interview; the interview will get you the job.

As a new graduate, it is best to focus on the quality of skills you have gained in college and through workplace experience. Remember that your résumé should highlight the relevance of your skills and knowledge to the job to which you are applying. You can give more detail in the cover letter and at your interview. You can emphasize assignments that you have done during your program that demonstrate a specific skill. For example:

- Demonstrated skills with medical office scheduling and billing [and bring the assignment with you to the interview if you get one]
- Proven, accurate keyboarding skills (60 wpm)

There are numerous formats for constructing a résumé and many helpful books on the market to give you ideas, three of which are listed at the end of this chapter. Choose the headings, the content, and the layout that will showcase your skills and experience in a manner that will appeal to the employer. Each time you apply for a job, review your résumé to make sure the format and content are suitable for that particular job.

In the header, include your name, address, a contact telephone number (home and/ or cell), and an email address. Ensure that the phone number is current and that it has a voice mail option. Your email address should be professional looking. If possible, get an email address that uses your name and your server, or something suitably neutral, such as yourname@getmail.ca. If your contact information changes after you have sent your résumé, contact any employer who may still be considering your application.

Electronic Résumés   Electronic résumés are popular, particularly with larger organizations such as insurance companies and large medical centres. Many jobs found on Workopolis require you to send in an electronic résumé (often referred to as an e-résumé). It can be constructed in much the same way as a paper résumé. Some organizations scan résumés for key words. Use words from the job description in your résumé because these are likely the key words the computer has been programmed to look for.

TIP

Have someone review your résumé and cover letter—preferably a person familiar with the type of job you are seeking. If you are asked for a "working interview," dress neatly, be prompt, and research the facility. Anticipate what needs to be done, and ask if you can help—even if it differs from the role you are applying for (e.g., a veterinarian on a working interview saw the technicians were very busy and pitched in to assist them). Be cheerful, professional, and approachable. Often staff members are asked for input as to who should be hired (from the short list of candidates). A friendly, sunny demeanour and the willingness to pitch in could make a difference in who they choose.

Job Search

Approach your job search with an organized plan and with a goal in mind. Focus your search on employment opportunities in the area of health care that most interests you rather than randomly applying for every job posted. Use available resources. Most colleges offer job banks through Student Services (or an equivalent), and they are usually free of charge. Student Services will ask you to provide the department with a current résumé and a summary of the type of job you are looking for. Student Services will then automatically send your résumé to prospective employers. Familiarize yourself with your college's policies related to giving out résumés, and keep in touch with Student Services if they have your résumé on file. Provide them with a new résumé if you update it. The process may vary with different colleges.

> **TIP**
>
> Be aware that when submitting an electronic résumé you should pay attention to your formatting. At times the résumé does not upload in the intended format (e.g., a text-based résumé may not show formatting done in other programs). The more simple the format the better. A poorly formatted résumé can adversely affect the employer's impression of you, in addition to making it difficult to read. Following are two weblinks with helpful advice for formatting an e-résumé:
>
> "Your E-Résumé's File Format Aligns with Its Delivery Model": www.quintcareers.com/e-resume_format.html
>
> "How to Format Your Résumé for Online Submission": www.ehow.com/how_2209105_format-resume-applying-jobs-online.html

Any of the professional organizations previously outlined offer access to lists of employment opportunities. Most hospitals keep a current list of job opportunities posted on their websites. Jobs are also posted internally for employees to respond to. If someone wants to move from one area to another, he or she can apply. It may be that a hospital employee without the proper credentials will apply. What happens then depends on hospital policy and the union. If policies are such that the hospital has an obligation to train that person, he or she may get the job (e.g., someone from housekeeping applies for a unit clerk position on a medical unit). Insurance companies also post available positions on their company website, and they usually require that you submit your résumé electronically.

Online job sites, such as Indeed (a comprehensive Canadian job site), Kijiji, or Workopolis, can be useful search tools. You can often select the region you want to concentrate your job search in and the type of job you are seeking.

If you want to work for government—for example, Health Canada—you can access the careers section of the relevant website. Provincial and territorial websites—ministries or departments of health—also have links to current employment opportunities. If there are government offices in your region, visit them and submit a résumé. These include regional health authorities, public health centres, Community Care Access Centres (CCAC) or the equivalent, or provincial or territorial billing offices (most provinces and territories have regional resource offices). Your local employment office will likely have listings. Government departments at the federal, provincial or territorial, and municipal levels usually list their employment opportunities with public employment offices.

Networking and cold calling are other choices that may help you find a position. Many jobs are secured by personal recommendation and word of mouth, or because an employer has your résumé on hand and met you when you dropped it off. Employers save time and money when they do not have to advertise a position (this can be done in most non-unionized organizations). Network by telling people about your qualifications, your skills, and the type of employment you are looking for. Tell your family doctor, your dentist, a medical secretary if you know one, or a nurse at the hospital. If you have completed a work placement with your college program, keep your eyes open for opportunities within the organization or with similar organizations. Individuals who excel in their work placement are frequently hired within the organization. Even if offered a casual position to start, take it; casual positions often result in full-time hours. If you are competent and professional, chances are the employer will seek you out or request that you leave a résumé with them in case a position becomes available. One cannot underscore the importance of professionalism enough. Do not sink to the lowest common denominator to feel part of a group. Be neat, professionally dressed, well groomed, and professional in manner (be respectful of others, do not gossip even if others do, use proper English, be helpful, and know your role).

Cold calling involves making contact with people you have not met before, but who you think may have a job you're interested in. Don't underestimate the value of checking with your local employment agencies either. Agencies in your area are in the telephone book under *Employment*.

Finding a job takes time and effort. It can be discouraging if you do not get immediate results. Keep your résumé current and tailored to the job you are applying for. Be choosy but flexible. Accepting a job that is not exactly what you want may lead to something more suitable. For example, accepting a position as a switchboard operator in a hospital may lead to a position as a clinical secretary. Volunteering to help with filing at a doctor's office can also lead to employment. Stay positive and unrelenting in your search.

An **externship**, or job placement experience, is part of many college programs and provides you with an excellent opportunity for applying theory to practice, often in the workplace setting of your choice.

externship a cooperative or workplace experience or period of training for a student that is provided by the student's educational facility.

>>> **POINTS TO PONDER**

Employers often look at a prospective employee's Facebook page to find out more about the job applicant. Items posted even several years back, if negative or controversial, will leave a negative impression with the employer. As a result, he or she may reject the applicant. Is there anything on your Facebook page that you would worry about a potential employer viewing?

Volunteer Work

If you do not have a job or a co-op placement through your college, volunteering is another way to obtain a variety of experiences and develop transferable skills. Volunteers are both needed and welcomed in almost every area. Everyone admires and respects the commitment of individuals who volunteer their time to community organizations. Volunteering not only develops skills but is also a rewarding personal experience and contributes to the organization and the people it serves. Volunteer work illustrates a commitment to and concern for others, initiative, and selflessness—all character traits that can only enhance an individual personally and professionally. You will gain concrete experience to show employers, as well as character references for such things as punctuality, commitment, and initiative.

Before applying for a volunteer post, consider how much time you have to commit. Many volunteer positions require commitment to a certain number of hours on a regular schedule. If school does not leave enough time for you to hold down a regular position, you could volunteer for special functions such as food drives, especially during the holiday season.

Volunteer opportunities may be found in hospitals, nursing homes, community organizations such as Meals on Wheels, mental health organizations, the Canadian Cancer Society, the Red Cross, medical offices, or hospices. You will get the most direct benefit from volunteering in an area related to your career path. You gain relevant experience in that area, are exposed to the general duties and responsibilities of other health care professionals with whom you may be working, and augment what you are learning at college.

If you are interested in working in a patient-care unit in a particular hospital, for example, apply to be a volunteer in the clinical setting at that hospital. If you think you would like to work in the medical records department, ask if they could use some help with filing or other general duties. If you want to work in a doctor's office, contact one (perhaps one that you have been referred to) and ask if you can help out for a few hours a week. Suggest something that you feel prepared to handle, such as filing.

List volunteer experiences in your résumé, noting why you chose to volunteer, your specific experiences, how you managed any difficult situations, and what you gained from the experience.

Applying for most volunteer positions is much like applying for a job: It is often a formal process that may require a résumé, personal and educational references, an application form, an interview, and a police background check. This is because the organization has an obligation to its patients to ensure that anyone working with them is suitable, safe, knowledgeable, honest, and trustworthy. Usually, a large organization such as a hospital has a volunteer coordinator who serves as a contact with applicants. An applicant would typically have an interview, much like a job interview, that covers interests and experience. Once accepted, a second interview is common to discuss specific placement. Training may also be required before assuming volunteer duties.

Simulated Office Experience

Medical office simulations are integrated into medical office administration programs in many colleges. The simulations not only provide practical exposure to activities that might be encountered on the job in a medical office, but also reinforce many of the topics covered in a medical office procedures course. Some programs interface with an IT program that offers a variety of learning experiences (such as Choice Learning Inc., which is affiliated with this book). Simulations are a valuable learning tool and will provide you with a working knowledge related to areas such as scheduling patients and billing.

Cooperative Work Experience

Some college programs have a workplace experience component, which may either be integrated into the program or placed at the end just prior to graduation. A workplace experience component may also be called a *co-op* (cooperative experience), *practicum* (practical application of skills), *consolidation* (an experience wherein the student consolidates acquired skills and theory), or *externship* (getting experience outside the college environment). The workplace experience involves a contractual agreement among the employer, the student, and the college. The time frame varies with the length and structure of the program. The purpose of this experience is to provide the student with the chance to put theory into practice—to apply the skills learned in college to the workplace setting. The student is able to assume some job responsibilities while still under the guidance of a **preceptor** or someone the student can turn to for guidance and advice.

preceptor a mentor who guides and supervises a student throughout a workplace experience.

In most co-op programs students can seek placement in an area of interest, assuming suitable opportunities are available and the experience offered matches program requirements. Most facilities require the student to apply for the experience in the same manner as one would for a job. Students thus gain experience with résumés and interviews. If more than one student applies for the same opening, the selection should be based on suitability, just as in any job competition. Do not take it personally if you are not selected—and make sure to apply for more than one position. Some programs do not use an application process; instead, the employer asks the program coordinator or a placement officer to select the best-suited student. Usually, student requests are an important part of any decisions made.

Here are just a few things that a cooperative work experience offers:

- An opportunity to apply what you have learned in college to a practical setting
- General work experience
- Personal insight into your own abilities, strengths, and needs for improvement
- An opportunity to develop a level of professionalism and professional ethics

Expectations and Responsibilities　The employer has the right to expect that the student involved in the experience is qualified (at an entry level) and will abide by the workplace's rules. In health care settings, for example, where health office professionals frequently have access to confidential patient records, students may be required to sign a confidentiality statement.

The college and the student have the right to expect that the employer will provide an experience that reflects the objectives and expectations outlined by the initial agreement. On occasion, an employer will view the student as merely an extra set of hands, forgetting that the student is there to complete a set of learning outcomes. Students should discuss such problems with their preceptors or employers and, if they remain unresolved, with their faculty advisors.

Student Preparation　Before entering a workplace experience, you must be prepared and organized. To ensure you start off on the right foot, you should meet with the employer and/or preceptor before accepting a position to review your own and the employer's expectations and to determine the duties and responsibilities of the position. Review all relevant materials, such as evaluation criteria, with the appropriate people. Discuss the evaluation tool itself and how often evaluations will take place. Most health care facilities require a visible liaison between the facility and the faculty advisor for the duration of the student's experience. Find out what type of contact will occur and how often; if possible, set up appointments in advance. Review your responsibilities to the college to ensure that there are no mix-ups or misunderstandings. Some colleges will expect you to send your faculty advisor weekly summaries or to submit a final paper on completion of the workplace experience.

Evaluation　Evaluations should be done at regular intervals during any cooperative experience—every two weeks is not unreasonable—to provide continuous feedback and to allow the student and the employer to discuss any problems as they arise. Positive feedback is equally important. Knowing that you are doing a good job provides you with confidence and a sense of accomplishment. If you feel that you are not getting positive feedback, tactfully ask for it: "What do you see as my strengths during these past two weeks?" "In what areas do you feel I am best suited to this experience?" Self-evaluations are also helpful and should normally resemble the employer's evaluation. If the two are very different, the reasons need to be investigated.

Employment Expectations　Any workplace or co-op experience should be viewed as if it were an actual job. Approach the experience with a positive attitude and a sense of commitment. Act like a professional in dress, manner, and attitude. Be punctual, and notify the employer if you are ill. Seek out new learning opportunities, complete tasks in a timely manner, demonstrate organizational skills, and try to work harmoniously with other team members. Although it is important to work as independently as possible, it is equally important to recognize your limitations, seek help appropriately, and work within your designated **scope of practice**, as previously mentioned. Not adhering to this can cause difficulties for you, your preceptor or employer, and perhaps others.

scope of practice working within the parameters of duties and responsibilities outlined by one's professional training and skill set.

A cooperative experience may lead to employment, but there is no guarantee, and you should not enter into it with that expectation. A positive cooperative experience will, however, provide you with a good reference to add to your résumé.

Continuing Education

Graduating from an accredited program as a health care professional is only the first step in the educational process. Most community colleges and independent educational centres across Canada offer courses in a wide range of clinical and administrative skills. You may be required to take courses to keep abreast of technological and communication advances within the administrative setting or to prepare you to assume a wider range of responsibilities in your current job setting.

Many colleges articulate with universities, offering advanced standing to college graduates wanting to pursue a degree in health administration. Athabasca University in Alberta is one such facility. The trend to expect multiple skills will continue to grow. Continued learning is not only a professional responsibility—a duty to yourself as well as your employer—but an effective way to broaden your career opportunities. Employers value self-motivation and the combination of experience and additional educational qualifications. Keeping abreast of the latest administrative procedures and technological advances makes you a valuable asset to any health care setting.

⟫⟫ WHAT TO WATCH FOR

- More administrative positions for physicians are within a group environment; you may work for one or several providers and be scheduling for an interprofessional health care team. Your role working in an interdisciplinary group setting may require you to rotate responsibilities—for example, answering the phone, scheduling lab and diagnostic tests, and billing.

- There will continue to be changes in the electronic office environment, making it necessary to keep your computer skills current and to know the program(s) you work with thoroughly.

- Be prepared to work with an increasingly diverse population; do what you can to understand the sociocultural needs of the individuals and families in your work setting. New Canadians, such as those from Syria, will need all the support, understanding, and guidance you can provide.

- You will see changing roles and responsibilities for the unit clerk/clinical secretary in the hospital setting with the introduction of computerized order entry. Order entry tasks will diminish, and your responsibilities will shift more to communication and administrative responsibilities.

SUMMARY

1. Job titles vary with the workplace setting, from medical secretary or medical administrative assistant in health offices to unit clerk and clinical secretary in hospitals. Occupational settings are diverse, from health offices to hospitals. Finding a workplace that suits your interests and competencies is important. Hospitals offer a variety of choices, from medical records and palliative care to working in a fast-moving, demanding area such as intensive care or on a surgical floor.

2. Professionalism in dress, appearance, and manner at all times is absolutely essential. Often you will be the first point of contact for a patient, and first impressions matter. Desirable attributes include a friendly, approachable personality, a sense of responsibility, flexibility, good judgment, and the ability to remain calm in stressful situations. Skills, while they may overlap with attributes, are generally learned. Communication skills are essential, including clear enunciation, excellent spoken and written grammar, sensitive listening, and the ability to express empathy and to understand and convey information clearly. Keyboarding, computer literacy, and the ability to understand, use, and write medical terms are also indispensable.

3. As a health care professional, you enter into a social contract with the public, your employer, and your colleagues. Given the nature of health care, expectations are high that you will perform your professional responsibilities with honesty, integrity, impartiality, and competence. Following a code of ethics based on the universal principles of autonomy, truthfulness, faithfulness, beneficence, and justice will promote trust, respect, and ethical practice.

4. When making ethical decisions, health professionals deal with a wide range of facts, concepts, contexts, principles, and people. Ideally, decision making is organized, includes all affected parties, and considers all the facts and the feelings of people involved. Ethical decisions often involve emotions, beliefs, and moral conscience. Following established steps will assist you in making fair and objective decisions.

5. Typical administrative responsibilities include greeting patients, managing communications, scheduling appointments, triaging patients, and billing. Clinical responsibilities may include doing patient interviews, assisting with medical examinations, taking vital signs, and educating patients.

6. Searching for a job can be time consuming and discouraging. Having a résumé that is professional in both content and format is essential. Most colleges offer students help in preparing résumés and getting prepared for job interviews. If you are applying online, follow the instructions carefully, and have someone review your résumé before you send it.

7. All work experience is valuable in developing transferable skills. If your program has a work placement component, treat it as though it is a job for which you have been hired. Be aware of your responsibilities as well as the obligations your workplace employer has to you. Generally, you are there to learn, not replace staff. Ask questions, be prepared, dress professionally, and follow policies and protocol. This experience could result in a job or an outstanding reference for a future job.

8. Membership in a professional organization offers a wealth of benefits, including opportunities for ongoing education, links to employment opportunities, and networking with other members of the profession.

KEY TERMS

administrative health
    professional (AHP) 3
allied health care 7
alternative health care
    (complementary health
    care) 8
attribute 10
autonomy 17
clinic 6
code of ethics 17

computerized physician order
    entry (CPOE) 3
core competency 15
duty 17
ethics 17
externship 30
licensure 25
medical assistant 6
medical office assistant 6
morals 17

patient 4
preceptor 31
regulated profession 24
right 17
scope of practice 33
triage 13
values 17
ward clerk 5

REVIEW QUESTIONS

1. Explain the controversy regarding the use of the term *patient* or *client* with regard to an individual seeking health care.

2. Differentiate between attributes and skills. Identify and discuss three attributes and three skills that are important in health office administration.

3. Define professionalism and discuss what it means for the health care professional.

4. What is meant by the term *triage*? How does effective triage relate to good judgment?

5. What are the main benefits of remaining calm in an emergency?

6. State the main advantages of belonging to a professional organization.

7. What is the purpose of a medical office simulation component, an externship, or a cooperative placement experience?

8. Identify the recommended font, spacing, and size and colour of paper when writing a résumé.

9. What is the advantage of networking with respect to a job search?

10. Compare and contrast the responsibilities and expectations of the student and the employer during a co-op or workplace experience.

11. What does working within your scope of practice mean?

12. List the benefits of ongoing education for the administrative health professional.

APPLICATION EXERCISES

1. Review the list of possible employment opportunities for the administrative health professional. Add any others you can think of or that are available in your community. Select two or three that interest you. Either individually or in a small group, list the duties and responsibilities you think would apply to each. Over the next week, interview individuals who work in these or similar settings, or research the jobs on the internet or at the library. Add any new information to your original list. Share your findings with the class.

2. Identify volunteer opportunities available in your community in the following settings (or in settings in which you would like to work). For each, describe the types of volunteer placements you could seek. Research the application process or other details regarding how you could become a volunteer in one of these settings.

   a. A pediatrician's office

   b. A medical records department

   c. An active patient-care unit in a hospital

3. Read the following scenario:
   Irum works in a busy medical office. A colleague, Molly, makes life miserable for her and the other staff members. She is uncommunicative, abrasive, and abrupt. She works in isolation, does not pass on messages, and refuses to work collaboratively. Information often is not passed on, appointments are mixed up, reports are not read or passed on to the doctor, and patients blame everyone in the office. What steps could you take to deal with this issue?

4. Construct a résumé suitable for applying for a part-time job, an externship, or a volunteer position. Ask the resource people available at your college to critique your résumé and suggest improvements. Keep this résumé in a file folder. Add all of your course outlines (learning outcomes) to this folder along with assignments that you are proud of.

Using tips from the websites provided at the end of this chapter, format your résumé to suit an electronic format. Use the internet to research résumé construction.

5. The following exercise is designed to help you identify the attributes you can bring to a job. This will help you set goals, present your strengths in a job interview, and develop a plan to build new strengths.

   a. In small groups or as a class, discuss each professional quality identified in this chapter as important for administrative health professionals. Add others that you feel are relevant. Analyze each quality, and list specific examples/ situations where you feel that quality would be an asset.

   b. From the preceding list, select some personal qualities that you think you possess. Under each quality, write a brief summary of ways in which you demonstrate that quality, including examples. Consider achievements you are proud of, in school, volunteer work, family life, or hobbies. What personal qualities, strengths, and motivators were instrumental in helping you make these achievements? Now ask a classmate or friend to select from the list qualities that he or she thinks you possess. How do the two descriptions differ? Can you explain these differences? Do you feel you are looking at yourself realistically? Do you come across differently to others from the way you see yourself?

   c. Compare your list and your friend's list with the list of qualities from part (a). Are there qualities you need to improve? Prepare a list of strategies for doing so.

   d. Identify three people you admire, whether they are people you know personally or public figures. Why do you admire these people? List the qualities you admire in them. Are they qualities you feel you have or ones you would like to develop?

e. Design the perfect job for yourself, specifying setting, employer, and responsibilities. What qualities do you think you would require for this job? How closely do they match the qualities you identified in part (b)? If you chose a fast-paced, hectic emergency department, do you feel that you work well under pressure? Do you have excellent critical thinking skills? If you chose an area such as medical transcription, do you pay attention to detail? Are there any areas where you think you need improvement? Make developing these a personal goal. You may choose a dental office—why? What aspects of the dental office environment do you think would better suit your skills and attributes compared with a doctor's office?

6. Using the ethical principles listed in this chapter as a foundation, develop a 10-point code of ethics for your profession. Work in groups of four or five. Discuss the rationale for each point. Have someone in your group record your final list. Identify a leader in your group to display your code of ethics, and as a class compare and discuss each list. Form a code of ethics for health office professionals by combining the best points from each group.

7. Independently or with a partner, conduct internet research for a recent story involving one of the five ethical principles discussed in this chapter, for example, the principle of autonomy and the patient's right to end his or her own life, which was made legal in Canada in 2016.

    a. Discuss the significant principles you feel are involved in the case you chose.

    b. What, if any, legal barriers exist? Consider the conflict between moral principles and the law.

    c. Describe what you would do in a similar situation, outlining your personal feelings and rationale. Use the steps of problem solving to reach your conclusion.

BOOKS ABOUT RÉSUMÉ WRITING

Kennedy, Joyce L. *Résumés for Dummies*. Hoboken, NJ: John Wiley & Sons, 2006.

Whitcom, Susan Britton. *Résumé Magic: Trade Secrets of a Professional Résumé Writer*. Indianapolis: JIST Works, 2006.

Brown, Lola M. *Résumé Writing Made Easy*. Upper Saddle River, NJ: Pearson Education, 2006.

WEBSITES OF INTEREST

Job Searching

http://jobsearch.about.com/od/findajob

Health Careers Interaction

www.healthcareersinteraction.com

This is a job search website for health professionals. Click on "Job Search and Career Planning" in the navigation bar.

Public Service Commission of Canada (employment opportunities)

www.psc-cfp.gc.ca/index-eng.htm

Canada Jobs

www.canadajobs.com/articles/category.cfm?Category=Job%20Search

Volunteer Canada

www.volunteer.ca

This site gives general information, lists special events, and allows you to register as a potential volunteer and browse a database of organizations.

Résumé Writing

http://jobstar.org/tools/resume/index.cfm

Medical Jobs Canada

www.jobcanada.org/medical.html

TELUS Health

https://telus.taleo.net/careersection/10000/jobsearch.ftl?lang=en&jobfield=160130090

QHR Technologies

www.qhrtechnologies.com/company/careers

eHealth Ontario

www.ehealthontario.on.ca/en/careers

OntarioMD

www.ontariomd.ca/portal/server.pt/community/work_with_us/733

Eluta.ca (Canada wide job search by province and job category)

www.eluta.ca/search?q=medical+secretary&l=&qc=

PROFESSIONAL ASSOCIATIONS

International Association of Administrative Professionals
www.iaap-hq.org

Association of Administrative Assistants
www.aaa.ca

Medical Office Assistants' Association of British Columbia
www.moaabc.ca

National Association of Health Unit Coordinators
www.nahuc.org/

Medical Group Management Association of Canada
http://mgmac.org/2013

Alberta Association of Clinic Managers
http://aacm.ca

Canadian Dental Assistants Association
www.cdaa.ca

Ontario Dental Assistants Association
www.odaa.org

Medical Secretary Salary Canada
www.livingin-canada.com/salaries-for-medical-secretaries-canada.html

Appendix 1A
Sample Résumé

JINATO LIAN

234 Anywhere Street ♦ Vancouver, BC V4Z W4T ♦ (604) 433-4444
♦ ljinato@donet.ca

KEY QUALIFICATIONS

- Detail oriented
- Excellent communic ation skills
- Proficient in MS Word, Meditec, and Visual Practice
- Demonstrated ability in order entry
- Proven knowledge base in terminology
- Medical Office Assistants of BC member
- Proficient with medical transcription and document editing.

RELATED SKILLS
ADMINISTRATIVE AND ORGANIZATIONAL

- Demonstrated proficiency with order entry
- Ability to prioritize and schedule laboratory and diagnostic tests
- Error-free dicta typing with a keyboarding speed of 55 wpm
- Proven ability to edit documents—hard copy and computer generated from voice recognition software
- Experience in organizing nursing schedules and finding replacements for ill staff members
- Solid knowledge of medical terminology, anatomy and physiology, pharmacology, laboratory and diagnostic tests
- Experience using various medical databases and managing electronic health records
- Familiar with ICD 10 coding strategies

COMMUNICATION AND INTERPERSONAL

- Ability to interact professionally and effectively with patients and patients' family members
- Highly ethical; professional in dress and manner
- Knowledge of privacy legislation and my related responsibilities
- Ambitious, seek new learning opportunities
- Work well independently and as a team member
- Work within my scope of practice, seek assistance when needed
- Reliable, honest, and trustworthy

EDUCATION

Health Office Administration Program, 2008–present, Douglas College,
New Westminster, BC General Arts and Science, 2002–2004, University of Waterloo,
Waterloo, ON

EMPLOYMENT HISTORY

Customer Service Representative, Maben Marketing, Calgary, AB, 2000–2002
Receptionist, Ribera Chiropractic, Saskatoon, SK, 2002–2004

VOLUNTEER EXPERIENCE

New Westminster Memorial Hospital, pediatric unit, 2002–present

Part II
Health in Context

Part II will give you the background that will serve as a common thread throughout the rest of the textbook. It discusses health and illness from the perspective of the individual in Canada's multicultural society. It then introduces you to Canada's health care system. Chapter 2 discusses health, health beliefs, and current concepts of health and illness, using the health–illness continuum. It explains how altered health and changes in role function affect patients and their families. You will learn how to respond constructively to patients and their families in sickness and in health and how to establish a trusting and supportive relationship with them. Chapter 3 builds on what you have learned in Chapter 2, with the introduction of cultural variation. Cultural barriers to health care are discussed, as well as the importance of accepting and understanding people from other cultures. This chapter will provide you with guidelines for effective cross-cultural communication, including using an interpreter. Chapter 4 will provide you with an overview of the structure and function of health care in Canada, including the principles and conditions of the Canada Health Act and primary care reform initiatives.

Chapter 2   Health and the Individual

Chapter 3   Culture and Health

Chapter 4   The Canadian Health Care System

Chapter 2
Health and the Individual

Tyler Olson/Shutterstock

LEARNING OBJECTIVES

On completing this chapter, you will be able to:

1. Explain the relationship between health beliefs and health behaviour.

2. Discuss the concepts of health and wellness.

3. Summarize the current health concerns of Canadians.

4. Describe the health–illness continuum.

5. Explain the typical responses to the stages of illness.

6. Discuss the effects of sick role behaviour on the patient and family members and the related implications for the health office administrator.

7. Discuss the effects of hospitalization.

Altered health has subtle and profound effects on a person and the person's family, friends, and social and work-related contacts. This chapter is designed to help you understand and recognize the behaviour patterns that altered health generates in those who are affected both directly and indirectly. Understanding why your patients act as they do can help you communicate more effectively and offer stronger support to them. If this chapter is not included in your curriculum, you will find it valuable supplemental reading to Chapter 8 on communication.

Behaviour is defined as a person's discernible responses and actions. It includes actions and reactions to people, situations, and emotions. Most people's behaviour is fairly consistent throughout their daily lives. Behaviour, however, changes in response to various stimuli. When upset, stressed, or angry, a person may react in an uncharacteristic manner. A stressful day at work can cause someone who is normally easygoing and friendly to become cross and snippy. Under excessive stress, a normally competent, organized person may become unable to focus or to function efficiently. Over time, most of us get to know how we respond to various stimuli. We develop coping strategies to modify and control ineffective behaviour or we simply avoid unpleasant or stressful situations.

behaviour a person's discernible responses and actions.

Illness is a stressor for most people. Illness affects people emotionally as well as physically, changing their behaviour patterns. An ill person may feel vulnerable, fearful, uncertain, and worried about the stress the illness is placing on others. The person may respond by becoming passive and dependent, withdrawn and uncommunicative, or short-tempered, outwardly angry, and critical.

Illness affects the behaviour of not only the ill person but also those close to him or her. Others' responses depend on a number of factors, including their relationship to the ill person (e.g., wife, husband, parent, friend), the nature of the illness, the treatment plan, the prognosis and recovery time, and the person's professional, social, and family roles.

Most of us value support and understanding in times of illness, especially from those who know us and understand how to offer reassurance. You cannot expect to know patients well enough to know how they respond under stress or how to support them as individuals. It is important, however, to have a general understanding of how people react and to know some helpful response patterns. You will often be the first point of contact for patients when they seek medical assistance. In the face of prolonged illness or investigations, you may have ongoing contact with the patient and the patient's family. When they call the office for information or to make appointments, or call the hospital for updates, a supportive and empathetic response will do much to comfort them. Responding effectively to patients and their families and offering empathy and appropriate support will help them feel valued and cared for and will contribute to their well-being and sense of security. It makes the experience of illness less stressful.

LO1 HEALTH BELIEFS

Health beliefs are things a person believes to be true about health, illness, prevention, treatment, and cure. A person's health beliefs are influenced by many factors, including culture and life experiences. Among health beliefs are people's understanding of their own susceptibility to illness and the effect of lifestyle on disease prevention and health promotion—for example, their estimate of self-imposed risks, such as smoking; a person may not believe that smoking causes lung cancer. Even those people who do may convince themselves that they are immune or that it will not happen to them: "I won't die of lung cancer. Grandpa Smith smoked two packs a day and lived to be 90." Even if people believe they may be susceptible to health problems, they may believe the benefits outweigh the risks (e.g., they enjoy smoking so much that they will take a chance— "Everyone dies of something").

One factor is something called *locus of control*: people's beliefs about whether their lives are shaped primarily by their own actions or by external forces. People with an internal locus of control believe they are responsible for what happens to them. People with an external locus of control believe they are victims or beneficiaries of luck, fate, or other people. A person with an internal locus of control is more likely to take responsibility for his or her own health: "I need to eat well and avoid smoking to maintain my health." Someone with an external locus of control tends to discount the effects of his or her own behaviour: "So I smoke. It's the only enjoyment I have. If I am going to get lung cancer, I will get it anyway. I might as well enjoy myself while I can." As this comment shows, beliefs also reflect how a person weighs immediate enjoyment against long-term effects.

Health beliefs also include attitudes to treatment options. Some people, for example, believe that doctors are powerful and generally have the answers. Others have lower expectations of the health care system and may be suspicious of doctors' recommendations. ("Oh, that doctor, she just likes to put everybody on pills. She doesn't really know what's wrong with me.") People also hold beliefs about the relative effectiveness of conservative and holistic approaches to medicine. Some view alternative therapies as an adjunct to the medical model of treatment, some view all forms of alternative medicine as quackery, and still others believe that alternative modalities can cure or prevent all diseases (including cancer). Health beliefs also influence attitudes toward decisions on end-of-life issues, such as whether to use life support and how aggressively to pursue treatment in the face of a terminal illness.

Health beliefs influence perceptions of health and health behaviour. Health beliefs can determine whether people actively seek to maintain health, how often they seek medical care, what treatment options they choose, and how they respond to illness.

HEALTH BEHAVIOUR

Health behaviour includes all the things a person does to stay healthy, physically and psychologically. For example, some people watch their diets, take vitamin supplements, try to exercise regularly, and may even try to avoid second-hand smoke. They may consciously create an even balance between work and relaxation—including making time for quality family life. Other people do such things sporadically. Still others may ignore diet and exercise but carefully avoid exposure to sick people. An individual's health behaviour is determined by his or her health beliefs, personality, health experiences, culture, and ethnicity, as well as the nature of an illness and the degree of understanding and support the person receives when ill.

One aspect of health behaviour is *illness behaviour*, also called *sick role behaviour* (discussed in more detail later). Illness or sick role behaviour refers to people's activities and behaviours in response to illness. It includes those behaviours from the point of believing that an illness exists through to recovery or death.

Many people take good health for granted. They may never have experienced serious illness and have no idea how they would respond.

>>> **POINTS TO PONDER**

Recently, an Indigenous child (Makayla Sault, an 11-year-old Ojibwa girl) was diagnosed with leukemia. During the initial round of chemotherapy Makayla suffered severe side effects, prompting her to beg her mother to stop the treatments and try traditional Indigenous medicine instead. Makayla was given 72 percent chance of survival with continued aggressive treatment. Understanding the risks, Makayla and her family opted to terminate the chemotherapy in favour of pursuing traditional Indigenous medicine and other alternative treatments. It was their belief that this was the best course of action for treatment, given the circumstances. Do you think the provincial government should have intervened, forcing Makayla to continue with the chemotherapy, or are you of the opinion that honouring the family's health beliefs was the right thing to do?

L02 CONCEPTS OF HEALTH AND WELLNESS

Health

Health, according to one definition, is "a relative state in which one is able to function well physically, mentally, socially, and spiritually in order to express the full range of one's unique potentialities within the environment in which one is living."[1]

A more recent definition[2] of **health** goes further to include spirituality as having an impact on our health. It considers each person unique, with specific abilities and capabilities. The inclusion of the phrase "relative state" indicates that health is individualistic and not constant. What Bob may consider to be good health, Maria may not. Today, concepts of health vary from person to person, but most people include such things as quality of life, happiness, and spiritual and intellectual components.

health according to one definition, "a relative state in which one is able to function well physically, mentally, socially, and spiritually in order to express the full range of one's unique potentialities within the environment in which one is living."

Wellness

Wellness is another word frequently associated with health. Generally, **wellness** refers to a state of physical and emotional well-being, as well as the practices that promote and maintain this state. Wellness, like health, is often defined personally. Usually it includes physical health, but it also embraces lifestyle, enjoyment of life, and intangible things such as happiness, contentment, and an overall quality of life. Some people may consider that they have achieved wellness even though they are not physically healthy. For example, a person with a chronic disease or disability may accept her limitations and be emotionally well. The disability or illness is then integrated into the person's concept of wellness. A person with multiple sclerosis may accept the disease and consider himself healthy. If his health continues to deteriorate, he might no longer define himself as being well; if, however, he accepts the degenerative nature of the disease, his sense of wellness might remain constant.

wellness a state of physical and emotional well-being, broadly considered.

The concept of wellness includes five dimensions that combine to shape our lives. Each dimension plays a different but important role. Consider a machine with five components: Take out one part, and the machine still runs. Take out two or three parts, and the machine may still run, but not efficiently. Take out four parts, and the machine stops. In a holistic understanding of wellness, all components must be working properly for a person to be happy and healthy. If one or two components need "adjusting," the person can still function but may seek assistance. Patients may seek health care because of physical problems or problems related to stress, anxiety, and depression. Always remember that people have many dimensions. Try to look at the whole person and not just the illness. Seeing your patients as whole beings will help you understand the many levels on which they respond to their problems. Your understanding and tolerance will help you interact more effectively.

Wellness is thought of in five dimensions: physical, emotional, social, intellectual, and spiritual.

Physical   The physical dimension refers to the body's health and functioning. Promoting physical wellness requires us to make intelligent choices relating to diet, exercise, risk-taking behaviours, and lifestyle.

Emotional   Emotional wellness involves recognizing one's own strengths and weaknesses, being able to analyze and deal with problems, and recognizing when one needs help. Emotional wellness means a person can manage stress appropriately and adjust to

---

[1]World Health Organization, 1943.
[2]*Miller-Keene Encyclopedia and Dictionary of Medicine, Nursing and Allied Health*, 6th ed. (Philadelphia: WB Saunders, 1993).

change. In today's world, stress is a part of daily life for most people. Stress can immobilize a person. The ability to manage stress, conversely, promotes both physical and emotional wellness. A positive outlook on life reduces stress, tension, and the risk of developing depression. Part of this is self-acceptance, self-confidence, and an inner feeling of well-being. It involves knowing who you are, striving to achieve your personal goals, and believing in yourself.

The link between physical and emotional wellness works both ways. On the one hand, such emotions as anxiety contribute to diseases, such as rheumatoid arthritis, hypertension, and stomach ulcers, and aggravate many chronic illnesses. Depression and stress can cause a wide range of physical symptoms. On the other hand, physical illness can result in emotional distress. For example, a thyroid imbalance can cause low or fluctuating moods. Illness can be saddening or deeply frightening. Ill patients' emotional reactions may cause them to make decisions that are not well thought out or analyzed.

Social Relationships and interactions are an integral part of everyday life. Our ability to connect with others contributes to our adaptive functioning. Most people strongly value healthy relationships involving trust and intimacy. Moreover, relationships provide a matrix of support in times of need. Research shows that people with partners and strong social networks are more likely to be physically healthy, and individuals with chronic terminal diseases live longer if they have a supportive social network. One reason women live longer than men (although the gap is closing) is that women are more likely to seek support in times of illness and stress.

People working in health care must interact in a positive manner and establish a trusting bond with patients. Patients who feel cared for and who trust and are at ease with the health professionals they interact with are more likely to have a positive attitude toward their health care. This attitude increases compliance with treatment, reduces stress, and promotes recovery.

Intellectual The intellectual dimension of wellness involves our cognitive ability to determine what is right and good for us and what is not. It involves assessment and analysis of what goes on around us and allows us to make choices to improve and educate ourselves.

People with physical limitations may compensate by using their intellectual abilities. Similarly, people with intellectual limitations can be helped to develop and achieve intellectual wellness to the level they are able.

Spiritual For some people, spirituality means a belief in and dedication to a higher power. Others experience spirituality as a personal, interior quality, tied to emotions, values, morals, and an ethical philosophy that guides them in their daily lives. In either sense, spirituality can give our lives purpose, direction, meaning, and structure. For many, it provides a sense of inner peace and harmony, and gives hope and strength in the face of adversity.

The spiritual needs of ill people are all too frequently ignored, which can increase their stress and undermine their ability to cope. Many of us look for something higher to believe in and seek comfort from when we are ill. Patients with a strong sense of spirituality tend to respond more calmly, more philosophically, and more positively to their illness, treatment, and potential recovery.

L03 CURRENT HEALTH CONCERNS OF CANADIANS

Most Canadians today are concerned about at least some aspects of their health care or the health care system at large. Some of these concern are shared nationally, others are specific to a province or territory, and still others are problematic at a local/municipal level. At the heart of most of these concerns is the fear that our health care system as we know it is not sustainable—that is, the system, primarily because of increasing costs and demands, will be unable to continue to deliver comprehensive, effective, equitable health care in accordance with the principles and conditions of the Canada Health Act (discussed in Chapter 4). Below we outline some of the most significant concerns for Canadians.

The Aging Population   An aging population poses significant concerns for both younger and older Canadians. Can the system meet the needs of an aging population? Will there be enough money and resources for transitional and home care? Will there be funds and resources for palliative care? What will the state of long-term care facilities look like in 10 years? Will human health resources be adequately trained to look after older Canadians? Younger Canadians are wondering what kind of health care will be available for them as they age. According to Employment and Social Development Canada, by 2036 10.4 million Canadians will be 65 or over, and by 2051 one in four Canadians will be over the age of 65. Newfoundland and Labrador is expected to have the highest ratio of older Canadians.

The High Cost of Prescription Drugs   A large number of Canadians do not have private drug plans or benefits from their workplace, making the high cost of prescription drugs a problem for many (after the age of 65, a person's prescription drugs, for the most part, are covered by his or her provincial/territorial health plan). An Angus Reid poll conducted in August 2015 revealed that one-quarter of Canadians or someone they knew could not afford to buy the drugs prescribed to them. The same poll found that that 91 percent of Canadians support a national pharmacare program. Although the provinces and territories provide some coverage to vulnerable populations (e.g., low-income individuals, older adults), Canada has neither a universal pharmacare program nor a national catastrophic drug plan (all jurisdictions have some form of catastrophic coverage, but eligibility criteria varies greatly). Canada is the only country with a universal health plan without a national drug plan. Pharmaceuticals take up the largest portion of Canada's health care budget.

> ### ⟫⟫ POINTS TO PONDER
>
> *Pharmacare 2020: The Future of Drug Coverage in Canada* is a research-based report that supports establishing a universal drug plan for Canada that, overall, would cost the provinces and territories less than under the current patchwork systems in place across the country. Many Canadians must pay for prescribed medications—and sometimes the cost is crippling. What do you see as the benefits and burdens of a national pharmacare program?

Antibiotic-Resistant Bacteria   According to the Canadian Antimicrobial Resistance Surveillance System Report 2015, the rise of antibiotic-resistant organisms poses a serious threat to the health of Canadians. This is particularly so for vulnerable population groups (older Canadians, children, and those with chronic illnesses or immunosuppressed systems) and for those in health care facilities. These organisms have also spread into the community setting. These organisms frequently cause life-threatening illnesses with limited treatment options available. The rising need to use expensive, last-resort antibiotics also increases the likelihood that even they will be ineffective against these organism. A significant cause of antibiotic-resistant organisms is overuse and misuse of antibiotics. For example, patients will frequently demand antibiotics even when they are not required, and physicians will often comply. Unfortunately, the development of new antibiotics is decreasing.

The 2003 SARS (severe acute respiratory syndrome) crisis initially made the health care community more acutely aware of the need to practise strict infection-control measures. This was also evident during the 2015 Ebola outbreak in Sierra Leone, Guinea, and Liberia. Even with perceived up-to-date infection-control measures, some health care workers treating infected patients in the United States were infected, showing the vulnerability of protocols in place in major hospitals. Most facilities in Canada (and elsewhere) are constantly looking for ways to improve their infection-control measures with ongoing emphasis on containing such communicable diseases as those caused by MRSA (methicillin-resistant *staphylococcus aureus*), VRE (vancomycin-resistant *enterococci*), and *C. difficile* (*Clostridium difficile*), which are almost always found in hospitals, nursing homes, other long-term care facilities, and now in the community setting. *C. difficile* is the most common cause of hospital-acquired diarrhea in the developed world. After a brief decline, in recent years it has reappeared as a hypervirulent strain. The result is increased morbidity and mortality rates. It is usually transmitted through the fecal–oral route, and there has been evidence of airborne transmission. Washing hands with soap and water has proven more effective than alcohol-based solutions in preventing transmission of this organism (see Chapter 5 for more detail).

MRSA and VRE are pathogens that, in many cases, have become resistant to the most effective antibiotics used to treat them (methicillin and vancomycin, respectively). These organisms usually cause symptoms in people who have other diseases or weakened immune systems (e.g., older people, those in hospital). Antibiotic resistance has become a major public health threat in Canada. As for *C. difficile*, according to the Public Health Agency of Canada it is the leading cause of infectious diarrhea in our hospitals and long-term care facilities. See Chapter 5 for more details on infectious diseases.

> ### ⟫⟫ POINTS TO PONDER
>
> Paxil presents at the office with his 3-year-old son, Amon. Amon has an ear infection, for which Paxil demands an antibiotic. Current best practices recommend not to treat ear infections symptomatically and not to use antibiotics unless absolutely necessary. Most ear infections in children resolve within a few days, even if the cause is bacterial in nature. Paxil does not want the hassle of looking after an ill child and thinks an antibiotic will shorten the course of the infection. What would you do in a similar situation?

Mental Illness   According to the Canadian Mental Health Association, mental illness is the leading cause of disability in Canada, with 20 percent of the population affected directly. There is a need for improved care for Canadians suffering from all forms of mental illness. Among other conditions, post-traumatic stress disorder (PTSD) continues to be an important health concern. It has been more readily recognized (or perhaps acknowledged) since Canadian soldiers have been sent abroad for combat missions. Hundreds of soldiers suffer from PTSD and are coming forward seeking medical help and, where possible, applying for disability related to PTSD. More recently, PTSD has been identified as problematic in other professions as well, such as first responders (police officers, paramedics, doctors, nurses) as well as prison guards. The Canadian Mental Health Association now recognizes PTSD as a mental illness. More information about PTSD and related support is available on the Canadian Mental Health Association website.

Chronic Disease   Two-thirds of deaths in Canada annually are attributed to chronic disease. These are a major health threats, especially among older Canadians. Partly because of our aging population, the majority of patients seen in a general practice present with one or more chronic diseases. It takes more time for the physician to assess and treat these individuals. There may be little time left for the other important elements of patient care—support, reassurance, and encouragement.

Access to Care and Wait Times   Although there are still a significant number of Canadians without a family doctor, this situation has improved significantly over the past two or three years. However, provincial governments differ in their views of how many physicians are required, and Ontario has recently cut residency spaces and enrollment into medical schools.

For the most part, wait times have improved, but not in all areas and not in all jurisdictions. Furthermore, wait times change from year to year. Each jurisdiction has its own benchmark time frames for procedures such as hip and knee surgery, cataract and bypass surgery, radiation treatments, and CT scans. For example, in Nova Scotia in 2014, only 44 percent of individuals requiring knee surgery received it within the province's benchmark time frame of 26 weeks. In Ontario, 86 percent received their require knee replacement within the Ontario benchmark time frame of 26 weeks. For some procedures the wait times are longer; this is attributed to increased demand for the related procedure. Benchmark time frames for radiation therapy in all jurisdictions is above 95 percent (based on 2014 statistics). A website listed at the end of this chapter provides links to wait times across Canada.

Leading Causes of Mortality and Morbidity in Canada

According to Statistics Canada (2014), malignant neoplasms (cancer) remain the leading cause of death in Canada, followed by heart disease and cerebral vascular disease (stroke).

In 2015, the Canadian Cancer Society estimated that two in five Canadians would develop some form of cancer in their lifetime, and one in four of those would die from the disease. Just over half of new cancers diagnosed will include lung, breast, colorectal, and prostate cancer. Eighty-nine percent of Canadians who develop cancer are over the age of 50. Thyroid cancer has the highest five-year survival rate, and pancreatic cancer has the lowest.

The Canadian Heart and Stroke Foundation reports that, currently, one-quarter of all deaths in Canada result from cardiovascular disease (heart disease and stroke), and these diseases were the leading cause of hospitalization in Canada in 2015. Cancer (all types) is the leading cause of disability in Canada, and more prescription drugs are used to treat cancer than any other condition. Interestingly, any death from heart disease up to the age of 75 is considered a premature death.

Diabetes is a major concern and affects almost every body system, in particular the cardiovascular system and kidneys, as well as being the leading cause of blindness. The Canadian Diabetes Association (CDA) claims that "diabetes is one of the greatest public health and health system challenges of the 21st century." The CDA reports that, in 2015, in excess of 10 million Canadians live with diabetes or pre-diabetes, and the cost to the health care system is enormous. Childhood obesity is a growing problem in Canada, which predisposes children to diabetes.

Impact on Canadians

Health care remains among the top three major concerns of Canadians—just behind the economy and the environment; it has been over 10 years since health was at the top of the list of concerns. The problems facing our health care system are caused largely by financial constraints, the management of health care resources, limited access to modern medical technology, and long waiting lists to see specialists and have surgical procedures. The shortage of doctors and nurses, as previously mentioned, which was a major concern five to ten years ago, is less of an issue now—except perhaps in more rural regions and in the North.

The length of hospital stays for almost all hospitalizations has been drastically reduced, partly because of financing concerns but also because of improved surgical techniques, including microscopic surgery. For example, discharge from hospital after hip and knee surgery is now a few days, not weeks. An uncomplicated gallbladder removal using microscopic surgery can now be done on an outpatient basis.

Most primary care groups and community health services offer clinics to follow and treat people with hypertension or diabetes. With advances in technology and connectivity between providers and patients, individuals at home can monitor their own blood pressure and blood sugar and send the information to their provider online for evaluation. In addition, there is an emphasis on prevention, such as enhanced access to prenatal care and screening programs for breast cancer. Some provinces have introduced incentives for family doctors to closely follow patients to ensure that their patients (as appropriate) are up to date on immunizations, Pap smears, screening for colorectal cancer, and so on.

Community-based care (or home care) also plays a significant role in reducing hospital stays. Hospitals are anxious to discharge patients who do not belong in active care beds, and home care is one solution, especially when long-term care beds are difficult to find. All jurisdictions have provincially funded home care programs that offer post-surgical care for the patient as well as supportive care for medical problems. Service providers may be offered by for-profit or not-for-profit organizations. In addition to support for individuals discharged from hospitals, community-based care programs provide a wide range of services that enable individuals to remain at home and out of long-term care facilities. Barriers to home care services include cost overruns and a shortage of human health resources (limiting a person to fewer hours than he or she may need). In most communities, however, if care hours paid for by the provincial/territorial plan are insufficient, a person can purchase more hours of care. But affordability is often an obstacle (as well as human health resources). A Statistics Canada report, *Canadians with Unmet Home Care Needs* (2014), found that nearly half a million Canadians requiring home care services went without. When community support is inadequate or even nonexistent, caring for an ill person often falls upon family members.

In the average Canadian family, both parents are working, making childcare a challenge. When middle-aged adults must take on the responsibility of caring for aging parents as well, it takes a toll on the family. Illness threatens not only an individual but also the economic and structural well-being of the family unit. Responsibilities of each family member change. If a child becomes ill, the parents—especially the mother—are forced to spend more time on care, which often disrupts their working lives and the lives of other children. Siblings may have to take on extra responsibilities or give up certain activities. A parent becoming ill can be even more disruptive and disturbing. It may mean a substantial loss of income—sometimes even a loss of two incomes if one spouse must care for the other. Again, children may have to take on extra responsibilities or may find themselves suddenly in new childcare arrangements. Children may also find it distressing to see a parent, who is supposed to be in charge, being incapacitated or dependent.

Most jurisdictions have developed minimum standards for family-care leave rights. As well, most jurisdictions have short-term leave programs allowing Canadians to care for health-compromised family members.

| Optimal Health | Good Health | Compensation | Poor Health | Serious Health | Premature Death/Death |

Probable direction of movement   Probable direction of movement

Figure 2.1 The health–illness continuum, with optimal health at one end and death at the other

L04 THE HEALTH–ILLNESS CONTINUUM

A continuum is a scale on which something can be measured. A continuum to measure health illustrates how a person's health status is constantly changing. Poor health moves a person toward death at one end, while optimal health is at the other end. An area in the centre is called *compensation*—most of us move between optimal health and compensation. Where a person places him or herself on the continuum is highly personal. Someone with a chronic illness or debilitating injury might still consider herself to be in good health, while another would place himself in compensation, perhaps closer to poor health. One's outlook and acceptance of one's health state (even death) has a great deal to do with where one places oneself on the continuum. (The continuum itself is simply a measurement tool.)

There are various health–illness continuum models, each with somewhat different interpretations and evaluation criteria. Figure 2.1 illustrates the continuum as a straight line, with optimal health and good health on the left, compensation near the centre, and poor health and eventually death on the right.

Optimal or good health, to the left on this continuum, is defined as the height of physical, emotional, spiritual, and intellectual health. Compensation is an area in the middle of the continuum, representing a person who may be experiencing altered health but is able to cope independently. People experiencing serious health problems (actual or perceived) usually move to the right end of the continuum. It depends, of course, on the person's response to a serious illness and how he or she adapts.

Death is viewed by some theorists as a natural part of the life cycle and therefore adaptive when it occurs in an older person, especially when the person accepts death. The death of a younger person, referred to as *premature death*, is not considered adaptive. In either case, a dying person who has accepted his or her plight would usually be placed at the extreme right end of the continuum.

L05 THE STAGES OF ILLNESS RESPONSE

Everyone responds differently to illness. The stages of illness response describe the process individuals go through when they face a potential or actual health problem.

Our state of health affects every aspect of our lives: how we feel, our level of energy, what we do and how we do it, our judgment and perception of people and things around us, and our interactions with others. A patient's response will affect how he or she adapts to an illness, choice of treatment, and ease of recovery. The patient's response also affects everyone close to him or her. Response to altered health depends not only on the nature and severity of the illness, but also on the patient's culture, social and family influences, beliefs, perceptions of health and illness, and personality. Responses vary from mild to extreme, and from adaptive to ineffective. An understanding of these stages will help you understand, anticipate, and deal with your patients' reactions. Although individual responses will vary in sequence and intensity, typical stages include the following:

1. Preliminary phase: the appearance of clinical signs
2. Acknowledgement phase: sustained clinical signs

3. Action phase: seeking medical intervention

4. Transitional phase: diagnosis and treatment

5. Resolution phase: recovery/rehabilitation or death

1. Preliminary Phase

Physical signs, although they may be vague, are the first indication that something is wrong. Many people consciously note the signs but attach no particular significance to them and carry on with their activities. Others may immediately begin to analyze the sign or behaviour and be concerned that it signals a change in their health pattern. Regardless of the response, at this stage most people keep the information to themselves.

If the clinical signs persist, the individual will give them increasing attention. Some people attempt to correlate the signs to an existing or previous condition or speculate on a cause, usually perceived as something that is not serious. They may or may not mention these signs in an offhand manner to someone else but are still thinking, "It's probably nothing." Others will think of a list of possibly serious conditions and may research possible causes. They may be thinking, "This could be serious. I am probably coming down with …" or, "I'll give it a bit more time." At this point, an element of denial remains.

2. Acknowledgement Phase

If signs of the illness persist, people will become more concerned. They may want someone to reassure them that nothing is wrong, or to validate that there is a problem. They often confide in someone close to them and whom they trust. If the perceived condition is potentially serious, an element of denial is more likely to persist. The person may attempt to rationalize symptoms: "I have stomach cramps because of all the Aspirin I took last week." "I was at the cottage and probably picked up something from the water there." "This chest pain is probably just indigestion. I should avoid those hamburgers." The patient may attempt self-treatment, perhaps with alternative remedies or over-the-counter medications. The short-term response is to wait and see. If clinical signs continue, the person will proceed to the next phase.

3. Action Phase

The next step is to contact a primary health care provider, usually the family doctor or a nurse practitioner. At this point, the person has most likely admitted that something is wrong but has little idea of what is wrong or how serious it is. At this stage, people may be unwilling to face the possibility of a major change in their health because they cannot cope with having to change their daily routines and roles.

Through the process of describing clinical signs and history to the provider, the person acknowledges the altered health pattern and is prepared to investigate probable causes. He or she becomes actively involved, cognitively and otherwise, in seeking a diagnosis.

4. Transitional Phase

Response to a diagnosis varies. If it is a simple problem, easily and quickly treated, the person will typically accept the diagnosis and begin the recommended treatment. If the diagnosis is more serious, resulting in protracted treatment with an undesirable or unpredictable prognosis, acceptance may be delayed. The person may seek a second opinion and experience denial, anger, and bargaining before coming to accept it. Some people never accept a really frightening diagnosis. This refusal often has a devastating effect on the family.

Once having accepted the diagnosis, the patient considers treatment options, makes a choice, and starts treatment. Most providers will invite the individual to participate in any necessary decision making. Often the provider will explain treatment options and will make recommendations, but will let the patient make the final decision. More decisions may be needed as treatment continues: for example, if the condition does not respond to the initial treatment, the patient and doctor may need to reassess and decide whether to try a different treatment. Decisions are rarely purely medical. Other factors come into play, such as pain or inconvenience, cost, time (how long a patient has to wait for treatment and how long treatment may take the patient away from normal activities), emotional factors (such as fear or distaste), and the effects of treatment on family members. Thus, family members may also be involved in making decisions.

5. Resolution Phase

Once treatment is initiated, the individual's focus shifts to recovery. If the problem is transient, treatment is usually short term and the patient quickly returns to his or her former position on the health–illness continuum. If the problem is more protracted, the patient will continue to focus on recovery. Recovery does not always mean a return to the former health state. For example, a patient facing a chronic illness may reach a resolution that involves some limitations and a change in lifestyle. Dealing with this new state takes some adjustment. Over time, most people do come to accept their altered health state. Others fluctuate between acceptance and denial, and some may never come to terms with what has happened to them. In the most serious cases, despite treatment, the final resolution may be death. This, too, often involves a series of stages, from learning the prognosis, through denial and anger or bargaining, to acceptance. When the patient faces long-term disability or death, family members, too, need to go through a process of assimilating the information and learning to accept it and rebuild their lives.

Implications for the Health Office Professional

By the time patients call the doctor's office for an appointment, they have acknowledged that a health issue exists, and most will be feeling some level of stress about their health state. A cheerful, positive, and caring manner will go a long way to comfort the patient. If you sense that the patient's condition warrants prompt attention or that the patient is very anxious, try to schedule an early appointment (see Chapter 9). In prioritizing appointments, a patient's emotional state can be as important as the physical complaint.

Patients who are diagnosed with a serious illness understandably experience prolonged stress and display different coping mechanisms. Some patients are initially in complete denial: "It's a mistake. Those test results can't be accurate. We should repeat them." Or, "This can't really be happening. I can't believe it's happened to me. I've done nothing to deserve this." The information they have been given may not register. Other patients may know intellectually that what the doctor has told them is true but may not believe it on an emotional level. Some patients may want a second opinion. If they ask you to make an appointment with another physician, gently refer them back to the doctor. Explain that this is something they must discuss with the doctor and that they must have a doctor's referral to see another physician. Though a second opinion is sometimes a good idea (and doctors themselves will sometimes ask for one), most territorial and provincial health plans will pay for a visit to a specialist for a second opinion only if the primary care provider requests a consultation.

> **TIP**
>
> Remember that illness affects everyone differently—including loved ones of the sick person. If a patient seems stressed, irritated, or angry, give them the benefit of the doubt. Be patient, remain calm, and be empathetic. *Most* of the time, a patient will respond in a positive manner and leave the office feeling valued and cared for.

Be sensitive to the patient's mood and emotional state. The range of responses is wide. A patient may not respond at all. He or she may pick up his or her belongings, smile, and leave the office. Another patient, usually pleasant and talkative, may become just the opposite. A patient may appear preoccupied, inattentive, or angry and resentful. Don't take such responses personally. Do your best to remain pleasant, empathetic, and helpful.

L06 SICK ROLE BEHAVIOUR

role a position in life that carries expectations of responsibilities and appropriate behaviour.

People assume social **roles** in life: positions that carry expectations of responsibilities and of appropriate behaviour. We have jobs and tasks we must perform, obligations to fulfill, and people who rely on us. Occupational roles determine how a manager and an employee should act; family roles determine how a mother, father, child, or sibling should act. Each of us plays more than one role in life. For example, Bob has roles as a father, a husband, and a teacher. As a father, he has responsibilities to his children. As a husband, he has responsibilities to his wife. As a teacher, he has responsibilities to his colleagues, his employer, and his students. Bob has also taken on roles as a member of the board of his local library and as a Scout leader, each of which involves certain obligations.

When people become sick, they are, to varying degrees, excused from their normal roles. When ill, it is acceptable for Bob not to go to work, not to play ball with his children, not to lead his Scout troop on a hike. In fact, being sick itself may be considered a role.[3] A person taking on this role, while exempt from normal responsibilities, is expected to behave in certain ways: to rest, to seek professional assistance, and to follow the doctor's advice. So far, this behaviour is adaptive.

sick role a particular social role that an ill person adopts, which involves giving up normal responsibilities and accepting care. May sometimes involve uncharacteristically passive behaviour.

However, the **sick role** can become ineffective. Some people, more commonly those facing a serious illness, develop a passive, submissive pattern of behaviour that may be quite unlike their normal attitude. Some people, often those with an external locus of control, seem to have continuous ailments and expect others to wait on and care for them. Others take on a passive role in the face of serious health problems, perhaps because of stress, fear, or uncertainty. They may prefer a physician or other health professional to make decisions for them because they trust that person's knowledge and experience or because the loss of their own familiar roles has undermined their sense of autonomy.

This abdication of responsibility is most common when a patient is hospitalized, perhaps because of the unfamiliar and highly controlled environment. When you are

---

[3]The concept of the sick role was first developed by sociologist Talcott Parsons as part of an attempt to define health and illness within a general theory of social action (T. Parsons, *The Social System*, Glencoe, IL: Free Press, 1951). Cited in Soma Hewa, "Physicians, the Medical Profession, and Medical Practice," in *Health, Illness, and Health Care in Canada*, 3rd ed., eds. B. Singh Bolaria and Harley D. Dickinson (Toronto: Nelson Thomson Learning, 2002).

dependent on others for your food, your mobility, and even your toileting, it can be hard to feel in control of your own life. A patient who, to all appearances, becomes immobilized by illness is difficult to deal with for both health professionals and family. The expectations placed on family members are overwhelming. The patient may become so passive that he or she will not participate in treatment, which impedes recovery. Health professionals must be careful not to cultivate patient dependence and should encourage patients to be actively involved in disease prevention, health maintenance, and the treatment of their own illnesses.

Always be sensitive to patients' responses to illness. Recognize that they may need support and encouragement. If a patient is cranky or whiny, be patient. If a patient seems angry and wants to blame others, be tolerant (within reason). Try to relate the behaviour to the nature, stage, and severity of the patient's illness.

Effects on Others

Response to illness is not confined to the person who is ill. Everyone who is closely associated with the sick person will be affected to some extent, spouses and children especially. How much the family is affected will depend on which family member is ill, how serious and how long the illness is, and what cultural and social customs the family has.

A sick person's role starts a chain reaction, affecting everyone who depends in any way on him or her. The severity of the effects depends on the nature and seriousness of the illness, as well as on the relationship to the sick person.

Consider Katya, a 35-year-old mother of three children. Her husband, Greg, is an electrician. Katya works part time for a busy obstetrician. She is a Girl Guide leader. She accompanies the church choir and is on the board of the library. Each of Katya's roles carries with it responsibilities, and there are people in each of those areas who depend on Katya to carry out those responsibilities.

Let's suppose that Katya comes down with bronchitis. The doctor prescribes an antibiotic and advises Katya to take a few days off. She calls her office to say she will not be in. She has to miss a library board meeting, which she was to chair. She has to cancel choir practice because they have no other pianist. She has to miss a Girl Guide field trip, which means the troop will be short one chaperone and must cancel the event. She is unable to take the kids to school or to pick them up.

Greg has to get the kids their breakfast and drive them to school, making him an hour late for work. Greg must also pick up the kids from school and put them to bed. He therefore must cancel an important meeting and miss his weekly golf game the next evening.

The kids are whiny because they miss their mother's attention. Dad does not know that Jamie likes porridge for breakfast, and he does not read the right kind of bedtime stories. Katya is not only in discomfort, but she also feels helpless and frustrated because she is bereft of her normal roles and guilty that she is letting everyone down. Greg is frustrated and feeling inadequate because the kids are not satisfied with the way he does things. He feels somewhat resentful that he has to miss his meeting and golf game. His supervisor is not happy that he came in late, which delayed an important job. The choir members feel under-rehearsed for their next performance. The library board is concerned because it postponed voting on an important matter until the next month ... and on it goes.

These examples show how illness affects not just the ill person, but everyone in that person's circle, especially the family. Effects on the family may include

■ changes in a person's duties and responsibilities,

■ increased stress because of anxiety related to the illness,

- conflict over unaccustomed responsibilities,
- financial problems,
- change in social patterns,
- loneliness (if the family member is hospitalized), and
- pending loss (if the illness is serious).

>>> POINTS TO PONDER

If you fell ill and required hospitalization for a week, what impact would that have on you, your family, and your close friends in terms of the shift in responsibilities that would occur?

Implications for the Administrative Health Professional

It is important to recognize that the whole family is affected when one family member becomes ill. You and other members of your team may have to support not only the patient but also family members during interactions. They may call or come into the office seeming angry, resentful, or just plain worried. Understanding what they are going through will help you put any unpleasant behaviour in perspective and maintain your calm and empathetic manner. It is helpful also to consider personality types.

Illness and Personality Types

Patients You Rarely See   Some patients deal with their health responsibly and rarely seek medical assistance. They are straightforward about their concerns, they know when to seek attention, and they follow the recommended advice. They are pleasant, easy to deal with, matter-of-fact, and accountable. Another group of patients puts off making appointments even when they should because they are shy and "hate to bother anyone." Other patients may avoid seeking medical attention because of nervousness about interacting with hospitals and physicians. Denial may be the motivating factor that keeps them from seeking help. These individuals can be their own worst enemies because their delays result in more protracted and serious illnesses.

Shy patients and nervous patients should be encouraged to seek medical help when necessary and to keep annual appointments for check-ups. Sometimes, encouraging them to call the office when they feel unwell keeps them in touch and provides a communication link.

Patients You See Frequently   Many doctors will tell you that 20 percent of their practice takes up 80 percent of their time. These patients are often the ones you and the provider may become impatient with. They are often sensitive to even the slightest alterations in their health. They may worry excessively, use home remedies, and call for medical advice or come to see the doctor frequently. They are demanding of the physician's time and apt to be critical when they think they are not getting enough of it. This is not to trivialize the patient's condition or complaints; for the most part, their concerns are very real to them.

It is important to remain polite to these patients and to be as accommodating as you can. It is up to the physician to speak to the patient about visits that are too frequent and to ask the patient to limit the discussion to what is causing the most distress. (Often the patient will come in with one complaint and then expect the doctor to address several, most of which are ongoing. Usually they become perceptive enough to assure you that they are only "coming in to see about the swelling in my ankles," for example, saving the rest of the list for the doctor.) Unfortunately, if the patient cries wolf often enough, a valid complaint may not immediately be taken seriously. When this type of patient calls the office, never ignore a complaint. Be especially aware of a new complaint or significant change to an established complaint. Listen to the tone of the patient's voice; is there an element of stress that is not usually there?

There is no real solution for the patient who wants more time and attention than the physician and administrative staff have to give. Seeking another physician these days is not a viable option for most patients, given the current shortage of doctors. Remain courteous and be as supportive as you can be.

L07 THE EFFECTS OF HOSPITALIZATION

Hospitalization is a major source of stress to the patient and family members, particularly now that hospital stays are reserved for the very ill. By the time a person is hospitalized, he or she has reached the treatment phase of the health response sequence. Usually the patient has already accepted the illness and the treatment regimen. However, in the face of more serious illnesses, the patient may go through a second stage of rejecting the diagnosis and choice of treatment. Some people accept their situation with a positive attitude; others may become overly passive and refuse to work toward recovery.

Hospitalization disrupts

- privacy,
- autonomy and independence,
- lifestyle,
- role function, and
- financial security.

Privacy

Privacy is important to everyone, in or out of hospital. Most people find comfort and security in having a space to themselves, especially introverts. Time to be alone to think and reflect provides a chance to regroup and renew. In the hospital, likewise, people need time to be quiet, to rest, and to think. They also need and have the right to physical privacy. Though some people can change or shower comfortably in the presence of others, others are very private about disrobing and doing personal hygiene. Their need for privacy does not disappear because they're in a hospital.

Privacy also relates to how close we let others get to us emotionally and physically. We all have emotional and physical comfort zones that others should not enter without permission. Culture, personality, gender, and religion influence the boundaries we set.

There is an old saying that when you enter a hospital, you leave your privacy at the front door. Often the crowded state of hospital wards makes privacy difficult to ensure, but sometimes it is just a matter of busy nurses and other health professionals taking a moment to think about it. It is difficult, especially in semi-private or standard accommodation, to maintain privacy in the presence of other patients and their visitors, hospital personnel with tasks to do, and the noise of the paging system. The nurses usually do their best to preserve patients' privacy by closing doors or pulling curtains when giving treatments and nursing care.

Sometimes you can help. If a patient requests quiet time, let the nurses know, or pull the curtains around the bed or close the door. This simple measure will at least give the patient a visual break.

If you know that a patient is going to have a meeting with a doctor, family member, or clergy, try to arrange for a quiet, private environment. You can book a conference room (if the unit has one) or suggest an empty room. If the patient cannot move out of the room, perhaps other patients in the room can.

If you need information from the patient —about insurance coverage, for example, or discharge arrangements—ask quietly. Never ask a patient to disclose potentially sensitive information within the hearing range of other people.

Autonomy

Autonomy is a person's independence, or ability to operate without outside control. Unfortunately, autonomy diminishes in the hospital environment. Patients are told when and what to eat, when to get up, when to go to bed, when to take their pills, and when they can have visitors. Many people find it difficult to adjust to this loss of control. Some struggle to retain what control they can. Others become almost dependent, allowing others to make decisions for them and take care of them. A family member may say, "I can't understand it. Fred is usually such an independent person." It could be that Fred is relinquishing control because he is simply too sick or discouraged to cope. It could be that he has given up. He may feel intimidated by the authority of hospital staff, or he may be enjoying the opportunity for a good rest!

The clinical secretary can help by allowing patients to do as much for themselves as possible. For example, offer a patient meal choices rather than suggesting something. If there is an insurance form to fill out, give it to the patient and let him or her do as much as she can by him or herself. If you need to help, ask the patient if you may sit down, offer to draw the curtains, and proceed to obtain the information, allowing the patient as much opportunity for expression as possible. Too many closed questions can make a patient feel like a robot, spurting out short "yes" or "no" answers with no opportunity to discuss anything.

Lifestyle

Hospitalization changes almost every detail of a patient's daily life—getting up, bathing, working, eating, socializing. They may miss simple things they took for granted at home, such as a portable phone or an electric razor. Patients with disabilities may miss their own assistive devices if these are not permitted in the hospital. A different walker, cane, or wheelchair can upset a patient and alter mobility. All this change makes many people uneasy: some may become withdrawn and uncommunicative, others may be openly resentful, and others may be downright angry.

Role Function

Though someone who is ill at home may be able to continue with some routine activities and function in some roles, the hospitalized patient experiences an almost total change in role function. Responsibilities are either taken over by someone else or put on the back burner. This creates stress and anxiety for the patient and family members. Some patients will push for discharge from the hospital before they are ready, which can result in complications and delayed recovery. On occasion, a patient will actually leave the hospital without the physician's permission.

Financial Security

The longer a patient is in hospital, the more likely it is that finances will become a problem, especially if the patient is the primary wage earner. Many people have some type of disability insurance or other coverage in the event of illness. For those who do not, the loss of wages can be a major blow. Families may also face additional expenses, ranging from childcare to transportation.

Implications for the Administrative Health Professional

Although clinical secretaries do not give patient care, they do frequently communicate with the patient, friends, and family members. If you understand the stressors for both the hospitalized patient and the family members, you can help ease them a little and communicate more effectively. You need to keep communication clear, accurate, and professional, while at the same time being supportive, understanding, and empathetic—not an easy task. It takes skill and patience to read the mood of the patient and to respond appropriately to the anxious husband, wife, brother, or sister. Trying to direct questions to the appropriate source or withholding confidential information from an inappropriate person can evoke angry, sometimes explosive, responses from individuals who feel that they are entitled to the information on the spot. Do not take it personally; it can help you stay calm and deal effectively with these individuals if you realize that most of them would not behave this way under less stressful circumstances.

Health Status

Health professionals, especially those working in hospitals, often field inquiries from family, friends, and acquaintances about a patient's health status. Family and friends will often call the hospital asking how a patient is doing on a particular day. Carefully follow federal and hospital guidelines for the release of such information. Usually, it is prudent to allow callers to speak to the patient's nurse, especially family members who are entitled to the details of the patient's condition. Otherwise, most facilities allow only general information to be released and sometimes not even that.

If you are allowed to give information, make sure it is up to date—an individual's health status can change from moment to moment. This information may be kept updated on the patient's chart (see Chapter 15). If you are asked to give general information, you will probably use the following standard terms:

Critical: The patient is hanging in the balance between life and death and is receiving active, intense intervention. The patient is often in the emergency room, operating room, intensive care unit (ICU), critical care unit (CCU), or recovery room.

Poor: The patient is near death but not receiving active intervention.

Guarded: The patient has moved from critical toward the wellness end of the continuum—but only just. The patient's condition is still volatile and easily subject to change.

Stable: This term is used once a patient's condition has steadied, typically after being considered critical. It is usually considered an improvement. Sometimes a patient will be reported as being critical but stable, meaning that although very serious, the patient's condition—at least for the moment—has not deteriorated. This is usually good news but does not necessarily indicate a sure recovery.

Satisfactory: The patient continues to improve and, usually, is out of danger. Although the position is optimistic, fluctuation or regression is still possible.

Good: The patient is believed to be on a firm footing and is expected to recover. Note, however, that it does not always mean the patient will return to the previous level of functioning. A stroke victim's condition, for example, may be described as "good" when she is not in danger of dying, although function may still be limited.

- Changes in both the job title and job descriptions for health office professionals/administrators. Continuing advances in IT software applications for health facilities require that you have a firm understanding of systems you work with.

- Movement toward a more collaborative approach to health care delivery—an interdisciplinary cooperation that ensures better access to comprehensive care.

- Pan-Canadian application of an electronic medical records system that is current, secure, and accessible.

- How Canadians respond to the 2015 Supreme Court decision that Canadians have the right to physician-assisted death, based on the premise that the "sanctity of life" also includes the "passage into death." This ruling creates a new constitutional right for an individual to have autonomy over his or her death.

- How the federal/provincial and territorial governments collaborate to create acceptable guidelines for physician-assisted death.

- Shorter hospital stays for patients, more care given in the community, and improvements to how community care is delivered.

SUMMARY

1. Behaviour is a person's observable responses and actions. Behaviour changes in response to stress, including both illness and hospitalization. Health beliefs affect our lifestyles and how we care for ourselves. Some people adopt self-imposed risks, such as smoking, sedentary habits, and poor diet, because they do not believe that they affect health or because they rationalize that nothing will happen to them. Others consciously work to improve and maintain their health and focus on prevention.

2. Definitions of health and wellness are individual. At one time, *health* was thought of as the simple absence of physical disease. Today, health is understood in broader terms. *Wellness* refers to the well-being of the entire person, embracing physical, emotional, social, intellectual, and spiritual components. All five elements interact: for example, anxiety can cause physical illness, and physiological disorders can also cause anxiety. At one time, health care was seen as a response to sickness, and people expected medical science to take care of them. Many people have now adopted a more preventive approach that emphasizes individual responsibility and healthier lifestyles. Recognition of the influence of social and economic factors has also grown.

3. Health care remains a concern for most Canadians at some level, including the sustainability of our public health care system as we know it in the face of current demands. For example, sufficient funding for mental health programs, home care for an aging population, and access to quality health care for Canada's Indigenous populations are some of the main concerns.

4. The *health–illness continuum* is a scale on which to measure a person's perception of his or her health state. Optimal health is at one end of the scale, and death is at the other. Two individuals with the same symptoms may place themselves at different points on the continuum. Most people, most of the time, place themselves somewhere in the area of optimal health or compensation, meaning they are experiencing some health problems but are coping on their own.

5. Although individuals respond differently to illness, there is a typical pattern of response. In the preliminary phase, people often ignore the first appearance of

signs or come up with their own explanations. In the acknowledgement phase, they acknowledge that there is a problem, and they may confide in someone else or try to rationalize the problem away. In the action phase, people respond to sustained clinical signs by contacting a health care provider and seeking a diagnosis. In the transitional phase, people accept or reject a diagnosis and then accept treatment offered or seek alternatives. The resolution phase may be brief or may involve adjustment to permanent changes.

6. People have many roles in life—as workers, family members, and members of a community—each involving responsibilities. Illness affects their ability to play these roles. It also affects the roles of others in their lives by shifting responsibilities to others, many of which the person assuming new responsibilities is unfamiliar with and unprepared for. Personality also affects response to illness. Some patients rarely contact the health office, either because they can handle their health on their own or because they are denying or ignoring health problems. The latter need to be encouraged to come in more regularly. Others are overly concerned with their health and demand a great deal of the physician's time. It is important to handle them firmly but tactfully and to recognize when they do report a new and serious problem.

7. Hospitalization is stressful for patients and their families because it disrupts privacy, autonomy, lifestyle, role function, and financial security. Although your contact with the patient will be mostly regarding administrative concerns, try as much as possible to preserve the patient's privacy and independence. When asked about a patient's health status, follow the facilities institutional policy on confidentiality, and make sure any information you do give is accurate and up to date.

KEY TERMS

behaviour   41
health   43

role   52
sick role   52

wellness   43

REVIEW QUESTIONS

1. Define the following:
   a. Health behaviour
   b. Health
   c. Wellness
   d. Health beliefs
   e. Self-imposed risk
   f. Role function

2. State the relationship between health beliefs and health behaviours.

3. List the five dimensions of wellness, and give an example of each.

4. What are the implications of the rise in antibiotic-resistant organisms to Canadians?

5. What is a chronic illness? What impact do chronic illnesses have on our society today?

6. Discuss the structure and purpose of the health–illness continuum.

7. Identify the five stages of illness and the typical responses at each stage.

8. What are the effects of illness on family members, especially with regard to changing role functions?

9. Explain the effects of hospitalization on patients and their families.

APPLICATION EXERCISES

1. List any self-imposed risks or risk-taking behaviours that you personally engage in. Research the health effects of one of these risks, and develop strategies to stop or reduce your risk-taking behaviours. Set goals for yourself. For example, if you smoke, you might decide that you want to quit or cut down to a specific number of cigarettes by a particular date. If you do not exercise, you might decide that you want to walk for 20 minutes three times a week.

Set a short-term goal (e.g., "By next Friday, I will reduce smoking by four cigarettes a day") and a long-term goal. List realistic steps you can take to achieve those goals. It may be helpful to brainstorm strategies with classmates with the same risk-taking behaviours.

Keep a daily log of your progress. If you have not met your goals, document why. Modify your plan accordingly. Each week for a month, take a few minutes at the beginning of the class to discuss your progress with your small group or partner. At the end of the month, review your goals. If you have made progress, you may want to continue. If not, you may decide to start over, modifying your goals or developing new strategies based on the information in your log.

2. Omar, a patient in your busy medical practice, has been diagnosed with terminal cancer. In addition, he and his family are personal friends of yours. The doctor has strongly recommended a course of chemotherapy for Omar as well as surgery. Omar has refused: "I believe I can have a higher quality of life with the time I have left if I don't undergo chemotherapy," he told the doctor. You know how committed he is to his family and that he values life and health immensely. You believe that Omar is making the right decision. The doctor (although he realizes this is typically not your role), however, has asked you to speak with Omar to try and persuade him to consent to treatment. The doctor feels that accepting treatment will prolong Omar's life by several months.

a. How would you respond in this situation?

b. Do you think Omar has the right to make his own decision without undue interference on the part of the doctor?

c. What do you think Omar means when he says he would rather enjoy a higher quality of life without the treatment as opposed to the few more months of life that the treatment may be able to offer?

3. Janet is a 34-year-old mother of two. She is separated from her husband and sends Susan, 5, and Matthew, 3, to daycare. She has no child support since her separation is still before the courts. Janet is a sales consultant at a local department store. She is on an anti-depressant. She volunteers at a local food bank but otherwise is not involved in community activities. She is new to the area and has only one casual friend. Janet smokes a pack of cigarettes daily. She belongs to a gym but does not go. Her favourite foods are hamburgers, fries, and wings, and she prefers Coca-Cola to milk.

Janet has noticed some blood in her stool for the past three months. She feels it is unimportant, likely due to hemorrhoids. One night she notices a substantial amount of blood in the toilet. She calls the office for an appointment, reluctant to come in that week. Tests reveal that Janet has a tumour of the ascending colon. She is hospitalized for a bowel resection. She is terrified of both the hospital and the impending surgery. She arrives on the floor tearful and frightened.

As the clinical secretary, you are asked to take Janet to her room and give her a brief orientation to the patient-care unit. Janet asks you to send down the nurse to help her get undressed and into bed. She asks you to bring her some water and to telephone her babysitter to see how the children are doing.

a. What is Janet's primary role?

b. Identify three other roles Janet plays.

c. What are Janet's attitudes toward health maintenance and disease prevention?

d. List three self-imposed risks that Janet takes.

e. Discuss Janet's behaviour up to and including her first physician's appointment in terms of the altered health response scale.

f. Describe Janet's behaviour on arriving at the hospital in terms of the sick role.

g. How should you deal with Janet? How can you calm her down?

h. What problems will Janet face regarding her children?

WEBSITES OF INTEREST

Health and Wellness in Canada

www.windfall.ca/healthwellness.html

Public Health Agency of Canada: Information on VRE, *C. Difficile*, and MRSA

www.phac-aspc.gc.ca/nois-sinp/vre-erv-eng.php
www.phac-aspc.gc.ca/id-mi/cdiff-eng.php
www.phac-aspc.gc.ca/id-mi/mrsa-eng.php

Public Health Agency of Canada: Healthy Living

www.phac-aspc.gc.ca/hp-ps/hl-mvs/index-eng.php

Wait Times for Health Care in Canada

http://canadaonline.about.com/od/healthcarewaittimes

Chapter 3
Culture and Health

kupicoo/E+/Getty Images

LEARNING OBJECTIVES

On completing this chapter, you will be able to:

1. Differentiate between culture and ethnicity.

2. Explain the benefits of cultural tolerance and understanding.

3. Discuss how to overcome cultural barriers to effective health care.

4. Understand differences in beliefs and practices.

5. Solve the problems that result from language barriers.

6. Select a suitable interpreter.

7. Summarize techniques and practices to deliver high-quality, culturally sensitive health care to an ethnically diverse population.

Canada is one of the most culturally diverse countries in the world. Every province and territory—indeed, every community—has a unique blend of cultural and social influences. Within each community there is great cultural variation, especially in large cities such as Toronto, Vancouver, and Montreal. Knowing about different cultures promotes understanding and acceptance and encourages adaptive rather than antagonistic relationships. As an administrative health professional, you can communicate with patients and support them if you understand something about their culture and how it shapes their health beliefs, behaviours, and expectations.

According to Statistics Canada, in 2011 20.6 percent of the total population was born outside of Canada. Between 2006 and 2011, the majority of immigrants came from Asia and the Middle East. Most of Canada's foreign-born population live in Ontario, British Columbia, Quebec, and Alberta, whose populations comprise more than 200 ethnic origins. Canada's linguistic diversity is evidenced by the approximately 200 languages spoken, with 20 percent of the Canadian population speaking a language other than French or English most of the time at home. For older newcomers who are unfamiliar with English when they arrive in Canada, learning the language—let alone understanding it—can be a challenge. This is especially true when discussing their health care needs and understanding potential treatment plans, whether in an office, clinic, or hospital. The most common languages spoken are Punjabi, Mandarin, Cantonese, Spanish, and Tagalog (according to the 2011 census).

Currently the focus for immigration is to keep Canada's economy strong, particularly after the recent recession. Statistics Canada shows that 60 percent of new immigrants came through the economic stream. This stream allows admission to the country based on the individual's ability to contribute to Canada's economic development (e.g., skilled workers, investors, entrepreneurs, those with high potential for self-employment). According to Statistics Canada, the immigration plan for the next few years will also include more admissions for spouses and children in the family category. These individuals will bring specific cultural needs with respect to health care, as well requiring access to family doctors and other health care services.

In 1971 Canada became the first country in the world to adopt a multiculturalism policy, illustrating a commitment to ethnic diversity. In 1986 the federal government passed the Employment Equity Act, and in 1988 it passed the Canadian Multiculturalism Act. The Canadian Multiculturalism Act directs the federal government to work toward equality in the economic, social, cultural, and political life of the country. The Canadian government has introduced a number of different programs over the years dictating immigration protocol. For example, as of January 2015, to come to Canada as a skilled immigrant, a person has to use a program called the Express Entry system. To apply for this, a candidate must create an online profile. This profile will be evaluated, and the candidate will be ranked and then placed in a pool with other candidates. Top candidates will be invited to apply online to become a permanent resident.

It is commonly said that while the United States is a melting pot, Canada is a mosaic. People are encouraged to join in Canadian life while retaining their own customs and cultural identity. And indeed this happens—sometimes. Walking along certain city streets, one has the sense of being in an international bazaar. Saris, babushkas, and dreadlocks mingle with business suits and faded denim; the cadences of many languages greet the ear; every imaginable food from every corner of the world seems to be on offer. Yet the mosaic is not without problems. Members of ethnic and cultural minorities report very different experiences: Some feel welcomed and cherished; others meet with discrimination and rebuffs. Some feel that multiculturalism is merely a tourist gloss on profound social division. Although governments can formulate policies, only people can make them work.

The 2015 refugee crisis in Syria provoked controversy across the country over Canada's immigration policies—many Canadians believe the country should drastically increase the number of refugees allowed in. One of the overarching concerns for many is security—admitting large numbers of refugees without detailed background checks. Another concern is the economic impact admitting a large numbers of refugees would have, including the cost of health care.

L01 WHAT IS CULTURE?

The term *culture* means different things to different people, as do many of the terms connected with it. Let us start by reviewing a few.

Culture may be defined as "the languages, beliefs, values, norms, behaviours, and even material objects that are passed from one generation to the next."[1] More broadly, culture refers to a collection of beliefs, rules, and practices that are shared by a group of people,[2] whether or not they are passed from generation to generation. These beliefs and norms are so basic to our lives that we are often unaware of them until we see people from other cultures following different norms. Our own culture becomes, in a sense, invisible to us. To people who have grown up that way, it simply feels natural to brush their teeth in the morning, eat three meals a day (rather than two or six), go to school, wear jeans, stand in line for movie tickets, say thank-you when given something, and listen to music on the radio. Yet none of these behaviours are natural—they are all learned as part of a culture. We often become aware of culture only when we see someone from another culture behaving differently. We may observe this behaviour as simply different or regard it as something we do not understand. Canadians often accept certain cultural variations, such as those in clothing and cuisine, and enjoy them as part of our rich, multicultural landscape. Yet it may be harder to recognize some of the subtler variations in culture. Seeing someone stand closer and speak louder than the Canadian norm or haggle over prices may make one dismiss the person as simply vulgar, loud, or cheap, without recognizing that he or she is simply following a different set of cultural rules.

> **culture** any combination of the languages, beliefs, values, norms, behaviours, and even material objects that are passed from one generation to the next.

Generally, culture is learned through imitation and observation rather than direct instruction. Culture affects people on personal, social, economic, environmental, and political levels. It may define appropriate behaviours for men and women (e.g., when and whom a person marries). Culture also influences attitudes toward older adults, family planning and parenting styles, social expectations and commitment, sexual practices, nutrition, and medical practices.

Though culture tends to be associated with a national or ethnic group, there are many variations. For example, the culture of a rural Maritimer will be a little different from the culture of an Ontario city dweller. A person who was born in Jamaica but grew up in Canada may share some cultural characteristics with Jamaicans but others with Canadians. Within a society can also be found many **subcultures**: groups that share many cultural aspects with the general society but have their own distinct cultural practices as well. There is, for example, a gay subculture, a biker-gang subculture, a rap subculture. Often, young people have a somewhat different culture from that of their parents, despite being part of the same broader culture.

> **subculture** the values and practices of a group that distinguish it from the larger culture.

Ethnicity

The word **ethnic** comes from the Greek term *ethnos*, "people." The dictionary defines *ethnic* as "relating to groups of people with a common racial, religious, linguistic, or cultural heritage." In this sense, we all have an ethnic origin. A fifth-generation Canadian of British ancestry is no more or less "ethnic" than an immigrant from Vietnam. Yet, in another usage, the term is used only for ethnic minorities and is sometimes used interchangeably with the terms *race* or *minority group*. Social scientists use the term, however, to refer to cultural characteristics. In this sense, a person's ancestry and

> **ethnic** relating to groups of people with a common racial, religious, linguistic, or cultural heritage.

---

[1] James M. Henslin and Adie Nelson, *Essentials of Sociology: A Down-to-Earth Approach* (Scarborough, ON: Allyn and Bacon Canada, 1997).
[2] Athena du Pre, *Communication about Health* (Mountain View, CA: Mayfield Publishing Company, 2000).

physical characteristics are not necessarily the same as their ethnicity. A black person who grew up in France will probably have a different ethnic identity from one who grew up in Trinidad, even if their physical characteristics are similar.

Race is often used to refer to groups of people with similar physical characteristics and a common ancestry. Some divide humanity into three races, others into four or more. However, most anthropologists have now rejected the categories as unscientific. Though human beings obviously have marked differences in physical characteristics, such as skin tone and facial features, there is no strong rationale for any particular lines of division among these variations. *Caucasian*, for example, is sometimes used as a synonym for *white* or *European*. Yet, as once used by anthropologists, the term denoted a race including not only white Europeans but also dark-skinned South and West Asians. Despite the inexactness of racial divisions, there are times when it is important in health care to note genetic and metabolic characteristics common to groups of people. For example, sickle-cell anemia is found mostly among blacks; Tay-Sachs disease is found mostly among people of European-Jewish ancestry (regardless of their ethnic identity or religion).

Ethnic identity is not the same as nationality. *Nationality* is manifested when a person belongs to a country, with all its legal benefits (such as the right to participate in elections) and social benefits (such as the right to health care and education). The person may gain citizenship by birth or may apply for citizenship in a new country. Many countries allow dual citizenship.

Ethnicity refers to the cultural characteristics of a particular ethnic group. It includes such things as traits, background, allegiances, and self-identification. Many minority groups find that their sense of ethnic identity fades over time as each generation becomes more immersed in the culture and practices of the country in which they live. For example, a family may move from India to Canada and faithfully practise their religion and related traditions. The children may retain their traditions and sense of identity while becoming more integrated into Canadian culture. When they have children of their own, who are born in Canada and exposed to Western culture from birth, adherence to traditional practices may be more difficult. Some people feel torn between two worlds; others quite comfortably establish their own cultural identity, blending elements of the new country and the old. In the case of mixed marriages and groups that have migrated, identity can be complex: "I am a Canadian Muslim from Uganda, of Gujarati background," or, "I am a Canadian, part Ukrainian and part Chinese."

Quebec is an example of a society that is actively trying to preserve its uniqueness and ethnicity. Laws in Quebec restrict the use of English in signage, business, and education. In France, too, such bodies as the Académie Française try to root out English colloquialisms, such as "le weekend."

Canada's Indigenous peoples are also trying to preserve their ethnicity and their culture by keeping their traditions, practices, and laws alive. This remains a struggle, especially for First Nations peoples. A large number of First Nations people still suffer from the devastating effects of residential schools where they endured isolation from their families, communities, and culture, as well as degradation, humiliation, and abuse (physical and sexual). These religious residential schools, supported by the Canadian government, were established to assimilate First Nations children into the Euro-Canadian culture. It was thought that assimilating the children would be easier than trying to change the adults (which is true, in that by the age of 10 an individual's cultural norms are firmly ingrained). It was thought that these children, when grown, would pass on the culture and lifestyle imposed on them to their own children, all but annihilating any remnants of their own culture.

These schools were established in the late 1800s by the Canadian government. The last school closed in 1996. Often referred to as "cultural genocide," the damaging effects of these schools on the First Nations population persist today. Many traditions have been lost or forgotten, some languages are on the verge of extinction, and for many the ability to be proud of their heritage has evaporated. Generations have lost their customs, languages, identity, and sense of purpose. The results primarily relate to the social determinants of health and include mental health problems, substance abuse, family violence, unemployment, and poverty. Having said that, it is true that attitudes vary. Some Indigenous (which collectively includes Inuit, First Nations, and Métis) people feel that preserving old customs is essential to their identity. Many feel free to pick and choose which aspects of traditional culture to embrace and resent the implication that they are less "authentic" if their lives resemble those of other Canadians in many ways. Indigenous cultures vary widely, and a person is less likely to identify with the broad category "Indian" or "First Nations" than with a specific cultural group, such as Cree, Inuit, or Ojibwa.

►►► POINTS TO PONDER

Residential schools are a dark part of Canadian history, and a part of history that many Canadians still remain unaware of. The Truth and Reconciliation Commission (TRC), whose mandate, in part, is to inform all Canadians about what happened, has increased public awareness of the unbearable suffering imposed on Canada's Indigenous population. How much do you know about residential schools and the TRC, the first phase of which was completed in December 2015?

Diversity

It is important to emphasize that cultural **diversity** includes more than just where a person comes from, their religion, or what language they speak. Other important inclusions are the LGBTQ community (lesbian, gay, bisexual, transgender, queer). Some would also include age, disability, income, and level of education. A **culturally competent** health care system provides services to anyone and everyone who needs them while respecting whatever differences exist. It is inclusive, and whenever possible, it tailors approaches and treatments to meet the needs of each person.

Regardless of ethnicity or culture, for example, transgender individuals face numerous societal barriers notwithstanding those related to obtaining unbiased health care (this may be more so for individuals who have experienced outright persecution in their country of origin). These barriers include fear of discrimination by and insensitivity of providers. Something as simple as using "he" instead of "she" for a transgender woman would be viewed as discriminatory. Transgender individuals may experience anxiety or even shame if they must have even a partial examination in a doctor's office. They may resist disrobing, and should never be forced to do so until they are ready. Within a health care facility, concerns may include the type of accommodation a transgender person is admitted to: Do you admit a transgender man to a female semi-private room or to a male semi-private room? Unless legally changed, the sex on the person's birth certificate is that person's sex for life, even if he or she has had sex reassignment surgery. In Canada, a transgender person can legally change his or her sex on a birth certificate regardless of having had or not had sexual reassignment surgery.

Transgender issues have become more public in the past couple of years, especially with the publicity generated by celebrities such as Caitlyn Jenner (who transgendered very publicly in 2015). More individuals seem to be questioning their gender identity, with many making the decision to seek reassignment surgery. When a transgender individual decides to have reassignment surgery, the process is long and difficult. Support

diversity differences and variety, including people from different ethnicities, sexual orientations, and social backgrounds.

cultural competence a set of behaviours, attitudes, and policies that work together to meet the needs of a cross-cultural population in a positive, culturally sensitive manner; individuals are culturally knowledgeable, are informed, and act without personal bias.

and acceptance from health care professionals goes a long way to making the process more tolerable.

According to the Canadian Professional Association for Transgender Health (2013), all provinces except Prince Edward Island and New Brunswick fund some combination of sexual reassignment surgery (also known as gender-confirming surgery, or GCS). Saskatchewan, for example, will cover the cost of a hysterectomy and mastectomy, but not the more specialized surgeries required, which are currently unavailable in that province. There is only one clinic in the entire country, located in Montreal, with two surgeons who perform the specialized surgeries needed to complete the transition. The total cost for the surgeries can be as high as $20 000.

Ageism is also on the rise and is experienced by many older Canadians. Some doctors are warning of a culture of ageism within the health care field, with health professionals treating older adults as though they don't deserve the same care as younger Canadians. Older Canadians are often viewed as a burden on the system, using up health care dollars that might be better spent elsewhere. Older people who are hospitalized and waiting for accommodation elsewhere (e.g., long-term care) are often referred to as "bed blockers." Older people, both inside and outside the health care system, are often ignored, patronized, or treated with disrespect. Perfectly competent older individuals are often treated as though they cannot think or make decisions for themselves. Something as simple as calling a person by his or her surname, for example, "Mrs. Smith, can I have your health card, please?" instead of "Mary, give me your health card, please" can go a long way. Many older people do not like someone to use their first name unless invited to. You could say, "Mrs. Smith, is it OK if I call you Mary?"

Finally, *multiculturalism* refers to people of various cultures living together in relative harmony and mutual respect. *Cultural diversity* implies maintaining distinct cultures within a broader society. The ideal is to celebrate differences without dwelling on them, in an atmosphere of understanding, respect, and tolerance.

Prejudice and Ethnocentrism

Prejudice means "prejudging" or coming to conclusions about a person or group on the basis of untested assumptions, without regard for the facts. Prejudice can be a negative or hostile attitude or thought based on intolerance and ignorance. It may just be felt internally or may be expressed. Prejudice may be expressed against any group, minority or not, and it may be found among any group. A common form of prejudice is *stereotyping*: assuming that all members of a group will be alike. Stereotyping may be applied to cultures and subcultures, age and gender groups, as well as occupations. For example, teenagers in groups may be viewed as a source of trouble; accountants may be stereotyped as "boring" and interested only in figures. We have all heard blonde jokes, based on the notion that fair-haired women are not very smart. Although prejudice is usually thought of as negative, positive prejudices are also possible (e.g., assuming that a black person will be athletic or a Welshman will be a good singer). There indeed may be behaviours that are more common among certain groups of people, but assuming that *everyone* in a perceived category has the same characteristics is inaccurate and harmful. An example from a health care perspective is the assumption that Asian women do not complain during childbirth while Italian women are very vocal.

Do not confuse prejudice with *discrimination*. Usually discrimination follows prejudice, but prejudice can occur without discrimination. Discrimination occurs when people are denied justice or treated unfairly because of their membership in a group.

More broadly, **ethnocentrism** is the tendency to use our own culture's standards as the yardstick to judge everyone. To some degree, this is inevitable. All people look at the world from the point of view of their own culture, and most of us naturally believe

ethnocentrism the tendency to use one's own culture's standards as the yardstick to judge everyone; the belief in the superiority of one's own group or culture.

that the values and beliefs with which we have been raised are right. But ethnocentrism can act like blinders, preventing us from seeing the big picture or from understanding another's point of view. At its worst, ethnocentrism leads us to view our own group and culture as superior to all others and leads to intolerance or condescension.

⫸ CULTURAL COMPETENCE IN THE HEALTH PROFESSION

A culturally competent health care system depends on culturally competent health professionals at all levels. Cultural competence is not something you can learn and leave. It is a process that is continually evolving, requiring you to change, adapt, and adjust almost daily. It is achieved by being open and honest with yourself and getting to know your own beliefs and value systems, and by asking questions of your patients and their family members as well as of yourself. It is about gathering knowledge and continually adjusting your own communication patterns, policies, and processes to meet the needs of the patients within your catchment area. The following are just a few recommendations:

- *Examine your own beliefs, values, and biases.* Understanding and acknowledging them will help you more effectively communicate with and assist others, even when differences incongruent with your own beliefs and values are apparent. Treat patients and their families in the same manner that you would want to be treated.

- *Never assume anything about a patient pertaining to values, beliefs, preferences, or health-related customs.* Take the time to find out more about a patient, developing a relationship that is individualized so you can better meet that person's needs. This is one situation where you should not treat every patient in the same way—you must adjust your communication patterns and treatment to meet his or her individual differences. Worth mentioning

is to never assume that someone who does not appear to speak English does not understand what is being said.

- *Be knowledgeable about cultures within the community where you work.* Develop a general understanding of the customs and expectations of various cultural groups. Familiarize yourself with resources available to you within your work environment and your community (e.g., interpreters, culturally specific support groups).

- *Develop a trusting relationship.* As an administrative assistant, you will not be diagnosing health problems, or providing treatment, but you will be the first person with whom patients interact when they either call or come into the facility. Develop a trusting relationship with your patients and their families, and do your best to meet their needs (e.g., scheduling appointments when it is convenient for them, perhaps accommodating family members at the visit, and answering their questions with respect and patience).

- *Work toward creating a welcoming environment.* Your clinic should be reflective of the community in which you work, and you should develop trustful communication patterns with your patients. For example, many communities across Canada have welcomed Syrian refugees—20 000 in 2016 alone. Addressing their medical and mental health needs in a culturally sensitive manner is essential; having an Arabic translator on hand would also be useful.

L02 THE NEED FOR INTERCULTURAL UNDERSTANDING

Never has it been more important to respect, learn to communicate with, and live in harmony with people from different cultures. Understanding is necessary from a social and humanitarian perspective, but also to ensure our economic and political well-being.

Immigrants and Refugees

Populations have become increasingly mobile. The beginning of this chapter discussed how varied the Canadian population is. Tourists and businesspeople from around the world also visit Canada, and sometimes they need health care here. Educational exchanges have increased in recent years. Students from other countries undergo the culture shock of dealing with a new country, culture, educational system, and language. Trying to understand their individual health beliefs and expectations, and how they interface with health care in their own country, is important. Canadians, too, travel frequently to visit friends and family and to do business. International trade agreements, such as the North American Free Trade Agreement, lead to job relocations (which will increase even more when the recent Trans-Pacific Partnership is finalized and implemented).

We often converse with people from other cultures and may not always understand the things they say, why they say them, or what they mean. For example, in an international chat group, a Swede was discussing his grandfather's peaceful end through euthanasia. A Canadian responded that euthanasia was nothing short of murder. Each was viewing the matter through the lens of his own culture. In Sweden, euthanasia has been legal for a number of years and is seen as an act of kindness when it respects the dying person's autonomy and wishes. In Canada, physician-assisted death became legal in 2016, but this legislation is still very new, and there is much discussion around the scope of the legislation. Many feel that it is too narrow in scope, in that a person seeking physician-assisted death must be in a situation where his or her death is considered "imminent." This excludes individuals who have degenerative diseases that will cause their quality of life to deteriorate to the point where they do not want to live (e.g., forms of dementia or neurological conditions such as amyotrophic lateral sclerosis [ALS]). The Canadian Medical Association is seeking consistency among jurisdictions regarding provincial laws dealing with physician-assisted death. Many Canadians, given the newness of this legislation, are unsure how they feel about it and what impact it may have on them and their friends or family members. Understanding and respecting another's point of view does not mean you must agree with it, but it does allow for fruitful discussion and enhances tolerance.

Recent global conflict and the threat of terrorism from groups such as ISIS (the Islamic State of Iraq and Syria) has generated fear and intensified intercultural intolerance. The first few years of the twenty-first century saw the September 11, 2001, attacks on the World Trade Center and the Pentagon, which changed the world and contributed to wars in Afghanistan and Iraq and escalated conflict in the Middle East. The past decade has seen ethnically motivated mass killings in Europe, Southeast Asia, and Africa. The brutal civil war in Syria, resulting from conflict between the Syrian government and Syrian opposition forces, and ISIS's operations in that country have resulted in the slaughter of thousands of Syrian citizens. In 2016, the refugee crisis (cited as the worst since World War II) saw tens of thousands of Syrians leaving their country, fleeing death and destruction and with many dying along the way. Some European countries have welcomed as many refugees as they can handle; others closed their borders. Germany accepted the most refugees, but other countries, including Canada, are opening their doors to accept refugees who are welcomed by some and regarded with suspicion by others. There is an underlying fear among many that accepting refugees may allow terrorists to enter the country, promoting mistrust and suspicion of newcomers to Canada. These tensions spill over to Canada's diverse society. On the whole, Canada has been welcoming, with many privately sponsoring refugee families either independently or through local organizations (e.g., churches and municipalities).

It is unrealistic to expect that all Canadians—new and established—will embrace every culture enthusiastically. People may find themselves living next door to someone from a group or culture they grew up learning to regard as a bitter enemy. Such feelings do not simply evaporate by virtue of being in a new country. Friends and adversaries alike immigrate to Canada, seeking business opportunities, proximity to family, and peace and freedom. In spite of these common goals, where prejudice exists it takes time for wounds to heal and for attitudes ingrained over generations to change. Long-time Canadians, too, can find it difficult to accept change and may regard newcomers as interlopers. Despite official goals of equality and acceptance, racial and ethnic prejudices are not uncommon among some groups in Canada.

In health care, cultural acceptance is a gateway to positive relationships that enhance effective care, patient health, and wellness. As an administrative health professional, you will play an important role in the delivery of this health care. You will, in many cases, act as an advocate for the patient. You can help break down cultural barriers and make the patient's health care experience more positive from both a medical and a personal perspective. As previously mentioned, you may be the first person an individual comes into contact with when seeking health care. A positive interaction is the first step toward establishing an adaptive and trusting relationship. The most important thing you can do is help your patient feel valued and respected. This, however, is not always as simple as it sounds. It may involve looking inward and coming to terms with your own thoughts, feelings, values, and attitudes. Make it a personal goal to understand your own attitudes toward various cultures and to work toward tolerance, understanding, and acceptance. Try to see people for who they are, understand where they are coming from, and develop a positive and caring attitude.

If you feel that a patient fears prejudice, you must do your best to reassure him or her by being consistently professional, warm, and friendly. Conversely, if you feel that a patient is prejudiced against you, for whatever reason, you must set aside your natural resentment and be patient. As you continue to behave in a professional and friendly manner, you will be helping to break down that prejudice.

Indigenous Peoples

Not only immigrants and refugees face challenges when it comes to health care. Cultural issues with health care extend to Canada's Indigenous population as well.[3] Disparities in socioeconomic conditions exist within Indigenous communities, which profoundly affect the health and well-being of this population group. In many communities available health care is woefully inadequate, with gaps among resources, organization, and delivery—this is especially true for remote communities.

Indigenous life expectancy is less than that for non-Indigenous Canadians. According to Statistics Canada (2011), this gap is approximately four to six years less for men and seven to ten years less for women. Social and health inequities for Indigenous peoples remain the highest in the country. These problems (particularly in northern communities) are perpetuated by isolation, high unemployment rates, poverty, food insecurity, inadequate housing, and substance abuse. Health concerns include high rates of mental illness, suicide, and chronic diseases, especially diabetes and sexually transmitted infections.

In smaller communities, health care is given at nursing stations, often by nurses or nurse practitioners, with distance support online, by telephone, via videoconferencing,

---

[3]Section 35 of the Constitution Act of 1982 recognizes First Nations and Métis as Indigenous populations. Indigenous more recently also includes Canada's Inuit population. Métis are people of mixed First Nations and European ancestry.

or from visiting physicians. Videoconferencing allows physicians to both see and interact with patients, perform examinations, diagnose problems, and prescribe treatment. Individuals with health problems that cannot be managed locally are transported, usually by air ambulance, to larger medical centres, most often a great distance from their community. Patients find this sudden move to a busy hospital intimidating. They also face the stress of being away from their own familiar environment and the support of family and friends. A lack of cultural understanding regarding traditional healing practices in favour of Western medicine is another obstacle.

That said, some centres are trying to address this problem by integrating traditional treatments with Western medicine. This requires that all members of the health care team be familiar with traditional healing practices. A good example of such a hospital is the Sioux Lookout Meno Ya Win Health Centre. As much as possible, the centre incorporates traditional practices, principles, and spiritual healing ceremonies such as vigils, smudging, and healing circles.

L03 BARRIERS TO CROSS-CULTURAL HEALTH CARE

Culture plays a role in shaping people's health beliefs—what health, wellness, and illness mean to them; who assumes responsibility for their health; their perception of illness and disease; and how they respond to medical intervention and care. Even the values attached to life and death are influenced by culture.

Dealing effectively with health care issues in an ethnically diverse population is difficult, even under ideal conditions. Problems within the health care system magnify these challenges.

Health Care Delivery

New Canadians, no matter what their country of origin or the type of health care they have been familiar with, will find the Canadian health care system different. Some individuals will be accustomed to readily available, comprehensive modern services covered by a universal health plan, while others may have had very little health care available to them and had to pay for services. Finding out what benefits they are entitled to will be among a newcomer's first concerns. Knowing a patient's immigrant status (refugee or immigrant) will enable you to clearly explain which health care services or benefits he or she is entitled to. You should also be able to direct patients to appropriate community services if there are gaps in their health care coverage.

In addition, taking the time to give newcomers (patients) the necessary clinic/office is important. Explain how to access their doctor and other members of the health care team, how and where to call to make an appointment, office/clinic hours, and what to do if they need a doctor after hours (e.g., if there is a clinic available or if they should go to the nearest emergency department).

As recently as 10 years ago, most doctors had more time to establish a closer relationship with patients, promoting both trust and understanding. That happens less frequently today. Although the number of family doctors in Canada is rising, there is still a shortage in many regions (particularly rural and northern areas). Finding a doctor may be difficult for new immigrants, unless a relative's doctor has agreed to assume their care. In spite of reforms in primary care, family doctors still have large practices and are treating patients with more complex health problems, resulting in less time to get to know their patients. Patients may feel frustrated, angry, and helpless. When cultural differences and language barriers further complicate the relationship, patients may feel that the provider does not view them as important or is giving them substandard care because of a lack of cultural knowledge and understanding or prejudice.

Interprofessional collaboration makes it possible for patients to have their health needs attended to by a variety of health care professionals (other than their physician). In some groups, the patient must be referred to another team member; in others the patient can make an appointment on his or her own (e.g., with a dietician). This practice may not be well received by some new Canadians. In many cultures, the doctor is seen as the only person with the knowledge and authority to make medical decisions and implement a plan of care. A patient may refuse to see any provider but the physician (e.g., nurse practitioners, midwives, counsellors, or nurses who are specialists in antenatal care or well-baby clinics). In desperation, they may go to a clinic or the emergency department to seek care. They will likely have a different physician each time, resulting in fragmented medical records and little or no continuity of care and follow-up. Frustrations related to the long waits to see specialists and to access diagnostic services also compound health problems for those dealing with cultural adjustments.

The Hospital Environment

To most of us, hospitals, nursing homes, and other patient-care facilities are a familiar part of the health care landscape. Admission to an acute-care hospital is common for a serious illness. Moving to a nursing home is becoming the norm for older adults who can no longer care for themselves and whose families cannot provide for them.

To some cultures, however, health care agencies, whether acute or long term, are frightening and unwelcome. Koreans, for example, may view admission to hospital as an imminent sign of death and a disharmony with the life forces of yin and yang. Many ethnic minorities will avoid hospitals at all costs, preferring to manage their illnesses at home.

Admission to a health care facility poses even greater problems. The thought of entering a nursing home, particularly for cultures where the norm is to care for seniors at home, is often repugnant. Asian cultures, such as Vietnamese and Chinese, typically have a tradition of caring for senior family members at home, with hospitalization being a last resort. An older adult may avoid or refuse hospitalization, fearing separation from family. Yet, in Canada, attempts to keep an older or ill family member at home may become problematic. Family members, despite their cultural norms, may be struggling with full-time jobs and raising a family as well as the stress of bridging two cultures. If they cannot manage with home care and other community support initiatives, the feeling of failure is twofold: Family members may feel they have not fulfilled their responsibilities, and the patient admitted to care may feel abandoned.

The pace of the hospital routine in itself may upset the patient. Latin Americans, for instance, take a more relaxed approach to life in general. They like to take their time, have things explained, and consider alternatives. The hectic pace of the hospital may so intimidate and confuse them that they may find it difficult to participate in their own health care. Likewise, in the health office they may not accept the urgency of a test and may try to fit it into their schedule rather than rearrange other appointments to make the test a priority.

Professionals' Attitudes and Lack of Knowledge

For the health care system to be fully effective, professionals must understand and adapt to the varied mix of cultural, racial, socioeconomic, and generational differences within their practices (including sexual orientation and diversity/identity issues). This is a complex undertaking that can't be achieved overnight. Lack of understanding may lead professionals to be condescending to patients or to otherwise treat them in a way they find disrespectful. Someone with a history of being discriminated against will be quick to perceive any slight and will be hurt. Even a simple error or misunderstanding can lose the patient's trust and respect. At worst, the relationship is so impaired that even patients' simple needs are not met.

Cross-cultural understanding has recently been identified as needing significant improvement for health professionals dealing with Indigenous peoples. There is a need to recognize the importance of both family roles and community responsibilities when rendering health care. As previously mentioned, health professionals need to respect traditional Indigenous medicine and the role of elders in the community.[4]

DIFFERENCES IN BELIEFS AND PRACTICES

Patients come to a health office bringing varied expectations that are shaped by a blend of their culture and their experiences. A person who grew up with a different health care system may be surprised at how things are done and may not understand much of what is done and why. People's culturally based beliefs also influence both their decision to seek treatment and their expectations of treatment. This section outlines a few culturally based attitudes that may affect health care. Keep in mind that this discussion is very general. You should never assume that all members of a cultural minority share the same beliefs, practices, and attitudes. This approach is stereotyping and is likely to lead to misunderstandings. Not only do cultures vary, but individuals vary too. Your own attitudes toward health might be quite different from your sister's or your best friend's, and they may change over the course of your lifetime as a result of your own life experiences. Be alert to differences in how individuals approach health care; be aware of their expectations, their compliance with medical treatment, and their understanding of issues affecting their health and treatment.

Recent newcomers (especially younger people) may adopt typical Western health beliefs, values, and expectations quickly. Others may incorporate a blend of Western beliefs and behaviours with those of their country of origin, while still others will not embrace Western culture at all. First- and second-generation Canadians are often at odds with their parents and grandparents regarding health beliefs and behaviours. This may promote disharmony within the family. You may at times feel that you are caught in the middle, attempting to honour the rights of the patient as well as those of the parents.

Confidentiality

The issue of confidentiality can be complicated by cultural expectations. It is not unusual for a parent to come into the office and demand confidential information about his or her teenage child or demand that a plan of care for a son or daughter be withdrawn or changed. In some cultures, it is expected that a parent will have access to this type of information, whereas in Canada the matter is usually between the teenage patient and the provider. Conversely, a grown child may come in demanding information about a parent. In some cultures, it is expected that the eldest son, for example, will assume responsibility for care of the parent and therefore have the right to all medical information. In Canada, the exchange of this type of information is not permitted without the patient's expressed permission. In such circumstances, it is best to remain neutral and to discuss the issue with the doctor.

---

[4]Janet Smylie, B.A., M.D., C.C.F.P., *A Guide for Health Professionals Working with Indigenous People* (Ottawa, ON: Society of Obstetricians and Gynecologists of Canada, 2000).

The Philosophy of Prevention

As we discussed in Chapter 2, a preventive model of health care currently predominates in Western culture. Individuals are encouraged to take responsibility for their own wellness. Virtually every community, in partnership with various levels of government, has agencies that promote health education and adaptive lifestyles. Doctors and other health care professionals have also assumed responsibility for health teaching related to health promotion. Members of some minorities may resist or may not understand this approach. Some cultures, such as those of some First Nations, see health and illness as matters of the "here and now." Visiting the doctor's office for an annual physical examination (as is recommended in many jurisdictions) is not a standard practice. This is not deliberate noncompliance or disregard for one's health, just a different perspective. Carefully explain to the patient the reasons for the examination. If this does not change the patient's attitude and behaviour, you may simply have to respect his or her perspective. Remember that you can accept and respect a person's point of view without agreeing with it.

The Concept of Illness and Treatment

Many cultures do not accept the concept of chronic illness. When people in these cultures feel better, they consider the illness to have been cured; if they feel poorly again, they consider that a new illness. To someone with this attitude, it is difficult to explain the cycle of **remission** and **exacerbation** that characterizes illnesses like multiple sclerosis (MS). With MS, there are usually periods when the patient feels better (remission) and may be completely symptom free. This is usually the result of a well-established treatment regime. Even with treatment, clinical signs or symptoms will generally reappear (exacerbation). Treatment is adjusted, and perhaps the patient will enjoy another remission. Patients who do not see this cycle as part of a chronic illness often stop taking their medication as soon as they feel well, which interferes with effective management of the disease. Consider a patient, Ana, with a urinary tract infection for which the physician has prescribed an antibiotic four times a day for 10 days. The doctor assumes she will take the medication as prescribed. As expected, the clinical signs disappear in a day or two. Four days later, Ana calls with complaints that should have been managed by the medication. As soon as Ana felt better, she assumed that she was cured and stopped taking the medication. The way to prevent this problem is to give patients a careful, detailed explanation of the importance of taking the medication until it is finished, even when they no longer experience symptoms, and to invite questions to make sure they understand.

remission the phase of a chronic disease characterized by a relief or absence of clinical signs or symptoms.

exacerbation the phase of a chronic disease characterized by a return of clinical signs or symptoms.

Explanatory Systems

Some cultures have systems of traditional or folk medicine that explain health and illness according to principles different from those of modern Western medicine. Some link health and illness with the supernatural or spiritual world. Some African Canadians, for example, believe in a direct connection between the body and the forces of nature. They may consider propitious dates, stars, and numbers in booking appointments or making decisions about their health care. Traditional Chinese medicine explains health and illness largely in terms of opposing principles. The causes of diseases originate from two sources, those operating from the outside and those operating inside. External causes relate to hot and cold. For example, some foods and some conditions are considered "hot" and others "cold." These terms do not refer to temperature but to inherent qualities of substances. People with a "hot" condition are advised to eat "cold" foods, and vice versa. First Nations and Inuit Canadians have a holistic view of health. They consider health to include a range of mental, physical, and emotional factors. Good health requires a balance among these factors. Healing can involve the use of herbal medicines, talking circles, sweat lodges, and teaching from elders.

You cannot ask patients if they believe in magic or in folk medicine, but you can find out about their beliefs by asking what they think is the cause of their symptoms. Such beliefs may influence anything from the food they eat to their level of activity and when they bathe. Respect where they are coming from. Remember that Western medicine does not know everything. Whether or not health beliefs have any basis in fact, people are more likely to do well if they are confident in and comfortable with their treatment. Comply with their requests whenever possible. In some cases, you may need to accept that the patient will not choose the treatment the health care provider deems best. There is no universal formula that will allow you to resolve the difference, but remember that the foundation of good health care is respect for the individual. Ultimately, it is the patient's health and the patient's decision.

Attitudes toward Mental Illness

According to Health Canada, mental illness affects one in five Canadians at some point during their lives. Those with mental health issues, disabilities, and addictions face multiple discriminatory barriers, from individuals as well as from institutions. This includes health care and law enforcement. In 2012, more emphasis was placed on police being better trained to deal effectively with mentally ill individuals and to work with social workers and mental health professionals.

Discrimination compounds the effects of living with mental illness. It makes it harder for individuals to seek appropriate treatment for their problems. Recovery is difficult because of limited support systems. Despite awareness campaigns and increasing acceptance, mental illness still carries a certain stigma in Western society. For example, although depression is a widespread diagnosis, and anti-depressants are commonly used, many people are reluctant to admit they have been diagnosed or are taking medication even to friends and family. In 2012 Bell Canada launched a campaign to initiate discussion about mental health issues called "Bell Let's Talk"; Olympic athlete Clara Hughes, who has suffered from depression, participates in the campaign. By 2016, the campaign had raised nearly $80 million. The money is used to support hundreds of mental health initiatives across the country.

The stigma of mental health problems is even stronger among people, such as Vietnamese Canadians, whose culture believes mental illness is governed by spiritual entities. Chinese Canadians and Hispanics also will often avoid seeking treatment for mental illness, feeling that such issues are personal and should be discussed only with family members. Followers of Scientology believe there is no such thing as mental illness and that treating perceived mental illness with therapy or drugs is useless if not unethical.

Be tolerant, understanding, and discreet with these patients and their family members when discussing related tests and treatment times and when booking referral appointments.

End-of-Life Issues

Advanced technology makes it possible to prolong life for terminally ill patients. Some individuals want every measure possible used to sustain life; others want little or no intervention. These decisions reflect cultural, religious, and experientially acquired beliefs and practices. Muslims, for example, generally find it unacceptable to prolong life with machinery unless the individual will be able to lead a satisfactory life.

The death of a family member affects families of different cultures in various ways. The Vietnamese may mourn a loved one for up to three years. They do not usually allow autopsies, believing that the body should remain intact. They may also be reluctant to register as organ donors.

In 2012, the CBC brought two cases to light regarding the termination of "extraordinary" life support measures at Sunnybrook Health Sciences Centre in Toronto. Two physicians are required to concur on the withdrawal of life support or other measures deemed extraordinary if they feel that these measures are futile. The decision of the physicians overrides the family's desire to continue these measures for whatever reason, whether cultural or the personal belief that their loved one will or can recover, even in part.

Childcare

In contemporary Western society, mothers often work full time outside the home, relegating childcare to a hired nanny or a daycare centre. Although many women make this choice for financial reasons, the practice is generally accepted. In some other cultures, however, such as many African and Indian cultures, mothers are more likely to seek work where they can take the child with them or to have extended family members take care of the child. Although these arrangements can be more difficult in Canada, it is not unusual to have grandmothers, aunts, or sisters care for children. When the child comes into the office, it is not uncommon for the mother as well as the child's other caregiver(s) to come for support. They may all want to be in the examination room with the child. Accommodate this wish if space allows and if there is no medical reason not to. You may want to ask who is coming in with the child so that you can use a larger examination room if one is available.

Modesty

In Western society, most people are only mildly uncomfortable about setting aside modesty for a physical examination. However, for people from some cultures, such as many Asian and Middle Eastern cultures, it is difficult and stressful to expose one's body to a stranger, even a physician. It is especially distressing for a woman to expose her body to a man because of the strong norm of modesty in these male-dominated cultures. For this reason, many South Asian women prefer a female provider. If you are aware that modesty is a concern, try to do what you can to make the patient more comfortable. If you are using the standard examination gowns that open at the back, give the patient two gowns, with the second facing the front. Let the doctor know that the patient is modest so that he or she can be careful to expose only one area at a time. In most Canadian offices it is typical for a nurse or office professional to be present during the examination, particularly for a pelvic examination and Pap smear. If the physician wants you to be present but you feel that your presence is uncomfortable for the patient, keep a distance and busy yourself with other work while being available to assist the doctor when required. If the patient wants to have a family member present, allow this.

Religious Constraints

People's religious beliefs may make certain medical treatments or procedures unacceptable to them. For example, Jehovah's Witnesses will refuse organ transplants or transfusion with blood or blood products. This decision must be respected when the patient is an adult. The issue becomes more complicated for children, and courts have considered cases in which parents have refused treatment that doctors felt was necessary for the children's survival. Hindus, Buddhists, or Jains may object to medical interventions that use animal products, as may Orthodox Jews (who do eat meat, but only if it meets the rules of *kashrut*). In general, see if an alternative is available when a patient is uncomfortable with any proposed treatment.

Number of Visitors

Many hospitals have strict rules regarding the number of visitors a patient may have in the hospital room, partly to avoid disturbing other patients. However, in some East Asian and South Asian cultures, the prolonged presence of family and friends is considered essential to an ill person's comfort, security, and well-being. The challenge here is how to adapt the rules to meet the needs of the patient. If you work in a patient-care unit, carefully explain the hospital policies regarding visitors to a family member, and at the same time try to find a compromise. One might be to move the patient to a private room. Another solution, if patients are ambulatory, is to ask them to visit in the reception area. If these options are not feasible and other patients are being disturbed, you might suggest a compromise: reducing the number of visitors, asking them to be as quiet as possible, and placing limits on visiting time while allowing a little more than the standard hours. If patients and their families see that you are trying to make compromises, they will feel valued and respected and will often be willing to meet you half way. However, rules created for public health reasons, particularly related to the spread of infectious diseases, place much tighter restrictions on visitors—including visiting times and the number of visitors allowed into a room (these may vary with situations). If your hospital has such rules, there is probably little you can do beyond explaining the rules and being sympathetic.

Childbirth

Cultures have different approaches to childbirth and parenting. For example, some South Asian and East Asian women are quite stoic when in labour. If such a woman calls the office to report that she is in labour, asking her if she is having much pain may not reveal much about how advanced the labour is. You may get a more accurate impression by asking how far apart her contractions are and how long she has had them.

Health professionals may get the wrong impression about a couple's relationship if the father seems to wish no involvement in the birth. It has become common in Western culture for fathers or significant others to be present for the entire birthing process. A Western man who shows no interest in the pregnancy and does not wish to be present for the birth *may* be indicating a lack of commitment to fatherhood. (Or he may just be uncomfortable with first-hand exposure to childbirth.) In some cultures, this disinclination simply reflects a cultural norm and says nothing about the man's love for his wife or his excitement about the coming baby.

It has also recently become common in the West for mothers to be sent home very soon after delivery, usually from 4 to 24 hours **postpartum**. The mother who is up and about and back to a reasonable level of activity quickly is admired for her quick recovery and tenacity. Some cultures, however, such as those in parts of India, encourage new mothers to recuperate for 40 days. During this period, a time for rest and spiritual and physical renewal, they are cared for by family members. Health professionals may worry needlessly about an Indian woman who spends a lot of time in bed after giving birth. She may not be a disinterested mother or suffering from postpartum depression; she may simply be following a cultural norm that calls for her to rest.

postpartum after delivery.

LANGUAGE DIFFICULTIES

L04
L05
L06

Communication is a significant cross-cultural barrier. Many Canadian immigrants do not speak English or French fluently, and some not at all. Some start learning rapidly as soon as they arrive, but others may live in Canada for years and never learn. Access to English- or French-as-a-second-language courses is limited in some communities, and some people find getting to classes difficult, perhaps because they lack time or child-care. Often, older adults do not even attempt to learn English because it is difficult and because they do not feel the need to do so. If they live with their family in an ethnic enclave, they can continue to speak their native language and manage quite well. Difficulties arise, however, when they interface with the health care system. Furthermore, even people with good second-language skills may revert to their mother tongue in times of stress or may lose some of their fluency and comprehension skills.

Language difficulties may cause a person to put off making an appointment, leading to worsening health problems and possibly a more stressful intervention. Although you cannot entirely remove this barrier, you can be consistently patient and friendly on the phone so that at least the patient need not fear embarrassment or rejection. Listen for halting speech or errors in usage or vocabulary; if the person's English appears to be limited, take a little extra time to speak clearly and slightly more slowly than usual. Make any instructions as uncomplicated as you can. Pause from time to time to allow the patient to ask for clarification. Avoid both medical jargon and idioms that may be obscure to someone with limited English. For example, if a patient asks you which of two laboratories to go to, don't say, "It's a toss-up," or "It's six of one, half-dozen of the other." The patient may just wonder, "What is being thrown?" "Six of what?" Instead, you could say, "You may go to either lab." If in doubt, have the patient repeat information for you. In fact, it is a good idea with any patient to have the patient repeat the appointment time for you. Calling the patient the day before the appointment can also clarify information that may not have been understood.

The same principles of clear communication apply in the office. For example, if you are explaining a diagnostic test to a patient, include details about the preparation, how the test will be done, how long it will take, and whether or not someone can come with the patient. Encourage the patient to ask questions, and answer as accurately as you can.

Speaking clearly does not mean lapsing into pidgin English. Nor does it mean raising your voice. Stick to correct, complete sentences in your normal tone. Some people try to make instructions clearer by omitting words. For example: "You go there for appointment. Girl, meet you at door." This can actually be more confusing as well as demeaning. Keep in mind that some people understand better than they can speak and will be bitterly insulted by baby talk. Instead say "Your appointment is on the third floor of the hospital. I will ask the receptionist to meet you at the door." When efforts at telephone communication appear too difficult, arrange for a family member or friend to act as an interpreter.

Using an Interpreter

In Canada, there is a requirement that medical practitioners provide their deaf patients with interpretation services. There is no such requirement for individuals with other language barriers. In some cases, language barriers (perhaps coupled with a profound sense of modesty or a belief that illness is an admission of weakness) will stop a person from seeking needed health care. Even if these patients do come, they will not understand anything about their condition or the treatment if you do not have a language in common. In many communities, access to interpreters is limited. Most hospitals keep a list of staff members who speak various languages. Of course, a second language is also an asset in the health office, but more often you will rely on family or friends as interpreters. If you feel an interpreter is needed, ask an appropriate person to come to each office visit. Some patients will be insulted, feeling that they are considered incompetent. Try to explain that you just want to make sure you understand each other clearly and that having an interpreter will benefit both parties. When patients understand the reason for certain requests and recognize that you care enough about them to take the time to explain, they will feel respected and cared for and will usually be more compliant. The friend or family member can also speak on the patient's behalf and can help the patient feel supported.

If you have a choice of interpreter, the patient will usually feel most at ease with someone of the same gender and approximately the same age. In Indian cultures, it is sometimes expected that the provider will give any information about the patient to a male member of the family, such as the father, the brother, or the son. A sibling or adult child may or may not be a good choice depending on whether the patient wants to keep certain things private. Usually a child or teenager is not the best choice; not only may young people lack the maturity to understand everything, but discussion may also expose them to matters they are not prepared to handle or that parents would rather keep from them. The down side of using a family member as an interpreter is that he or she may not be entirely objective or accurately translate what either the provider or the patient is saying; instead the family member may mould what is said to suit what he or she thinks should be said or done.

Book a longer appointment for a patient who will be using an interpreter. Information will have to be repeated by the interpreter and perhaps restated by the provider for clarification. The interpreter should be at the same physical level as the patient—if the patient is lying in bed, offer the interpreter a chair beside the bed. Always face the patient, not the interpreter, and make eye contact, even though the patient will have to look to the interpreter for the information. The inability to effectively communicate affects the health professional as well as the patient. Be patient. While you may be getting frustrated, keep in mind that the patient is equally frustrated and may also be anxious and may feel inadequate, which undermines self-esteem. The importance of effective communication cannot be overemphasized. See the following box for suggestions on cross-cultural communication in the health office.

⟫⟫ HOW TO IMPROVE YOUR CULTURAL COMPETENCE

A culturally competent health care system depends on culturally competent health professionals at all levels. Cultural competence is not something you can learn and leave. It is a process that is continually evolving, requiring you to change, adapt, and adjust almost daily.

On a day-to-day level, keep these tips in mind:

- *Smile, especially while greeting someone.* Almost all cultures appreciate smiles, as long as they are appropriate to the situation.

- *Speak softly, but loudly enough to be heard.* A loud voice may be perceived as aggressive. Remember that speakers of other languages are not deaf and will not understand better if you speak louder.

- *Always greet a patient you do not know by surname.* Switch to first names only at the patient's invitation. Though many North Americans like the informality of first names, it can be considered intrusive in many cultures. Even in North American culture, many seniors consider uninvited use of the first name a sign of disrespect.

- *If a language barrier exists, speak slowly and clearly.* Use simple words and avoid medical jargon. Watch for nonverbal cues: facial expressions, body language, and gestures. Do not assume that a nod or smile means the patient understands or accepts what you say. Sometimes a patient is confused but is trying to be polite. On the other hand, never assume that someone who does not appear to speak English does not understand what is being said.

- *Keep in mind that some languages, such as Chinese and Arabic, place the family name first.* Some people retain this format; others switch to the English style. If you are not sure, ask. Use the same approach if you do not know how to pronounce the name—do not guess: "Excuse me, I'm not sure how to pronounce your name." Some people will not correct you if you guess incorrectly.

- *Observe carefully how the patient looks at you.* Most North Americans consider direct eye contact a sign of self-confidence and forthrightness. Many cultures, including some Asian and some First Nations cultures, consider direct eye contact domineering and disrespectful. If you notice the patient avoids eye contact with you, stop looking directly. Looking at the patient quickly and then away is usually acceptable. Sustained eye contact is more likely to offend.

- *Try not to appear impatient or rushed.* This is difficult when you are responsible for a busy office. However, being rushed will increase patients' anxiety and can interfere with their ability to communicate.

- *Be aware that different cultures have different comfort zones that regulate how close to stand to someone in conversation.* If you feel that a patient is intruding in your personal space, try to decide whether he or she is being confrontational or simply following a cultural rule. If it is the latter, try to ignore it. Conversely, if a patient takes a step back from you, do not take it personally; you may have entered his or her personal space.

- *If a patient extends his or her hand, take it.* Although shaking hands is not usual in Canadian health offices, refusing an offer to shake hands may be taken as a slight and as evidence of prejudice.

- *Show genuine interest in the patient, and always demonstrate a friendly, warm attitude.*

- *Be receptive to any culturally based requests and do what you can to honour them.* If appropriate, tell the patient you will discuss the request with the doctor. Even if the patient's request does not seem feasible, do not reject it outright. Compromise is much easier if the patient feels you have made an effort.

- *Involve the patient in decision making when you can.* This affords a feeling of control, which is particularly important when a patient is feeling otherwise overwhelmed.

- *When booking tests, ask patients when the best time is.* This may hinge on when a family member or interpreter is free to accompany them.

- *Write down instructions.* Printing is usually easier to understand. If possible, have the interpreter write the instructions down in the patient's first language. Many laboratories have patient instructions in different languages. Highlighting the area that the patient will be referring to will help avoid confusion.

⫸ REMEMBER THE SMILE PRINCIPLE

Sensitivity. Be sensitive to the needs of the patient.

Mutual respect. The patient who feels respected feels valued and will respect you in return. Mutual respect enhances communication and promotes trust.

Interest. Showing interest in the patient keeps the lines of communication open and helps make the health care experience positive.

Language. Assess language barriers and adapt accordingly. Are you communicating clearly with the patient, or do you need an interpreter?

Explanation. Explain clearly to the patient and family.

⫸ WHAT TO WATCH FOR

- How immigration standards and practices have evolved and responded to the need to accommodate large numbers of refugees from war-torn countries.

- How accepting Canadians are as a whole to refugees, or whether bias and discrimination become more prominent.

- Implementation of legislation related to physician-assisted death across Canada and how Canadians react to this legislation.

- The impact of accepting large numbers of refugees into the country on health care (how the system adapts to give proper, culturally sensitive care to refugees in accordance with the terms and conditions of the Canada Health Act).

SUMMARY

1. Canada is an increasingly multicultural country. Being responsive to the differing needs and expectations of people from different cultures is essential to effective health care. Culture affects our attitudes and behaviours and almost every aspect of our lives. It is so ingrained that we are often unaware of its influence. Ethnocentrism can cause us to fail to see another's point of view and can impede understanding.

2. Cultural understanding is more important than ever in a shrinking world, but international conflict has exacerbated tensions. Cultural acceptance in the health office is essential to a trusting, positive patient relationship.

3. A shortage of doctors means less time with patients, making it more difficult to establish relationships and overcome cultural barriers. Many immigrants to Canada are unable to find doctors. Immigrants may also be daunted by medical technology and hospitals and may meet with disrespect or condescension from some health professionals.

4. People from some cultures may not accept preventive health care, considering health to be something in the "here and now." Some do not accept the concept of chronic illness, viewing each exacerbation as a new illness. Some have explanations of health and illness that differ from those of modern Western medicine, and some attach a strong stigma to mental illness. Though it is important to be alert for these differences, it is equally important not to make assumptions about a patient's attitudes. Treat each patient as an individual.

5. Differing attitudes toward childcare, childbirth, schedules, modesty, and visiting practices can require flexibility from the health care professional. Try to accommodate patients' requests whenever possible.

6. Language often poses a barrier. If the patient's English is limited, speak clearly and slowly, avoid medical jargon and colloquialisms, check for comprehension, and encourage questions. If you are unable to communicate clearly, try to arrange for an interpreter, who may be a hospital staff member or a friend or relative of the patient.

KEY TERMS

cultural competence 65
culture 63
diversity 65

ethnic 63
ethnocentrism 66
exacerbation 73

postpartum 76
remission 73
subculture 63

REVIEW QUESTIONS

1. Define culture, and explain the various components of culture.
2. Explain the relationships among culture, ethnicity, race, and nationality.
3. Explain how changes in the Canadian health care system have adversely affected immigrants and their access to health care.
4. Outline some of the problems related to hospitalization that are experienced by ethnic minorities.
5. How can the administrative health professional protect the privacy of a very modest patient?
6. Explain some steps the administrative health professional can take to overcome language barriers.
7. Describe three techniques that will enhance communication with a patient who has limited English-language skills.

APPLICATION EXERCISES

1. **a.** In groups of two or three, select and interview someone from a different culture about his or her experiences with health care in Canada. Develop a picture of what health care was like in that person's country of origin, and compare it with that in Canada. Ask the person to identify problems he or she has encountered and what steps could be taken to resolve those problems.

   b. Prepare a short oral presentation on the basis of the information gathered from your interview. Research health care in that person's country of origin to create a more complete picture of the differences from and similarities to the health care system in Canada. Make a list of the person's recommendations for change, adding any that your group can think of. Try to include such things as communication with the person (e.g., making an appointment with the physician or for blood work and diagnostic tests), providing an interpreter, clarifying what is covered under their provincial/territorial plan, references to required community agencies, and issues related to hospitalization.

2. Review physician-assisted death protocols in your jurisdiction. Discuss the criteria for someone who wants to apply for physician-assisted death. Does it differ from current federal legislation? Identify amendments that have been made to the 2016 legislation, if any. In a small group, discuss your personal views, concerns, and preferences. Try to find middle ground within your group and make a list of recommendations.

3. Identify the two prevalent cultures in your area. Summarize key cultural expectations related to the health and health care of these groups. In small groups, create a scenario in which patients and health professionals have different expectations. (Use your research summary to identify these expectations.) For example, a patient refuses a physical examination or a patient in hospital refuses to ask her eight family members to leave after visiting hours are over. One student should role-play the patient and one the administrative health professional. Ask the class for suggestions on how to resolve the disagreement.

4. Panaji Singh is a 13-year-old female born in Canada who has come to see the doctor wanting birth control pills. She has a boyfriend and is sexually active. Her parents resent the relationship and do not know Panaji is sexually active. Panaji's parents are traditional and believe their daughter should follow cultural and family rules—sex before marriage is not one of them. They also believe that that any health concerns their daughter has must be shared with them, thus patient–physician confidentiality (as it is understood in Canada) is an issue. A week later, Mrs. Singh calls the office wanting to know why her daughter came in. She wants to make an appointment with the doctor to discuss her daughter's visit and subsequent treatment—without Panaji present.

   a. How would you respond to her on the phone?

   b. How do you feel about patient–physician confidentiality and Panaji's rights when culture is involved?

   c. Outline what you believe to be the rights of the parents and Panaji's rights.

   d. What kind of a dilemma does this put the doctor in?

5. In groups of two or three, choose a province or territory and explore the status of its Indigenous population. Consider cultural details, demographics such as population distribution, access to health care, overall health, and social issues.

6. Using the internet, research the problems of the First Nations community of Attawapiskat. List the main problems; identify the strategies laid out to address the problems, and by whom; and describe the progress to date. What solutions would you suggest?

WEBSITES OF INTEREST

Evaluation of the Provincial Nominee Program

www.cic.gc.ca/english/immigrate/provincial

Immigration and Ethnocultural Diversity in Canada

www12.statcan.gc.ca/nhs-enm/2011/as-sa/99-010-x/
99-010-x2011001-eng.cfm

White Coat, Black Art Podcast on Physician-Assisted Death

www.cbc.ca/radio/whitecoat/pastepisodes/quebec-canada-
and-the-right-to-die-1.3351725

National Council on Interpreting in Health Care

www.ncihc.org/faqs-for-healthcare-professionals

Chapter 4
The Canadian Health Care System

Sam Spiro/Fotolia

LEARNING OBJECTIVES

On completing this chapter, you will be able to:

1. Summarize the history of the health care system in Canada.

2. Explain the five principles and two conditions of the Canada Health Act.

3. Understand how Canadian health care is structured and administered.

4. Describe the settings in which primary care is delivered in Canada.

5. Discuss the structure and function of primary care delivery models in Canada.

6. Examine how health providers are remunerated in Canada.

Health care in Canada is provided to all eligible residents under provincial and territorial health insurance plans, regardless of income, employment, or health. Although our health care system has had its share of problems, most Canadians want it to be preserved. Most agree that continued initiatives to promote and maintain cost-effective, high-quality care are essential if our health care system is to survive. This chapter includes a brief overview of significant events in the history and development of health care in Canada to help you understand the basic structure of the system, how it functions, and some of the challenges it faces. Table 4.1 contains a chronological

TABLE 4.1 Chronology of Legislation and Regulations Affecting Health Care Coverage in Canada

1946	Citizens of Swift Current, Saskatchewan, establish the first public health insurance program in North America, making health services available to all residents.
1947	Saskatchewan's CCF government, led by Tommy Douglas, introduces the first provincial hospital insurance program in Canada.
1948	The Liberals introduce a National Health Grants Program to assist provinces and territories with construction of new hospitals, keeping their promise to introduce cost-shared social programs.
1957	The federal government introduces the Hospital Insurance and Diagnostic Services Act to encourage the development of hospital insurance plans.
1961	All provinces and territories have public insurance plans in place for in-hospital care.
1962	Saskatchewan extends health insurance to include out-of-hospital coverage for physician services.
1965	A Royal Commission, headed by Emmett Hall, calls for a universal, comprehensive, national health insurance program with minimum standards set across the country.
1966	Under the National Medical Care Insurance Act, Ottawa agrees to pay 50 percent of provincial and territorial health costs.
1972	All provincial and territorial insurance plans cover physician services.
1977	Trudeau's Liberals replace 50/50 cost sharing with five-year block funding that gives provinces and territories more control over health spending. The Established Programs Financing program combines health care transfers with educational transfers.
1984	The Canada Health Act is passed unanimously by the House of Commons, allowing Ottawa to withhold funds if provinces and territories do not comply with the five principles. This bill bans extra-billing and charging for insured services.
1985–1993	Federal share of spending on health under the Mulroney government drops from 30.8 percent in 1985 to 23.5 percent in 1993.
1995	Canada Health and Social Transfer (CHST) brings massive cuts in transfer payments to health and social programs.
1995–1999	Federal-to-provincial/territorial transfer payments continue to drop, and provincial and territorial expenses continue to grow. Hospitals are closed and services are slashed.
2000	All levels of government agree to new reforms in primary care, management of pharmaceuticals, management of health records (electronic in particular), health infrastructure, as well as an increase in federal-to-provincial/territorial cash transfers.
2002	The federally commissioned Romanow Report recommends increased federal health spending and sets out guidelines.
2002	The Kirby Report recommends a dedicated health care tax and guaranteed limits to waiting times for medical services.
2003	The premiers reach an accord to implement a new health plan. The federal government agrees to provide $34.8 billion over five years to go toward a Primary Health Reform Fund, drug coverage, and updated diagnostic and medical equipment.
2004	The provinces and territories negotiate a 10-year, $41 billion health accord with Prime Minister Paul Martin. Under the accord, the federal government increased annual funding while setting a series of guidelines for improving and expanding health care coverage and delivery across the country. In January 2004, Prime Minister Paul Martin pledges $2 billion in health care funding to the provinces and territories and participation in continued discussions for a long-term action plan for health care.
	The provincial and territorial leaders also agree to establish a new public health agency that will be similar to the Centers for Disease Control and Prevention in the United States to deal with infectious diseases.
2004	Introduction of PIPEDA—federal legislation protecting personal information. This affects some health care organizations. In the 2004–2005 fiscal year, the CHST was split into the Canada Health Transfer and Canada Social Transfer.
2006	The Public Health Agency of Canada receives royal assent on December 12, 2006. This establishes the agency as a separate organization within the health portfolio. The agency's directive is to assist the federal minister of health to complete his or her duties.

(continued)

TABLE 4.1 (*continued*)

2011	The Canadian government put forth a new accord for the funding and management of health care for the provinces and territories. According to the new agreement, the federal government will guarantee the provinces and territories 6 percent health care funding increases until the 2016–2017 fiscal year. After that time, the annual finding will be tied to gross domestic product (GDP). Unlike previous accords, the new accord did not contain the federal government's parameters for spending—the provinces and territories are free to use the money at their own discretion. The ministers of health hope to stimulate negotiations with respect to this accord. The federal government estimates that health care spending will rise from $30 billion in 2013 to $38 billion in 2018. The accord contains a "no strings attached" policy, in that the federal government will not interfere with any province that experiments with or expands private delivery of publicly funded care. However, the core principles of the Canada Health Act are maintained in that user fees, fully private care, or other major violations of the act will still result in clawbacks.
2016	Legislation is passed by the federal government setting out the terms and conditions for physician-assisted death in Canada.
	The federal health minister begins negotiations for a new accord with provinces and territories, with an emphasis on home care (the 2004 accord was not renewed by the Harper government).

summary of significant events in the evolution of legislation and regulations that have led to the public health care system we have today.

L01 L02 THE CANADA HEALTH ACT

The Canada Health Act (1984) is the current federal insurance legislation. It replaced previous legislation and consolidated all components of health insurance. Each province and territory is responsible for the delivery and administration of its own health services. The federal government contributes a designated amount of money to health care. The provinces and territories pay the balance of what is required to deliver health care within their own jurisdictions.

The Canada Health Act comprises five principles and two conditions that all provinces and territories must meet to receive the health-related transfer payments from the federal government. Under the act, the federal government can impose various other penalties if these conditions are not met. These conditions and principles provide the foundation for health care delivery in Canada.

√Principles

1. Public Administration

Health care in each province or territory must be

- managed by a public authority (may not be privately operated),
- managed on a not-for-profit basis, and
- subject to federal inspections and financial audits.

2. Comprehensiveness

- Each province and territory must ensure that those who are eligible receive all services designated medically necessary by doctors and hospitals.
- This includes coverage of any surgical dental procedure that is considered necessary from a medical/dental perspective and that must be carried out in hospital.
- Where the law permits, the plan must cover the insured person for additional insured services rendered by other health care **providers**.

provider any person or group of persons who delivers a health care service.

3. Universality

- Every resident of each province and territory is entitled to fair and equitable public health insurance coverage.

4. Portability

- The province or territory must grant insurance coverage to an eligible person within three months.

- The plan must provide coverage for insured individuals who are travelling outside their resident province or territory. Host-province rates apply to health care provided in other provinces or territories. The individuals must be covered by their province of origin during any waiting period imposed by any other province or territory.

- Out-of-country coverage must be provided according to established guidelines.

5. Accessibility

- Each province and territory must provide fair and reasonable access to all insured health services through uniform terms and conditions. Residents of all regions are entitled to the same medical care and benefits.

- The plans must make reasonable compensation to all providers for insured health services.

Conditions

There are also two conditions that must be met under the Canada Health Act:

1. Each province and territory must provide information and statistics on insured health care to the federal government.

2. Each province and territory must formally recognize the financial contribution of the federal government.

 RESPONSIBILITIES AND FINANCING

The federal government works in partnership with provincial and territorial governments to finance and deliver national health care. The provinces and territories themselves are constitutionally responsible for administering and delivering health care services within their jurisdictions. They decide, among other things, how much money to spend on health care systems, where to locate hospitals, how many physicians they will need, and which supplementary health services to cover. For example, although not required by the Canada Health Act, most provinces and territories cover the costs of medication and nursing care for seniors managing at home.

Federal Government Responsibilities

- Setting, administering, and monitoring all national standards for medicare

- Making payments to provinces and territories for health care under the Canada Health and Social Transfer Act

- Financing and delivering services to specific groups, including veterans, First Nations peoples living on reserves, military personnel, and inmates of federal penitentiaries; Royal Canadian Mounted Police officers, formerly covered by the federal government, are now covered by the jurisdiction in which they live (see Chapter 12)

- Providing leadership in health promotion, protection, and disease prevention, including public education

Provincial and Territorial Responsibilities

- Delivering health services to eligible residents
- Funding and managing insured hospital, physician, and allied health services
- Managing and evaluating cost-effective delivery of health services
- Managing components of prescription care and public health services

Financing

Health care in Canada is funded, for the most part, by the federal, provincial and territorial, and municipal governments through a blend of personal and corporate taxes, and by workers' compensation boards. Some provinces also use revenue from sales taxes and lotteries. British Columbia and Ontario require eligible residents to pay health care premiums, although this is not a requirement mandated by the Canada Health Act. Moreover, it is estimated that about 30 percent of health care costs are paid for by the private sector. This is primarily at the municipal level through volunteer and private organizations. Many of these groups contribute funding to the construction of new hospitals, diagnostic services, and other services deemed necessary within a community. They also support services to individuals within a community, such as Meals on Wheels and home care. Although private insurance covers many unpaid services, individuals pay out of pocket as well (e.g., for home care when the person requires more hours of care than allotted to them).

The federal government transfers funds to the provinces and territories in the form of both cash and tax points, which are calculated using a complex formula. There are two main transfer programs: the Canada Health Transfer and the Canada Social Transfer. As well, the federal government, under Territorial Formula Financing, provides funding to the territories (using three different funding formulas) that considers the unique needs of each territory. Among other things, these funds can be used for health care.

Equalization payments are unconditional payments (based on a three-year national average of GDP) made by the federal government to less prosperous jurisdictions to ensure they can deliver an acceptable level of health care. These payments are unconditional in that the provinces can spend the money they receive at their own discretion, as long as it relates to health care. Any province that falls below the national average is eligible for equalization. In fiscal 2015–2016, Ottawa distributed $17.3 billion in equalization payments to six provinces (often referred to as the "have-not" provinces): Quebec, Ontario, Manitoba, Nova Scotia, New Brunswick, and Prince Edward Island. Based on the funding formula, Alberta, Saskatchewan, and Newfoundland and Labrador, provinces that have all had significant downturns in their economies (because of the drop in oil prices) in 2016–2017, did not receive equalization payments. It is expected that the "have-not" provinces will soon change (e.g., Alberta will receive equalization payments, and Ontario will pay into them).

Benefits covered by provincial/territorial plans vary from one jurisdiction to another. In all jurisdictions certain benefits are available only to individuals with specific financial or health needs. Private health insurance covers many supplementary or uninsured health services. Many private and group health insurance policies are paid, at least in part, through employee benefit packages. See Chapter 10 for more detail on coverage.

In Canada, 95 percent of hospitals are not-for-profit and publicly funded. Some long-term care and specialized facilities are operated for profit. These facilities are regulated by provincial and territorial governments.

Some provinces and territories have a single authority responsible for all health care. Others have an overall responsible body but two administrative bodies, one to handle hospitals and health care facilities and the other to handle medical care. These organizations negotiate remuneration and other policies with professional bodies, such as the College of Physicians and Surgeons in each province, the Canadian Association of Optometrists, the Ontario Medical Association, the Newfoundland and Labrador Dental Association, the Medical Society of Nova Scotia, and the Manitoba Medical Society.

All provinces and territories, with the exception of Prince Edward Island and Alberta, have regional health authorities throughout the province/territory that assess the needs of a given community and allocate funds accordingly (as outlined by their respective Ministry of Health). For example, in Ontario these organizations are called Local Health Integration Networks, or LHINs. These LHINs have autonomy over the allocation of funds to various health services within their regions. (In 2012 they were given the authority to fund primary health organizations.) The Northwest Territories has eight health organizations called Health and Social Services Authorities. Health Prince Edward Island is that province's sole health authority, under its Department of Health and Wellness.

Restructuring in 2007, Alberta Health Services is now the single provincial health authority responsible for overseeing both the planning and delivery of health care in the province. This includes hospitals, continuing care and mental health facilities, clinics, and community health services. Alberta Health Services is the largest health authority in Canada and is organized into five geographic zones. The Alberta Health Services Board governs Alberta Health Services.

Payment of Premiums

In Canada, there are two models for paying provincial and territorial premiums: (1) residents pay insurance premiums; and (2) the government covers health care costs through blended taxation.

British Columbia and Ontario residents pay insurance premiums. In all other provinces and territories, health care is paid for by tax money from the federal, provincial or territorial, and municipal governments, including sales taxes, employer levies, and property taxes. Coverage is universal for legal residents, regardless of employment status.

British Columbia All premiums paid are based on family size and income. Starting January 1, 2015, based on an annual income of $30 000, a single person would pay a monthly amount of $72.00, a family of two would pay $130.00, and a family of four would pay $144.00. Those with an income under $22 000 pay no premiums.

Ontario The Ontario Health Premium is income based. Those with taxable income of $20 000 or less are exempt. Above that, premium levels rise with taxable income. The premium is deducted from employee pay and pension cheques through Ontario's personal income tax system.

⟫⟫ POINTS TO PONDER

Ontario and British Columbia require their residents to pay health care premiums. Do you personally think this contravenes the principles of the Canada Health Act?

Health Care Delivery

Several models of health care delivery and remuneration are used in Canada. Over the past few years, the number of practising physicians in the country has increased, but many Canadians still have no family doctor. Primary care reform initiatives across Canada have, for the most part, moved to a multidisciplinary, interprofessional team approach to health care. Thus, family doctors are increasingly working in groups or family health organizations with other providers, such as nurse practitioners, physician assistants, pharmacists, dietitians, and social workers. Some providers work in educational facilities, hospitals, clinics, community health centres, or public health facilities. Several methods of payment are used to compensate Canadian physicians, but most are paid using a blended formula (e.g., capitation-based funding and fee-for-service).

Health care structures and settings are quite similar across Canada, both in and out of hospitals. Experimentation with various primary care models of delivery continues across Canada. It has become evident that there is no "one model to fit all." Different physicians in different groups want different things. In most jurisdictions, the governments are flexible with respect to the models they fund. Other questions remain: What services should be covered? How are these services best delivered? What can be done to improve access? What is the best approach to reducing wait times? Is private health care part of the answer? These issues are continually reexamined in the search for a balance between cost and quality.

L04 PRIMARY HEALTH CARE

primary health care (1) integrated health care by a provider who addresses the majority of a patient's health concerns; (2) treatment administered during the first medical contact for a health concern.

Primary health care is the provision of integrated health care services by providers who address the majority of a patient's health concerns. Primary health care also refers to treatment administered during the first point of contact for a particular health concern. Usually, family physicians (also called family practitioners or general practitioners, GPs) deliver primary care along with nurse practitioners and, secondarily, a team of health professionals, including pharmacists and physiotherapists. In some regions other providers, such chiropractors and naturopaths, are part of this team. In Canada, specialists are not considered primary care providers because a patient must have a referral from a family doctor to be seen by one (for a consultation). In other words, a person cannot call the office of a specialist and ask for an appointment without a referral from their family doctor.

TIP

If you are coordinating appointments among primary health providers, be sure that consultation reports are sent to the appropriate providers. This can be accomplished by listing the individuals to whom copies should be sent with the original consultation request.

Physicians within a *family practice* provide *primary care* and thus are primary care providers. However, family physicians provide a range of services well beyond the scope of what is defined as primary care services. Emergency departments or urgent care clinics provide primary care in emergencies but do not provide the full range of services offered in a family practice.

The family physician is an MD (medical doctor) whose postgraduate specialty is in family medicine. Family physicians are generalists—they look after the general medical needs of patients from babies to seniors. Primary care includes health promotion, disease prevention, health maintenance, counselling, patient education, and diagnosis and treatment of acute and chronic illnesses in a variety of health care settings (e.g., office, hospital, critical care, long-term care, home care, daycare). In addition to having a general practice, a number of family doctors also work in other areas (with special training); these include emergency medicine, anesthesiology, or sports medicine. In such circumstances the doctor would only work as a general practitioner for two or three days a week, often sharing the practice with another physician. A **locum tenens**, often simply called a "locum," is a doctor temporarily taking over another doctor's practice, such as during vacations. If the practice is specialized, the locum must have the same specialty. Primary care physicians often use a locum when they travel.

Specialists and Primary Care

Specialists (also called consultants) are not considered primary care physicians, although some specialists do render some primary care services. (For example, many obstetricians provide the same type of prenatal primary care assessments that family physicians do; patients are referred to them either because they are high risk or because their family physician does not deliver babies—which is the case with most family physicians.) If an obstetrician is doing "normal" deliveries, the patient may see her family doctor until she is in her sixth month of pregnancy, after which point the obstetrician will assume care her until the baby is delivered. After that, unless there are complications, mom and baby return to the care of their family doctor.

Most family practitioners quickly realize what conditions they are equipped to handle and when they should refer to a specialist for diagnosis or treatment. For example, Amina, who is 12 weeks pregnant, goes to see her family doctor for a routine prenatal check-up and follow-up on a glucose tolerance test the doctor had ordered. (Amina has a family history of diabetes.) The results of the test indicate that Amina has gestational diabetes. The family doctor then refers Amina to an obstetrician and an internist, both of whom will follow her through her pregnancy, labour, and delivery. The family doctor will be kept within the circle of care—all test reports and consultation reports will be sent to the family doctor to keep him or her informed about Amina's condition. The family doctor will provide care for her after she has delivered and her condition has stabilized. He or she will also provide care for any unrelated health problems that occur in the meantime, such as an ear infection. Likely a pediatrician will look after the baby, at least for the first few days of life. As well, a midwife could be involved if the mother so chooses, at least at the beginning; but because Amina is considered a "high-risk" pregnancy, the midwife would most likely turn care completely over to the specialists.

Primary Health Care Settings in Canada

Solo Practice   Solo practice refers to a physician practising independently, with staff members who may include a health office professional, a nurse, or both. The physician in solo practice may share a call schedule with other doctors to provide extended coverage for patients. Physicians in solo practice are becoming few and far between.

Group Practice   A group practice involves several physicians who may or may not share office space, expenses, and support staff. Depending on the mix of providers, they may also share a call schedule. A group practice is usually, but not always, made up of providers within the same specialty, but the group may not be incorporated. The physicians may have a group number for provincial or territorial billing purposes. Often the services of the group's physicians are provided through the group, and are billed in the name of the group, and the resulting revenues are treated as receipts of the group.

Partnership   Strictly speaking, a partnership is a business formed by two or more individuals who are jointly and separately financially liable for the operation of the business. Some physicians form such legal partnerships. Although they submit fee-for-service claims individually and do not have a group billing number, their income, net of expenses, is considered by the Canada Revenue Agency to be personal taxable income of individual partners. Other physicians simply share certain expenses of the practice through an informal or formal agreement. Each physician has clearly defined responsibilities, rights, and obligations. Note that physicians will often speak loosely of colleagues with whom they share a call schedule as "partners," although they are not actually members of a partnership.

Professional Corporation   A professional corporation is a legally incorporated business that allows professionals to reap many of the benefits of a for-profit corporation. A medical professional corporation must be organized for the sole purpose of rendering medical services, and the shareholders must be licensed physicians. The corporation may simply handle expenses, with each physician otherwise practising independently. Alternatively, the physicians may be employees of the corporation along with others, such as administrative staff. Services within a corporation vary. They may include physiotherapy, laboratory and diagnostic facilities, and alternative modalities, such as acupuncture and chiropractic. The main advantages are financial. Health maintenance organizations (discussed subsequently) are one type of corporation.

Primary Care Groups   Corporations are becoming more popular as primary care reform models move to the team approach to health care. The size, structure, function, and makeup of these groups vary from one jurisdiction to another. Remuneration formulas also vary.

Names for primary health care models include family health teams or family health networks or organizations (used in Ontario), family health clinics and primary care networks (used in Alberta), and primary health care cooperatives (used in Saskatchewan). They differ slightly in structure and care delivery format. In such organizations, there is often a separate "corporate" component headed by one or two individuals who oversee and manage the business end of the enterprise—including components of human health resources and IT support. The providers function independently alongside or at arm's length from the corporation. This model is used for both legal and business purposes. In some jurisdictions the government provides significant funding to start and maintain primary care groups—most of which use a multidisciplinary team approach to care.

Many groups of this nature prefer a central setting—one building where the "team" resides and there is central management of administrative and support staff as well as clinics related to the group. This model is appealing to patients as everything is close by, easily accessed, and details of their care are readily available to all team members. This model also attracts new doctors who are looking for a "turn-key" operation and coverage, allowing them a more normal lifestyle.

Clinics   A clinic is a health care setting that offers services to outpatients. A clinic can be managed by one physician or a group of physicians or a nurse practitioner (particularly in rural areas). They may offer services ranging from the simple diagnosis and treatment of complaints to therapeutic or preventive treatments. Some clinics offer a range of services under one roof, such as laboratory, physiotherapy, and consultations with specialists. There are also specialty clinics, such as prenatal, oncology, or orthopedic. Clinics may be privately owned, government sponsored, or organized by a group of doctors who share space and staff but bill separately. Clinics vary in name and in services offered. The following descriptions are general.

Some provinces have clinics (e.g., Alberta's Primary Care Network Clinics) that provide a medical home for individuals without family doctors or nurse practitioners.

The Mosaic Medical Clinic in Calgary is an example. The clinic, whose mission statement is "Better Health for All," provides both routine and complex care to its patients, including the management of chronic diseases like diabetes. They also offer free workshops on topics ranging from happiness to stress, anxiety, and weight loss.

- *Walk-in clinics* (also called *after-hours clinics* or *ambulatory care clinics*) offer medical services to patients, usually without an appointment. Sometimes a group of family physicians will offer after-hours care for **orphan patients** (patients who do not have a regular doctor) or for patients who, for whatever reason, could not see their own physician during office hours. A walk-in clinic may or may not treat urgent complaints, such as fractures and lacerations. Some facilities may combine services, such as the Coventry Hills Family Care Centre in Calgary, which operates as both a walk-in clinic and a family practice centre.

- *After-hours clinics*, most typically, are organized by physicians within a community to ease the stress on local emergency departments and are operated on a fee-for-service basis, with the physicians sharing office and administrative costs. As with walk-in clinics, they are likely to accept any patient. This differs from Ontario after-hours clinics operated by formal groups, such as family health networks, family health groups, and family health organizations, where services are restricted to patients who are rostered with the physicians belonging to the group. Although this is a contentious issue with patients, a number of these clinics prefer the patient to call to make an appointment rather than just showing up, although exceptions are made. Sometimes these clinics are managed by a nurse practitioner, with a family doctor available, should the need arise. In Alberta, most after-hours clinics clearly differentiate themselves from walk-in clinics, stressing that patients must first call the provincial Health Link information service to be referred to a clinic.

- *Urgent care clinics* also offer services without an appointment. The main difference is the focus on immediate care of urgent but not life-threatening complaints, such as lacerations or fractures. An urgent care clinic may also offer diagnostic and perhaps pharmacy services.

- *Outpatient clinics*, often located at or connected to a hospital, provide medical services to patients who have been discharged from the facility, as well as to others who need their often-specialized services. Clinics may or may not require appointments. Examples of types of outpatient clinics include oncology, diabetic, and orthopedic.

Emergency Departments Emergency departments (emergency rooms, ERs) do provide nonurgent primary care, but they are supposed to be reserved for patients in acute distress, such as chest pain, stroke symptoms (numbness or tingling in a limb, severe headache, visual disturbances), or breathing difficulties. Others are encouraged to see their family physician or seek medical care elsewhere. However, many patients go to ERs for health concerns that could easily be managed elsewhere, exacerbating overcrowding. Educating patients in a general practice setting about the appropriate use of an ER is important. This overuse of ERs results partly from the large number of orphan patients across the country. If there are no available ambulatory care clinics, an orphan patient has nowhere else to go.

Not every hospital offers emergency services, and ERs in different hospitals may render different levels of care. Some ERs, for example, lack the capacity to deal with major trauma cases. All hospitals, however, will have procedures in place to direct emergencies, including evacuating patients to appropriate trauma centres. A fully active ER is open 24 hours a day, seven days a week, and is equipped to deal with almost all emergencies.

orphan patient a patient who does not have a family physician and must get medical services from clinics and emergency departments.

Managed Care Managed care is a set of strategies, procedures, and policies designed to control the use of health care services. Such strategies include a review of medically necessary services, enticement to use certain providers, and case management. The goal is to conserve health care expenditure while maintaining quality by reorganizing health care delivery within a community. Managed care techniques are most often practised by organizations and professionals who assume responsibility for the population of a geographic area. A health maintenance organization is an example of a managed care organization.

Health Maintenance Organizations (HMOs)
HMOs offer prepaid, comprehensive health coverage for hospital and physician services. Most commonly, HMOs combine a group practice with a payment or funding arrangement. Examples are community clinics in Saskatchewan and in Sault Ste. Marie, Ontario. Ontario offers such care in the form of health service organizations and community health centres. Community health centres are primarily small clinics on a **global budget**, with salaried physicians and a range of other health professionals offering centralized primary care. Quebec has *centres locales de services communautaires* throughout most of the province that provide an impressive range of health care services.

LO5 PRIMARY CARE DELIVERY IN CANADA

Reforms to primary care delivery (often called *primary care renewal*) began approximately in the year 2000 when the federal government committed $800 million over five years through the Primary Health Care Transition Fund to improve primary health care in Canada. Renewed funding ended in 2008, after which time the provinces and territories assumed continuing costs. The objective of primary care reform was (and remains) to improve the basic structure of primary care funding, organization, and delivery. Since then all jurisdictions have implemented a variety of health care delivery models that continue to evolve.

Current concerns include how to effectively provide care to an aging population, manage chronic diseases, provide mental health services at a primary care level, and coordinate care with home care and community services. The integration of computerized electronic health and medical records is an ongoing challenge, meeting the ultimate goal of a workable, confidential, and efficient pan-Canadian system.

In Alberta, family doctors in primary care networks (PCNs) work collaboratively with other health professionals to deliver primary health care. The number and mix of health professionals in a PCN can vary. As well, they can be in one location or in several clinics in a geographic area. The Alberta government provides funding for the PCNs to hire a mix of health professionals; each PCN has the flexibility to determine what services best suit the community they are in. Under this model, patients can approach the clinic with a variety of complaints or questions and could be seen by a number of different providers; for example, a doctor, nurse, physiotherapist, or even a mental health professional, depending on the nature of the problem. PCNs are usually physician led and are funded on a per capita basis. Alberta also offers access to primary care services through family care clinics. These differ from PCNs in that individuals can access a variety of health care practitioners without an appointment. They provide a hub of family-centred care and are patient driven.

Ontario continues with its mix of primary health care models, often referred to collectively as patient enrollment models. These models require participating physicians to be part of a group practice or practice network. As of 2012, two-thirds of Ontario doctors worked within this type of framework, with 72 percent of Ontario's population enrolled.

The Particulars of Patient Enrollment Models

Most of these models require patients to enroll with a physician in the group. The models are commonly called patient enrollment models, or PEMs. Family doctors moving to a PEM must notify their patients of the process and explain the purpose and benefits of enrollment. The process itself is called *rostering*. This means the patients sign a form agreeing that they will seek all of their primary care services from that group or from one physician within that group.

Patients who enrol with a group are entitled to extended services. Enrollment is based on the following principles:

- Patients are free to choose their physician.
- Patients agree to seek all care from that physician.
- Patients sign a contract with one primary care physician at a time.
- The signed contract outlines patient–provider responsibilities and provides for enrollment termination.
- Enrollment is not automatic on conversion of a physician's practice. Physicians must invite patients to enroll in the group. Most of these reform models can have both enrolled and uninvolved patients. Thus, patients who do not want to sign this agreement may continue to see their doctor under the fee-for-service system. For example, a university student living away from home would probably maintain a fee-for-service arrangement because, under the terms of most primary care reform contracts, the family physician would be penalized every time the student saw the campus doctor. This, of course, would depend on the type of primary care reform group his or her family doctor belonged to—not all require rostering.
- Only eligible registrants of the provincial or territorial health plan will be accepted as enrolled members.

Patients agree to

- receive all primary health care from network providers, except in medical emergencies or when travelling;
- maintain valid health insurance and obtain a photo health card, if necessary;
- advise the physician of any change in address or telephone number; and
- allow the release of certain information to the Ministry of Health, such as preventive care history (e.g., mammograms or screening colonoscopies).

The physician agrees to meet all the patient's primary health care needs.

Many primary care reform models/groups use blended funding. This includes a **capitation or population-based funding** model in which the province or territory pays physicians a set amount per year for each patient enrolled, regardless of the type and number of services the physician provides for each patient. Under this model, a physician receives more money for patients who are statistically more likely to require frequent services, such as older patients with multiple medical problems.

capitation or population-based funding a funding system that pays a physician a given amount per patient enrolled, regardless of the number of services performed.

Advantages of Primary Care Reform Models

Primary care reform models may offer patients a number of advantages. Office hours may be extended depending on the needs of a particular practice and community. Continuity of care is enhanced because physicians involved share more information with one another, as well as with specialists, diagnostic and laboratory facilities, and other community services. Doctors are more actively involved with discharge planning, outpatient services, and home care services. The model may be able to offer both patients and providers access to a wide range of health educational materials. Also, a phone system can offer advice and triage for patients who are unsure about what kind of care to seek, especially outside of regular hours. For example, a patient who calls with chest pains would be told to go to the nearest emergency department, perhaps by ambulance. A patient with a sore throat might be advised to wait and see the doctor the next day. A mother with a feverish child might be advised to go to the nearest walk-in clinic or to see the physician on call. There is also a doctor available to advise the patient if the nurse on the telephone needs more advice.

The funding for PEM models is complex, although capitation-based funding and fee-for-service remain the primary methods of remuneration. In these models, certain services are bundled together in what is called a "basket" of services and included under the capitation payment plan. These services are primarily preventive in nature, such as mammograms, childhood immunizations, influenza immunizations, Pap smears, and screening for colorectal cancer (fecal testing for occult blood).

Doctors are paid bonuses for achieving certain milestones related to these services. For example, for immunizations the doctor would be paid one amount for immunizing 60 percent of those eligible in the practice, a higher amount for 70 percent, and so on. These bonus payments for most PEMs are paid annually. There are tracking codes that the doctor's office can use to tabulate how many services are rendered in each category. In Ontario these tracking codes are one group of "Q" codes. Doctors are also paid for "signing up" or enrolling patients. Other services they are paid for include diabetic management, smoking cessation, and mental health management. These are all billed using various "Q" codes. Premiums involve annual payment to the provider for goals met under the specific model guidelines and the completion of accurate records.

Implications for the Administrative Health Professional

Converting a practice from the fee-for-service model to a PEM model requires teamwork between the physicians and the administrative staff. If the model includes **rostering**, initially all of the patients within a practice must be enrolled—that is, invited to sign a contract with the physician or group. In most jurisdictions, the Ministry of Health assists with the rostering process, at least initially. Patients must make an informed decision on the basis of an understanding of the rights and responsibilities of both parties. Patients should be given information sheets and the opportunity to discuss any concerns with either the physician or the office staff. You must keep track of all registered patients and the date on which their agreement was signed.

Running a primary care group also entails ongoing administrative responsibilities for the health office professional. Most provinces and territories require practices to continue to track services (see the section on "Shadow Billing"). You will also continue to submit claims for services excluded from the capitation agreement, such as house calls and hospital visits to patients. The services that the provider bills for vary with the specific framework of the model he or she practises within.

Working in a PEM has a number of other challenges you might not encounter as frequently in a smaller office or clinic, particularly if it is newly formed or undergoing changes. This includes establishing one's job description and scope of practice. Any new environment suffers growing pains—a time when individuals involved grow and adjust to the environment's needs and required responsibilities. Not many PEMs (new or established) have formal job descriptions for administrative staff. Responsibilities are often left to staff members to sort out. This can foster discontent and frustration among staff members, cause disorganization within the office or clinic, and lead to further frustration on the part of providers.

rostering establishing a list of patients who agree to participate in a primary health network according to the rules of the province or territory.

Tips for Working within a Health Organization

- Try to define roles for each person working within your office or clinic setting or on your team; this should be done collaboratively.

- Balance responsibilities fairly, taking into consideration an individual's expertise and preferences, if possible. This results in staff members feeling involved, valued, and respected.

- Address problems early, openly, and in a tactful and objective manner. Have the facts and, if possible, a solution to offer. Speaking out in a professional manner clears the air, brings problems to the forefront, and usually results in a satisfactory settlement.

- Collaborate with the physicians and other providers when problems arise and their input or direction would be beneficial. Remember that the providers are affected when problems occur in the administrative domain. This may cause them discontent and frustration as well, which could result in negative relationships with you and other administrative staff.

- Ensure that you have the proper training for tasks you are asked to assume. For example, if you are asked to summarize charts for conversion to the EMR/EHR format, you should have specific guidelines set out by the physician and work through a number of charts with someone trained in that area.

- Be prepared to stand your ground—you are an educated, knowledgeable, and valuable member of the health care team. At the same time, recognize that compromise is important as long as the solution is sound, fair, and workable—and one you are comfortable with.

- Do not form alliances with other members of the team that will result in a "us–them" situation. Treat every member of the team with respect, always. Remember that some personalities are more difficult to work with than others. This includes all of those with whom you work, from physicians and nurse practitioners to physiotherapists, pharmacists, and administrative staff. Try to build on their strengths.

- Do not underestimate the stress that a negative or uncomfortable work environment can cause—particularly on a continued basis. It is not uncommon for team members—from administrative staff to providers—to succumb to stress and require time off. The stress can be that high.

L06 PAYMENT OPTIONS FOR PHYSICIANS

Fee-for-Service

There are a large number of physicians that still bill their provincial/territorial plans on a **fee-for-service** basis, either exclusively or as part of a blended remuneration system.[1] Each province and territory has its own fee schedule detailing insurable services and fees. (These schedules will be covered in more detail in Chapter 11.) In most jurisdictions payment is based on the specific type and extent of service, including the complexity of the service. Other considerations may contribute to how much the provider is paid. For example, in British Columbia the amount payable for a service also relates to the age of the patient.

fee-for-service a system under which a provider is paid by public health insurance for each insured service rendered to an insured patient. These providers are considered "opted-in" to the public payment system.

Example Dr. Harvey sees 25 patients on Monday. His health office professional submits claims to the provincial health plan for each encounter. On Tuesday, Dr. Harvey

---

[1] *The Medical Post*, January 22, 2008. The National Physician Survey is Canada's largest census survey of Canadian doctors.

sees only 15 patients. He is paid for 15 services. In some provinces, the specific service rendered for each visit would determine how much the doctor is paid for each service. Suppose Mr. Jones has a sore throat, Mrs. Marchese has a skin rash, and Mr. Kirschen has abdominal pain. In Ontario, Dr. Harvey would be paid a different sum of money for each patient on the basis of the complexity of each assessment. (See Chapter 11 for more detail.) In British Columbia, Dr. Harvey would be paid a certain amount if Mr. Jones were 90 years old and a different amount if he were 35, regardless of the nature or complexity of the assessment.

Shadow Billing

primary care groups (PCGs) a variety of structurally similar groups of physicians or other health professionals working collaboratively under an organizational framework to deliver primary health services. The health professionals may or may not be in one physical location.

Shadow billing is used in some **primary care groups (PCGs)** to allow direct comparison of the cost effectiveness of capitation and fee-for-service. Claims are submitted as if the physician were billing fee-for-service but are marked with a special identifying code and a zero balance. Thus, a record is produced of how much would have been spent on rostered patients if each encounter had been billed fee-for-service.

Example   Dr. Chen is working in a primary care reform group. In one calendar year, she was paid $300 000 under the capitation formula to take care of 2000 patients while providing extended hours and other health care services to her patients. The shadow billing for her practice year showed that under the fee-for-service system, she would have billed the Ministry of Health $350 000. In this case, capitation saved the ministry $50 000.

Remuneration Options for Opted-In/Opted-Out Physicians

opted-in (of a physician) billing the provincial or territorial plan for health services rendered.

opted-out (of a physician) billing patients for services rendered; patients pay the fee to the doctor and submit a claim to the health plan. Very few physicians chose to opt out. This may change, however, if private health care becomes more prevalent and patients can buy private insurance for medically necessary services.

It is important to note that rules governing direct and extra-billing for **opted-in** and **opted-out** physicians vary. Some jurisdictions allow opted-in providers to bill the patient directly, some do not; some jurisdictions make extra-billing an offence, others indirectly deter extra-billing by eliminating any public insurance available for the services supplied by opted-out physicians or for the services supplied by opted-in physicians who try to extra-bill.

Direct Billing

As mentioned previously, physicians who bill their provincial or territorial plan for services rendered are referred to as being opted-in to the provincial/territorial health plan. Opted-out physicians operate outside of the public plan and bill their patients directly for a service (this is also called *direct billing*). The patient pays the physician, and the health plan reimburses the patient. There are very few opted-out physicians, because provincial/territorial plans either disallow the practice or have implemented restrictions that render the practice unprofitable.

Extra-Billing and User Fees

extra-billing charging a patient more than the amount paid by the provincial or territorial health plan for a medically necessary service.

clawback the amount, dollar for dollar, that the federal government cuts health transfer payments to a province or territory that permits extra-billing.

Extra-billing occurs when a physician or other entity charges the patient more for an insured service than the provincial or territorial plan will pay. The practice is not allowed under section 18 of the Canada Health Act. The federal government imposes penalties on any jurisdiction that allows extra-billing. It estimates how much money practitioners in a particular province or territory have extra-billed patients in each fiscal year, then it withholds that amount dollar for dollar from its health transfer payments to that province or territory. This penalty is called a **clawback**. There are, however, some jurisdictions that allow extra-billing by doctors who are opted-in or -out of the public systems. For some individuals, private insurance will cover the additional costs incurred by extra-billing, but this coverage may be subject to legal restrictions depending on what province or territory they live in.

User fees are different than extra-billing fees. A user fee is any charge, other than extra-billing, for a health service; for example, a charge to use the emergency department of a hospital, or a charge to visit your family doctor. The person is charged to use a service, not for the service itself. Jurisdictions allowing user fees are subject to the same penalties as for allowing extra-billing. Charging patients reasonable fees for enhanced and uninsured services (discussed subsequently) is *not* considered extra-billing or imposing user fees.

Be aware that you may be held liable for knowingly participating in extra-billing. Be careful not to inadvertently bill a patient for any insured service. If you suspect that your provider is extra-billing, speak to your provider to clarify the issue or seek legal counsel.

Salaries

A salaried doctor is paid a set fee for all services rendered during a designated time frame; thus hours, workload, and remuneration are clearly defined. Salaries are usually paid for a full-time position. Many physicians at universities are salaried to perform a mix of research, teaching, and clinical work. Physicians in many community health centres are salaried but, to date, remain a small part of the population. Several provinces, such as Newfoundland and Labrador, have salaried district medical officers.

Global Budget

A global budget is a lump sum given to doctors in a group or corporation for services performed. Most academic health sciences centres receive a global budget from the provinces or territories and, out of that funding, may pay physicians in a number of ways. Physicians may be paid on a global budget to practise in a remote area; vacation time, professional development, and relocation fees may be offered as additional incentives.

Sessional Payment

Sessional payment is similar to a salary but is not usually for a permanent position. A physician on sessional payment is employed or contracted to perform designated services for a certain time frame. The contract may be renewed or renegotiated at the end of the term.

Capitation

Most provinces and territories use capitation to some degree. Capitation provides a fixed payment for all medical services a patient may require in a given time frame. The physician may be paid more for individuals who are at higher risk for more health problems, such as seniors. A drawback of this payment plan is that it does not provide a **physician incentive** to extend the services he or she offers to patients. Many provinces have voiced concern about the 2011 health accord proposed by the federal government in that federal-to-provincial/territorial payments will be capitation based. This will leave smaller provinces with less income.

physician incentive when physicians are monetarily remunerated for maximizing services related to preventive medicine (e.g., immunizations, Pap smears, mammograms). This involves encouraging their patients to have screening tests.

Indirect Capitation

Indirect capitation occurs when an organization is given a set amount of money to manage health care for a designated population base; for example, a regional health authority or a managed care organization. With this funding, the organization must manage its health care responsibilities (staff, services, administrative costs, capital expenditures, etc.) within the confines of its budget.

Blended Payment

There are numerous combinations of salary, fee-for-service, and capitation. Blended payment plans are increasingly popular among physicians, particularly those entering into primary care reform groups, in which capitation usually provides the funding base.

For example, a doctor could be employed by a university but charge fee-for-service in a private practice. Or a physician with a fee-for-service practice may also receive a part-time salary or sessional payment for seeing patients in a nursing home. Another example would be the coroner in a community. The coroner is paid a salary by the ministry or the local health authority but is often also a family physician in private practice.

Fees for Uninsured Services

Physicians may charge patients directly for services *not covered* under their provincial or territorial health insurance plan. Such services may include renewal of a prescription over the telephone, filling out insurance forms and documents associated with medical assessments, writing notes for someone who has been ill, filling out a passport form, or conducting certain patient-related interviews. Some physicians offer an arrangement in which a patient pays a lump sum of money (referred to as a *block fee*) for an individual or a family for a range of uninsured services over a period of time—usually not more than 12 months. Some patients feel more comfortable with a block fee than with having to pay separately for uninsured services. Block fees are particularly appealing to older patients who often need telephone advice or to patients on numerous medications who frequently need one renewed. Some primary care reform groups include a basket of uninsured services for rostered patients, and thus block fees are unnecessary.

The College of Physicians and Surgeons in each province and territory has set out rules for the block fee model. You must ensure that these guidelines are posted in a prominent place in the health office. Similarly, fees for all uninsured services should be posted in the office or clinic. Patients must be aware of what the fee is before an uninsured service is rendered.

Other Uninsured Services   A large number of medical services in Canada are uninsured and privately paid for. Private services include most dental services (more than 20 percent), medical and diagnostic services provided at private clinics, drugs (more than 30 percent), and much of the cost of long-term care. Remember, only *medically necessary* services are covered under the Canada Health Act. That leaves gaping holes in the health service spectrum. According to Statistics Canada, private funds (including private insurance and out-of-pocket payment) represented more than 30 percent of Canada's overall health care spending in 2007.

Patients may also pay for enhanced services. An example is for cataract surgery at a private facility. The surgery itself is covered by the provincial or territorial health plan, but the patient may purchase a superior lens and pay for additional levels of postoperative care. The same is true of hip replacements. The patient can pay for a superior-quality hip joint. Some provinces allow payment for an MRI (magnetic resonance imaging). The rationale is that although an MRI is deemed medically necessary within a "reasonable" time frame, an earlier MRI can be considered an "enhanced" service, and therefore a facility can legally charge anyone who is willing to pay for one. In many jurisdictions, a pregnant woman can pay for a 3D ultrasound of her unborn child.

Providers Eligible to Bill Fee-for-Service

In all provinces and territories, physicians and dentists may bill the health plan if they meet that province's or territory's criteria. Other providers may also bill fee-for-service with specific limitations and restrictions. This varies across the country.

Optometrists   Optometrists are graduates of a four-year degree program. There are two schools of optometry in Canada: one in Waterloo, Ontario, and one in Montreal. In most provinces and territories, optometrists may bill their provincial or territorial plans with certain restrictions on fees and frequency of services. Most provinces and territories do not cover routine eye examinations for prescription lenses. The scope of practice of the optometrist and the ophthalmologist can be confusing. The optometrist renders much of the primary eye care required by patients but refers certain problems to an ophthalmologist (an MD specializing in the care of the eyes). For example, if an optometrist diagnoses a condition such as macular degeneration in a patient, she will refer the patient to an ophthalmologist for further investigation and staging of the disease. She might also provide the patient with information about current treatments for the disease, such as vitamin therapy and the option of other treatments such as photobiomodulation therapy (which is not covered by provincial health insurance).

Dentists   Dentists are also graduates of a four-year degree program. Across Canada, dentists and dental surgeons may bill their provincial or territorial plans for dental work that is both deemed medically necessary and carried out in a hospital. Other criteria vary across the country. No provincial or territorial plan covers the cost of all dental services for everyone, but many provinces and territories provide some dental care for individuals receiving social assistance. Newfoundland and Labrador provides basic dental services for children 12 and under, as well as for adolescents under 17 who are receiving income support. In most provinces and territories, dental associations have their own fee schedule and liaise with the Ministry of Health.

Chiropractors   Chiropractors complete a four-year postgraduate degree program at a chiropractic college. Provincial and territorial coverage for chiropractic care varies because of different interpretations of the Canada Health Act as to what is medically necessary. At present, only Manitoba, Saskatchewan, and Alberta offer limited health plan coverage. Such policies are subject to change; to confirm your province's or territory's coverage, consult the websites at the end of this chapter. Across the country, workers' compensation boards and many insurance companies offer extensive coverage for chiropractic services. Chiropractic care is covered extensively by third-party players.

Physiotherapists   A physiotherapist is a graduate of a four-year degree program. (Soon a master's degree will be the criteria for entry to practise.) Many physiotherapists are employed by hospitals and are therefore salaried. Some work in the community, primarily in physiotherapy clinics. Most provincial and territorial plans cover physiotherapy for in-hospital patients. Some provinces cover designated services outside the hospital.

Osteopaths   These providers diagnose and treat injuries and diseases of the musculoskeletal, circulatory, and nervous systems. Treatment modalities include manipulation, physiotherapy, medication, and surgery. Osteopaths train abroad and complete a one- to three-year internship before they are licensed to practise. Some provinces cover osteopath services.

Podiatrists Podiatrists and chiropodists treat diseases and deformities of the foot. Treatment strategies include the use of braces, splints, shields, physiotherapy, medication, and surgery. Although many podiatrists train outside Canada, community colleges in some provinces offer three-year diploma programs.

Midwives Midwifery is a rapidly growing profession in Canada. Legislation and models of midwifery care are diverse across the country. The only jurisdictions in which midwives are not regulated are Prince Edward Island, Yukon, and Newfoundland and Labrador. The process to regulate midwives is underway in Newfoundland and Labrador but is expected to take two to seven years. In New Brunswick, legislation to license midwives was adopted in 2010. Despite this, the New Brunswick Health Department withdrew funding to the Midwifery Council of New Brunswick, making it impossible for midwives to practise because they could not get a licence. In 2014 the council was reinstated, but the government claims there is no funding to hire midwives.

Midwives render antenatal, intrapartum, and postpartum care to their patients. They also help look after the baby for the first six weeks or so. Midwives can deliver babies in the hospital if they have admitting privileges, or at the patient's home. Many cities have birthing centres that provide a home-like environment for the birth of a baby, with seamless access to a hospital should the need arise. Midwives can order some laboratory tests and ultrasounds. If a midwife suspects that her patient is at risk, she will send the patient back to the family doctor or request a consultation. If the midwife deems it necessary she can, in most jurisdictions, seek a consultation with a specialist and transfer care of a mother considered to be high risk. The family doctor must be notified, as he or she will assume care for both mom and baby after they are discharged from the midwife's care.

There are seven midwifery programs in Canada, one in British Columbia, one in Alberta, three in Ontario, one in Quebec, and one in northern Manitoba. Completion of one of these accredited programs leads to a baccalaureate-level degree in midwifery.

Other Providers

Other providers are not yet allowed to bill fee-for-service but are, to a large extent, funded by the ministries through various payment plans.

Nurse Practitioners Nurse practitioners (NPs) are practising in almost every jurisdiction across Canada. NPs have a scope of practice well beyond that of a registered nurse. They can conduct physical examinations, assess patients for routine problems like earaches, and write prescriptions for certain drugs. NPs can specialize in such areas as primary care, cardiology, and pediatrics—the latter two working in hospitals. NPs are primarily salaried with allocated funding coming from the federal or provincial/territorial governments, depending on where they work. Fee-for-service has not been deemed a viable model for remuneration. Some jurisdictions have initiated nurse practitioner–led clinics (NPLC). In such clinics, the NPs are the primary care providers leading an interprofessional team of health care professionals and administrative staff.

Physician Assistants Initially confined to the Armed Forces, physician assistants (PAs) are skilled health professionals who support physicians in a range of health care settings, from doctors' offices (generalists as well as specialists) to emergency departments. They work alongside physicians, nurses, NPs, and other members of the interprofessional health care team. Enabling legislation for PAs as well as educational programs are increasing across the country. The Canadian Association of Physician Assistants website listed at the end of this chapter provides a current and more detailed look at the role and scope of practice of the physician assistant. At this point, PAs are not allowed to bill their provincial or territorial plan for services rendered.

FINDING A FAMILY DOCTOR

Almost daily you will get calls asking if the doctor is willing to take new patients. For the most part, the answer is no. However, some family doctors quietly accept new patients; for example, relatives or friends of current patients, or friends who have moved to town. If a new doctor moves into the community, it does not take long for him or her to have a full complement of patients. Physicians can decide just how large a practice they want, limiting the number of patients they take (or enroll) to a specified number (see Chapter 8).

It is a good idea to ask for guidelines regarding how to handle these requests. As a rule of thumb, suggest that the caller ask other health professionals—for example, their optometrist or dentist—if they know of anyone taking patients. Sometimes the emergency department at a local hospital will keep a list of "open" practices. A reliable resource is the provincial/territorial College of Physicians and Surgeons or College of Family Physicians. There should be a "Find a Doctor" link on the college's website. See the website of the College of Family Physicians of Canada listed at the end of this chapter.

⟫⟫⟫ WHAT TO WATCH FOR

- The way in which the federal, provincial, and territorial governments respond/adjust to providing health care for the large numbers of new Canadians arriving in Canada starting in 2015.
- Ongoing changes in how primary care is delivered in your jurisdiction.
- How your province or territory adjusts to meet the continuing needs of an aging population; for example, with home care resources and cost restraints.
- Changes made by the federal government to the current health accord, and improvements to health care access and delivery for Indigenous peoples.
- Restoration of health care for refugee claimants.
- Steps taken to provide Canadians with a universal drug plan.
- Implementation of physician-assisted death.

SUMMARY

1. In 1947, Saskatchewan was the first province in Canada to establish some form of provincial health insurance. The Canada Health Act, passed in 1984, was the beginning of a formalized national health care plan.

2. The Canadian health care system is built on the five principles and two conditions of the Canada Health Act. The principles are public administration, comprehensiveness, universality, portability, and accessibility. These principles are meant to ensure that all Canadians have free access to all medically necessary health care services. The act outlines conditions that the provinces and territories must meet to receive health funding from the federal government.

3. The federal and provincial or territorial governments share responsibility for health care, although the federal government is responsible for certain sectors (e.g., veterans). The federal government sets national standards and, through a mix of funding formulas, partially funds health care. The provinces and territories may use the funds to deliver health care at their discretion. In British Columbia and Ontario, residents pay premiums for health insurance; in all other provinces and territories, coverage is paid for by tax revenues.

4. Primary care settings in Canada include solo or group family practices, clinics, emergency departments, and managed care arrangements, including health management organizations. A clinic is a health care setting that offers services to outpatients. Clinics are popular in most jurisdictions and help alleviate overcrowding and misuse of the emergency department. Nurse practitioner–led clinics are increasing in number, particularly in rural areas. Most NP-led clinics have a variety of health professionals to coordinate and deliver care. Examples of clinics include after hours, walk in, urgent care, and outpatient.

5. The manner in which primary care is delivered in Canada is similar in many respects, but each jurisdiction has adapted delivery models to meet the needs of its residents. Names, size, mix of health professionals, hours of operation, and services offered differ. Interprofessional collaboration has been key to the successful delivery of patient-oriented health care, effectively using the specific skills of each health professional. Some jurisdictions (e.g., Ontario) enroll patients into practices, which carries benefits and obligations for both patient and provider.

6. Fee-for-service is still a widely used method or remuneration in Canada. However, a growing number of family physicians are paid using a blended formula (e.g., capitation-based funding and fee-for-service). Physicians may also be hired on salary or through a sessional contract. Some have blended sources of income. Almost all specialists in private practice bill fee-for-service. As well as physicians, providers who may bill health plans include (depending on the province or territory) optometrists, dentists, chiropractors, physiotherapists, osteopaths, podiatrists, nurse practitioners, and midwives.

KEY TERMS

capitation or population-based funding 93
clawback 96
extra-billing 96
fee-for-service 95
global budget 92

locum tenens 89
managed care 92
opted-in 96
opted-out 96
orphan patient 91
physician incentive 97

primary care groups (PCGs) 96
primary health care 88
provider 84
rostering 94

REVIEW QUESTIONS

1. When was the first health care legislation passed in Canada?
2. Which province had the first provincial health plan?
3. What is the purpose of the Canada Health Act, and when was it passed?

4. What are the five principles of the Canada Health Act, and what do they mean?
5. What are the responsibilities of the provincial or territorial and federal governments regarding health care?

6. Have the main principles of the Romanow Report been implemented in your jurisdiction?

7. What constitutes a primary care setting?

8. What are the main objectives of primary care renewal, and how do reform initiatives change the organization of primary care?

9. What are the advantages and disadvantages of rostering patients?

10. Differentiate between fee-for-service and shadow billing.

APPLICATION EXERCISES

1. In small groups, research how primary care is delivered in your province or territory. Describe the structure, function, and services of three different groups/modes of delivery. Interview three to four patients from different delivery models, asking about services offered, level of satisfaction, and what improvements they feel could be made. Are there plans to change primary care delivery in your community? Describe.

2. Research the types of providers in your province or territory who are allowed to bill the provincial or territorial plan. Choose three of these providers, and identify any billing restrictions placed on them.

3. Wait times in all provinces and territories differ, as do the number of orphan patients. Strategies for addressing these problems also vary. Investigate these issues in your own jurisdiction.

   a. What are the wait times for hip, knee, cataract, and cardiac bypass surgery? MRIs?

   b. Have wait times improved or become longer over the past five years? If they are not improving, why? What steps is your government taking to address this?

   c. How many individuals in your jurisdiction are without family doctors? Is the situation different between urban and rural areas? How is the province or territory and municipality trying to fix the problem?

4. What home care services are offered in your community? Research how they are delivered, how they are financed, and how efficient these services are. (Are there long wait lists? Do individuals have to pay for services themselves?)

5. Emily is 84 years old and is admitted to hospital with a broken hip; she is also showing early signs of dementia. Following surgery, it is determined that she could no longer manage at home. Research the services available in your community for Emily and the steps Emily or her family must take to access these services. What type of long-term care facilities are available? What is the wait time for a facility of Emily's choice? What are the costs involved?

6. Divide into small groups. Research the types of private health care services available in your province or territory. Suggested elements to address include opted-in/opted-out options, direct billing, extra-billing, and the legality of private insurance covering publicly insured services. As a class, compile a list of private services offered, including those that are financed in part by the public plan (e.g., private diagnostic clinics, physiotherapy clinics, corporate groups).

WEBSITES OF INTEREST

Canada Health Act

www.hc-sc.gc.ca/hcs-sss/medi-assur/cha-lcs/index-eng.php

Provincial Health Care Plans and Systems
Newfoundland and Labrador

www.health.gov.nl.ca/health

Prince Edward Island

www.gov.pe.ca/health

Nova Scotia

http://novascotia.ca/DHW

New Brunswick

www2.gnb.ca/content/gnb/en/departments/health.html

Quebec

www.msss.gouv.qc.ca

Ontario

www.health.gov.on.ca

Manitoba

www.gov.mb.ca/health

Saskatchewan

www.saskatchewan.ca/government/government-structure/ministries/health

Alberta

www.health.alberta.ca

British Columbia

www.gov.bc.ca/health

Yukon

www.hss.gov.yk.ca

Northwest Territories

www.hss.gov.nt.ca/health-landing

Nunavut

www.gov.nu.ca/health

The Canadian Association of Physician Assistants

http://capa-acam.ca

College of Family Physicians of Canada

www.cfpc.ca

Part III gets down to basic information about quality and standards, diagnostic testing, and pharmacology that applies to any health-related occupational setting. Chapter 5 introduces the principles of quality, standards, and safety in health care. Essential topics, such as occupational health and safety legislation, Workplace Hazardous Materials Information System (WHMIS), asepsis, infection control, and Standard Precautions are discussed in detail. You will learn effective risk-management techniques appropriate to your role in health care. Environmental safety, both for health professionals and patients, is also discussed. Chapter 6 will introduce you to diagnostic testing, including laboratory tests and diagnostic imaging, and your role in the process. You will be instrumental in requisitioning these tests, accurately and responsibly reporting test results to the appropriate people, and booking appointments for patients. You will also inform patients about preparing for tests and what to expect. Chapter 7 will provide you with a knowledge base about pharmacology suitable to your related responsibilities. You will gain an overview of types of drugs, drug effects and side effects, and routes of administration. You will learn how to deal with prescriptions in the health office and how to direct patients to appropriate resources when they have questions related to their medications.

Chapter 5   Standards and Safety in Health Care

Chapter 6   Diagnostic Tests

Chapter 7   Pharmacology

Chapter 5
Standards and Safety in Health Care

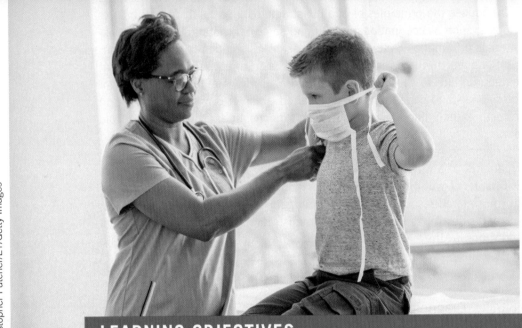

Christopher Futcher/E+/Getty Images

LEARNING OBJECTIVES

On completing this chapter, you will be able to:

1. Examine the role of quality assurance in health care.

2. Discuss the spread of infectious and communicable diseases.

3. Implement strategies related to medical and surgical asepsis.

4. Identify strategies to prevent and control the spread of infection.

5. Apply the principles of Standard Precautions.

6. Provide a safe health office environment for staff and patients.

When you go to a restaurant, you expect your food to be of high quality and prepared according to certain standards. When you purchase a shirt or a car, you likewise expect the product to reflect a certain quality. Even dealing with a bank, you expect that the individuals who manage your money will be appropriately trained and will know what they are doing. Health care is no different. It is a service; its scope and nature vary, and it is provided by individuals whom you expect to be appropriately trained and knowledgeable. You also expect the services you receive to be of a certain quality. As a health office professional, you must be aware of the standards of care and service that you and your facility are expected to provide. You must participate in ongoing evaluation and ensure that you maintain a high standard of service.

LO1 QUALITY ASSURANCE IN HEALTH CARE

Quality assurance is any systematic process that checks if a product or service is meeting requirements. Quality assurance also includes establishing, promoting, and maintaining a safe occupational environment. Industry and other occupational settings embody specific goals and criteria in their quality assurance initiatives. Industrial settings often have a full-time quality control officer.

quality assurance any systematic process that checks if a product or service is meeting specified requirements. In health care, it is a systematic assessment to ensure that services are of the highest possible quality using existing resources.

Quality assurance in the health care environment is an orchestrated and methodical approach of continuously scrutinizing, evaluating, and improving the quality of health services. Patients should expect nothing short of excellence in assessment, diagnosis, treatment, and ongoing care. They are entitled to prompt diagnosis and treatment, punctual reports on laboratory tests, accurate prescriptions, reasonable waiting times, timely access to emergency services, and proper follow-up. Quality assurance is particularly critical when budgets are limited and resources scarce.

Quality assurance in health care is the responsibility of both employers and employees. Large facilities usually have a formal quality assurance committee. In small practices, you, as the health office professional, play a large role. To do so effectively, you must understand the principles of quality assurance and safety, including infection control. You must be conscious of both your own and the patients' safety in the office.

It is vital to maintain a safe environment in the health office—one that reduces risk of harm to both patients and staff. In the health office, you will encounter people from all age groups, with varied health problems, altered emotional and physical needs, and a wide range of abilities and disabilities. You have a responsibility to protect not only yourself but also those who cannot protect themselves against injury, fire, and infection. A website at the end of the chapter gives a detailed summary of precautions to control infection in a doctor's office.

Hospitals

Hospitals and other health care facilities participate in a process known as *accreditation* (discussed in Chapter 14), which demonstrates that they meet provincial or territorial standards. Health care providers, such as doctors, nurse practitioners, and midwives, must go through a peer-review process of *credentialling* to establish and maintain privileges to admit and care for patients at a health care facility. Health care facilities conduct routine reviews of facility policies, procedures, and quality of care; this is usually the responsibility of the department called risk management or quality assurance. The following are some of the problems frequently reviewed that cover policies, procedures, documentation, and actual patient care:

- Patients who are readmitted to hospital within a certain number of days after discharge
- Deaths occurring within the hospital
- Unscheduled returns to surgery
- Infections contracted within the hospital
- Falls, medication errors, and other irregularities

Investigations of these problems will hopefully lead to improved patient care.

Health Offices

Many smaller health offices do not have a formal quality assurance plan. If your office does not have such a plan, you may want to propose establishing one. However, quality assurance is addressed informally each time an action is taken to correct a problem or improve services to patients. Remember that a quality assurance plan can only be as good as the people who initiate and practise it. A quality assurance review should follow the following principles:

- In a large enough setting (e.g., the health department of a large factory), a committee should be designated to oversee the review. This may require formal training of some or all of the committee members. In a smaller health office, ideally all staff members would work together as a team.

- Keep it positive. A review is not meant to punish those who make errors, but rather to find the causes of problems and correct them. Stress the goal of enhancing performance and patient service.

- Actively involve all staff so that everyone "owns" the process. A collaborative effort generalizes problems, avoids pinpointing blame, and promotes working toward the common goal of improved service and care.

All services in the office should be open to review, with more thorough investigation of trouble spots, including the following:

- Errors in writing prescriptions
- Mislabelling test specimens
- Multiple needle-sticks by staff
- Frequent long waiting periods for patients in the reception area
- Inadequate or delayed follow-up on abnormal test results
- Protracted delay in returning phone calls
- Not answering the telephone within a reasonable time frame
- Patient complaints of staff members being rude, discourteous, or displaying bias
- Inaccurate or incomplete documentation and charting
- Patient concerns about involvement in selecting treatments
- Patient concerns about the type and length of treatment offered

Once areas of concern have been identified, measures to address each must be outlined and implemented. Periodic review is needed to assess progress. A suggestion box in the waiting room may help identify patient concerns and generate valuable ideas.

The Incident Report

An incident report is formal documentation of any lapse in acceptable procedure, protocol, or policy that results in undesirable effects. Most large agencies, such as hospitals and busy clinics, design their own incident reports, containing generic information plus anything specific to the agency itself. All work-related injuries require completion of a workers' compensation board accident form and perhaps an agency incident report as well. Some organizations have an employee incident form separate from the general incident report.

The incident report has long been dreaded as an instrument that brings blame and punishment to those perceived to be responsible. More recently, incident reports have taken on a more positive role, focusing not on assigning blame, but on identifying problems, determining why they occurred, and suggesting corrective steps. Often, incidents are not the fault of one person but the result of a combination of events.

The format of an incident report will vary with the agency. However, most include the following elements:

- Date and time of the event
- A summary of the event
- A detailed account of events leading up to the incident
- Who was present initially, and anyone else involved in the incident
- Who was notified of the event (e.g., coordinator, clinical leader) and when
- Any untoward consequences (e.g., a bruise, a cut from a fall, or altered consciousness from being given the wrong medication)
- Any action, medical or otherwise, taken as a result of the event (e.g., physician ordered an X-ray after a patient's fall)
- An evaluation of the incident
- Recommendations for preventing a similar occurrence

The person discovering the incident should initiate the report. This may or not be the person responsible for the incident (if anyone is specifically responsible). The person immediately in charge of the area where the incident occurred must be promptly notified—a doctor, charge nurse, or supervisor, for example. That person will likely assume responsibility to notify other individuals as required and oversee report completion.

Consider Mr. Dodhia, who fell out of bed because someone left the side rail down. He sustained a cut to the side of his forehead and complained of a sore arm. Nema, a unit clerk, found Mr. Dodhia on the floor beside his bed. Nema notified a nurse, who settled Mr. Dodhia back into bed. Nema also notified the charge nurse. An incident report was initiated. The doctor was called and, after examining Mr. Dodhia, determined there were no serious injuries. Preliminary investigation found that a nurse, Andrea, had taken Mr. Dodhia to the washroom and forgot to put up the side rail. Mr. Dodhia's family was glad his injuries were minor and left it at that. The completed report was signed by those involved and forwarded to the appropriate department (e.g., risk management or quality assurance). In such cases, further investigation, if required, would be conducted by risk management or quality assurance. If appropriate, all findings, conclusions, and recommendations would be communicated to administration and perhaps the board of directors.

TIP

If an incident report needs to be filled out in your occupational setting, prepare the report to the extent that you can and include essential information, like the patient's name. Keep the process confidential. Remain nonjudgmental and refrain from discussing the incident with anyone. If you are involved in the incident, be honest, objective, clear, concise, and brief with your documentation. View the completion of an incident report as a positive move that may prevent a similar occurrence in the future.

An incident report is not kept on the patient's chart. In most cases, duplication of the report is prohibited, and those involved must refrain from discussing the incident inappropriately. An incident report can hold information that is potential ammunition for a lawsuit.

Occupational Health and Safety

Occupational health and safety boards are responsible for ensuring that necessary safety standards are met in the workplace. Safety standard requirements vary depending on the workplace environment. Each province and territory has its own occupational health and safety legislation. Employment and Social Development Canada is responsible for occupational health and safety in federally regulated workplaces.

The Workplace Hazardous Materials Information System (WHMIS) is federal legislation administered through the Canadian Centre for Occupational Health and Safety that educates employers and employees about workplace hazards. You can learn more about WHMIS and the centre from the websites listed at the end of the chapter.

Workers' Compensation

Workers' compensation is a form of social insurance. When a work-related injury (or an occupational disease) occurs, a claim is submitted by the injured party; workers' compensation decides if the injured party is entitled to financial compensation. Once a claim is approved, workers' compensation will work with the injured party and his or her medical team to assess, treat, and rehabilitate the person. The priority is to return the injured person to work as soon as possible, sometimes on a modified work plan. Consider Nathan, a registered nurse who hurt his back lifting a heavy patient. Nathan reported his injury, the appropriate forms were completed, and Nathan was assessed by his physician. Nathan was off for three weeks, during which time he received physiotherapy. After three weeks, Dr. Tamblyn recommended that Nathan return to work as long as no lifting was involved for three months. Nathan was assigned to administrative duties for that time frame.

Each province and territory has its own workers' compensation boards/commissions with the exception of the Northwest Territories and Nunavut, where one board oversees both jurisdictions. In some jurisdictions, workers' compensation boards/commissions administer occupational health and safety legislation (or components of it). In other jurisdictions, a department within the provincial/territorial government is responsible for this legislation. Federal legislation covers employees of the federal government as well as Crown corporations across Canada (e.g., banks, federal government departments). Employees of the federal government receive benefits and services (through workers' compensation) that are reimbursed by the federal government through provincial or territorial workers' compensation boards.

Employers pay premiums to workers' compensation boards, which are gathered into a common fund out of which benefits are paid to workers injured as a result of their employment. In exchange, employees relinquish the right to sue employers for on-the-job injuries. Each province and territory has a workers' compensation board or equivalent that administers funding and adjudicates cases.

L02 INFECTION PREVENTION AND CONTROL: HOW INFECTIONS SPREAD

Infection prevention and control (IPC) measures are usually the responsibility of a team of health professionals who develops, implements, and evaluates strategies and programs to prevent and manage infectious diseases. Although important in all health care environments, IPC is a major focus in hospitals and long-term care facilities. This is particularly so with the growing number antimicrobial organisms (so-called superbugs) that are resistant to previously effective antimicrobial medications. Antimicrobials include antibiotic, antifungal, and antiviral medications. Any setting that cares for ill people will naturally have increased risks of **infection**, which can result in serious illness and even death for both health professionals and patients, especially vulnerable groups such as the very young, the elderly, and those with compromised immune systems. According to the Public Health Agency of Canada (PHAC), the total annual cost of treating antimicrobial infections in 2015 was more than $1 billion.

The 2003 SARS (severe acute respiratory syndrome) outbreak in Toronto and Vancouver, the 2009 H1N1 (also known as the swine flu) **pandemic**, and the 2014 Ebola crisis in West Africa demonstrate how difficult it is to identify, isolate, and contain infectious diseases, even with the most modern infection protocols and equipment available. Health providers in modern U.S. hospitals were infected with the Ebola virus even when using strict isolation techniques. It was also found that the Ebola virus can survive in a "cured" patient for up to nine months, making the person still infectious. These outbreaks also demonstrate the ongoing need for collaboration regarding IPC management at both the national and international levels. Responding to international health alerts requires a harmonized effort on the part of the World Health Organization (WHO) and its member states. Each country has its own response management procedures.

All hospitals, long-term care facilities, and seniors' centres have IPC resource manuals (health offices and clinics may not have an IPC manual, but will have basic protocols in place, which are discussed later in this chapter). Everyone who works in a health care facility must adhere to IPC policies. One break in protocol can have devastating consequences. It is not uncommon for a floor in a hospital or nursing home—or sometimes the entire facility—to be under quarantine because of an influenza or gastroenteritis outbreak. Specific isolation procedures and protocols come into play until the outbreak is contained and no new cases appear within a designated time frame.

> **infection** a disease process that results from the entry and spread of a microorganism.

> **pandemic** a global outbreak of a specific disease that does or has the potential go affect a large population.

⟩⟩⟩ POINTS TO PONDER

Most health facilities stress the importance of all employees getting the flu shot, although they cannot legally force individuals to do so. Those who are not immunized pose a risk to patients and others. Do you think that employees in the health care field have a moral obligation to be vaccinated?

An infectious disease is one that is caused by a **microorganism**—that is, an organism too small to be seen with the naked eye. Infectious diseases are generally, but not always, **contagious or communicable**, meaning that they can be transmitted from one person to another (although some are transmitted more easily than others). Communicable diseases range from the familiar common cold to more serious illnesses, such as strep throat, tuberculosis, malaria, and acquired immune deficiency syndrome (AIDS). Some are serious enough to cause permanent disability or death. Some can be prevented through immunization, and many can be cured with medication. Most infections caused by bacteria, fungi, or parasites can be treated effectively with antimicrobial drugs, while most viral infections, like the common cold, cannot be treated effectively using current agents.

Infections may be classified in several ways. In terms of extent, they may be local (confined to a specific part of the body) or systemic (affecting the whole body). In terms of the pattern of development, they may be acute (immediate and time limited), chronic (persistent), latent (dormant between recurrences), or opportunistic (occurring in response to poor **immunity**). Of special concern for infection control are nosocomial infections, which are infections that patients pick up in a health care setting. As

> **microorganism** an organism so small that it can only be seen under a microscope.

> **contagious or communicable disease** a disease that is spread from person to person.

> **immunity** an individual's ability to fight off disease.

many as 10 percent of hospitalized individuals will develop a nosocomial infection. These infections can be debilitating or fatal.

Patterns of Infection

An infection can occur anywhere in the human body, internally or externally. It can affect parts of the body or the body as a whole. An infection may be referred to as a **local infection** if it is limited to a specific part or area of the body, usually external. An incision line, a scratch, or a cut can become infected, or an eye can become infected. Local infections may be evidenced by redness, swelling, or increased warmth in the affected area. Local infections can be treated with **topical** antibiotic creams or with oral antibiotics. Some local infections can become systemic if not treated properly.

Systemic infections affect the entire body in some manner, although the source of the infection may be limited to one part of the body. For example, a kidney or bladder infection, although located in a particular organ, is likely to produce more generalized clinical signs, such as fever, increased pulse or respiratory rate, fatigue, loss of appetite, and generalized aches. Colds and strep throat are also considered systemic infections. Even **otitis media** (middle ear infection) can cause systemic responses, such as fever. **Septicemia**, or blood poisoning, is a disease caused by pathogens in the bloodstream that involves the whole body.

Acute and *chronic* refer to the onset and duration of an infection. Many familiar infections, such as bad colds and otitis media, are often **acute infections**. The course of the illness is usually short, and the patient may recover with or without treatment. Some acute infections, however, can be serious, leading to long-term damage or even death. A **chronic infection** occurs when the microorganism that causes it is present for a long period of time, sometimes persisting for life. The person may have signs or symptoms continuously or may have asymptomatic periods. Periods without symptoms are known as **remissions**; periods when symptoms occur again are called **exacerbations**. The organism may be transmitted even if the patient is **asymptomatic**. An example of a chronic infection is hepatitis B. Although the person may show few symptoms or be completely asymptomatic, the person still carries the virus and can pass it to others. A **latent infection** is one in which the clinical signs disappear and recur, although any infection lasting more than two weeks may be called a chronic infection. Most chronic infections show little change over their slow progression. For example, in herpes simplex virus 1 (HSV 1), after the initial infection the virus can lie dormant for long periods until some stimulus, such as fatigue or stress, reactivates it. When clinical signs and symptoms reappear, the infection becomes an **active infection**.

A *primary infection* is the original or initial infection a patient displays. It is not always the patient's main medical problem. A *secondary infection* is one that occurs when a bacterial infection follows or complicates a condition already present. For example, Ms. Valdez develops viral pneumonia. This is the primary infection. Several days later, because of a buildup of mucus in her lungs, Ms. Valdez develops another infection caused by a bacterium. This is a secondary infection.

A **recurrent infection** is sometimes confused with a relapse or the reappearance of an initial infection. A recurrent infection is a repetition of an infection after recovery. It is a distinct episode; pathogens involved may be the same as or different from those responsible for the initial infection. A **relapse** involves a flare-up of the initial infection after it appears to have subsided. A relapse is caused by the same organism as the original infection.

A person does not get sick every time a microorganism enters his or her body. A healthy person with a fully functional immune system can resist many of these disease-causing agents. An **opportunistic infection** is one that occurs only under certain

---

local infection an infection that is confined to a specific region of the body, for example, a finger.

topical applied to the skin or affected area.

systemic infection an infection that has spread to more than one region of the body.

otitis media infection of the middle ear.

septicemia an infection in the blood stream that can worsen rapidly and is often life threatening.

acute infection an infection that is time limited.

chronic infection an infection that is persistent over a long period, perhaps for life.

remission a period in which a chronic infection shows no symptoms.

exacerbation a period in which a chronic infection shows symptoms.

asymptomatic without clinical signs or symptoms.

latent infection an infection in which the symptoms disappear and recur, but the disease-causing agent remains in the body.

active infection an infection in which signs and symptoms are present.

recurrent infection a distinct episode of an infection after recovery from the initial infection; may involve the same pathogens or different ones.

relapse the reemergence of an initial infection after it appears to have subsided but has not been cured.

opportunistic infection an infection that does not ordinarily cause disease but does so under certain circumstances, for example, in compromised immune systems; so called because it takes advantage of an "opportunity."

circumstances, such as when the person's immune system is compromised. For example, people whose immune system has been weakened by AIDS are susceptible to otherwise rare types of pneumonia and fungal infections that would not affect them if their immune system were healthy.

Patients come to health care facilities to become well, so it is particularly distressing when the facility environment makes them ill. Yet **nosocomial infections**, those acquired in a health care facility, are not surprising. Patients who are hospitalized are often ill, and their body's defences may be weakened. In addition, there are likely to be more infectious organisms in a patient-care facility than in other places, and these organisms can be carried from one patient to another by a variety of items or by health care professionals. Nosocomial infections range from minor to life threatening.

nosocomial infection a hospital-related infection; one that is not present or incubating when a patient is admitted to a hospital or health care facility.

Microorganisms

A microorganism is a microscopic life form too small to be seen by the naked eye, such as a bacterium or virus. A microorganism that can cause disease or infections is called a **pathogen**. If an infection develops, it may be local or systemic. The severity of an infection will depend on the nature and **virulence** of the infectious organism. This is determined by the strain of organism present, the number of these organisms present, and how potent these organisms are.

Not all organisms cause disease; those that do not are called **nonpathogenic**. Normal flora typically present in various parts of our body, such as the intestine or the bladder, is a nonpathogenic organism. It is worth noting, however, that normal flora found in one part of the body can cause an infection if transferred to another. For example, normal flora found in the bowel can cause an infection if it is transferred to the bladder.

pathogen a microorganism that causes disease.

virulence the power of a microbe to produce disease in a particular host.

nonpathogenic not causing disease.

Bacteria   Bacteria are single-celled organisms that multiply by cell division. Most bacteria are nonpathogenic, but some types of bacteria are major causes of infectious diseases. They may be categorized by their demand for oxygen or their shape. **Aerobic bacteria** require oxygen to live and multiply. **Anaerobic bacteria** can live and multiply without oxygen. Both types thrive on moisture, darkness, warmth, and the presence of nutrients.

aerobic bacteria bacteria that require oxygen to grow.

anaerobic bacteria bacteria that do not require oxygen to grow.

Viruses   A virus is an organism that cannot be seen with a regular microscope. Viruses may cause illnesses such as the common cold, influenza, and infectious mononucleosis. Viruses are difficult to treat and do not respond to antibiotics; they do, however, respond to some vaccines, such as those that cause childhood diseases like measles, mumps, chicken pox, and whooping cough. In 2016, the Zika virus was declared a global public health emergency, prompting travel advisories to areas where the virus was spreading; the WHO even advised countries not to collect blood donations from people who had travelled to Zika-affected regions. The virus is thought to affect the brain development of unborn babies, a condition called *microcephaly*, and neurological problems in adults. Pregnant women are especially at risk, and it is now believed that men infected with the virus can pass it along to unborn children at the time of conception. A number of athletes withdrew from the 2016 Olympics in Rio de Janeiro because they were concerned over contracting the virus. Scientists are trying to develop a vaccine, but there is little hope for finding one in the near future.

The Chain of Infection

To understand the transition of an individual from a healthy state to an infectious state, one must examine a series of events known collectively as the infection cycle.

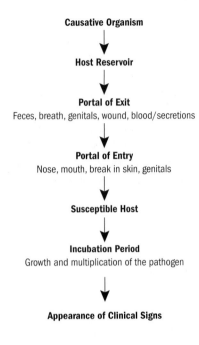

Figure 5.1   The chain of infection

The infection cycle has been compared to the links of a chain. All of the links in the chain must be present for infection to occur (see Figure 5.1). These steps include the following:

- A causative organism
- A host reservoir
- A portal of exit
- A mode of transmission
- A portal of entry
- A susceptible host

Causative Organism   To initiate an infection, the microorganism must be a pathogen.

Host   A host (also referred to as a host reservoir) is where the pathogen is initially found. The host can be a person, an animal, or an environmental habitat, such as soil, feces, water, or food. The host must be capable of providing an environment in which the microorganism can live, grow, and multiply.

Portal of Exit   The pathogen must have an exit from the host reservoir. In humans, this could be through the bowel, nose, or mouth, or in blood, semen, or saliva.

Mode of Transmission   After the organism leaves the host reservoir, it needs transportation to the new host, or recipient host (the person receiving the organism). Methods of transmission include the following:

- *Direct contact*: Transmission from person to person. For example, Jenny has a pathogen in her throat and kisses Jake, transmitting the organism to Jake.
- *Indirect contact*: Transmission from a person to an object (such as a tissue) to a person. For example, a health office professional touches infected body fluid and accidentally transfers it to the new paper sheet on the examination bed. The pathogen in the fluid is transferred to the next patient.

- *Droplet transmission*: Transmission by coughs or sneezes. Infections are commonly spread this way in the health office, especially during the cold and flu season. During influenza outbreaks, hospitals and nursing homes will often limit or ban visitors to reduce the spread of influenza.

- *Vehicle route*: Transmission via food, water, or blood and body fluids. Human immunodeficiency virus (HIV) and hepatitis can be transmitted via body fluids. This mode of transmission is similar to indirect contact, except that the object is the host itself.

- *Airborne transmission*: Transmission through dust, evaporated droplets in the air, or airborne particles of hair and skin. Microorganisms carried in this manner can be dispersed widely by air currents, ventilation systems and fans, and may be inhaled by people at some distance. Transmission by evaporated droplets differs from droplet transmission in that the residue of the evaporated droplet remains suspended in the air for long periods. Dust from linens containing the infectious agent would be another example. The organisms are inhaled by or dropped on the recipient host.

- *Vector transmission*: Transmission in which a bird, animal, or insect (called the *vector*) carries the infectious agent. Malaria and West Nile virus are transmitted this way through mosquitoes.

Portal of Entry After the organism has left the host reservoir via some means of transmission, it must find a route into the recipient host. The common portals of entry are through the respiratory, gastrointestinal, or genitourinary tract or by direct entry through an open wound, scratch, cut, or any other break in the skin. A wound infection usually results from the entry of a pathogenic organism through a break in the skin.

TIP

Ensure that your vaccinations are up to date. Get your flu shot! Consider the pros and cons, but getting this vaccination can prevent you from spreading the virus to a vulnerable population.

Susceptible Host The *recipient host* is the person to whom the organism is transferred. An infection does not occur every time a pathogenic organism invades a host. The susceptibility of the host depends largely on the person's immune system and defences.

Vaccines

There are numerous types of vaccines, differing in how they are made and how they are stored. They work because the body responds in the same manner to an **antigen** whether it is exposed to it naturally or via a vaccine. Vaccines are scientifically prepared, rigorously tested, and predominantly safe. A small percentage of immunized individuals suffer serious adverse effects—far less than those associated with the disease.

In the health office, some of your patients may opt not to have themselves or their children vaccinated. This is a personal decision that must be respected. Some jurisdictions require certain vaccinations as a condition for school attendance, although there may be exemptions for children with certain medical conditions. Individuals who are unvaccinated are at risk of both acquiring an infection and passing an infectious disease

antigen a pathogen or any other substance that induces an antibody response.

to others. Many vaccine-preventable diseases thought to be eradicated (e.g., measles, mumps, chicken pox, whooping cough) are reappearing. This is likely due to unvaccinated people spreading diseases and the failure of some vaccine protocols, such as the whooping cough vaccine, which may lose its effectiveness over time.

Storing and Handling Immunizing Agents   Proper storing and handling of vaccines is essential to preserve their potency. It may be your responsibility to oversee the proper storage and handling of immunizing agents. Every office must follow the PHAC's guidelines for storing and monitoring vaccines. Each manufacturer will print storage guidelines on the package. Most recommendations specify that vaccines be stored at temperatures from +2°C to +8°C.

Most vaccines must be protected from light as well (e.g., MMR, varicella, BCG, and flu vaccines). Keep them stored in the packages they come in. If a vaccine is reconstituted but not used, immediately return it to the fridge and dispose of it if not used within the manufacturer's recommended time frame. Your local public health authority will likely make routine checks on your office to ensure that vaccines are properly stored.

Pay attention to expiry dates, and adhere to the following procedures:

- Use a frost-free refrigerator.
- Have a designated person monitor the fridge temperature at the same time daily.
- Use a commercially available maximum–minimum thermometer, placed in the middle of the fridge. A large plastic bottle filled with water placed in the fridge will help maintain a stable temperature.
- Immediately place newly delivered vaccines in the fridge (even 20 minutes is too long to leave them sitting out).
- Store vaccines in the middle of the refrigerator to avoid extremes of temperature.
- Make sure the electrical cord is in a place where it will not easily become disconnected (you can use a safety lock plug).
- Keep vaccines with the earliest expiry date in front.
- Don't store lunches or other items (such as specimens) in this fridge.
- Remove vaccines right before use and refrigerate them as soon as the nurse/doctor has finished with them (they may do this themselves, but you can act as an extra check). It is easy to leave a vaccine out, especially during busy times, such as the influx of patients for their flu shots early in the flu season.
- Ensure the doctor uses an insulated carrier for vaccines equipped with a freezer pack (the vaccine should not be in direct contact with the freezer pack).
- If you discover your fridge is not working, transfer the vaccines to another fridge as soon as possible. If the time frame of the failure is unknown, you may have to discard the vaccines.
- If there is a power failure, four hours is the accepted limit after which you must transfer the vaccines to another refrigerator.
- If you suspect the cold chain has been compromised, public health will assist you to make decisions regarding whether or not the vaccines are safe to use.

Recommended Vaccines for Patients   You should know the recommended immunization schedules for patients (especially children) in your jurisdiction so that you can schedule the patients' appointments appropriately. Some of these vaccinations are given in conjunction with a well-baby check-up. A child who is sick with a fever should have the immunization postponed until the child is better. Parents may be anxious (particularly new parents) when their baby receives an immunization, fearing the child will react or, at the very least, be "out of sorts" for a day or two. Provide the parents with as much information and support as you can. The most common side effect from a childhood immunization is redness and tenderness at the injection site. A small child might also be cranky and fussy for a day or two. The Public Health Agency of Canada's website listed at the end of this chapter will provide you with detailed information on recommended vaccines as well as common questions patients may ask. It will provide you with a current list of child and adult immunizations recommended by the PHAC for your own jurisdiction.

Recommended Immunizations and Tests for Health Professionals In health care settings, you will naturally be exposed to more sick people than in other workplaces. Therefore, you should be immunized against the infections that present common threats. People object to vaccinations for a variety of reasons: they are too busy, they dislike "shots," they misinterpret minor local reactions as allergic reactions, or they believe vaccines cause serious complications like autism—a belief proven to be entirely false. The reality is that immunizations not only protect you but also your patients. If you contract an infection, you are likely to pass it on to patients, some of whom are particularly vulnerable.

> **TIP**
>
> If you are entering completed vaccinations into the computer, you will be asked for the type of vaccine, its manufacturer, and its expiry date for every entry. Have the package handy or write down the expiry date of each vial so you are not fishing for the information every time you make an entry.

Check with your doctor to see that your routine immunizations are up to date. Some childhood vaccinations will protect you for life, but many others require boosters to maintain immunity. Many facilities have a specific list of immunizations required for employees and often for volunteers and students on externships. For some diseases, you may have the option of having **antibody** titres done, which would test for immunity. Some colleges may also require immunizations for health office administration students and will provide opportunities to receive all necessary shots.

antibody a protein specific to a certain antigen that weakens or destroys pathogens.

Influenza In most parts of the country, the influenza vaccine is readily available (usually in the fall), and it is generally recommended that everyone, including children over the age of six months, be immunized. Health care professionals are at risk for contracting the flu and are potential host reservoirs for passing the infection to someone else. Health professionals are strongly urged to get the influenza vaccine. Otherwise they can easily pass on the virus to a population at risk.

In 2012, Health Canada recommended that children between 6 and 23 months of age receive a full dose of influenza vaccine. Research shows that the full dose is both safe and more effective. Some jurisdictions may still give children in this age category two injections of 0.25 millilitres (half the adult dose) at least four weeks apart. As well, it has been ascertained that an allergy to eggs is no longer a reason for people to refrain from getting the influenza vaccine.

Hepatitis A and B Hepatitis A and B are serious, sometimes chronic or deadly viral infections of the liver. Transmission of these viruses can occur in a health care setting as a result of an accidental prick with a contaminated needle or other sharp instrument. Although there are separate vaccinations for hepatitis A and B, Twinrix is a popular vaccine that provides protection from both hepatitis A and hepatitis B. Side effects are rare for these immunizations, although most practitioners recommend that patients stay in the office for at least 15 minutes in case of a reaction. The routine schedule for Twinrix is three doses—the second injection at least one month after the first, and the third injection six months after the first. However, an accelerated schedule of four doses is an option for those with time constraints. Some facilities make this immunization a condition of employment. The vaccine provides protection for 10 years, and probably for lifetime if the series is completed. There are currently no recommendations for booster shots of this vaccine.

Measles, Mumps, Rubella (MMR)   Although most Canadians are immune to these diseases (older people because they had the diseases as children, and younger people from childhood immunizations), another dose may be recommended. The MMR vaccine is a combined preparation given in one needle. Contraindications include pregnancy, receipt of **immunoglobulins**, or a sensitivity to eggs or neomycin. There is controversy over individuals who have a sensitivity to eggs. Only life-threatening reactions are considered to be a firm contraindication; people with the potential for such reaction can be tested with a weaker version of the serum.

immunoglobulin a serum that contains antibodies that can help protect an exposed person from contracting the disease.

Hepatitis C   Hepatitis C also causes a chronic liver infection that can be deadly. Research for a hepatitis C vaccine is currently underway. Individuals often do not realize they have hepatitis C for years, until they become symptomatic. Health professionals, on the other hand, can seek both diagnosis and treatment if possible exposure to hepatitis C (e.g., a needle prick) has occurred. There are new drugs on the market to treat individuals with hepatitis C, some recently approved by Health Canada (e.g., Victrelis, Harvoni, Sovaldi). Drugs are selected based on the particular strain (or genotype) of virus infecting the person. Recommended drugs, course of treatment, and effectiveness will depend on the person's condition.

Pneumococcal Infections   Although health care professionals are not considered to be at higher risk than the general population for pneumococcal infections, some facilities recommend this immunization for their employees' own protection. It is particularly recommended for health professionals with chronic illnesses such as diabetes, heart disease, or disorders of the immune system.

Diphtheria/Tetanus/Pertussis   Booster shots are recommended every 10 years after primary immunization has been given for these infections. Health care professionals are not considered to be at higher risk than the general population.

Meningitis/Varicella/HPV   Other vaccines in current use include Menjugate (to prevent meningococcal infection) and Varivax (to prevent infection from the varicella zoster virus, which causes chicken pox). A vaccine (Gardasil) for the human papillomavirus (HPV) is currently being promoted by the PHAC.

Tuberculin Testing   Tuberculosis (TB) is a disease that is constantly being monitored. In Canada, after several decades of decline, the annual incidence rate of TB has remained about the same for the last 10 years, with an estimated 1700 to 2000 new cases reported annually. TB is not declining, primarily because of immigration and international travel to and from areas where it is prevalent, including East, Southeast, and South Asia; sub-Saharan Africa; parts of South and Central America; the Caribbean; Eastern Europe; and the former Soviet Union. Indigenous peoples also have a higher incidence of TB, as do individuals with HIV and those living in poor economic circumstances. Recently a resistant form of TB emerged, causing global concern. The strain is resistant to both first- and second-line drugs. In 2007, several of these cases were reported in Toronto. These are called MDR-TB (multi-drug resistant) and account for an estimated one in four cases.

Infectious Diseases of Particular Concern

As mentioned earlier in the chapter, hepatitis A and B are infectious diseases that can be contracted by health professionals. The other disease to note is HIV.

HIV and AIDS are not the same thing—AIDS is the advanced stage of the disease caused by HIV. Not all HIV-infected individuals go on to develop AIDS. AIDS is now considered a chronic disease, managed by a cocktail of medications. Health care workers are most commonly exposed to blood-borne infections such as hepatitis or HIV through accidental injury from a needle or sharp instrument contaminated by blood or contact with body fluids through a break in the skin. This can occur within a number of contexts, including cleaning up trays and equipment after a treatment with an HIV-positive patient. Because HIV does not survive well outside the body, it cannot be transmitted through the more routine routes discussed earlier. Normal daily contact with an infected person poses no risk.

Steps to Take if Exposure Is Suspected   If you suspect that you or someone you are working with has been exposed to an infectious disease, follow agency protocols for reporting and responding to such an incident. Once the exposure incident has been medically assessed, the physician will determine an appropriate course of treatment. In the case of hepatitis B, vaccination at the time of exposure followed by a second injection of hepatitis B immune globulin is indicated. The vaccination series must be completed. In most jurisdictions, post-vaccination testing is recommended six to eight weeks after completion of the final vaccination series. Testing is strongly recommended even if the person has been previously vaccinated.

Procedures should also be in place for potential HIV exposure. The exposed person should immediately be referred to an emergency department for medical assessment because antiviral treatment, if recommended, is most effective when administered within two hours of HIV exposure.

Exposures to such infections that occur in the workplace are considered workers' compensation injuries. It is important to report any incident immediately, seek prompt treatment, and ensure that the appropriate forms are completed.

L03 L04 PREVENTING THE SPREAD OF INFECTION

Even if you are not directly involved in patient care, your actions can either transmit pathogens or prevent their transmission. An understanding of **asepsis** is essential.

The first line of defence, in both the hospital and the health office, is personal cleanliness. You can easily carry microorganisms into the work setting or back home on your clothing and body. If you carry pathogens home, you can become ill or spread illness to your family. If you carry pathogens to the hospital or office, you may spread infection to vulnerable patients. For this reason, some health care facilities ask direct-care staff members to leave their uniforms and shoes at work. Although this policy does not usually apply to administrative staff, it is a still good idea. Wearing a uniform or lab coat only at work limits the chance of transmitting harmful organisms both at work and outside. A uniform or lab coat also looks professional, is easy to launder, and protects your own clothes.

asepsis a state in which pathogens are absent or reduced. There are two principal types of asepsis: medical and surgical.

Medical Asepsis

Medical asepsis is killing germs *after they leave* the body. The purpose is to reduce or control the number of microorganisms; it does not completely eliminate them. We practise medical asepsis in our daily lives every time we wash our hands, use a tissue when we cough or sneeze, or clean countertops with a disinfectant after preparing food. Medical asepsis should be practised in every health care setting.

Handwashing   Handwashing is probably the single most important component of medical asepsis and the *single most effective method of protecting yourself and others from infection*. How often you wash your hands will depend on the scope of your nonadministrative duties. Wash your hands after breaks and before and after preparing an examination room, assisting with a procedure, or assisting a patient. Wash them before and after using gloves or handling specimens, waste, or potentially soiled instruments or other articles. Figure 5.2 illustrates the proper handwashing technique.

To wash your hands, properly, you need

- soap,
- running water,
- a clean towel, and
- a garbage can.

It does not matter what type of soap you use. Soaps and detergents are not disinfectants. They emulsify, reducing surface tension to facilitate the removal of soil and

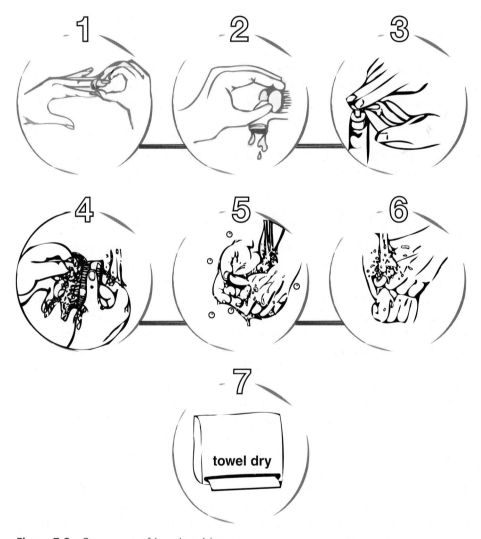

Figure 5.2   Sequence of handwashing

organisms. Hands can be cleaned but never sterilized and will always harbour some organisms. Here are the steps for proper handwashing technique:

1. Remove all jewellery, such as rings and watches, as these items can harbour bacteria and other organisms, preventing effective washing. Also, look for breaks in your skin, which provide a portal of entry/exit for organisms. If there are any skin breaks, you should wear gloves.

2. Turn on the water, and adjust it to a comfortable temperature.

3. Add enough cleansing agent to your hands to create suds.

4. Wet your hands, rubbing all areas vigorously. Ensure that you clean nails, fingers, between your fingers, and the front and back of the hands up to the wrist area. Nails need special attention, as do the areas between your fingers. Nail polish, especially if chipped, will also provide a hiding place for organisms. If you frequently touch patients, instruments, or other articles used in patient care, avoid wearing nail polish in the office and keep your nails reasonably short.

5. Scrub, using good friction, for one to two minutes.

6. Rinse off all soap, preferably by putting your hands under the running water fingers first and moving your hands up under the running water.

7. Dry your hands beginning at your fingertips and patting them dry up to the wrist.

8. Using the towel, turn off the taps.

9. Discard the soiled towel.

Remember: It is the friction and the running water that does the job.

The steps earlier describe a medical hand wash. A surgical scrub uses a slightly more effective cleansing agent, takes longer, and uses a more thorough technique.

Although handwashing is the most effective method of preventing the spread of infectious organisms, there are other steps you can take.

The Health Office   The office and reception areas must be kept scrupulously clean at all times. You should provide the office cleaning service with guidelines for cleaning, including the use of disinfectants, as required. The more specific the guidelines, the better. A checklist for the cleaning staff to tick off will ensure that all required areas are cleaned and will document what has been done.

The reception area should be well ventilated, and seating should place patients at a comfortable distance from one another. If possible, have two or three groupings of chairs. Ask patients with known infectious conditions not to visit the office or, if they must be seen, book them at the end of the day. Do not book patients who are susceptible to infections at the same time as someone who may have one, such as a person who thinks she or he might have the flu. There are times, however, when this information is simply not available. You can only do your best to keep infectious patients away from others, especially older patients and children. *Note:* Do not book a pregnant patient at the same time as someone who might have rubella. The rubella virus can be **teratogenic** to the fetus in the first trimester of pregnancy.

teratogenic causing abnormalities in the fetus.

Properly clean all instruments, such as stethoscopes, otoscopes, ophthalmoscopes, and thermometers. Some articles must be sterilized and others disinfected (discussed in more detail later in this chapter). Carefully clean the examination rooms between patients. Wipe down the examination bed and counters between patients if you suspect they have an infectious disease or if there has been contamination with any body fluid. Dispose of garbage frequently and properly.

Provide tissues and an adequate number of wastebaskets, and consider putting up a sign asking patients to use tissues when they cough or sneeze. The only children's toys suitable for the office are those that can be wiped down daily with a disinfectant. Books for small children are often available in materials that can be wiped clean.

Specimens left in the washroom, such as urine samples, should be handled with gloves. Wipe the counter and any visible spills after a specimen has been removed. Do not leave specimens sitting in the washroom where another patient may spill them or come in contact with them.

Health Care Facilities Follow the principles outlined earlier, as well as facility guidelines on specific situations, as previously mentioned. Nosocomial infections (even those that respond to antimicrobial medications) are a serious problem in hospitals, leading to considerable morbidity and mortality, particularly among patients who are coping with other illnesses or recovering from surgery.

Hospital Infections Several infections are particularly concerning in the hospital setting. Infections occurring in the hospital (nosocomial infections) are troublesome; they can easily spread, causing long-term illness or death. Hospitalized patients are usually more susceptible to infection because of compromised immune systems, age, surgery, immobility, or the nature of the illness itself.

Containment and control of infectious outbreaks begins with adherence to strict handwashing guidelines and other protocol on the part of *all staff* in the hospital. Some hospitals limit or track the transfer of patients from one facility to another or within one facility. Many hospitals across the country screen selected patients for the presence of infectious organisms on admission, particularly VRE, MRSA, and *Clostridium difficile*. Individuals with these infections are placed in isolation (segregating the patient in a private room). There are different levels of isolation dictating which precautions staff and visitors are required to take. The type of isolation depends on the seriousness of the infecting organism and how it is spread (e.g., droplet, airborne, direct contact). Details describing a specific isolation policy will be in the hospital's procedures manual. Polices may involve wearing a mask, gown, and gloves when entering the patient's room, for example. Here is some information on each of these infectious organisms:

■ *MRSA. Staphylococcus aureus* is usually a harmless bacterium found in healthy people. MRSA stands for "methicillin-resistant *Staphylococcus aureus*." It occurs when the staph organism is resistant to methicillin. Vancomycin is an antibiotic sometimes used to treat MRSA, but there has recently been evidence that strains of *Staphylococcus* are also resistant to this antibiotic—called vancomycin-resistant *Staphylococcus aureaus* (VRSA).

■ *VRE.* Vancomycin-resistant *Enterococcus* is another bacterium that is cause for concern in health care facilities. It occurs when *Enterococcus* mutates and becomes resistant to vancomycin, the primary antibiotic used against it. *Enterococcus* infections can occur in the urinary tract, blood, and wounds, including surgical wounds. Emerging strains that are resistant to previously effective antibiotics are very difficult to treat.

■ *Clostridium difficile.* Known more commonly as just *C. difficile*, this bacterium is one of the most common causes of often-deadly infections in hospitals and long-term care facilities. It is normally present in the gastrointestinal tract. It commonly emerges in the hospital setting as a pathogen in people who have had the normal balance of flora in the gastrointestinal tract altered. It can cause serious illness in immunocompromised individuals and older adults.

General Precautions The janitorial staff clean most hospital areas thoroughly and regularly. They almost always wear gloves. Garbage cans are emptied frequently, and all areas, including patients' rooms, are dusted and wiped. A thorough *terminal cleaning* is done when a patient is discharged.

Staff members who have potentially infectious diseases are encouraged not to come to work, and the general public with infectious conditions are asked not to visit hospitalized patients. Staff members in some facilities are strongly encouraged to receive the flu vaccine annually and keep other required immunizations current. This can be a contentious issue for employees who do not wish to have the flu vaccine, as most hospitals are firm about this policy; organizations cannot force an employee to get the flu vaccine. Providing information about the flu vaccine is the best way to encourage employees to get immunized.

When a facility imposes visiting restrictions, you may be required to inform visitors and to help enforce restrictions. It is not uncommon for long-term care facilities to be **quarantined** if there is an outbreak of the flu or other infectious disease. This may include a total ban on visitors to a single patient-care unit or to the entire facility. Such events are stressful for everyone. Patients become anxious about illness and miss the contact with family and friends. They may become demanding and bad tempered. Family members may dismiss the need for quarantine and insist on visiting. They may be upset, argumentative, rude, and sometimes even aggressive. Staff are caught in the middle and may also be coping with increased workloads and longer workdays if some staff are ill. Infected patients may be isolated (see discussion later in this chapter) in an attempt to contain the infection.

> **quarantine** isolating or separating a patient, patient-care unit, or facility.

⟫⟫ POINTS TO PONDER

Some hospitals have a policy forcing staff who refuse the flu vaccine to wear masks despite lack of proof that this prevents viral transmission. Unvaccinated individuals have a much higher probability of spreading the virus; most health care workers deal with vulnerable population groups for whom a case of the flu could be fatal. If there is no medical contraindication, do you think health care workers should receive the flu vaccine? Should there be consequences if the health care worker refuses?

Surgical Asepsis

Surgical asepsis is an extension of medical asepsis, otherwise known as sterilization. The goal is to destroy all pathogens before they can enter the body. An example is the sterilization of surgical instruments before an operation. No pathogens remain on the instruments, so none are introduced into the body.

Sterilization uses physical or chemical procedures to destroy all microbial life, including highly resistant bacterial endospores. Sterilization of various objects and instruments is the primary method used in health care to protect patients from **contamination** with pathogens. Without this process, a patient's risk of developing infection would be very high.

> **contamination** the presence of pathogens on an object.

If you work in a hospital, you may be responsible for ordering sterile equipment and maintaining stocks of sterile supplies. In some health care offices, one person, often a nurse, is responsible for disinfecting and sterilizing instruments and equipment for reuse. In many practices, however, all staff share this responsibility. Some articles are sterilized and others are disinfected. In either case, the first step is thorough cleansing.

Sterile Technique All health procedures need to be carried out, and all sterile material must be handled in such a way as to prevent contamination. This is called **sterile technique** (**sterile** means completely free from pathogens). For example, a nurse

> **sterile technique** methods to avoid contamination of sterile materials.
>
> **sterile** completely free of pathogens.

changing a surgical dressing would use sterile technique when opening the dressing tray, handling the instruments, and cleaning and redressing the wound. He or she might wear sterile gloves, depending on the technique used, but would scrupulously avoid touching any part of the instruments or dressing considered sterile.

Sanitizing, Disinfecting, and Sterilizing

Three levels of hygiene are generally used in health care facilities: **sanitization**, **disinfection**, and **sterilization**. These terms can be confusing because definitions overlap. *Sanitization* and *disinfection*, for example, are sometimes used interchangeably. To disinfect, by definition, is to free an article or a substance from harmful organisms. Sanitization, disinfection, and sterilization all destroy microorganisms, but disinfection is more effective than sanitization in destroying a wider variety of more resistant organisms. Sterilization is a process that kills virtually all organisms and is the highest level or most effective cleansing process. Surgical instruments must be sterilized.

The specific health setting determines how many and what types of instruments require sanitization, disinfection, or sterilization and how often. In a dental office, for example, you may have to process instruments through all three levels of cleansing several times daily; a simple check-up may require treating a variety of instruments. A family physician's office, which uses fewer instruments, may sanitize and disinfect articles daily but sterilize only certain instruments every couple of days. All offices using nondisposable equipment will have a protocol for cleaning, disinfecting, and sterilizing instruments, but protocols, solutions, and methods of sterilization will vary with the type of practice.

Disposable instruments and examination and dressing trays are popular and reduce the need for sterilization. For example, most health care facilities use temperature-taking devices with disposable components. Offices and facilities using disposable tools must consider their effectiveness and convenience against the cost.

Sanitization   The word *sanitary* means "clean," and it comes from a Latin root meaning "health," showing the importance of cleanliness to maintaining health. Sanitizing is the first step in the cleansing process. It is necessary to sanitize instruments and other devices used in patient procedures. As well as removing some pathogenic organisms, sanitizing articles removes blood, other fluids, tissue, and debris from surgical instruments and is crucial in preparing instruments to be sterilized. Articles that come in contact only with intact skin—with the exception of mucous membranes—may require only sanitization; however, that does not prevent a health office from using higher-level disinfectant solutions. (If an article has been used on a patient with an infectious condition, more thorough cleansing is needed.)

Sanitizers (solutions used for sanitizing) are specially formulated, nonabrasive, low-sudsing detergents with a neutral pH. These detergents are effective in removing fats and oils and help remove bacteria and other debris. Stronger detergents can damage instruments and other articles.

Sanitize instruments as soon as possible after use to prevent fluids from crusting or drying. If you do not have time to sanitize immediately, rinse instruments under cold water (hot water may cause blood to solidify) and place them in an appropriate solution, such as an enzyme detergent with anti-rust properties. Always wear gloves when sanitizing instruments.

Start by rinsing articles thoroughly and carefully in cold water. To avoid injury, always check for sharp instruments (referred to as **sharps**), such as scissors, scalpel blades, and needles. Properly dispose of scalpel blades and needles in a special container (discussed later). Separate other sharp instruments, such as scissors, curettes,

sanitization removal of gross contaminants and some microorganisms from instruments, skin, and so on; the lowest level of medical hygiene.

disinfection a more thorough removal of contaminants than sanitization but less thorough than sterilization.

sterilization the process of destroying all microorganisms, including bacterial endospores and viruses. This is the highest level of cleanliness.

sanitizer a substance that significantly reduces the bacterial population in an inanimate environment but does not destroy all bacteria or other microorganisms.

sharp any instrument with a sharp edge or point, such as a scalpel, scissors, or a needle.

and pointed forceps. Clean each instrument separately. Make sure that you clean all surfaces of each instrument. (Any debris left on an article will impede sterilization because it blocks part of the instrument's surface area from the sterilizing agent.) Open movable instruments, such as forceps and scissors, and carefully check all surfaces. A small brush, such as a toothbrush, is helpful. The instruments may be slippery, so concentrate on what you are doing and do not rush. Place each sanitized instrument carefully in a designated area, still separate from the other instruments, to dry.

Disinfection   As previously noted, disinfection is a term that can be broadly used in health care to refer to the removal of organisms from objects. Usually it refers to the process of further removing pathogens from articles that have been sanitized. Disinfection uses stronger **disinfectant** solutions/chemicals than those used for sanitization. Become familiar with solutions used in your occupational setting, and follow office policy and manufacturers' directions when disinfecting items.

disinfectant a chemical substance that destroys or eliminates specific species of infectious microorganisms. It is not usually effective against bacterial spores.

Chemical Disinfection   Chemical disinfection is used for heat-sensitive equipment that may be damaged by high temperatures. Chemical disinfection is not as reliable as boiling or sterilization. All instruments immersed in a chemical disinfectant must be absolutely clean and dry; wet instruments will dilute the solution, and debris may impede complete exposure of the instrument to the chemical, thus rendering the disinfection process ineffective. Exposure to air can also interfere with the action of some solutions, so containers for soaking instruments should have a lid. It is easy to forget to replace the lid when you add an instrument, but an open container can mean ineffective disinfection. Pay particular attention to the disinfectant solution itself. It must be stored at the proper temperature and used and diluted accurately according to the manufacturer's directions. All solutions have a shelf life, after which they begin to lose their disinfecting properties. Diluted solutions should be carefully dated and replaced appropriately.

Any instruments that have been chemically disinfected must be thoroughly rinsed before they come into contact with human tissue. If the level of disinfection must be maintained, sterile water is used to rinse them. After proper disinfection, if an instrument (e.g., an oral thermometer) needs only to be clean for subsequent uses, it may be rinsed under tap water before each use.

There are disadvantages to chemical disinfection. There is no way to verify the level of disinfection achieved, and the solutions are often hard on the instruments. However, it is effective for instruments that cannot withstand high-temperature methods of sterilization.

Antiseptics and Disinfectants   *Disinfectant* and **antiseptic** are another pair of terms that can be confusing. Disinfectants and antiseptics both destroy microorganisms. A disinfectant solution, however, is usually considered more potent (i.e., it can kill a wider variety of microorganisms) than an antiseptic and is not suitable for use on human tissue. An antiseptic destroys some microorganisms but is not too harsh to use on the skin. Handwashing removes microorganisms from our hands. There are solutions used in health care that are more effective for killing microorganisms than regular soap but are still suitable for use on human tissue. Antiseptic solutions are sometimes referred to as disinfectants, but unlike true disinfectants, they are suitable for use on skin and mucous membranes. (See Table 5.1.) Antiseptics are considered **bacteriostatic**, meaning they reduce or inhibit the number of microorganisms, while disinfectants are considered **bactericidal**, meaning they kill microorganisms. Isopropyl alcohol, for example, is an antiseptic frequently used to swab the skin before giving an injection. (*Note*: There is some controversy over the effectiveness of this practice, but most providers use some sort of cleansing agent; some use normal saline.) Antiseptics are also

antiseptic a cleansing agent that can be applied to living tissue to destroy pathogens.

bacteriostatic reducing or inhibiting the number of microorganisms.

bactericidal killing microorganisms.

TABLE 5.1	A comparison of antiseptics and disinfectants
Antiseptic	**Disinfectant**
Bacteriostatic	Bactericidal
May be used on skin and mucous membranes	Not used on skin or mucous membranes
Weaker	Stronger
Examples: isopropyl alcohol, iodophors	Examples: hydrogen peroxide, bleach

used to prepare a patient's skin before surgery. Betadine, povidone, and Savlon are other commercially used solutions.

In a health office, alcohol or another topical antiseptic is often kept in a dispenser with a retractable lid. Depressing the lid with a cotton ball saturates the ball with the solution. The container must be cleaned frequently and thoroughly and the solution replaced appropriately. Labelling the container with the date the solution was changed and when it should be changed will help you to remember when to change the solution. Other offices will use single use/packaged alcohol swabs, but these are more expensive.

Bleach remains a popular disinfectant and is known as the universal disinfectant. Javex is a familiar brand of bleach. Although most of us have come in contact with household bleach and suffered no skin damage, bleach is irritating, and repeated exposure can damage tissue. A 10 percent solution of bleach and water is effective for a number of uses. It appears to be effective against most viruses, including HIV. Bleach solutions have a short shelf life when diluted and have corrosive properties.

Sterilization   The method of equipment sterilization varies with facilities. The steam autoclave (see Figure 5.3) is one of the most common sterilizers used in health care. There are many varieties and sizes available that are suitable for health offices and health care facilities. The **autoclave** works on the principle of steam under pressure. Temperatures reach 124°C. This kills all pathogens, including spores. The autoclave is safe, convenient, dependable, and inexpensive to operate. The main disadvantage is

autoclave a device using steam for sterilization.

Figure 5.3   The steam autoclave

Medicshots/Alamy Stock Photo

that a number of instruments cannot withstand the high temperatures. Autoclaving also dulls instruments and causes deterioration of some rubbers and plastics. There are specific ways in which instruments and other equipment must be prepared, placed in, and removed from the autoclave to ensure that all items are sterile. If you are responsible for sterilizing equipment, you will be given instructions specific to the process used in your workplace.

L05 STANDARD PRECAUTIONS

Standard Precautions protect both health professionals and patients from cross-contamination from a variety of pathogens, primarily those transmitted through blood and other body fluids. Standard Precautions, developed by the Centers for Disease Control and Prevention in the United States, are internationally implemented. These guidelines expand on similar standards developed in the 1980s, called Universal Precautions, and incorporate another system called Body Fluid Precautions.

Standard Precautions stress that it is virtually impossible to determine who is and is not infected with pathogens. Even patients who have tested negative for infections, such as HIV infection, may turn out to have the disease. Therefore, you should apply Standard Precautions *at all times regardless of the patient's age, gender, diagnosis, or your level of familiarity with the patient*. Consider blood and all body fluids, except sweat, as potentially infectious. Major concerns include HIV, hepatitis B, and other blood-borne infections, such as hepatitis A and C.

Standard Precautions involve the use of protective barriers, such as gloves, gowns, aprons, masks, or protective eyewear, to reduce your risk of exposure to infection. Not all measures are intended for all health professionals. As a health office professional with primarily administrative duties, you are at lower risk than are other health professionals. Your risk will vary, however, with your job setting and responsibilities. Specific sources of potential contamination for the health office professional are discussed later in this chapter. You must assess your own risk factors and follow the appropriate guidelines. Remember that a single exposure can result in serious consequences. It is better to be safe than sorry.

Use Standard Precautions (summarized in Table 5.2) when you expect to come in contact with any of the following:

- *Blood.* Be mindful of the presence of blood not only when it is visible (e.g., cleaning up spilled blood) but also when cleaning instruments and dressing trays or disposing of needles, linens, and gowns. Wear gloves whether or not you can see blood.
- *Body fluids.* Avoid contact with all body fluids, secretions, and excretions, with the exception of sweat. Urine, feces, nasal secretions, tears, sputum, saliva, and emesis

Standard Precautions a set of internationally accepted infection control measures, policies, and procedures used in health care facilities to prevent the transmission of diseases that can be acquired by contact with blood, body fluids, nonintact skin (including rashes), and mucous membranes. These measures protect both health professionals and patients.

TABLE 5.2 Standard Precautions

Gloves: Wear gloves before coming in contact with blood, mucous membranes, nonintact skin, or body fluids. Change them after each procedure.

Handwashing: Wash hands after glove removal, between patients, or after coming in contact with any body fluids or potentially contaminated surfaces.

Gown/Apron: Wear gowns or aprons during procedures in which you may be splashed with body fluids.

Mask/Eye Protection: Wear masks and eye protection during procedures in which you may be splashed with body fluids.

Scoop: Do not recap needles by hand. Recap needles by scooping the cap off the surface with the needle itself.

Sharps: Use designated sharps disposal containers to dispose of all needles, scalpel blades, or other sharp objects.

Wastes/Linens: Dispose of all wastes and linens in accordance with local policies and law.

Resuscitation: Keep mouthpieces and equipment on hand to use for emergency resuscitation to minimize direct contact.

(vomited material) can all be possible sources of infection. The risk is intensified if they are contaminated with blood.

- *Nonintact skin.* If you or a patient has a cut, scratch, or any other break in the skin, the potential for contamination is greater. Any break in the skin is regarded as a breach in the body's first line of defence.

- *Mucous membranes.* Be aware of any possible situation where you might be exposed to a patient's mucous membranes or to tissues, dressing materials, and so on that may have been contaminated with secretions from mucous membranes.

Gloves

When should you wear gloves? In some situations, it is your decision, based on your comfort level. Some health professionals wear gloves for nearly all patient contact, others only when there is a more specific reason. Gloves may offend some patients who feel you are labelling them as unclean. However, as gloves have become more common in health care, people are getting used to them. You can explain that wearing gloves protects the patient as well as yourself. There are a few guidelines about gloves:

- Wear gloves when touching body fluids, secretions, excretions, and contaminated items.

- Change gloves between patients, between tasks and procedures on the same patient, and after contact with material that may contain infectious organisms. *Never* simply wash your hands with your gloves on and proceed to another task or patient.

- Remove gloves after use and before touching uncontaminated items and surfaces. Wear gloves for a specific task, not for an extended length of time.

- Dispose of gloves appropriately, taking care to remove them without touching the outside surface (see Figure 5.4).

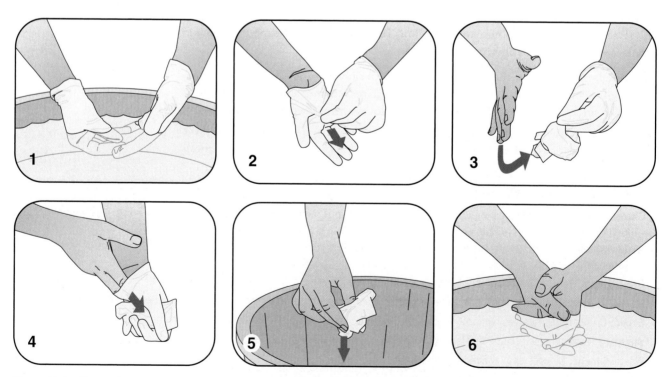

Figure 5.4 Removing gloves

Be alert for latex allergy. Clinical signs include the following:

- Skin rash
- Hives
- Flushing
- Itching
- Symptoms of asthma, such as shortness of breath, itchy red eyes, and runny nose

If you or a patient is allergic to latex, switch to nonlatex gloves.

Wearing gloves may pose difficulties when picking up instruments, cleaning them, and disposing of sharps because the gloves may alter your sense of touch and reduce your dexterity. Work carefully and methodically when performing tasks with gloves on. Remember that, even if you are wearing gloves, a puncture is a potential portal for infection.

Procedure for Removing Gloves   Never touch the outside surface of the gloves you are wearing if there has been contact or even potential contact with a contaminated substance. Once you touch the outside of the glove, you are no more protected than if you had not worn gloves at all. It is important to wash your hands after removing your gloves. Do not rely on gloves alone to protect you from infectious contact.

1. *Optional*: If your gloves are soiled with blood or other secretions, some recommend rinsing them before removal. Others argue that wetting the gloves only makes it more likely that you will transfer contaminants to your hands during removal. It is your decision.

2. Grasp the glove on your right hand by the cuff. Slowly pull the glove down over your hand, turning it inside out. (The contaminated portion of the glove is now on the inside. The part of the glove that was against your uncontaminated hand is on the outside.)

3. Holding the removed glove in your left hand, grasp the inside of the other glove just below the cuff, taking care not to touch the outside.

4. Pull the glove off and over the first glove, which you are still holding in your left hand. Now, the second glove is covering the first glove. Only the outside portion of the second glove is visible.

5. Dispose of the gloves in an appropriate receptacle.

6. Always wash your hands after removing gloves.

Mask, Eye Protection, and Face Shield

You may require this type of protection if you work in a dental office and are cross-trained to assist at the chair-side—otherwise, the use of this equipment is not likely necessary. However, do wear these devices if you think you are at risk of being splashed or sprayed with blood, body fluids, secretions, or excretions. Conceivably, it could happen if you are washing contaminated materials or instruments.

Keep mouthpieces, resuscitation bags, or other devices with your emergency equipment in case you need to give mouth-to-mouth resuscitation.

Gowns or Aprons

Protect your skin and clothing if you are helping with any procedure that is likely to generate splashes or sprays of blood or other body fluids. Remove the soiled gown immediately after use and, as with gloves, dispose of it according to office/agency guidelines, again avoiding contact with the exposed surface. (Touch only the part that was against your body.)

Equipment Used for Patient Care

Handle any equipment that may have touched blood and other body fluids carefully—remember that contamination might not be visible. Instruments commonly used in a physician's office include various types of scissors, suture equipment (e.g., needle-driver), and a variety of forceps. Be especially careful when handling anything sharp, such as suture needles, injection needles, and scalpel blades. Always remove a scalpel blade with forceps, and *never* try to recap a contaminated needle by hand (holding the needle in one hand and the cap in the other). Dispose of the needle in the proper needle disposal unit without capping it. Most needles used today have a safety mechanism to protect the person disposing of the needle. Some models have a sheath over the needle; in other models the needle retracts into the barrel of the syringe. There should be a disposal unit in every examination room. When full, these units must be properly disposed of following guidelines for biohazardous waste. Do not overfill sharps containers. If you must walk with a needle or other sharp instrument in your hand, point it away from your body and away from other people.

Specula, which are used for Pap smears, should be rinsed and cleaned only when wearing gloves and then put into an appropriate solution until they are sterilized.

If there is broken glass anywhere, wear gloves to sweep it up; *never* pick it up with your hands.

TIP

It is the responsibility of the user to dispose of sharp instruments, such as lances and needles. However, do not assume that the provider has done so. Always look carefully for anything sharp, and isolate or dispose of it before you clean up a tray or anything else that has been used for a patient procedure.

Linen

Properly handle, transport, and process used linen soiled with blood and other body fluids, ensuring that you avoid contact with your clothing and other surfaces. When changing the linen or paper on an examination bed, wear gloves and roll the sheet up and away from you. Hold it at arm's length when carrying it to the nearest disposal area. Some offices double-bag linens in specially marked laundry bags.

The Health Environment

Use the recommended disinfectant to wipe all potentially contaminated surfaces: for example, countertops, the examination bed, chairs (if soiled), the sink, and taps. Throw out all contaminated paper towels in the appropriate container, usually a plastic bag that is marked "biohazard."

Assisting with Examinations/Procedures

Some physicians may ask you to assist with a variety of assessments, examinations, and procedures that are potential sources of infection. Assess each situation carefully, and use protective barriers, such as gloves, appropriately.

Well-baby assessments, for example, could involve weighing an infant and perhaps taking measurements, such as length and head and chest circumferences. This could cause exposure to urine, feces, and other body substances. Another possible risk for contamination may occur if you are assisting with a procedure and are required to receive contaminated instruments from the physician.

Obtaining and labelling specimens is a potential source of contamination. Urine specimens left in the bathroom or in the examination room must be labelled, requisitioned, and prepared to be sent to a lab or tested in the health office. You may be asked to do routine dipstick testing (to measure sugar, protein, and ketones), to obtain a finger prick for hemoglobin or blood sugar, or to assist in taking a Pap smear, throat swab, sputum specimen, or stool sample.

Cleaning up instrument trays may be a routine responsibility for you. Never underestimate the importance of avoiding pricks from needles, scalpels, and other sharp instruments. Any needle or blade may have microscopic amounts of contaminated blood. Do not assume that the person using the instruments or needles has disposed of them properly. Be responsible for checking for forgotten or misplaced sharps. The following is a story of an actual occurrence in a health care office:

> Lina worked for a busy pediatrician, Dr. Gonsalvez. Holly, a 16-year-old single mother, brought her five-day-old son in for a check-up and blood testing. Holly was staying at a women's shelter, had no fixed address, and was not known in the community. Lina was cleaning up after Holly and the baby left. In gathering up some cotton swabs left on the counter, she pricked her finger with a lance that had been accidentally left under the cotton swabs. The lance had been used to obtain blood from the baby's heel for a test. Lina's finger was bleeding. Although Holly was in a high-risk category (due to factors such as a history of drug abuse), she had refused to be tested for HIV. Lina had little choice but to submit to a regimen of prophylactic treatment for potential exposure to hepatitis and HIV.

TIP

Be especially mindful of any contact with potentially infected sources if you have sores, open lesions, cuts, or chapped hands.

LO6 PREVENTING INJURY IN THE HEALTH OFFICE

To keep your patients safe, ensure that the physical arrangement of the office is safe and that safe practices are in place (e.g., proper supervision of children). The first step is to understand factors that put people at special risk.

Personal Risk Factors

Childhood   Every growth and development stage has certain typical characteristics. Understanding these patterns will help alert you to potential dangers.

Infants   Infants are helpless and depend on others to meet all of their needs, including safety. They are curious, like to explore their environment, and have no concept of danger. Infants love to touch and taste; they will grab anything they can reach and put it in their mouth. They are at risk of aspirating foreign objects, poisoning, and falling.

- If you are weighing a baby, do not take your eyes off him or her. Even turning your back for a second can result in a fall.

- Never leave an infant unattended, even in an infant seat.

- If you notice a parent or caregiver turning his or her attention away from the baby (e.g., when the baby is on the examination table), gently remind him or her of the dangers.

- Keep dangerous objects out of the baby's reach. An object is dangerous if it is
  - small enough to swallow,
  - sharp or pointed, or
  - toxic.

(Keep paper out of the baby's reach, too. It probably will not harm the baby, but it will do the paper no good.)

Young Children   As children learn to stand and walk, they greatly increase their mobility. But their sense of danger lags behind. They are curious, imitative, and enjoy navigating new environments, including open doors and stairways. Their ability to climb puts them at risk of falling, and increasing problem-solving skills allow them to reach places you might have thought were secure. They love to investigate drawers and cupboards and will often find dangerous objects. Many will still put anything in their mouth, leading to choking or poisoning. They like to mimic others; for example, a child may find a soiled needle and use it to imitate the doctor.

Never allow a young child (under the age of eight) to be in an examination room alone. Watch the child who can open doors and wander off. Keep the lower shelves in the examination room locked or free of anything that might cause injury to a child, such as instruments, sharp objects, and items that can be ingested. Be alert for chairs that the child might climb on to reach a counter, shelf, or examination bed.

If the parent is with the doctor, someone should be available to watch the child either in the examination room or in the reception area. All too often, parents will leave their children in the reception area, feeling that they are safe because they are occupied with a toy or a book. But children are mercurial, and when the toy loses their interest, they may take up something more dangerous. It only takes a moment for an injury to occur. Normally, you will not have time to assume the responsibility of watching a child.

> **▶▶▶ POINTS TO PONDER**
>
> A mother has left her three-year-old child unattended in the reception area while she speaks with the doctor. The phone is ringing and another patient is waiting to check in. How would you handle this situation?

All toys in the reception area or examination room should meet provincial or territorial safety standards and should be safe for children under three.

School-Age Children   School-age children are more aware of danger but, depending on their age and upbringing, often lack the knowledge and awareness to meet all of their own safety needs. Their increased motor skills put more objects within their reach; however, they are increasingly receptive to explanations of danger. Keep in mind, however, that children with developmental delays may be at increased risk.

Visual and Hearing Impairment   Older adults are particularly prone to diminishing vision and hearing, but these difficulties can occur at any age. Do not assume that only senior patients suffer from these impairments. Often, people will underplay their disabilities, putting themselves at risk of injury.

Mobility Impairment   Mobility difficulties can range from the most obvious to the subtlest of impairments. The patient may, for the most part, manage well and independently, but sometimes anxiety or a current health problem can turn a normally manageable impairment into a problem. Be especially alert for patients with impaired balance, weakness, or an unsteady gait.

Any patient who has had a procedure requiring sedation should be assessed for the ability to navigate independently. Sedation may leave patients with slower reflexes so that they are unable to move quickly to avoid injury. Pre-existing mobility problems increase the risk. For procedures requiring sedation, always suggest the patient bring along a family member or friend.

Altered Cognition   Some older, ill, or developmentally delayed patients may tend to be confused. What may normally be only mild confusion may be compounded by anxiety and stress in the health office. Whatever the cause, confused or very anxious people may not take in information properly or may misinterpret instructions. They may have poor judgment and fail to recognize danger. For example, a patient may forget an assistive device and fall.

Fatigue   When people are overtired, accidents happen. People lose dexterity and agility and are more likely to drop things or stumble. Patients may misunderstand instructions or take the wrong medication.

It is not only patients who can become overtired. Try to show up at work rested. If you are tired, be doubly careful about handling sharp, heavy, or delicate objects, and double-check your work. If you sense that you are reaching the point where you can no longer work reliably, tell your employer. It is not heroic to keep working through your fatigue if you make a potentially dangerous mistake, such as handing someone the wrong medicine or dropping a sharp into the wrong container.

Overconfidence   Some people, particularly older adults with recent impairments, think they can do more than they really can. For example, a person with impaired balance might insist on walking out to the taxi or car without assistance. An understanding, tactful offer of help may be easily accepted.

Environmental Risk Factors

You will be largely responsible for maintaining a safe environment in the health office and reception area. Make sure the environment meets the needs of your specific patients; a pediatrician's office will have different safety needs than a gerontologist's. Be continually alert for areas you can improve upon, and listen to patients' complaints or suggestions.

Lighting   Dim lights in the reception area and halls may predispose patients to falls. Find a balance between dimness and bright, glaring lights.

Noise Level   Children and teens do not appear to mind a noisy environment, but loud noise may be irritating and distracting to adults and may hurt older people's ears or interfere with hearing aids. It may also reduce their ability to concentrate or understand instructions. If you play music, keep it quiet enough so that people can be heard clearly without raising their voices.

Providing a Safe Environment

- Keep the floors clean and dry, especially during rainy or winter weather. It is fine to post a sign asking patients to remove their boots—but few will. No one wants to remove their boots to walk on a cold and perhaps wet or damp floor. Older people are at increased risk of falling because of mobility problems, poor balance, slower reflexes, and osteoporosis.

- If spills occur, clean them up without delay.
- Pay extra attention to patients with altered vision or mobility problems.
- Periodically check the reception area for scattered books, magazines, and toys.
- Avoid loose scatter rugs. Patients can easily slip and fall or trip over the edges. If you must have an area rug, have a smaller one that fits under a coffee table or some other heavy, fixed structure.
- Arrange furniture, such as coffee tables, out of the way of traffic.
- Do not rearrange the room too often. The unfamiliar layout can be a barrier to patients with poor vision.

⟫⟫ WHAT TO WATCH FOR

- How Canada, through the Public Health Agency of Canada, responds to any new pandemic alert (e.g., influenza), and how efficiently and effectively the PHAC, working with the WHO, meets the needs of Canadians.

- Trends regarding the number of people who refuse vaccinations both for themselves as well as their children and the reemergence of potentially fatal childhood diseases.

- The prevalence of "superbugs" resistant to antimicrobial medications, including what steps Canada and the international community are taking to deal with this (e.g., reducing the overuse of antibiotics, incentives for drug companies to bring new drugs to market).

- Changes in risk-management programs in health care facilities to manage the alarming rise in nosocomial infections.

- How our health care system adapts to accommodate the refugees coming to Canada, including the identification, control, and treatment of potentially infectious diseases.

- New vaccines that emerge (e.g., for hepatitis C) and changes in vaccine protocols that may occur in your region for both adults and children.

SUMMARY

1. Quality assurance is a systematic process of checking to see whether a product or service meets requirements. Excellence in the health care environment includes prompt treatment and reporting of laboratory tests, accurate prescriptions, reasonable waiting times, guidance in emergencies, and proper follow-up. Hospitals have formal quality assurance plans; health offices may use a more informal system.

   Workers' compensation and occupational health and safety legislation together provide a safe environment for employees. Workers' compensation sets out rights and responsibilities for employers and employees, including the conditions under which an employee may refuse work perceived as unsafe. WHMIS is federal legislation ensuring that employees are knowledgeable about hazardous materials in the workplace.

2. Health care settings pose risks of infection for both professionals and patients, some of whom are particularly vulnerable. Infection prevention and control (IPC) is a major focus in hospitals and long-term care facilities, particularly with the rise of antimicrobial-resistant organisms. Knowledge of the chain of infection and adhering to facility IPC protocols is essential. Remember that simple handwashing is one of the most effective ways to reduce the spread of infection.

3. Levels of hygiene range from sanitization through intermediate-level disinfection to sterilization. The required level depends on the material and conditions of use. Proper procedure must be followed to ensure disinfection or sterility.

4. Health professionals should keep routine immunizations up to date and should be vaccinated for common diseases, including the flu and hepatitis A and B.

5. Standard Precautions protect both health professionals and patients from cross-contamination from a variety of pathogens, primarily those transmitted through blood and other body fluids. These precautions should be applied at all times, not only for individuals you suspect of having an infectious condition that may put you or others at risk.

6. Consider the risks for injury to your patients, particularly young children, seniors, and those with physical or cognitive impairments. Ensure that all instruments, solutions, and medications are out of children's reach. Never leave a baby alone on a table or scale. Make sure children are supervised. Use proper lighting, and arrange furniture to reduce the risk of falls and other injuries.

KEY TERMS

active infection 112
acute infection 112
aerobic bacteria 113
anaerobic bacteria 113
antibody 117
antigen 115
antiseptic 125
asepsis 119
asymptomatic 112
autoclave 126
bactericidal 125
bacteriostatic 125
chronic infection 112
contagious or communicable disease 111
contamination 123

disinfectant 125
disinfection 124
exacerbation 112
immunity 111
immunoglobulin 118
infection 111
latent infection 112
local infection 112
microorganism 111
nonpathogenic 113
nosocomial infection 113
opportunistic infection 112
otitis media 112
pandemic 111
pathogen 113
quality assurance 107

quarantine 123
recurrent infection 112
relapse 112
remission 112
sanitization 124
sanitizer 124
septicemia 112
sharp 124
Standard Precautions 127
sterile 123
sterile technique 123
sterilization 124
systemic infection 112
teratogenic 121
topical 112
virulence 113

REVIEW QUESTIONS

1. What is meant by quality medical care?
2. Discuss the relevance of quality assurance in the health office.
3. What is the purpose of an incident report, and who would initiate it in any given situation?
4. Draw a diagram illustrating the chain of infection, and explain each step.
5. Describe how the administrative health professional should deal with used needles, soiled linen, and dirty surgical instruments.

6. Discuss strategies to implement medical asepsis in the workplace.
7. Why are nosocomial infections considered so dangerous?
8. In what circumstances should you wear gloves?
9. How can you reduce injury to small children in the health office?

APPLICATION EXERCISES

1. In small groups, list and discuss all the services and policies you think are important for a high-quality general practice. Consider both patients' and professionals' perspectives in the office. On the basis of your discussions, draw up a quality assurance manual for the office.

2. Using the Public Health Agency of Canada website found at the end of the chapter, prepare a reference chart that a health office professional could use for determining when children should be scheduled for immunizations. Research the benefits and risks of childhood immunizations.

   a. Joyce, who has a one-month-old baby, decides not to have the child immunized. Discuss your own feelings about this decision. Do you think she is right or wrong in making that decision? Give reasons for your stand.

   b. Compare Ontario's schedule to those used in Alberta and British Columbia. In a three-month period, a 13-month-old and a 2-year-old have joined your Alberta practice from British Columbia. Another child, aged 6 years, came from Ontario. What adjustments would you have to make to merge the two protocols? What adjustments would you have to make for the same children in your practice to accommodate only the Ontario changes, that is, to ensure that the child's immunizations were complete in accordance with the current protocol?

3. Visit a health care setting of your choice. (Alternatively, your professor may divide the class into groups and assign a variety of settings.) Prepare by researching the basic elements of WHMIS so that you know what to look for. Find out what materials in each setting are under WHMIS guidelines. How are staff informed about WHMIS? Where do they keep their Material Safety Data Sheets (MSDS)? (If a visit to an occupational setting is not possible, see what you can find by doing an internet search on the setting of your choice.)

4. In small groups, choose a health office setting (dentist, optometrist, urgent-care centre, family physician). Visit one or more offices (perhaps your own physician or dentist), noting the layout of the reception and office areas. Now design an ideal office, specifying layout and types of furniture. Take into account safety from injury and fire, employees' comfort, and safety from cumulative stress injury.

5. In small groups, review the workers' compensation board website in your jurisdiction, and in particular review the online forms. Contact your family doctor's office to see what forms they use most frequently. Create a fictitious case of a workplace injury where someone has to make a workers' compensation claim, including information from the person's family doctor. Download the forms you will need and fill them out using the information in the "case" you created.

6. Research the risks scientists associate with the Zika virus. Do you think Olympians were justified in opting out of the 2016 Summer Games because of health concerns? Would you travel to an area where you could potentially be infected? Why or why not?

WEBSITES OF INTEREST

WHMIS Overview

www.hc-sc.gc.ca/ewh-semt/occup-travail/whmis-simdut/index-eng.php

An Online Course on WHMIS

www.whmis.net

Canadian Centre for Occupational Health and Safety

www.ccohs.ca

Canada's National Workplace Health and Safety Website

www.canoshweb.org

Association of Workers' Compensation Boards of Canada

www.awcbc.org/en

Public Health Agency of Canada: Canadian Immunization Guide

www.phac-aspc.gc.ca/publicat/cig-gci/index-eng.php

IPC in Clinical Office Practice

www.publichealthontario.ca/en/eRepository/IPAC_Clinical_Office_Practice_2013.pdf

Chapter 6
Diagnostic Tests

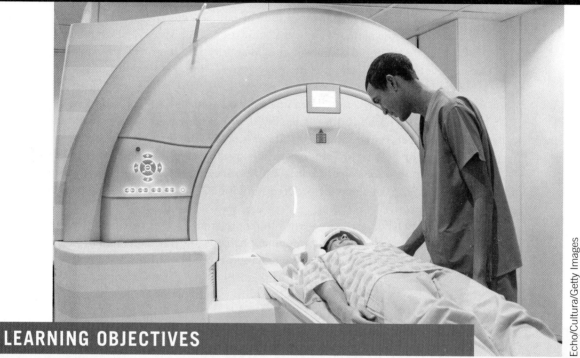

Echo/Cultura/Getty Images

On completing this chapter, you will be able to:

1. Describe the role of diagnostic tests in patient care.

2. Identify the departments of a laboratory, and outline the roles of allied health professionals and physicians who work in laboratory and diagnostic medicine.

3. Describe commonly ordered laboratory diagnostic tests.

4. Educate patients about laboratory and diagnostic tests.

5. Demonstrate how to fill in requisitions with the required information.

6. Discuss how to receive and organize test results in the office and in hospital settings.

7. Explain how to deal with abnormal results.

This chapter gives an overview of diagnostic testing and highlights common tests. The purpose is to make you aware of the more commonly ordered tests and of your related responsibilities. Detailed information can be obtained from any laboratory and diagnostic manual. Specific tests are also discussed in context throughout this book.

L01 PURPOSE OF DIAGNOSTIC TESTING

Medical practice is based on information gathered from a variety of sources, including patient history and physical examinations. Diagnostic testing done by laboratory and diagnostic imaging departments provides another valuable source of information to establish a diagnosis and monitor a patient's progress and response to treatment. Tests can visualize and analyze body structures, tissues, and fluids. Tests are an important part of health promotion and disease prevention in that they screen for disease, detect problems early, and facilitate prompt treatment. Diagnostic testing can also be used to establish baseline results for patients undergoing treatment or surgery. It may also be used for legal purposes. Results of lab tests are interpreted by a physician in the context of the patient's clinical examination and history. The results may validate or invalidate an initial diagnosis, they may lead the doctor to adjust or change the patient's treatment plan, or they may provide the welcome information that the patient is healthy.

A healthy body is said to be in a state of homeostasis, equilibrium, or balance. Each part of the body that is analyzed or examined has what is called a normal range, or a **reference range**. Results of tests are compared with this range. If they fall above or below this range, further investigation is often warranted. Various abnormal tests may, together with a physical examination and patient history, lead to a diagnosis. Tests may be ordered individually or as groups, sometimes referred to as test profiles.

reference range the normal range; the values expected for a particular test.

Different laboratories may use different reference ranges depending on the analysis type, reagents used, and patient population. Thus, the normal ranges presented in this chapter may not be exactly the same as those used at any given laboratory. Always assess any lab result in the context of that laboratory's normal range.

All laboratories should provide normal ranges with test results and flag abnormal results.

L02 TESTING FACILITIES AND PROFESSIONALS INVOLVED

Diagnostic testing is done in licensed clinical laboratories and diagnostic imaging facilities, both private and within hospitals. A limited number of tests are performed in physicians' offices.

Private laboratories are widespread in Canada. They may be centrally located, with satellite labs in medical buildings or large ambulatory/urgent-care clinics. These facilities offer clinical laboratory services, including routine testing on blood and other body fluids and tissue analysis. Smaller satellite labs in some provinces and territories are referred to as specimen collection labs, and they simply collect specimens (e.g., blood, urine, stool, sputum) and send them to a central laboratory for analysis. Both private and hospital-based diagnostic imaging facilities offer such services as X-rays, **computed tomography (CT)** scanning, **magnetic resonance imaging (MRI)**, **ultrasonography**, and **mammography**. Diagnostic imaging provides a detailed view of structures beneath the skin. Continuing and rapid technological advances in this field have added to its versatility, diagnostic capabilities, and complexity. Advances in diagnostic medicine have contributed significantly to the rising cost of health care in Canada, resulting in long waits for many of these tests.

computed tomography (CT) a type of X-ray that produces three-dimensional images of cross-sections of body parts.

magnetic resonance imaging (MRI) a diagnostic tool that uses a magnetic field to produce images of body structures and organs.

ultrasonography a procedure that uses high-frequency sound waves directed at an organ or object to produce a visual image.

mammography a specialized X-ray of the breast.

Canada has national and provincial or territorial laboratories that provide specialized services. The Public Health Agency of Canada has two national laboratories—the National Microbiology Laboratory in Winnipeg and the National HIV and Retrovirology Laboratories in Ottawa—that provide specialized services to all provinces and territories as requested. The labs can respond quickly to any health emergency, working collaboratively with other resources, and are linked to a government-wide emergency response system. The national laboratories conduct research as well as analyze specimens sent from across the country. The National Microbiology Laboratory was the first in the world to decode the genetic makeup of the H1N1 flu virus. The Winnipeg lab is one of 15 centres worldwide equipped with facilities to deal with biosafety issues, including the most deadly infectious organisms. It is a facility where scientists and researchers can share and discuss information as they study established, emerging, and reemerging diseases in both human and animal populations.

In most provinces and territories, hospitals have clinical laboratories and diagnostic imaging services. The larger the hospital, the more complex and varied the testing services it offers. Hospital facilities serve inpatients, outpatients, and the general public. An average-sized hospital typically offers the following laboratory departments:

- Hematology
- Blood bank or blood transfusions
- Chemistry
- Microbiology
- Histology/pathology/cytology

Larger hospitals also offer the most complete range of diagnostic imaging services. An average-sized hospital would likely offer the following radiographic studies:

- Routine/plain film X-rays
- Contrast techniques
- Fluoroscopy
- Computed tomography (CT)
- Magnetic resonance imaging (MRI)
- Ultrasonography

Cardiac and respiratory diagnostic services are also offered primarily by hospitals. Larger hospitals offer the most complete range of diagnostic imaging services.

Sometimes the test may be performed at one facility but is sent elsewhere to be processed and evaluated, often to another city or to a provincial or territorial lab. It may take several days to a week for the results to come back. Let your patients know when you expect the results back. This alleviates the anxiety of waiting and wondering why you have not called, particularly if the patient expects undesirable results.

Patients often think that they must go to a hospital to have a test done if it is to be covered by their health plan. Provincial and territorial health plans cover most diagnostic services deemed medically necessary, regardless of where they are offered. Examples of exceptions in some provinces include PSA (prostate-specific antigen, a blood test used to diagnose prostate cancer); BAT (bioavailable testosterone, used to investigate erectile dysfunction); and the *Helicobacter pylori* test (used to isolate a specific bacterium involved in stomach ulcers). Physicians' offices and laboratories will have a current list of uninsured lab and diagnostic tests. It is important that patients are informed before they have tests if they will have to pay for them. This is the provider's responsibility, but the patient may ask you for clarification.

Recent recommendations by the Canadian Task Force on Preventive Health Care (2014) are not to routinely do PSA tests to screen for prostate cancer on healthy men of any age. The rationale is that the risks do not outweigh the benefits (the test is painful and often includes unnecessary biopsies and treatments). Knowing that this test can be helpful in diagnosing prostate cancer, do you think it should still be done?

Allied Health Professionals

The primary duty of a *phlebotomist* is to draw blood specimens from patients. A phlebotomist may also collect specimens, prepare and maintain equipment, and do related data entry and clerical tasks. Phlebotomists are often trained on the job but may come from related health professions. They are employed in a public or private laboratory or a hospital. Medical laboratory technologists, medical technicians, or medical laboratory assistants frequently assume this duty as part of their general responsibilities.

A registered *medical laboratory technologist (MLT)* is knowledgeable in all areas of clinical laboratory work and can carry out specialized tests. MLTs have a three-year college diploma or a bachelor's degree. An MLT makes independent decisions concerning the quality of laboratory results. Responsibilities often include education of peers, students, and subordinates; research and development of new techniques; and laboratory supervision.

A *medical technician* or *medical laboratory assistant* usually graduates from a college program with a certificate and performs more routine laboratory procedures, often under the supervision of a medical technologist.

Physician Specialists

Physicians who specialize in various areas of diagnostic testing work in almost every laboratory department.

A *hematologist* is a physician who specializes in the diagnosis, treatment, prevention, or investigation of disorders primarily of the blood and lymphatic systems. A hematologist may work in general practice or in a laboratory.

autopsy the examination of a body to determine the cause of death or to identify disease processes.

A *pathologist* is a medical doctor who examines tissue samples and interprets results. A pathologist also performs **autopsies**.

Radiology is the study of images of the human body, and a *radiologist* is a physician who specializes in interpreting these images. A radiologist may specialize in evaluating one particular area of the body. With diagnostic tests becoming more sophisticated, specialists are narrowing their fields to the interpretation of highly specialized tests.

COMMONLY ORDERED TESTS

You need a general understanding of the commonly ordered tests, including where and how to order them and the type of information you need to book them. Your patients depend on you as a resource for information.

If you work in a hospital, you may be asked to obtain test results for the physician or to requisition a test that has been ordered. Knowing which laboratory department to call will save you both time and frustration. You should also be aware of **critical values** of common tests and how to read reports and note abnormal results. Rereading your notes or texts from any anatomy and physiology courses you have taken will help you understand these tests. Table 6.1 lists some of the more common test abbreviations you will come across.

critical value a test result that indicates a life-threatening situation and requires immediate attention.

TABLE 6.1 Abbreviations for commonly ordered laboratory and diagnostic tests

ABGs	arterial blood gases	LDH	lactic dehydrogenase
AFB	acid-fast bacilli	LDL	low-density lipoprotein
APTT	activated partial thromboplastin time (see PTT)	LP	lumbar puncture
BE	barium enema	LS	X-ray of the lumbosacral spine
BUN	blood urea nitrogen	MCH	mean corpuscular hemoglobin
C&S	culture and sensitivity	MCHC	mean corpuscular hemoglobin concentration
C&T	cross-match and type (for compatible blood; see T&S)	MCV	mean corpuscular volume
CBC	complete blood count	Mg	magnesium
CK	creatine kinase	MRI	magnetic resonance imaging
CO_2	carbon dioxide	Na	sodium
CRP	C-reactive protein	O&P	ova and parasites (often in stool specimens)
CSF	cerebrospinal fluid	OB	occult blood
CT	computed tomography	P	phosphorus
CXR	chest X-ray (PA: posterior-to-anterior; Lat.: lateral)	Pap	Pap smear
ECG	electrocardiogram	PCO_2	partial pressure of carbon dioxide
ELISA	enzyme-linked immunosorbent assay	PFT	pulmonary function test
ERCP	endoscopic retrograde cholangiopancreatography	PSA	prostate-specific antigen
EMG	electromyography	PT	prothrombin time
ESR	erythrocyte sedimentation rate	PTT/aPTT/APTT	partial thromboplastin time (see APTT)
FBS	fasting blood sugar	RBC	red blood cell
GB/GBS	gallbladder series	S&A	sugar and acetone
GTT	glucose tolerance test	SGOT	serum glutamic-oxaloacetic transaminase
HbA1c	glycosylated hemoglobin	SGPT	serum glutamic-pyruvic transaminase
Hb	hemoglobin	T3	triiodothyronine
HBV	hepatitis B virus	T4	thyroxine
Hct	hematocrit	T&S	type and screen (for compatible blood; see C&T)
HDL	high-density lipoprotein	TSH	thyroid stimulating hormone
HIV	human immunodeficiency virus	UGI	upper gastrointestinal series
INR	international normalized ratio	US	ultrasound
IV-GTT	intravenous glucose tolerance test	VDRL	venereal disease research laboratory
IVP	intravenous pyelogram	VMA	vanillylmandelic acid (usually a 24-h urine test)
K	potassium	WBC	white blood cell count
KUB	X-ray of the kidney, ureter, and bladder		

Hematology

Literally translated, *hematology* means the study of blood. In the laboratory, hematology deals with the processing and evaluation of blood and blood components. The average human body contains five to six litres of blood. Blood is composed of serum, or plasma (the liquid portion of blood in which blood components are suspended), red and white blood cells, various proteins, hormones, antibodies, and other elements that perform specific functions. (Tests on blood plasma are usually done by the chemistry department.) Cells are examined and analyzed for their size, shape, functional ability, and numbers. The following are some of the more common hematological tests.

Complete Blood Count   One of the most common and useful tests is the complete blood count (CBC). A CBC may be ordered to help the physician establish a diagnosis or as part of a routine medical examination for screening purposes. It can provide valuable information about the blood and blood-forming tissues (especially the bone marrow) as well as other body systems and the patient's overall health. A CBC typically includes the following tests to analyze the various types of blood cells:

- Red blood cell count (RBC)
- Hematocrit
- Hemoglobin
- White blood cell count (WBC)
- Differential blood count (diff)
- Platelet count

There are, however, variations among laboratories; some, for example, do not include differential or platelet counts unless specifically ordered. Table 6.2 shows sample reference ranges for the main tests included in a CBC.

Red Blood Cell Count   This test counts the number of red blood cells in a specific volume of blood. Most counts are performed using an automated system. Results of this test are closely linked to the patient's hemoglobin and hematocrit. It is usually repeated at designated intervals in patients experiencing continued bleeding problems,

---

TABLE 6.2   Reference ranges for the common elements of a complete blood count (CBC)

RBC
male: 4.7–6.1 $\times$ 10^{12}/L
female: 4.2–5.4 $\times$ 10^{12}/L

WBC: 4.0–10.6/L
May be referred to as a leukocyte count (LC)

Hematocrit
male: 0.40–0.50/L
female: 0.36–0.44/L

Hemoglobin
platelet count: 100 000–450 000
male: 138–172 g/L
female: 121–151 g/L

Note: Reference ranges vary with testing methods. Use the ranges supplied by your laboratory. Some laboratories may also use different units of measurement; for example, hemoglobin is sometimes measured in mmol/L instead of g/L.

and it plays an important role in diagnosing and evaluating patients with anemia. As with other tests, the normal range for RBCs varies with age and gender. Normal ranges may also vary slightly with the lab performing the test. Normal values might vary between 4.7 and 6.1 $\times$ 10^{12}/L for adult males and between 4.2 and 5.4 $\times$ 10^{12}/L for adult females.

Red blood cell indices are completed as part of most automated RBC analyses. They provide information about the size, weight, and hemoglobin concentration of RBCs. The mean corpuscular volume (MCV) reflects the average size of an RBC. The mean corpuscular hemoglobin (MCH) is a variation on the MCV measurement and indicates the average amount of hemoglobin in a single red blood cell. The mean corpuscular hemoglobin concentration (MCHC) determines the average hemoglobin concentration per 100 mL of packed red cells. The cell's weight is assessed by a test called random distribution of RBC weight (RDW), which measures the red blood cells for consistency in size. This index is available only on automated cell-counting equipment. Cell counters categorize erythrocytes by volume as they are counted.

Hemoglobin (Hb) Hemoglobin is a protein on the red blood cells that attaches to oxygen in the blood and carries it throughout the body. It also removes carbon dioxide. Hemoglobin gives blood its red colour and is the main content of the red blood cell. The amount of oxygen in the blood is determined by the concentration of Hb in the blood. Abnormal results indicate that something is wrong. Two common problems associated with a low Hb are anemia and hemorrhage. The normal range varies with gender and age and the altitude at which a person lives.

Hematocrit The term hematocrit (Hct) comes from roots meaning "to separate blood." This test reflects the percentage of the total volume of blood occupied by cells. An Hct is almost always done together with an Hb as both are usually affected by the same underlying pathology. A low Hct may result from a diminished production of red blood cells, blood loss, or the abnormal destruction of the cells. In the case of hemorrhage, the results are most accurate several hours after the event. Often, the Hb and Hct are determining factors when doctors decide to give a person a transfusion with blood or blood products. Note that a low Hct in pregnant women is considered normal (within limits) because pregnancy involves extra blood volume without a corresponding increase in red blood cells.

Red Blood Cell Morphology Red blood cell morphology describes the appearance of the red blood cells on a blood film. This report may diagnose a condition like malaria or suggest the need for further testing. A report of oval macrocytes, for example, suggests a vitamin B_{12} or folate deficiency.

White Blood Cell Count The white blood cell (WBC) count determines the total number of white cells in the blood sample. White blood cells are the body's primary means of fighting infection. There are five main types of white cell, each of which plays a different role in responding to the presence of foreign organisms in the body. These cells are examined in the differential count (see below). Elevations in the WBC count can result from stimuli, such as having a baby, stress, and infections. The normal WBC count varies with age. It is higher in babies and decreases as a person gets older.

Differential Count A differential count estimates the different types of white blood cells as a proportion of the total WBC count. This count is valuable in determining what kind of disorder a patient has (e.g., viral infection, bacterial infection, allergic response). It is usually split into neutrophils, lymphocytes, monocytes, eosinophils, and basophils.

```
RS LABORATORIES AND DIAGNOSTIC SERVICES
223 Lakewood Ave.
Vancouver, BC
V5R 6M1
```

Physician	Client: Perreault, Anne
Dr. D Singh	DOB: 11/4/56
43 Rundle Ave	Sex: F
Vancouver, BC	PH: 604-321-2232
	MCP # 4323432255
	Subscriber's Initial: A
	Date of Service: Sept 2/08
	Date Printed: Sept 3/08

Report Status: final

Test Name	Result	Abnormal	Reference Range	Units
Hematology				
WBC*	13.7×10^9/L	H	(4.5–11.0)	
RBC	3.81×10^{12}/L	L	(3.90–5.60)	
Hct	0.3480 L/L	L	(0.3500–0.4700)	
MCV	91 FL		(0.78–100)	
MCH	31.0 PG		(27.0–32.0)	
LYMPH	0.32		(0.20–0.45)	
NEUT	0.65		(0.25–0.80)	
MONO	0.02		(0.01–0.10)	
EOSIN	0.00		(0.00–0.06)	
BASOP	0.00		(0.00–0.03)	
PLATELETS	NORMAL			
ESR	31		(0–20)	

* note WBC
Call for repeat of CBC stat. See me Thurs.

Figure 6.1 Hematology report (note that values vary slightly from one laboratory to another)

Figure 6.1 shows a printed report of a complete blood count. Note that for each result the normal values are listed as the "reference range." Abnormal readings are listed under the abnormal column. In this report, the RBC and Hct are flagged as L for low, and the WBC is flagged as H for high. Results posing considerable concern are also marked with an asterisk and addressed at the bottom of the report. The doctor has added notes for the administrative health professional (AHP). He wants to have the CBC repeated *stat* (immediately) and to see the patient. The AHP should arrange the test and book the appointment, initial the request to indicate this has been done, and note what has been done on the patient's chart.

Platelet Count   The platelet count is an actual count of the number of platelets, or thrombocytes, in a given volume of blood. Platelets, the smallest blood cells, play a vital role in the blood clotting system. A low platelet count may indicate a bleeding disorder.

Erythrocyte Sedimentation Rate   The erythrocyte sedimentation rate (ESR), or sedimentation rate (sed rate), is a measure of the settling of red blood cells in a saline or plasma solution over a specific period of time. Doctors often use this test to evaluate the condition of a patient with nonspecific complaints or symptoms. An elevated rate is not usually diagnostic of any particular disease or condition or the involvement of any particular organ, but it does indicate that an underlying disease may be present, perhaps infection, cancer, kidney disease, or rheumatoid arthritis. This test is most frequently used along with others to monitor a patient's condition or response to treatment.

Coagulation Studies These tests measure the clotting time of the blood. They are used in particular for individuals on blood thinners or anticoagulants.

Partial Thromboplastin Time (PTT)/Activated Partial Thromboplastin Time (APTT/aPTT)

PTT/APTT/aPTT tests are used to evaluate a component of the clotting (coagulation) system. Coagulation depends on the action of substances in the blood called *clotting factors*. Measuring the PTT helps assess which specific clotting factors may be missing or defective. The APTT is a variation of the PTT, giving similar results that can be used interchangeably. Some consider these tests synonymous. Sometimes a test ordered as a PTT will come back as APTT or aPTT, depending on the variation of the test the lab uses. These tests are also used to monitor therapy with **heparin**, an anticoagulant that prolongs the time it takes for the blood to clot. It is important to monitor the patient's clotting time to keep the dosage within a therapeutic range. Too much heparin could cause bleeding problems; too little could lead to a blood clot. Critical values for either of these tests would be phoned in, and the doctor should be notified as soon as possible. Normal APTT/aPTT is usually between 28 and 38 seconds (varies with the lab). The therapeutic range for heparin administration is 60 to 85 seconds.

> **heparin** an anticoagulant (blood thinner) given to people who are at risk for developing blood clots.

International Normalized Ratio (INR)

The international normalized ratio is a system established in part by the World Health Organization for reporting the results of blood coagulation tests. All results are standardized. For example, Dr. Wong has a patient taking warfarin (brand name Coumadin). The patient travels to another province but is to have his INR levels done three times a week and to let Dr. Wong know the results (or have the lab call her with the results) so that she can adjust his warfarin dose. With the standardization of the INR, this patient could have a blood test done anywhere, and Dr. Wong would know that the results are the same as those she would get in the lab she usually uses (unlike some of the values, for example, a CBC). The normal reference range is 0.9 to 1.1. The therapeutic range for someone on warfarin therapy is 2.0 to 3.0.

More recently, low-molecular-weight heparin (a new class of anticoagulant) is being used both prophylactically and to actively treat individuals for actual and potential clotting issues and related conditions. As a prophylactic, low-molecular-weight heparin is as effective as standard heparin or warfarin but requires no monitoring (APTT or INR).

Blood Bank/Blood Transfusion

Blood and blood products are supplied to health care facilities in Canada by the Canadian Blood Services (CBS), a not-for-profit organization that screens and collects blood used for all transfusions across Canada. The organization also manages the Canadian Bone Marrow Donor Registry. The CBS screens every donor and tests each unit of blood or blood product for a variety of transmissible diseases.

A hospital's blood bank or blood transfusion department tests to ensure that blood or blood products given in transfusions are compatible with the patient's blood type. Transfusion of mismatched blood can result in a serious reaction, even death. The process of matching blood is called *blood typing*, *cross-matching*, or *cross-typing*.

There are four main blood types: A, B, AB, and O. These letters represent antigens on the red blood cell. If you have the A antigen, you are type A; if you have the B antigen, you are type B; if you have both the A and B antigen, you are type AB; if you do not have any antigen, you are type O. Each blood type carries antibodies to antigens present in the blood plasma of the other blood types. For example, if you are type A, you have anti-B antibodies and would react to any blood with the B antigen in it. If you are type B, you would have anti-A antibodies, therefore reacting to any blood with the A antigen in it. If you are type AB, you do not have any antibodies, making you the universal recipient. Each person's blood can also be categorized as either Rh-positive or Rh-negative. The rhesus, or Rh, factor is an antigen on the surface of the red blood cell. If you have it, you are positive; if you do not, you are negative. These factors must also be analyzed in the process of finding compatible blood or blood components for a patient.

Patients are usually cross-matched if they present with a significantly low Hb/Hct resulting from a pathological process, before any major surgery, and in the event of hemorrhage. In emergency cases, the order would be stat. If there is no time for a cross-match, the doctor would order type O negative blood, which is also known as the universal donor. Type O negative blood has no antigen (A or B) and no Rh factor and, therefore, will not react with other blood types.

A related test that may be done by the blood bank is the Coombs' test indirect, which measures a person's antibodies against red blood cells. This test is done for mothers who are Rh negative to determine whether they have developed antibodies against a possible Rh-positive baby. A Coombs' test direct is done on the baby after it is born and tells the doctor whether the baby has been sensitized by its mother's blood and, if so, how seriously. A baby with high levels of antibodies needs intensive observation for a condition causing pathological jaundice, which, if serious enough, requires exchange blood transfusions.

3 Chemistry

The chemistry department deals with tests on urine, blood plasma, and other body fluids. These include a variety of tests for blood sugar levels, electrolytes, blood urea nitrogen (BUN), creatinine, electrolytes, cholesterol and triglyceride levels, and various enzyme tests (microbiology). Timed and random urine tests are also completed in this department. Figure 6.2 shows a chemistry report. Note that the urea is considered abnormally high and appears under the abnormal column. This value may be given on a lab report as urea or as BUN. In either case, it measures in the blood the level of urea, a byproduct of metabolism that builds up in the blood and is cleared by the kidneys. Diseases that compromise the function of the kidneys frequently lead to increased blood urea levels. Normal values range from 3.5 to 7.0.

Creatinine   *Creatinine* is a byproduct of creatine phosphate, a compound found in skeletal muscle tissue that is produced continuously and excreted by the kidneys. An increase in **serum** creatinine (the level of creatinine in the blood) indicates possible renal dysfunction. Levels can also become elevated as a result of some muscle diseases and congestive heart failure. Normal adult serum creatinine values range from 55 to 115 mmol/L for a female and 62 to 120 mmol/L for a male, depending on the lab. Creatinine and BUN may be ordered together to assess kidney function, although creatinine alone is usually a better test.

serum the fluid portion of the blood. Often used in phrases describing levels of blood components, as in serum creatinine.

Electrolytes   Electrolytes are elements that are found in body tissues and blood in the form of charged particles. An order for electrolytes includes testing for levels of sodium, potassium, and chloride. Normal ranges for sodium are 135 to 145 mEq/L; for potassium, 3.5 to 5.0 mEq/L; and for chloride, 99 to 108 mEq/L. These will vary with laboratories. Electrolytes are discussed in more detail in Chapter 17. Chloride is not often ordered routinely these days.

RS LABORATORIES AND DIAGNOSTIC SERVICES
223 Lakewood Ave.
Vancouver, BC
V5R 6M1

Physician	Client: Perreault, Anne
Dr. D Singh	DOB: 11/4/56
43 Rundle Ave	Sex: F
Vancouver, BC	PH: 604-321-2232
	MCP # 4323432255
	Subscriber's Initial: A
	Date of Service: Sept 2/08
	Date Printed: Sept 3/08

Report Status: final

Test Name	SI Result	Flag	Reference Range
Chemistry			
GLUCOSE-RANDOM	12.2 mmol/L	H	3.6–7.8
PC BS	4.8 mmol/L		3.8–7.80
UREA	10 mmol/L	H	3.5–7.0
CREAT	60 mmol/L		50–110
SOD	137 mmol/L		135–145
POT	3.0 mmol/L	L	3.5–5.0
CL	104 mmol/L		99–108
Cholesterol*	5.03 mmol/L		< 6
Triglycerides	2.03 mmol/L		0.6–3.60
TOTAL THYROID (TOTAL T4) 0.30 mmol/L			60–155
T UPTAKE 0.30			0.22–0.34
FREE THYROXINE INDEX (FTI) 30			13–53
THYROTROPIN (SENSITIVE TSH) 2.34			0.50–5.00

*moderate risk category: cholesterol 5.20-6.20

Book for 5hr gtt. Note on chart diet counselling
DS

Figure 6.2 Chemistry report

Blood Glucose Levels   Blood glucose (sugar) levels are used to diagnose metabolic diseases, such as diabetes mellitus, and to monitor diabetics and adjust their medication. There are a number of tests for monitoring glucose levels. They differ depending on the time of day they are performed and what the patient has had to eat or drink, as both factors affect glucose levels. One of these tests is a fasting blood sugar (FBS), meaning that the patient must remain NPO (eat nothing) for at least eight hours before the test. (On occasion, a physician may allow a patient to have sips of water or to take an important medication.) In hospital, this means delaying a patient's breakfast until the test is completed. Blood is usually taken early in the morning so that breakfast does not have to be delayed long. The clinical secretary would also put an NPO or FBS notice at the patient's bedside the night before the test. In the health office, make sure patients understand that not eating and drinking is important for accurate results. This test gives a value for blood sugar levels when they have not been immediately affected by food. Normal range for an FBS is 3.9 to 6.1 mmol/L for an adult and 3.3 to 5.5 for a child. An FBS of less than 2.0 is considered critical.

Another common test for blood sugar, taken two hours after eating, is called a two-hour postprandial glucose level (2 h PC BS or 2 h PPG) and is used to diagnose early diabetes mellitus. Diabetics usually have elevated glucose levels two hours after eating, whereas the levels would return to normal within two hours in a person without the disease. Normal reference range for adults is 3.3 to 7.8 mmol/L.

A random blood sugar may be taken any time. This is not as valuable a test as the FBS or the two-hour PC BS but will certainly reflect abnormal glucose activity.

Glycosylated hemoglobin is a test used to measure blood sugar control over an extended period in individuals with diabetes mellitus, and it is especially valuable in assessing a person's compliance with or response to treatment. It measures a component of hemoglobin known as A1c (which is on the RBC) that binds with glucose in the blood and indicates how much glucose has been in a person's blood during the previous two to four months (the average being 120 days). The test is usually ordered as an HbA1c, GHb, or glycohemoglobin. No fasting is needed for this test. Normal levels range between approximately 4.5 percent and 6.5 percent. It is also used now to diagnose diabetes if the level is over 6.5.

You should be aware of critical blood sugar values, check reports diligently for abnormal results, and report levels that are a concern to the provider at the first opportunity. Critical levels would be telephoned to the office or hospital and should be given to the doctor as soon as possible. If the provider is unavailable, notify the doctor on call.

Glucose Tolerance Tests   The most common test in this category is the oral glucose tolerance test. This test, a more detailed test to diagnose diabetes, assesses the body's ability to use glucose by measuring blood glucose levels at specified intervals after the person has ingested a set amount of a glucose solution. The test is most often done on an outpatient basis and must follow specific dietary recommendations. The patient should be on a carbohydrate diet (at least 150–200 grams per day) for at least three days before the test, and then remain NPO for 10 to 14 hours before the test. The outpatient patient should be given a handout describing the dietary preparation. Fruits, breads, cereals, grains, and potatoes are some excellent sources of carbohydrates to recommend. As well, some facilities ask the patient to refrain from strenuous exercise and smoking 8–10 hours prior to the test. The procedure takes anywhere from 2 to 4 hours depending on the number of readings you want.

For the hospitalized patient, you or the nurse would post an NPO notice by the patient's bedside. Delay or cancel breakfast on the morning of the test. The patient must not eat, drink coffee or tea, or smoke after drinking the glucose solution until the test is finished.

Cholesterol/Triglycerides   These tests measure types of fats (also called lipids) in the blood. The two main lipids measured are cholesterol and triglycerides. Cholesterol is a waxy fat produced by the liver and is essential to the production of some hormones and to cellular growth. Cholesterol combines with proteins and is circulated throughout the body. In the circulating form, it is referred to as lipoprotein (and often appears on lab requisitions under this name). There are two types of cholesterol: high-density lipoproteins, or HDL (called "good cholesterol" because it does not clog vessels and removes extra cholesterol from the body), and low-density lipoprotein, or LDL ("bad cholesterol," which clogs arteries, increasing the risk of heart attack and stroke). The reference range for HDL is 1.0 to 1.8 for an adult male and 1.2 to 2.4 for an adult female; the reference range for LDL for an adult is 1.4 to 4.0.

Triglycerides are also lipids and are beneficial as long as they remain within normal ranges. Elevated levels are associated with heart disease, arteriosclerosis, and atherosclerosis. It is considered good control if a patient's triglyceride level remains below 1.7 mmol/L. (Most lab values vary somewhat with gender and age.) Patients with high levels of either cholesterol or triglycerides may be advised to eat a low-fat, low-cholesterol diet. In Figure 6.2, the cholesterol result of 5.03, while within the normal range, is considered to present some risk for the patient. The physician has noted on the bottom of the report that the patient is to be booked for diet counselling.

Heart (Cardiac) Enzymes   When a person has a heart attack (also called a myocardial infarction, or MI), heart muscle is damaged. As a result of this damage, cardiac **enzymes** are released into the bloodstream. Measuring these enzymes can tell the

enzyme a protein capable of initiating a chemical reaction that involves the formation or breakage of chemical bonds. When muscle damage or death occurs, enzymes within the muscle cell are released into the circulating blood.

doctor if a heart attack has actually occurred and, if so, how extensive the muscle damage is. Sometimes measuring the enzymes is definitive in the diagnosis of a heart attack when ECG findings are absent or nonspecific. The enzymes most commonly measured are creatine phosphokinase (CPK, also known as creatine kinase [CK]) and troponin. The normal or reference range for total CK is 39 to 174 U/L for an adult male and 26 to 140 U/L for a female.

Urinalysis

Urinalysis: Urine for Routine and Micro   A urinalysis is a valuable routine diagnostic and screening test that provides preliminary information about the kidneys and related processes. It may be ordered as "urine for routine and micro," or R&M. Routine testing includes examining the specimen for colour, clarity, specific gravity, pH, protein, glucose, and ketones. Microscopic analysis of the specimen involves numerous tests for the presence of red and white blood cells, casts, crystals, bacteria, yeast cells, and parasites—all not normally present. The microscopic part is not done routinely much any more unless asked for since the routine testing is usually adequate. (See Figure 6.3.) Doctors order this test frequently, sometimes as a screening test, sometimes in response to either specific or vague symptoms, because it provides information on a wide variety of potential problems. Some hospitals do this test on all admissions; others do it only if there are specific indications. Some facilities use the term *urinalysis* to mean only a routine test; others use it to mean a urine test for routine and micro. Note, as discussed below, that a routine and micro is a different test from a urine ordered for culture and sensitivity—although you frequently see these ordered together for example, "urine for R&M and C&S."

RS LABORATORIES.
223 Lakeway Ave.
Vancouver, BC
V5R 6M1

Physician	Client: Perreault, Anne
Dr. D Singh	DOB: 11/4/56
43 Rundle Ave	Sex: F
Vancouver, BC	PH: 604-321-2232
	MCP # 4323432255
	Subscriber's Initial: A
	Date of Service: Sept 2/08
	Date Printed: Sept 3/08

Report Status: final

Test Name	Result Abnormal	Reference Range	Units
URINALYSIS: CHEMICAL			
COLOUR	NORMAL		
APPEARANCE	TURBID		
GLUCOSE	NEGATIVE		
KETONE	NEGATIVE		
SPECIFIC GRAVITY	1.015		
BLOOD	TRACE		
PH	5.0	(4.5–8.0)	
PROTEIN	NEGATIVE		
NITRITE	NEGATIVE		
RBC	0	(0–6.0)	
WBC	0	(0–6.0)	

Figure 6.3   Routine urinalysis report from biochemistry

Timed Urine Collections Timed urine collections (also ordered as 24-hour urine collections) are quantitative tests done on urine collected over 24 hours. This test provides information about cumulative elements in the urine. Substances, such as hormones excreted by the kidney, are not excreted uniformly throughout the day, so a 24-hour collection provides the physician with a more accurate picture of kidney function. Timed collections are analyzed for such things as creatinine clearance, protein, and hormone levels. The patient is given a large bottle to put the urine in. The patient should void in the toilet upon waking up. Thereafter, the patient collects all urine up to and including the first void the next morning.

For example, if the test is to begin at 8:00 a.m., the patient empties his or her bladder then, but does not collect that urine. All the urine produced in the next 24 hours is collected in a clean container. At 8:00 a.m. the next day, the patient collects the final sample. A 12-hour sample may also be ordered. For timed urine collections, stressing the procedure is vital. Even one discarded void will invalidate the test, as it is quantitative in nature. Every drop of urine counts.

Specifics regarding the urine collection will vary with the type of test. For example, the bottle may contain special solutions, be clear or opaque, or require refrigeration or protection from sunlight. To ensure accurate results, patients must follow instructions precisely. Urine specimens are best refrigerated or taken to the lab as soon as possible. The longer they sit around, the more likely it is that the results will be inaccurate. Labelling them immediately reduces the chance of mixing up specimens.

You may need to call the lab to order the large sample bottles. In a hospital situation, ensure that the lab has sent the appropriate bottles (the patient sometimes needs more than one) to the floor, and that they are clearly labelled.

Random Urine Collection A random urine specimen is one that is obtained any time, often in the doctor's office. A random test is usually done for preliminary screening purposes. Urine is collected in the same container as for routine and micro.

In the hospital setting you would make the necessary arrangements with the dietary department. The patient may need assistance refrigerating the urine. If so, that is the nurse's responsibility. If you see the sample bottle sitting out, let the nurse know—or refrigerate it yourself if that is something you are allowed to do.

Early Morning Specimens Most often, a physician will ask the patient to bring in a first morning void for a urine specimen. This specimen is preferred because it has a more uniform volume and concentration, and its lower pH helps preserve the formed elements. Abnormalities are easier to detect. These specimens are used, among other purposes, to diagnose and monitor pregnancies. Pregnant women are usually asked to bring in a specimen for testing with each prenatal visit. It is tested, usually in the office, for such elements as glucose, ketones, and protein.

TIP

If you are asked to transport a urine test for culture and sensitivity to the lab, make sure you take it immediately or refrigerate it until you can transport it there. Left out, organisms can grow and invalidate the test. Likewise, if you see a sample sitting around, check with the nurse or refrigerate it.

Microbiology

Microbiology studies body fluids and tissues for infectious organisms, such as bacteria, viruses, parasites, and fungi. These organisms can be detected in a number of ways. A common type of test is culture and sensitivity (C&S). This is a two-step process in which any organism present in the specimen is grown in a controlled environment, and then the susceptibility or resistance to various antibiotics is determined. Suppose the culture grew a pathogen, for example, *E. coli*, and the antibiotics used for the sensitivity portion of the test were amoxicillin, Bactrim, and Ciprofloxacin. Test results showed that the *E. coli* was resistant to the amoxicillin but sensitive to Bactrim and Cipro. This tells the doctor that treating the patient with either Bactrim or Cipro would be effective but that treatment with amoxicillin would not be effective against that particular strain of *E. coli*.

When a patient has a suspected infection potentially treatable with an antibiotic, it is usually best for the provider to have the results of the C&S before initiating antibiotic therapy. It is hard to make patients understand this, especially if they are in pain. Treating a sore throat with antibiotics when test results show the infection is viral is absolutely useless (and expensive). Prescribing an antibiotic that the organism is resistant to is also ineffective. Needless use of antibiotics contributes to the development of antibiotic-resistant organisms. Patients who understand the rationale behind waiting for test results may be less impatient to have the physician prescribe something. If an acute infection (such as a bladder or kidney infection) is suspected, it may be important to start treatment as soon as possible; in this case, the doctor will take a specimen but start the patient on antibiotics without waiting for results. When the results are back, the doctor may change the prescription if indicated by the results.

Midstream Urine Tests Urine specimens for culture and sensitivity are often ordered by the physician to diagnose urinary tract infections (see Figure 6.4). They are usually **midstream urine specimens (MSU)**, also called clean catch urine specimens, obtained by following specific instructions. Many offices use disposable specimen kits that include these instructions. To obtain a midstream urine specimen, the patient must carefully wipe the area around the urethra with a cleansing solution. The solution used varies; often, washing with just soap and water is recommended. The patient must start to void into the toilet, then stop and collect the middle part of the urine in a sterile container. Most people find it nearly impossible to void into a small bottle, so many kits supply a larger sterile container in which the person can catch the middle part of the urine stream. This is then emptied into the sterile bottle, taking care not to contaminate the urine or the container edges, and the lid is applied.

midstream urine specimen (MSU) also called a clean catch urine specimen; a urine specimen collected after cleansing oneself and discarding the first part of the urine stream to avoid contamination; used for culture and sensitivity tests.

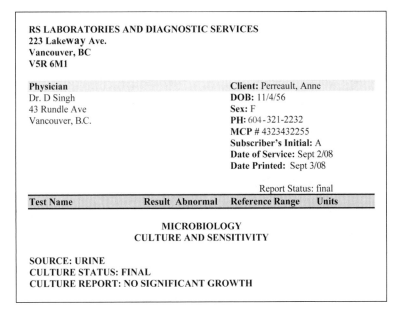

Figure 6.4 Normal urinalysis report for culture and sensitivity

Urine specimens for C&S *must be taken to the lab immediately or refrigerated*. If a specimen sits at room temperature, bacterial growth will interfere with the accuracy of test results. The lab will reject a specimen that has not been handled properly. Sometimes a patient will be asked to obtain a midstream urine sample at home. It is very important for the person to understand the importance of refrigerating the specimen.

Sputum Tests

Culture and sensitivity may be used to diagnose the cause of a chest infection, such as bronchitis or pneumonia. Sputum tests are also used to diagnose fungal infections, lung cancer, and tuberculosis. If a patient is providing this specimen at home, be sure to tell him or her to produce an early morning specimen and to try to cough it up deep from the lung passages. Phlegm from the upper airways and throat are unacceptable specimens. Also advise the patient not to use mouthwash prior to obtaining the specimen as antibacterial properties in the mouthwash will interfere with test results.

Chapter 20 discusses these tests as they relate to the hospitalized patient; there is important information about these tests with respect to order entry procedures.

Blood Cultures   Cultures done on blood are ordered if a patient is suspected of having septicemia, a blood infection. Infection can spread from various organs or result from surgery. Particularly dangerous is a condition called endocarditis, an inflammation and infection of the lining of the heart or heart valves. Although this infection is not common, people who have prosthetic heart valves or prosthetic joints are at increased risk. Blood cultures might be ordered on a patient (in or out of hospital) with the onset of a high and otherwise unexplained fever. These are often ordered in groups of two or three to ensure the accuracy of the tests. They may be collected all at once or at designated intervals.

Stool Culture and Analysis   A stool culture or analysis is done to diagnose certain conditions affecting the digestive tract, including infection, poor absorption, or cancer. Lab analysis includes microscopic analysis and chemical and microbiological tests for such organisms as bacteria, fungi, parasites, and yeast. Other elements, such as mucus and blood, are also identified. A common test is stool analysis for occult blood (OB). Stool specimens are often ordered in groups of three, which would be separate samples, perhaps one each day. It is sometimes difficult to keep track of specimens obtained in the hospital, so the nurses usually note on the patient's electronic or traditional PI screen/eKardex (discussed in Chapter 19) when they have obtained a specimen. Most facilities provide disposable kits for patients to obtain stool specimens. Depending on the test, patients may be instructed to collect the sample in a container, scoop a small portion into a vial, or smear a small amount on special test paper.

Lung Function Tests

Spirometry   Spirometry is a test used for lung function screening and is one of many pulmonary or lung function tests. It is administered using a portable device called a spirometer. This easily administered, noninvasive test measures the air capacity and function of the lungs. The patient breathes into a mouthpiece attached to a spirometer. The tests measures the volume of air exchanged, how fast it is exchanged, and the compliance of the respiratory muscles.

Spirometry is often ordered preoperatively to assess a person's surgical risk with regard to having an anesthetic, particularly for individuals who are older, who smoke, or who are morbidly obese. The test is also often done in conjunction with related physiotherapy procedures to determine patient progress. Postoperatively, patients are sometimes given a portable spirometer to keep at the bedside and use to measure lung function after surgery as well as to encourage the patient to practise deep-breathing exercises. A more detailed test called plethysmography is sometimes ordered if more accurate information is required.

Arterial Blood Gases An arterial blood gas (ABG) assessment is done on a patient to determine the amounts of oxygen and carbon dioxide dissolved in the blood. The test also calculates the blood's pH, or acid/base balance. The test is ordered on people who are hypoxic, often as a stat test. In many hospitals this test is done in the respiratory department—and usually for emergency patients or inpatients. For that reason, details regarding this test are discussed in Chapter 20.

Lung Scan A lung scan is performed in the nuclear medicine department to diagnose pulmonary embolism (lung blockage) and to evaluate lung disease. This is a two-part test. First, the patient inhales very small particles of radioactive material for three to five minutes through an aerosol. Then technicians take pictures of the lung fields with a special camera to record the distribution of the radioactive material. For the second part of the test, the patient receives an IV injection of radioactive material. X-rays are then taken of the lungs, with the patient assuming various positions. A CT for pulmonary embolus is probably now the test of choice, if available.

Diagnostic Imaging

What was once the X-ray department in most facilities is now called the diagnostic imaging department because X-rays are only one of the imaging tools available. Other imaging techniques include CT scans, MRI, and ultrasonography.

X-Ray An X-ray is a visual test in which an image of a selected body part or region is created by using low doses of radiation reflected on film or fluorescent screens. X-rays can be used to diagnose a wide range of conditions, from pneumonia to a fractured bone. Common X-ray tests include chest X-rays, often ordered as "chest X-ray PA and lateral." This means the doctor wants a front and side view. (See Figure 6.5 for a normal chest X-ray report.) An X-ray can be done on almost any body part, for example, the abdomen to evaluate trauma or a blockage of the bowel, or the bones to assess for fractures. Most X-rays require little or no preparation, but you will likely have to book an appointment for a patient to have one done, although you can specify how urgent it is. (See Chapter 9 for booking procedures.) In the hospital, if a patient is acutely ill or cannot be moved, the doctor may order a "portable," or you may request a "portable" if the nurses deem it best for the patient. The technologist will come to the patient's room with a portable X-ray unit. However, they are not of the same quality as that done in the radiology department.

TIP

"Portable" X-rays are done when the condition of the patient is such that he or she is unable to be transferred to the diagnostic imaging department. Keep the requisition on the floor and call the diagnostic imaging department. This should be treated as an urgent or stat order.

Chest X-ray A chest X-ray is used to evaluate the status of the lungs, heart, and surrounding anatomy. It can diagnose conditions including pneumonia, heart failure, pleurisy, and lung cancer, and it can pick up heart abnormalities, especially in small children.

```
RS LABORATORIES AND DIAGNOSTIC SERVICES
223 Lakewood Ave.
Vancouver, BC
V5R 6M1
Diagnostic Imaging Dept.
```

Physician	Client: Perreault, Anne
Dr. D Singh	DOB: 11/4/56
43 Rundle Ave	Sex: F
Vancouver, B.C.	PH: 604-321-2232
	MCP # 4323432255
	Subscriber's Initial: A
	Date of Service: Sept 2/08
	Date Printed: Sept 3/08

Report Status: final

Examination Required

CHEST X-RAY – bilateral

The inspiration was suboptimal. The heart is not enlarged. The C/T Ratio is 15.5/26 cm, with a suboptimal inspiration. There is a 1 cm calcified granuloma in the left lower lobe. The lungs and the pleural spaces are otherwise clear.

U/S ABDOMEN

Examination was suboptimal as the client was not cooperative. Grossly, the gallbladder, liver, proximal abdominal aorta, interior vena cava, kidneys, spleen, and head and body of the pancreas are unremarkable. Distal abdominal aorta and tail of the pancreas are not imaged. The common hepatic duct is not dilated, measuring 5.9 cm in calibre.

V.ss   Y.J. Henry MD, Radiologist

Figure 6.5 Report of a chest X-ray and an abdominal ultrasound

Endoscopic Retrograde Cholangiopancreatography (ERCP) An ERCP is a test that uses an endoscope to visualize the liver and bile ducts. The patient is required to remain NPO for eight hours before the test. Because a contrast dye is used, it is important to ask the patient about related allergies. Many contrast dyes contain iodine, so a history of allergies to iodine or past dye tests would be important. Patients find this test very uncomfortable. Despite a local anesthetic, and often an intravenous relaxant, gagging, nausea, and vomiting may occur when the endoscope is passed down the throat.

Cholecystography For this test, the patient must be given a contrast dye that helps visualize the gallbladder 12 to 14 hours prior to the test. Alternatively, the dye can be given intravenously just prior to the test. In preparation for either test, the patient should remain NPO after the pills are taken or after 2200 hrs (10:00 p.m.). As well, for either test, written consent is usually requested. Anyone with a previous reaction to a contrast dye or who is allergic to iodine or seafood should not be given the dye. This test is rarely done now since an ultrasound reveals more.

Barium Enema A barium enema visualizes the lower portion of the bowel. Barium is inserted through the rectum prior to the X-rays.

Protocols vary for preparing patients for this test. Some doctors order a fibre-restricted meal at noon the day before the test, followed by a clear fluid supper. Others require a full-fluid, low-fibre diet the whole day prior to the test. Still others have the patient consume a special supplement up to two days prior to the test. Most patients are asked to take a laxative the night before. A common one is magnesium citrate, which is very salty. Many patients will tell you that the prep is worse than the test. Those who have experienced it suggest taking the laxative ice cold or sucking on a lemon afterward.

For the hospitalized patient, you must put the patient's existing diet orders on hold and initiate the preparatory diet orders. Make sure that the dietary department is aware of the changes. In some computerized environments, the dietary department is notified that a patient is having a barium enema and automatically adjusts the diet. In some facilities, you must post a sign at the patient's bedside about diet changes; for example, it might read "clear fluids" or "NPO."

Barium Swallow   A barium swallow is an X-ray of the throat and esophagus visualized using a contrast medium that is ingested as a drink with the consistency of a milkshake. The passage of the barium through the esophagus and stomach is monitored on a fluoroscope. Pictures are taken with the patient in different positions to maximize the view of the gastrointestinal (GI) tract. The test takes 30 minutes to 1 hour to complete. Similar tests may be ordered as a GI or upper GI series, which focus more attention on the stomach and duodenum.

The patient must be instructed to remain NPO for eight hours prior to the test and may be placed on a restricted diet for two or three days prior. It is very important for the patient to follow these instructions. Even swallowing a pill may interfere with the examination.

Patients must be advised to take a laxative following the test because the barium can be highly constipating. Let patients know that the first two or three bowel movements may be a greyish-white colour.

When booking both a barium enema and a barium swallow, whether for an inpatient or outpatient, you must book the barium enema first. Otherwise the barium from the swallow will interfere with the accuracy of the barium enema.

Ultrasonography   Ultrasonography (US), frequently referred to simply as an "ultrasound," is an imaging method that uses sound waves with frequencies above detection by the human ear to produce pictures of structures within the body. It is particularly effective in analyzing soft-organ tissue, such as the gallbladder, liver, kidneys, ovaries, and bladder. (See Figure 6.5 for an ultrasound report of the abdomen.) Ultrasonography is popular for pregnant women and is the most common investigative procedure in obstetrics and gynecology.

Usually, the AHP will book an appointment for a patient's ultrasound. An ultrasound of abdominal organs, particularly for a pelvic examination, may require an empty stomach and a full bladder. The patient is instructed to drink about six glasses of water one hour before the test. This fills the bladder, resulting in better visualization of some abdominal structures, especially the uterus. A full bladder is very uncomfortable (whether pregnant or not), and some patients find drinking that much water difficult. Advise patients not to go to the bathroom even if they feel they must. If the bladder is not sufficiently full, the test may be postponed or the patient may be asked to drink more water and wait until the bladder is full enough.

Proton Emission Tomography (PET)   This is a type of nuclear medicine imaging. The PET produces three-dimensional images of functioning body parts, such as a beating heart or blood flow. It is often done in conjunction with CT scans or MRI. The patient is given a radioactive substance intravenously, by mouth, or by inhalation. There is no special preparation, but patients are asked to leave all jewellery at home. If they don't, it will be removed prior to entering the diagnostic area. It is presently only available in larger centres and is reserved for specific indications.

CT or CAT Scanning   Computed tomography, also called computerized axial tomography (CAT) or a CAT scan, is a technique using X-rays and a computer to produce cross-sectional images of any part of the body. It often provides more detailed information than conventional X-ray techniques. Common investigations include those of the head, spine, thorax, abdomen, pelvis, and joints. Not every facility has a CT scanner, so you may need to arrange for a hospital patient to have the test done elsewhere.

The part of the body being visualized is positioned inside a cylinder that tilts and rotates to facilitate various views. Claustrophobic people may not be good candidates for this test. The test is, however, less confining than an MRI. Examinations usually take between 20 and 40 minutes. The patient may need to arrive an hour early. Dye may be used to accent organs, but renal function and certain nephrotoxic drugs have to be monitored if used. The CT requisition will often ask a series of questions related to renal function.

Magnetic Resonance Imaging (MRI)   The MRI machine produces a strong magnetic field. When a patient is placed inside this field and the body is exposed to short radio frequency pulses, some of the protons within the cells of the body realign with the external magnetic field. Cells from different parts of the body behave in different ways. Using modern high-speed computers, an analysis of this process can be used to produce images of different parts of the body. MRI is invaluable in diagnosing a wide range of conditions throughout the body and is particularly useful in diagnosing disorders of the brain, spine, and joints.

On older MRI machines, which are closed in, the test involves moving the patient into a tunnel approximately one metre in diameter. Most tests require the patient to hold fairly still. Patients who are claustrophobic are poor candidates for the older model MRIs. Patients with metal devices in their bodies are also unable to have an MRI because of the strong magnetic field used for the scan. The doctor needs to know about pacemakers, metal pins or clips, tattoos (many contain lead), metal in the eye or a history of grinding metal, and IUCDs (intrauterine contraceptive devices). On occasion, a contrast dye may be used, which does not contain iodine. Still, known allergies to any type of dye are important to note.

MRI is not readily available in many communities across Canada. In some regions, the wait for an MRI can be longer than other tests. If you have a patient who is booked several weeks in advance for an MRI, make a note on your calendar or computer to give the patient a reminder call a week or so before the test. Patients forget tests and appointments that are two weeks away, let alone several months. Many MRI machines are operated 24 hours a day to reduce waiting time. If a patient does not show up, a resource that could have been used for someone else is wasted.

Mammography   A mammogram is an X-ray of the breast that can be used as a screening mechanism to detect early-stage cancer. Most provincial and territorial plans will pay for periodic mammograms at certain ages, usually for older women and those with family histories of breast cancer, who are considered at increased risk. This test must be booked, but waits are usually not long. The test takes about 10 minutes. Many women find the pressure used to compress the breasts painful. Patients may be advised to avoid caffeine for up to two weeks before the test to reduce breast sensitivity. It is also helpful to have the test a week after the patient's period, when the breasts are less tender. Women having the test for the first time are often quite apprehensive and may ask you if it will hurt. Remember that pain is a subjective and individual experience. Some women talk of feeling nothing but pressure; others describe the experience as excruciating. Avoid using the word "pain." Advise the woman that there is certainly pressure and that the level of discomfort varies from person to person.

Figure 6.6 is a report of a mammogram noting some irregularities. In light of the patient's history of a breast lump, the radiologist recommends further investigation.

Bone Mineral Density Test   A bone mineral density (BMD) test uses small doses of radiation to check the density of bone in the spine and hip. It is used to detect early

DIAGNOSTIC IMAGING DEPT

Physician	**Client:** Perreault, Anne
Dr. D Singh	**DOB:** 11/4/56
43 Rundle Ave	**Sex:** F
Vancouver, BC	**PH:** 604-321-2232
	MCP # 4323432255
	Subscriber's Initial: A
	Date of Service: Sept 2/08
	Date Printed: Sept 3/08

Report Status: final

Examination Required

MAMMOGRAM

The breasts are mildly dense bilaterally.
Benign-appearing calcification is demonstrated in the left breast. Both breasts are relatively symmetrical in appearance and appear unchanged when compared to previous mammogram of January 4 of last year. However, clinical history mentioned a lump in the left breast. It would be helpful to include a diagram of the left breast including the area of suspected lump so that it may be further analyzed with the ultrasound modality, as it is possible for a clinically suspicious lump to be overlooked on plain mammography.

V.ss   Y.J. Henry M. Radiologist

Book for appointment this week.
DS

Figure 6.6 Mammogram report

osteoporosis and to monitor patients with osteoporosis. The exam takes about 20 minutes. Patients may be instructed to wear clothes without metal buttons, zippers, or buckles. Some facilities will delay a BMD if the patient has had a barium swallow or enema or other radioactive studies within the preceding one or two weeks.

Other Tests

Colonoscopy   A colonoscopy is a visual examination of the entire large intestine, from the lowest part—the rectum—all the way up through the colon to the lower end of the small intestine. The procedure is used to look for early signs of cancer in the colon and rectum. It is also used to diagnose the causes of unexplained changes in bowel habits. A colonoscopy enables the physician to see inflamed tissue, abnormal growths, ulcers, and bleeding.

Preparation for this test involves dietary restrictions for one to three days before the test. Often, only fluids are allowed on the day prior to the test. The patient must also be instructed to take a laxative the night before and perhaps the morning of the test and to be NPO (except for the laxative) for eight hours prior to the test. It is usually done in the hospital on an outpatient basis. The patient will likely have an intravenous (IV) tube and receive sedation for cramping. The patient can expect to be in the hospital for about four hours. A patient who receives sedation should not drive for at least 12 hours and will need someone to provide transportation.

Some diagnostic centres now offer a virtual colonoscopy (CT colonoscopy), which does not require sedation or anesthesia. This test still requires a full bowel prep and does not allow for a biopsy if a polyp is found. If there are any suspicious or abnormal results, a full/routine colonoscopy is still required.

Gastroscopy   Also called an *endoscopy*, this is a common procedure in which the lining of the esophagus, the stomach, and the first part of the small intestine are viewed using a flexible instrument called an endoscope, which is passed through the mouth and into the stomach. Most gastroscopies are carried out using a local anesthetic throat spray, sometimes supplemented by intravenous sedation. The patient may feel like gagging when the scope is inserted. The test takes about 20 minutes. The patient should have someone to drive him or her home in case sedation is required.

Tests for the Cardiovascular System

Electrocardiogram   An electrocardiogram (ECG or EKG) is a noninvasive test that records the electrical activity of the heart via electrodes placed on the chest, arms, and legs. This test helps the doctor evaluate a person's cardiac condition, including determining whether the person has had a heart attack and, if so, what part of the heart has been damaged. An ECG can also detect an irregular heartbeat and the presence of **ischemia**, a lower concentration of red blood cells because of a blockage.

ischemia a local lack of red blood cells because of mechanical obstruction of the blood supply, usually caused by arterial narrowing.

Holter Monitoring   Holter monitoring is a continuous tracing of heart activity. Electrodes are placed on the chest area with leads attached to a small transportable recorder. The patient keeps a record of his or her daily activities and any relevant symptoms, such as chest pain or angina. This may be ordered for one or several days. After the test, a computer and subsequently a cardiologist examine the recording. This test is ordered by a physician and may be done in the hospital or on an outpatient basis. The equipment is usually hooked up in the cardiopulmonary services department, in an independent lab, or in the hospital, and the patient is given instructions. Holter monitoring is usually done on an outpatient basis. If the appointment is scheduled while the patient is still in hospital, record it on the patient intervention (PI) screen (discussed in Chapter 15). Make sure the patient has all the relevant information for the test prior to discharge.

Stress Test   Sometimes called an exercise ECG, this test measures the heart's response to the increased demands for oxygen caused by increased activity. The patient is asked to walk on a treadmill (or ride an exercise bike) at various speeds. The test usually lasts about half an hour. Some patients experience such symptoms as angina or shortness of breath, so a physician and a technician should be present during this test and the patient should be carefully assessed afterward. This test is ordered by a physician and can be done on an inpatient or outpatient basis. Book the appointment with the lab, and record the information on the PI screen.

Doppler Ultrasound   The Doppler ultrasound is used, among other purposes, to assess peripheral pulses that are difficult to hear. The ultrasound unit has earpieces like those of a regular stethoscope. However, instead of a standard bell and diaphragm, the cord is attached to an audio unit with an audio transmission device called a transducer. This transducer picks up and amplifies the sounds of blood moving through vessels. The Doppler ultrasound is also used to detect a fetus's heartbeat. Similar devices are used to detect **bruits** (unusual sounds) that are not easily picked up by auscultation, such as the sound of blood passing over a rough spot in a blood vessel. Doppler tests are usually carried out by cardiopulmonary services. You need to book an appointment and arrange to have the patient go to the department.

bruit a sound, especially an abnormal one, heard on auscultation or by ultrasound.

Echocardiogram   An echocardiogram is a noninvasive procedure that uses ultrasound waves to evaluate cardiac function and structure. An echocardiogram is essentially an ultrasound of the heart. Often referred to simply as an "echo," this test can display a cross-section of the beating heart, visualizing the chambers, valves, and major vessels.

There is no special prep for this test, and it can be done in a doctor's office or in the hospital. Gel is applied to the chest, and a wand-like apparatus called a transducer is moved over the chest area to produce images that are recorded and visible on a screen.

Cardiac Catheterization   Also called a "heart cath" or an angiogram, this procedure is performed in a special lab. A thin wire called a cardiac catheter is inserted through an artery, usually in the thigh, and threaded into the heart and coronary artery. A dye is injected, and X-rays are taken. The patient usually requires some sedation. Smaller hospitals may not offer this test, so the patient may have to be transported to a larger hospital.

LO4 HEALTH TEACHING

The AHP's role in diagnostic testing will be primarily administrative and includes completing and giving out requisitions, reporting and filing results (discussed later in the chapter), and educating patients. To fill this role, you need to recognize and understand the laboratory tests commonly ordered in hospitals and health offices. Patients need to know where to go for the test, how to prepare for it, and what to expect. They have many questions in mind: How long will it take? Exactly what will happen? Can someone come with me? Will I have sedation? How much discomfort will I feel? Will I be able to drive afterward? Do I have to do anything special afterward?

Patient education is the single most important factor in successful tests. Tests can be accurate only if patients understand how to prepare for them. It may take you a few more minutes to explain clearly and carefully, but the time is well worth it. A patient who does not understand the instructions may call the office several times to have them clarified. A well-informed patient is likely to be less apprehensive, more compliant with preparation instructions, and more cooperative at the time of the test. For example, if a patient does not realize that the test involves an IV, she may be frightened and require prolonged persuasion, throwing off the lab's schedule. She may even refuse the test. Other tests may have to be cancelled if the patient has eaten; for example, a fasting blood sugar will not give accurate results unless the patient has fasted for 8 to 12 hours. Other procedures, such as a barium enema, an upper GI series, or a colonoscopy, also require that the patient remain NPO, as food in the stomach could cause vomiting and gagging during the test. Most tests requiring sedation also require that the patient be NPO because of the potential for aspiration (if the patient vomits and inhales the vomitus into the lungs), because respiratory arrest and death can result. Likewise, some tests, such as a colonoscopy, require a laxative or enema the night before or the morning of the test. If the bowel is not properly evacuated, the colon cannot be adequately visualized, resulting in an invalid test that has been a waste of everyone's time (not to mention the cost of the test). Sometimes, medication must be discontinued for a specified time before a test. Other medications essential to the patient's well-being may be permitted even for a patient who is to be NPO.

Providing the patient with written as well as oral instructions is helpful. Most laboratories keep handouts explaining the test preparation. If they do not, develop your own and give them to your patients as required. Although some diagnostic facilities do not mind the patient calling them for instructions, it is better if you can give all the needed information. Figure 6.7 shows a teaching handout for an echocardiography, a diagnostic tool used to visualize and assess the structure and function of the heart muscle, valves, and pericardium.

THE ECHOCARDIOGRAM

Description of the Test

An echocardiogram uses ultrasound waves to assess the motion of the heart. A technician places a device, called a transducer, at different locations on the chest and directs sound waves toward the heart. These sound waves reflect back and create a picture on the monitor, which is recorded on video. This picture will be reviewed by a specialist. The picture shows the valves and the blood as it passes through the heart and shows how the heart muscle functions. This test takes about 1½ hours to complete.

Preparation

None. You may bring someone with you if you wish. You will not receive any sedation and will be able to drive if you so choose.

During the Test

This test is not painful. You will be required to lie down for the test. A gel is applied to your chest to facilitate the transmission of the ultrasound waves. The transducer will be moved over your chest to look at various portions of your heart. You will experience no pain, but often the transducer is pressed firmly against the chest wall and you may feel some pressure or tenderness.

After the Test

The technician will wipe off the gel. You may leave as soon as you are done.

Risks of the Echocardiogram Test

None; ultrasound is harmless.

Report

A detailed report of your echocardiogram will be sent to the physician who ordered the test.

Figure 6.7 A teaching handout

LO5 REQUISITIONS

Almost all tests require a requisition, except those done right in the doctor's office, such as a hemoglobin or dipstick urine. These would be recorded on the patient's chart. Tests ordered in the doctor's office, other than routine blood work and urinalysis, may have to be booked. The protocol for booking tests is discussed in Chapter 9. It is essential to fill out the requisition accurately and completely. Always recheck the requisition to be sure that it is complete and correct.

Include the patient's demographic information, health card number, physician, test required, and any additional information requested on the requisition. In the hospital, the physician's name may be electronically added or may appear on the patient's addressograph. If it is not (e.g., if a consultant orders the test), add the name of any doctor who should receive test results. Usually, results are sent to the ordering physician's office, to the family doctor, and for an inpatient to the patient's chart. If you work for a specialist, add the family doctor's name to the requisition, unless otherwise requested, to ensure that the lab sends the report to the family doctor as well as to the specialist. If the patient is booked for surgery, indicate the date and time. A requisition for an electrocardiogram will ask you to list any heart medication or fluid pills the patient is taking, sometimes including the dose and frequency. This information is relevant to the interpretation and, sometimes, the processing of the test. If the test is for a culture and sensitivity, you may be asked to identify any antibiotics the patient is currently taking as these may affect the results. In a hospital, you would find this information on the patient's medication administration record in the computerized

CONESTOGA GENERAL HOSPITAL ELECTROCARDIOGRAM REAQUISITION	
Patient's Name: Health Card # Hospital #	Address: Version Code: Unit: Room: Bed#
Requisition Date	Appointment Date/Time
Elective O Priority O Stat O	Patient Ambulatory O Portable O Surgery Yes O No O Procedure: Date: Time:
Referring Physician (MRP)	
Phone and Fax No.	Other:
Copies To	Patient's Ht. Patient's Wt. (actual not stated)
Clinical History Patient's Ht.	Patient's Wt. (actual not stated)

Figure 6.8 Electrocardiogram requisition—paper format

environment, in the electronic Kardex, or in a separate field that lists the patient's current medications. (See Figure 6.8, which illustrates an ECG requisition for a hospital inpatient.) Also include any specific reporting instructions, such as "Call doctor with results."

Other information required may include the date and time the specimen was collected (or time to be collected) and, sometimes, the name of the person who collected the specimen. In the computerized environment, if specific information is requested, a mandatory field will appear when you requisition the test. The physician usually orders the test, but several members of the health care team may be in a position to collect it, or the patient may collect the specimen him or herself (e.g., a urine specimen). If it is not readily identifiable, the lab may want to know the exact source of the specimen and how it was obtained. For example, a swab could come from a wound, the throat, the ear, or elsewhere; a urine specimen may be a voided specimen or obtained from a urinary catheter; a sputum specimen may be coughed up by the patient or obtained through a suction catheter. Figure 6.9 shows a requisition for a routine urinalysis,

URINALYSIS REQUISITION

HOSP. NO. DR.	DATE COLLECTED / NURSE
PATIENT SURNAME / GIVEN NAME / INITIALS	☐ ROUTINE ☐ URGENT ☐ PRE-OP (O.R. DATE:) (O.R. TIME:)
ROOM (ADDRESS)	24h COLLECTION: START TIME / FINISH TIME; RANDOM COLLECTION: TIME
FAMILY / REFERRING PHYSICIAN(S) / DATE OF BIRTH: DAY MONTH YEAR	
DATE / TIME SPECIMEN RECEIVED / INITIAL / LAB NO.	CREATININE CLEARANCE ONLY: PATIENT - HEIGHT .... WEIGHT ....

☐ ROUTINE		REFERENCE RANGE	OHIP: ☐ YES ☐ NO			24h VOLUME .... mL		
COLOUR AND APPEARANCE					✓	TIMED COLLECTIONS		REFERENCE RANGE
GLUCOSE		Negative	LEUKOCYTES / hpf			CREATININE		7.1-15.8 mmol/d
KETONES		Negative	ERYTHROCYTES / hpf			CREATININE CLEARANCE		1.24-2.08 mL/s
SPECIFIC GRAVITY (S.G.)		1.010-1.030	EPITHELIAL CELLS / hpf			CALCIUM		< 7.50 mmol/d
BLOOD		Negative	CAST / hpf			PROTEIN		0.01-0.1 g/d
pH		5 - 8				AMYLASE		< 1100 u/d
PROTEIN		≤ Trace	MUCOUS THREADS/hpf					
NITRITE		Negative	AMORPHOUS CRYSTALS / hpf					
LEUKOCYTES		≤ Trace	CRYSTALS / hpf					
☐ BILIRUBIN		Negative	BACTERIA / hpf					
☐ UROBILINOGEN		≤ Trace	YEAST CELLS / hpf			PREGNANCY TEST		

FORM #2214 REVIEWED MAR/90 DATE OF REPORT TECHNOLOGIST

HEALTH RECORDS

Figure 6.9 Urinalysis requisition—paper format

Huron Perth Healthcare Alliance

which could be used in an office or a hospital. Note that the requisition asks whether the test is urgent, routine, or preoperative. In-hospital requisitions often ask about the urgency of the test. Some are needed **stat**, meaning immediately; some may be *urgent*, meaning soon but not necessarily immediately; and others are *routine*, meaning they can be done the next time the lab normally sends someone around to collect it. Computerized requisitions usually address this with a mandatory field.

In the office, the physician usually identifies the tests he wants done on the requisition, as well as relevant patient information, leaving the AHP to fill out the rest. In the hospital setting, you will be filling out the entire requisition, either manually or electronically. Absolute accuracy is imperative.

Many paper requisitions have two or three copies. One can be kept for the patient's chart as a record that the test has been requisitioned. This is especially useful in the hospital setting. If a specimen gets lost, it provides some measure of proof that it was indeed ordered. In the computerized environment, the computer will keep a record of all such transactions and tests can often be booked online so there is no paper required.

In the doctor's office, make a note on the patient's chart that a test has been ordered and, if applicable, the time for which it was booked. The physician may note that the test has been ordered under "plan" or "treatment" on the chart, in which case you would only add the date and time. A patient may call you because she or he forgot when the test was booked. This information is also useful if a specialist calls wanting a certain test done before he sees the patient or wanting to know what tests were ordered. Sometimes a diagnostic facility will call about a previously ordered test.

In computerized facilities, such as hospitals, lab tests are electronically ordered and therefore paperless. If a test is ordered stat, telephone the appropriate service to ensure they are aware of the order. Electronic requisitions are sent to an "inbox" in the appropriate department and are only checked at specific intervals. If a stat test is electronically ordered at 1300 hrs (1:00 p.m.) and the next routine check of the inbox is at 1700 hrs (5 p.m.), the stat order would be missed. Because stat orders for tests often require a technician to come to the floor to collect the specimen, it is more efficient to print the requisition on the floor so that it is there when the technician arrives. (See Chapter 15 for more on electronic requisitions.)

Figure 6.10 illustrates a biochemistry/hematology requisition for a patient in hospital. If you were transcribing a doctor's orders, you would tick off all the specific tests ordered by the doctor.

PREPARING AND HANDLING SPECIMENS

It is unlikely that you will be asked to have much to do with actual testing. In the doctor's office you might, however, be asked to collect and label some specimens, such as urine specimens. The patient will probably leave the specimen in the washroom or examination room. Some patients may bring the urine specimen to the office with them. It is essential to label the specimens promptly and correctly. If there are two bottles of urine in the bathroom and you are not absolutely certain which belongs to whom, you must discard them. The requisition itself should be filled out, at least in part, by the doctor. You may be asked to complete the patient information. The requisition must be placed in a bag with the specimen or otherwise attached to it. The specimen container itself must also be individually labelled. Most labels have an adhesive backing so that they can be affixed to the container. Labelling the actual container before the test is sometimes a good idea. In the case of a urine specimen, sticking the label on after the specimen collection prevents the label from becoming soiled. Remember to refrigerate midstream urine specimens until the lab picks them up.

STRATFORD GENERAL HOSPITAL MULTI-REQUEST REQUISITION

IMPRINT PLATE (PRINT IF NO PLATE) IF STAT ATTACH STICKER

OTHER HOSPITAL

DIAGNOSIS

SPECIMEN	MO	DAY	TIME
IF URGENT PRINT PHONE NO.	COLLECTED BY		
	ORDERED BY DR.		

CHECK TEST(S) REQUESTED

SCREEN 1 — BIO-CHEMISTRY	SCREEN 1 — BIO-CHEMISTRY	SCREEN 3 — HAEMATOLOGY
1 ☐ BLOOD SUGAR – FAST	37 ☐ DIGOXIN	8 ☐ DIFFERENTIAL – NEUT
2 ☐ BLOOD SUGAR – PC	39 ☐ T4 FREE	9 – BAND
3 ☐ UREA	40 ☐ TSH	10 – LYMPH
4 ☐ CREATININE	**SCREEN 2 — BIO-CHEMISTRY**	11 – MONO
5 ☐ ELECTROLYTES – SODIUM	1 ☐ BLOOD GAS – pH	12 – EOSIN
6 – POTASSIUM	2 – pCO_2	13 – BASO
7 – CHLORIDE	3 – pO_2	14 – META
8 – TOTAL CO_2	4 – BICARB	15 – MYELO
9 ☐ CALCIUM	5 – SATURATION	16 – COMMENT
10 ☐ PHOSPHORUS	6 ☐ PROTEIN ELECTROPHORESIS	17 – COMMENT
11 ☐ MAGNESIUM	7 ☐ ACETAMINOPHEN	18 – COMMENT
12 ☐ TOTAL PROTEIN	8 ☐ ETHANOL	19 ☐ PLATELETS
13 ☐ ALBUMIN	9 ☐ LITHIUM	20 ☐ ESR
☐ URATE	10 ☐ DILANTIN	21 ☐ RETIC
☐ CHOLESTEROL	11 ☐ SALICYLATE	22 ☐ PT
16 ☐ TRIGLYCERIDES	12 ☐ THEOPHYLLINE (TIME)	23 ☐ PT – CONTROL
17 ☐ HDL CHOLESTEROL	13 ☐ GENTAMICIN – TROUGH (TIME)	24 ☐ PTT
18 ☐ BILIRUBIN – TOTAL	14 ☐ GENTAMICIN – PEAK (TIME)	25 ☐ PTT CONTROL
19 – DIRECT	15 ☐ AMMONIA	27 ☐ FIBRINOGEN
20 ☐ AST	18 ☐ Hb A1C	28 ☐ FDP
21 ☐ CK	19 ☐ OSMOLALITY – SERUM	29 ☐ THROMBIN TIME
22 ☐ LD	20 ☐ OSMOLALITY – URINE	30 ☐ LAP
23 ☐ CK–MB	24 ☐ CORTISOL	32 ☐ MONO TEST
24 ☐ LD–1	25 ☐ HCG – S	33 ☐ RA
25 ☐ GGT	P3 ☐ ROUTINE URINALYSIS	34 ☐ CRP
26 ☐ ALP	**SCREEN 3 — HAEMATOLOGY**	36 ☐ ASTO
27 ☐ ACP–T	1 ☐ CBC – WBC	37 ☐ ANA
28 ☐ ACP–P	2 – RBC	38 ☐ IgA
29 ☐ AMYLASE	3 ☐ HEMOGLOBIN	39 ☐ IgG
30 ☐ IRON	4 – Hct	40 ☐ IgM
31 ☐ TIBC	5 – MCV	**SCREEN 4 — BIO-CHEMISTRY**
32 ☐ VITAMIN B12	6 – MCH	9 ☐ CARBAMAZEPINE (TEGRETOL)
33 ☐ FOLATE – SERUM	7 – MCHC	28 ☐ PHENOBARBITAL
☐ FOLATE – RBC		39 ☐ VALPROIC ACID (DEPAKENE)
35 ☐ FERRITIN	TEST(S) NOT LISTED ABOVE	P5 ☐ THYROID ANTIBODY
36 ☐ ALT	ENTER ON MISCELLANEOUS FORM LA-007	

LA-45 1994-03   MOORE SPEEDISET 3 OIC MOORE CLEAN PRINT 9 Quality 3010 PATENTED 1962 1964 1975 O

Figure 6.10 A multi-request paper requisition for a hospitalized patient. Also used for outpatients.
Huron Perth Healthcare Alliance

Most laboratories will have a courier who picks up specimens and delivers them to the lab. *Remember to use Standard Precautions* (as described in Chapter 5) *when handling all specimens.*

[L06] [L07] RECEIVING AND RECORDING TEST RESULTS

In both the hospital and the health office, the medical secretary may be responsible for receiving and filing test reports (electronic or otherwise). In the health office, reports of laboratory and diagnostic tests are usually sent electronically or faxed (hard copy). Urgent or critical results will almost always be telephoned to you and followed up with a faxed or electronic report. A critical result has a slightly higher priority than urgent results, depending on the situation. You must relay these results to the physician as soon as you get them (in person, by phone, or messaging him or her electronically—flagged as critical or urgent). Sometimes a nurse from the hospital will call with a lab result, wanting orders from the doctor (e.g., if a patient's blood sugar is high, he or she may want the doctor to adjust the patient's insulin order). Put these calls directly through to the physician. Both electronic and printed reports will make note of abnormal results. Review Figures 6.1 and 6.2 for an example of a WBC count and an elevated glucose level result in a test report. Many offices also call patients with normal results to alleviate their concerns. A number of labs now give patients a code they can use to access their test results online. Patients may call with questions about their results.

When receiving a phoned report, you must be absolutely sure you have the correct patient. Take the patient's first and last names and date of birth to check against your records. The date of birth is valuable when there are two or more patients with the same name in a facility or practice. If the patient is in hospital, also check their hospital number. Always repeat all reported information back to the caller, including the patient's identifying information, the type of test, and the values/results. A misplaced decimal point or transposed numbers can have serious consequences. Even if you are certain that you recorded the numbers correctly, remember that the person giving you the report may have made a mistake reading them to you. Reading the values back can catch both kinds of error. Take the name of the caller as well. Faxed reports will have to be scanned into the patient's electronic medical record. Again, be sure you upload it to the correct chart. Uploading a report to the wrong chart can have serious consequences, both for the intended patient and the patient whose chart the report was incorrectly uploaded to.

TIP

Report abnormal or critical values to the physician immediately. If the lab calls the doctor's office with a critical result, put the call through immediately.

Recording Results for the Preoperative Patient

When a patient is booked for surgery, inevitably there will be routine blood work that must be completed first, as well as other specific tests. Many hospitals have a comprehensive checklist to be completed before a patient goes to the operating room (see Chapter 15). This list will include lab results, medication, mental status, and a note on where documentation is to be found for such things as consent, physical history, and consultations. The form may also note preop preparation, including not only whether the patient is NPO and has voided or been catheterized, but also such details as removing contact lenses and dental work. You will be required (perhaps in collaboration with a nurse) to ensure that all the appropriate lab work is on the chart. If a test has not been ordered for the patient, mark the line "NA" for "not applicable." Never leave it blank. The surgeon may assume it was not done but was necessary. Sometimes, especially with emergency surgery, test results may not be back yet. In this case, tick "call OR." Either you or the lab is responsible for ensuring that the results are telephoned to the operating room. Some tests results are very important for surgeons to have prior to operating. Without certain test results, surgery may be cancelled.

- Changes in recommendations with respect to tests that used to be done routinely but may not be now, such as the PSA for prostate cancer, and further whether these recommendations extend across the country.

- Improvements or delays in patient access to diagnostic tests, especially CT and MRI screening.

- Increases in genetic testing as it relates to genes causing or predisposing the patient to illness using DNA or RNA as a biomarker for clinical testing (e.g., under development in Sweden and showing promise is an RNA test of blood platelets that can detect, classify, and pinpoint the location of cancer).

- The cost of diagnostic tests and how these costs factor into decisions on what tests to order; many physicians are only ordering tests they deem necessary to be more financially responsible.

- More widespread access to lab and diagnostic test results for patients, receiving the results electronically on computers or smartphones. In British Columbia the successful trial is a free "my ehealth" serviced rolled out by Excelleris Technologies, a division of LifeLabs.

SUMMARY

1. Diagnostic tests are ordered by a physician or other provider and give valuable information to diagnose and monitor patients' conditions.

2. Tests are processed by medical laboratories, which may be part of a hospital or be independent. Laboratories have specialized departments, such as hematology (blood work), pathology (tissue samples), and diagnostic imaging (X-rays, ultrasound).

3. Among the more common tests are complete blood count, electrolytes, blood glucose levels, cholesterol and triglycerides, and culture and sensitivity (C&S) tests for the presence of pathogens in blood, urine, or swabs from wounds, ears, or the throat. Diagnostic imaging includes conventional X-rays, barium swallows or enemas, ultrasound, CT scanning, MRIs, mammograms, bone mineral density tests, and endoscopies.

4. Clear, concise, and complete patient information saves time in the long run and is essential for effective, accurate testing.

5. Tests usually require requisitions and must often be booked. Make sure that requisitions include all necessary information, which often includes the patient's medication and the urgency of the test.

6. You will likely receive test results both as printed and as phoned-in reports. Notify the doctor immediately of abnormal and critical values. File results with the most recent ones on top.

KEY TERMS

autopsy 140
bruit 158
computed tomography (CT) 138
critical value 140
enzyme 148
heparin 145

ischemia 158
magnetic resonance imaging (MRI) 138
mammography 138
midstream urine specimen (MSU) 151
reference range 138

serum 146
stat 162
ultrasonography 138

REVIEW QUESTIONS

1. Identify three professionals who work with lab and diagnostic facilities, and explain what they do.

2. What role does diagnostic testing play in health promotion and illness prevention?

3. What tests are usually included in a CBC?

4. What are the most common tests ordered on a microbiology requisition?

5. What tests usually require a patient to fast?

6. Discuss the basic information needed when booking a lab test.

7. What is the advantage of thorough patient instruction about test preparation?

8. Why must the dietary department be notified when a hospital patient is NPO for a test?

9. What is meant when a test is ordered *stat*?

10. What is the appropriate way to handle a midstream urine sample taken for culture and sensitivity?

APPLICATION EXERCISES

11. Contact a local laboratory facility or doctor's office and identify what lab and diagnostic tests are uninsured in your area. Why are they uninsured? State the purpose of these tests and the cost to the patient.

12. Choose four of the following diagnostic tests. Construct a patient teaching handout for each. Include such information as how the test is done, what it is for, how long it takes, whether the patient should have someone to take him or her home, any medications involved, and other specifics related to preparation for the test.

- CT scan
- Glucose tolerance test
- Abdominal ultrasound
- Gastroscopy
- Colonoscopy
- Other (your choice)

WEBSITES OF INTEREST

Mammogram Instructions and Explanation

www.imaginis.com/mammography/diagnostic-mammography-2

Midstream Urine

www.healthcentral.com/encyclopedia/adam/urine-culture-clean-catch-4019967/overview

Links to Explanations of Various Diagnostic Tests

https://medlineplus.gov/diagnostictests.html

Click on the test/category of interest for further detail.

Information on Lab and Diagnostic Tests

www.labtestsonline.org/map/index.html

This website provides links to look up screening tests and tests specific to a range of conditions. This site will also take you on a virtual tour of a lab—Click on "Features," then under "Inside the Lab," select "Follow That Sample: A Short Lab Tour."

DNA Solutions: DNA Testing—Canada

www.dnacanada.com

Chapter 7
Pharmacology

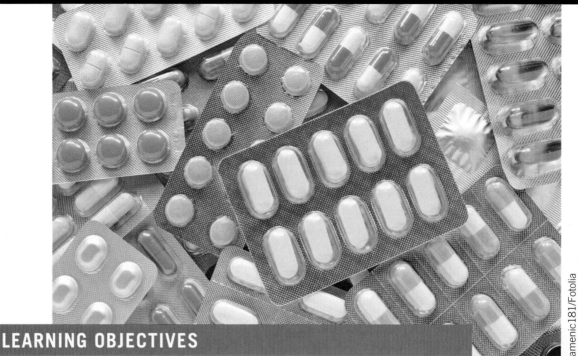

amenic181/Fotolia

LEARNING OBJECTIVES

On completing this chapter, you will be able to:

1. Communicate effectively with various members of the pharmacy team.

2. Discuss four major sources of drugs and related names.

3. Describe Canadian legislation controlling drugs.

4. Understand the way prescription and over-the-counter medications are dispensed.

5. Identify the major classifications of drugs and routes of drug administration.

6. Explain the elements of pharmacokinetics, including side effects and allergic responses.

7. Within your scope of practice, educate the patient about the appropriate use of herbal, over-the-counter, and prescription drugs.

8. Properly handle prescriptions and know how to store and dispose of drugs in the health office.

pharmacology a biological science and academic discipline that deals with the properties, uses, and actions of drugs and chemicals in living beings.

Pharmacology is the study and description of drugs, including their composition, actions, and effects. Pharmacology involves research into the therapeutic and adverse effects of drugs on living beings, their curative potential, and their interactions with other medications. In short, pharmacology examines the effects drugs and chemicals have on living things. A basic knowledge of pharmacology is important for all health care professionals. A *pharmacy* is a licensed business involved in dispensing drugs. *Dispensing* involves compounding, packaging, labelling, and selling or delivering a drug in response to a prescription written by a qualified health provider. Your responsibilities for medications will be varied. You may be asked to phone a prescription to a pharmacist, take phoned-in requests for repeats from a pharmacy or a patient, and copy dictated medical reports. In the hospital, you will process physicians' medication orders.

One component of pharmacology is *pharmacokinetics*, which deals with the effects drugs have on people. It considers how the drug is taken and absorbed into the body, how the body metabolizes it, or breaks it down, and how it is distributed and excreted. *Pharmacodynamics* looks at the small scale: It is concerned with the study of molecular and physiological effects of drugs on cellular systems and how they act on these systems. *Toxicology* concerns the adverse effects of drugs and chemicals used for therapeutic purposes as well as in agriculture and industry. *Clinical pharmacology* is the study of various drugs and their effects on people. It includes the study of how they work, how they interact with other drugs, and their therapeutic effects on diseases and disease processes.

As a health office professional, you need a basic knowledge of pharmacology. You will often be the intermediary between the patient and the physician, the patient and the pharmacist, and the pharmacist and the physician, ordering new prescriptions, dealing with repeats and renewals, and passing on information. Patients will have questions about their prescriptions and about over-the-counter (OTC) drugs, vitamins, supplements, and herbal medications. You should be able to respond to basic questions knowledgeably; more importantly, you need to know when to direct the patient elsewhere for answers.

You need to understand the components of a prescription, the information needed for renewals, which medications the physician may order over the telephone, which require a faxed or written script, and when the patient should see the physician about medications. In both the hospital and the health office, you need to be familiar with the more common medications, their spelling, and classification. Table 7.1 lists some drugs commonly prescribed in Canada. It is also important to know what time of day drugs should be taken, which medications should be taken with food, and which should be taken on an empty stomach. In the hospital or long-term care facility you will be responsible for transcribing medication orders accurately to the appropriate medication administration record. You must understand the terminology that accompanies the medication order. You also need to understand the pharmacist's role in your setting and how to work effectively with the pharmacist.

LO1 THE PHARMACIST

Pharmacists are the experts in drug information. A pharmacist is a health professional who is trained in the art of preparing and dispensing drugs. Licensing standards for pharmacists are set by the provinces and territories but are similar across the country. Pharmacists must graduate from a university program recognized by their governing body and must have practical experience. Provincial and territorial regulatory authorities grant pharmacists licences, assess the competency of pharmacists, and ensure public safety. Pharmacists dispense drugs in response to prescriptions

TABLE 7.1   Some drugs commonly prescribed in Canada

acetaminophen and oxycodone (Percocet)	glyburide (Diabeta)	olanzapine (Zyprexa)
alendronate (Fosamax)	heparin	omeprazole (Losec)
amlodipine (Norvasc)	hydrochlorothiazide/HCT (Hydrodiuril)	oxycodone (OxyNEO; replaces OxyContin)
amoxicillin (Amoxil)	hydromorphone	paroxetine (Paxil)
atorvastatin (Lipitor)	hydroxyzine (Atarax)	phenytoin (Dilantin)
azithromycin (Zithromax)	insulin preparations (Humulin, Novolin)	pioglitazone (Actos)
budesonide (Pulmicort, Symbicort)	ipratropium bromide (Atrovent; also solution for nebulizer)	pravastatin (Pravachol)
celecoxib (Celebrex)	irbesartan (Avapro)	prednisone (Winpred, numerous generics for many of these drugs)
cephalexin (Keflex)	ketorolac (Toradol)	pregabalin (Lyrica)
ciprofloxacin (Cipro)	lansoprazole (Prevacid)	propranolol hydrochloride (Inderal)
citalopram (Celexa)	levofloxacin (Levaquin)	raloxifene (Evista)
clopidogrel (Plavix)	levothyroxine (Synthroid, Eltroxin)	ramipril (Altace)
codeine (comes in 15, 30, & 60 mg tabs)	loratadine (Claritin)	ranitidine (Zantac)
diazepam (Valium)	lorazepam (Ativan)	Rh (D) immunoglobulin IV/IM (WinRho SDF)
digoxin (Lanoxin, Toloxin)	losartan (Cozaar)	risedronate (Actonel)
dimenhydrinate (Gravol)	losartan and hydrochlorothiazide (Hyzaar)	risperidone (Risperdal)
donepezil (Aricept)	low molecular weight heparin (LMWH)	rosuvastatin (Crestor)
enalapril (Vasotec)	meloxicam (mobicox)	salbutamol inhalation (Ventolin)
escitalopram (Cipralex)	meperidine (Demerol)	sertraline (Zoloft)
esomeprazole (Nexium)	metformin (Glucophage)	sulphamethoxazole-trimethoprim (Septra, Bactrim)
ethinyl estradiol and levonorgestrel (Min-Ovral, Alesse, Triphasil)	metoprolol (Lopresor)	tamsulosin (Flomax)
fentanyl patch	morphine (MS Contin)	terbinafine (Lamisil)
fexofenadine (Allegra)	naproxen (Anaprox, Naprosyn)	Tylenol #3 (acetaminophen/ codeine)
fluoxetine (Prozac)	nifedipine (Adalat)	venlafaxine (Effexor)
fluticasone and salmetrol (Advair, MDI)	nitrofurantoin (Macrobid)	warfarin (Coumadin, Taro-Warfarin)
fluticasone oral inhalation (Flovent)	nitroglycerin transdermal (Nitro-Dur, Minitran, Trinipatch)	terbinafine (Lamisil)
fosinopril (Monopril)		zyloprim (Allopurinol)
furosemide (Lasix)		

written by physicians, dentists, or other designated health providers. They are also an important resource for patients, physicians, and other health professionals. Although most medications are accompanied by explanatory literature, patients often do not understand the sheet or seek more information. Pharmacists will answer their questions, simplify written explanations, and provide more detail, as required. Patients may be confused about when to take a medication, whether it will interact with other medications they are taking, and its side effects. Pharmacists can reinforce physicians' information. They will also give advice about OTC drugs and herbal products. Medications are one of the fastest-changing components in health care: As fast as some are removed from the market, new ones are approved and introduced to the market. Even if a drug has been on the market for many years, there is still much new information about potential uses, adverse effects, and actions on the body that is learned each year.

A pharmacist will review the patient's medication profile (based largely on the pharmacy's own records, the patient, and information from the doctor) when filling a prescription and will notify the doctor of potential adverse interactions or of more effective medication. The pharmacist is often the first to pick up on misuse or abuse of prescribed medications and, depending on the situation, will either speak to the patient or notify the physician. Some provinces will pay the pharmacist to complete basic and advanced medication reviews for specific groups of patients following specific timelines (e.g., annually or biannually).

The pharmacist will advise the physician of new medications, more economical alternatives, changes in dosage recommendations, and alerts about medications. He or she collaborates with all levels of health professionals to effectively and safely manage patients' medications and will act as an information resource for you, clarifying medication orders in the hospital and supplementing information in the health office.

Emerging Responsibilities for the Pharmacist

Currently, the scope of practice for pharmacists is expanding across Canada. To assume most of the extended responsibilities the pharmacist must have special training. Added responsibilities include giving flu shots and other immunizations (in Canada, British Columbia, Alberta, and Nova Scotia are leading this initiative), emergency prescribing (of previously prescribed medication), offering pharmaceutical opinions (e.g., advice on an existing or potential drug-related problem as well as suggesting possible interventions), ordering lab tests (to manage a patient's response to drug therapy), authorizing refills (during a physician's absence or for individuals in long-term care facilities or with chronic diseases), prescribing certain medications, and making adaptations to prescriptions (e.g., dose, duration). Pharmacists receive special training for giving immunizations. The other responsibilities require collaboration with the patient's doctor(s) and depend on inclusive electronic medical records (EMR) access. As well, pharmacists can refuse to fill a legally completed prescription. This would occur if the prescribed treatment is deemed inappropriate by the pharmacist based on information available at the pharmacy (and would require consultation with the physician). Saskatchewan pharmacists were the first in Canada to receive provincial payment for assessing approved "minor ailment conditions" that result in a drug prescription. Currently approved treatable minor conditions include acne, insect bites, and cold sores.

Other members of the pharmaceutical team are *pharmacy technicians* and *pharmacy assistants*. Both work under the direction of a pharmacist. Assistants package medication and assist with other dispensary duties and clerical functions. Technicians have greater responsibilities and more extensive training, usually a one- or two-year postsecondary program. They procure supplies, maintain inventories, and help dispense and distribute medications. Regulated technicians can independently perform and sign off on the filling of a prescription. A pharmacist is required to sign off on its therapeutic appropriateness.

L02 DRUGS: AN EXPLANATION

A drug may be defined as "a chemical substance that affects the processes of the mind or body, and any chemical compound used in the diagnosis, treatment, or prevention of disease or other abnormal condition."[1] In common speech, *drugs* are sometimes thought of as illegal substances, and drugs taken for health reasons are more commonly referred to as *medicines* or *medications*.

Drug Sources

Drugs are derived from a variety of sources.

Plants   Much of the current knowledge about drugs came from herbalists, who used plants and herbs in years gone by. They knew through trial and error what herbs, plants, and plant derivatives were effective for various conditions. We use many of their concepts and discoveries in conventional medicine today. Drugs can be obtained from fungi and from the leaves, seeds, sap, stems, fruit, and roots of various plants. The willow tree, for example, contains a component originally used in the production of Aspirin. Digitalis is an extract from the leaf of the purple foxglove. Morphine is derived from a gummy substance extracted from the seed pod of the opium poppy. Other products of plants include **fixed oils**, such as castor oil, and **volatile oils**, such as peppermint and cloves.

fixed oils (also called base or carrier oils) oils, extracted primarily from plants, that do not evaporate.

volatile oils oils, extracted primarily from plants, that evaporate

Animal Sources   Animals are a natural source for some medications, such as hormones. Originally, insulin was obtained from the pancreases of slaughtered animals, primarily pigs and cattle. Some estrogen is obtained from the urine of pregnant mares. (Synthetic and plant-based forms of estrogen are also available.)

Minerals   Minerals also supply of wide variety of natural drugs, such as potassium and iron supplements, milk of magnesia (a commonly used antacid and laxative derived from magnesium), and lithium carbonate (a salt used to treat bipolar disorder).

Semi-synthetic   The term *synthesis* means that something is chemically reproduced. A semi-synthetic drug results when a drug from a natural source is combined with synthetically produced compounds to alter the effect of the medication. The net result of such combinations is a single new chemical formed from some reaction between those ingredients. For example, heroin is a semi-synthetic variant of morphine.

Synthetic   Synthetic drugs are completely formulated in the laboratory. Some are produced using chemicals and others by copying genetic activity in a living organism. Examples of synthetic drugs include diazepam (Valium), acetylsalicylic acid, ibuprofen, and fluoxetine (Prozac). Synthetic forms of insulin were introduced in 1981. Today, there is widespread use of insulin produced from genetically modified bacteria and yeast.

---

[1] *Miller-Keene Encyclopedia Dictionary of Medicine, Nursing and Allied Health*, 6th ed. Philadelphia: W.B. Saunders, 1997.

Drug Names

A single drug can have up to four names. Each refers to the same drug but from a slightly different perspective. These names are

- chemical,
- generic,
- trade, and
- botanical.

Chemical   The chemical name of a drug represents its exact formula. For example, the chemical name of bupropion (marketed as Wellbutrin or Zyban) is 1-(3Chlorophenyl)-2-[(1,1-dimethylethyl)amino]-1-propanone. The familiar acetaminophen (Tylenol) is N-(4-hydroxyphenyl) acetanamide. Not surprisingly, these names are seldom used, except by pharmacists and manufacturers in the context of chemical interactions and perhaps in research.

Generic   The generic name of the drug is the nonproprietary name given to a medication, or the official name assigned to it. Generic names for new compounds are given out by an international body to ensure that no two products have the same generic name. The name is much simpler than the chemical name and is not owned by anyone; it does not have protection by copyright. A pharmaceutical company can manufacture a drug (prescription or OTC) under its generic name and put its own trademark on it. Generic names are always spelled in lowercase. Some examples of generic names are

- acetaminophen (one trade name is Tylenol),
- digoxin (trade names are Lanoxin, Toloxin), and
- warfarin (one trade name is Coumadin).

Trade Name   When a pharmaceutical company develops a new drug, it applies to the government for a patent, which gives it the right to sell the drug without competition for a designated period, usually 20 years. (However, it takes roughly 10 years from the time a pharmaceutical company applies for a patent until the drug is approved for use, reducing the effective patent life of the drug to 10 years.) This system is designed to allow the company to recover its investment in researching and developing the drug and to encourage continued research and development. Most manufacturers select a proprietary (trade) or brand name for a drug once it has been approved for sale. This name receives a registered trademark and is, in most cases, legally protected forever. A brand name may be registered only in certain countries. Anyone can reproduce a drug once the patent has expired but cannot use the original company's trade name. The second company can manufacture the drug under its generic name or can apply for a trademark for a name of its own choosing. It takes a manufacturer two to three years to develop a generic, chemically identical copy of a patented drug at a cost of about $1 million.

Trade names are always capitalized. Often, the trade names are more familiar than the generic name: people are more likely to have heard of Valium than of diazepam or of Tylenol than of acetaminophen. However, the use of generic names is encouraged over trade names to avoid confusion.

Generic drugs are generally less expensive than brand name drugs, partly because the producer of the generic drug is covering only the costs of manufacturing, not of research, development, and extensive advertising. For example, generic acetaminophen is less expensive than Tylenol. Generic ibuprofen is less expensive than Advil, which is the trade name under which one manufacturer produces the same medication. Some companies claim that the trade name drug is of better quality than a clone with a generic name, and some of these claims may be valid. The exact ingredients may differ, resulting in an altered absorption and excretion rate and a slightly different therapeutic effect.

Even when a medication is prescribed by its trade name, the pharmacist may be legally obligated to fill the prescription with a less expensive generic form of the medication unless the doctor or patient specifies "no substitution." If a drug plan is contributing to cover some of the costs of the prescription, they may only pay for the cost of a generic product. The patient might have to pay for the difference if a particular brand name product is requested.

Interchangeability in Ontario is regulated by provincial legislation. Interchangeability allows the pharmacist some autonomy in choosing which brand to dispense. The ODB (Ontario Drug Benefit) Formulary/CDI (Comparative Drug Index) identifies which products are interchangeable. If a product is not listed as interchangeable, the generic version cannot be dispensed in place of the brand prescribed without first receiving the approval of the prescriber. This applies in all provinces and territories.

Botanical   This is the name used to refer to the natural substance or substances that a drug is made of. An example of this is *Digitalis purpurea*—herbs from which digitalis is derived.

L03 DRUGS AND THE LAW

The regulation and control of drugs in Canada is achieved jointly by the federal and provincial and territorial governments.[2] The Health Products and Food Branch of Health Canada is responsible for drug quality, safety, and efficacy. It regulates the manufacture and importation of drugs for sale in Canada, as well as their distribution, including conditions of sale. The federal Food and Drugs Act and other regulations control the testing and introduction of new drugs to the Canadian market. Federal legislation covers all drugs and chemical substances, legal and illegal. Provinces and territories also have regulations governing the dispensing and control of medications.

In response to concerns about inconsistencies among provinces and territories, in 1995 the National Association of Pharmacy Regulatory Authorities (NAPRA) proposed a national drug scheduling prototype to standardize regulations across the country. Provinces and territories are in various stages of adopting these regulations. NAPRA's system sets out three schedules, explained in the next section.

The federal government issues standards and regulations, under the Controlled Drugs and Substances Act (CDSA), that govern the use of controlled substances in Canada. Certain drugs are defined as **controlled drugs** under the CDSA. These are typically drugs with a high potential for addiction and abuse, often narcotic analgesics. Special rules, discussed later in this chapter, apply to prescribing, administering, handling, and storing these drugs.

controlled drugs drugs defined by federal law that special rules apply to because they are liable to be abused.

L04 DISPENSING DRUGS

There are two methods of dispensing drugs: by prescription and over the counter.

Prescription Drugs

Federal laws make drugs that are dangerous, powerful, or habit forming illegal, except if prescribed by a licensed physician or other qualified health provider who is to monitor the patient's condition. (These drugs correspond to NAPRA's Schedule I.)

---

[2] Material for this section has been contributed by Steve Chapman, author of *Drug Control in Canada: A Chemical and Legislative Compendium*. Toronto: Isomer Design, 1993.

A prescription is an order written and signed by the practitioner for a particular drug to be dispensed to a particular patient.

The pharmacist can dispense most controlled drugs only with a written and physically signed prescription or a signed faxed prescription that can be verified as originating from the prescriber. The use of fax technology by prescribers to transmit new prescriptions to a pharmacy is now commonplace. A pharmacist can receive any type of prescription from a prescriber by fax, including a straight narcotic or controlled drug.

A prescription is usually filled by the pharmacist and given or delivered to the patient. In some cases, doctors ask the pharmacist to prepare ahead of time medication packs, which contain limited amounts of the medication and corresponding directions. They are then used when a pharmacist is not available to dispense drugs, for example, at night in an emergency department in a smaller hospital. A doctor may prescribe a pain medication and give the patient a night pack to last until the next day when the pharmacy is open.

Over-the-Counter Medications

OTC medications are those considered safe for individuals to take without the specific advice of a physician. They are available in pharmacies and a variety of retail outlets. Remember that even OTC drugs can be harmful if used incorrectly. For this reason, most provinces and territories have categorized these drugs to provide some control over access. Note that because some private insurance plans cover only prescribed drugs, physicians will sometimes prescribe some medications, even though they are available over the counter.

Pharmacy Only: Restricted Access   Drugs in this category are available only from a pharmacist (though no prescription is required) and are kept behind the counter. Use of the drug may delay recognition or mask the symptoms of serious disease. The drug may cause important adverse reactions, including allergies, or interact with other drugs, foods, or disease states that cannot be adequately addressed through product labelling. Intervention by the pharmacist is necessary to assess patient risk to prevent such problems for an individual patient through interpretation and clarification of labelling. These drugs correspond with Schedule II of the NAPRA guide.

Pharmacy Only: Under Supervision   Other medications are available only in pharmacies and are sold in a self-serve section of the pharmacy. The initial need for these drugs is normally identified by the patient, physician, or pharmacist, but chronic, recurrent, or subsequent therapy can be monitored by the pharmacist. The availability of the pharmacist to provide advice can promote appropriate use of the drug, and the pharmacist can direct the patient to a practitioner for assessment if the treatment period has been inappropriate or the therapy has been ineffective. Medications in this category include those that could present risks to certain people if used without adequate knowledge. These drugs correspond to Schedule III of the NAPRA guide.

Sold Anywhere: No Restrictions   Other medications can be sold in any retail outlet—corner stores, department stores, gift shops—without any professional supervision. ASA (acetylsalicylic acid), acetaminophen, antacids, and other common drugs are in this category. These drugs are considered "unscheduled" in NAPRA's guide.

Patient Education   Most OTC preparations have instructions and indications for use clearly outlined on the package label, but additional patient education better ensures correct and safe usage. Any medication can be harmful if used incorrectly. Nonprescription medications can interact badly with prescription medications the patient may be taking, with foods, or with disease states.

Patient information becomes even more important as a number of former prescription drugs have been granted OTC status. Examples include vaginal creams, such as Monistat for yeast infections; Benadryl for allergic reactions; and the anti-inflammatory Motrin. Some drugs, such as ranitidine (Zantac), used for stomach problems, are available at lower doses than those prescribed by a doctor. There is always the danger that a person who needs to see the doctor will instead self-treat with OTC medications. A pharmacist can provide advice to promote appropriate use or can direct the patient to a practitioner for assessment. Patients must be encouraged to have any persistent problems checked out medically.

L05 CLASSIFICATION OF DRUGS

Drugs can be classified by function (how they act), by effects, or by body system. Because a medication may be used for more than one purpose and on more than one body system, categories often overlap.

Classification of Drugs by Use

Desired effects or uses of drugs include the following:

- Therapeutic
- Diagnostic
- Curative
- Replacement
- Prophylactic

Therapeutic Drugs   Therapeutic medications—whether prescribed or OTC—are taken to relieve symptoms. They are used to treat a wide range of conditions from life-threatening ones to minor ailments, such as a cold or a headache. Many of the drugs you deal with will fall into this category, especially in the office setting.

Diagnostic Drugs   Diagnostic drugs are used to perform diagnostic tests. Examples would include the barium in a barium swallow or the contrast media used in nuclear medicine.

Curative Drugs   Curative drugs are given to overcome a disease, infection, or other conditions. Antibiotics are a common example.

Replacement Drugs   Replacement drugs are taken to "replace" a hormone or other normally present substance that the human body can no longer produce. For example, people whose thyroid glands do not function well, or who have had the thyroid gland removed, take l-thyroxine (Synthroid, Eltroxin) to replace the thyroxine they lack. People with diabetes may take insulin to replace the insulin their pancreas cannot produce. Female hormones, such as estrogen and progesterone, are other examples.

Prophylactic Drugs   This category of medications is given either to prevent a condition or to decrease the severity of a condition. Examples of prophylactic drugs are immunizations, such as the measles, mumps, rubella (MMR) vaccine.

Classification by Action or Function

- *Adrenergic.* Causes blood vessels to constrict and augments the strength and rate of the heart and opens airways. Used for such conditions as bronchitis, asthma, and various allergies. Examples include epinephrine, adrenalin, salbutamol (Ventolin), and xylometazoline (Otrivin).

- *Analgesic*. Relieves pain. Analgesics include controlled or narcotic drugs, such as morphine sulphate (MS Contin), and non-narcotic drugs, such as acetaminophen (Tylenol, Anacin, Atasol, Tempra).

- *Anesthetic*. Reduces or obliterates pain by reducing sensation. Can be given for local or systemic effect. When given locally, the patient is conscious. General anesthetics put the patient to sleep, such as during major surgical procedures. Local anesthetics include lidocaine (Xylocaine) and bupivacaine (Marcaine).

- *Antacid*. Reduces acidity in the stomach and gastrointestinal (GI) tract. May be used for dyspepsia or heartburn. Examples include aluminum hydroxide and magnesium carbonate (Maalox, Diovol).

- *Anxiolytic or anti-anxiety*. Reduces stress levels and feelings of anxiety. Examples include diazepam (Valium), alprazolam (Xanax), and lorazepam (Ativan).

- *Anti-arrhythmic*. Controls abnormal heartbeats, known as arrhythmias, which affect the electrical conduction of the heart. Examples include amiodarone (Cordarone), verapamil (Isoptin), and propafenone (Rythmol).

- *Antibiotic*. Given to fight bacterial infections. Drugs that destroy bacteria in a person's body (Apo-Pen VK, ciprofloxacin [Cipro]) are known as bactericidal; those that inhibit the growth of bacteria, such as tetracyclines, are known as *bacteriostatic*. Erythromycin can be cidal or static depending on the concentration and the bacteria susceptibility.

- *Anti-cholinergic*. Blocks the neurotransmitter acetylcholine. Blocking this transmitter can cause constipation, dry mouth, and dry eyes. Medications that increase acetylcholine action are used in the treatment of Alzheimer's disease and dementia and can have side effects of diarrhea and excessive salivation. Examples include benztropine mesylate (Cogentin). Other drugs, such as antihistamines and anti-depressants, also have anti-cholinergic properties.

- *Anti-coagulant* Commonly called blood thinners these drugs are given to prevent blood clots. Warfarin (Coumadin) is an example of an oral anti-coagulant. It is most commonly used to reduce the risk of stroke in atrial fibrillation. Heparin and LMWH are most often used following surgery. The NOACS (new oral anti-coagulants, which include Xarelto-rivaroxaban) are often used post-surgery (e.g., after a knee replacement). These drugs should not be taken with ASA and certain herbal medications, except under the specific direction of a physician.

- *Anti-convulsant*. Given to prevent, control, or relieve seizure activity, such as in an individual who is epileptic. Examples include carbamazepine (Tegretol) and phenytoin (Dilantin).

- *Anti-depressant*: Used in the treatment and control of clinical depression. Examples include bupropion (Wellbutrin), amitriptyline (Elavil), fluoxetine (Prozac), and venlafaxine (Effexor). These must *not* be taken with St. John's Wort, a herbal anti-depressant, because of the potential for serious interaction.

- *Anti-diabetic/Anti-hyperglycemic*. Used to control diabetes mellitus. Insulin is a parenteral hypoglycemic used for type I or insulin-dependent diabetes; oral anti-hyperglycemics, used for the initial stages of type II or non-insulin-dependent diabetes, include glyburide (Diabeta) and repaglinide (Gluconorm), which increase insulin secretion. Anti-diabetic medications have different mechanisms. Some anti-hyperglycemics stimulate the pancreas to produce more insulin. Other medications, such as metformin (Glucophage), pioglitazone (Actos), and rosiglitazone

(Avandia), work to improve the body's use of insulin and decrease the amount of glucose released by the liver.

■ *Anti-diarrheal.* Given to stop or control diarrhea. Perhaps the most common of these today is loperamide (Imodium).

■ *Anti-emetic.* Given to control or prevent nausea and vomiting. Dimenhydrinate (Gravol) is often given to prevent nausea after surgery. People also take it to prevent motion sickness.

■ *Anti-fungal.* Used to treat fungal infections, either locally (e.g., athlete's foot) or systemically. Examples of topical anti-fungals include miconazole nitrate (Monistat) and clotrimazole (Canesten). Oral anti-fungals include terbinafine (Lamisil) and ketoconazole (Nizoral).

■ *Antihistamine.* Used to relieve allergies. The drug blocks histamine, which is released when a person has an allergic reaction. A common side effect is drowsiness, although there are antihistamines on the market that avoid this side effect. Examples include diphenhydramine hydrochloride (Benadryl) and loratadine (Claritin).

■ *Anti-hypertensive.* Taken to lower and control high blood pressure. There are a wide variety of anti-hypertensives on the market with different modes of action. Some of these medications act to impede vasoconstriction or to cause vasodilation, increasing the ease of blood flow in the body. Others slow the heart rate and decrease the force of the heart's contraction. Others act on a hormone produced by the kidney called angiotensin that affects blood pressure. Examples of anti-hypertensives include propranolol (Inderal), lisinopril (Zestril), amlodipine (Norvasc), and ramipril (Altace).

■ *Anti-inflammatory.* Controls various inflammatory processes in the body, such as joint inflammation and pain. NSAIDs, or nonsteroidal anti-inflammatory agents, include ibuprofen (Advil) and naproxen (Anaprox). Prednisone, a steroid, also has anti-inflammatory properties, but because of the high potential for adverse effects, especially with long-term use, it is used only for serious conditions.

■ *Anti-neoplastic.* Used in the treatment of some forms of cancer. Examples include cyclophosphamide (Procytox).

■ *Anti-pyretic.* Reduces fever. Examples include ASA (Aspirin) and acetaminophen (Tylenol).

■ *Anti-spasmodic.* Relieves muscle spasms (e.g. in the lower back) that result from either injury or disease. An example is Robaxin (methocarbamol) for back muscle spasms.

■ *Anti-tussive.* Controls or relieves coughing. Very few anti-tussives will totally eliminate a persistent cough, but they usually provide enough relief to allow the patient to sleep or rest. Many of these medications are Schedule I or II medications. An example is a drug containing codeine or dextromethorphan, such as Benylin (Delsym) or Novahistamine DM Expectorant, which combines guaifenesin and pseudoephedrine. Some common pediatric anti-tussives containing these ingredients have been reformulated or withdrawn from the market altogether following an American Academy of Pediatrics study showing that many children were being accidently given too much medication by well-meaning caregivers (including parents), resulting in overdoses and serious side effects.

■ *Bronchodilators.* Used primarily to treat chronic obstructive pulmonary disease (COPD) and asthma, these medications cause the bronchial passages to relax and ease breathing. An example is salbutamol (Ventolin).

- *Cardiogenics*. Strengthens the heart muscle and heartbeat. Effective in some patients in relieving the symptoms of congestive heart failure. Digoxin (Lanoxin) is an example.

- *Cathartic*. Another broad term for laxatives, such as Magnolax, which combines magnesium hydroxide and mineral oil emulsion, magnesium hydroxide (milk of magnesia), and bisacodyl (Dulcolax).

- *Contraceptive*. Used for birth control. Most common are oral contraceptives ("the pill"), such as Triphasil and Min-Ovral, which combine progesterone and estrogen. Various vaginal creams and suppositories also fall into this category.

- *Decongestant*. Used to alleviate sinus and nasal congestion. These medications act by reducing swelling of the nasal passages. Some of these drugs are also controlled, or kept behind the counter in pharmacies, because they contain pseudoephedrine, which is a precursor for the illegal manufacture of methamphetamine. Some examples of these medications include xylometazoline (Otrivin) and pseudoephedrine (Sudafed). Patients should be cautioned that nasal sprays and eye drops should be used for three to seven days only, depending on the medication. Longer use can cause a rebound reaction, which means that stuffiness and swelling can actually increase as the blood vessels enlarge even more than they did before taking the medication. Oral decongestants do not cause the rebound reaction.

- *Diuretic*. Aids in the excretion of excessive body fluid, which can relieve symptoms of hypertension and congestive heart failure. An example is furosemide (Lasix).

- *Emetic*. Used to induce vomiting, such as in the case of a drug overdose. Ipecac syrup is an example.

- *Hormone*. Used primarily to replace hormones that the body can no longer produce. Insulin (Humulin, Novolin) and levothyroxine (Eltroxin, Synthroid) are examples. Hormones are also used to treat symptoms of menopause and in individuals who are seeking sex changes.

- *Hypnotic*. Used as sleeping pills or for their sedative effects. Most of these drugs are controlled. Examples include zopiclone (Imovane) and temazepam (Restoril).

- *Immune system modulating agents*. Alters the body's immune system. These drugs are used in the control and treatment of certain autoimmune diseases, such as rheumatoid arthritis and systemic lupus erythematosus, in which the body attacks its own tissues and organs. They are also used to deal with transplant rejection. Examples are prednisone (Apo-prednisone) and methotrexate.

- *Miotic*. Used by ophthalmologists and optometrists to constrict the pupil of the eye. Pilocarpine is an example. It is also used to treat glaucoma.

- *Mydriatic*. Dilates the muscles of the eye, such as for an eye examination. Some are long lasting (up to 24 hours). The patient becomes very photosensitive and should not drive. An example is atropine.

- *Narcotic*. Acts on the central nervous system, causing pain relief. In large doses, it can depress the respiratory system. These drugs have a high potential for addiction and abuse and are usually controlled. Examples include hydromorphone (Dilaudid), and OxyNEO, the drug replacing painkiller OxyContin in Canada.

- *Purgative*. More powerful than routine laxatives, these drugs are often taken by patients preparing for diagnostic tests, such as a colonoscopy. Sodium phosphate (Fleet enema, Phosphosoda) is an example.

- *Vasodilator*. Causes the blood vessels to dilate, lowering blood pressure. An example is amlodipine (Norvasc).

- *Vasopressor.* Induces vasoconstriction and raises blood pressure. May be used for patients in hemorrhagic shock. Examples include epinephrine (adrenalin) and mitodrine, which is used to correct hypotension in people with Parkinson's disease.

Classification by Scope of Action

Drugs can be described as local, systemic, or cumulative on the basis of the scope of action.

Local A local, or topical, effect occurs when the drug is stored and produces an effect only at the site of application. A local anesthetic, for example, reduces sensation in the body area to be worked on. Creams used for a rash, such as a steroid cream, would be considered local.

Systemic Systemically acting drugs circulate in the bloodstream to produce a general effect, such as a central nervous system stimulus or depressant. Most oral drugs have a **systemic** effect. Some drugs are ingested and carried by the circulatory system to the entire body but affect primarily one area or one body system. Some drugs are stored preferentially in certain areas to produce a desired effect. For example, antibiotics used for a genitourinary infection might affect the renal system more than other systems.

systemic circulating through the bloodstream to produce a general effect on the body.

Cumulative A cumulative effect happens when the drug accumulates in the body faster than it can be metabolized or excreted and exerts a greater effect than the initial dose. These heightened concentrations can cause drug toxicity, damaging the kidneys, liver, or other organs. Most drugs have a therapeutic window of blood levels in which they work most efficiently and safely. What varies is how wide that safe range is. Gentamicin, for example, has a narrow therapeutic window and has to be carefully dosed and monitored. Higher levels cause damage to the balance and auditory organs and kidneys. In contrast, amoxicillin and ampicillin can be given in a wide range of doses, depending on the severity of the infection, without the patient developing toxicity.

There are times when a cumulative effect is desirable. Sometimes a "loading dose" of an antibiotic is given at the onset of an infection to achieve therapeutic blood levels quickly. For example, azithromycin (Zithromax) might be prescribed at 500 mg day 1, then 250 mg daily days 2 to 5.

Classification by Route of Administration

Drugs may be administered via many different routes (listed later) and can be manufactured in different forms for a number of reasons. Some drugs can be given in only one way. For example, insulin is ineffective given orally and must be injected or given intravenously. When more than one route is possible, the choice is determined by the action the doctor wants—for example, an intravenous medication may (not always) take effect faster than an oral medication—and by how the patient is able to take it. For example, the oral route is unsuitable for a vomiting patient. Medications given intravenously or by injection start acting faster and are therefore best for medical emergencies, such as a heart attack, or for relief of intense pain. When transcribing medication orders in the hospital, make sure that the route of the medication is entered accurately.

Topical/Transdermal Route Medication may be applied to the body surface to be absorbed through the skin or the mucous membranes. The effects may be local or systemic. For example, a steroid cream may be applied to treat a local dermatitis or an antibiotic cream to treat a localized infection. A hormone patch or a cream absorbed through the skin can have a systemic effect in hormone replacement therapy. A fentanyl patch applied to the skin can give systemic pain control. Patches are commonly used for heart medication. The recommended sites of application are important and application to nonrecommended sites alter the absorption and action.

Transdermal Patch   A transdermal patch consists of bandage fabric that contains medication. An adhesive outer layer holds the patch onto a selected spot on the skin surface. The structure of the patch facilitates sustained and controlled delivery of the medication. Patches are commonly used for heart medication, pain control, motion sickness, and smoking cessation. It is important that patients understand the proper use of the patch. For example, to prevent overdose, any existing patches should be removed before applying a new patch or patches. Patches usually have specific storage instructions.

Ointments and Lotions   An ointment is usually an emulsion of semisolid consistency used externally. Most ointments use lard, petrolatum, white wax, or paraffin for a base. The other ingredients depend on the use of the ointment. Lotions are ingredients contained in a water base that are normally patted on. Calamine lotion used to treat itching is an example. A liniment is in a liquid base but contains more oil than a lotion. Compresses are applied on a pad of gauze or other material.

Inhalation Route   Drugs may be administered into the airway to be absorbed through the mucous membranes of the respiratory system. This route is used primarily to treat conditions of the respiratory tract, such as asthma and COPD. A variety of inhalation delivery devices, called puffers or metered dose inhalers (MDI), dispense a suspension by one of two different delivery systems. MDIs are propellant driven. The device will dispense a specific dose of the medication each time the patient activates it. A dry powder device relies on the patient to forcefully pull or inhale the drug from the device into the airway. Spiriva is an example of a medication in the powdered form. Medication can also be delivered by air or oxygen using a mask device with a reservoir for the medication that is diluted in a vehicle, such as normal saline (salt water). Sprays are often used for their local effects on the nose, throat, and lungs. An example is xylometazoline hydrochloride (Otrivin), used as a nasal decongestant.

otic via the ear.

Otic Route   Medications may be placed directly in the ear (the **otic** route) for local ear infections, such as otitis externa (infection of the outer ear canal, also referred to sometimes as swimmer's ear). They are usually in the form of drops, either in solutions or suspensions. Oil is sometimes carefully instilled into the ear canal to soften wax that is plugging the canal.

Ophthalmic Route   Eye drops or ointments are used to treat a number of conditions, including glaucoma. Antibiotics in the form of eye drops are applied via the **ophthalmic** route as a precaution after laser surgery.

ophthalmic relating to the eye.

Nasal Route   Medications may be sprayed or inhaled via the nostrils. Atrovent is a decongestant spray used for rhinitis. Systemic effects may also be achieved; pain medications, such as butorphanol tartrate (Stadol), may be given by nasal spray. Flonase is a topical anti-inflammatory steroid for treating seasonal allergic rhinitis.

Sublingual or Buccal Route *Sublingual* means under the tongue, and *buccal* means between the cheek and the gum. This is a relatively quick-acting route and does not necessitate swallowing. Examples of medications designed to be absorbed under the tongue include the tranquilizer lorazepam (Ativan) and nitroglycerin, which is used to relieve angina.

Vaginal Route Suppositories or creams are applied vaginally to treat local yeast or bacterial infections. Prostaglandin E is administered vaginally to induce labour in pregnant women who are well past their due date or who, for various reasons, need to deliver early. A variety of contraceptive creams and foams are also designed to be administered vaginally.

Rectal Route Rectal suppositories dissolve and are absorbed by the lining of the intestine. The effects may be systemic or local. Suppositories are rocket- or oval-shaped to ease insertion. They melt at body temperature, and the medication is absorbed into the bloodstream. Suppositories are useful when a patient cannot take drugs by other means. For example, a drug to combat nausea may be given as a suppository if a patient is likely to vomit an oral medication. The effect of this would be systemic. A suppository such as hydrocortisone for hemorrhoids would have a local effect. Enemas for evacuating the bowel are also administered rectally. Another example is the use of 5-ASA products to treat inflammatory bowel disease at the distal end of the colon.

Oral Route The most common means of administering medication is oral—by mouth. Oral medications are absorbed by the gastrointestinal system and can be ingested in a variety of forms. The effects of oral medication are influenced by a number of factors, such as the characteristics of the medication, the motility of the bowel, and the presence or absence of food in the gastrointestinal (GI) tract. Medications given orally are manufactured to achieve desired effects.

Pills *Pills*, to most people, mean any type of solid oral medication, whether it is a tablet, caplet, or capsule. Historically, pills are pressed, usually round, solid medications. Many of them are *scored*, or marked, so that they can be easily divided to give half or quarter doses.

Pills are difficult to swallow for many people, who find they seem to stick in the throat. Doctors may recommend that pills be crushed and taken with something like jam or apple sauce. This is contraindicated for some pills, as they may lose effectiveness or harm the patient; the pharmacist would identify which pills should not be crushed. Many older people take calcium, and you may hear some refer to the large pills as "horse pills." Calcium comes in more easily ingested forms.

Enteric-coated medications are covered with a smooth coating that prevents the medication from dissolving until it is further down the GI tract, bypassing the stomach. This is useful for medications that irritate the GI tract, especially in individuals with a history of ulcers or gastrointestinal problems. Enteric coating is also designed to release the medication at a specific target, for example, Asacol for inflammatory bowel disease. ASA is commonly enteric coated. Enteric coating also protects some medications from destruction by stomach acid and allows release further along the GI tract where absorption can occur.

Sustained Release Medications of various shapes and forms may also be encased in or mixed with substances that cause a delay in the active absorption of the medication to ensure slow but sustained action. This allows once-daily formulations, which enhance adherence to therapy in chronic conditions, such as hypertension. An example is metoprolol SR (Lopresor SR). It also allows for sustained pain control and prevention of the emergence of pain (Hydromorph Contin).

Caplets   A caplet is usually an oval-shaped solid medication, either with an outer coating or compressed. Some people find them easier to swallow than tablets.

Capsules   A capsule is essentially a medication in a powdered or liquid form encased in a hard or soft shell or outer coating, usually a form of gelatin. Capsules mask the taste and odour of medications. Some people also find capsules easier to swallow. Many time-release medications come in capsule form. Controlled-release capsules contain pellets of a drug in a protective coating that dissolve slowly in the intestinal tract. Release time of the medication can be spread over hours.

Liquid   Many drugs are available in liquid form. Any medication that is not solid or semisolid is considered to be a liquid preparation. The main advantage of liquid preparations is ease of ingestion, especially for children or anyone who has difficulty swallowing. They may be ordered or referred to as a *suspension*, meaning that small particles are suspended in the liquid base. Suspensions must be shaken before ingestion. An *emulsion*, which consists of droplets of oil and water mixed together, must also be shaken vigorously before use.

An *elixir* (ordered as such) contains alcohol, sugar, water, and sometimes an ingredient to flavour the medication. Syrups are a concentrated solution of sugar in water and do not contain alcohol.

Parenteral Route   **Parenteral** refers to the administration of medications by various types of injection or intravenously. Medications delivered parenterally achieve the fastest and most accurate effect. The most common variations in giving medications by injection include the following.

Subcutaneous Injection (s/c)   This type of injection deposits a small amount of solution under the skin for absorption into the bloodstream. Some immunizations, such as the flu shot, are given subcutaneously, as are some drugs, such as morphine. Medications given subcutaneously are absorbed more slowly than those given into the vein or into the muscle. For this type of injection, a subcutaneous needle and syringe are used. The needle size is shorter (about 1.5 cm) and narrower (usually a 25 or 26 gauge) than those for other intramuscular injections. The barrel of the syringe usually holds about 2 to 3 cc of the medicine.

Insulin is usually given subcutaneously using specially designed syringes calibrated in insulin units or a pen injector device, devised specially for insulin administration.

Intradermal Injections   The objective of an intradermal injection is to inject a small amount of solution between layers of the skin, usually at a 10- to 15-degree angle. Medications given intradermally include steroids for a skin rash and tuberculosis vaccination. Allergy testing is often done intradermally. Intradermal amounts range from 0.1 cc to 0.3 cc. Often a tuberculin syringe is used for this injection; this is the smallest syringe available and holds only 1 cc. Needles are 27 or 28 gauge and are about 1 cm long.

Intramuscular Injections (IM)   This type of injection is given directly into a muscle. Medications given using this route are absorbed faster than those given subcutaneously and slower than those given intravenously. Larger amounts of medication can be given intramuscularly than by the s/c route. IM injections are given into larger muscles, such as the deltoid in the upper arm or the vastus lateralis, which is located on the upper lateral aspect of each leg. Injections in the hip, or gluteal muscle, have become less common because of the risk of damaging nearby nerves. The needle used is larger and longer, usually a 22-gauge needle 4 cm in length.

Z-Track   Occasionally the physician will write an order for a Z-Track injection, a specific technique for intramuscular injections, used for medications that may irritate or stain the skin—usually iron. The skin and muscle are pulled to one side, the injection given, and the skin released. This techniques seals the medication in, preventing it from oozing back when the needle is withdrawn.

Intravenous Medications administered intravenously—that is, straight into the vein—are more effective and faster than those by any other route. Therefore, this route is used in emergencies. Medication may be administered from a syringe or through intravenous tubing (referred to as an IV push). It can also be diluted in intravenous solutions and given slowly by way of a minibag or add-a-line, or closely through a special chamber called a buritrol (see Chapter 17) when doses need to be monitored.

L06 PHARMACOKINETICS

As noted earlier, pharmacokinetics deals with how the body processes and uses a drug, including the absorption, metabolism, distribution, and excretion of the drug.

Absorption

Absorption includes the processes by which a medication is taken into the body and released from the dosage form. Factors include how the drug is taken into the body (route), the form in which the drug is taken (e.g., ASA with an enteric coating is absorbed differently from plain ASA), and whether the medication is taken on a full or an empty stomach. Some foods or liquids interfere not only with the absorption of the drug but also with its therapeutic effect. The presence of food may also enhance the absorption and action of other drugs.

absorption the process by which a medication is taken into the body, broken down, and transformed into a form the body can use.

Metabolism

Many drugs are administered in their active form; some (e.g., enalapril) require transformation into active metabolites for effectiveness. Various organs in the body are responsible for **metabolism** or breaking down a medication further into these particles or metabolites. This is accomplished by various body enzymes. Age and health affect the process. The liver plays a major role in transforming drugs into a form that can be excreted from the body; for this reason, someone with liver disease may be unable to take certain medications. The kidneys, lungs, intestines, and other tissues also metabolize some drugs.

metabolism the process of breaking down a drug or other substance into metabolites used by the body. Metabolism is also the altering of a substance so that it may be inactivated and excreted from the body.

Distribution

The drug metabolites are then transported or "distributed" to various parts of the body. **Distribution** also determines how long it takes for a medication to begin acting, when the action of the drug is at its peak, and when the action/effects of the drug decline. A number of factors affect the distribution of a medication, including by which route it was administered, the physical characteristics of the drug itself, and the age and health state of the patient.

distribution the process by which metabolites are transported to various parts of the body.

Excretion

Excretion is the process by which the body disposes of a drug. This is accomplished primarily by the kidneys. Some medications are excreted by the GI tract. Medications can also be excreted in smaller amounts in saliva, tears, sweat, and breast milk. Although there are some legitimate concerns, nursing mothers are sometimes too afraid of medication and forgo necessary therapy because of fear of potential adverse effects on the baby. The efficiency of excretion is affected by the health and function of the kidneys and liver and by interactions with other medications. If a medication is not excreted efficiently, it can accumulate and produce adverse effects. This is sometimes called *drug toxicity*. Testing is commonly done for toxic and therapeutic levels of many drugs, such as digoxin and gentamicin sulphate.

EFFECTS OF DRUGS

Therapeutic Action

Every medication has a method of action. For example, an antibiotic may work by preventing bacteria from reproducing. A tranquilizer affects the part of the brain that deals with the transmission of nerve impulses. A *therapeutic action* is one considered desirable—the purpose for giving the drug.

Side Effects/Adverse Effects

Every drug has potential side effects. There are two main types: (1) those that are expected to occur as part of the pharmacological action and (2) those that may be *unpredictable* in occurrence. Most people develop a tolerance for common side effects or use strategies that help deal with them. Rarely will a person have to discontinue a medication for common, less serious side effects. Before making a decision, the patient and doctor should consider how important the drug is for the patient and how frequent, uncomfortable, or unmanageable the side effects are. Patients should not stop taking a prescribed medication without consulting the doctor.

Unpredictable events are much less common but could potentially be fatal. They may range from neurological responses to anaphylactic shock. It is important that patients report serious adverse effects quickly so that the physician can respond accordingly. Their attention should be drawn to the list of side effects that should be reported immediately.

Most drug resource manuals outline the side effects that may be experienced from taking each drug. Some list them by system and others by frequency of occurrence and severity. All pharmacies give out information about the drugs they dispense, including a list of potential side effects. Sometimes patients will read the side effects and decide they do not want to take the medication. It is important to explain to patients that many listed side effects are quite rare and to explain the strategies that help prevent an anticipated side effect. For example, if it is important for the patient to take a drug likely to cause nausea, he or she should be taught how to control the nausea. In some cases where the drug is for symptomatic relief or where other treatment options are available, it may be quite reasonable for the patient to choose an alternative. In most cases, it should be pointed out that the benefits of taking the drug almost always outweigh the chances of developing minor side effects.

Allergies

It is important to differentiate allergies from side effects. A side effect might be an upset stomach or diarrhea. An allergy would be a serious reaction, such as chest pain, a skin rash, or ultimately anaphylaxis, which is life threatening. It is important for the patient to clearly describe and document reactions so that the doctor can decide whether the patient can safely use the drug again. For example, codeine makes some people sleepy and gives others nausea, but these are not allergic reactions. Nausea and diarrhea are not contraindications for using an antibiotic again. In contrast, a patient who experiences hives, shortness of breath, blood pressure alterations, or circulatory collapse should *never* use that drug again, unless careful testing under an allergist's supervision establishes that a reaction was not allergic or that the patient has outgrown the allergy.

Food allergies are also important to note. An allergy to nuts, for example, is a contraindication for taking some medications. It is worth noting that Atrovent's reformulation does not contain soy lecithin, so there is no longer a cross-reaction with nuts.

Any allergies must be clearly indicated on the patient's chart, either in the office or in the hospital. Allergies are also recorded at the pharmacy if the patient is registered there. For this reason, as well as to maintain continuity of care, it is a good idea for patients to regularly use a single pharmacy. Patients should be fully aware of their allergies and should realize that the drug they are allergic to may have different names.

A patient who has had severe allergic reactions should wear a MedicAlert bracelet or equivalent. Most pharmacies have information about these devices, which can be purchased in the form of attractive jewellery. They may give information on conditions (such as diabetes), current medications, and severe allergies, including food allergies. Because the devices can carry only a limited amount of information, patients have to select the information most important in an emergency. For example, knowing that a person has diabetes or is taking an anti-coagulant could change a paramedic's response to an emergency, but knowing that the patient has arthritis would not. If patients ask you whether they should have a bracelet, where they can get one, and what should be on it, consult with the doctor before advising them.

Factors that Influence a Drug's Therapeutic Effect

Body Weight   The patient's body mass is an important factor in calculating the appropriate dose. If a patient weighing 40 kilograms took 10 mg of diazepam, the effects would be far greater than on a patient weighing 100 kilograms.

Age   Older people and small children respond differently to medications from those in the middle, not only because of differences in body mass but also because their body systems process medications differently. Older people and very young children are less able to excrete drugs and so may reach toxic levels more quickly. Older children have livers that work even better than those of adults, so the calculated dose of a particular drug may be higher than for adults.

As well, developmental factors are sometimes a concern. For example, quinolones generally are not used in pediatric patients because of concerns that the drugs cause premature closure of growth plates. Tetracyclines are avoided in pregnant women (they can inhibit bone growth of the fetus) and children under 12 because of their effects on teeth.

Gender   Some drugs may affect men and women differently, not only because of differences in body mass but also because of different relative muscle masses and because of hormonal and metabolic differences. Pregnancy is important to consider; hormonal changes may alter drug effects, and drugs can present a risk to the fetus.

Time of Day   The time at which medications should be given is affected by the patient's normal body rhythms, food intake, and level of activity. A fluid pill, for example, is best given earlier in the day so the patient is not up all night going to the bathroom. Some drugs are short acting and others long acting; thus, some are taken once a day and others several times a day. Some drugs, such as warfarin, should always be given at the same time each day. Antibiotics should be given at regular intervals to maintain therapeutic levels.

Some medications will be absorbed more slowly if taken on a full stomach than on an empty stomach. Drugs that should be taken on an empty stomach include some antibiotics, such as penicillin. The acid environment of the stomach degrades penicillin G, for example. The actual action of some drugs is affected by certain foods. For example, tetracycline should not be taken with milk products or antacids. Some cholesterol-lowering agents and many other drugs should not be taken with grapefruit juice or after eating a grapefruit, which increases blood levels of the medication. (It is important that patients avoid all forms of grapefruit at all times when taking these medications because the effects on the medication are long lasting.) A medication may also interact with other drugs taken at the same time. For example, calcium and iron may bind to many other medications to prevent their complete absorption.

Consider all these factors when transcribing medication orders. Most facilities will have a protocol to follow.

L07 NATURAL HEALTH PRODUCTS

The Natural and Non-prescription Health Products Directorate (NNHPD) regulates natural health and nonprescription products in Canada. These products include vitamins, minerals, herbal remedies, and homeopathic medicines. Natural heath products are available and advertised freely, citing cures and relief of symptoms that are "natural" and "drug free." (Note that the term *natural* is used somewhat arbitrarily; many powerful prescription drugs are derived from plants and are, thus, natural.) Many of these drugs (and they are drugs) do have therapeutic effects. Some trials have shown that many of these drugs do work as indicated, but many herbal medications have never been tested in sound scientific studies, and many claims remain unsupported.

The Natural Health Products Regulations in Canada came into effect in 2004 with 53 recommendations to regulate NNHPDs. In its expanded role, the directorate is now responsible for nonprescription and disinfectant drugs as well as natural health products. These responsibilities include product licensing, manufacturing practices, product labelling (including recommended use and cautionary statements), reporting of significant side effects to Health Canada, and the implementation of clinical trials.

Licensing of NNHPDs requires the manufacturer to apply to Health Canada for a product licence. Once granted permission to market, the producer must label the product with the letters NPN followed by an eight-digit product licence number. Homeopathic medicines have the product number preceded by the letters HM. Encourage patients to look for the product number since it indicates the product has been approved for safety and effectiveness by Health Canada.

Many people are unaware that herbal remedies, like other drugs, can have side effects or unpredictable effects, interact with prescription medication, or cause adverse effects with some medical conditions. Ginkgo biloba, for example, can cause bleeding. Ephedra has been reported to cause insomnia, increased nervousness, high blood pressure, and an irregular heartbeat.

Patients are often reluctant to tell their physician they are taking natural health products for fear that he or she will admonish them for doing so. They are more likely to tell you or the nurse. A positive, open-minded response will put the patient at ease. This approach will facilitate the patient's use of natural products effectively in conjunction with any other medications they may have been prescribed, and it will reduce the chances of unfavourable drug interactions.

Interactions with Prescription Medications

Many herbal medications will interact in some way—sometimes adversely—with certain prescription drugs. It is important for doctors to ask patients about herbal medications and for patients to report accurately. Unfortunately, many doctors are not well informed about these substances.

St. John's Wort, for example, has been shown by some studies to be effective in treating mild to moderate cases of depression, but it should not be combined with other anti-depressants because one potentiates the action of the other. Toxicity and undesirable side effects may result.

With the number of medications many people (particularly seniors) are taking, and with the mix of acute and chronic conditions people live with, the use of herbal medications must be carefully monitored. This is not a case where "more is better"— more might be fatal.

Here are some examples of herbal products that interact badly with certain prescription drugs:

Echinacea	Not to be used with prednisone or other corticosteroids, or in conditions where the immune system is involved (e.g., AIDS, rheumatoid arthritis, cancer).
Gingko biloba	Contraindicated in people who take Aspirin. Many individuals do take Aspirin prophylactically to prevent heart attack or stroke and when a mild anti-coagulant action is deemed advantageous. Other anti-coagulants, such as warfarin, should not be mixed with this herb either.
Garlic	Potentiates the action of insulin and of hypoglycemics, such as sulphonylurea. Also contraindicated in patients taking blood thinners.
Valerian	(Recommended for calming effects.) May potentiate the action of tranquilizers, such as diazepam (Valium), lorazepam (Ativan), other benzodiazepines, and barbiturates.

PATIENT EDUCATION

Ask patients to bring all medications to selected office visits. Stress that OTC and herbal remedies are medications and must be included for the physician to complete an accurate drug profile. All drugs should be brought in their original bottles for verification. A dosette with the pills in it is not suitable, unless all the drugs are labelled on the dosette.

Pharmacies will dispense medications in weekly dosettes or sealed blister packs, with labels indicating when to take each. This is important for people, especially older people, who have memory problems or who have difficulty organizing and taking multiple medications.

Many people stop taking drugs when they feel better, take them inappropriately, or discontinue them if they have minor side effects. Again, patient education is important. For example, antibiotics must be taken for the full period prescribed.

Some physicians advise patients to carry a list of their drugs with them at all times in case they are in an accident. You can help by periodically reviewing the list with the patient to ensure that it is current and correct. (Keep the list of a patient's medications up to date; the use of an electronic chart facilitates this.) You could also prepare the list for a patient who has difficulty doing so.

People often feel embarrassed to ask questions about their medications, particularly if they feel the provider is busy or unapproachable. You can help by encouraging patients to write down their questions before they come in for an appointment. Many doctors want their patients to bring their medications with them for each office visit.

If the patient appears confused about medications or asks you questions, take the time to direct the patient appropriately. If you can answer the questions competently, do so; if it is a matter of clarifying written instructions, do so. The patient may need to have the provider or the pharmacist review the medications again. Although most pharmacies do provide excellent instructions, some offices give out their own pamphlets on some medications (e.g., warfarin). These may cater to patients who speak another language, reinforce important points noted in the pharmacy handout, or include specific information related to the patient's individualized plan of care.

Drug Resources

The *Compendium of Pharmaceuticals and Specialties* The most common drug reference for professional offices and health care facilities is the *Compendium of Pharmaceuticals and Specialties* (CPS), published annually by the Canadian Pharmacists Association and distributed to health care practitioners. There is an online version that is more practical to use, and kept current. It contains an updated list of most drugs used with detailed information on actions, indications and contraindications, and side effects. However, the information is not exhaustive, and at times it may be advisable to consult other references, the primary literature, or a drug information centre. The CPS is intended for professionals and is not meant for laypeople. Information for the patient is available only in the online version.

Other There are a variety of drug/pharmacology books on the market. Some are geared more to nurses and others to health professionals, such as you. If you deal frequently with prescriptions or transcribing medications, you may want your own reference book. You can become familiar with it and add your own notes and markers. Most software used in hospitals and other facilities contain essential information about prescribed drugs. They will monitor drugs and doses prescribed and flag drugs that may induce drug-to-drug interactions, as well as those the patient is allergic to.

L08 HANDLING PRESCRIPTIONS

Prescription drugs are so called because they can be dispensed only by authorized prescribers, including not only physicians but also nurse practitioners, pharmacists, and some optometrists. If the patient is in the office, the doctor is most likely to fax the prescription from his or her computer directly to the desired pharmacy, so the patient does not handle the prescription at all. If this is not possible, the doctor will write the necessary prescription and give it to the patient to take to the pharmacy. Either way, the doctor will ensure that the details of the prescription are recorded on the patient's electronic medical record.

In Canada, faxed prescriptions are accepted as the equivalent of written prescriptions. Any prescriptions faxed must be sent in a secure manner and in accordance with jurisdictional guidelines. For example, prescriptions for narcotics may be faxed to only one pharmacy, must contain all relevant information, must be signed by a qualified provider, and may not be refilled or transferred. If a patient requires a refill, the prescription must be reordered by the provider. After successful transmission of a prescription, the original prescription must be invalidated and kept with the patient's chart (paper or electronic). Faxes can be accepted from a practitioner registered to practice anywhere in Canada.

An e-prescription is the electronic preparation and transmission of a prescription by a qualified provider to the pharmacy of a patient's choosing using software facilitating the secure transmission of data.

Prescription Forms

Although more prescriptions are written online, most doctors still have prescription forms or pads headed with their name, address, and other necessary information. Figure 7.1 shows the elements of a prescription. Figure 7.2 shows a prescription written in a formal format (e.g., with the words "sig" and "mitte" written in); Figure 7.3 shows a prescription written informally, with the names of the elements left out.

Prescription forms must be kept safe because of the danger of theft and forgery, primarily by people who want narcotics, sleeping pills, and tranquilizers. Keep prescription pads out of sight and secure.

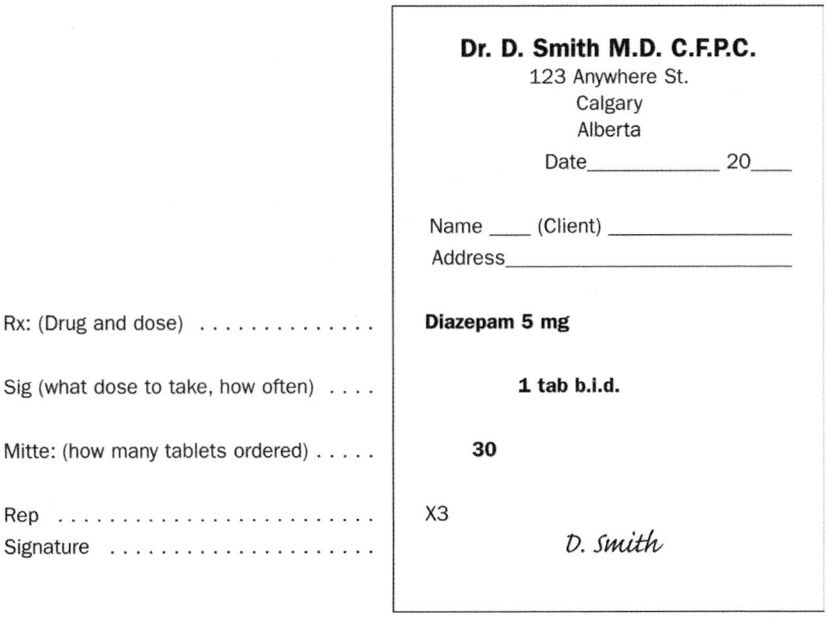

Dr. D. Smith M.D. C.F.P.C.
123 Anywhere St.
Calgary
Alberta

Date_____ 20____

Name ____ (Client) _____
Address_____

Rx: (Drug and dose) . . . .   **Diazepam 5 mg**

Sig (what dose to take, how often) . . . .   **1 tab b.i.d.**

Mitte: (how many tablets ordered) **30**

Rep X3

Signature . . . .   *D. Smith*

Figure 7.1 Parts of a prescription

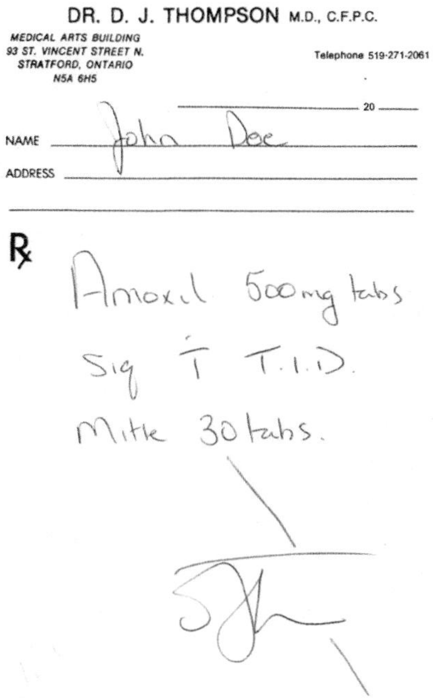

Figure 7.2 A formal prescription

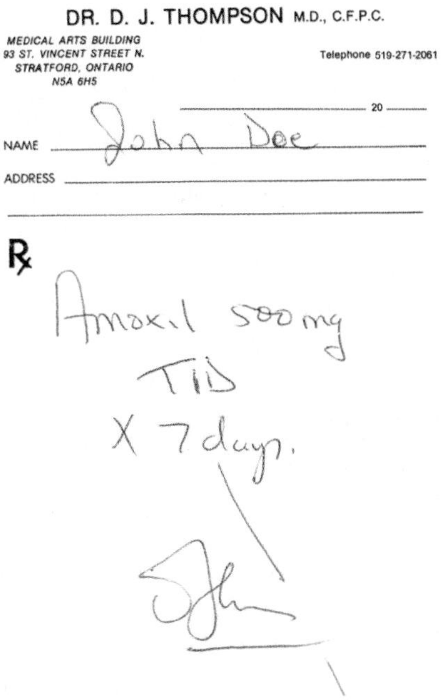

Figure 7.3 An informal prescription

TABLE 7.2 Common abbreviations used in medication orders and prescriptions

Ad lib	as needed by the patient
bid	twice daily
cap	capsule
c̄	with
d/c	discontinue (can be mistaken for discharge)
gtt	drop
hs	bedtime (can be mistaken for half strength)
hs prn	as required at bedtime
od	daily (discouraged because of the potential to interpret as "right eye")
prn	as necessary, or as required
qhs	every bedtime
qs	quantity sufficient
q ___ h	every ___ hours (q4h: every 4 hours; q6h: every 6 hours; etc.)
qd or od	every day (every day; q2d every 2 days; etc.; also discouraged)
qid	four times daily
stat	immediately
tab	tablet
tid	three times daily
po	by mouth
IM	intramuscular injection
s/c	subcutaneous injection
IV	intravenously
SL	sublingual

Note: Although these abbreviations are used frequently in the health care sector, the Institute for Safe Medication Practices Canada warns that many are frequently misread and can result in harmful errors. When possible, providers are encouraged to write out the instructions in full. If in doubt when interpreting an order, always check with someone and look at the context in which the abbreviation is written.

To convey most instructions on prescriptions, doctors use a set of standard abbreviations, listed in Table 7.2.

Repeats and Renewals

Some prescriptions, such as antibiotics, are usually issued for a defined period of time. Once the specified period is over, the prescription is no longer needed. Medications for chronic conditions, such as diabetes, hypothyroidism, or hypertension, may be renewed many times. However, the doctor will want to review the patient's condition and the dose from time to time. Prescriptions are often written with a certain number of repeats available (see Figure 7.1). If the patient is starting a new medication or a new dosage of a medication and the doctor wants to check on the patient's progress and response to the drug, he or she may write a prescription with no renewals, requiring the patient to come in for an assessment or blood work.

Repeats and renewals differ slightly, although some people use the terms interchangeably. Repeats are continuations of long-term medications, while renewals are extensions of prescriptions that have run out, often of one-time or short-term medications. Medications for chronic conditions are usually prescribed with instructions that the prescription can be repeated or refilled a given number of times before a new prescription is necessary. For example, Dr. Gifford prescribes Brenda thyroxine (a medication for hypothyroidism, a lifelong condition) with three repeats. This means Brenda can call the pharmacy three times and have her medication request filled without contacting the doctor. When the three repeats have been used up, the doctor must be contacted to authorize a renewal of that medication. The doctor may simply "renew" the prescription order or ask Brenda to come in for an assessment before he does that. As mentioned earlier in the chapter, in some provinces, the pharmacist may be allowed to renew the medication or order a related lab test before doing so.

Policies for prescription renewals vary with the physician. Some doctors will not renew any prescription over the telephone but insist that the patient come in for an assessment—particularly when the medication is a new one. This is prudent at times because physicians are responsible for any reactions or adverse effects of the medications they prescribe.

In most cases, when doctors first write a prescription, they will include what they feel is an appropriate number of repeats at the time. When the repeats have been used up, it is time for the patient to be seen and reassessed. For example, Dr. Gifford may feel it is time to do some blood work on Brenda to see whether her thyroid medication is effective or whether the dose needs to be adjusted. Likewise, birth control pills are routinely prescribed for a year. At the end of that time, the doctor may want to give the patient a Pap smear and do a gynecological examination.

Prescriptions for narcotics, sleeping pills, or tranquilizers will not normally be renewed without an office visit and assessment. You will likely be told to make appointments for patients in such situations.

Some patients resent the inconvenience of having to see the doctor for a prescription renewal. They may feel that it is a money grab on the part of the physician. Actually, the doctor can charge more for a telephone renewal than for a minor assessment. It may be necessary to educate the patient about the benefits they receive from regular assessment.

Most physicians will also refuse to order antibiotics without seeing the patient. This is the responsible thing to do. Most often a swab or other test is done to determine the cause of the infection and to identify the most appropriate antibiotic for the patient. Some patients, however, will call stating that they have a sore throat and want an antibiotic to make them better. It is helpful to explain why the doctor wants to see the patient before ordering or renewing an antibiotic. As explained in Chapter 5, antibiotics are not effective against viruses. Different antibiotics are also effective against different groups of bacteria. Putting a patient on an antibiotic for an infection it cannot cure wastes money and leads to needless side effects. Worse, the bacteria in the patient's body can develop resistance to the antibiotic and can then be passed on to others. The overuse of antibiotics has become a major public health issue as antibiotic resistance increases.

Sometimes when requesting a renewal or a repeat, a pharmacy will simply fax the original prescription that the doctor had written along with a copy of the information put on the bottle at the time the prescription was filled.

A pharmacist may refuse to fill a prescription because he or she feels it is outdated. There are no hard-and-fast rules, but many pharmacists consider prescriptions outdated a year after they are written. A reassessment by the prescribing health professional would be in the patient's best interest. Some controlled substances do have a legally imposed time frame within which they can be filled.

Phoned and Faxed Prescription Requests

In the health office, you will receive calls about prescriptions from patients, pharmacies, and facilities such as nursing homes. Most will deal with medication renewals. Physicians will have different protocols on how to manage these calls.

Regardless of who is calling, you need to record all information clearly and accurately. Keep a system for recording information—usually on the computer. You will likely be required to enter the information regarding medication requests (renewal or repeats) directly into the patient's EMR. If the patient is calling, you need to get the following information, most of which you will have online if you are able to access the patient's chart. To ensure you have the correct patient, ask for his or her date of birth as well as full name; check the date of birth with that on the patient's eChart (electronic chart). You can message the physician electronically with requests if the pharmacy does not do so directly.

- Patient's first and last names
- Address and phone number
- Medication (ask for the spelling if you are not sure. Even one wrong letter can identify a different medication)
- Prescription number
- Dose and frequency (e.g., 5 mg TID)
- Date issued
- Preferred pharmacy
- Pharmacy's location and phone number (or you may keep the numbers of local pharmacies handy)

You may also want to ask

- if the patient wants the medication delivered or will pick it up;
- when the patient will pick up the prescription or will be home for deliveries;
- how the patient plans to pay (e.g., charge, cash on delivery); and
- whether the patient has a drug plan.

Some health offices leave it up to the pharmacy to arrange payment and pickup or delivery. Others pass on the information with the approval. You want to ensure that someone will be home when the medication arrives. Sometimes patients will ask that the medication be left in a mailbox or between doors. Currently, in most jurisdictions, a prescription must be delivered into the hands of the recipient or a designate. This is especially so for certain medications (controlled substances, tranquilizers). Ontario, for example, requires that the pharmacy obtain a signature of acceptance for receipt of delivered prescription items, so delivered medication must be received by a person. If the patient cannot find the delivered medication, the pharmacy assumes no responsibility for medications that are left according to the patient's instructions.

When a pharmacist calls, you can assume that the pharmacy already has some of this information. However, you still need to get

- the patient's first and last names,
- name of the medication (correctly spelled),
- the dose and frequency (e.g. 5 mg TID),
- the date issued, and
- the pharmacy's phone number (if you don't have it).

Write the pharmacy's phone number on the request to make it easy for the doctor to call if he or she has a question.

The doctor should personally review all prescription requests. Many doctors review renewal requests last thing in the morning, or just before starting office hours in the afternoon, and again late afternoon. Do not leave it too late, though: Some pharmacies may be closed, or patients may be unable to pick up the medication. If you think a request is urgent, take it to the doctor as soon as possible.

More often than not, a patient will call the pharmacy instead of the doctor's office for renewal of medications. (Some doctors ask their patients to do so.) The pharmacist then requests permission from the doctor, often by fax. You should give the fax to the doctor and note any changes in the patient's eChart. For example, the doctor may want to see the patient before authorizing a refill on the faxed medication request. The physician may authorize just enough of the medication until the patient can come into the office. Once the doctor has approved or rejected requests, telephone or fax the designated pharmacy with the information. Remember, there are special policies to follow for prescriptions for controlled substances.

Physicians who have patients in nursing homes must review a resident's medications at designated time frames—for example, every three months. Often the nursing home will fax the resident's medication profile to the physician, who will review it, make the necessary adjustments, and ask you to fax the changes back. Figure 7.4 is an example of a form the physician may use.

LINCON PHARMACY

CONDITIONS / DIAGNOSES:				ALLERGIES:	
				DIET:	

ADMISSION NOTICE / BEST POSSIBLE MEDICATION HISTORY (BPMH) FORM-DISCONTINUE ALL PREVIOUS ORDERS

MEDICATIONS	TIME	RECONCILIATION	☐ NEW ADMISSION ☐ RE-ADMISSION
		☐ Continue ☐ Discontinue _____ ☐ New	LAB WORK ORDERS/OTHER ORDERS:
		☐ Continue ☐ Discontinue _____ ☐ New	
		☐ Continue ☐ Discontinue _____ ☐ New	
		☐ Continue ☐ Discontinue _____ ☐ New	
		☐ Continue ☐ Discontinue _____ ☐ New	**REASON TO DISCONTINUE CODE:** A. Adverse Drug Reaction D. Duplicate Therapy B. Not Needed E. No Supporting Diagnosis C. Changed F. Other:_____
		☐ Continue ☐ Discontinue _____ ☐ New	**MEDICATION LIST SOURCES (Check Minmum 2):** ☐ LTC MAR - Name of Facility: _____ ☐ Hospital Discharge - Name of Facility: _____ ☐ Physician - Name & Phone #: _____
		☐ Continue ☐ Discontinue _____ ☐ New	☐ Resident/Family ☐ Review of Vitals ☐ Community Pharmacy ☐ CCAC LOA with most responsible person and medication: ☐ Yes ☐ No

FAX TO PHARMACY: 416-555-8874 or 1-800-555-7777
NURSE: PLEASE CHECK "SEND" BOX IF MEDICATION IS REQUIRED

NAME OF PHYSICIAN:	
SIGNATURE OF PHYSICIAN:	DATE:

Figure 7.4 Prescription authorization form

Drug Measurements

There are three measurement systems used in pharmacology that physicians may use when writing medication orders. Canada generally uses the metric system; others sometimes use, at least in part, the apothecaries' measure or the household (imperial) system. You will not be asked to calculate doses, but you do need to recognize measurements so that you interpret and transcribe them accurately.

SI Units   The metric system, with which you are familiar, is also referred as the *Système Internationale* (SI). Drugs are commonly prescribed in milligrams (mg), millilitres (mL), or cubic centimetres (cc). A cubic centimetre is the same as a millilitre; the terms are used interchangeably. The abbreviation "eq" stands for equivalents, a unit of measure used in laboratories; "meq" stands for milli (1000 smaller). Drugs may also be prescribed in micrograms (μg; sometimes also mcg). Be careful not to misread micrograms as milligrams—there is a tenfold difference.

Be acutely aware of the presence of decimals. If in doubt, check. To avoid misreading, written orders involving decimals should use a 0 to precede a measurement: for example, instead of .5 mg, write 0.5 mg. It is too easy to miss a decimal point and transcribe .5 mg as 5 mg. Prescribers should *not* use a 0 on the right-hand side of a decimal point. For example, write 5 mg rather than 5.0 mg, because 5.0 mg can easily be read or transcribed as 50 mg.

Household Measurement   Household measurements refer to imperial measurements, such as teaspoon, tablespoon, cup, and drop (gtt), once the standard household and commercial measurements in Canada and still the standard for lay uses in the United States. These measurements often make more sense to patients, especially older patients. Table 7.3 shows common imperial measures and their metric equivalents.

Most of us think of body weight in pounds and ounces. You rarely hear a mother say, "My baby weighed in at 4500 grams." However, doctors usually use metric measurements in tracking body weights and calculating doses. Medications are often ordered as so much "per kg body weight," so doctors like to have an up-to-date record of patients' weights, especially for children. You can tell a patient his or her weight in pounds, but record the weight on the patient's chart in kilograms, or in grams for babies.

Apothecaries' Measure   You may occasionally come across the apothecary system, which uses minims, fluid drams, and fluid ounces for volume, and grains, scruples, drams, pounds, and ounces for weight. Note that this system overlaps with

TABLE 7.3   Household measurements and metric equivalents

Household Measurements			Metric
Volume	1 teaspoon (tsp.)	= 60 drops (gtt)	= 5 cc = 5 mL
	1 tablespoon (tbsp.)	= 3 tsp.	= 15 cc = 15 mL
	2 tbsp.	= 1 fluid ounce (oz. or fl. oz.).	= 30 cc = 30 mL
	8 fl. oz.	= 1 cup	= 240 cc = 240 mL
Mass (weight)	1 ounce (oz.)		= 28.349 g
	1 pound (lb.)	= 16 oz	= 454 g = 2.2 kg

TABLE 7.4 The apothecaries' measure

Mass		Volume	
Symbol	**Measure**	**Symbol**	**Measure**
gr.	grain	min.	minim
sc.	scruple	fl. dr.	fluid dram
dr.	dram	fl. oz.	fluid ounce
oz.	ounce	pt.	pint
lb.	pound	qt.	quart
1 grain = 60 mg = 0.06 grams		480 min. = 1 fl. oz. = 30 mL = 30 cc	

the household system. Occasionally, a doctor will write a drug order using grains. For example, you may see a prescription for phenobarbitol written as "phenobarb gr. 1/2." Since one grain is equivalent to 60 mg, this means 30 mg of phenobarb. Or you may see "morphine 1/4 gr." (equivalent to morphine 15 mg) or "ASA gr. 5" (325 mg). You may see an order or prescription for 1 oz. of Magnolax. One ounce equals 30 cc or 30 mL. Do not do the conversion yourself; read or transcribe the order as written, and let the pharmacist interpret it. Table 7.4 summarizes the apothecaries' measure.

International Units   Some drugs (e.g., insulin) and nutrients (e.g., vitamin A and vitamin E) are measured in international units (IU). Each 1 mL of insulin contains 100 IU. In Canada, physicians write insulin orders using IU or the symbol U⁻. (The Institute for Safe Medication Practices recommends writing the word "units" because many errors have occurred because of the use of these symbols. For example, if a U looked like a 0, 6U became 60 units.)

HANDLING DRUGS SAFELY

Because drugs are potentially dangerous substances, they must be handled with special care, especially controlled substances.

Storing and Handling Drugs

■ Keep all medications in their original containers until they are administered or dispensed. (This is not likely your responsibility, but if you see medications sitting out in unlabelled containers, consult with the nurse or physician, or discard them.)

■ Check the manufacturer's storage recommendations.

■ Some drugs must be kept in dark containers or dark areas. Do not leave any drug for long in the sun or bright light.

■ If noted on the label, keep drugs refrigerated. Monitor the refrigerator temperature. If there is a power outage, transfer medications to a working refrigerator.

■ Do not open bottles unnecessarily. Some drugs, like older forms of nitroglycerin, lose potency if opened frequently.

■ Once a drug (such as a pill) is removed from its container, do not return it. This is a basic safety precaution employed by many facilities. There is the danger that it has been contaminated or a chance that another medication could be returned to the container.

- Keep drugs and solutions for external use well separated from those used internally.

- Store disinfectants and cleaning agents well away from medication.

- Store drugs in an ordered arrangement: by classification or alphabetically by drug name.

- Store medications with the ones expiring first at the front of the cabinet or shelf. (All medication bottles should have expiry dates on the label.)

- Discard unused expired medication such as samples or those returned by patients. For safe disposal, return to a pharmacy. Do not place in the garbage or flush down the toilet. It can then be directed to disposal companies that incinerate surplus medications at high heat.

- Never leave medications out in an examination room. If the doctor leaves samples out, put them away before the next patient comes in.

Controlled Drugs

Special rules apply to the use of controlled drugs, as defined by the CDSA. These involve drugs with a high potential for addiction and abuse, such as fentanyl and other narcotics. They are typically medications in pure form. For example, codeine is a controlled drug. However, combination drugs containing smaller amounts of codeine are not controlled. If controlled drugs are kept in a medical office, special precautions apply, including the following:

- Keep a special record of controlled substances dispensed, administered, or prescribed, either in a daily log or arranged by type of drug. For each entry, check that the physician has included the patient's name and address, the name and quantity of the drug, the diagnosis, and the purpose for which the drug was provided. Keep records for at least two years.

- Store all controlled substances in a safe or an immovable locked cabinet. Make sure it is locked after use.

- Be alert to the risk of break-ins. Although most providers do not keep narcotics in their medical bags, on their person, or in their offices, they, their offices, and their vehicles are frequent targets for thieves looking for narcotics.

- Report the loss of any controlled substances immediately to the local legal authorities.

Narcotic Control Records and Tracking Controlled Medications

In the few facilities (e.g., long-term care) where controlled medications may still be tracked manually, when a nurse gives a controlled substance to a patient (e.g., fentanyl), he or she must record the patient's full name, room number, time, dose, and route by which it was given in a designated book such as a narcotic control book or binder. These stock medications are counted at the end of every shift by two nurses. The nurses must sign that all controlled medications are accounted for. When required, the pharmacy department replenishes these medications. It is important to note that in the majority of facilities controlled drugs of any kind are carefully dispensed, tracked, and monitored by the pharmacy.

Hospitals have abandoned the manual system for dispensing all medications and now use barcode-enabled systems that receive medication orders, sort, and automatically distribute the medications. Doses may be individualized for each patient. Narcotics and other controlled drugs are also dispensed and tracked by the system—thus, the need for a narcotic book has been eliminated. Controlled drugs are still counted at regular intervals, for example, weekly. A nurse must scan his or her index finger or enter a password to access narcotics and, in some facilities, the patients' routine medications.

Disposing of Medications

As mentioned earlier, expired or unneeded drugs in the office as well as patients' medications should be disposed of by an authorized agency (such as a pharmacy) and in an appropriate manner. Most pharmacies accept unused and outdated medications and dispose of them properly. Dumping drugs down the drain or the toilet is not acceptable because of the potential cumulative environmental effect.

Some patients save their medications and take them when they think they need them, for example, for a cold or sore throat. This often involves misuse of antibiotics. Others share their leftover medications with friends and family members. Explain to patients that these habits are dangerous. Their friends may be allergic to the drug or may be taking another drug that will interact badly with the new drug. If the doctor changes or discontinues a patient's medication while a quantity of the original remains, encourage the patient to bring the leftover medication to your office or to a pharmacy for disposal. Pharmacies often have certain days when they invite patients to bring in expired or unneeded drugs for disposal. Some patients see this as "wasting" money or medications and are reluctant to part with them.

It may be a good idea for family members to occasionally survey the medicine cabinet or medication box of older people and dispose of outdated medications as well as those the person is no longer taking. One woman found 30 or 40 bottles of unused medications in her grandmother's cabinet. She said that her grandmother would take some occasionally to self-treat. "Grandma thought that if a little is good, more would be even better, and different kinds might cure things that haven't even happened yet." This story is not unusual.

Preventing Drug Abuse

The abuse of prescription drugs in Canada is increasing at an alarming rate, particularly among our youth. The misuse of prescription drugs is defined as taking a medication that was not prescribed for you or taking a prescription drug in a way in which it was not prescribed. There is a host of scenarios wherein prescription drug abuse occurs. For example, patients may sell their prescription drugs, then attempt to obtain more from the physician. They may seek early renewal of their prescription, or present with complaints they think will influence the doctor to write a new one. Two of the most commonly abused prescription drugs are opioids, such as fentanyl, which are used to treat pain, and benzodiazepines, such as lorazepam, which are used to treat anxiety.

Most often you will receive the call from a patient asking for a drug renewal. The pharmacy may also call with a request from a patient, particularly if pharmacy employees are suspicious about the request. Be alert for behaviours that may indicate a drug-seeking or drug-abusing patient. Often a person will ask for medications to be renewed early, perhaps saying the pills were lost, stolen, or spilled. Keep a record on the patient's EMR of such calls and the reasons given. You will be able to access a patient's pharmacological history, review it for a pattern of asking for early renewals, and alert the doctor.

Physicians prescribing drugs with a high potential for abuse to unfamiliar patients usually prescribe a limited supply. Pharmacies will often dispense only small quantities at a time. Be suspicious of patients who plead for larger quantities of such medications stating that it is either too expensive or too difficult for them to get the prescription refilled.

Be wary also of anyone who walks into the office off the street, perhaps stating that they are visiting from out of town and forgot their medications at home or had them stolen. Other individuals will present with complaints of a severe, perhaps recurrent pain and will name the exact drug they need to relieve it. They sometimes suspiciously have allergies to any drug of lesser potency. "Tylenol does nothing for me, doctor, but Percocet does." Or "I am allergic to codeine, but Demerol really helps."

>>> **POINTS TO PONDER**

A Word about Fentanyl
Fentanyl is an opioid, a class of painkillers that also includes oxycodone and morphine. It is powerful and often deadly when used improperly. The illegal use of fentanyl has reached crisis levels in many parts of Canada, especially British Columbia and Alberta, and is responsible for an alarming increase in drug-related deaths. Some jurisdictions are passing legislation to make take-home kits containing naloxone (an antidote for narcotic overdose) available to residents without a prescription. British Columbia was the first to do this, and Alberta the second (in May 2016). Although individuals can access fentanyl legally, it is important to keep an eye on patients this drug has been prescribed to, both to monitor for the possibility of addiction as well as the potential for illegal use. Do you think health care professionals can help minimize the frequency of fentanyl overdoses? If so, how?

Avoiding Drug Errors

Any error in drugs or dosages can be serious, even fatal. A number of factors can contribute to medication errors; you can help prevent some of these.

Errors are more likely when orders are taken orally (e.g., over the telephone) than when they are provided in writing or electronically. It is all too easy to mishear or to have a slip of the pen. In most health care facilities, only a registered nurse can receive oral orders (medication or other) from a physician, although this is changing. For example, in nursing homes a practical nurse may be allowed to accept an oral order.

Errors can also occur in transcription because of poor handwriting (by physicians and other professionals), confusion between drugs with similar names, misuse of zeroes and decimal points, confusion of metric and other dosing units (see "Drug Measurements"), and inappropriate abbreviations (see Tables 7.2, 7.3, and 7.4).

Thorough knowledge of the spellings, pronunciations, and typical ordering methods of medications, as well as measurements and symbols, will help you be accurate in reading orders aloud, writing down phoned-in information, and transcribing.

Be alert for drugs with similar names, when speaking about them, writing down phoned-in information, or transcribing. If you are responsible for arranging medications in a doctor's office, write the generic name as well as the brand name on the container. Post a list of drugs that could be confused, such as Accutane and Accupril; Atarax and Ativan; Benadryl and Benylin; or Atrovent and Alupent.

TIP

Transcribing drug orders is a task you must take very seriously. Check and double-check to ensure that you have transcribed the order properly. Many drug names are similar. A mistake in the drug name, symbol, short form, or dose designation can result in a serious error. Do not expect the nurse to catch these errors—you must take responsibility for the work that you do. The Institute for Safe Medication Practices website listed at the end of the chapter will provide you with excellent information that will keep you from making transcription/order entry errors. If order entry is one of your responsibilities, keep a hard copy of these resource sheets with you at work.

Check your work. As mentioned earlier, when you take a prescription request over the phone, read it back to the caller. If you phone in information or orders, ask the person on the other end of the line to read it back to you.

⟩⟩⟩ WHAT TO WATCH FOR

- Advances in pharmacogenomics (personalized medicine)—the development of safe, effective medications and doses that will be tailored to a person's genetic makeup (e.g., chemotherapy).
- What steps the medical community will take to deal with the increasing rise in antimicrobial-resistant organisms (e.g., providers prescribing fewer antibiotics, public education so that individuals do not demand antibiotics).
- Incentives encouraging pharmaceutical companies to research newer antimicrobial medications.

- More widespread use of secure portals offered by physicians giving individuals access to their own health records, including their medication profile, allergies, and medical history, such as vaccinations and previous medications. Educational materials regarding their medications will also be available.
- Continued implementation of pharmacy service portals providing a variety of self-serve pharmacy services. Kiosks will be placed in various locations (e.g., a clinic). The patient can log in and, among other services, choose their pharmacy location as well as the time and date they want to pick up their prescription.

SUMMARY

1. The pharmacy team works together to educate their patients and prepare and dispense prescriptions. It is important that you recognize the various responsibilities of various team members to maximize effective communication regarding patients' prescriptions, including reordering and renewals.

2. Drugs are derived from several sources, including animals, plants, and natural minerals; they may also be partly or entirely synthesized in a laboratory. Regardless of the source of a drug, they are organized into four name categories: chemical, generic, trade or brand, and botanical. The generic and trade names are used most frequently. The generic name is nonproprietary; the trade name is assigned by the manufacturer and has patent protection for up to 20 years.

3. The federal Controlled Drugs and Substances Act determines which drugs are illegal and places controls on narcotics and other drugs considered hazardous. Regulations for controlled drugs are stringent; despite this, practitioners and pharmacists must be vigilant to minimize inappropriate use of narcotics.

4. Regulations set out which drugs may be dispensed only by prescription and which may be purchased over the counter. Provincial and territorial regulations may vary slightly and may follow NAPRA guidelines. Some OTC drugs may be sold anywhere; some may be sold only in pharmacies; and some must be kept behind the counter in the pharmacy.

5. Drugs can be classified by use (e.g., curative, replacement, or prophylactic), by action or function (e.g., anti-hypertensive, anti-emetic), by scope of action (local, systemic, or cumulative), and by route of administration. All drugs are administered by a particular route—by mouth, by injection, or intravenously, for example. The route by which a drug is administered is ordered by the provider based on what type of therapeutic action is best for the patient as well as the patient's condition.

6. Pharmacokinetics describes four stages in the body's use of a drug: absorption, metabolism, distribution, and excretion. Age, weight, gender, health, time of day, and presence or absence of food can alter the processing of a drug. All drugs have side effects, which are sometimes mistaken for an allergic reaction. Although some side effects can be bothersome enough to require the patient to stop taking the drug (e.g., fatigue or diarrhea), they are less severe than an allergic response, which usually means the patient should never take the drug again.

7. Natural health products can be effective but, like all drugs, can have side effects and can interact, sometimes adversely, with other drugs. Many patients do not consider herbal medications to be real drugs and do not report them to their health care provider. Encourage patients to be upfront about what OTC and herbal medications they are taking. Educating the patient as to why this is important and interacting in a nondiscriminatory manner is essential; patients often feel uncomfortable disclosing that they take herbal medications (particularly to a doctor).

8. Security in terms of medications kept in the office may be your responsibility in part or in whole. Ensure that they are stored properly and out of sight. Narcotics should be in a locked cupboard (although they are rarely kept in a physician's office). Keep prescription pads out of sight, number them, and use only one at a time. Store medications correctly, refrigerating those that require it. Keep medications in their original containers, and make sure labels are legible. Encourage patients to return partially used prescription drugs to the pharmacy, where they will be properly disposed of.

KEY TERMS

absorption   183

controlled drugs   173

distribution   183

fixed oils   171

metabolism   183

ophthalmic   180

otic   180

parenteral   182

pharmacology   168

systemic   179

volatile oils   171

REVIEW QUESTIONS

1. Differentiate between pharmacokinetics and pharmacodynamics.

2. What are the roles of the pharmacist and the pharmacy assistant?

3. Describe four drug sources.

4. Explain the four categories of drug names, giving examples for each.

5. What are four routes by which medications are given? Describe each.

6. What are three factors that can interfere with the therapeutic effects of a drug?

7. Differentiate between allergies and side effects. What should you do if you learn that a patient has a medication allergy?

8. Why is it important to encourage patients to report any herbal medications they are taking?

9. Why is it important for a patient to bring current medications when coming to the office for an examination?

10. Describe proper methods for keeping medications in the health office.

11. List the factors contributing to medication errors and the steps you can take to prevent them.

APPLICATION EXERCISES

1. Divide into groups of three or four. Divide the list in Table 7.1 into as many sections as there are groups. List each drug in a table similar to the one later. Use a drug reference manual (you may have purchased one for your course) or the websites listed at the end of this chapter. For each drug in your group's section, list the trade and generic name, the action of the drug, the typical adult dose (if your instructor wishes), three to five major side effects, and helpful patient teaching. Put the group lists together to compose a master list to distribute to the class.

Generic Name	Trade Name	Therapeutic Category	Typical Dose	Side Effects	Health Teaching

2. Ask a sales consultant in a local health store for a list of commonly sold natural health products. Individually or in small groups, select one product or a group of related products from the list. Research this product at the library or on the internet. Make sure to assess the reliability of your sources, especially on the internet. Develop a teaching pamphlet for patients in a family physician's practice about the potential benefits and risks of this product and, if applicable, the dangers of taking this medication with prescription drugs (e.g., St. John's Wort with anti-depressants).

3. Drug abuse in Canada is an ongoing problem, to the point where some jurisdictions are calling it a public health emergency. Research the severity of illegal drug use in your area. What drugs are of most concern? What is the incidence of drug-related deaths? Are there safe-injection sites in your area (such as those in Vancouver and Toronto)? Do you agree or disagree with these initiatives? What benefits and drawbacks do you see related to safe-injection sites?

WEBSITES OF INTEREST

MediResource

www.mediresource.com

MedicineNet

www.medicinenet.com/script/main/alphaidx.asp?
p=a_pharm

MedBroadcast

www.medbroadcast.com

Drug Index

www.rxlist.com/script/main/hp.asp

Health Canada (follow links for natural and nonprescription health products)
www.hc-sc.gc.ca

National Association of Pharmacy Regulatory Authorities
http://napra.ca

Institute of Safe Medication Practices Canada
www.ismp-canada.org

Controlled Drugs and Substances Act
http://laws-lois.justice.gc.ca/eng/acts/c-38.8

Part IV of the textbook gives more detail on the administrative aspects of work in the health office. If you work in a health office, you will likely be the first person many patients see and interact with. Effective communication and patient relation techniques are vital.

In Chapter 8, you will learn appropriate verbal and nonverbal communication techniques to use in person and on the telephone. You will also gain strategies for dealing effectively with difficult or dissatisfied patients. The chapter also discusses effective handling of mail and other written communications and how to deal effectively with peers and other health professionals. Chapter 9 applies what you have learned in Chapter 8 to effective management of scheduling. It deals with how to schedule patient appointments and the principles of triage. You will learn how to assess the urgency and nature of a patient's health complaint and schedule the patient appropriately. Various scheduling systems are discussed, along with the challenges patients present with when they want to see the doctor.

Chapters 10, 11, and 12 prepare you for provincial/territorial billing. These chapters outline the principles behind provincial and territorial billing in Canada, discussing the common elements apparent in most provinces and territories. Chapter 10 explains how provincial and territorial health care plans work. Chapters 11 and 12 detail the elements of a health care claim and the process of billing, emphasizing electronic billing. The Ontario system is used to demonstrate the billing process; however, most exercises can be adapted to the structure of any provincial or territorial billing plan. Chapter 12 also discusses the principles and procedures for billing patients, insurance companies, and others for uninsured services. Chapter 13 provides an overview of health records management. Topics include the life cycle of the medical chart, basic chart content, security and confidentiality, and common filing systems.

Chapter 8
Communicating for Health

Monkey Business Images/Shutterstock

LEARNING OBJECTIVES

On completing this chapter, you will be able to:

1. Effectively manage fax, email, and mail within health care settings.

2. Apply the principles of plain language in health communication.

3. Coordinate the use of communication devices in the health office.

4. Manage and respond properly to incoming and outgoing calls, including maintaining confidentiality in the health care setting.

5. Conduct yourself professionally in all types of face-to-face interactions with patients.

6. Communicate appropriately with difficult or angry patients.

7. Discuss strategies to effectively interact with health professionals.

Communication in the health office takes many forms, including the telephone, cellphones, computer messaging, emails, the internet, and facsimile machines. Advances in communications technologies, such as the implementation of electronic medical records (EMRs) and electronic health records (EHRs), allow physicians to access their patients' health information from almost any location as long as they have internet access and a computer.

If a physician's patient has been seen by another provider during an evening or weekend, the physician can receive notification of that visit—usually within hours of the visit—as well as a detailed record of the visit, which enhances the continuity of patient care. Other digital communications solutions, such as the Canada Health Infoway's Telehomecare service, help patients manage chronic diseases from the comfort of their own home, using self-monitoring tools along with professional coaching. This reduces office visits and hospital admissions. Yet any information exchange system is only as good as the people operating it, from their knowledge base to their ability to communicate effectively.

Excellent communication is critical to good health care delivery in any setting. Although this chapter focuses on communication in a family doctor's office, the same skills and approaches apply whether you work in a specialist's office, a clinic, a hospital, or a dentist's office. In the health office, many of the responsibilities of the administrative health professional (AHP) revolve around using the telephone and the computer as well as face-to-face communication to collect and relay information, interact with patients, and coordinate activities. Communication affects patient care, treatment plans, appointment scheduling, patient education, and interchanges between professionals. Effective health communication is challenging both for patients and for health professionals. Your skill as a communicator is essential not only to make sure everyone gets the information they need, but also to make people feel more comfortable.

It would be helpful to review Chapter 1 at this point, which details the importance of professionalism with respect to dress, general appearance, and manner (emphasizing the importance of professional communication with others).

L01 THE OFFICE AND THE FAX MACHINE

Despite the use of sophisticated medical office software, the fax machine is still used a great deal in many offices. Pharmacies, hospitals, and long-term care facilities in particular will fax certain reports, test results, and requests for medication repeats or refills. Doctors and dentists will fax requests for consultations and consultation reports. The number and types of reports faxed will, of course, vary depending on the use of both EMRs and EHRs in a given community.

Note that if you are in the position of purchasing a fax machine for your office, consider purchasing the accompanying maintenance agreement. The vendor will maintain and repair the fax machine and help resolve problems with the related telephone line.

Receiving/Sending Faxes

When you receive a fax, check that you have the number of pages noted on the cover sheet; call the sender if you are missing pages. When you send a fax, specify the number of pages on the cover sheet. Keep a log of all fax transmissions, noting the same information as on the cover sheet. This serves as a record in case a transmission is lost. Most machines will print out a report that the transmission went through, giving the date, time, and destination. These reports should be filed as a confirmation of faxes sent and received. Your facility and phone number should be on the cover sheet. It is not uncommon for someone to send a fax to the incorrect destination, especially when working with a large volume of material that must be sent.

Sending and receiving reports must be done to protect the confidentiality of all documents. Often, fax machines are used by a number of people, and some are shared by more than one office or hospital department. It is easy for someone to scoop up a bunch of faxed documents and take someone else's material by mistake. To minimize this risk at your end, try to place your fax machine in a secure area. Fax machines usually have a distinctive ring that you will recognize. This will alert you that faxed material has arrived. Most faxes arrive randomly any time of the day or night. It is a good idea to check for faxed material periodically, as well as first thing in the morning. When you receive faxed reports, pick them up as soon as you can. Even better, some fax machines come with mailboxes accessible only by code. The sender punches in a code to designate where the fax is being sent. The receiver then punches in the code to activate the printer and receive the message.

Prescriptions and Pharmacies

Pharmacies typically fax the doctor for requests for prescription renewals (remember from Chapter 7 that a *renewal* occurs when there are no further *repeats/refills* authorized on an existing prescription). You can fax the request form back to the pharmacy, once renewals have been authorized, altered, or declined. (See Figure 7.4 in Chapter 7.)

You must then scan that information into the patient's EMR. The doctor usually needs to see the patient's chart when he or she is renewing a prescription or prescribing something new—for example, to review the patient's medication profile or look up test results that may influence what is prescribed. Using EMRs, the doctor can patch directly into the patient's chart. If you are using paper charts, pull the chart and put it on the doctor's desk along with the prescription request.

In an EMR environment, with the required equipment the doctor can also send prescriptions directly to the pharmacy from his or her computer, eliminating the need for a paper prescription. Be sure that you know what pharmacy the patient wants the script sent to, and update the information on the patient's EMR if it has changed. You will likely have a drop-down menu on your software showing various pharmacies to choose from. See Figure 8.1.

Prescriptions for narcotic and controlled drugs can be faxed or sent as digitalized image files in most jurisdictions. Electronic signatures may be acceptable if they meet the guidelines set out by the jurisdiction's College of Pharmacists Guidelines. For example, the electronic signature must be a unique, clearly identifiable, life-size image.

Figure 8.1 A drop-down menu showing a list of pharmacies to choose from
Used by permission of Choice Learning, Inc.

In hospitals where physicians still write orders, if medications are involved you must fax the order to the pharmacy (they then fill the medication order and modify the patient's electronic medication administration record). Once you have finished faxing the order sheet, place it safely in the patient's chart or elsewhere according to protocol. Be sure to recheck the patient's name on the order sheet to ensure that it is filled in correctly.

Specialty Appointments and Related Consultation Reports

Faxing and receiving consultation reports still requires significant use of the fax machine. If a patient requires an appointment with someone (e.g., a specialist, physiotherapist, or dietician), the physician must complete a request for consultation detailing relevant portions of the patient's medical history pertinent to the reason for the consult request. You would fax this information to the appropriate destination—for example, the specialist. They would receive the consultation request, make an appointment, and fax back the appointment information. You would then call the patient with that information. Once the consult is completed, the specialist's office will fax you a completed consultation report. This report must be scanned and uploaded into the patient's EMR.

> **TIP**
>
> When scanning and filing a report to a patient's EMR, you must be sure you have the correct chart. Validate this by looking up the patient's EMR by both name and date of birth (DOB). You may have patients with the same name, so using the DOB as well is an additional safety check.

Faxed Reports and Scanning

In environments with EMR and EHR connectivity, reports can be sent right to the doctor's computer and can then be directly filed into the patient's EMR. Reports may come from a hospital, pharmacy, or public or private lab, for example. Otherwise, all faxed (paper) reports must be scanned and uploaded to the patient's chart. This is time consuming, especially when dealing with multiple reports, where you must scan the reports into a batch or file. You would then select the patient's electronic chart and categorize the report. To avoid filing a report into the wrong EMR, you must recheck the name on the report with the EMR you are dumping it into, and then file it appropriately. Categories you can choose for filing the report include imaging, operative, consultations, letters, hospital discharge, hospital diagnostic reports, history and physical, internal reports, and external reports.

EMAIL

Email is used in many health offices and other health care settings for messaging purposes, but *not* for sending confidential health information. Some practices make appointments and send patients' messages via email. Even if you make all appointments by phone, it is a good idea to have an email address as another way to contact the patient. You should have the patient's consent to use email for medical exchanges.

If you are sending email messages that contain confidential information, you should have security features in place: Encrypt the message and label it confidential.

Never use a web-based email service. When receiving email, do not leave anything confidential showing on your screen or accessible to anyone for whom it is not intended.

If you send letters or reports by email, use the same standards as you would for any professional written communication. Use proper spelling, grammar, and capitalization. Too many people have become sloppy with email, treating it as casual conversation. That may be all right for a quick note to a friend, but not for professional messages. When formality is more appropriate, send a properly formatted letter by email attachment. When replying, consider eliminating previous information so that if the email does get lost or accidentally sent to the wrong person, the amount of information is minimized.

There are rules to follow for proper email protocol:

■ Ensure you have the proper email address. When you start entering the address, the auto function will insert the address the computer "thinks" you want. It is easy to accept the wrong address, particularly if you are in a hurry. Try adding the email address before you write the message. Check it again before you send the email.

■ Always use a subject line. Some computer security software programs will prevent you from sending an email without one. As well, the subject line is handy to use for filing, retrieving, and tracking email. When you use the "reply" option, the subject field retains the original subject line—ensure it reflects the current content of the message.

■ Keep the message short and to the point. In a busy office, reading (and writing) longer messages takes time.

■ Do not use email "lingo." Use proper grammar and punctuation. Improper abbreviations, jargon, and mistakes reflect poorly on you and your organization. Most email software has a spellcheck option—use it!

■ Answer promptly. Prioritize email messages and respond accordingly. Always reply. Delayed responses make you appear inefficient and discourteous. If you do not have the information the sender requires immediately, let them know there will be a delay. For example, a message saying, "I received your message and will follow up within two days when I have the information you require" is better than letting someone think you are slow or didn't receive the message. Respond to all of the questions in the email. Not answering questions requires unnecessary follow-up and wastes time.

■ Keep the message thread intact. Keep the original message in your email reply. Do this by using the reply option, not the new message option. The original message serves as a reminder in case you forget the details of the original message. If you are sending the original email to others (using the "cc" option), however, ensure that there is nothing sensitive or confidential in the original message thread before you do so.

■ Proofread your email. Always reread your email—just as you would any written document. You have a last chance to check wording, clarity, format, grammar, spelling, and punctuation.

■ Be aware of security. Do not open email attachments if you do not recognize the source. Add a disclaimer to your email. A disclaimer should include a statement regarding virus transmission and breach of confidentiality. A confidentiality disclaimer can protect your office or organization against the improper use of confidential information. The recipient of the email could be held liable for misusing the information.

Patient Portals

More providers now offer their patients secure portals, which is another communication tool. A patient portal is a secure website that gives an individual 24-hour access to his or her personal health information. To access the portal the person requires a secure user name and password. Some portals allow people to exchange emails with members of their health care team; request medication renewals; schedule, cancel, or confirm appointments; review educational material; and make payments for services not covered by their provincial/territorial plan. Patient portals benefit the patient as well as the health team. For example, using the portal reduces phone calls to the office (e.g., for information about immunizations) and incidents of playing telephone tag with patients.

Patient portals offer varying features. When a patient wants to use a portal for the first time, clearly outline the steps needed to access the portal, what features the portal offers, and what he or she can expect from each feature. Emphasize the importance of security features to ensure that health information is kept confidential.

Most portals have an audit trail—that is, patients can see who accessed their chart, when, and what changes were made. Note that many hospitals also offer patient portals offering patients access to selected portions of their health information (from their eChart), including demographics, reports, medications, hospital visit histories, and upcoming outpatient/clinic appointments.

WRITTEN COMMUNICATION

Printed communication in the health office has decreased with the use of the fax machine, email, and EMRs. However, even with electronic tools, you will often still need to fill out insurance forms, process return-to-work notes, and prepare dictated consultation reports, depending on the type of health office you work in. Many health offices use medical transcription or voice recognition software for creating reports, and then fax them to their destinations.

If you are responsible for typing letters and reports, you need a thorough knowledge of medical terminology, anatomy, physiology, spelling, grammar, and formatting. Reports must be accurately reproduced, be professional in language and appearance, and follow the standard format used at your facility. The provider may use a digital dictation transcriber (wherein you must retrieve and type out the information) or voice recognition software.

You will likely be expected to edit written communications for grammar, punctuation, correct word choice, and clarity. Documents created using voice recognition software must be checked for words that were not recognized properly. For example, one report dictated and sent out—unedited—said, "The baby died." It should have read, "The baby cried."

For forms and letters you frequently use, it is a good idea to use **templates**. Templates can be formatted to suit the written communication needs of the provider you work for. For a family doctor, templates are suited for sick notes, consultation requests, invoices, and missed appointments. These templates can be retrieved as a macro.

Some offices send out quarterly newsletters that include information about the practice, updating patients on policies and new treatment options. Sometimes they also include significant events about the professional staff—those who leave, new staff members hired, and so on. This creates a friendly bond with patients and is, in part, a marketing tool. Marketing in offices (other than a doctor's office) is a vital component in building and maintaining a patient base. You may also be responsible for creating patient teaching information. Such material must be clear, relatively simple, and organized to make it easy to read. Remember that many laypeople have limited knowledge of medical concepts and terminology. Avoid jargon. If it is simpler to use specialized terms, explain them on first usage.

template a computerized file with a predesigned and customized format that can be designed for specific functions (e.g., letterhead, formatted letters, scheduling purposes).

Using Macros in the Health Office

Any technology you can use to simplify written communication is worthwhile mastering, such as the use of macros. A *macro* is a sequence of commands or functions that, when combined and saved, can be recalled with a single key stroke or combination of key strokes. The use of macros saves time when used to perform a series of functions or tasks you use frequently. As well, macros eliminate the need to remember multiple steps that may be required to perform a complicated function. It is a user interface that you create to meet the specific needs of the office—from administrative purposes to ordering groups of tests (by the provider) to provincial/territorial billing.

Often a doctor has to submit several claims related to one visit. Many visits are repetitive and involve the same claims submissions. Well-baby visits, for example, occur at regular intervals, such as at one, four, and five months. Each visit involves an assessment and, depending on the visit, designated immunizations. For example, Dr. Hussain, who bills fee-for-service, sees Abby for a two-month well-baby visit/assessment in Ontario.[1] Here, you would bill for a well-baby assessment—2 month (A007)—and the immunizations, which typically include pentacel (G841), Prevnar (G846), and rotavirus (G538). Instead of writing in these claims separately for every two-month well-baby visit the doctor completes, you can create a macro that will display all of the claims together (e.g., Alt + F4). You would then submit the claims according to protocol. This macro can be used for all two-month well-baby visits (see Figure 8.2).

Likewise, a macro can be used to simplify ordering a grouping of lab or diagnostic tests (a grouping of lab tests is also called a *lab panel*); for example, if a diabetic patient comes in for an assessment, the physician may have a routine set of tests he or she orders, such as a CBC, creatinine, AC ratio, A1c, lipids, thyroid, and ECG. By using a macro, the

Figure 8.2   Using a macro for a billing claim for a well-baby assessment
Used by permission of Choice Learning, Inc.

---

[1] If Dr. Hussain worked in a primary care network (PCN), he would also bill a premium code for assessment of a baby less than two years of age, which is Q015. (See Chapter 11.)

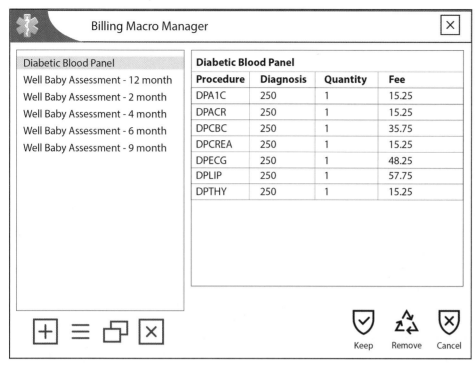

Figure 8.3 Using a macro to order blood work for a routine diabetic assessment

Used by permission of Choice Learning, Inc.

stroke of one key can order these tests as a group. If billing as an intermediate visit, the service code A007 (or the equivalent in your area) would be used with the diagnostic code of 250. If the visit was a quarterly diabetic check for a physician working in a PCN, the service code would be K030 with a diagnostic code of 250 (see Chapter 11 and Figure 8.3).

Macros can be applied to a variety of templates used for documentation and correspondence, maximizing functionality and saving time. Examples include static templates (e.g., letterhead, sick notes, back-to-work notes) and macro templates, which contain information that can be inserted into multiple locations (e.g., active medications and allergies, physician signatures).

Signs

If there is something you want all your patients to know, it often makes sense to put a sign in the reception area or at the front desk. For example, you may want to ask patients to call at certain times to schedule appointments (see Figure 8.4). You may want to let them know about office policies, charges for uninsured services, or dates when the office will be closed. You may want to remind them to take off their boots, to show their health cards, or to wait in the office after an allergy injection. It is important to note that all primary care reform groups must clearly post signs related to office and clinic hours. Any other services that are part of the group benefit package must also be clearly conveyed to patients—telephone helplines and services included in and

PLEASE CALL AFTER 10:00 A.M. TO MAKE OR
CANCEL APPOINTMENTS.

THANK YOU FOR YOUR COOPERATION.
Dr. D. Thompson

Figure 8.4 An office sign

excluded from the "basket of services" for which the provincial or territorial plan will pay. The sign needs to convey the message clearly while being appealing and leaving a friendly impression. A few suggestions follow.

- Make the sign large enough to be noticed.
- Make the lettering large enough for people with limited vision to read.
- Make the sign simple but attractive. A simple border can help, as can a little colour. Rounded, open fonts are usually more appealing than narrow, heavy ones. Do not use ornate fonts.
- Keep the words brief and to the point.
- Be clear. Ask several people what the sign means to make sure it cannot be misinterpreted.
- Keep a friendly tone. Such phrases as "Please," "Thank you," and "We appreciate" are more courteous than simple commands or words like "must" and "don't."
- Try a little humour. But make sure your wording is not confusing or offensive to anyone.

Incoming Mail

In most offices, mail is delivered daily and arrives either by courier, special delivery, or regular post, which includes priority post and registered mail. You will probably be responsible for sorting and dealing with the mail according to office guidelines. Like phone calls, most incoming mail falls into certain categories.

Medical Reports   Electronic reports may be received regarding consultations, operations, home care, lab results, or radiology reports, with fewer now provided as a hard copy. Many are still faxes—these must be scanned into the patient's EMR. Occasionally lab reports may arrive by courier. Any lab reports (regardless of format) should have abnormal or marginal results flagged (electronic reports may have them highlighted in red). Depending on the degree of connectivity, the lab may notify the doctor electronically. The lab will almost always call the office if the results are alarming. You would either put the call through to the doctor or message him or her (send a flag to a computer or tell him or her yourself). Alternatively, the nurse may be able to handle the call. Diagnostic reports (such as radiology or ultrasound) will be sent electronically. With respect to lab results, of immediate concern are abnormal blood sugar and blood coagulation results (e.g., INR, APTT, BS). Usually the doctor will ask you to contact the patient regarding abnormal test results of any description. You may be asked to schedule an appointment for the patient to discuss the problem or instruct the patient—at the request of the doctor—to alter the dose of a medication (e.g., withholding a dose of warfarin if the INR is too low). This may be the responsibility of the office nurse if there is one.

Insurance Reports   Insurance reports are the bane of most physicians' lives—and of yours. Completing insurance forms takes an inordinate amount of the doctor's time. They are sent by numerous sources, including private insurance companies, workers' compensation boards, and government agencies. You should fill out as much of these forms as you can, which is usually limited to demographic information. For example, you can fill in the name, address, DOB, health card number, and claim number (if there is one). Many of these forms require detailed medical information that only the doctor can provide. Often the patient will come in with a wad of forms to be filled in, thinking that the doctor can do it while he or she waits. Patients often do not understand the time factor and that the doctor cannot simply abandon his or her current schedule to sit down for half an hour to prepare the forms.

Every insurance company has its own forms. The commonly used ones include those requiring a physical assessment of the patient, functional assessment forms, return-to-work forms, and disability assessment forms.

Once the doctor completes and signs the forms, you will send them back. You may have to individualize a reply or attach such documents as medical reports. Where consent is required, do not forget to include the signed form. Dental, chiropractic, and optometry offices have a higher volume of insurance forms, because most of their services are covered by third-party carriers (rather than the provincial or territorial health plan). Most insurance forms are completed at the point of service and faxed to the carrier by the administrative assistant.

TIP

Organization is efficiency: When you receive an insurance form for the doctor to complete, fill out as much as you can, make an appointment for the patient for the necessary assessment if required, tell the patient when he or she can expect the report to be completed for pickup (or if/when it will be mailed/faxed), and be clear about charges the patient is expected to pay if applicable. Follow the doctor's protocol for filling out reports—he or she probably would like the forms to be neatly stacked on his or her desk so they can be completed throughout the day. Some forms require online completion, but most are done by hand.

WCB/WSIB Forms   You can view samples of the workers' compensation board (WCB; in Ontario this board is called the Workplace Safety and Insurance Board [WSIB]) forms you will likely be dealing with most frequently on your provincial/territorial WCB/WSIB website. Look for a link such as "Forms for Health Professionals" (or a similar phrase). In Alberta, the link is under "Health Care Providers," for example. Familiarize yourself with the forms most frequently used, such as Form 8 in Ontario (used for all patients claiming WSIB benefits for work-related illness or injury) and forms C050 (first report) and C151 (progress report) in Alberta. In British Columbia a commonly used form is Form 8/11, Physician's Report (to see this report, follow the link provided at the end of the chapter to find the WorkSafeBC website).

In most jurisdictions, basic claims require a functional abilities form be completed prior to the patient returning to work. Looking at the forms commonly used in your jurisdiction will give you an idea as to how lengthy and time consuming they will be for you and the physician to complete. WCB/WSIB claims may require you to photocopy parts of the patient's chart—you can claim payment from the WCB/WSIB for this, as the cost is about 40 to 45 cents a page. You also bill for the amount of time it takes for the physician to complete the form, usually by the half hour and in increments of 15 minutes. The payment changes if the report is accompanied with a medical opinion versus one without. The WCB/WSIB and patients are always in a hurry for prompt return of these forms, as claims cannot be adjudicated without them. There is sometimes discord between the physician and patient regarding the initiation and continuation of disability claims—both WCB/WSIB claims and others—which can be unpleasant for all involved. For example, the doctor may feel that from a medical perspective the patient can return to work, perhaps with work restrictions, but the patient feels he or she is not ready. Also, the employer may not want to accommodate work restrictions. Such situations may require the physician to fill out additional forms, make further assessments, or perhaps meet with WCB/WSIB officials and the patient.

You can submit WCB/WSIB claims by fax, mail, or electronically if your office has registered to do so. If you submit forms electronically, you should keep a copy in the patient's file and print a copy of the recommended pages for the patient to keep. Keep a record in the patient's file of when forms were completed and sent (if the form is completed in paper format, scan a copy to keep in the patient's EMR). In many jurisdictions the WCB/WSIB pays the physician more for electronic submissions, probably to encourage this mode of submission. Typical forms include the Health Professionals Injury Report (in Ontario, Form 8) and a report detailing the injured person's ability to return to work (e.g., a functional abilities form, or FAF). This form does not usually contain any diagnostic or confidential information. To bill for this form, you would be required to fax specified portions of this form to the WCB/WSIB.

Personal Mail Place any letters or documents marked "confidential" and any letters you recognize as personal on the doctor's desk unopened.

Educational Materials Educational materials can be for the doctor, for the staff, or for patients. If the patient-oriented material seems generally useful, you can put it in a rack in the reception area. Some material may be suitable for specific patients only; it can be placed in the treatment and examination room or left with the doctor. It is best to give this type of material to selected patients as appropriate. Educational materials for the doctor include a never-ending supply of medical journals, notifications of seminars, updates on drug therapies, and medical newspapers; the doctor should sort through these. Always replace outdated materials.

Magazines for the Reception Area Many medical offices receive subscription magazines for the reception area. Some of these are promotional and sent free of charge; others may be ordered by the doctor or office staff. You may be tempted to "borrow" the magazines that appeal to you. It is fine to read them, but make sure they find their way to the reception area while they are still current. If your doctor does not subscribe to any magazines, you might suggest it (the cost of subscriptions can be written off as a business expense). Reading material in the office should reflect general interests, keeping in mind your patient population. For a medical office, cater to various interests with a selection of lifestyle magazines, such as *Canadian Living*, and magazines covering sports, health, travel, science, or culture. For younger patients, include storybooks at various levels. If you work for a gynecologist, you might have a similar selection but with more focus on women's interests. If you work for a pediatrician, you will want more picture books. Have a few board books or washable fabric books for babies. If you are working in a dental office specializing in aesthetic dentistry, you might consider some magazines highlighting smile makeovers.

Outdated magazines are a standing complaint among patients. Remove shabby or outdated magazines (generally more than three months old). Decline patients' offers to bring in old magazines unless they are relatively current. Some offices offer notepaper and pens so people who see a recipe or any other interesting item in a magazine can copy it rather than tearing out pages or taking away the magazine.

Junk Mail As with any household or business, you will receive your share of flyers, notices, and other forms of junk mail. This clutters the office and, for the most part, is inappropriate for a health care setting. Sort and discard such material as it comes in. If you shelve it to sort through later, it will pile up. Some doctors like to look over pharmaceutical advertising; if yours does not, it, too, is junk mail.

Cheques Depending on the type of office you are working in, you will receive cheques and other forms of payment for deregulated services or other things the doctor charges for. You will also receive third-party payments from insurance companies and workers' compensation boards (see Chapter 12). Many AHPs will open envelopes containing cheques and place them on the doctor's desk to review.

In many dental, chiropractic, or optometry health offices, the patient is asked to pay at the point of service and is reimbursed by the insurance company. The patient may have a policy whereby the insurance company pays the doctor directly. This is called assignment of benefits, but it is not often used. It is an arrangement between the patient and the insurance carrier whereby the patient gives written permission for the carrier to send a cheque directly to the provider. When this occurs, there may be a portion of the fee that the insurance does not cover; thus the health office must also collect money from the patient. A credit card or cheque is the preferred method of payment.

Usually, cheques are marked for deposit only and are added to the provider's account according to your office routine. Keep a careful log of all payments received—from whom, the date, and the amount. Accurate bookkeeping is a must.

Holiday Mail   Often, the office stays open even when the doctor or other provider is on vacation. Sometimes a locum looks after the practice, or other members of a group practice or clinic cover for the doctor. In most primary care reform groups, the office remains open and patients are booked for appointments at the group's central clinic. Continue to sort the mail and review lab reports, radiology reports, and so on. Make sure you have clear instructions on contacting a doctor with any abnormal results or correspondence that requires immediate attention, such as time-sensitive insurance reports. If you cannot contact a doctor, call the correspondent, explain that the doctor is away, and make suitable arrangements to attend to the matter. Prioritize remaining correspondence so that the doctor can deal with the most important or immediate concerns promptly when he or she returns.

Outgoing Mail

The amount of mail actually sent by doctors is rapidly decreasing. What outgoing mail is sent must be prepared and sent promptly. Much of the material that was once mailed—medical reports, lab reports, radiology results, insurance reports—is now routinely faxed, emailed, or viewed online. Sometimes an original copy is needed; for example, insurance companies processing a claim usually require forms hand-signed by the doctor. Often, a report may be faxed and the original mailed. Keep and file a copy of all outgoing documents.

Patients who are moving to a new city or otherwise changing doctors will need a copy of their chart sent to their new health care provider. The patient must sign a consent form before any medical information can be sent. Since most health offices have completely moved to electronic charts, information required is usually summarized, downloaded, and faxed to the new provider, or transferred to a disc and mailed. If you work in an office that still has paper charts, you will find that the offices will keep the original chart and either mail or fax the information. Sometimes only a summary of the information in the paper chart is sent. The amount a patient is charged for a chart transfer varies (see Chapter 11).

Outgoing mail may include notices to patients, such as formal notification of missed appointments and an invoice charging for the missed appointment. Very few offices will mail out appointment reminders to patients, emailing or telephoning instead. Family doctors, as a rule, do not contact their patients with appointment reminders, although there is newer software that will automatically generate a reminder and email it directly to the patient. Reminder letters/calls are more common in the offices of chiropractors, optometrists, dentists, and some specialists.

Some primary care providers send out reminders related to preventive care, such as for flu vaccines, stools for occult blood, and Pap smears. Reminders for mammograms in many jurisdictions are sent out by the provincial/territorial breast-screening program.

Ending a Doctor–Patient Relationship   Occasionally, a doctor (or other provider) and a patient part ways because of differing values and expectations regarding the patient's health and care. Either the doctor or the patient may initiate the separation. If a doctor feels that he or she cannot continue to provide quality care for a patient, it is in the interests of both parties to terminate the relationship. This is not something a doctor will do lightly or just because a patient is difficult. Usually, all efforts will be made to preserve the professional relationship. However, sometimes doctors feel they can no longer work with patients who refuse to follow advice. Or the doctor may be uncomfortable with patients who demand ongoing care that the doctor does not feel is necessary, especially if they demand that the doctor, against his or her professional judgment, declare them unfit for work so they can receive insurance payments or workers' compensation. In other cases, the patient may leave because he or she mistrusts the doctor's diagnosis and wants the kinds of treatment the doctor cannot provide. In a dental office, a patient may be noncompliant with a treatment regime, such as wearing braces; in a chiropractic office, the patient may refuse to wear a brace or do recommended exercises. Sometimes personalities just clash. Usually the decision is mutual: If the doctor has done all he or she can for the patient and the patient wants more or different care, the patient will be just as eager to find a new doctor as the doctor is to be relieved of the responsibility of caring for the patient.

Nevertheless, a parting of ways is tricky and must be handled with discretion, sensitivity, and an eye to legal liability in case the patient sues, possibly alleging discrimination or negligence. A doctor withdrawing services must notify the patient in writing and must continue to provide care until the patient has found another doctor. With the shortage of doctors in most parts of the country, this can be a long time. Figure 8.5 shows a sample letter "firing" a patient.

Send such a letter by registered mail to ensure that the patient receives it. Put a copy in the patient's chart. If the patient calls after getting the letter, document all contacts in the chart. If the patient wishes to speak with the doctor about the situation again, have the doctor call the patient back.

Dear Mr. Dykstra,

I am writing to notify you that I am withdrawing as your family doctor. I feel that I am unable to continue to provide you with quality medical care as a result of our differing expectations and your refusal to follow my medical advice.

I will be happy to provide you with any medical care you need until you find another doctor.

You may also use the walk-in clinic if you require medical care.

Please contact us to let us know where you want a copy of your medical records sent. You will be required to sign a release form before your medical records can be transferred.

Sincerely,

M. Adams, MD

Figure 8.5   Sample letter ending a client–doctor relationship

LO2 PLAIN LANGUAGE

A communications movement called plain language is making its way into health care from the business and legal communities.[2] Plain language principles, although developed for writing, also lead to effective, clear oral communication.

Plain language is speaking and writing so that your patients understand you. It is organizing and presenting information that focuses on your patients' needs. It is keeping them in mind when you write letters, memos, phone messages, or instructions. Always ask yourself three essential questions when communicating with a patient:

- What do they need to know?
- What do they already know?
- How will I present it to them so that they understand?

Plain language means asking, "Is this clear?" as you explain something on the phone or in person. It is watching for nonverbal clues from your patients and paying attention to what they are telling you.

Why Plain Language?

Before you start, ask yourself what barriers might keep your patients from understanding you. These include the following:

- Literacy problems
- Language and culture
- Educational level
- Stress and self-esteem issues

Consider the following:

- A significant number of adult Canadians have trouble with literacy tasks, such as filling out a form, following instructions, or calculating a tip in a restaurant. Language barriers or medical terms further complicate this.

- Seniors are one of the fastest-growing population groups in Canada. Many have limited vision and require large print and simple graphics. Literacy problems are also somewhat higher among older Canadians because of previous limited educational opportunities.

- Some Canadians whose second language is English often have difficulty understanding written and spoken instructions, especially when the content is technical.

Using plain language is especially important in the health care field because misunderstandings can be serious. Patients need to fully understand what you are telling them. For example, if you are referring them to a specialist, they need to understand why they are going, what they need to bring with them, and the date, time, and location. If they are getting a test done, they need to understand the purpose of the test and how to prepare for it. Clear instructions the first time will often eliminate the need for the patient to call back.

When you help people understand what they are supposed to do—keep an appointment, follow medication orders, fill in a form—you help them be responsible for their health care.

---

[2] This section has been contributed by Susan D. Milne, Plain Language Consultant.

Using plain language also shows respect for patients. It tells them you will work with them to achieve their goals. No one likes to admit they cannot understand something, but lack of understanding can cause frustration and confusion. Using plain language and checking for understanding will avoid this.

Keep in mind, though, that there is a difference between plain language and talking down. As mentioned in Chapter 3, no one likes to be talked down to. Although clarity is always good, sometimes trying too hard to keep your language simple can alienate people. For example, one educated mother was given a prescription for her daughter by a specialist. When she expressed concern about possible side effects, the specialist told her, "It's good medicine. It's safe for children." She felt that the doctor was not taking her seriously and she was not reassured. Later, her family doctor told her, "This medication has been shown by large-scale studies to be highly effective, and it has an excellent side-effects profile." Although the family doctor said essentially the same thing as the specialist, the mother was reassured when she heard a reasoned explanation in the kind of language she was used to. If you are a good conversationalist, you will learn to listen to patients, gauge their vocabulary and verbal sophistication, and tailor your own style to suit.

Plain Language Tips

Here are some tips you can apply to your written and spoken communications with patients:

1. *Write as you speak, using a conversational tone.* Use "you" and "we" to make your communication friendly and direct. It is easier for patients to figure out what to do if you address them directly.

   Instead of   Patients should complete the forms before seeing the dentist.

   Try   Please complete the forms before you see the dentist.

2. *Include one main idea per sentence.* Keep sentences short (around 10–15 words or fewer). The first example that follows contains three ideas and is 34 words long. The second example is easier to understand because each main idea gets its own sentence, and the sentences are shorter.

   Instead of   This prescription gives you 30 days' worth of medication, and the doctor would like to see you before you finish the medication, so can we set an appointment for about three weeks from now?

   Try   This prescription gives you 30 days' worth of medication. The doctor would like to see you before you finish the medication. Can we set up an appointment for about three weeks from now?

3. *Use active verbs most often.* The subject of an *active verb* performs the action ("Joanne called the clinic"). The subject of a *passive verb* is acted upon ("The clinic was called by Joanne"). Often, the doer of the action does not appear at all in a sentence with a passive verb ("The clinic was called"). Sentences with active verbs are more direct and easier to understand because the people doing the action are named at the beginning of the sentence.

   Instead of   The application form was processed by human resources. (passive)

       All decisions pertaining to the payment of medical claims over $500 are the prerogative of your insurance company. (passive, unclear as to who decides)

       This medicine is to be taken before every meal. (passive, unclear as to who takes the medicine)

Try   Human resources processed the application form. (active, direct)

                   Your insurance company will decide whether it will pay medical claims over $500. (active, clear as to who decides)

                   Take this medicine before every meal. (active, clear as to who takes the medicine)

4. *Group related information together.* Finish with one topic before you begin another. In writing, guide the reader through the material by using lists and descriptive headings. Think about how the design of your document can help make it easier to read. For example, notice the use of lists, headings, and tables in this book. Do they help you understand the information and find sections more easily?

5. *Tell people what to do, instead of what not to do.*

Instead of   We will not reimburse you for your dental expenses unless you provide us with all necessary receipts.

Try   Give us your dental receipts, and we will reimburse your expenses.

6. *Get rid of jargon and acronyms, wherever possible.* If you must use a technical term, explain it. And remember, some acronyms have more than one meaning, so write them out in full (or explain what they mean) the first time. Professional communication is about being clear, not about impressing patients with how much you know.

accomplish	do
advise	tel
designate	name
due to the fact that	because, as
have a responsibility to	must
influenza immunization	flu shot
in the amount of	for
per annum	a year
pursuant to	following
remittance	payment
subsequent to	after
terminate	stop, end
to the extent that	if, when
with reference to, regarding	about

Plain language is a common sense revolution in business and health communications. It is being driven by patients reacting to websites they cannot figure out how to use, statements and contracts they cannot interpret, forms they cannot complete, and health care instructions they cannot follow.

L03 THE TELEPHONE

The telephone remains one of the most important communication devices you will use in any health care setting. The telephone still provides a vital link among health professionals, patients and their families, and health resources. How you communicate with people on the phone is as important as face-to-face interactions. People often get their first impressions of you and the practice on the phone. If you learn to use the phone effectively, you will project a positive image of yourself, your employer, and the practice.

Telephone and Messaging Equipment

If you are choosing equipment for your office, you need to be aware of the choices on the market and choose those that suit your office's clientele and administrative style. You need to be familiar with the equipment in your office: how it works and its capabilities and limitations. This may involve some initial training. Although the principles are the same, each telephone system is different. Most systems include the ability to put a caller on hold and to transfer a call to an extension.

The typical health office has an ordinary touchtone telephone with two or three extensions: one in the doctor's office and perhaps one in the lab or workroom, if you have one. Larger multi-doctor practices will have more telephone lines, usually one or two for each provider. The telephone in the front office may receive several lines. In larger practices, often, one staff member is assigned the principal responsibility of answering the phone. This person usually uses a headset, leaving her hands free to access the computer, pull charts, and receive messages. There are also wireless telephone systems that offer even more freedom and flexibility.

Rarely will you find a telephone or even an intercom in an examining room. For the most part, examination rooms are equipped with a computer, or the provider will have an iPad or portable Android device that he or she keeps with him or her for communication purposes. The provider can message other staff members as the need arises. Doctors can also complete requisitions for lab and diagnostic tests while still with the patient; they will be printed and either given to the patient or faxed to the appropriate facility. Because the main telephone line is so busy with incoming and outgoing calls, most offices also have a second "private" line with an unlisted number. This allows doctors to make and receive calls when they need to and is useful in an emergency. The private number is given to only a few individuals, such as the doctor's family and selected health professionals.

The second line is sometimes used for the fax machine as well, although many practices have a dedicated line for that purpose. Most telephone companies can provide you with a separate number for the fax machine on the same telephone line. If a fax is coming into the office, the fax machine answers that number after the first or second ring. If your system is programmed that way, do not answer that line until after the second ring. Other systems may use a separate line for the fax only or may signal a fax with a different ring.

Other optional services your office can purchase include call answer, universal messaging, call waiting, call display, call privacy, voice mail, and ident-a-call. These features may or may not suit your office.

Call Answer/Voice Mail   This service will take messages 24 hours a day, seven days a week, even when the telephone is in use. You can retrieve the messages at your convenience. You need a touchtone phone to use this service. You are signalled that there is a waiting message either by a flashing light or by an interrupted dial tone when you pick up the receiver. Most doctors opt not to have the option for leaving messages. Voice mail places the onus of contacting the patient on you or the physician. This is time consuming and sometimes frustrating.

Universal Messaging Some doctors prefer the consolidated services of universal messaging. Universal messaging delivers phone messages, faxes, and emails to one place. This internet-based solution transforms media messages into digital files and sends them to an email box. The receiver can access them via email or through a private webpage. Messages can be sent on a delayed basis and provide a confirmation that a message has been received.

Call Waiting This service allows you to receive calls while you are talking on the telephone. You will hear a soft beep. You ask the other party to hold, and press the flash button while you answer the incoming call. To return to your initial call, you press the flash button again. Some offices have visual call waiting, which shows the name and number of the caller, allowing you to decide which calls you wish to answer.

Call Display With a compatible telephone, you can see the name and number of the caller. This is not used extensively in health facilities but is useful in some.

Ident-a-Call This service allows you to have two additional telephone numbers on one line, each with its own distinctive ring. Some practices offering multiple services within the practice will use this feature.

Automated Attendant With this service, callers outside the practice can dial directly to an internal extension without going to the receptionist first.

Automatic Call Distribution This gives you the ability to set up a call centre for incoming calls, which is practical for receptionists in a medium or large practice.

Conference Calling This connects three or more people for a group call. The usefulness of this feature is related to the practice style of the physician.

Electronic Medical Record (EMR) Integration A telephone system can be programmed to integrate with an EMR system so that information from patients' EMRs appears on the computer screen when they call in.

Call Forwarding This feature allows you to transfer incoming calls from one phone to another where you can be reached or where someone else can take a message. This is helpful in an office where extensions are limited. If you are in an area where there is another telephone, you can have calls from the main office line forwarded to the telephone within your reach.

Automated Routing There are a number of automated routing devices on the market. Some are designed for larger facilities, such as hospitals, while others are tailored to small- and medium-size offices. These devices will answer each call, offer the caller a selection of options, and direct the call accordingly. An office with four doctors could separate calls by doctor. For example:

> "Good morning, Hudson Medical Centre. Please choose from the following four options: for Dr. McArthur, press 1; for Dr. Santorelli, press 2; for Dr. Lisowski, press 3, for Dr. Feinberg, press 4."

The device allows a single number to link to four offices. It is efficient and remains relatively uncomplicated. Routing devices can be programmed to meet your office's needs. Most can direct callers who simply want routine information, such as office hours, to recorded messages. This saves you time since you do not need to take those calls. However, the more options you have available, the more complex the system becomes and the more frustrating for some of your patients. Many health care consumers feel that the automated routing device in a health office is just one more step away from personalized care.

Telephone Answering Options

Every facility must have some method of answering the telephone when the office is closed or you are not available. A number of things must be considered when choosing which option works best for a practice. Whatever option you use, it is vital that the communication remains professional and friendly and meets the needs of your patients.

The Answering Service   An answering service employs operators who answer calls for a broad range of clientele, ranging from doctors to churches and private companies. These operators usually have some training in dealing with medically related calls and have a protocol to follow. Use of an answering service has declined significantly in favour of automated answering options and electronic devices such as pagers.

Answering Devices   There is a wide selection of answering machines on the market, in both analogue and digital format. Make sure the device is of good quality and is reliable. Some answering machines are used only to give a message to the caller. The message can be changed as required. Others allow callers to leave messages.

Another option is an automated service provided by telecommunications companies such as Bell, TELUS, or others (such as call answer, discussed earlier). This option eliminates the clutter of an answering machine.

TIP

If you change from one answering system to another, or the options offered to your patients change, expect some confusion on the part of those in your practice. Be patient and reinforce the changes that have occurred. You may even want to provide a short explanation as a handout for patients.

Patients needing emergency or urgent care are directed to the nearest appropriate clinic or emergency department. The family doctor may not be involved at all. Thus, there is no need for any exchange of information. A recording in the doctor's office can give callers a simple message, directing them to the emergency department or after-hours clinic. Family doctors with EMR capabilities should receive an electronic summary of their patient's visit to the clinic or the emergency department as soon as the information is entered by the attending physician. This does not always happen, contributing to fragmented patient care.

In all provinces and territories, those who want phone advice can call government-run services, such as HealthLine in Saskatchewan, Health Link in Alberta, Telehealth in Ontario, and HealthLink in British Columbia and Newfoundland and Labrador, which offer medically approved information on a variety of topics. Calling 811 will connect a BC resident to a nurse anytime. At designated times, a person can also connect with a dietician or a pharmacist. Some jurisdictions require the patient to give his or her health number when accessing this type of service. Most provinces/territories offer translations in several languages (e.g., Saskatcwan's HealthLine offers translations in about 100 languages).

▶▶▶ POINTS TO PONDER

Some jurisdictions have rolled out apps that will tell the public the estimated wait times at various emergency departments. These apps are updated frequently (e.g., every 15 minutes). What are the benefits and potentially negative aspects of using these apps?

Across Canada, provincial/territorial telephone help lines have been established for anyone to call for prompt, confidential advice and direction regarding health concerns. In most instances, a doctor is on call to handle situations referred to them by the nurse/person handling the call service. Sometimes the patient must wait for a call back from the help line—this should occur within a designated time frame. This service may be offered during selected hours or on a 24-hour basis. Services of this type may also be referred to as tele-triage. In jurisdictions where patients are rostered, primary care groups may offer a similar and parallel service to their rostered patients.

Some offices combine an answering machine with an answering service. For example, a practice's phone line may be answered with the following message:

> You've reached the office of Dr. McMichael and Dr. Bodnarchuk. The office is now closed. If this is an emergency, please call 911 or go to the nearest hospital emergency department. If you would like to speak to a doctor on call, please call the answering service at 905-555-5555. You may also call ONcall Healthline at 1-866-000-0000. If you wish to make an appointment, please call during office hours, which are 9:00 to 5:00 Monday to Thursday, and 9:00 to 12:00 on Friday.

Using an Answering Device

Most offices activate the answering machine over the lunch hour and when the office closes for the day. The message that you leave on the answering machine should be friendly, clear, and concise.

Messages can be worded generally and left the same from day to day. Some offices prefer to create a new message for each day.

Closing Messages

1. "Dr. Thompson's office is closed until 9 o'clock tomorrow morning. If you have a medical emergency, please go to the emergency department at Stratford General Hospital."

2. "Dr. Thompson's office is closed until 9 o'clock tomorrow morning. If you have a medical emergency, please go to the emergency department at Stratford General Hospital. Dr. Thompson's office hours are Monday, Tuesday, and Thursday, 9:00 a.m. to 5:00 p.m., and Wednesday, 9:00 a.m. to 12:00 noon. The family health clinic, located in the Jenny Trout Centre, 123 Erie Street, Suite 4, is open for nonurgent medical matters weekday evenings from 5:00 p.m. to 8:00 p.m. and Saturdays from 9:00 a.m. until noon."

3. "Dr. Jones's office is closed until tomorrow at 8 o'clock in the morning. If you have a dental emergency, please call the dental emergency number, 403-111-2222, or leave a message and someone will return your call as soon as possible."

Lunch-Hour Messages

Most medical offices close over the noon hour, allowing staff members and the doctor time to rejuvenate from the morning's activities. Messages for over the noon hour are fairly straightforward:

> Dr. Thompson's office is closed for lunch and will reopen at 1:15. If you have a medical emergency, please go to the emergency department at Stratford General Hospital.

Using the Answering Device at Other Times

Every office will be busier at certain times than others. Do not be afraid to use your answering machine or service for brief periods when you are very busy with other responsibilities. The volume of incoming calls usually peaks first thing in the morning or before the doctor begins to see patients in the afternoon. You may be meeting with the doctor to review the day's schedule, dealing with mail or incoming lab test results (which come by courier or are faxed), and so on. Leave the answering machine on for an extra 15 to 30 minutes.

> Good morning. This is Dr. Thompson's office. The office is open, but we are unable to answer the phone at this time. Please call back after 10:00 a.m.

You will be more organized in the long run and better able to deal with calls and other duties if you are not trying to juggle several things at the same time. Your patients will soon get to know what time you are ready to accept calls. If there is an emergency, they will call the appropriate facility as per your taped message. Callers with nonurgent agendas will call later.

In recording any message, speak clearly and at a moderate pace. Keep all messages as simple as you can. Directions should be simple, clear, and concise.

Pagers

Very few providers still carry pagers, also known as beepers. These small portable message devices are a critical component of a communications network. They allow people who need direct access to the doctor to contact him or her directly, eliminating the need for an answering service. Often the doctor gives the pager number to a short list of health professionals, hospital units, and facilities where he or she has patients.

Mobile Phones

Cellphones (or smartphones) have become as important to most doctors as their pagers—often replacing the pager. There is a wide selection of such devices on the market that allow the doctor to respond to messages swiftly and conveniently. He or she can use text messaging and access email, the internet, and a number of other web-based tools.

The mobile number should be given out only by the doctor. Some doctors still prefer to be reached by pager; many leave their mobile phones turned off. They prefer to use their mobile phone, if necessary, to return calls. Most hospitals do not allow the use of mobile phones inside the building. Current research, however, indicates that the use of mobile devices in hospitals is not as disruptive as many believe.

Communicating across Time Zones

You may be required to contact patients or agencies in other jurisdictions. Be aware of differences in time zones across Canada, as shown in Table 8.1.

TABLE 8.1	Time zones across Canada	
Time Zone	**Location**	**Time**
Pacific	Most of British Columbia, Yukon	1:00 p.m.
Mountain	Alberta, Northwest Territories, Northeastern British Columbia, and western part of Nunavut	2:00 p.m.
Central	Saskatchewan, Manitoba, part of northwestern Ontario, and central part of Nunavut	3:00 p.m.
Eastern	Most of Ontario, most of Quebec, and eastern part of Nunavut	4:00 p.m.
Atlantic	New Brunswick, Nova Scotia, Prince Edward Island, most of Labrador, and easternmost part of Quebec (south of Labrador)	5:00 p.m.
Newfoundland	The island of Newfoundland and southeastern Labrador	5:30 p.m.

L04 TELEPHONE SKILLS AND TECHNIQUES

Handling telephone calls appropriately and efficiently is primarily the AHP's responsibility. You need to control the volume of incoming calls, and triage and direct callers while maintaining a positive, patient-oriented atmosphere. Effective management of these calls is essential not only to the well-being of your patients, but also to the management of your office. It is a challenging task that requires skill, knowledge, patience, and excellent communication skills. Dealing with the public in any situation can be both rewarding and challenging. When this is coupled with health care issues, the challenge is even greater.

Improving Your Telephone Manner

Your attitude, mood, and stress level are clearly conveyed on the phone. People will react to the tone of your voice, your choice of words, and your response to them. If your manner is positive, chances are the telephone conversation will be positive. Even a grumpy, irritated patient is apt to be easier to deal with when there is a pleasant, patient person on the other end of the line. This, in turn, will make your life easier and reduce job stress.

As with face-to-face interactions, effective telephone communication is a skill. Some of us are more natural communicators, readily perceived as warm, caring, and friendly. Think of someone you have spoken with who made you feel good. How did you feel? What made you feel that way? The tone of voice? Inflections? Choice of words? Was the person empathetic and supportive? How did that person show empathy?

When conversing with such people, you can feel their warmth and almost see them smile. You look forward to speaking with them. That is what you want to achieve in the health office. If you are one of those natural communicators, you bring a wonderful asset to your job. If not, you can develop your "telephone self" through practice.

- When the phone rings, stop what you are doing to answer the phone. This will help you focus on the call.

- Take a deep breath, and concentrate on the call.

- If someone comes into the office while you are on the telephone, make eye contact, nod, or wave, but remain focused on the caller. When you finish the call, you can attend to the newly arrived patient.

- Do not push your mouth up to the mouthpiece of the telephone. This muffles your voice. Have you ever heard someone talk with his or her mouth on a microphone? A mouth on the mouthpiece produces a similar effect.

- Do not chew gum, eat, or drink when you are speaking on the telephone.

- Smile when you answer the phone, even if you do not feel like it. Some people claim that a smile will make you less tense and more patient and impart a lift to your voice.

- Practise speaking into a tape recorder with various telephone greetings. You might be surprised at how you sound.

- If you have a soft, quiet voice, practise putting more energy into your voice.

- Speak in a lower voice. A lower tone is more soothing and more easily heard and understood.

- Speak more slowly than you usually do. This gives the person at the other end time to take in what you are saying and adjust his or her thoughts.

- Pronounce each word clearly. Space your words carefully to avoid running them together and sounding garbled.

- Be expressive, avoiding a monotone. This gives interest and meaning to what you are saying and adds appropriate emphasis.

- Do not be embarrassed to use gestures when you are on the telephone; it may enhance the tone and organization of speech. Watch someone talking on the telephone to see how it works. For example, in giving driving directions, many people will sketch the turns in the air; this helps them sequence what they are trying to explain.

Your choice of words is also important (as it is in face-to-face interactions). Use proper grammar and sentence structure and choose your words appropriately. Though proper English usage has relaxed substantially over the last few years, slang and poor grammar have no place in professional conversation. "It don't," "youse guys," "her and I," and "I seen" are some of the errors that will make you sound uneducated and unprofessional. Older people, in particular, will notice this, and in almost every practice today, older people make up a large part of the clientele. If you are not sure about English grammar, take a remedial English course or work through an exercise book. People often fall into error when trying to speak properly. For example, people taught to avoid saying, "Me and Jane are going to the show" may compensate by avoiding "me" entirely and may end up with sentences like "Please return it to Jane or myself"—which is just as bad.

TIP

Answering the Phone: The Six Ps

Prompt

Polite

Precise

Professional

Positive

Patient

Sound confident. Avoid muttering "I guess," "I'm not sure," "ummmm," or "I, uh, like, you know." Such vagueness makes the caller wonder whether you are a reliable source of information. If you are asked something that you cannot answer, simply say, "I will have to check that with the doctor," or "I will recheck that policy, Mrs. Rubinoff, and call you right back." You want to convey the idea that if you do not have the information at hand, you know where to get it and will do so promptly.

Answering the Phone

Promptness Try to answer the telephone before the third ring. This may not always be possible in a busy office, but making a conscious effort will pay off. You may tell yourself that the task you are completing will only take a moment, but it could be seven or eight rings later when you get to the telephone. The caller at this point may be disagreeable and upset or, worse, it may be an emergency. Usually, it is better to answer the telephone and then get back to what you were doing. *Not* making answering the phone a priority may become a habit that will cause endless irritation for patients.

Greetings   Review the examples that follow. Which one appeals to you the most? The least?

- "Good morning, Dr. Tremblay's office. Lise speaking."
- "Dr. Tremblay's office, Lise speaking. How may I help you?"
- "Dr. Tremblay's office, Lise speaking."
- "Dr. Tremblay's office."
- "Doctor's office."

Most patients prefer the first, with the second and third ones close behind. The first greeting is complete and courteous. It identifies the doctor's office and the speaker, as do the second and third.

Giving your own name is not only friendly but helpful. The patient may know you by name and feel more comfortable speaking with you. Furthermore, the patient may be following up on an earlier phone call or visit and want to speak to the same person as before. Having to explain the reason for the call to someone else is frustrating and could waste your time as well as the patient's.

"Doctor's office" is impersonal and lacks warmth. It also does not rule out a wrong number; it could be a different doctor's office. How can you name the doctor if you work for a number of doctors? Some group practices solve this problem with a different line for each doctor. If you have separate lines, answer each with the doctor's name. If you have a common line, answer with the name of the group or clinic:

"Rankin Medical Centre, Andrew speaking."

> ### ⟫⟫⟫ POINTS TO PONDER
>
> Administrative staff in a number of doctor's offices answer the phone with "Doctor's office," claiming not giving a name saves time. But does it? How often does the caller respond, "Is this Dr. Heine's office?" and then, "Is this Diane?" or " Is it you I was speaking with earlier about my ultrasound?" Usually it saves time to establish identification immediately so that the patient can get right to business. What do you think?

Handling Incoming Calls

Dealing with Volume   You can reduce the number of calls you receive in the office by asking patients, other professionals, and agencies to fax information, if appropriate. Faxes are particularly useful for prescription renewal requests (see Chapter 7) and test results (see Chapter 6). A fax gives you a printed copy of the information or request and leaves the phones free for other calls if you have a separate fax line. Some offices are asking that people use email. This is efficient to a point but can become time consuming.

The Morning Rush   Be aware of peak times for incoming calls in your office, and make an effort to change some of these patterns. For example, many patients will call for an appointment first thing in the morning. This is likely a busy time for the office staff. You can ask your patients to call for appointments at certain times of the day or post a sign to that effect. (See the discussion of signs earlier in this chapter.)

Appointment Cancellations   You certainly want patients to call if they have to cancel an appointment. However, to reduce the volume of incoming calls, some health offices have a telecommunications system that asks patients who are calling to cancel or reschedule to leave a message. These messages must be checked at regular intervals.

Patients Calling for Clarification of Instructions   A common type of call will be from patients seeking information. You can help reduce this type of call by clearly and concisely explaining any instructions to the patient about tests and appointments (see Chapter 6). Whenever possible, give out printed instructions, and highlight relevant areas. Avoid medical jargon that might confuse the patient. It is worth taking a couple of extra minutes to explain something thoroughly if it saves having to explain it again over the phone.

Patients Calling for Test Results   Try reversing the process. Tell patients that you will call them if there is any concern about the test results. If patients want to know either way, tell them you will call with results within a certain time frame. This obviously depends on the type of test; results from simple blood work can be back within 24 hours, while biopsy results may take a week. You could also advise patients to call the office if they have not heard from you by a certain date. This still gives you the opportunity to call, but does not leave the patient sweating for weeks if you forget or the test is delayed.

Handling Typical Calls

Most calls in a doctor's office fall into certain defined categories. Your first decision is regarding which calls to handle yourself and which to pass on to the doctor. If there is a nurse, she can take a number of the calls that you would otherwise route to the doctor. The nurse and the doctor should agree just what types of calls the nurse can handle—usually questions about immunizations and other health-related issues. If the nurse takes a call that he or she does not feel qualified to handle, the nurse will direct the call to the doctor or have the doctor return the call when he or she is available. Most providers put aside a designated time for returning calls.

Table 8.2 assumes that there is no nurse in the office and divides typical calls into three categories: those that you or another AHP can usually handle, those that should be directed to the doctor (either immediately or as a message to call back), and those that fall into a grey area. The ones in the middle column of the table you may be able to handle after consultation with the doctor, or you may be able to handle in part before leaving a message for the doctor. The doctor should establish clear policies on how to handle different types of calls.

Drug and Supply Representatives   Drug reps are people employed by drug companies to promote their company's line of medications. They visit doctors' offices to discuss their products and sometimes leave samples. The reps may call for an appointment or simply arrive at the office. Most doctors set specific times—perhaps every Friday from 11:30 a.m. to 12:00 p.m.—when they will meet with the rep. You need to know the policy, make sure the drug reps know it, and adhere to it. Encourage reps to call the day before to confirm the appointment. Remember to notify drug reps as well as patients if you have to cancel appointments.

Supply representatives also visit all types of medical offices. For example, dental supply representatives are employed by dental supply companies who provide equipment,

TABLE 8.2 Routing typical calls

Calls You Can Handle	Calls You Might Handle with Consultation	Calls to Direct to the Doctor
Drug reps	Patients asking for medical advice	Other doctors wanting to speak to your doctor (always put through another doctor unless specifically advised otherwise)
Patients calling to make appointments	Patients calling to request the results of lab tests	The hospital wanting orders on a patient who has been admitted or asking to change or renew an order
Patients calling for information about family	Calls relating to prescription renewals/repeats	The hospital calling about a change in a patient's status (always put this through; it may be an emergency)
Patients wanting to talk to staff members	Patients wanting to speak with the doctor	Community agencies calling to speak with the doctor about patients under their care
Individuals looking for a doctor	Laboratories calling with test results	Personal calls for the doctor
Laboratories or diagnostic facilities calling to confirm or change appointment times		

sundries, and service support to the dental office. The representative will visit the office to collect orders, demonstrate new products, arrange for learning seminars for the dentist and staff, and arrange for equipment servicing. It is more efficient if these reps have an appointment rather than arriving unannounced.

Patients Calling to Make Appointments This type of call is generally straightforward, and the AHP would handle it. The only time you may want to check with the doctor would be if the patient had spoken to the doctor with a special request for a visit outside of office hours. Unless the doctor had told you about this, you would confirm with him or her.

Remember that when patients call to make an appointment, it is for a reason, usually related to a health concern. One cannot overemphasize the importance of a pleasant telephone manner in this situation. Be positive and helpful. Try to accommodate the patient's request, but remain in control by offering choices. Never use barrier words, such as "I can't," "you can't," "it's impossible." Instead, try the following:

> Mr. Li, which would be better for you, morning or afternoon? I'm sorry, Mr. Li, I don't have anything for late morning. I can fit you in on Wednesday at 9. I realize that's somewhat early for you, but the advantage is that you won't have to wait. Later in the morning, on Wednesdays in particular, we get very busy and often run a bit late. Now, I could give you an appointment next Monday morning, but that's six days away. Would you prefer that?"

You are maintaining control while offering Mr. Li choices.

Appropriate use of triage is essential. Anyone whose problem sounds urgent should be seen immediately or sent to the emergency department. Anything like chest pain, shortness of breath or other breathing difficulties, loss of consciousness, profuse bleeding, loss of function of body parts (e.g., inability to effectively move one side of the body), or loss of sensation must be dealt with immediately, as should earaches, high fever, or a UTI (urinary tract infection). The doctor should provide you with criteria for triage both in the office and over the telephone. Remember that it is not your responsibility to make medical decisions, but you should know how to direct patients with health concerns. You will gain experience at triage, but never second-guess a patient in distress. When in doubt, err on the side of caution and assume it is an emergency: Check with the doctor immediately and/or send the patient to the nearest emergency department. A needless emergency visit or a little disruption is better than a preventable death or permanent disability.

Patients Asking for Medical Advice   The best advice here is "Don't." An exception is triaging obvious emergencies. Your employer may also define certain areas of knowledge and experience within which you may give advice. For example, if a mother calls asking when to bring her child in for the next well-baby check-up or for a set of immunizations, you should be able to answer by consulting a schedule of routine visits and the patient's chart. However, if a child is ill and the mother wonders about going ahead with an immunization, check with the nurse or doctor if you have not been given clear guidelines.

If you have an office nurse, direct advice calls to her unless office policies dictate otherwise. If you do not have a nurse, make a note of the concern and tell the patient that the doctor will call back, or make an appointment for the patient to discuss the concern with the doctor.

Patients Asking about Costs for Dental Treatment   Don't give quotes unless you have explicit guidelines and instructions. It is best to explain to the patient that the cost will vary from person to person. Because each person's mouth is unique, it is difficult to quote for dental services. The dental office policy may be that you could present to the calling patient a range of fees; you might say, for example, "The cost of a dental cleaning varies depending on how many teeth are present and how much time is spent on your cleaning. The average range is between $75 and $150."

TIP

Think a smile, be upbeat and enthusiastic, negotiate, but remain in control while letting the patients think that they are making the decisions.

Patients Calling for Lab Test Results   The doctor should have a policy on which results you can give over the phone. Most policies allow you to give normal results on the phone. The doctor usually discusses an abnormal result with the patient as it will probably require treatment or explanation. Some doctors may ask you to call the patient, let them know of the abnormal result, and set up an appointment.

Patients Calling for Information about Family Members   The doctor more commonly delivers this type of information because it involves confidentiality issues, assessments, and perhaps a prognosis. Sometimes the doctor may ask you to pass on straightforward information. Remember that information must not be given without the patient's express permission. The exception is parents discussing a minor child— and this becomes a grey area as the child gets older. Generally, a doctor would not share information about a teenager without the teenager's permission, especially if it involved sexual activity or birth control.

Be polite but firm. You might suggest that the family member speak directly with the patient. If he or she cannot, then probably the patient wishes to keep the information confidential. For example, you could say, "I am sorry, Mrs. Smith, but I am not authorized to give you that information. If you are able to supply us ⟨permission⟩ to release that information, you could come in and d⟨iscuss it⟩ with Dr. Thompson. Perhaps if you speak to your son, he will ⟨answer⟩ your questions."

Or you may simply say, "I cannot provide you with that info⟨rmation; it is confi-⟩dential. I can have the doctor call you."

Personal Calls for the Doctor   Assume that the doctor's s⟨taff and family⟩ members would not call unless it is important. Ask if they wis⟨h to speak to the doc-⟩tor immediately or if he or she can call back. For the most p⟨art, family and⟩ friends would text or email the provider and not call the mai⟨n office.⟩

Other personal calls may be to give the doctor informat⟨ion and not require you to⟩ speak with the doctor. Unless it is urgent or the doctor h⟨as asked that the call be⟩ put through, take a message and telephone number. As w⟨ell, give the caller an⟩ approximate time for the return call, and ask if there is a be⟨tter time to call.⟩

Patients Wanting to Speak with the Doctor   Try to determine why the p⟨atient⟩ wants to speak to the doctor. Most patients will give at least a general reason. You may be able to handle the call yourself, or it may be best for the patient to make an appointment to see the doctor. If the patient is seeking nonurgent medical advice and you have a nurse in the office, direct the call to him or her. If a patient refuses to give a reason, do not press the matter. Respect the patient's right to privacy, and have the doctor call back. Take the person's name and the phone number where he or she can be reached at the time you expect the doctor to return the call. Repeat the number back to the patient to ensure accuracy. Pull the patient's chart and leave it with the doctor.

Unless the case is urgent, most doctors will return calls after they have finished seeing patients for the day. If a patient insists on speaking to the doctor at once, explain that the doctor is with a patient. Be polite but firm. Remember that you are the filter between the doctor and the outside world. Ultimately it is the provider who will make the decision as to when to return a call.

New Patients   You need to know the doctor's policy on new patients. There are still a number of Canadians without a primary care physician. Family physicians realize that if they take on more patients than they can handle, they will not have enough time to offer high-quality medical care to anyone.

Some doctors have an iron-clad policy of not accepting any new patients. Others will accept relatives of families already in their practice or will make the occasional exception. Sometimes a doctor will be asked personally to take on a new patient or family. He or she may agree and then forget to tell you. If someone calls for an appointment saying that the doctor has agreed to accept him or her as a patient, check with the doctor.

If your practice is not accepting new patients, say so: "I am sorry, but Dr. Suzuki is not accepting any new patients at this time." Be firm but polite. It is also helpful to put a sign in the reception area to this effect. If there are doctors in your area accepting patients, you could add their contact information to the sign. All jurisdictions have a website where individuals can add their names to a wait list for a doctor in their area. Make this information available.

A newly established doctor will take new patients, usually until a certain patient number is reached. If you work in such a practice, find out the doctor's policies. Some primary care delivery models may stipulate the relative number of patients a physician should have in his or her practice. Some doctors interview patients before deciding to accept them. This has highly discouraged in all jurisdictions; the practice is sometimes called "cherry picking" and leads to troublesome ethical questions such as discrimination.

accepting new patients, you will have to initiate a patient chart and speak to the patient about transferring records from the former provider.

Unlike physicians, dentists are abundant in most communities. Most dentists welcome new patients and depend on a referral program. Dental offices have incorporated marketing strategies as a way of attracting new patients. Using a combination of both internal and external marketing has become the norm for today's practices. Individuals can call a general dentist and some dental specialists without a referral. Optometrists and chiropractors also take patients without referrals.

Laboratories Calling with Test Results   Most of the time you can take these calls. Remember, accuracy is paramount when recording lab results. One mistake when writing down lab values—transposing two numbers, for example, or putting a decimal point in the wrong position—can change the value from critical to noncritical and vice versa. For example, suppose the lab phoned with a hemoglobin level of 12.4 (which is normal) but you wrote down 4.12 (which is critically low). The doctor would probably order needless follow-up tests and alarm the patient. Writing down lab values for the wrong patient can also have disastrous consequences. You might be telling the doctor that Mrs. Strugnel, 65, has tested positive for pregnancy.

- Have the caller spell the patient's name if you are not sure.
- Always read the test results back to the caller. For example, "The Hb was 14.5, the WBC 13.000, the INR was 7.5, and the blood sugar 9. The patient was Mr. Michael Cook." Asking for the date of birth is an added safety check. (This information is on most requisitions and therefore would be available to the caller.) There may be more than one patient in the office with the same last name and first initial or even the same first name. The date of birth may be the only unique piece of identifying information.

Calls Relating to Prescriptions   A significant number of the incoming calls in a doctor's office concern prescriptions—although with most pharmacies faxing prescription requests, these calls are decreasing. These calls may be placed by the patient, the pharmacy, or a health care facility and may be requests for a renewal or a repeat of a prescription or, in some cases, for a new prescription. Attention to detail and accuracy is essential. Doctors will have different policies on how to handle these calls, but all prescription requests should be personally reviewed by the doctor. See the section on prescriptions in Chapter 7 for more detailed information.

Calls from Other Doctors   Under most circumstances, you would put a call from another doctor through to the doctor unless the caller is content just to leave a message.

Calls from the Hospital

Order Requests   An order is a directive provided by the doctor, usually to a nurse, concerning the care of a hospitalized patient. Patients must have doctor's orders provided on admission and on discharge, as well as during their stay. These orders change, sometimes several times a day, depending on the patient's needs and condition. If the nurse calling tells you the order is needed urgently, put the call through right away. For example, a patient who is in pain may require an order for an analgesic, or a patient with a critical test result may require insulin or an anticoagulant immediately. Even if not urgent, hospital order requests should be dealt with fairly quickly, but the doctor would probably prefer to deal with them between patients. If the nurse leaves a message to have the doctor call back, take the name of the hospital, the patient-care unit, the patient's first and last names, the diagnosis, the name of the nurse calling, and, if given the information, what the order is needed for.

Often, a hospital unit will call wanting discharge orders for a patient. It is not uncommon for a doctor to tell a patient he or she can go home and then forget to write the order. The patient packs up and goes to the nursing station to announce he or she is leaving only to find that no discharge orders have been written. Sometimes a doctor will write a discharge order for a new mother but forget to write one for the baby. The patient is usually asked to wait until the nurse receives the discharge order. In these situations, if at all possible, put the call through to the doctor.

Report of a Change in a Patient's Condition The hospital will call if a patient's condition takes a turn for the worse or becomes unstable. Put such calls through immediately. Hospitals do not often call to let the doctor know that the patient's condition has improved unless the doctor has requested such information for a very ill patient.

Notification of a Surgery Date You can handle these calls. Make note of the surgery date on the patient's chart, and make a note for the doctor, who may be required to assist with the surgery. Make sure that a preoperative assessment has been completed on the patient if required. (You may be responsible for booking this assessment.) Call the patient with all necessary information. Make any other necessary arrangements, such as booking a pre-admission routine, which requires the patient to complete forms and have required blood work done ahead of time.

Community Agencies Wanting to Discuss a Patient with the Doctor Usually, you should put this call through to the doctor unless the caller says the matter can wait. Often it is related to a matter that the agency is dealing with at the time of the call. The office nurse, if you have one, may be able to handle this type of call.

The Telephone and Confidentiality

Conversations in any office are easily overheard. You will often be discussing confidential information with patients, perhaps peers, and other health professionals. Assess the potential for breach of confidentiality, and use your ingenuity to avoid problems. Try to speak in a low voice. If you are in an office with a window area that can be closed off, do so. Say as little as possible if it involves confidential information, and let the person on the other end of the telephone do most of the talking. Take or make highly confidential calls in a location that can be private. If your office has no such location, you may have to reserve some telephone calls for times when the reception area is empty (e.g., noon hour, just before closing), or use a phone in the doctor's office when he or she is out.

Remember that it is against the law to release any medical information about patients without their written permission or that of their designated authority. (This applies to any means of exchanging information. You cannot, for example, transfer medical records to a new doctor without the patient's written permission.)

You can give information to specialists to whom the patient has been referred or to anyone else directly and actively involved in the patient's care. Give only the information needed. A physiotherapist probably needs to know about a patient's hip problem, but not her obstetrical history or the fact that she was on anti-depressants several years ago. You are not at liberty to discuss a patient's condition with even another staff member, for example, just because the patient is a mutual acquaintance or has an interesting case history. Even good news is confidential. It can be easy to slip into giving out confidential information, so think carefully. For example, Fatima was working in a hospital in a maternal/child unit. She went down for coffee. Renée (who worked in a medical unit) sat down beside her, and they began discussing mutual friends:

"I heard that Tia came in last night in active labour. Did she have her baby yet?"

Fatima thought for a minute and responded, "I can't give you that information, Renée. I am sure that Tom (Tia's husband) will get around to notifying everyone when the time is right."

"Give me a break, Fatima, we're not talking life and death here. I won't tell anyone."

"Sorry, I can't," Fatima replied. "I have to get back to the floor. See you later."

Fatima did the right thing. It can be tempting to share this kind of information with a friend or colleague, especially if you are pressured, but to do so is unprofessional, unethical, *and* against the law.

Never leave a message containing medical information about a patient with another person (other than, of course, a child's parent on matters where confidentiality is not an issue) or on an answering machine unless special arrangements have been made. There are conflicting thoughts on how to leave messages. Even a simple message to call a doctor's office could be a problem if someone chose to impersonate the patient in order to get the information. Besides, the patient may not want others to know that she has been to see the doctor. Even if confidentiality is not an issue in the patient's home, a patient waiting for test results could become anxious, especially if he or she has to wait until the next day or after the weekend to call you back. One option is to simply leave a message to "call Laura" (using your first name).

Most health facilities will require that you sign a confidentiality form when you are hired. We will look at confidentiality in the hospital in Part V.

Taking Telephone Messages

Record everything that requires action or a call back—the most efficient way to do this is to use your computer messaging/task feature and send the message to the appropriate team member. *Do not trust anything to memory*. In a busy office, it is too easy to forget something. Never write a message on a scrap of paper—there is a fair chance that the piece of paper will get lost. If you do write things down, keep a notepad or notebook and a pen in a convenient location.

Every message recorded on paper or electronically requires the following:

- Name of the caller
- Name of the patient, if different from the caller
- Telephone number
- Date and time

Name   Be sure that you write down the caller's name accurately. If you are in doubt, ask. If you are embarrassed to admit that you do not remember a patient's name, ask for the spelling:

> Regan, could you spell your last name for me?
>
> T-h-o-m-p-s-o-n
>
> Thanks. I wasn't sure if you spelled it with or without a p.

If someone is calling on behalf of a patient, get the patient's name as well. Ask whether the doctor should return the call to the caller or the patient.

Caller's Telephone Number   Read the telephone number back to the caller to ensure that it is correct. Make sure your writing is legible. If you are in a hurry, your "3" might look like an "8," for example, or you might transpose numbers. Try to approximate what time the doctor will return the call. This can be difficult with a doctor's uncertain schedule, but it is unreasonable to expect the caller to wait around indefinitely. Ask the caller for the number where he or she can be reached at the time you expect the doctor to return the call. Also, ask the caller to try to keep the line free at that time. It is frustrating to a doctor who is trying to return a call several times only to find the line busy each time; the doctor may not have the time to keep trying.

Date and Time   This is important because return calls are sometimes overlooked or delayed. Knowing the date and time the call was received will help the doctor return the call within a reasonable time frame.

Content of the Message   The types of messages you take will vary. The most common are requests for prescription renewals (discussed in Chapter 7) and the results of lab tests (discussed in Chapter 6). Repeat the message to ensure accuracy, especially if it involves numbers, such as a lab result. You can summarize a more general message, but make sure you include all important points.

Signature or Initials of the Message Taker   This is important in a large office. If the doctor has any questions about the message, he or she needs to know who took it. Including your signature also ensures that you take responsibility for what you have written.

Electronic Messaging

Most medical software systems have a messaging platform (or a message board) that can be used to perform numerous types of communication tasks as well as task management and communications functions. These include sending a message to any team member with the option to prioritize the message (e.g., normal, urgent, or very urgent). "Very urgent" messages will, on some systems, pop up on the recipient's screen (see Figure 8.6). Some programs will also colour code prioritized messages.

A message board or task manager platform can be used in several situations:

- By the doctor to asking you (or other staff members) to perform various tasks, such as "Call Mrs. Woodrow and tell her she needs to have an INR done tomorrow."

- You might get a call from a patient requiring a drug renewal. You would message the doctor "Mr. Edgar Buckland would like his Advil renewed." When the doctor has finished renewing or not renewing Mr. Buckland's Advil, he or she will message you back to say the task is completed. You would post that into the patient's chart.

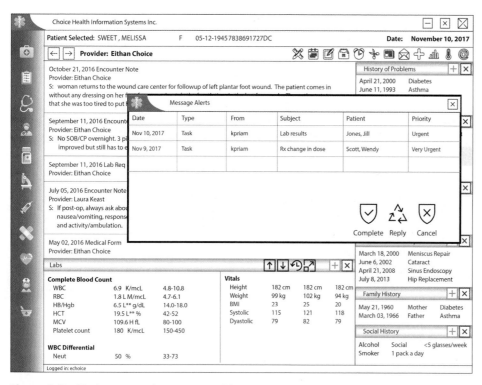

Figure 8.6 Tasks messaging screen with message marked "Very Urgent"
Used by permission of Choice Learning, Inc.

- If you have to call a patient and there is no answer, you can leave a note "left message, no answer." The task will stay active until you mark it as completed. At that point, the completed action will be filed in the patient's EMR (e.g. "Mrs. Woodrow has been notified to have an INR done tomorrow").

- You can also attach phone messages to the patient's chart—some will require a response from the doctor, others might be information only. For example, Mrs. Bastone called to say her husband had coughed up some bright red blood. You inform the doctor, and he or she tells you to bring Mr. Bastone in that afternoon, but when you call, Mr. Bastone refuses to come in, preferring to wait. Posting a phone note on the chart is prudent for legal as well as informational purposes. The doctor may try calling Mr. Bastone himself or let him make his own decision.

Personal messages for the doctor are usually still done electronically. Leave the "patient box" unchecked. The system also functions as an employee intranet.

Handling More Than One Call

If there are two lines into the office or clinic, it is inevitable that sometimes they will both be ringing at once or you will be on line 1 when line 2 rings. If you are the only person available to answer the phone, you need to deal with both calls and find out if either represents an emergency. Suppose you were talking to Mrs. Felipe on line 1 when line 2 rings:

> Excuse me, Mrs. Felipe, may I put you on hold for a minute? (Answer line 2)

> Dr. Patel's office, Theresa speaking. Are you able to hold? (Wait long enough to hear the answer. Imagine a patient complaining of acute chest pain or stroke symptoms only to be put on hold! If the caller hesitates, ask, "Is this an emergency?" If the caller identifies an emergency, then you must deal with it. If this necessitates a long delay, briefly return to line 1.)

> I'm sorry, Mrs. Felipe, I have an urgent situation to deal with and will call you back as soon as I can. (Don't say "something important to deal with," which suggests she is not important.) (If the caller on line 1 agrees to hold, go back to line 2 and complete the urgent call. Then return to line 1.)

> Hello, I'm sorry to have kept you waiting. How can I help you?

TIP

Making Effective Calls

- Make the call at an appropriate time.
- Be sure that you are the best person to handle the call. For example, are there likely to be questions that only the doctor can answer? Are you in conflict with the person?
- Know whom you wish to speak to and if someone else can take the information. Place the call when the appropriate person is most likely to be available.
- If confidentiality is a concern, place the call from a phone with privacy.
- Have the information you need handy, such as a calendar, the doctor's appointment schedule, or the patient's chart.
- Plan what you want to say.
- Write a list of information you need.
- If you are retrieving information, especially medications and lab values, write it down and read it back for accuracy.
- Be polite but brief and to the point. Avoid long social conversations.

The caller may not want to hold for reasons other than an emergency. He or she may be calling long distance or may be busy. These calls should be returned as soon as possible.

Ending a Call

Always bring some type of closure to the conversation. Thank the person for calling, or end with some other pleasant phrase, for example, "I look forward to seeing you on Thursday," or "I appreciate your calling with that information." Always say goodbye, and allow the caller to hang up first.

Handling Outgoing Calls

Most AHPs will tell you that there is no ideal time to make outgoing calls. Dealing with patients, answering the telephone, finding reports and charts, and responding to doctors' requests leave little uninterrupted time. But effective management of outgoing calls is an essential component of practice management.

You can eliminate the need for some calls by using other methods of communication. If fax or email will work well, use it. This usually saves time and provides a printed record.

Being organized and prepared will make your outgoing calls more effective and help you manage time. Have a plan for each call that you make. Outgoing calls, like incoming calls, tend to fall into certain categories:

- Scheduling appointments for patients at other facilities
- Notifying patients of test results or appointment times
- Responding to insurance companies or lawyers
- Arranging file transfers
- Arranging meetings or speaking engagements for the doctor
- Responding to requests by the doctor (calling patients, other facilities, finding reports, etc.)

Keep Needed Numbers Handy Looking up numbers wastes time. If your telephone system has an autodial feature, program in frequently called numbers, such as hospitals, consultants you frequently refer to, pharmacies, laboratories and other diagnostic facilities, and community care agencies. Or you can create a file on your computer. Keep your telephone numbers up to date. Otherwise, you will forget and have to look the number up or call the operator. This applies to your patients' files as well. When you swipe a patient's health card, check to see whether the address and telephone number are current.

When you are making appointments, write the patient's daytime phone number or email address in the appointment book so that if you have to cancel, you will not need to look up numbers. Some offices skip this step because it takes time, but looking up 20 or 30 phone numbers (even on the computer) is considerably more time consuming.

Ensure that your numbers are current. Every few months, specifically ask the patient if his or her phone number is still the same: "Mr. Kim, your number is still 647-444-4444 at work, and 647-333-3333 at home?"

Plan the Timing Make the call at the appropriate time. For example, unless the matter is urgent, do not call a hospital unit at 10:00 a.m., when nurses are likely giving out medications, or between 3:00 and 3:30 p.m., when some of the nurses are likely to be taking reports as shifts change. You will likely get a busy signal or an answering machine and just have to call again. Obviously, you cannot always time your calls, but you would be surprised how much time you save by doing so when you can. Prioritize calls, and make time-sensitive ones as soon as you can. Make the rest of your outgoing calls in a clump during a less busy time of day. Try to avoid interruptions. If there is a more secluded phone, use it, especially if there is a concern about confidentiality. If you are in the front office, close the window leading to the reception area (if you have one). If possible, have someone else (another AHP or an office nurse) receive patients while you make the calls.

Be Prepared Have handy all the information you are likely to need. For example, if you are booking a consultation or a test, have the patient's chart beside you so that you can answer questions. Also, find out beforehand when the patient is available so you do not waste time rebooking. (You could ask the patient to rebook, but some facilities prefer to deal with the office.)

Make Reminder Calls, if Needed Many specialists, dentists, optometrists, and chiropractors, who often have appointments set up well in advance, have the office routinely call the patient the day before an appointment with a reminder. Family doctors' offices are usually too busy. However, if you have a patient who is repeatedly late or has difficulty remembering appointments (perhaps because of cognitive impairment), it might be worth your while to make that call.

Stay on Track When you have the time, a brief social conversation is pleasant and helps build relationships with patients and other professionals. However, a few minutes here and there can really add up. If you are pressed for time, after a brief greeting, get right to the point of the call and end it politely but promptly.

Leaving Messages If the person you are calling is not home, leaving a message—either with another person or on an answering machine—requires thought and adherence to confidentiality standards. Avoid leaving medical information unless explicitly asked to do so by the patient. Simply ask the patient (or designated person) to call the office back. Remember to speak slowly and clearly and repeat your number at the end of the message. Rarely is it a good idea to call the patient at work unless you have the patient's permission to do so. If confidentiality is a real concern, arrange for the patient to call you if he or she is expecting a test result.

Controlling Telephone Time

Time on the telephone can easily get out of hand, especially if patients feel that you are free for a social conversation. A patient may be lonely or may just like to talk. A brief social exchange is friendly and appropriate, but longer conversations will eat away at your workday. Be polite, but keep the caller on track. "You wanted the results of your lab test, Mrs. Pinder." Or, "Mrs. Pinder, when did you want that appointment for? I have an opening tomorrow afternoon." You can also politely indicate that you are ending the conversation. "Thank you for calling, Mrs. Pinder. I'll see you next week." Usually, the caller will get the message and facilitate ending the call.

TIP

Remember, as discussed in Chapter 1, professionalism is essential. This includes your dress, attitude, and manner. Always address others with the utmost respect, whether in written or oral communication. This includes your nonverbal communication, the tone of voice you use, and the words you choose.

L05 FACE-TO-FACE COMMUNICATION WITH PATIENTS

Communicating face to face draws on the same skills and attitudes as telephone communication. However, face-to-face encounters bring the added dimension of vision. You are now communicating not only with your voice and words, but with your facial expression, body language, and even dress and presentation. Your responses to people are more perceptible. You may be able to modulate your voice to disguise distaste for a person or anger at a situation on the telephone. In person, you also have to control your facial expression, eye contact, and demeanour to create a positive impression. Some people find it easier to relate to people in person; others find the telephone easier. You need to learn to be comfortable with both. You will probably spontaneously establish an easy, pleasant relationship with most patients. You may feel no rapport with others and find still others irritating or difficult. There will always be a segment of the practice that takes up more of your energy and time because of personalities, needs, or maybe loneliness. There is an old saying among doctors: "Twenty percent of your practice will take 80 percent of your time." This applies to your time as well. These patients may call for appointments regularly or simply show up expecting to be seen. Some come to see the doctor for human contact, reassurance, and support. At times it will be difficult to smile and be pleasant, but your job requires you to do so. You can improve patient management by developing strategies to help you maintain a consistently professional and friendly manner.

Greeting the Patient

What Not to Do   "The Doberman at Desk A" is a reputation you do not want! Whether you interact with individuals on the telephone or in person, you are almost always the first point of contact for anyone entering or calling the office. While you have a duty to the physician to screen calls and visits, you are also responsible for being polite, reasonable, and approachable to patients and the public. This applies to any medical facility, whether you work in a lab, in a family doctor's office, or for a specialist, and for any type of interaction: handling an appointment request, giving out information to a patient, or directing a referral. Regardless of the situation, there are proper and polite ways to respond. Do not be responsible for a negative reputation either for yourself or the facility in which you work, where individuals are remiss to call or come in because of perceived Doberman-like characteristics: ferocious, snappy, protective, and impatient.

Appropriate Greetings   If possible, acknowledge each patient as he or she enters the office. Always greet the patient with a smile. If you are on the telephone when a patient arrives, make eye contact, smile, nod, or use other appropriate nonverbal signals of recognition. When you are finished with the call, greet the patient and ask for his or her health card. Briefly answer any questions, and let him or her know approximately how long it will be before he or she sees the doctor. The exchange does not have to be a long one and may save you time in the long run. Give the patient your undivided attention, even if for less than a minute. Have a brief conversation with the patient about safe topics. Certainly, you do not want to discuss his or her latest round of radiation therapy or visit to the psychiatrist. For example, it would be inappropriate to comment to a newly arrived patient, "Good morning, Robert. You look like you've finally lost some weight!" Or, "Your sister-in-law was in this morning. I think her ulcer is clearing up." Thoughtless comments like these embarrass patients and breach confidentiality.

Develop strategies to personalize your patient interactions. One way is to keep notes on a patient's chart (sticky notes on a paper chart or incidental notes on an electronic chart) about the patient's interests, hobbies, or family events. Imagine how valued the patient will feel when you ask about his recent scuba diving trip or how her new granddaughter is doing. You will not always have the information or the time to do this, but when you can it adds a personal touch and can make someone's day. For example,

> Mrs. Janssen, may I have your health card please? Thank you ... how is that new granddaughter of yours doing? She would be ... what ... six months old now? Here's your card, Mrs. Janssen, please have a seat. The doctor is running pretty much on time today.

The extra minute you take to inquire about her granddaughter establishes a warm, friendly feeling. You do have to keep the conversation short, though. If Mrs. Janssen starts telling you in detail about her daughter's struggles with childcare, you can smile sympathetically and say, "Yes, it's a challenge. Here's your card, Mrs. Janssen."

Addressing the Patient

Use the patient's name whenever possible (but do not repeat it so often as to sound insincere). It personalizes the encounter and makes the patient feel respected. There is a trend today, in stores, restaurants, and professional settings, to call everyone by their first name. Some patients are comfortable with first names; others are not. Older patients, in particular, and patients from certain cultures may find the familiarity disrespectful and impolite. For example, a clinical secretary came around the corner into the reception area of a hospital radiology department with a chart in hand. "Betty, Betty," she called, her voice getting louder, "is Betty here?" An elderly woman moved forward, dressed in a neat suit and a hat and using a walker. She looked at the secretary and said coldly, "Don't you have any manners? What gives you the right to be so familiar with me?" Other patients may feel the same resentment even if they do not express it. If you do not know the patient, initially use Mr., Miss, or Mrs. (Glance at the next-of-kin section on the chart; a married woman will usually give her husband as next of kin; if the next of kin is a parent or sibling, you can try Miss or Ms.) For example, in the previous situation, the clinical secretary might have said, "Mrs. Sheridan ... Mrs. Sheridan ... is Mrs. Sheridan here?" Mrs. Sheridan might reply, "Please call me Betty." Or she might correct, "That's Miss Sheridan." If she does not, the secretary may ask her how she prefers to be addressed. When you meet a new patient in an office, always ask about preference. Write the patient's answer on the front page of the chart as a reminder to other staff members. Some people write their full names on their forms but prefer to be addressed by a nickname; others hate them. Some women prefer Ms. to Mrs. or Miss; others, especially older women, dislike the title.

It is also important to try to pronounce the patient's name properly. If you are unsure of how to pronounce the name of a new patient, ask the patient to help you rather than mangling the name. Then, write down the name *the way it sounds, using phonetics*.

The Wait

If the doctor is running late or has been unexpectedly called away on an emergency, inform the waiting patients. Their time is just as valuable as the doctor's. Often, people take time off from work, get babysitters, and otherwise rearrange their schedule to come see the doctor. A long delay may disrupt their arrangements. Letting patients know about delays shows respect and often avoids the frustration of an indeterminate wait. Offer alternatives, depending on how long the delay is. If the delay is short, you can tell the patient, "David, Dr. Levesque is running about 15 minutes behind." For a longer delay, you might suggest they go for a coffee, do some shopping, and come back at a certain time. Patients may have to alter some plans—perhaps phone the babysitter, the hairdresser, or the person picking them up. If the delay is more than half an hour, it is reasonable to give the patient the choice of waiting or booking another appointment. You may also be able to avoid such waits by getting in touch with patients before they leave for the doctor's office to inform them of the delay and reschedule, if necessary. (See Chapter 9 for a discussion on scheduling.)

Escorting Patients to the Examination Room

Escorting patients to the examination room provides another opportunity for conversation. If your office has a nurse, this may be his or her responsibility, or it may be done by whoever is free. This applies to most health offices. In the dental office, for example, it could be the administrative assistant, dental assistant, hygienist, or dentist. Watch the traffic flow. If you see a patient leaving, you will know that the examination room is empty. If you are alone in the office, prepare the room for the next patient *before* you usher him or her in. If there is a nurse who is busy elsewhere, check the room first; the nurse may have already prepared it. Take the patient's chart, call the patient, and walk beside, not in front of, him or her to the room. Walking side by side feels more equal and allows conversational exchange. Stop just outside the door, and allow the patient to enter first. It may be your duty to obtain a brief history about why the patient has come to see the doctor and record the information on the chart. You would then instruct the patient on how to prepare for the examination and provide a gown, if appropriate. Usually, only a complete physical requires that the patient remove all clothing. For an examination of the upper body (such as the chest/lungs), patients are usually asked to remove everything from the waist up. The abdomen may be examined with clothing on, depending on the doctor's preference. If a woman is having a pelvic examination or a Pap smear, she would be required to remove everything from the waist down. Most patients appreciate privacy while undressing.

If you are simply escorting the patient to the room, try to keep the conversation light and general. Answer any questions you can, and let the patient know how long the doctor will be. Put the chart in the designated place, usually a chart holder outside the door of the examination room or on the doctor's desk.

When the Patient Is Leaving

Unless patients have to book an appointment or a test, they often leave without saying goodbye. They may be feeling confused about the instructions they have been given or disturbed about some information the doctor has given them. Acknowledging their departure gives you the opportunity to pick up such cues and respond accordingly, answering questions or offering a comforting comment if appropriate. A smile, "Goodbye," "It was nice to see you," or even a wave is good patient relations if you can manage it. In many dental offices, the patient is asked to stop at the administrative desk after the appointment, either to pay for dental services or make another appointment—even for a check-up or cleaning that is six months away.

Communication with Patients with Altered Mental Health

For the most part, individuals with mental illness are the same as anyone else, and thus you communicate with them as you would with anyone. Mental illness, however, as with any illness, can occur at varying levels. Individuals with a mental illness that is more clinically evident may indeed have altered communication patterns. These may include a short attention span, higher levels of frustration/impatience, or an inability to internalize what is being said. This would require on your part patience, understanding, and perseverance. Understanding the typical behaviours and needs of the more common mental disorders, such as psychosis and schizophrenia, is helpful. Individuals coping with clinically evident psychosis, for example, can exhibit thinking disturbances. Thoughts may be unclear, following a conversation may be difficult, and the patient may appear unresponsive or uncooperative; some of these patients may also experience delusions or hallucinations. Schizophrenia affects perception, thinking, feeling, and behaviour. Some communication techniques include speaking calmly and clearly, and maintaining eye contact. Phrases such as "I would really appreciate it if you would …" are helpful.

It is important to remember that mental illness has nothing to do with a person's level of intelligence. Treat these individuals with the same level of respect and honesty that you would any other person. Trust, as with any patient, is an essential ingredient to successful communication. Individuals with a mental illness may not like to be reminded of it, and certainly do not want to be branded as "sick" because of it. Being understood, respected, and valued is of great importance, especially if the person feels that having a mental disorder stigmatizes him or her.

Many are fearful of individuals with more pronounced mental illnesses. Having a mental illness does not increase the likelihood of offensive or violent behaviour (unless compounded by something like substance abuse). If you are working in an established medical practice, you will get to know the needs, attitudes, and communication styles of individual patients. There may be specific strategies for dealing with an individual, including "triggers" and topics to avoid. If the person's condition is complicated with substance abuse, interaction may become difficult. Seek the assistance of the health care provider if you feel the conversation is getting out of hand.

LO6 DEALING WITH DIFFICULT SITUATIONS

You must be prepared to interact effectively, both in person and on the telephone, with patients in a variety of situations. Inevitably, some patients will be angry, rude, or just plain difficult. They may be upset, anxious, stressed, or confused. How people react will reflect a combination of personality factors and the situation they find themselves in.

If not handled sensitively, an angry and upset patient may become increasingly louder and sometimes aggressive. Your challenge is to maintain your composure and try to contain the situation. Waiting to see the doctor is an ongoing source of irritation in many health offices. Some patients relax with a book, others mutter good-naturedly, and still others become openly resentful. Other issues upset patients as well: a lab test result that they were not notified about, a long wait before they can see a specialist, a mix-up in appointment dates, problems with prescriptions, or unmet expectations of health care. Sometimes patients' distress about bad news may turn to anger.

Often anger begets anger. Have you ever come home in a good mood only to find an argument in progress? You probably found that your own mood deteriorated quickly. If a family member confronts you angrily, how do you respond? Most people will become defensive and show their own annoyance in word and gesture. But what can this entirely natural reaction lead to? An escalated argument.

Businesspeople often say, "The customer is always right." In a sense, the same principle applies to health care. As discussed in Chapter 1, we no longer deal with *patients* who are expected to passively receive care, but with individuals who are active consumers of health care. If your practice is patient driven, your goal is patient satisfaction and retention. Dealing effectively with difficult situations goes a long way toward achieving patient satisfaction.

The key to dealing with angry or upset patients is to show genuine warmth, respect, and empathy. If you are taking or have taken a communications course, you will be familiar with these variables. Apply them to health care situations.

Warmth is difficult to define but makes a world of difference. It can be displayed through words, voice, facial expression, and eye contact. Over the telephone, a soft tone of voice can convey warmth, as can words that express concern for the patient. Emphasizing some words can also display warmth:

> Mr. Martinez, I am so sorry that you were kept waiting so long.

Being treated with *respect* is a fundamental human right and is especially important in health care. A patient who feels respected will be better able to calm down and deal with issues. One way to show respect is simply to pay full attention as you allow the patient to express his or her thoughts and feelings. If the complaint is long, acknowledge that you are listening with the occasional "Uh huh" or "I see." You may also ask for clarification: "Miss Hakimi, I'm not sure I understood that last part. Would you repeat the part about the X-ray getting lost?" Using the patient's name also signals respect for the individual.

Empathy is the ability to put yourself into the patient's situation. Understanding where the patient is coming from does not have to mean that you agree, but it does give you a deeper appreciation of how the patient is feeling. If you can show that you understand where the patient is coming from, without judging, the patient will feel more accepted and valued. Try such phrases as the following:

> I understand how you must be feeling, Mr. Amadou.

> You seem very worried, Ms. Carr. Let's look at the options we can consider here and find out what would be best for you.

Met with warmth, respect, and empathy, most people have a hard time staying angry. Certainly, their problem does not disappear. However, the level of anger and anxiety may subside, paving the way for meaningful dialogue about solutions.

The Aggressive, Unpleasant Patient

Remain calm. Remind yourself that the anger is not aimed at you personally. When people are angry, they often take it out on the nearest person. Separating yourself from the situation helps you keep your emotions in check. Speak as slowly as usual, and do not raise your voice, even if the patient is shouting. The last thing you want is a shouting match. A technique that sometimes works is to actually lower your voice. The patient will have to stop talking to hear what you are saying.

It is important to retain control of the conversation. Be firm, but do not argue with the patient. Do not give the patient something more to argue about; stick to the issue at hand. Sometimes, a response such as "I'm so sorry. That sounds like it was very upsetting for you" will take the wind out of the aggressive patient's sails. Remember, often the patient really does have a valid concern or complaint. If the complaint is justified and the office is at fault, acknowledge it and apologize. Try to find a way to rectify the problem immediately. In some situations, all you can do is apologize. If there is a reasonable explanation for the error, tell that to the patient. It will not right the wrong, but it might help him or her understand why it happened. If there are steps you can take to prevent a similar error from occurring again, assure the patient that you will take them.

As discussed in Chapter 2, sometimes the patient's perspective may be altered because of illness or an emotional reaction to the illness of a loved one. That does not make the issue any less real for the patient. Regardless of the situation, if you make clear to the patient that you will work *with* him or her, you will usually get somewhere.

Ask the patient what he or she sees as a possible solution. People will often calm down when they feel they have input and are listened to. If you have several options to deal with the issue, offer all of them, and ask the patient which he or she thinks is most appropriate. If the issue is something that you cannot rectify, assure the patient that you will look into the matter and get back to him or her with an answer or direct him or her to someone who can help. Give a time frame. "I understand, Mr. Premsyl. I will talk to Dr. Matthews when she gets in after lunch and call you back before four o'clock, if that's convenient for you."

Sometimes, writing down the concerns may help a patient calm down and refocus. Assure the patient that you will give what he or she has written to the appropriate person.

If the patient is rambling and you cannot get a word in edgewise, try raising your hand into the stop position. The patient's eyes will follow your hand and, usually, he or she will stop talking for a moment. Use this opportunity to interrupt: "Celina, I think I understand what you are saying. Let me rephrase the problem, just to be sure. I don't want to miss any of the facts here." This response requires the patient to pay attention to what you are saying and lets the patient know that her complaint has been heard and that you are taking steps to deal with it.

Remember, when you were little, how you felt when your mother said, "No!" or "You can't," or "I won't allow you," or "Never"? You probably felt backed into a corner and more determined than ever to do whatever you were not allowed to do. To an angry person, these words are like a red flag to a bull. Instead, use conciliatory and nonjudgmental language.

The Threatening Patient

If you are facing an angry or aggressive patient across your desk, stand up. If you are sitting and the patient is standing, that puts the patient in a position of power, physically as well as emotionally, and makes you seem more vulnerable.

On a rare occasion, you will face a situation you cannot deal with. It is no shame to admit it. Remember that you matter, too. Patience has its limits; you should not tolerate being abused or threatened.

Some sources will advise you to put a disruptive patient into a separate room, such as an empty examination room or the doctor's office. Although this might work in some situations, in your particular situation use your good judgment. If possible, call the doctor out to support you and perhaps take control of the situation. Never enter a room alone with a patient who makes you feel threatened. Do not let the patient stand between you and the door of the room. If you ever feel that your safety is threatened, tell the patient that you are going to call the police—then do it.

The Anxious Patient

Skill and patience are also needed in dealing with anxious patients. Speak to them especially warmly and gently. People who are stressed, anxious, and preoccupied with thoughts of, for example, an illness or the prospect of an operation are less able to take in and retain information. This temporary loss of capacity will compound forgetfulness and confusion in anyone (elderly or not) with cognitive impairments. If you see that a patient is anxious, carefully explain whatever he or she needs to know about medications, treatments, and subsequent appointments, and reinforce the information by writing it down.

The Patient Wanting a Prescription Renewal

Patients will frequently call wanting a prescription renewal. You can look up the patient's prescription history in his or her EMR. This will tell you when the prescription was last filled, how many repeats, and how many pills the doctor ordered. For the most part, this is an easily handled call. However, there are those who are seeking medications inappropriately—usually those drugs with addictive properties. The patient is on a mission and will have every possible excuse: The medication was accidently flushed down the toilet, I forgot my medication in a cab, the dog knocked them over and ate them (poor dog), they were vacuumed up by accident, I am away and forgot them at home, I threw them out by mistake, I lost them, I had to take more because of increased pain—almost anything. The patient is likely to become angry if you stall or suggest that he or she come in to see the doctor, saying that it is office protocol and the doctor will not renew without a visit (which is usually the case). Be polite but firm—you are in control. Ask the patient to call later for an appointment if the conversation is going nowhere.

Know Your Limits

Throughout this section, we have emphasized the need to make the patient feel important. But you are important, too. You are human, and you, too, have emotions. There will be times when your own concerns make it difficult to maintain the calm, warm, unruffled manner you would like. If the problem is work related, try to resolve it promptly. The tension of an unresolved conflict in the office cannot help but affect how you relate to others. Approach the person(s) involved and tactfully address the matter. If you do not feel the parties involved are able to deal with the issue fairly and responsibly, try to get a third party to help resolve the conflict, perhaps the office manager or the doctor.

TIP

Dealing with Difficult Patients

- Keep calm.
- Do not take it personally.
- Listen to the complaint without interrupting, and then restate it.
- Use the patient's name from time to time.
- Keep your voice quiet, even if the patient is shouting. Try lowering your voice.
- Try to put yourself in the patient's shoes.
- Acknowledge the patient's anger or frustration.
- Do not blame the patient.
- Assure the patient that you will do everything you can to help. Offer options.
- Never argue with the patient or use provoking words or phrases, such as *never, can't, won't,* or *you're mistaken.*
- If the complaint is justified and the office is at fault, acknowledge it and apologize.
- If the patient becomes verbally abusive, swears, or threatens, simply say, "Mr. Leung, I cannot help you if you continue speaking to me like that."
- If a caller continues to be abusive, say, "Mr. Leung, I will not listen to that kind of language. Please call back later. Goodbye." Then hang up.

>

- If you cannot resolve an issue, consider passing it on to the doctor. Some patients feel that the doctor is the ultimate authority and that they have won the battle by being able to discuss the issue with the doctor.
- Document the complaints on the patient's chart as soon as possible while the details are fresh in your mind. Do not record impressions or intangibles. Whenever possible, use direct quotes.
- Tell the doctor what occurred. The doctor may need to deal with the occurrence the next time the patient comes into the office. It is important to work as a team. Even if you or the doctor is in the wrong, acknowledging the fact together reinforces your office's commitment to good patient care.

Personal issues likewise cause strain and undermine your ability to deal with other people and their problems. If possible, deal with personal issues at home, and shelve them while at work. But recognize that this is not always realistic. You are not doing yourself or anyone else any favours if you ignore your personal problems when they adversely affect your performance. You have to balance your own physical and emotional health needs with the demands of your job, even if it means taking time off.

L07 PROFESSIONAL COMMUNICATION

You may want to review the principles of professional dress, appearance, and manner discussed in Chapter 1. In this chapter, so far, we have emphasized the importance of communication with patients. It is equally important to communicate effectively with other health professionals. Even within the office, miscommunication can turn an otherwise pleasant workplace into a minefield.

What undermines good communication in the office? Stress, of course, is a factor. However, staff members who have a good working relationship will not take the occasional stress-induced flare-up to heart. Territorialism also leads to trouble when staff members guard their own job responsibilities so jealously that they resent anyone who tries to help. A health care setting requires a certain amount of sharing. Teamwork is the backbone of any successful enterprise. If you see that a colleague is feeling pressured or overwhelmed, offer to help, if possible; it can make a huge difference.

Each staff member will have a certain level of expertise in a given area. Sometimes people, especially if they are insecure or lack self-confidence, will not ask for help because they do not want to acknowledge that someone else might know more than they do about a particular subject or procedure. Office professionals can end up working alone in the same office, isolated by defensive attitudes and not benefiting from cooperation. It is so much more effective to give each person credit for what he or she does well and to share knowledge and experience.

Always treat others with respect. Comment positively on what a co-worker does well. If you see someone doing something you think you could do better, assess the situation before you speak. Sometimes it is better to keep quiet. If you feel you must offer advice, do so constructively. Ask for help if you need it. Most of us are pleased to share knowledge with someone who appreciates it.

You may meet with a cold shoulder in a new job. Try not to take it personally. The other staff members may feel threatened by your arrival or resent the hiring of another staff member. They may miss the person you are replacing or may simply not adjust well to change. Sometimes, you just have to tough it out. However, if you are patient, polite, and persistent, usually a constructive relationship develops. Be positive. Be aware of your limitations as well as your strengths. Learn all you can from the staff members who have been there before you. They know the routine and are invaluable sources of information. Show respect for their knowledge and a desire to learn.

Never arrive in a new job setting, even if you are hired as the manager, and attempt to rearrange the office and its administrative structure on your first day. It may end up being your last day as well. Remember the saying, "You catch more flies with honey than with vinegar." Staff members need to get used to you, and you need to get to know them. Allow them to show you the ropes. If you must make changes, go slowly. Listen for clues about things they are satisfied with and those they are not. If someone complains about something, pick up on it. Ask the staff member to explain and to suggest improvements. Involve the staff members, make group decisions, and give credit for good suggestions. In the following example, Kamala has just been hired as office manager. Ellen, a long-time employee, does the appointment bookings.

Ellen: "That appointment book frustrates me sometimes."

Kamala: "Why, Ellen?"

Ellen: "It's so small. There just isn't enough space to write things in."

Kamala: (who had thought the appointment book was too small from her first day) "What kind of book do you think would be better?"

Ellen: "Well, I don't know. We've had this one forever. Natalie, the former manager, liked it, but her writing was almost microscopic."

Kamala: "It doesn't leave much space, I agree. Would you mind looking for something more suitable?"

Note that Kamala initially said nothing about her observation. When Ellen complained, instead of jumping in with a decision, which Ellen might have resented, Kamala drew out Ellen's opinion. Kamala showed Ellen respect by supporting her views and acknowledging her ability to choose something that would work for her. Kamala is secure enough not to need to show power; instead, she shares responsibility, which gives Ellen confidence and a sense of autonomy.

In the next example, Rita has just been hired by a busy pediatrician. She is partway through her first morning at work when Gail, the senior office professional, notices that Rita is having trouble filing a pile of claims. Consider these two responses:

Rita, you've made a mess of those claims. Let me do that.

Rita, I know that filing those claims can take forever. I used to hate doing it. You're faster than I was at first. I found a shortcut that really speeded up the process. Would you like me to show you?

In the second response, Gail notes Rita's difficulty in a neutral tone. Rather than criticizing Rita, she puts herself in Rita's position and shares her own past difficulties. She keeps her tone conversational and does not claim superiority. Instead, she gives Rita a "warm, fuzzy feeling" that helps establish a connection and boosts Rita's confidence. Then she offers a suggestion and gives Rita the choice of accepting or rejecting it.

INVENTORY

Maintaining adequate office supplies is both a demanding and a precise task requiring excellent organizational skills. It will be your responsibility to contact the appropriate resources to ensure that office supplies and other items are ordered as required. This will include everything from paper, labels, and pens to toilet tissue and cleaning supplies. In addition you will have to order such medical supplies as syringes, Pap smear kits, swabs, histology containers, fecal occult blood test kits, immunizing agents (vaccines), and patient information pamphlets. Keep information for reordering handy. Many offices fax reorder forms to the supplier.

Try to keep costs down by occasionally looking for better deals (for paper type products in particular, since for medical supplies there may be limited choices). Sometimes your local office supply store may be your best option. Remember, though, that the best price may not mean the best product.

TIP

Take time every day to check inventory. Create a list of supplies on a spreadsheet. Analyze inventory for several months so you can adjust levels, reordering accordingly. If possible, order online. If using a purchasing order, keep the orders filed so you can check your buying history. Always check delivered supplies against the purchasing order to ensure everything is there. It is best for one person in the office to be responsible for inventory.

⟫⟫ WHAT TO WATCH FOR

- Increased use of web-based tools, such as portals, to facilitate patient access to their EMRs as well as communication with health team members (other offices, hospitals, and pharmacies).
- Secure email, which is being used more frequently for patient contact in practice settings.
- Improvements in the pan-Canadian initiative for EHR technology, improving prompt, efficient, and secure access to patient records at any point of service across the country.
- Virtual office visits or communicating via the internet (which is already being piloted in some jurisdictions).
- Advances in technology initiated by the Canada Health Infoway (EHR integration across Canada and the implementation of other technologies for patient care, thus reducing office visits and hospital admissions).

SUMMARY

1. Technology has, to a large extent, replaced written forms of communication. The fax machine and the telephone, however, still play a large role in facilitating communication in the health office and the hospital, and each require a working knowledge to maximize efficiency and confidentiality. The use of postal mail, although decreasing, still plays a role in many offices (e.g., invoices for missed appointments and preventive care notices).

2. Effective, professional communication, oral and written, is central to any health care facility. Excellent grammar, a command of medical terminology, the ability to interact with others, and the ability to maximize the use of technology are essential skills. For example, the use of macros and templates can save time and reduce errors. Both oral and written communication should be clear, concise, and succinct.

3. The cellphone, pagers (to a lesser degree), the computer, and answering devices are all used in most offices and health care facilities. There may be office/facility protocols that apply to some of these applications. Proper use of the computer system (e.g., a message board) to facilitate communication will result in efficient, confidential exchanges among staff members and patients, and within the community.

4. Managing both incoming and outgoing phone calls will be one of your most important and challenging responsibilities. Triaging patients, managing health information (e.g., what you can or cannot disclose), and scheduling appointments keeping time management in mind requires skill and patience.

   You must ensure that all health information is handled in a secure and confidential manner—from oral exchanges within the health office/facility to the use of email, fax machines, and messaging. Each jurisdiction has privacy laws you should be aware of.

5. Face-to-face communication includes the element of visual interpretation of a message. Your facial expression—if you smile or do not smile, if you look serious, worried, or disinterested—can easily alter how a message is perceived. Nonverbal communication includes gestures as well. It is important to remember that with face-to-face communication you are communicating not only with your voice and words, but with your facial expression, body language, and even dress and presentation.

6. Responding effectively to angry patients or family members requires excellent communication techniques, objectivity, and patience. The proper applications of techniques to prevent a situation from escalating as well as dealing with ones that do are important. Do not hesitate to use the doctor's name or to ask for him or her to intervene if you feel a situation is escalating to a point where you feel out of control or endangered.

7. Interprofessional communication is an area that should not be ignored, because it is equally important to communicate effectively with other health professionals. Even within the office, miscommunication can turn an otherwise pleasant workplace into a minefield.

KEY TERMS

template 209

REVIEW QUESTIONS

1. Discuss the term *professionalism* as it applies to telephone communication.

2. Identify some strategies to enhance a positive impression over the telephone.

3. List four telephone services available today, and discuss how they would be useful in the health office setting.

4. Compare and contrast the advantages and disadvantages of an answering service and an answering machine in the health office.

5. Discuss confidentiality concerns relating to fax, email, cellphones, and pagers.

6. List the information that is essential when taking a telephone message.

7. List eight types of incoming calls to the health office. Discuss the appropriate methods of dealing with them and the rationale for each.

8. Describe the appropriate strategy for handling more than one telephone call at the same time.

9. Identify and discuss six methods to enhance efficiency when dealing with outgoing calls in the health office.

10. Discuss four ways to effectively deal with an angry patient.

APPLICATION EXERCISES

1. Review the following directives. Think of a patient-friendly way of putting these into a sign.

   a. Take off your boots at the door.

   b. There is a $30 charge for missed appointments.

   c. Notify reception when you arrive.

   d. You must show your health card at every visit.

   e. The doctor does not give out prescriptions over the phone.

2. In groups of three, create three scenarios of telephone conversations. They do not have to be related to health care issues, but each should involve one person calling and one answering who must direct, explain, or deal with a complaint or request. Examples:

A customer calls the bank wanting to know her balance. The teller refuses.

A patient calls the doctor's office complaining because he was sent a bill for a missed appointment.

3. The responder should rate her own telephone personality, the caller should give her impressions, and the third group member should give a rating. Switch roles and repeat twice. How does your self-evaluation differ from others' evaluation of your style? What strengths do you have? What areas do you need to improve?

4. Jennifer accidentally opened a personal letter addressed to Dr. Ward (who is married with two young sons). It was from a patient in the practice. Jennifer read the letter even though she knew she should not. The patient, an 18-year-old female, was thanking the doctor for a wonderful evening out. She went on to say that she cared for him and was looking forward to continuing the "relationship." Horrified, Jennifer put the letter back into the envelope and stuffed it into her pocket. She didn't know what to do. This is an ethical situation with potentially legal implications. What would you do? Using the problem-solving steps suggested in Chapter 1, outline a course of action for Jennifer.

5. Suppose you work in a busy family practice office. You receive the following calls. Respond to each call in what you think is the best manner. Think about how you should handle or direct the call and whether you need additional information. If the call is for the doctor, should you put it through? How should you respond to the caller's questions or demands? You may work alone or in small groups to complete this assignment. If you work alone, compare your responses with someone else's. Think about ways to improve your responses.

1:00 p.m.
- "My mother, Bertha Waters, was in to see Dr. Marino yesterday. She has been upset ever since. She won't talk to me about it. I want to know what's going on."

1:10
- Hi, this is Rosa from labour and delivery at the hospital. I have Mrs. Stein here, and I think she's in labour. Could I speak with the doctor?"

1:15
- "Hello, this is Sandra Moscati calling. I would like to make an appointment to see the doctor. I am having some chest pain, and I find it hard to catch my breath."

1:17
- "This is Wilson Meyers. I have an appointment for Thursday afternoon to see the doctor, but I am not going to be able to make it. I thought you would like to know."

1:20
- "Hello, this is Ella. I would like to make an appointment to see the doctor. I had my X-ray yesterday, and oh, what an experience, I must tell you. First, I had a hard time getting down to the hospital. Then I got lost trying to find that X-ray department, but this nice lady ..."

1:25
- "This is Jim Cameron. I want to have my prescription for Valium renewed. You can phone it in to Lakeside Pharmacy. I will pick it up after 6:00 p.m."

1:30
- "I have been trying to get through to you for the last half hour. What's the matter with you people? Do you leave your telephone off the hook? Don't you realize that there are sick people wanting to get in touch with you? Can't you afford another telephone line? This is ridiculous, just ridiculous."

1:32
- "Hello, this is Rob Bruni. I am a drug rep with Abbot. I would like to drop in later with some samples and see the doctor."

1:34
- "Hello. This is Bill from MDS. I have some lab results on Martha Bowman:
Hb 12.1
WBC 15.00
Blood Sugar 12.5. That's high, I thought you should know."

1:40
- "This is Raj Anand. Could I speak to the doctor, please? It's important."

1:45
- "Good afternoon, this is Dr. Mason. Dr. Marino, please."

1:50
- "I would like to have some pills renewed. Would you ask the doctor to do that for me?"

2:00
- "This is three north at the hospital calling. I need some orders on Mr. Walsh."

2:04
- "This is Ayesha Mahmoud. I was wondering if you could give me the results of my Pap smear. It was done last week, and I'm feeling a little anxious."

2:10
- "This is Stephanie Pichette. I need my birth control pills renewed. I only have about three pills left."

2:15
- "This is Denise Olson. My son Kyle has a sore throat, and I would like the doctor to phone in a prescription for an antibiotic."

2:20

- "This is Jake Ellis. I have a bone to pick. You told me that Dr. Marino would call me back yesterday after hours, and he didn't. I waited for two hours for that call. I want an explanation!"

2:35

- "My name is Samantha Kovacs. I am a relative of Josh Lemke. He's a patient of the doctor. I just moved to town, and I need a doctor. Josh said it wouldn't be a problem."

WEBSITES OF INTEREST

Health Communication

www.healthypeople.gov/2020/default.aspx

Workers' Compensation Boards across Canada

www.awcbc.org/en/linkstoworkerscompensationboardscom-missions.asp

Written Communication Skills

www.skillsyouneed.com/writing-skills.html

Chapter 9
Scheduling Appointments

kurhan/Shutterstock

LEARNING OBJECTIVES

On completing this chapter, you will be able to:

1. Use the basic features of scheduling software, and explain the importance of keeping health information secure.

2. Discuss basic scheduling procedures, related terms, and scheduling strategies.

3. Determine the appropriate length of time for various appointments.

4. Cope effectively with difficult patients and disruptions in scheduling.

5. Schedule special appointments, consultations, diagnostic tests, and surgeries.

Efficient and organized scheduling is vital to the success of any medical practice. In fee-for-service settings in particular, proper scheduling and billing generate the main sources of provider income. Proper scheduling also improves service to your patients. Scheduling appointments is one of the main tasks of health office professionals and requires effective communication skills, people skills, good judgment, a general knowledge of medical diseases and conditions, and an understanding of the physician's own style of management. It is essential that you understand all components of the scheduling software you use to maximize its potential. In an office with several staff members, one person may be assigned the responsibility of scheduling, sometimes on a rotational basis; thus, everyone in the office should be able to perform this important duty.

L01 TOOLS FOR SCHEDULING APPOINTMENTS

The telephone and the computer are your primary tools for scheduling appointments. The number of computers and their location will vary with the needs of the office. Most offices have two or more computers in the administrative area: one in the doctor's private office and one in each examination or treatment room. How "electronic" your office is affects scheduling, charting, and billing procedures in the practice. Many offices also use laptops or tablets to facilitate scheduling. When booking appointments, the interfaces you will use the most are various components of the scheduling, patient registration, and claims submission modules.

Basic Features of Scheduling Software

Most medical office software systems offer a wide range of features that can be adapted to suit the needs of any provider. Paramount is ease of use, defined by an organized and logical approach to the various modules in the system. At the heart of any medical software system is the scheduling module. This module will interface with other modules in the system, including the patient's electronic medical record (EMR), pharmacy, patient registration, billing, chronic disease management, forms and documents management (including templates for forms and letters), task management, and internal messaging. Following are some of the essential features any software system should offer.

A scheduling software module should enable you to do all of the following:

- Schedule appointments for single- and multi-provider formats
- View appointment screens for a day or a week at a glance (see Figures 9.1 and 9.2)
- Pre-edit the provider's schedule (showing when the provider is unavailable to see patients); see Figure 9.1
- Schedule two patients into the same time slot (double booking) (see Figure 9.2)
- Create appointments from a single interface, thus enabling you to select the required date for an appointment and access the patient's name and information from a search tool on the scheduling screen (see Figure 9.3a)
- Track patient flow by flagging the appointment status—when the patient has checked in or whether the patient is a no show; this information should be available to the provider and other staff members involved with the patient's visit (see Figure 9.3b)
- Enter appointment details, including the reason for the appointment
- Create and apply templates for specific types of visits
- Attach notes to the appointment as well as enter notes into the patient's chart regarding missed appointments, requests for prescription renewals, phone calls and how they were handled, or other information relevant to the patient's care
- Edit/change appointments (change the appointment date, time, or length) with the option to load the same appointment details
- Select the frequency of recurring appointments (e.g., every month) and navigate dates within the scheduler
- Search for a patient's appointment (e.g., Mary calls, forgetting when her appointment is) as well as compile a patient's appointment history

Figure 9.1 Weekly schedule showing physician availability; slots are left open for same-day urgent appointments

Used by permission of Choice Learning, Inc.

Figure 9.2 A daily schedule featuring a double-column daily schedule for two physicians and examples of double booking

Used by permission of Choice Learning, Inc.

- Recall patients (e.g., the doctor asks you to have André come back to discuss his lab results)

- Create, add, edit, and remove templates (e.g., for visit types, counselling, physical examinations, well-baby visits, prenatal); this is often achieved using colour coding

- Schedule rooms and equipment and link them to providers' schedules and patients' bookings, which is especially helpful in a busy clinic setting

- Use and print day sheets (appointment summaries) in either a single or multi-physician practice (see Figure 9.4)

Figure 9.3 (a) Short registration screen with the patient's demographics on the right and appointments listed on the left

Used by permission of Choice Learning, Inc.

Figure 9.3 (b) Status of an appointment

Used by permission of Choice Learning, Inc.

- Create patient-specific lists for various functions, such as contacting patients to get their flu shots

- Manage provincial/territorial and third-party billing from a variety of entry points

Few providers work in a single physician office (except perhaps for specialists), opting to combine two, three, or four physician practices—even if part of a primary care group. Administrative staff, therefore, may be scheduling appointments for two or more physicians. Scheduling software will allow you to toggle between/among providers' schedules as well as offer various screen views of each provider's schedule (day/week/month). Figure 9.1 shows a weekly schedule for one physician, with times when the physician is not available to see patients noted (e.g., for meetings and when the office closed when he is away). It also shows slots left open for urgent patients. A weekly view allows you to quickly assess when you can book a patient for either doctor.

Day Sheet

Laura Keast

November 10, 2017

Time	Patient			Reason	Billing Codes/Diagnosis
9:00 AM	HAIRSTON, ALBERT M 05-12-1945	5267299078	905-552-4589	BP	A001/401
9:15 AM	BURDETT, ALLEN M 11-10-1995	4731312132	905-552-4590	Flu	A007/487
9:45 AM	VALERIO, AMY F 14-05-2012	2890707574	905-552-4591	Abdominal Pain	A007/787
10:15AM	MERRIMAN, ANDREW M 21-04-1954	5870324976	416-552-4592	Back Pain	A007/847
10:45 AM	SCHULZE, CYNTHIA F 03-12-1984	9138291322	905-552-4593	Birth Control	
11:30 AM	HAUGEN, ELLEN F 16-05-1994	9710664778	416-552-4594	UTI	
11:45 AM	MATHIS, HELEN F 15-04-2000	5138627465	416-552-4595	Sore Throat	
1:00 PM	MCGUIRE, ISOBEL F 18-04-1965	2499861356	647-552-4596	Headaches	
1:30 PM	FULLER, JUDI F 28-07-1986	2925747220	416-552-4598	Diabetes	
2:30 PM	MESSINA, MARION F 13-04-2006	4720753543	647-552-4599	CPX	

Appointments 10

Printed by: kpriam

Figure 9.4 Day sheet

Figure 9.2 is an example of a day's schedule for two physicians showing two columns with some patients double booked (discussed later in the chapter). If you work in a team environment (e.g., in a primary care setting) you may be required to book appointments for a variety of providers, including a nurse practitioner, counsellor, dietitian, or physiotherapist. Most scheduling modules will allow you to manipulate the features it offers to suit the specific needs of each provider—from booking availability to templates for different types of appointments.

In Figure 9.3a you can see an appointment scheduler with the patient search option opened. The demographic information from the selected patient is visible on the right-hand side of the screen. In most systems you can click and drag and drop the patient's name into the required appointment slot.

You have the option of booking appointments from the registration screen or from a screen called "short registration." Using the short registration screen allows you select a patient, view his or her demographic information, make an appointment, and update patient information quickly.

You can track patient flow by also clicking to update the status of the appointment: for example, "confirmed" when the appointment is made, "arrived" when the patient checks in at the time of the appointment, or "no show" if the patient skipped the appointment (this ensures the information is added to the patient's chart). If you are at all concerned for the patient's well-being (i.e., why he or she missed the appointment), you should follow up appropriately. Figure 9.3b shows a patient has arrived for her appointment.

Day Sheet

The day sheet is a computerized summary of the provider's appointments for the day (see Figure 9.4). Because you can access other functions from the day sheet, it can be used for several purposes, including billing. For example, let's say you want to perform an action or actions for a particular patient; from the day sheet you can send a follow-up message (make an appointment for Anita when the biopsy results are back), or make note of a task you must complete (send a consultation letter to a specialist, or book a diagnostic test). You can also submit billing claims from the day sheet; if there are numerous claims for the same procedure/visit type and diagnostic code, you can access an existing (or create a new) macro to complete the claim.

Many offices print a hard copy of the day sheet for referral purposes and for keeping notes (for both the administrative staff and the physician). If you work in a multi-physician office, make sure you have the proper day sheet selected. Nurses may keep their own copy to help them organize their day, keep notes, and write down billing information for such things as injections and other procedures they carry out themselves. It is also handy if your computer system is down. This is not uncommon, particularly with more complex systems connected to a variety of other providers and organizations. If you can't use the computer, you do not have access to the scheduler. The day sheet can be invaluable in such situations. The doctor can keep his or her copy in the office and refer to it throughout the day (the doctor will likely be using his or her computer for encounter-related purposes, not looking at the appointment schedule). The day sheet helps the doctor keep on schedule and gives him or her an idea of how many patients are left to be seen and who is to be seen next. If you include the reason for the patient's appointment, it also informs the doctor what he or she will be dealing with ahead of time. Some providers also use the day sheet to record notes, reminders, and claims information, such as the type of visit, diagnostic code, and so on, whether the office is computerized or not.

If a patient cancels an appointment or you have to fit in an emergency, mark the change on the day sheet, adding it to the appointment schedule when you have access to the computer again. Alternatively, the doctor may keep track of scheduled patients and add notes using his or her own computer or tablet. Any changes you make on the electronic schedule immediately show on the doctor's computer/tablet. (The doctor will have to click the "refresh" button to see the changes.)

Appointment Cards

Appointment cards help reduce the number of patients who miss their appointments or show up on the wrong day or at the wrong time. They also save you time, because fewer patients will call and ask when their appointments are. The doctor's phone number is on the card, which encourages patients to call if they are going to be late or miss their appointments. See Figure 9.5 for an example of an appointment card.

Dr. D. J. Thompson, M.D., C.F.P.C.
Medical Arts Building
93 St. Vincent Street North
Stratford, Ontario
N5A 5H5

Name:_____ has an appointment on
Date:_____ Time: _____a.m./p.m.

Please call if you are unable to keep this appointment.
There is a $20 charge for failure to notify this office
within 24 hours of an appointment cancellation.
Ph. 519-271-1111

Figure 9.5 Appointment card

Reminders

As mentioned in Chapter 8 some health care providers—usually not family physicians, but specialists, optometrists, chiropractors, and dentists—will contact patients to remind them of upcoming appointments. There is software available that will email out reminders right to the patient's smartphone. Many providers charge for appointments that are missed without at least 24 hours notice. If this is the case, you will be required to charge the patient accordingly—either the next time they are in the office or by mailing them a bill. You should provide the patient with a written receipt.

Confidentiality and Scheduling

Keeping all health information confidential and secure is mandated by both ethical principles and the law. You have unprecedented access to the health information of all the patients that your provider deals with. Even the fact that a patient has scheduled an appointment must be kept confidential.

With an electronic scheduling appointment system, place the monitor at an angle that does not allow patients to read it. Turn the monitor off when you are not using it. Although many offices, clinics, and other health care facilities still have paper charts, most information is stored on the patient's EMR. During the period of transition from paper to EMR, any information not uploaded into the EMR must be kept for a designated period of time. Paper charts must be kept secure and must be accounted for. Computerized information (a patient's EMR) should only be available to appropriate individuals (those directly involved in the patient's care, which is sometimes referred to as the *circle of care*). You can "lock" the patient's chart if need be, which can be done from the day sheet on most systems. For example, if a patient arrives and you load the patient's chart to change some demographic information, you can lock the chart until it is needed by someone else. When the nurse or physician wants to access that chart, they can log in and do so. Keep all passwords confidential and, if written down, stored securely. Most systems require that you change your password at regular intervals. A password that is alphanumeric (letters and numbers) is advised.

The appointment schedule is a legal electronic document and must be backed up and filed. If you make a mistake or change appointments, keep a record of the changes. In a manual situation, do not erase an appointment; instead, draw a neat line through the error and write in above it. An alternative for computerized systems is to note no-shows and cancellations on the daily appointment schedule or day sheet. You should also note this information on the patient's EMR or paper chart. Note that most physician-governing bodies across the country require you to keep a record of all appointments for 10 years.

If you are using an actual appointment book, keep it out of view of patients, and at the end of the day put it in a secure place. Otherwise, it can innocently be seen by the cleaning staff and anyone else with access to the office.

L02 SCHEDULING PROCEDURES

Pre-editing the Provider's Scheduler

It is important to set aside a time to update the doctor's electronic scheduler. This applies to any other provider who is seeing patients (e.g., nurse practitioners, dentists, hygienists). Filling in the times you know the provider to be unavailable is called *scheduling by exception*. Most systems will allow you to do this "behind the scenes" on a separate calendar that interfaces with your patient appointment scheduler. Some systems will provide an option wherein you will be physically unable to book a patient appointment at a time when you have the doctor scheduled as unavailable. This saves time and prevents you from accidentally bringing in a patient only to find that Dr. Smith is away at a conference. This is easily done in a hectic office environment. Pre-editing the doctor's time can be done a month or so in advance and updated accordingly. You should review the doctor's schedule with him or her frequently to ensure accuracy. All too often the doctor will forget to tell you that he or she will be away at a meeting or is leaving early for an appointment. Items should include the following:

- Routine times when the doctor is not in the office (many physicians take Wednesday afternoons off)
- Routine commitments, such as hospital rounds or medical seminars (often conducted weekly, usually around 7:00 a.m.)
- On-call schedules, which are usually available several months in advance (it is vital that this schedule is accurately recorded. Doctors sometimes switch calls with another doctor and may forget to tell you. Discuss the doctor's call schedule at least every few days to ensure any changes are noted.)
- Assigned days in the clinic or the emergency department (most primary care reform groups have a clinic that operates five days a week, including evenings. Doctors from the group staff the clinic on a rotational basis. How often depends on the number of doctors in the group.)
- Variable meetings and appointments
- Statutory holidays (you can do this for an entire year, which helps to avoid confusion; your software may do this automatically)

If you are working for a multi-provider practice, ensure that you carefully edit each provider's schedule. In a dental or optometry office where allied health professionals are seeing patients, schedules depend on one another. For example, if a hygienist is off, the dentist's and dental assistants' schedules may also be affected.

Scheduling Templates

You can create scheduling templates to suit specific types of patient visits, specifying the amount of time the visit should take (see Chapter 8). Examples include prenatal examinations, counselling sessions, or physical examinations. It may be the physician's preference to have such visits on certain days of the week and to limit the number.

Standard Terminology

To save both time and space (few appointment schedulers have enough space for long notes), use standard terms and abbreviations in scheduling as shown in Table 9.1. Though these abbreviations are fairly standard in physicians' offices, not all dental practices use the same abbreviations.

Scheduling Considerations

In scheduling appointments, consider first the patient's health concern. How soon should the patient be seen? How long an appointment will the doctor need to deal with

TABLE 9.1 Common medical abbreviations used in scheduling

V/S	vital signs check	Can	cancellation	Ref	referral
CPx	physical examination	NS	no show	ECG	electrocardiogram
A/CPx	annual physical	FUp	follow-up	Lab/w	lab workup
AHE	annual health examination	RS	reschedule	US	ultrasound
		A/S	allergy shot	WB	well-baby
PN	prenatal	Imm	immunization	Pap	Pap smear
PP	postpartum check	F/S	flu shot	Con	consult
NP	new patient	Inj	injection	BP	blood pressure

the concern? If possible, try to accommodate the patient's individual needs as well. For example:

- See school-aged children after school or on professional development days. High school students may have variable schedules.

- A mother of school-aged children may prefer to come in while the children are at school, as long as she can be home for their return.

- Patients with busy schedules and work-related commitments during the day may prefer appointments first thing in the morning before delays occur.

- Older patients or those who take a great deal of time with the doctor might best be seen at the end of the morning or afternoon.

- Never book an appointment for a pregnant woman back to back or even close in time with a patient who may have rubella (German measles). Avoid even same-day bookings if you can. If a pregnant woman who is not immune to rubella contracts the disease, especially in the first trimester, the consequences to the unborn baby could be serious. If a child has symptoms suggesting rubella (rash, fever, crankiness), check your appointment scheduler to see if you have a prenatal appointment booked.

- Patients with disabilities might depend on others to get them to and from the office and therefore may need special consideration regarding their appointment times.

- Patients who need interpreters usually require a longer appointment. Schedule this at the end of the day or morning so that if the visit takes longer than expected other patients are not kept waiting.

If you are making an appointment for a new patient or someone with whom you are not familiar, try to determine if they have special needs so that you can accommodate them as much as possible. I once made an appointment over the telephone for a patient who had never been to the office. She arrived in her wheelchair only to find that the office was not wheelchair accessible. She had to return home without being seen. (The doctor made a house call later in the day.)

Pre-office Conference or Information Update It is good to get into the habit of reviewing the day's appointments with the provider, using a day sheet or viewing the electronic schedule. An excellent time is at the beginning of the day or before the doctor starts seeing patients in the afternoon. Some physicians also like updates mid-morning and mid-afternoon. This quick meeting facilitates good communication and helps the day run smoothly. It lets the doctor know what is happening and how heavy the day is and gives both of you the opportunity to talk about other matters. You can ensure that the doctor knows about any activities he is scheduled for that day; he may have forgotten about a commitment made weeks ago. Also, ask if the doctor has anything to add to the schedule; she may have forgotten to tell you about something that came up at the last minute. Doctors have been known to encourage a patient to "just drop in this afternoon," which plays havoc with your appointment schedule. You have to deal with these patients, try to fit them in, and often make scheduled patients wait. You need to communicate clearly with the doctor about the problem; you can request that he not do this, except in special circumstances. If he does, he should at least let you know so that you can pull the patient's chart and be prepared. If patients are expecting to pick up forms, you can give them to the doctor or remind her to complete them. You can also present any abnormal lab tests to the doctor, receive instructions on dealing with them, and ask any questions you may have about other issues or reports. Bear in mind, the need for a preconference will vary with the type of setting you work in. In busy multi-physician practices, a preconference may be impractical. Instead, you can message the physician with any important information about the day's activities. You can also send messages regarding any particular patient by attaching a note to the patient's chart.

TYPES OF SCHEDULING

A number of different scheduling methods are currently used in health care. Each has its own advantages and disadvantages and suits some types of practice better than others.

Fixed Office Hours, or Open Scheduling

With this method, the facility is open at certain hours, and patients can come whenever they like within those hours without an appointment. Few family practices use this method, but it is used in some group practices and is the norm in walk-in and urgent care clinics based on the principle of providing care to patients when they need it. Patients first see the administrative health professional (AHP), have their health card validated, and explain the purpose of the visit. Patients in urgent need of care are seen first; otherwise, patients are seen in the order in which they arrive. The patient must understand that, barring an emergency, they will be seen on a first-come, first-served basis.

This method eliminates the work of maintaining schedules and the problems of missed or cancelled appointments and late arrivals. It suits some patients with busy and irregular schedules.

One obvious drawback to this method is the unpredictable variations in workload. There may be very slow periods, in which staff time is not used effectively, and times when both you and the doctor are so busy that it is difficult to cope. Another drawback is that you have no time to pull the patient's chart ahead of time, no opportunity to validate the health card, and no idea what the presenting problem is. You have no time to prepare for procedures required for particular complaints, such as syringing an ear.

If you are working in a walk-in or urgent care clinic, the patient is unlikely to have a chart there. All information is recorded on a facility admission sheet and perhaps a progress, multidisciplinary, or fact sheet. You will take the necessary patient information, process the health card, and record the reason for the visit. The physician will record the details of the visit on the appropriate record. Forward duplicates to the patient's family physician.

Wave Scheduling

Wave scheduling is a compromise between open scheduling and scheduling by appointment (stream scheduling). This method is so named because patients come in

wave scheduling scheduling several patients for the same block of time, typically an hour.

groups, like waves hitting a beach. A certain number of patients are booked to see the provider within a given time frame; for example, four patients booked at the beginning of each hour, or three every half hour. Although this type of scheduling can occur in general practice, you are more likely to find wave scheduling in the office of an allergist or an endocrinologist. First, determine how many patients the provider can see in the time frame. (See the discussion later in this chapter.) For example, if Dr. Meiros usually sees one patient every 10 minutes, he will see approximately six patients in one hour. You would then ask six patients to come in between 9:00 and 10:00 a.m., and another six between 10:00 and 11:00 a.m. They are not given specific times. The premise is that some patients will come earlier than others. It allows patients some flexibility, while still offering some structure and control. You can view charts and validate health cards ahead of time. The drawback is that if all the patients in a wave arrive at the same time, some will have to wait longer. It can also create issues as to who is seen first if patients arrive at the same time.

Modified Wave Scheduling   Modified wave scheduling uses a basic block of time, as does wave scheduling. However, patients are given narrower time slots to control traffic flow more closely. For example, you might ask two patients to arrive between 1 p.m. and 1:15 p.m., another two to arrive between 1:15 and 1:30, and so on.

Affinity Scheduling

affinity, cluster, categorization, or analogous scheduling scheduling similar appointments together, for example, scheduling physical examinations on a certain day.

Affinity scheduling, also called **cluster, categorization, or analogous scheduling**, involves scheduling patients in clusters on the basis of the type of service or reason for seeing the doctor. Many dental offices, as well as some medical practices, use this method. For example, the dentist may see patients who need check-ups on Monday and Wednesday mornings and those who require uncomplicated fillings on Tuesday and Thursday afternoons. Monday and Wednesday afternoons may be surgery days, and Fridays may be reserved for orthodontic procedures. A general surgeon might see all patients with breast lumps on a certain day, those with abdominal complaints another day, those who need follow-up assessments another day, and so on. Primary care physicians do not usually use this method of scheduling exclusively.

In some primary care reform groups using alternative payment plans, affinity scheduling is becoming more popular. Doctors in primary care groups are given bonus or incentive payments for meeting certain service milestones (e.g., completing a certain number of Pap smears and immunizations). Affinity scheduling allows the physician to efficiently schedule individuals that help him or her meet these criteria.

Affinity scheduling maximizes the use of special equipment that may be needed for certain procedures and makes it easy to determine how much time to allow for each appointment. It is helpful and saves time to use appointment templates for affinity scheduling. However, the repetition of affinity scheduling can become boring for the provider. Furthermore, in a given week, the range of patients' problems may not fit the affinity schedule. This form of scheduling also leaves fewer choices for patients.

combination or blended scheduling a combination of affinity and random scheduling.

Combination or Blended Scheduling   Often, a medical practice will use a mix of randomly scheduled appointments with affinity scheduling to create what is called **combination or blended scheduling**. Many physicians will do annual physicals and preoperative examinations at certain times, perhaps Monday and Wednesday mornings. They may see prenatal patients and do well-baby examinations on Tuesday and Thursday mornings. Individuals who require allergy injections may be asked to come in on Tuesday and Friday afternoons. The doctor must be in the office when a patient has an allergy shot in case there is an adverse reaction, but if there is a nurse to give the injection, the doctor does not usually have to see the patient. The rest of the time is open for any type of complaint. Of course, other patients can be fit in or double booked any time, as the need arises.

Advantages to this type of scheduling include organization and making optimum use of specialized equipment. Annual medicals, for example, take anywhere from 20 to 30 minutes. Doing them on specific days allows the rest of the week to be used more efficiently for more routine encounters and avoids delays caused by lengthy appointments. Scheduling an annual examination in the middle of a busy afternoon when the reception area is full and you are already running 45 minutes late will only add to the stress for you and the waiting patients.

Assess the scheduling pattern in your practice. You may be able to introduce some changes that enhance efficiency.

Double Scheduling, or Double-Column Booking

Double scheduling or double-column booking is rarely used as the *primary* scheduling method in any facility. However, when a busy office or clinic already has a full schedule and has to accommodate emergencies, double booking can lend a semblance of order to what could be a scheduling nightmare. The additional patients' names are entered into the same time slot, or a second column or row beside or beneath the names of the regularly scheduled patients. Most systems, by default, will show a single column for booking patients, with the option of adding another column for any particular day. For providers that routinely double book you would adapt the scheduler to show two columns by default (see Figure 9.2). On the computer screen sometimes it may look as though the doctor will see both patients at the same time. Double booking will work reasonably well as long as you double book a patient with one who can be seen quickly. In this case, each patient is estimated to take 5–7 minutes (a brief or minor assessment). An example might be a skin rash or a re-check of vital signs or an incision. Allergy shots and other injections are also appropriate for double booking. If there is a nurse in the office who gives injections, the physician will often not see the patient at all (although the doctor must be in the office in case the patient has an adverse reaction). How effective double booking is in part also depends on the availability of examination rooms and by the physician's ability to manage his or her time.

Double scheduling is discussed later in this chapter with reference to times allowed for patients to see the provider. Explain the situation to regular patients who end up waiting, and thank them for their cooperation.

> **double scheduling or double-column booking** scheduling two patient appointments at the same time, on the assumption that one of the appointments will involve little of the doctor's time.

Stream Scheduling

Stream or fixed-interval scheduling is the most common method of scheduling appointments in medical offices. With this manner of scheduling, each patient has a fixed, or specific, appointment time, and patients are supposed to come in a steady stream. In a well-organized office, patient flow should be fairly smooth most of the time. Some disruptions and delays are unavoidable. However, if delays are chronic, a review is needed. There may be several causes:

> **stream or fixed-interval scheduling** allotting a specific, unique time slot for each patient appointment; the most common method of scheduling.

- You may be allowing insufficient time for each patient.
- The doctor may spend longer than he or she should with each patient. You cannot change how the provider operates—although you can discuss it with him or her—but you can book more time with each patient and fewer patients in the day. This will affect revenue and might motivate the provider to use his or her time more efficiently.
- Patients may be in the habit of mentioning one complaint when they book but present with additional ones when they arrive at the office. Remind patients that

time scheduled with the provider is based on the original complaint. Offer to schedule another appointment for any other problems.

- ◼ Perhaps you are allowing too many walk-ins. Post a sign that clearly states that, except in emergencies, patients will be seen by appointment only—and stick to that policy.

- ◼ Patients may be bringing the whole family along to be seen "because I was coming anyway." If concerns are not urgent, book another appointment for the other family members. Remind them that if they want back-to-back appointments next time, they must request two appointments when they book.

The success of stream scheduling is contingent on accurate estimation of appointment times.

Same-Day/Advanced Access Scheduling

Timely access to physicians and other members of the health care team is essential to efficient and effective health care. That, however, is the exception to the rule; many Canadians wait days if not weeks to see their doctor for nonurgent conditions—and even longer for a physical examination. Advanced access scheduling accommodates appointment requests within one or two days (preferably one day) regardless of the reason (urgent, routine, or preventive) and limits scheduled appointments to a predetermined percentage of the day's bookings. This is to accommodate those who require the predictability of a scheduled appointment (individuals the physician must see at a given interval for clinical reasons, disabled people who require transportation that must be arranged in advance, etc.). Most jurisdictions are encouraging physicians to move at least in part to this model.

Same-day appointments increase patient satisfaction and, depending on the setting, increase the likelihood of the patient seeing his or her own doctor.

To move to a same-day appointment model takes time (from weeks to several months) and can be both difficult and complicated depending on the size and configuration of the practice. First, you must clear the backlog of booked appointments as far ahead as you have them scheduled. This requires that you explain what you are doing to the patients and listen to any concerns they have. Change can be difficult, especially for those that predict they will have challenges with the new system. As the backlog clears, you can begin offering patients same-day appointments. When patients come in, instead of telling them to make an appointment to come back in, for example, three weeks, the physician should advise them to call back in about three weeks. This holds for any reason the patient is required to come back. A woman may ask for an appointment for her next prenatal examination due in a month. Tell her to call in about a month, expecting to get in on the day she calls. Just what strategy the practice employs to achieve an advanced scheduling model will vary, and the process will be a learning curve for everyone.

Some elements of scheduling will not change. When patients call, you should still ask the same questions regarding the reason for the appointment so you can schedule the right amount of time. If the patient has complex or multiple problems to present at that visit, knowing what they are in advance will allow you to schedule the patient time with other members of the health care team if appropriate, ensuring that as many of the patient's complaints as possible are addressed during that visit. You would also still triage patients and prioritize those with urgent problems. Unlike many practices, where there are designated rooms for certain types of visits, it is helpful to have all of the examination rooms equipped in the same manner so that each room can accommodate any type of visit (well-baby visit, gynecological examination, etc.). In a traditional practice, your appointment schedule will have a degree of predictability, especially if you use templates, and use affinity scheduling (at least in part). With open access scheduling you do not have quite that level of control over who comes in and when. You will find that the busiest time is in the morning, with calls for appointments decreasing after lunch and slowing down even more as the afternoon progresses. Patients calling after 4:00 p.m. are likely best moved to the next day, depending on the time the office closes.

Digital Self-Scheduling

Self-scheduling through an internet portal is becoming popular. Patients are given access to the physician's booking schedule through the internet. They must create a password and log in, and when they click on "Scheduling," only available appointments will be visible. The patient can choose the health provider he or she wishes to see (if the physician practices in a team environment; for example, a nurse, a counsellor, a podiatrist, or a physiotherapist). Next the patient chooses the type of appointment required. This is usually from a drop-down list, and the choices will vary with the provider. Choices can be specific, such as a well-baby visit, a prenatal check-up, a blood pressure check, an allergy injection, a physical examination, and so on; or they may be more general in nature, such as minor assessment, intermediate assessment, or a combination of these choices. The visit choice will determine the length of the appointment.

Figure 9.6(a) shows a patient booking an appointment with a physiotherapist. Here, there is a charge for the visit noted. The patient answers a few questions (e.g., whether this is a first visit) and notes the reason for the visit. In Figure 9.6(b) you can see the appointment in real time in the clinic calendar view, which also displays the patient's comments.

Some physicians will have a designated number of digital appointment spaces each day. The rest would be reserved appointments made in the traditional manner. Dr. Pellizari's office, for example, allows for six spaces/day for digital self-scheduling, accounting for about an hour's worth of appointment time. You would be responsible for monitoring these appointments so that you know who is coming in and when. Some offices have two screens for you to work from, allowing for constant monitoring of appointments that were self-scheduled.

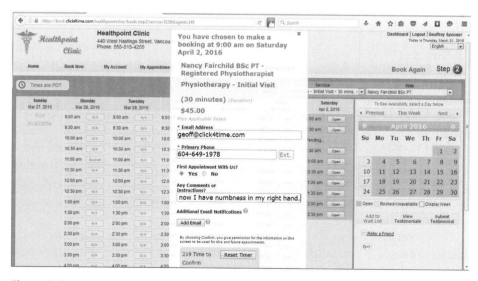

Figure 9.6 (a) A self-scheduling screen showing a patient booking an appointment with a physiotherapist (part of the medical team)

Used by permission from Click4Time Software Inc.

Figure 9.6 (b) The new appointment shows in real time in the clinic calendar view, which also displays the patient's comments.

Used by permission of Click4Time Software Inc.

Advantages of self-scheduling include time saved (calling for an appointment can take several minutes just to get through to the office); the ability to schedule, cancel, or change an appointment outside of office hours; appointment reminders generated by some software; electronic communication with providers offered by some systems/providers, and fewer calls for office staff to deal with. Some systems will include access to the patient's appointment history as well as his or her EMR.

Specialized software is available for self-scheduling and related purposes. Click-4Time Software Inc. is one online appointment and resource booking system that is growing in popularity and is sanctioned by Canada Health Infoway. In addition to patients being able to book and manage their own appointments, the system allows family physicians to refer patients to specialists, whereby required forms are electronically attached to patient appointments and referring doctors receive automated notification of cancelled appointments and no-shows.

The major laboratories in Canada now offer websites where patients can book appointments for lab tests online (e.g., LifeLabs), making the process easier and more convenient for both physicians' offices and patients. A first-time user would log on by creating a password that can be used for future encounters. As with many facilities using digital self-scheduling, there are certain tests that must be manually booked—these are listed on the lab's website.

Few disadvantages of self-scheduling have been noted. Perhaps you have less control in terms of preparing for the specific needs of each patient, but that can be addressed by having very specific online scheduling options—for example, a drop-down menu from which the person can choose the type of appointment. Routine visits for a minor or intermediate assessment (e.g., for a sore throat, rash, indigestion, arthritis) do not usually require special preparation or use of a specific examination room.

Online scheduling, as with open access scheduling, is not for everyone. Many older Canadians are unfamiliar with computers, let alone the internet. Others may have health issues that prevent them from making appointments digitally. Therefore, all offices must offer the option for patients to make appointments by phone. Moreover, patients with urgent medical problems (not requiring a 911 call or a trip to the emergency department) are more likely to call the office or to just show up.

L03 STANDARD TIMES FOR APPOINTMENTS

How much time a doctor spends with a patient will depend on several things:

- The doctor's practice style
- The type of practice (e.g., specialist, primary care physician, optometrist, chiropractor)
- The type and number of individuals in the office helping the provider (e.g., dental assistants, hygienists, chiropractic assistants, nurse practitioners, optometry assistants)
- The reason for the visit

In a family doctor's office, most appointments are scheduled every 10 to 15 minutes. Some doctors take more time with patients than do others. Some very busy doctors may double book two or more examining rooms every 15 minutes. The doctor may see the patient briefly but have a nurse, nurse practitioner, or assistant do a lot of the preliminary workup, health teaching, and part of the examination. If the assistant has done some testing, the provider would review the results with the patient and complete any necessary parts of the examination.

Categories of Assessment

The reason the patient has come to see the provider determines the length of time the doctor should spend with him or her. For example, it would take the doctor less time to assess a patient with a sore throat than one who was complaining of abdominal pain. Each province or territory has different terms to categorize visits. Ontario terms are used here, as outlined in the chapter on health plan billing, but the principles are the same everywhere.

A *minor assessment* is something that the doctor can deal with relatively quickly and that may only require a quick look or a verbal investigation. An *intermediate assessment* takes more of the doctor's time. A *complete assessment* refers to an investigation of most (usually all) body systems, or a complete physical examination, and takes 20 to 40 minutes or more, depending on the provider.

The following list covers the most common types of visits to a family physician, with approximate recommended scheduling times:

- Minor assessments (usually limited and done quickly), 5–7 min.
- Intermediate assessments (requiring moderate amount of time), 10 min.
- Initial prenatal examination, 20–30 min.
- Subsequent prenatal examinations, 10 min.
- Well-baby visits (progress check for a healthy baby), 10–15 min.
- Partial gynecological examination (e.g., Pap smear), 10 min.
- "Talks" or counselling, 30–60 min. (usually billed as units of time)
- Annual health examinations or complete assessments, 20–40 min. (sometimes longer if the patient is a senior or has multiple health problems)
- Allergy shots/flu shots: often no appointment needed, especially if there is a nurse to give the injection
- Immunizations: usually given to children during routine check-ups; no separate appointment is needed. (It may sometimes happen that immunization and check-up dates do not coincide; in this case, the nurse can give the immunization without the patient seeing the doctor.)

How to Determine the Type of Visit

It is important to know the reason for the appointment so that you can book the appropriate amount of time. If a patient seems reluctant to tell you, explain that you can better accommodate him or her if you know how much time is needed with the doctor. The patient may then give you some indication: "I need to talk about a personal problem," "It won't take long, it's something simple," or "The doctor knows what to do, this only takes a few minutes." However, if the patient still refuses to tell you, do not make an issue of it; just assume an intermediate assessment.

The majority of appointments in a family doctor's office are intermediate assessments, which require a moderate amount of time. An intermediate assessment involves a moderately detailed history and examination of one or more body systems. When you think about it, even an earache involves more than a transitory conversation and a quick look at the ear. The doctor must take a history related to the complaint, look in the ears, check the throat and neck for lymphadenopathy (elevated cervical nodes), and examine the chest to rule out related respiratory problems.

As discussed earlier, double booking works well for certain types of visits. For example, if Amanda is coming in for an allergy shot but does not have to see the doctor, the nurse will give her the shot while the doctor is seeing Matysio for a well-baby visit. Likewise, the nurse can remove Mark's sutures and complete the charting. Unless there are complications, Dr. Devour will only need to spend a brief amount of time with Mark. (Remember that one examining room will be tied up while the nurse is removing Mark's sutures.) Thus, you can book him alongside Lillian, who is coming in for a follow-up to see if the antibiotic has cleared up her ear infection—usually a quick check. Dan, who has a rash, does need to be seen by the doctor, but the visit will probably be brief, so he can also be double booked. Determining the type of visit is not as easy with open access scheduling or self-scheduling, but offices seem to adapt.

Scheduling for Other Providers

If you are scheduling appointments for an optometrist, you need to be familiar with the various procedures and examinations done in the office so that you can book appropriate times. A complete eye exam usually includes dilating the patient's eyes. This necessitates a 20- to 30-minute wait after the drops are instilled until the pupils are sufficiently dilated to conduct the examination. The optometrist would see other patients during that wait time. Often, staff members can complete some preliminary examinations, such as an automated refraction, so patient appointment times can overlap at certain points.

Scheduling for a dentist involves the same principles. The patient can come in at a specific time to see the hygienist and then see the dentist. Likewise, the dentist may inject freezing before filling a patient's tooth, then fill a tooth for another patient while the freezing is taking effect. Dentists book using units of time, usually 15 minutes. Certain procedures would take two units of time, others perhaps three or four.

A chiropractor may complete an adjustment and then have the patient move to another room for some physiotherapy but see the patient again before he or she leaves the office. If the chiropractor uses acupuncture, the patient may have to remain in the office for half an hour or more. In the mean time, the chiropractor would see other patients.

Information Needed to Book an Appointment

Some offices that use a manual scheduling system take more information than others do. The more complete the information (within reason), the easier it is to get in touch with the patient if you need to cancel or change the appointment or for any other reason. Record first and last names of the patient and pertinent phone numbers (e.g., work, home, cell). You need to have the patient's permission to call them at work. Some patients may prefer to be contacted using their email address.

TIP

Some patients may be evasive if you ask them the reason for the visit. The reason may be something personal. Explain you want to ensure that you schedule the appropriate amount of time with the doctor and have any equipment or materials the doctor may need ready. If this doesn't work, try to get a general sense as to what the reason is. "Do you think the visit will require a physical examination of any kind?" or "Do you think that you will require a fair bit of time talking with the doctor?"

An electronic scheduler allows you to easily access contact information, usually by clicking on the patient's name and then accessing the patient registry database.

Some offices do not ask the reason for the appointment. This information, however, helps the AHP not only book the appropriate length of appointment but make any special preparations for the visit. For example, if a patient has a sore throat, the doctor will probably want to take a throat swab. You or the nurse could put out the needed equipment, making the visit more efficient. Likewise, if a patient is coming in to get her prescription for birth control pills renewed, the doctor will probably do a Pap smear if it has been a year since her last visit. You would need to know this so that you or the nurse can prepare a speculum and put the patient into the appropriate examination room. A well-baby check needs to take place in the examining room where the baby scales are located. If you have to reschedule an appointment for a physical examination, you would want to choose another day when the doctor is doing physical examinations. Knowing the reason for the visit is necessary for affinity scheduling or if you are using scheduling templates.

Triage

Triaging patients in an office setting, clinic, or the emergency department has become the norm. Triage refers to assessing the urgency patients need to be treated and responding accordingly. Triage trumps the first-come, first-served philosophy. In an emergency department, a person with a more minor complaint (a sore throat) may sit for hours if more urgent cases come in, even long after they have arrived. This may be disconcerting for the person waiting, but for the person in need of immediate care it could save his or her life.

Occasionally, a patient will just show up at the office wanting to see the doctor. If a patient is in distress or clearly has an urgent need to see the doctor, let him or her in immediately or as soon as possible, even if it means making others with scheduled appointments wait. Otherwise, treat the patient the same way as a patient who phones in and book the earliest available appointment, which may be on another day. If patients in this situation are not satisfied, advise them that they can wait but you cannot guarantee that the doctor will be able to see them and that next time they should call for an appointment. If you handle the incident in this manner, most patients will only do it once. If you squeeze these patients in, there is no incentive for them to change their behaviour. Why should they? It gets them what they want.

If a patient telephones the office wanting to see the doctor right away, the urgency of the situation must be assessed. A nurse or the physician would most likely do this. In some health offices, however, the AHP would be given triage guidelines. Direct acute emergencies, such as chest pain, difficulty breathing, profuse bleeding, or stroke symptoms, should be directed to the nearest emergency department. If in doubt, involve the doctor or nurse in making this decision. Never make decisions without clear guidelines, and never make decisions you are unsure about without appropriate consultation. Health advice is the domain of the doctor or the nurse.

What about the patient who wants a same-day appointment when your schedule is already full? Determine the reason and assess the need using the triage guidelines, or ask the patient to speak to the nurse. If the problem is not serious enough to justify a trip to the emergency department but still sounds quite urgent, double book the patient. High temperature, earache, and urinary tract infections are usually considered urgent. For example, if a mother calls about a baby with a fever who is pulling at his ears, tell her to bring him in. This child must be seen. Generally, ailments involving small children should be assessed as soon as possible. On the other hand, an adult who has had a cough and a sore throat for a couple of days, in the absence of other serious clinical signs, is probably not an emergency. You need to be firm. It is not reasonable to make other patients wait to accommodate this patient. If you allowed every patient who asked for an immediate appointment to get one, chaos would result. Give the patient the earliest available appointment. If he or she remains insistent, suggest a walk-in clinic. Make sure that you do not, in any way, imply that the complaint is trivial. The patient may be worried and upset; to him or her, the complaint is troublesome. Show that you are concerned and are doing your best to help. One strategy that appeases patients is to offer an appointment several days away initially and then one a little sooner. For example:

> Mr. McIvor, I am sorry, the earliest opening I see here is Friday afternoon at 2:00 p.m., but let me see if there is anything I can do (pause). Actually, I think I can squeeze you in on Thursday morning at 10:30. Would that be better for you?

Or

> Mr. McIvor, I am sorry, but the earliest available appointment I have is Friday afternoon at 2:00 p.m. What I can do is make a note that you want to get in as soon as possible and call you if I get a cancellation. Now, what is the best number to reach you at?

You are offering alternatives and asking the patient for input. At the same time, you are sticking to your guidelines.

If squeezing someone in makes other patients wait, explain that an urgent problem has come up without going into details. If the doctor is going to be delayed by more than half an hour, ask the waiting patients if they want to schedule another appointment.

L04 MANAGING DISRUPTIONS TO THE SCHEDULE

As the great Scottish poet Robert Burns said, "The best-laid schemes o' mice and men gang aft agley." I wonder if Burns ever worked in a health office! The most organized office manager cannot predict what the next hour or the next phone call will bring. Contingency plans are necessary to keep the office running efficiently and, in some cases, to ensure the well-being of your patients.

Catch-Up Time

It is a good idea when pre-editing the appointment book for the week to set aside some catch-up-time slots, or buffer zones. These vacant time slots give you some flexibility to do the following:

- Let the doctor catch up if he or she is running late
- Provide a much-needed coffee break (although that rarely happens, except for quick gulps between patients and phone calls)

- Give the doctor an opportunity to return important phone calls or to review messages and prescription requests
- Squeeze in patients who need immediate attention

Cancellations

A cancellation represents lost revenue if the slot is not filled—a concern, especially if it is a long period, as it may be in a specialist's or a dentist's office. In a specialist's office, you would likely fill the slot from a wait list. In a dental office, you may also have a wait list of patients with a toothache or a filling that has fallen out. If not, you may call patients to see if they would like to move up their appointment. In a family physician's office, the spot can usually be filled almost immediately with patients calling for appointments or walking in. Indeed, in the family physician's office, a cancellation is usually a welcome opportunity to catch up. Draw a neat line through the patient's name and write "can." beside it.

No-Shows

Sometimes a patient does not show up for an appointment and does not call to let you know. As with cancellations, in a manual environment draw a neat line through the patient's name in the appointment schedule and write "N/S" beside it. On a computerized system, check "no show" so that it is recorded on the appointment screen and day sheet. Add the information to the patient's EMR. If a patient misses an appointment, it is not only lost revenue for the provider (a physician cannot bill the public plan for missed appointments), but it also forfeits an appointment spot another patient could have used, thus "wasting" an appointment. This is especially problematic when it involves providers for whom there is a long wait list (e.g., specialists). You rarely have time to offer the slot to patients who may be on a long waiting list, which you would if the patient called a day ahead to cancel the appointment.

No-shows can also be worrying. In many work settings, you will get to know your patients. Some people are chronically forgetful or late. If the patient is usually punctual, missing an appointment may signal trouble. A good example is an actual one when an older diabetic gentleman, usually reliable, did not show up for an appointment. The office manager called his home. Not getting an answer, she called a relative. The man was found unconscious in the bathroom, having experienced an insulin reaction. Without prompt treatment, the outcome could have been very serious. Though few causes will be this serious, it is always a good idea to at least call the patient. You can use this opportunity to rebook the appointment, which will help the patient get the health problem looked after and will help the provider maintain revenue (especially for those not funded provincially/territorially). As discussed earlier in the chapter, many providers charge patients for missed appointments.

>>> POINTS TO PONDER

Richard, a disabled man, called a mobility transfer company to book a ride to his doctor's office for an appointment at 1:00 the following afternoon. The driver said he could pick Richard up at 12:30—the soonest his schedule would allow. Upon reviewing the timeline, Richard called the doctor's office to say he would be 15 minutes late. The office said that was fine. Richard's ride arrived at 1:00 p.m. Richard called the office again to say he would not be in. The office charged Richard a staggering $300 for the missed appointment (which was lengthy and involved some tests). Was this fair? Who bears the responsibility for this incident? How could Richard have avoided this situation?

Chronic offenders are difficult to deal with. Posting a sign indicating that there will be a charge for missed appointments may motivate some individuals to call ahead or to simply show up. Most offices that charge for missed appointments require 24 hours' notice unless the reason for missing is beyond the patient's control. Family doctors are less likely than specialists and other providers to charge for missed appointments. However, if this is your office policy, you must follow through and charge the patient. Some offices do let the patient off with one warning, but only one. If you have time, a reminder call the day before may help. Many optometrists, dentists, specialists, and chiropractors do give reminder calls, but the majority of family physicians do not.

The Family Visit

Often a patient will make a single appointment and then come in with another family member (or two) in tow expecting the doctor to see them all. For example, a mother may make an appointment for one child and then bring one or two more. "Kyle has an earache, and Jessica has this rash on her arm. It will just take the doctor a minute to have a peek." You must discourage this behaviour. Unless the other complaints are urgent, you could respond with, "I am sorry, Mrs. Miklos, Dr. O'Brien is already running late and simply does not have time to see both Kyle and Jessica today. I do have an opening tomorrow afternoon, though." If you see that a patient prefers to bring the whole family together, you can ask when she calls next, "Did you want to combine your appointment with the follow-up visit for Kyle? I have two appointments available back to back next Tuesday, if you prefer."

The Patient with Multiple Complaints

Patients sometimes make an appointment to see the doctor about a specific problem. When they arrive, that problem has blossomed into several. When you are recording the patient's presenting problem, tell the patient that the doctor has only enough time to deal with the original problem. If the other complaints are not urgent, tell the patient that you would be happy to book another appointment. The doctor should also be firm about this. If he or she relents and deals with each issue every time, all of your efforts will be to no avail. Patients will get away with what they can because "The doctor doesn't mind. She always has time for me." Perhaps, but at the expense of other waiting patients. A united front, with physician follow-through, is essential. If the patient tells you that he or she has two problems to see the doctor about, an alternative is to book a double slot if one is available.

TIP

Sticking to Policy

You must establish a policy with the doctor regarding issues such as the family visit or the patient with multiple complaints. Your aim is to maintain patient flow according to the schedule and avoid backlogging patient appointments. The result is a heavy day, frustrated patients waiting for their appointment, and offenders who will repeat the behaviour. The doctor must be on board with you—too often, once the patient gets into the examining room the doctor will see other family members or deal with more than one complaint despite the fact that you have told the patient otherwise. This tells the patient that what you say doesn't really matter and undermines your intended role and authority. Discuss this with the doctor in a straightforward and firm manner. Most physicians will attempt to adhere to office policy, even if they "slip" occasionally.

Patients Who Refuse to See Team Members

In many primary care settings, various members of the health care team see patients for specific complaints (e.g., a nurse practitioner, a registered dietitian, a nurse). Some patients initially get angry and upset at the prospect of seeing someone other than the physician. Consider the patient's background when you try to reason with him or her. Explain the advantages of seeing another team member, stressing the fact that the person is well qualified and can (in most situations) spend more time with him or her. Also stress that it is a team environment, that the doctor is still part of the team, and is there if he or she is needed. Many offices have nurses do a Pap smear, for example, and may take a medical history from the patient, or a nurse practitioner will do a physical examination, or a registered dietitian will council the patient on weight loss and nutrition. If the patient remains resistant, have the doctor speak with him or her. Usually, after patients have seen another team member, they become comfortable with an interdisciplinary approach to their care, recognizing the expertise of other health care providers.

Physician's Absence

Occasionally, the physician may be called away or be unable to come into the office at all. You are then faced with a scheduling nightmare: cancelling appointments on short notice and rescheduling.

If the physician is called away suddenly, perhaps to the emergency or delivery room, first try to contact patients who may not have left for the office yet. If the reason for the visit is fairly urgent, refer the patient to another physician—the group's clinic, if there is one, or a walk-in clinic. Reschedule the rest as soon as conveniently possible. When you call patients, explain the physician's absence (in general terms) so that they realize the situation is beyond anyone's control. Most patients are good-natured about the inconvenience. Offer the same explanation to patients already in the office, apologize, and reschedule their appointments. Inevitably you will not reach all the patients. All you can do is apologize when they arrive and reschedule. Do not leave a message at a patient's workplace unless you have permission to do so.

L05 SCHEDULING VARIATIONS

New Patients

Ask new patients to come 15 to 20 minutes before they see the provider to fill out a questionnaire or health history sheet, which gives the physician important information. Practices that are more or less paperless may offer the patient a tablet with a questionnaire he or she can complete electronically. The physician or other health professional should carefully review the history sheet with the patient to ensure that the information is complete and accurate. Some offices have the AHP fill the form out online while interviewing the patient. Others scan the completed form and add it to the patient's EMR. Patients may leave a question unanswered if they do not understand it, or they may give an incomplete answer. For example, a patient may answer the question, "Have you had any previous surgeries?" with a simple "Yes." A review can elicit more useful information. Obtain demographic information, add the patient to your computer records, and start a chart. If you do not have the patient's medical records, ask him or her to sign a release so you can get them from his or her former doctor. It is important for the doctor to have this information to ensure continuity of care.

For some providers, the first appointment is long because the provider needs to take a complete history and discuss diagnosis and treatment plans. Some providers, such as an orthodontist or a chiropractor, may also need a long second appointment because they review X-rays and other data gathered from the initial examination to construct a treatment plan and explain it to the patient on the second visit.

Some practices have a sheet or booklet containing information about the practice, such as the office hours, policies, charges for uninsured services, the doctor's on-call schedule, and where to go or call in an emergency. If your office does not have such a booklet, consider creating one. It prevents confusion, saves everyone time in the long run, and helps the patient feel comfortable. Some practices call patients the day before the appointment and remind them to bring any medications they are taking. If patients have difficulty communicating, perhaps because of language difficulties or cognitive problems, ask that someone who can provide information accompany them.

Appointments for Patients' Forms

In any practice, there will be forms for the doctor to fill out: private insurance forms, sick notes, back-to-work/school notes, workers' compensation forms, forms for place-ment in long-term care facilities, home care forms, and physical examination forms for work, school, summer camp, and so on. Most forms require the doctor to examine the patient, either partially or completely. Filling out these forms can be time consuming and frustrating for the doctor. Rarely will the doctor have time to fill them out on the spot—a problem that many patients don't understand. Explain that the doctor will complete the form as soon as possible, and give a time frame: "May I tell Dr. Amiri that you will be in Thursday afternoon to pick up the completed form?"

Most practices charge to prepare such forms and notes. Post a sign in the recep-tion area listing the cost of all such services. See Chapter 12 for a discussion on collecting payments.

Appointments for Drug Representatives

Drug representatives were discussed in Chapter 8. If the doctor sets aside time to meet with drug reps, remember to slot them in when pre-editing. If you do not know a drug rep, take his or her business card so that you can call to cancel if you have to.

House Calls

Many but certainly not all family doctors will make house calls when they consider it necessary, perhaps when a patient with limited mobility or a patient recovering from an accident or illness cannot leave home. However, most other patients who want the doctor to come to their home are asked to go to the emergency department, by ambulance if necessary. It is a reasonable assumption that ambulatory patients will come to the office unless their complaints are fairly serious. The doctor can assess the patient more efficiently and effectively with access to a hospital's equip-ment and diagnostic services.

If a patient requests a house call, gather all relevant information about the patient's presenting problem and check with the doctor before scheduling a house call. If the doctor agrees to see the patient at home, clearly write down the patient's name, address, phone number, and, if possible, directions to the house. Give the patient an approxi-mate time when the doctor will come. If the patient is immobile, request that someone be at the house to let the doctor in. It is often best for the doctor to have another per-son in the house for legal reasons. One doctor made house calls to an older patient who began giving him gifts and behaving in a suggestive manner. When this pattern became clear to him, he asked that someone be present for all visits. The doctor may want a printout of the patient's health profile and a record of the patient's latest medications and lab reports. In a manual setting, pull the patient's chart. The doctor may want to review the patient's medical history or take the chart along. Remember to note all house calls on the physician's electronic scheduler.

Appointments with Specialists

A family doctor usually refers a patient to a specialist for a more thorough investigation into a health problem that requires specialized, detailed attention. Appointments with specialists are likely to last from half an hour to an hour. Specialists therefore see fewer patients in a day than do family physicians. You will often make the appointment with the specialist. As noted in Chapter 8, most consult requests are faxed to the specialist; they will schedule the appointment and fax the information back to you. You will then have to contact the patient. This may take up to a day. If the appointment date/time is unsuitable for the patient, they can call the specialist's office and rebook. Alternatively, you could ask the patient if there is a specific day he or she is unavailable and note that on the consult request prior to faxing. Given the long waits for appointments with specialists, most patients have enough time to shift their schedule. Across Canada, waits to see specialists average four to six months. Specialists triage, so if the patient's needs are urgent tell the specialist's office. If an early appointment is not available, you can ask that the patient be added to a wait list in case of cancellations.

Over the telephone, give basic information (or fax the information). If you have a secure internet connection, you can send the information electronically, including the following:

- The patient's name
- Telephone number
- Address
- Diagnosis

As well, you may fax or mail other medical information:

- Consultation request form letter
- Relevant previous test results
- Tests the family doctor has ordered in preparation for the consultation
- Relevant history

Make sure that the information reaches the specialist's office before the appointment. Add the specialist's name to any test requisitions so that the laboratory will send the specialist a copy of the test results. Call the specialist's office to ensure that the results have been received. Advise the patient of anything else he or she should bring, such as medications or X-rays. Ensure that the patient has the specialist's phone number and directions to the office.

Because specialist appointments may be made weeks or months in advance, it is easy for patients to forget. Given the long waiting periods, this is a wasted opportunity, as well as a loss of revenue for the provider. Some specialists' offices call the patient the day before the appointment. Some family doctors' offices will do this instead. With computerized appointment scheduling, you can enter a reminder to yourself to call the patient. The note will automatically appear on your screen on the appropriate day. If for any reason the patient cannot keep the appointment, make sure he or she calls the specialist in advance. When you schedule the appointment, ask about charges for missed appointments. If the specialist has such a policy, you must notify the patient in advance.

If you work for a specialist, notify the family doctor if a patient cancels an appointment or fails to show up. The family doctor's AHP should note this on the patient's chart and let the doctor know. The family doctor can then investigate the reason and will not be awaiting a letter from the specialist.

Appointments for Tests

Physicians routinely order procedures or laboratory tests for patients. All tests require a requisition, as discussed in Chapter 6.

Blood Work   Routine blood work does not usually require an appointment with the lab. However, the patient may need directions to the laboratory and the hours of operation. The patient may have a choice of laboratories, which may be either in-hospital or a private facility. If your office is in a medical building, you may have a laboratory on site (sometimes called a satellite lab). Provincial and territorial insurance covers the cost of most tests at any lab. The patient can choose whichever is more convenient. You can give the requisition to the patient, fax it, or send it electronically to the lab. Sending the requisition reduces the chance of the patient misplacing it.

TIP

Most software will allow you to record when patients have appointments with specialists or tests with a pop-up reminder option. Use this option and call the patient a week prior to the test. An appointment that is six months away is easily forgotten.

Diagnostic Tests   Diagnostic tests are more likely to require appointment times, and some require special preparation. (See Chapter 6.) Before scheduling the appointment, ask the patient for a range of convenient days and times. The exception is for such tests as MRIs, which, in some parts of the country, currently have waiting periods of up six months for nonurgent cases. In this case, take whatever appointment you are offered. Once the appointment is made, give the patient written verification of the date and time. Send or fax the requisition to the appropriate facility.

Scheduling Patients for Surgery

A patient who is scheduled for surgery has already been to see a specialist to determine the nature of the surgery required. The surgeon's AHP will book the procedure with the appropriate facility. The surgeon's office may notify the patient of the date or may notify the family doctor's office, in which case you would relay the information to the patient. Often this is done by fax. You will also provide the patient with details about the admission. Depending on the procedure, the patient may be booked for day surgery (in and out the same day) or as an inpatient. Most often inpatients are asked to come to the hospital the morning of the surgery and are admitted at that time. Preoperative preparations are completed in a pre-admit clinic, then the patient goes to surgery, and then postoperatively to a patient-care unit.

Some basic information is needed in scheduling surgery:

- The patient's name
- Address

- Phone number
- Date of birth
- Provincial/territorial health plan number
- Private insurance coverage, if any
- Type of accommodation requested if an overnight stay is required (standard/ward, semi-private, private room)
- Referring physician's name
- Surgeon's name
- Provisional diagnosis
- Name of the procedure (e.g., hysterectomy, left total hip replacement, laparoscopy)

A patient may have a **provisional diagnosis** of an ovarian cyst and be booked for a laparoscopy. The procedure may reveal that she has an ectopic pregnancy. The postoperative diagnosis then would be an ectopic pregnancy.

You may need to book an appointment for a patient to come in to the family physician's office for a preoperative assessment. In some provinces and territories, if the patient has had an annual physical within a certain number of days prior to the surgery, he or she will not have to have a preop assessment repeated. Patients having a major operation must have a complete assessment to provide current information about their medical conditions and to determine if they are a good surgical candidate. Most hospitals have a preop teaching program, usually outpatient, for surgical patients. The patient will have to make an appointment at the hospital to have an orientation, fill out some preliminary forms, and be told what to expect before and after the operation.

> **provisional diagnosis** a tentative diagnosis made before a procedure is done, which may be confirmed or changed by findings.

⟫ WHAT TO WATCH FOR

- How primary care practitioners schedule appointments, including the move to open access scheduling. What are the drawbacks? Is it really more efficient?
- Improvements to and increased use of digital self-scheduling—how well it works, and what settings it is best suited for.
- More emphasis on interdisciplinary collaboration in primary care—health professionals working together to see patients, sharing the responsibilities to improve patient care.
- The use of improved technology to post wait times to see providers in offices, clinics, and hospitals (some facilities already do this).

SUMMARY

1. To apply the principles and protocols of effective scheduling, you must be familiar with the scheduling features of your software system. Most systems have similar capabilities, allowing you to work in a single or multi-physician practice, easily access information to schedule appointments, pre-edit the schedule, apply templates, message within the practice setting, and use the day sheet effectively.

    Keeping health information secure is essential. This means keeping the computer screen out of view of others, locking the computer when the need arises, changing passwords appropriately, and keeping oral exchanges involving patients private (e.g., out of the hearing range of patients in the waiting area).

2. Knowledge of scheduling procedures/protocols (e.g. using templates, pre-editing the scheduler), along with the ability to determine the proper length of an appointment will contribute to an organized practice environment and contribute to efficient patient flow.

   Ambulatory care and urgent care clinics usually have open scheduling within fixed hours. Specialists may prefer affinity booking—grouping appointments for similar purposes—and family doctors may blend affinity with random scheduling. Double scheduling is used to cope with a busy day; it assumes that some patients will take less of the doctor's time. Stream scheduling, in which each client is assigned a specific, unique time slot, is the most common. Each method has advantages and disadvantages. You may be able to modify your office's scheduling method to enhance efficiency.

3. The time required for an appointment depends on the type of practice, the provider's style, and the reason for the visit. Typically, a minor assessment may take 5 to 7 minutes, an intermediate assessment 10 to 15 minutes, and a complete assessment or annual health exam 20 to 40 minutes or longer. You need to ask the reason for the visit to book appropriately.

   The principles of triage are applied in all health care settings—urgent cases are seen first. In the office setting you should have a protocol to follow, both when a person calls for an "urgent" appointment and for walk-ins. At no time should you make decisions related to who should be seen without clear guidelines or without consulting the nurse or doctor if you have concerns about what to do.

4. Rarely does an office run smoothly. There will be daily disruptions that interfere with the best-laid plans. Being flexible and having the ability to take a deep breath and deal with disruptive situations calmly is key. Having two or three "catch-up" slots will help—they allow time for nonscheduled patients who need to be seen, give you and the provider breathing space if not used, and ease backlogs in the schedule. Sticking to office protocol is important, such as limiting patients to one complaint and discouraging patients who come in expecting family members to be seen at the same time.

   In any practice there will be variations to routine scheduling. This includes drug reps, new patients, and making arrangements for the provider to make house calls (if he or she does house calls). A new patient, for example, should be asked to come 20 or 30 minutes ahead of time so that required forms can be filled in (usually a history questionnaire). Drug reps are often seen before the office opens or over the lunch hour, depending on the provider's preferences.

5. When scheduling specialist appointments and diagnostic tests, first find out when the patient is available. Make sure the specialist gets all necessary information and that the patient knows the date, location, and what to bring. In scheduling surgery, you may need to schedule a preop assessment.

KEY TERMS

affinity, cluster, categorization, or analogous scheduling 262
combination or blended scheduling 262
double scheduling or double-column booking 263
provisional diagnosis 277
stream or fixed-interval scheduling 263
wave scheduling 261

REVIEW QUESTIONS

1. How can the use of scheduling templates improve office efficiency?

2. What steps can you take to ensure that the appointment book remains confidential?

3. Compare and contrast the advantages and disadvantages of open access scheduling with fixed (routine) scheduling.

4. What is meant by *double scheduling*?

5. List the advantages of using catch-up or buffer zones in the daily schedule.

6. How should you handle a patient who walks into the office complaining of a sore throat and cough and wants to see the physician immediately?

7. What information should you take when scheduling an appointment both in the office and for a house call?

8. Describe the administrative steps you take when a new patient first arrives in the office.

9. How would you respond to Mrs. Garlinski, who wants to come in for her follow-up blood pressure check but refuses to be scheduled to have this done with the nurse?

10. What information is necessary when scheduling a diagnostic test, such as a mammogram?

APPLICATION EXERCISES

1. **a.** Design an appointment schedule on your computer, that is suitable for the office of a primary care physician.

   b. Pre-edit the next week, using the following information:

      i. Dr. Schumacher does hospital rounds from 8:30 a.m. to 9:30 a.m. every day.

      ii. He likes to do physical examinations in the morning on Tuesdays and Thursdays, but no more than two per day.

      iii. On Thursday he has a patient-care conference from 11:00–11:45 a.m. in his office.

      iv. He must be out of the office by 5:00 p.m. on Thursday for another meeting.

      v. He is seeing a drug rep from 10:00–10:15 a.m. on Friday.

   c. Book the following appointments. Assume that Dr. Schumacher's style is to take an average length of time with patients or just a little longer. For each patient, consider

      • what level of assessment is needed (minor, intermediate, major),

      • how long an appointment to book, and

      • the best time to book it.

      i. Mr. Reynolds wants to have his annual physical examination. H: 416-432-4444; email: reynolds@sunshine.on.ca. Retired. At home most of the time.

      ii. Donna Kim needs an appointment for her first prenatal visit. W: 416-332-3432, H: 416-343-3333. She works full days and has three other children.

      iii. Elaine Yang is due for her allergy shot. She does not have to see Dr. Schumacher. She is at school full time. H: 416-332-3332.

      iv. Maya Appleton has had a cold and sore throat for three days. She has experienced a pain in her left ear for the last 24 hours. She is 13 years old. H: 416-222-2222.

      v. Jessica Zehr has a rash on her left forearm. Home-maker. H: 416-333-2222.

      vi. Mihail Reznikoff complains of diarrhea and abdominal cramps that he has had for 24 hours. H: 416-333-3333, W: 416-333-2222.

      vii. Elisabeth Walker, who is a diabetic, has been having trouble with regulation of her blood sugar level. She states she has been hypoglycemic twice in the past three days. She also has a sore on her left foot.

      viii. Rachel Desmond is planning to become pregnant. She is coming in for advice and genetic counselling. She prefers Thursday.

      ix. Marnie McLaughlin needs an appointment for a well-baby exam for Karen, who is three months old. H: 416-222-5555. Marnie is on maternity leave. Wednesdays work best, she says.

      x. Emily Lawton is coming in for a physical examination. She is 88 years old. H: 416-111-2222.

      xi. Mr. Anatoly wants an appointment. His left knee is swollen, and he is having difficulty walking. H: 416-234-3333, W: 416-943-9969. Thursdays are good.

      xii. Mrs. Hazel calls and wants an immediate renewal for her Valium. H: 416-323-4444, W: 416-321-0222.

      xiii. Cathy Evans needs an appointment to discuss placing her aged mother in a nursing home. Any day is good.

xiv. Jeremy Karsch wants an appointment for what he thinks is a recurrence of his bronchitis. Email: jhewitt.@sympatico.ca.

xv. Mario Liotta wants to see the doctor. He is complaining of redness and swelling in his left leg. H: 416-432-3233.

xvi. Phil Ioannou needs an allergy shot. H: 416-111-2441.

xvii. Georgina Gould wants an appointment for a gynecological examination, Pap smear, and insertion of an intrauterine contraceptive device. Any day but Mon./Tues. works for her. H: 416-426-9214.

xviii. Gary Janacek was asked to come in today for a blood pressure check. H: 416-421-6666.

xix. Betty Nguyen calls with vague symptoms of fatigue. H: 416-944-2111. Wants Tues. appt.

xx. Shaundra Ladouceur comes in complaining of a plantar wart (a wart on the sole of the foot). H: 416-111-9472. Any day is OK.

d. In groups of three to four, compare your appointment schedules. Do your partners see any problems with your scheduling? In particular, note any differences in how long an appointment each of you assigned to a given patient. Was this because you came to different conclusions about what level of assessment was needed? Decide as a group which level is accurate. Adjust your schedule to solve any problems pointed out by your partners.

2. Dr. Hanoi has just opened a medical practice. She is part of a primary care reform group who rosters patients. She instructs you to begin scheduling appointments so she can begin her "interview and screening" procedures. Dr. Hanoi tells you to find out a little about the person before you schedule an appointment. She gives you criteria of people she is not prepared to interview: those over 40, individuals with chronic health problems, people on workers' compensation claims, or those on social assistance. You feel very uncomfortable about this process, and you are unsure you want to be a part of this. In small groups, discuss the ethical and moral implications of this policy. Is the doctor upholding her code of ethics? Are her actions violating the rights of health consumers? Are her actions morally or legally right or wrong? Try to find out whether the College of Physicians and Surgeons in your jurisdiction has guidelines about this type of action. Are you obliged to comply with Dr. Hanoi's wishes? What courses of action do you have?

WEBSITES OF INTEREST

Booking Same-Day Appointments

www.aafp.org/fpm/2000/0900/p45.html

A Guide to the Personal Health Information Protection Act

www.ipc.on.ca/images/resources/hguide-e.pdf

Chapter 10
Health Care Plans

Monkey Business/Fotolia

LEARNING OBJECTIVES

On completing this chapter, you will be able to:

1. Differentiate between insured (medically necessary) and uninsured medical services.

2. Discuss supplementary services covered at the discretion of provinces and territories.

3. Determine how the value of various services is determined in accordance with provincial/territorial fee schedules.

4. Outline health care coverage, considering eligibility, the application process, and timelines.

5. Explore the role of private insurance in health care coverage.

This chapter expands on the information in Chapter 4, giving details about the structure of territorial and provincial health care plans and the system of remunerating physicians. It will give you the background knowledge you need for Chapter 11, Preparing for the Billing Process, and Chapter 12, Billing. Chapter 4 also lists the types of eligible providers who can bill provincial or territorial health care plans on a fee-for-service basis.

To be eligible to submit claims, providers must be licensed by and in good standing with their professional college and be registered with their province or territory. **Provincial or territorial billing** begins with the province or territory issuing billing numbers to providers, either as individual providers or groups, which must be cited on all submitted claims. In some provinces, a provider cannot bill under another provider's number. Other provinces allow a locum to bill under the regular doctor's number. The provider whose number appears on the claim assumes responsibility for that claim.

provincial or territorial billing the process whereby a health care provider submits a claim to a province or territory for insured health services rendered.

LO1 INSURED AND UNINSURED SERVICES

The Ministry of Health in your province or territory (or a division of the ministry) is essentially the insurance company that is responsible for claims assessment and payment. Health care plans pay only for **insured health care services**—normally those they also define as *medically necessary*. Both the list of services considered medically necessary and the fees for these services are negotiated by the ministry and representatives from provincial or territorial medical associations. Services covered under workers' compensation or certain other federal legislation are excluded, although some provinces act as payment agencies for workers' compensation claims (discussed later in this chapter). For the specific services insured in your province or territory, consult your ministry's website. Lists of services are updated annually.

insured health care services medically necessary hospital, physician, and surgical-dental services provided to insured individuals.

The Canada Health Act defines *physician services* as "medically required services rendered by medical practitioners." A service includes the physician's time and expertise. The physician must maintain appropriate and detailed records of every service rendered, unless otherwise noted.

Services considered *assessments* generally include direct physician–patient contact. For example, Darlene came into Dr. Atkins's office for a blood pressure check-up. The nurse took Darlene's blood pressure and recorded the results. If Darlene then left without seeing the doctor, Dr. Atkins could not legally claim that visit as an assessment because he did not see Darlene. In some provinces the blood pressure check-up could be billed, but not as a physician encounter. The physician must be present, either directly supervising or available, and the procedure must be appropriately documented with a record of who performed it. If Dr. Atkins came into the examination room and discussed Darlene's blood pressure with her, even briefly, he could submit a claim for the related assessment.

Naturally, the extent of the assessment will vary with each encounter. Normally, an assessment requires that the physician examine the patient or take a history, make a diagnosis, implement appropriate treatment (including giving advice and support or counselling), and make an appropriate record. (See Chapter 11.) It may or may not include a procedure, such as an injection.

medically necessary referring to those services or supplies that are essential to the care and treatment of an illness or injury and that could not have been omitted without adversely affecting the patient's medical condition or the quality of the health care rendered under generally accepted professional standards of medical practice at the time and place incurred.

The term **medically necessary**[1] has not been formally defined by the Canada Health Act. Though the parameters of "medical necessity" are constantly debated, the Canadian Medical Association defines a medically necessary service as "one that a qualified physician determines is required to assess, prevent, treat, rehabilitate, or palliate a given health concern or problem." Services considered medically necessary in a given province or territory at a given time may not be considered so in another province or territory or at another time.

For example, if Jacob went to the physician with a sore throat, he would be examined and perhaps have a swab taken. The physician might choose to put Jacob on an antibiotic or give him advice on how to relieve the pain. This whole process would be

---

[1] Library of Parliament, Parliamentary Information and Research Branch, The Canada Health Act: Overview and Options (94-4E). www.parl.gc.ca/information/library/prbpubs/944-e.htm.

considered a *service* and the visit by the patient an *encounter*. The assessment, diagnosis, and treatment, including any tests and follow-up, would be covered because they are considered medically necessary. If Jacob went to see the physician to get a note to return to school after being absent, the visit or encounter would *not* be considered medically necessary and would therefore not be insured. Patients can expect insurance coverage only for services deemed medically necessary as outlined in the provincial or territorial fee schedule.

Another common insured physician service is called a *consultation*. This service in most provinces and territories is provided by a specialist (also called a consultant) only upon written request from a referring physician, usually the primary care physician or other provider such as a nurse practitioner. This occurs when the referring provider feels that he or she does not have the expertise to deal with a particular health problem or if the patient requires surgery, for example. Levels of consultations will be discussed in Chapter 11.

Though each province and territory has some latitude in deciding what services to insure, the Canada Health Act sets out categories of services that must be covered, specifically medically necessary physician, hospital, and surgical-dental services (the latter includes only those that must be performed in a hospital). Insured health services include physician services, including home and hospital visits and inpatient services, provided in an approved hospital facility.

Insured services are also referred to as regulated services. Ministries review services regularly to consider whether they should continue to be insured and whether the fee should be adjusted. A service that is no longer insured is removed from the fee schedule, or **deregulated**. For example, a few years ago routine infant circumcision was removed from the Ontario fee schedule because it is not considered medically necessary.

deregulated when a service is removed from a province's or territory's fee schedule so that it is no longer insured under that jurisdiction's health plan.

Hospitals and physicians also provide services that are not defined as medically necessary and are not covered by provincial or territorial insurance. These services, whether performed in a hospital, clinic, or physician's office, must be paid for by the patient or by private insurance.

Long-Term Care/Residential Care Facilities

All jurisdictions offer residential care to provide a variety of living options to those who need them. The names for residential facilities vary: Lodges, nursing homes, and long-term care homes are the most widely used terms. These organizations may be stand-alone facilities or connected to other types of care, including hospitals. For example, in some jurisdictions long-term care facilities can expand on and diversify not-for-profit services in areas of housing, geared-to-income shelter, or life leases. Most long-term care facilities also have a secure section, or what they call "cottages," for people with Alzheimer's disease and other forms of memory loss.

A long-term care facility provides 24/7 nursing care and supervision as required to individuals unable to remain in their homes because of illness or disability. All provinces and territories have residency criteria that must be met—Alberta has the most detailed. All jurisdictions subsidize the cost of the facility based on an income/assets analysis. There are differences in coverage. For example, Ontario and British Columbia consider only annual income (not assets) when a person applies for a subsidy. New Brunswick considers both assets and annual income. Long-term care is fully subsidized in Nunavut. In most jurisdictions, if an individual is eligible for a subsidy it is for basic accommodation only—if their entire income goes toward their basic accommodation, the person must be left with a nominal amount of money to cover the cost of personal and other items (e.g., television, telephone, sundries). Until recently a four-bed room was considered basic accommodation, but as facilities are renovated and new ones built, four-bed rooms are being phased out in favour of private or "preferred" private rooms (two-bed rooms with a partial wall dividing them).

It is important to note that there are privately owned, provincially licensed facilities across Canada, most offering levelled care, but these are not publicly funded. This care ranges from independent living to full 24/7 nursing care. Individuals can purchase the services they need as they require them (e.g., meals, laundry and housekeeping services, or medication administration). Full nursing care can cost up to or exceed $10 000 a month. For example, Sunrise of Vancouver, which is a privately owned and operated home, is licensed by the province to provide long-term care. In Ontario, long-term care is provincially funded and regulated. In any private facility, an individual can still apply for transfer to a provincially funded long-term care facility, but there is usually a lengthy wait list.

Hospital Services

Insured hospital services include medically necessary services to inpatients and outpatients. Insured inpatient services include the following:

- Standard ward accommodation and preferred accommodation, if medically required
- Meals
- Nursing services (including private nursing care, if deemed medically required and ordered by the physician, or as determined by the nursing staff for the patient's benefit)
- Drugs and related preparations when administered in the hospital
- Use of an operating room, delivery room, or case room and anesthetic facilities
- Laboratory, radiological, and other diagnostic services, along with the necessary interpretations
- Use of other therapies, such as physiotherapy, occupational therapy, speech therapy, and audiology
- Medical and surgical equipment and supplies
- Services provided by individuals who receive remuneration from the hospital

Insured outpatient services vary across provinces and territories but typically include the following:

- Laboratory, radiological, and diagnostic procedures
- Physiotherapy, speech therapy, occupational therapy, diet counselling services (if considered medically necessary)
- Renal dialysis (in hospital and at home, including equipment)
- Medications for patients with specific conditions, such as cystic fibrosis
- Administration of rabies vaccine

Hospitals also offer services that are not insured. These also vary by jurisdiction but typically include the following:

- Private or semi-private accommodation (many Canadians have private insurance to cover the additional cost)
- Private duty nurses, unless ordered by the physician
- Grooming services, such as a pedicure or a haircut
- Telephone and television
- Accommodation for cosmetic surgery (not deemed medically necessary)
- Medications to take home (there may be some exceptions)

To contain costs, some facilities are asking patients to bring personal items they might expect to be provided, such as tissues and soap. On some obstetrical units, new mothers are asked to bring diapers, breast pads, and sanitary supplies.

Physician Services

The following services are insured across the country:

- Physical examinations, when done to investigate symptoms or for disease prevention/screening (with some conditions—not all provinces cover annual preventive general assessments)
- Home visits and physician visits to other health care facilities (with some conditions)
- Major and minor surgeries
- Obstetrical services
- Complaint-driven office visits

Provinces and territories may cover other services, but Table 10.1 lists some common services that are *not* usually covered. One major variation is the handling of physical assessments of well adults. Ontario recently deregulated the annual health

TABLE 10.1   Services that are usually uninsured

■ Back-to-school/work notes/certificates	■ Preparation or provision of a drug, an antigen, or an anti-serum used for treatment that is not used to facilitate a procedure (hepatitis B vaccines, WinRho for RH-negative mothers)
■ Physical examinations requested by a third party (e.g., for school, camp, driver's licence) or in preparation for travel	■ Allergy treatments (generally, the doctor's or nurse's service is covered, but the serum is not)
■ Completion of insurance/disability forms	■ Drugs used in infertility treatments
■ Transfer of files when a patient changes physicians (includes the physician's time as well as photocopying, faxing, or mailing costs)	■ In most cases, psychoanalysis
■ Legal proceedings	■ Circumcision of male newborns (unless deemed medically necessary)
■ Telephone advice/consultations (with certain exceptions, such as the supervision of ongoing medication)	■ Reversal of vasectomies
■ Charges for long-distance calls related to the patient's treatment	■ Reversal of tubal ligations
■ Assessment relating to fitness to continue employment	■ Gastric stapling or gastric bypass (covered in some provinces and territories depending on the patient's condition)
■ Missed appointments/procedures	■ Removal of superficial veins for cosmetic purposes
■ Renewal of prescriptions when the patient does not see the physician	■ Removal of warts other than plantar and venereal warts
■ Any duplication of service that is contrary to the guidelines outlined in the fee schedule	■ Immunizations not considered medically necessary (criteria vary with jurisdiction and from time to time. Often, provinces cover immunizations to groups deemed at high risk. Where immunizations are not fully covered, usually the patient must pay only for the serum.)
■ Devices, such as an intrauterine contraceptive device (IUCD)	■ In some provinces, interviews not considered medically necessary
■ The newer types of removable fibreglass cast (standard plaster casts are covered; the more expensive, lightweight, waterproof fibreglass casts are considered a convenience, not a medical necessity)	■ Alternative therapies, such as acupuncture, even if provided by a physician

examination, replacing it with a less comprehensive assessment called a periodic examination. Most jurisdictions now only cover assessments that are complaint driven.

You need to be aware of the services not covered in your area. These services may be covered by private insurance or may be paid for by the patient. (As discussed later, patients must be notified in advance of charges.) Physicians may charge patients directly for services not covered under their provincial/territorial health insurance plans. (This is not to be confused with illegal user fees for insured services.) How much the physician is allowed to charge varies with the province or territory and the situation, but it is usually based on the nature and complexity of the service (and the amount of physician time it requires) and the qualifications of the provider. For example, a specialist may charge more than a primary care physician would. The physician may also charge associated costs (plus taxes where applicable) and a reasonable markup to cover administrative costs incurred as a result of the service. Some provincial and territorial medical associations have recommended fees for uninsured services, which may often be found on the association's website.

Fees may be collected from third parties and directly from patients. Procedures for collecting fees from third parties and directly from patients are discussed in Chapter 12. Patients may pay for other types of services and facilities, such as home care, which may be partially covered by a provincial/territorial plan. As discussed in Chapter 4, patients may also pay for enhanced services or so-called enhanced products; for example, if Mike broke his arm, he could opt for a plastic cast instead of a plaster one, which would be covered by his public plan.

L02 OTHER HEALTH BENEFITS

Most provinces and territories cover a range of related health services, although programs vary.

Travel Assistance

Canadians who must travel great distances for medical treatment are often compensated. For example, patients who live in designated areas of Northern Ontario are eligible for compensation from the Northern Health Travel Grant to offset some of the cost if they must travel more than a given distance to access a medical service. The grant pays a specified amount of money per kilometre travelled, after a deductible distance (e.g., 100 kilometres), but does not cover the costs of meals or accommodation. The patient must go to the nearest provider who can render the required service and must have a letter from a physician, dentist, optometrist, chiropractor, midwife, or nurse practitioner giving the reason for the referral. Other examples include the Medical Transportation Assistance Program in Newfoundland and Labrador, which provides financial assistance for residents who incur substantial costs when travelling for insured medical services, such as cancer treatment or surgery, and the Travel Assistance Program in British Columbia.

If your area has such a grant program, make sure your patients know about it. A surprising number of people who could use the help do not know about it. Keep up to date on program criteria and eligibility, which change often.

Drug Benefit Plans

catastrophic drug plan a plan that would cover overriding drug costs causing impending financial hardship on individuals.

Canada is the only country with universal health care that does not have a national Pharmacare program that would cover the cost or prescription drugs. Moreover, at present there is no national **catastrophic drug plan**. However, each province and territory has a drug benefit plan for seniors and other designated groups. Eligibility for such plans will vary, and criteria often change.

PharmaCare in British Columbia provides income-based financial support to eligible BC residents (which includes all residents registered with the Medical Services Plan) for a range of specified prescription medications and medical supplies. Fair PharmaCare is a specialty plan offering income-based benefits to families who need it the most; the coverage is more comprehensive than the PharmaCare program, and many families do not have a deductible under the Fair PharmaCare plan. Families who do have deductibles have the option of paying for those costs under a monthly deductible payment plan.

Manitoba also calls its drug benefit program Pharmacare (as does Nova Scotia); benefits are based on a family's income and the amount paid for eligible prescription drugs. Under Newfoundland and Labrador's Prescription Drug Program, a new program called the Access Plan also provides more comprehensive coverage to eligible low-income residents.

▶▶▶ POINTS TO PONDER

In 2016, Manitoba enacted legislation making it necessary for individuals to have a prescription to obtain any drug containing codeine. Pharmacies are recognized as providers and can write prescriptions for this type of medication. All information will be recorded in a provincial database so that individuals wanting a medication with codeine (e.g., Tylenol 2) can be tracked. This means that those on a drug benefit program may have access to this type of medication (formerly purchased over the counter and paid for personally). Do you think this is a good idea? Do you think it will cut down on drug abuse?

The Ontario Drug Benefit (ODB) Program covers, among other groups, seniors and residents of long-term care facilities. Ontario's Trillium Drug Program covers part of the cost of drugs for individuals not eligible for the ODB but who have high prescription drug costs in relation to their income. Some provinces and territories use annual **deductibles**. For example, if the cost of a family's drugs were $2000 and the deductible was $500, the family would pay the $500 and the province or territory would pay the remaining $1500. Another method used by some provinces and territories is called a *co-payment*. This requires that the patient pay a portion of the cost of each drug prescribed.

deductible the portion of a benefit that a beneficiary must pay before receiving coverage.

The Drug Benefit Formulary

Most provinces and territories have a formulary that lists selected prescription and nonprescription drugs covered by drug benefit plans. The formulary may sometimes include a variety of medical supplies and devices. Each province and territory has a committee that reviews new drugs on the formulary and recommends additions to and deletions from the formulary. Purdue Pharma is the drug company that made OxyContin, a highly addictive but widely used painkiller (also called hillbilly heroin). In April 2012 the company stopped making OxyContin and introduced OxyNEO, a supposedly less addictive replacement. Ontario, with other jurisdictions following, has delisted OxyContin from its drug benefit plan. In another attempt to curb the abuse of drugs, jurisdictions across Canada are changing their policies on covering higher doses of opioids. For example, in 2016 the Ontario Ministry of Health and Long-Term Care announced that all opioids that exceed the equivalent of 200 milligrams of morphine a day will be delisted from the province's drug formulary. This has been controversial, with fierce opposition by some physicians, especially those involved in palliative care, where effective pain control for patients involves the use of higher doses of these drugs.

If the physician feels the patient should have a drug not on the formulary, he or she can seek approval for funding the drug for that patient. This is called a restricted listing drug. The physician must fill out a form requesting the drug for the patient—sometimes called a limited use (LU) form. There are other drugs not on the restricted-use list. For these drugs, the physician must write a letter requesting the drug or submit another form. There are still more drugs that are entirely off limits to those on provincial/territorial drug plans; the only option for use of these would be the patient paying for them. These are the newer, more expensive drugs.

A physician would seek use of a drug not on the formulary for a couple of reasons. The first is if the patient is allergic to or otherwise cannot tolerate the available drug. The second is a situation wherein the patient doesn't respond favourably to the available drug. For example, Sandra is on a hypoglycemic agent (from the formulary list), but it isn't controlling her blood sugar properly. The physician feels that a newer drug on the LU list would be more therapeutic, so she requests permission to use that. If that drug fails to control Sandra's blood sugar levels properly, the physician would then seek permission to use a drug that isn't on the LU list.

Patients sometimes wonder why their physician does not prescribe specifically requested medications. Encourage them to ask the physician for clarification. You should be aware of patients who are on provincial/territorial drug benefit plans and of any special forms (such as for restricted listing drugs) the physician must fill out.

Physiotherapy

Coverage of physiotherapy varies across the country. Generally, physiotherapy services provided in a hospital are covered by provincial/territorial health insurance plans, whereas community-based services may or may not be. Most jurisdictions cover this service for outpatients in an approved clinic. In provinces and territories that cover physiotherapy, the patient must be referred by a physician, and the service must be considered medically necessary.

Ambulance Services

Most provinces and territories completely or partially cover emergency ambulance services, whether ground or air, and ambulance transfers from one facility to another to obtain medical services. Services include medical and paramedical personnel deemed necessary on a particular trip. The patient may have to pay part of the cost. This is called a co-payment. Some provinces and territories completely cover ambulance services for designated groups. In some jurisdictions, municipalities pay most of the cost of ambulances; some have banded together to jointly cover the cost. Ambulance services are staffed by paramedics who are highly trained first responders.

Optometry

Many provinces and territories have reduced the optometry services they will insure. Across Canada, the majority of individuals from age 20 to 64 have no provincial or territorial coverage for eye examinations. (This varies; for example, in British Columbia coverage is available up to the age of 18.) In most jurisdictions, individuals in the 20 to 64 age category are partially covered for eye exams if they have a traumatic eye injury or certain medical conditions, such as diabetes, glaucoma, macular degeneration, or cataracts (conditions where an optometric examination is deemed medically necessary to treat or monitor disease progression). If a person goes to see his or her primary care physician with an eye condition that is within his or her scope of practice, it would be covered under the provincial/territorial plan. For example, Kevin, who lives in Alberta, wakes up in the morning with conjunctivitis and makes an unexpected visit to his family doctor, a walk-in clinic, or the nearest emergency department. Fees for eye examinations done by an optometrist are set by the optometrist. Some provinces, such as Alberta and Quebec, have had that policy in place for several years. In British Columbia, the Medical Services Plan currently covers $46.38 for a full eye exam and $29.48 for a minor or follow-up examination. Services not covered include those related to contact lens, corrective laser surgery, and devices such as eye glasses, eye medications, and visual aids for those with low vision. Most jurisdiction will partially cover low vision aids under other plans. No province or territory will cover even part of the cost of devices or surgeries to enhance vision out of country. For example, the London Eye Hospital in London, England, has a revolutionary new intraocular lens called the EyeMax that greatly improves vision for individuals with conditions such as macular degeneration. The cost to a Canadian seeking to have this device implanted would be over $10 000 per eye.

If you work for an optometrist or oculist and your region's health care plan restricts eye examinations, you need to keep accurate records and notify patients when they are due for a routine assessment. If patients request assessments earlier than allowed, you have to let them know that they are responsible for payment. For example, suppose Ashley, who is 19 years old, had a complete oculo-visual assessment on July 15, 2016. Because she is going away for the summer, she wants to have her next check-up done in June 2017. It is your responsibility to explain that because it is less than 12 months later, she will not be covered. Her choices are to have the assessment in June and pay for it herself (considered an assessment requested for personal reasons) or to wait until she gets back. "Aw, come on," she may say, "why don't you just do the check-up in June and send the bill in July?" Altering data like that is illegal; if it were discovered, the plan would not pay the fee, and you could be charged with an offence. The same principle applies to any service with a time restriction, such as annual physical examinations.

L03 DETERMINING THE VALUE OF AN INSURED SERVICE

Each insured service is assigned a monetary value, reflected in a service code, item code, or fee code (they all mean the same thing) that determines how much the provider can charge for the encounter. How this value is determined varies across the country. Most systems take into account the nature or complexity of the patient's problem and the depth of the assessment or the age range of the patient. Other elements (sometimes combined) considered may include

- the time the physician spends with the patient,
- the patient's age,
- any additional interventions rendered at the time of the service, and
- special circumstances, such as where and when the service is rendered.

Complexity of the Assessment

Generally, the time spent with a patient depends on the complexity of the assessment (which will be discussed in more detail in Chapter 11). Many provinces and territories have two or three categories based on the complexity of the assessment and time spent with the physician. A visit of a type that usually requires minimal time with the doctor would be considered a minor assessment. In Ontario, a minor assessment usually includes a brief history and examination of the affected body part or region, a brief examination and history of a mental or emotional disorder, and brief advice or information regarding health maintenance, diagnosis, treatment, or prognosis. An intermediate assessment is more complex and requires a history of the presenting physical, mental, or emotional complaint and an inquiry about and examination of the affected body part or system to establish a diagnosis. The physician would receive a higher payment for a complete physical examination, either symptom driven or done for preventive assessment. In British Columbia, the categories are somewhat different: The category of partial or regional examination includes what would be called minor and intermediate assessments in Ontario. British Columbia has special categories for emergency care, which are divided into level I, II, and III assessments.

Time-Based Services

Fees for some services, such as counselling, surgery, and providing anesthesia, are based, at least in part, on the physician's time. The physician is paid so much per unit of time (e.g., 15 or 30 minutes) spent rendering the service. Different jurisdictions calculate units slightly differently. Time-based payment may apply after an initial base fee. For example, suppose a surgeon is paid a set amount to remove an appendix. However, if the surgeon runs into complications and takes longer to complete the procedure, he or she could bill the province or territory for the extra time spent in the operating room. Some jurisdictions also allow physicians to charge extra if they are required to spend extra time assessing, treating, or monitoring a patient. These claims are usually reviewed individually. For example, in Ontario, if a physician is required to spend more than 30 minutes on what should have been a minor or intermediate assessment, he or she can submit this claim for special consideration for time-based remuneration. Most jurisdictions require physicians to note start and end times.

The Patient's Age

Most provinces and territories assign different service codes bearing higher fees for the same service depending on the age of the patient. For example, there may be a premium code attached to the fee code for services to older adult patients. In British Columbia, assessments have different fees for patients in five different age groups.

Additional Interventions

Providers in all provinces and territories can bill for diagnostic and therapeutic procedures, ranging from complex to minor, such as taking a urine sample or giving an injection. (Procedures considered a routine part of an assessment, such as a Pap smear as part of a woman's complete physical, may not be billed separately.) These services are billed using what many jurisdictions call a *procedural code*. Procedures done in conjunction with a physician visit are billed at a lesser amount than those done separately. For example, if a patient visits the doctor for an assessment and also gets a flu shot, the doctor charges for the visit (service code) and for the flu shot (procedure). If the patient comes into the office only to get a flu shot (whether from the doctor, a nurse, or a medical assistant), the physician does not submit a service code but can charge a slightly higher amount for the procedure.

Time, Location, and Special Circumstances

Most fee structures make allowances for services that must be provided at inconvenient times and locations. For example, a premium may be charged in addition to the regular fee if the physician has to travel to another facility or the patient's home or if a service must be done outside of office hours. Services provided after midnight often have higher premiums. A premium may also be chargeable if the physician has to cancel office appointments to provide emergency service out of the office.

Independent Consideration

In most provinces and territories, some services do not have a fee attached to them. Remuneration for these services vary with the situation, thus the provincial or territorial payment agency reviews each submission independently. These services are marked with a region-specific identifier.

The Fee Schedule

Every province and territory has a manual that outlines its rules and regulations regarding billing for insurable services. This resource manual is often referred to as a *fee schedule*. The proper name of this resource varies. In Newfoundland and Labrador, it is referred to as the *Medical Payment Schedule*; in Saskatchewan, the *Physician Payment Schedule*; and in Ontario, the *Schedule of Benefits*.

Your province's or territory's fee schedule is a valuable resource. It is provided to physicians and facilities at designated intervals or can be purchased at most government bookstores. *Schedules are now available on the internet*, and as a student, you may legally download for study purposes your province's or territory's fee schedule or only the components used in your program.

L04 HEALTH CARE PLANS: ELIGIBILITY, HEALTH CARDS, AND APPLICATIONS

Eligibility for Health Care Plans

Although there are some variations from one jurisdiction to another, generally, people who are Canadian citizens or landed immigrants and are permanent residents of a province or territory are eligible for health insurance in that jurisdiction (they are called **beneficiaries**). Some jurisdictions also extend eligibility to temporary residents in certain categories, such as temporary workers, holders of a minister's permit, foreign students, and refugees whose status has been confirmed by the Immigration and Refugee Board of Canada. Provincial and territorial health plans do not cover certain designated groups for which the federal government is responsible:

beneficiary a person eligible to receive insurance benefits under specified conditions.

- Indigenous Canadians living on reserves
- Members of the Armed Forces
- Members of the Royal Canadian Mounted Police (but not their families)
- Inmates of federal correctional institutions

Payment of Premiums In Canada, there are two models for the payment of provincial and territorial premiums: (1) residents paying insurance premiums, and (2) government covering health care costs through blended taxation.

As mentioned in Chapter 4, only British Columbia and Ontario residents pay insurance premiums. In all other provinces and territories, health care is paid for by tax money—including sales taxes, employer levies, and property taxes—from the federal, provincial/territorial, and municipal governments. Coverage is universal for legal residents, regardless of employment status.

Health Cards

All provinces and territories give eligible individuals a health card (in some provinces it is referred to as a care card or a service card). This card must be presented each time the person seeks any insured health service. It is required across Canada that the user have a valid health card at the point of service. Some facilities enforce this policy more stringently than others, so follow your employer's policy. Even if your employer is willing to provide treatment to patients without cards, encourage the patients to remember to bring the card next time. A posted notice in a prominent place also helps remind patients. Some patients do not believe they need the card; they feel that you know them and can simply look up their information. That may be so in your office, but you are doing patients a disservice if you let them develop the habit of leaving the card at home. Sooner or later, they will probably be refused a nonurgent service at some other facility.

You may be able to convince patients that the health card is necessary by comparing it to a credit card. Suppose a customer went to buy a pair of shoes in a department store, but at the cash register she said, "Sorry, I left my credit card at home. I'll take the shoes now and pay you next time." Or suppose she presented an expired credit card. It is unlikely the cashier would let her walk out with the shoes unless she paid cash. A health card is no different.

Card formats vary, but generally a health card includes the person's name (the card must be changed if the person's name changes), health number (in many jurisdictions this is assigned for life), and expiry date. (See Figure 10.1.)

Health Numbers Each health card has a personal identification number on it. Depending on the province or territory, this number ranges from 7 to 12 digits. (See Table 10.2.) This number may be referred to as a health card number, a care card number, or a personal identification number. Some jurisdictions issue a separate health number for each eligible individual; others issue family numbers. In Manitoba, only adults are issued a health card, which contains the name of each family member and their own personal health number. It is particularly important with a family number to report changes in family status, such as marriage and divorce.

All jurisdictions issue a health number, but some also issue a separate account number. In 2013, British Columbia moved to replace the provincial health card with a Services Card, which has a unique lifetime identification number; this card is integrated with a person's driver's licence (if he or she has one) and is used to access any government service. Most eligible adult BC residents (ages 19 to 75) will be required to renew their enrollment in the Medical Services Plan before 2018. Manitoba is also implementing a similar card. In 2017, Manitoba started issuing all-in-one Identification Cards that combine a person's health card with photo identification, driver's licence, and travel identification. Driver's licence information will appear on the front of the card, and the person's health number will be on the back. Other jurisdictions are also considering a combination identification card.

Alberta, too, uses both unique personal health numbers and family account numbers for billing purposes. On turning 21, a person must apply for a different billing account number but retains his or her personal health number. In Ontario, each person has a health card number for life; there is no account number.

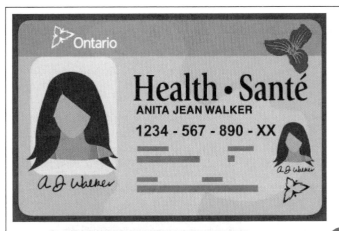

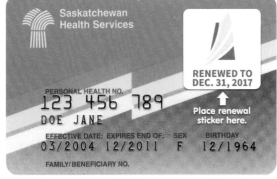

© 2012, Government of Saskatchewan

Ontario Ministry of Health and Long-Term Care

JONATHAN FREDERICK JOHNSTONE
123 456 789 001
Card Expires: 2011.03.31

Date of Birth	Gender	Valid From
1967.11.11	**M**	**2007.04.01**

Government of Newfoundland and Labrador, Department of Health and Community Services

MCP Identification Card

This card identifies the person whose name appears on the reverse side as being registered under MCP.

THIS CARD MUST BE PRESENTED EACH TIME YOU RECEIVE MEDICAL SERVICES

Please notify the Newfoundland and Labrador Medical Care Plan of any change of address. Forms are available from MCP, physician's offices, or http://www.gov.nl.ca/mcp/ Toll free # 1-800-563-1557

Figure 10.1 Sample health cards from Ontario, Saskatchewan, Prince Edward Island, and Newfoundland and Labrador

Saskatchewan Ministry of Health; Ontario Ministry of Health and Long-Term Care; Prince Edward Island Department of Health and Wellness; Government of Newfoundland and Labrador

Expiry Date/Renewal Date   In some jurisdictions, health cards have an expiry date noted right on the card. After the expiry date, the health card is invalid and must be renewed. In some jurisdictions, cardholders are notified by mail when the expiry date is approaching. Record the expiry date on the patient's chart, and if the patient comes in close to that date, remind him or her that the card will soon expire. Although renewal is the patient's responsibility, you will not only be doing the patient a service but also saving yourself the time and trouble of claim rejections because of an invalid card. Many office software programs will alert you when a patient's card is nearing its expiry date when you swipe it. In all jurisdictions where health cards are assigned to temporary residents, the card will have an expiry date.

TABLE 10.2 Abbreviations and formats for health numbers in Canadian jurisdictions

Jurisdiction	Abbreviation	No. of Digits	Registration Unit
British Columbia	BC	10 or 11	Individual
Alberta	AB	9	Individual
Saskatchewan	SK	9	Individual
Manitoba	MB	9	Subscriber/family group
Ontario	ON	10	Individual
Quebec	QC	10	Individual
New Brunswick	NB	9	Individual
Nova Scotia	NS	10	Individual
Prince Edward Island	PE	9	Individual
Newfoundland and Labrador	NL	12	Individual
Yukon	YT	9	Individual
Nunavut	NU	9	Individual
Northwest Territories	NT	7 + 1 letter	Individual

Version Code   On the newer Ontario card, the version code is represented by two alpha characters that follow the health number. The purpose of this code is to reduce health card fraud. If a card is lost, the replacement card will bear the same health number but a different version code. If someone tried to use the lost or stolen code, it would be immediately picked up when the card was checked.

Privacy and the Health Card   A health card (unless it is a combined health/ID card) is an important personal document that must be treated as private and confidential. It is to be used for health care purposes only. It is illegal to ask someone to show a health card for identification purposes (e.g., cashing a cheque, applying for a charge card, proof of age). An exception is that seniors in Ontario may use their health card as proof of age for seniors' discounts. Showing the card, however, is voluntary. This does not hold true in all provinces and territories.

Registering for Provincial or Territorial Health Insurance Coverage

You will likely be asked about registering for health coverage. Although the information is publicly available, it is helpful to understand the process so that you can explain it to patients.

Each province or territory has its own application form, which is usually available at doctors' offices, hospitals, and ministry offices in cities and larger towns. Many jurisdictions have the application form online as well. Figure 10.2 shows an application form for Prince Edward Island. In some jurisdictions, the form may be mailed, faxed, or brought in to the approved location along with the appropriate identification and citizenship or immigration documents.

Each applicant must supply the ministry with specific information and validate this information. This information is stored in a central electronic database and is confidential. The insured person must supply accurate, current information.

Stress the importance of bringing all the required documentation. Without it, applications will not be processed, which will lead to delays and frustration. Patients are often surprised at what is accepted as documentation. Applicants need documentation

Health PEI

Personal Health Card Application
•
Carte santé personnelle Formulaire de demande

Santé Î.-P.-É.

PO Box 3000
126 Douses Road, Montague
Prince Edward Island, C0A 1R0 Canada
Telephone: (902) 838-0900 / 1-800-321-5492

C.P. 3000
126, chemin Douses, Montague
Île-du-Prince-Édouard, C0A 1R0 Canada
Téléphone : (902) 838-0900 / 1-800-321-5492

Please print all information clearly.
Complete in full and return to above address.

Prière d'écrire clairement en lettres moulées.
Veuillez remplir en entier et renvoyer à l'adresse ci-dessus.

For Office Use Only • À usage interne seulement

Document No. • *Document n°*	Household No. • *Ménage n°*
Date eligible • *Date d'admissibilité*	Status • *Statut*
Day • Jour Month • Mois Yr. • Année	
Date entered • *Date de saisie*	Entered by • *Saisi par*
Day • Jour Month • Mois Yr. • Année	
Date approved • *Date d'approbation*	Approved by • *Approuvé par*
Day • Jour Month Yr. • Année	

Name (surname, first name, initials) • *Nom (nom, prénom, initiales)*

Birth Date • *Date de naissance*	Sex (M/F) • *Sexe (M/F)*	Country and Province of Birth *Pays et province de naissance*	Personal Health Number *Numéro de la carte santé*
Day • Jour Month • Mois Yr. • Année			

Mailing Address • *Adresse postale*	City/Town • *Ville*

Postal Code • *Code postal*	Telephone No. • *Téléphone*	
	Home • *Maison* ( )	Work • *Travail* ( )

Spouse (surname, first name, initials) • *Conjoint(e) (nom, prénom, initiales)*

Birth Date • *Date de naissance*	Sex (M/F) • *Sexe (M/F)*	Country and Province of Birth *Pays et province de naissance*	Personal Health Number *Numéro de la carte santé*
Day • Jour Month • Mois Yr. • Année			

1. Dependant (surname, first name, initials) • *Personne à charge (nom, prénom, initiales)*

Birth Date • *Date de naissance*	Sex (M/F) • *Sexe (M/F)*	Country and Province of Birth *Pays et province de naissance*	Personal Health Number *Numéro de la carte santé*
Day • Jour Month • Mois Yr. • Année			

2. Dependant (surname, first name, initials) • *Personne à charge (nom, prénom, initiales)*

Birth Date • *Date de naissance*	Sex (M/F) • *Sexe (M/F)*	Country and Province of Birth *Pays et province de naissance*	Personal Health Number *Numéro de la carte santé*
Day • Jour Month • Mois Yr. • Année			

3. Dependant (surname, first name, initials) • *Personne à charge (nom, prénom, initiales)*

Birth Date • *Date de naissance*	Sex (M/F) • *Sexe (M/F)*	Country and Province of Birth *Pays et province de naissance*	Personal Health Number *Numéro de la carte santé*
Day • Jour Month • Mois Yr. • Année			

4. Dependant (surname, first name, initials) • *Personne à charge (nom, prénom, initiales)*

Birth Date • *Date de naissance*	Sex (M/F) • *Sexe (M/F)*	Country and Province of Birth *Pays et province de naissance*	Personal Health Number *Numéro de la carte santé*
Day • Jour Month • Mois Yr. • Année			

See other side • *Voir au verso*

Figure 10.2 Application for health coverage in Prince Edward Island (*Continued*)

Used by permission of Health PEI.

Residential Status • *Résidence*

☐ New Resident
Nouveau résident

☐ Returning Resident
Résident de retour

☐ R.C.M.P., Armed Forces, Penitentiary
G.R.C., Forces armées, établissement pénitentiaire

| | | |
Day • *Jour* Month • *Mois* Yr. •

(Please indicate release date if any of the above apply • *Veuillez indiquer la date de libération, le cas échéant*)

Province/Country of last residence • *Dernier lieu de résidence (province ou pays)*

Mailing Address • *Adresse postale*	City/Town • *Ville*	Country • *Pays*	Postal Code *Code postal*

Former Provincial Health Care No. (if applicable) • *Ancien numéro de la carte santé provinciale (le cas échéant)*

Reason for coming to Prince Edward Island • *Raison de la venue à l'Île-du-Prince-Édouard*

☐ Internship
Stage

☐ Student
Études

☐ Employment
Emploi

☐ Other
Autre

(Please specify • *Veuillez préciser*)

Length of stay on Prince Edward Island • *Installation à l'Île-du-Prince-Édouard*

Permanent • *Permanente*
☐

Temporary • *Temporaire*
☐

Date of arrival on Prince Edward Island • *Date d'arrivée à l'Île-du-Prince-Édouard* _____ | _____ | _____
Day • *Jour* Month • *Mois* Yr. • *Année*

Citizenship Status (must attach copy of immigration record or proof of Canadian citizenship before applications may be processed)
Citoyenneté (*La demande ne sera traitée que sur la foi des dossiers de l'Immigration ou d'une preuve de citoyenneté canadienne.*)

☐ Canadian Citizen
Citoyen canadien

☐ Working Visa
Visa d'emploi

☐ Canadian citizen returning from another country
Citoyen canadien de retour de l'étranger

☐ Landed Immigrant
Résident permanent

☐ Other
Autre

(Please specify • *Veuillez préciser*)

I hereby authorize the details of this application may be discussed with the Federal Department of Employment and Immigration Canada.
J'autorise par la présente la discussion des détails de la présente demande avec le ministère fédéral de la Citoyenneté et de l'Immigration.

Signature _____

Declaration • *Déclaration*

I hereby state that I am legally entitled to remain in Canada, I am permanently residing and making my home in Prince Edward Island and I understand that it is an offence to give false information in this application.

Je déclare par la présente que je suis légalement autorisé à demeurer au Canada, que je réside en permanence à l'Île-du-Prince-Édouard et que je comprends que de fournir des renseignements faux dans la présente demande équivaut à commettre une infraction.

Signature _____ | _____ | _____
Day • *Jour* Month • *Mois* Yr. • *Année*

Figure 10.2 (*Continued*)

from three categories, a fact that confuses many people. Applicants must bring one document from each of the three following categories (detailed lists of specific examples of documents are on your provincial/territorial Ministry of Health website):

1. Proof of Canadian citizenship or immigration status
2. Proof of residency in the province/territory (this varies somewhat; check the local form)
3. Proof of personal identity (i.e., that you are who you say you are)

Temporary Health Cards In most jurisdictions, a paper health card similar to the plastic card is issued for patients who need a card immediately (e.g., those whose cards are lost or stolen) or who are eligible for coverage for only a short period of time. In some provinces, a validated copy of the application form accepted by the ministry serves as a temporary card.

Registering Newborns When a baby is born, the birth must be registered. Newborn registration must be completed before a birth certificate can be issued. Newborns are covered immediately by the provincial or territorial health insurance plan of the jurisdiction in which at least one parent is eligible to receive health care. In some jurisdictions, including Ontario, hospitals and midwives have forms with preassigned health numbers that they complete when a baby is born. There is a tear-off portion that serves as the baby's health card until an actual health card is issued. In Ontario, the ministry will enter the baby's name and information into the system and should send a health card for the infant within three months after receiving the completed top portion of the form. When the baby's card expires, the parents will be asked to show a birth certificate when they make an application for a new health card. In jurisdictions that do not use preassigned health numbers, parents should apply for coverage for the child as soon as possible. (See Figure 10.3.) In Alberta, coverage is provided from the date of birth if notification is received within one year. Otherwise, coverage begins on the first day of the month in which notification is received. In British Columbia, either parent must complete a registration of birth form (given to the mother at birth) and return it to the Vital Statistics Agency within 30 days of the baby's birth. In British Columbia and other provinces and territories, parents can apply for a SIN (social insurance number) for the baby at the same time.

Registering Adopted Children Adopted children are normally registered for coverage in the same way as babies. The adoption process requires the collection of sensitive information, including the birth mother's identification. Even if an adopted child already has a health card, his or her adoptive parents would apply for the child as a new registrant. This approach prevents accidental disclosure, since identifiable information will not be on the application form.

Updating and Correcting Cards

It is important to ensure that health cards are kept current and information is up to date, which in some jurisdictions means renewing them from time to time.

Name Change In most jurisdictions, insured individuals who change their names must fill out the appropriate form to ensure that health coverage eligibility is maintained. You can find the relevant form on the Ministry of Health website for each province or territory. For name changes because of marriage, applicants must provide one of the following:

- Marriage certificate
- Certified statement of marriage

NEWBORN / ADOPTED CHILD REGISTRATION FORM
Please Print

MAILING ADDRESS

Street/P.O. Box	City/Town		
Province	Postal Code	Telephone Number (Home)	Telephone Number (Work)

PARENT OR GUARDIAN

MCP Registration Number	Surname	Given Name and Initials	Birth Date (YY/MM/DD)

CHILD/CHILDREN TO BE REGISTERED

Surname	Given Name and Initials	Sex (M/F)	Birth Date (YY/MM/DD)

DECLARATION (It is an offense to give false information for the purpose of obtaining coverage under the Newfoundland and Labrador Medical Care Plan)

I hereby declare that the information given is correct and the person(s) listed on this form are residents of Newfoundland and Labrador.

Signature   Date

REQUIRED DOCUMENTATION

If registering a child/children through adoption, a copy of the official adoption papers, or the birth certificate, is required for each child.

If the surname of the child/children is different than the registering parent or guardian, a copy of the birth certificate is required for each child.

Medical Care Plan		Medical Care Plan
22 High Street, P. O. Box 5000		57 Margaret's Place, P. O. Box 8700
Grand Falls-Windsor NL Canada A2A 2Y4		St. John's NL Canada A1B 4J6
Tel: 1-800-563-1557 Fax: 709-292-4052	*http://www.gov.nf.ca/mcp*	Tel: 1-800-563-1557 Fax: 709-758-1694

Figure 10.3 Application to register a newborn or adopted child in Newfoundland and Labrador
Government of Newfoundland and Labrador

■ A record of marriage form (it must be the original, signed by the person who conducted the marriage [e.g., clergy], and must include the name of the spouse, date of the marriage, and marriage licence number)

For other name changes, the applicant would supply a change-of-name certificate. Marriage is, of course, the most common reason for name changes—at least for women. After getting married, a surprising number of women begin to use their husband's name without thinking about their health registration. You can help by asking any woman you know who is getting married if she is changing her name and, if so, tell her that she needs to have her health card changed. If a male or female patient asks you to use a new surname, or if you hear that a patient has taken Canadian citizenship, you can also explain that a new card is needed.

In Ontario, if the individual still has the old-style red-and-white card, he or she will need to register for a photo ID health card at the same time, bringing documents of the same type needed to apply for a new card.

Some newly married women, although they are using their married name, continue to use their old card for a while. Keep both names on your computer system and records to avoid confusion when looking up the patient's information. Keep in mind, however, that not all women change their names when they marry. When spouses have different surnames, it is usual to cross-reference family units by making a note on the patients' charts and linking them in the computerized database.

There is a similar process to follow if the marriage dissolves and the patient wishes to return to her original name. Details can be obtained from your ministry. Usually, a copy of the final divorce certificate is required.

Address Change   Residents changing only their address can usually do so as follows:

- Fill out and mail a change-of-information form obtained online and either mail or fax it to the nearest provincial/territorial service office
- Complete the form and mail it in
- Update the card at a kiosk (in jurisdictions that offer kiosk services); the patient will need the new postal code and the health cards of all family members

When you find out that patients have moved or plan to move, remind them to update their cards. Increasingly, health care facilities are refusing to accept health cards that lack current information. Manitoba, for example, specifically states that any change in location or family status, such as marriage, birth, adoption, death, divorce, or separation, must be reported to the Insured Benefits Branch. A patient with an incorrect card will not be refused the service but may be required to pay and seek reimbursement from the ministry. New Brunswick specifically requires that individuals report any incorrect spelling of names, wrong date of birth, and out-of-province or out-of-country moves by one or more members of a family.

If you are dealing with another province or territory, be sure to check the specifics. For example, if you work in British Columbia and one of your patients is moving to Nova Scotia, check with the ministry in Nova Scotia before advising your patient about how to apply for health care registration in that province.

Lost or Stolen Health Cards

Health cards should be kept as secure as credit cards. Across Canada, health card fraud is a concern. If one of your patients loses a health card or has it stolen, advise the person to report it immediately to the appropriate government office. Usually, there is a toll-free number. In Ontario, patients who had a photo health card will be issued a new photo card. Patients who had a red-and-white card will have to go to a ministry office to register for a photo card. Any replaced card will have a different identifier—in Ontario, a new version code will be issued, and in other jurisdictions the accounting number will change (many jurisdictions have a permanent health number).

New Brunswick has a specific form for replacing lost or stolen cards. Some other jurisdictions use the same form as for the original application. Prince Edward Island charges a replacement fee, with a maximum amount per family.

The Three-Month Waiting Period

Moving from Outside the Country Individuals moving to Canada, or Canadians returning after living out of the country, have a three-month wait before they are eligible for provincial health insurance if they move to Ontario, British Columbia, Quebec, or New Brunswick. These individuals should be encouraged to apply for private health insurance for that period. Many private health insurance companies will not provide coverage unless the applicant purchases the insurance within five days of moving to Canada.

Refugees, refugee claimants, and immigrants from "humanitarian designated classes" who live in those provinces can receive emergency and essential health services through the Interim Federal Health Program. People moving from out of the country to the other provinces and territories are eligible for health coverage immediately.

Note that the recent refugees Canada has accepted (and is continuing to accept) have permanent residency from the moment they land in the country and are not subject to the three-month wait.

Moving within Canada People who move from one province or territory to another will face the three-month waiting period before their new health coverage comes into effect. They will still be covered by their province of origin. Unless they are moving from or to Quebec, providers in the new province can be paid through the reciprocal agreement (discussed later).

The three-month waiting period does not generally apply to individuals discharged from the Canadian Armed Forces or the RCMP or to people moving to become residents of homes for the aged, nursing homes, homes for people with disabilities, or other homes designated as charitable.

Absences from the Province or Territory of Origin

Provincial or territorial health insurance plans provide coverage for residents during absences both within and outside Canada. Criteria may differ with each region. Residents are generally covered for vacations and for absences for education or work for a specified length of time. In some provinces, "snowbirds" who spend the winter in warmer climates must reside in the province for at least six months plus a day each year to be eligible for continuous coverage. Long absences—for extended vacations, employment, academic studies, and missionary work with approved charities—should be reported to the health care plan with supporting documentation. In Ontario, this is done on the change-of-information form. With approval, coverage may be extended as long as five years for employment.

Out-of-country medical services are usually paid at the rate that would be paid for the service in the resident province or territory. If the provider charges a higher fee, the patient may be responsible for the difference. Usually, the patient must pay when receiving the service and then submit receipts to the provincial or territorial health plan for reimbursement.

What is considered an insurable service in one jurisdiction may not be in another, perhaps providing incentive for residents in one jurisdiction to seek an otherwise uninsured service in another jurisdiction. This is not normally permitted. For example, a patient whose home province does not cover routine infant circumcision cannot get it covered by travelling to a province that does cover the procedure.

Patients sometimes have elective surgery done in the United States to avoid long waits in Canada. Many have applied for authorization for such out-of-country surgery and been refused. On occasion, however, provinces or territories will authorize payment for a medically necessary procedure to be done outside the province/territory or country when the treatment is not available there or within the time frame considered medically necessary.

Billing for Out-of-Province/Territory Patients

A **reciprocal agreement** among all the provinces and territories, except Quebec, allows providers to bill their own ministries for services rendered to insured residents from other parts of Canada. This covers medical and related diagnostic services. (Hospitals are covered by a similar separate agreement.) Prior approval is not normally needed. Physicians will normally be paid at the fee rate in their own province or territory.

Quebec has not signed a reciprocal agreement with any other province or territory for insured physician services. If you work for a provider in Quebec, charge out-of-province/territory patients directly and advise them to keep the receipts and seek reimbursement from their own health plan. If patients mention that they will be travelling in Quebec, let them know that they should be prepared to pay for any medical services, and remind them to keep the receipts. Physicians outside Quebec who render services to Quebec residents should take all the patient and diagnostic information, charge the patient, and provide a receipt and record of the service provided. The patient can claim reimbursement from the Quebec Ministère de santé et des services sociaux. Ontario has provided patients from the Outaouais Region of Quebec with services unavailable in their region. Until 2015, submissions have been made on cards; they are not automated. Claims will be processed upon receipt and will be paid in the next billing cycle provided they are received by the monthly claims cut-off date. Supporting documentation is usually required.

reciprocal agreement an agreement among provinces and territories (with the exception of Quebec) that allows providers to bill their own ministries for services rendered to insured residents from other parts of Canada (e.g., a person from Manitoba visiting a doctor in Nova Scotia).

L05 PRIVATE INSURANCE

Although medically necessary hospital and physician services in Canada are covered primarily by public health insurance, private health insurance plays a significant role in covering services not eligible under provincial or territorial plans. Private insurance becomes increasingly popular as government health plans drop services once covered, such as routine eye examinations and chiropractic services in most jurisdictions. Many general insurance companies offer health insurance. However, a few companies specialize in it.

Blue Cross and Liberty Health Insurance are two of the larger companies in Canada that provide supplementary health care insurance. They cover services ranging from home nursing care and health care aids to semi-private and private hospital accommodation and a television and telephone while in hospital. They may also cover co-payments and deductibles for services only partly covered by the government, such as prescription drugs, alternative therapies, and accommodation in long-term care facilities, such as nursing homes. The extent of the coverage is reflected by premiums paid. Many companies provide health insurance through group policies, often included in employee benefits packages. These policies may cover alternative health care services, such as chiropractic, massage therapy, and acupuncture, as well as comprehensive dental and eye care and medications.

Blue Cross was organized in 1939 as a not-for-profit prepaid health insurance plan. Policies can be obtained through independent member benefit plans in each province or territory. Like other companies, they provide supplementary benefits, dental benefits, prescription drugs, medical care outside Canada, and critical illness coverage.

Liberty Health is another major player in the health care industry. The company's main business is group insurance through employers, but they also offer health insurance for individuals and families, as well as life and disability insurance. Liberty Health offers drug and dental insurance in various packages, with higher-premium plans paying a higher percentage of potential expenses, as well as coverage for paramedical services, ambulance services, physiotherapy, vision services, and additional hospital coverage.

Most insurance companies will require medical information from the claimant's physician. This may be directly related to the reason for the claim or involve additional

```
┌─────────────────────────────────────────────────────────────────┐
│         CONSENT FOR DISCLOSURE OF PERSONAL HEALTH INFORMATION     │
│                                                                   │
│   I _____ (name of patient) give Dr. _____ (full name of │
│   physician) permission to disclose the following health information: │
│                                                                   │
│   _____ │
│   _____ │
│   _____ │
│   _____ │
│   _____ │
│   _____ │
│   _____. │
│                                                                   │
│   To (name of recipient of the information): │
│                                                                   │
│   _____ │
│   _____ │
│   _____ │
│                                                                   │
│      I understand the purpose of disclosing this health information, and that I am signing this │
│   document of my own free will and I can refuse to sign this form. The reason for disclosure of │
│   this health information, how it will be used, and the benefits and consequences of disclosing │
│   this information has been explained to me in terms that I understand and accept. │
│                                                                   │
│   My Name: _____ │
│   Address: _____ │
│   Home Tel.: _____     Work Tel.: _____ │
│   Signature: _____     Date: _____ │
│   Witness Name: _____     Address: _____ │
│   Home Tel.: _____     Work Tel.: _____ │
│   Signature: _____     Date: _____ │
└─────────────────────────────────────────────────────────────────┘
```

Figure 10.4 Sample of a release of personal health information form

information. Release of this information requires a release of personal information form, completed by the doctor and signed by the patient. Figure 10.4 is a generic example of such a form.

Motor Vehicle Insurance

Insurance for injuries sustained in motor vehicle accidents is carried by most large insurance companies. Such claims can represent a significant portion of those you deal with in the office. In British Columbia, for example, the Insurance Corporation of British Columbia is a provincial Crown corporation providing, among other services, auto insurance to many BC motorists. Forms you will be required to deal with include those requiring a physical assessment for special drivers' licences as well as those related to injury-generated claims. Forms for each company will have common elements, for example, the demographic information you can fill out for the physician. Ensure that the patient has completed any release of medical information forms, and keep a note of when forms have been completed and sent and to whom. If medical information is to be faxed or mailed directly to the company, explain this to the patient, who may be under the assumption that he or she can take the information and send it him or herself. There are situations wherein this is contraindicated.

Workers' Compensation

Workers' compensation is another type of insurance in Canada. (See Chapter 5.) Every jurisdiction has a workers' compensation board (WCB), although names vary somewhat: In Ontario, the board is called the Workplace Safety and Insurance Board (WSIB); in Yukon, it is the Yukon Workers' Compensation Health and Safety Board; and in British Columbia, it is called WorkSafeBC. Through premiums paid by employers, WCBs insure workers against work-related injuries, paying partial replacement of wages as well as covering medical and other health care expenses resulting from injuries. Services covered under the Workers' Compensation Act are usually billed directly to the Ministry of Health, which is then reimbursed by the WCB. There are exceptions that vary somewhat by jurisdiction (see Chapter 12 for more detail). An injured worker must sign a form allowing the treating physician to release medical information relating to the claim to the WCB. See Chapter 8 for details regarding common forms and links to these forms.

⟫⟫ WHAT TO WATCH FOR

- An increase in deregulated services as jurisdictions attempt to cut costs.
- Collaboration between the federal and provincial governments for a possible agreement to implement a national pharmacare program.
- A national strategy for mental health.
- Changes in strategies for community-based and long-term care to provide proper care for an aging population.

SUMMARY

1. Licensed physicians and other providers in good standing are eligible to receive fee-for-service payment from provincial or territorial health plans. All jurisdictions' health plans cover hospital services and physician services deemed medically necessary.

   Uninsured services vary but usually include back-to-school/work notes, completion of forms, transfer of files, telephone advice, and infant circumcision (unless medically necessary). Some jurisdictions cover preventive physical examinations; others do not. It is helpful to post a sign listing the more common services that are not covered in your jurisdiction, along with the charge for each.

2. Extended benefits vary. Most jurisdictions have a drug plan, long-term care coverage, ambulance coverage, travel assistance when necessary medical services are at some distance, and some optometry coverage. You should be able to inform patients about such benefits.

3. Many provinces and territories base physician payment on the complexity of the service performed, while some pay higher fees for older patients. Fees may be higher for services performed under special circumstances.

4. Canadian citizens (including the RCMP since 2013) and landed immigrants, as well as foreigners meeting certain criteria, are covered by provincial or territorial health plans. Health cards in all jurisdictions contain similar information; some jurisdictions have photo ID cards integrated with drivers' licences. For example, in 2017 Manitoba will be issuing all-in-one photo identification cards that combine a person's health

card, driver's licence, and travel identification. Most health and integrated ID/health cards must be renewed at designated intervals (often five years). Canadians moving within the country retain coverage from their province/territory of origin for a period of three months unless the jurisdiction they are moving to waives the three-month wait for coverage. Ontario, New Brunswick, and British Columbia are the only provinces that enforce a three-month wait for individuals moving to Canada; babies have immediate coverage.

5. Many Canadians have private insurance to cover services that provincial or territorial plans do not cover, such as preferred accommodation in the hospital, additional nursing care, drug and dental benefits, optometry, and chiropractic.

KEY TERMS

beneficiary   291
catastrophic drug plan   286
deductible   287
deregulated   283

insured health care
   services   282
medically necessary   282

provincial or territorial
   billing   282
reciprocal agreement   301

REVIEW QUESTIONS

1. List and explain six hospital and medical services that are *not* covered under most provincial or territorial plans.

2. What is the purpose of a drug benefit plan, and what segment of the population are such plans generally created to support?

3. What does a health office professional have to consider in scheduling vision checks?

4. List the three categories of documentation a person must present when applying for health care coverage, and give three examples from each category.

5. Describe the process of registering a newborn for health care coverage.

6. What province does not participate in the reciprocal agreement? How does that affect patients from that province and patients travelling in that province?

7. List four groups of people who are exempt from the three-month wait for health coverage in some provinces.

8. Describe the process to follow if your health card is lost or stolen.

9. What can you do in the health office to reduce fraudulent use of health cards?

10. What are three organizations that provide private insurance for Canadians, and what types of services do they cover?

APPLICATION EXERCISES

1. Using the internet or other resources, develop a list of the extended health services covered in your province or territory. Explain who is eligible for this coverage and the range of services offered.

2. Research how ambulance services are managed in your own province or territory and three others. Make a list comparing what is covered in each jurisdiction and the cost to the ministry and to the patient.

3. Amrini, who arrived in your province/territory two months ago, has two part-time jobs and is supporting a wife and three children. He has not applied for health insurance, not knowing how to do so or where to go. His combined salaries give him about $24 000 a year. One child, aged 6, is diabetic, the other, aged 12, is asthmatic, and his wife is six months pregnant. He can't afford to pay for the medications. He doesn't know where to turn for help. He has paid cash for services at your office (family medicine). You suspect his wife has used his sister's health card for prenatal

check-ups at a walk-in clinic. Describe the steps you would take in this situation. Include corrective measures, such as helping Amrini access your provincial/territorial health plan. Review the drug benefits in your jurisdiction, and identify which plan would best suit his needs. List the necessary steps Amrini would have to follow to register. You can start at http://healthycanadians.gc.ca/health-system-systeme-sante/cards-cartes/health-role-sante-eng.php#card.

4. Hinder has injured her back at work. She is diagnosed with a slipped disc and must be off work for at least three weeks. Outline the steps she would take to

- report her accident initially,

- obtain the forms she would require the physician to fill out, and

- apply for compensation (include the location of the nearest workers' compensation office).

WEBSITES OF INTEREST

Canada's Health Care System

www.hc-sc.gc.ca/hcs-sss/medi-assur/index-eng.php

Canada Health Act

http://laws.justice.gc.ca/en/C-6

Canada Health Act Annual Reports

www.hc-sc.gc.ca/hcs-sss/pubs/cha-lcs/index-eng.php

Provincial/Territorial Ministries of Health

http://healthycanadians.gc.ca/health-system-systeme-sante/
cards-cartes/health-role-sante-eng.php

This site lists provincial and territorial Ministries of Health. It
includes a link to information regarding eligibility and acquisition of health cards in each province and territory.

Alberta's Five-Year Health Action Plan

www.health.alberta.ca/documents/Becoming-the-Best-
2010-Highlights.pdf

Globe and Mail Catastrophic Drug Coverage Series (Week of
April 4, 2011)

www.bestmedicines.ca/node/152

Catastrophic Drug Coverage in Canada

www.lop.parl.gc.ca/Content/LOP/ResearchPublications/2016-
10-e.html?cat=health

Chapter 11
Preparing for the Billing Process

contrastwerkstatt/Fotolia

LEARNING OBJECTIVES

On *completing this chapter, you will be able to:*

1. Discuss the purpose, benefits, and management of health card validation.

2. Categorize commonly used services into general, intermediate, and minor assessment.

3. Describe the structure and purpose of the physician's billing number.

4. Apply the principles of claims submission using diagnostic and billing codes.

5. Properly prepare and submit claims containing premium, diagnostic, and therapeutic procedural codes.

6. Identify which forms are commonly used in claims submission.

7. Understand the health claims review process.

Chapter 10 gave an overview of health coverage, especially provincial or territorial coverage. This chapter explains the principles of billing. General rules and policies are similar across Canada, as are definitions for such things as an *encounter*, a *consultation*, and a *comprehensive visit*. All provinces and territories use physician numbers, service codes, and diagnostic codes, which are discussed in this chapter. Chapter 12 will describe specific billing procedures used in the submission of claims to the ministry. Ontario codes are used from time to time to illustrate how to use diagnostic, service, and procedural codes when completing a claim; you would simply insert the codes used in your jurisdiction. You will find some of the information in this chapter reinforced in Chapter 12, where you learn how to organize claims to send to the ministry/payment agency. Table 11.3, later in this chapter, illustrates commonly used International Classification of Diseases (ICD-9) diagnostic codes.

INITIATING A CLAIM

A claim *begins* with the submission of a claim for services rendered. The payment agency then reviews the claim. The cycle ends with payment to the provider for all valid claims. The payment agency examines each claim submitted to ensure the following conditions:

- Provider has a valid billing number
- Service claimed is authorized by provincial or territorial guidelines
- Fee claimed is the one determined by the fee schedule
- Patient has a valid health card
- Claim is submitted in a technically correct manner

All claims must be submitted in a certain format (usually electronically) and within a designated time frame.

L01 HEALTH CARD VALIDATION

Some provinces and territories try to control health card fraud by using health cards that have expiry dates and incorporate photographs and version codes. Only Alberta, British Columbia, and Manitoba have not required health card renewal. As mentioned in Chapter 10, British Columbia and Manitoba have moved to an integrated Services/Identification Card with photo ID. These cards will have to be renewed at designated intervals. As emphasized in Chapter 10, individuals should *always* be asked to present their health card before receiving a medical service.

Health card validation means checking the card to make sure it is authentic, current, and matches your information for the patient. This confirms that the patient is eligible to receive the service. All jurisdictions have methods for validating health cards.

You may feel that validating every card is a waste of your time and the patient's time. However, the process offers real benefits for both the provider and the health care system. The health care system benefits because validation reduces the fraudulent use of cards. The provider benefits because validation significantly reduces rejected claims. (Invalid cards are one of the most common reasons for claims rejection.) Validation improves your provider's cash flow and saves the time and expense of sorting out and resubmitting rejected claims. During validation you are prompted to verify the patient's current address, which keeps your records up to date. In some jurisdictions validating the health card will provide supplemental information; for example, in Ontario you will receive the date of the patient's most recent oculo-visual assessment, bone mineral density measurement, or sleep study date of service. This occurs only if you are validating the card using web-based health card validation or interactive voice response validation options.

Note: Any health card validation system needs to be secure because it grants query access to a secure database, which contains confidential information. Ministries require that users have a password, which must be changed periodically. *Keep track of when your password expires, and change it before it does.* Keep it confidential; if you write it down, ensure that only you have access to it.

Methods of Validation

In most jurisdictions, there are several ways you can validate a patient's health card; most are classified as real-time validation methods. The method that suits your facility the best will depend on the size of your practice or clinic, the speed of response required, and whether your patients are mostly long term, transient, booked in advance, or walk-in. Efficient validation methods are part of most primary care initiatives. The following is a summary of the more commonly used validation systems.

Web-Based Validation Most offices/clinics use a health card validation service that works with a web browser and existing software. The server establishes a secure connection to the ministry through which information is transmitted over the internet. You can highlight one patient or several, right-click, and choose "validate" from a drop-down menu. Feedback is provided within seconds. This web-based option is the easiest and fastest method of validation. (See Figure 11.1 and Figure 11.2.)

Interactive Voice Response Interactive voice response (IVR) is a popular choice for smaller practices with a low patient volume. It is an automated method of health card validation that is available 24 hours a day, seven days a week, using a touchtone phone to call a toll-free number. IVR validation is completed with the following steps:

1. Key in your personal identification number. This ensures that the information exchanged remains confidential.

2. You will then be asked to key in the health card number and the version code of the card you are validating.

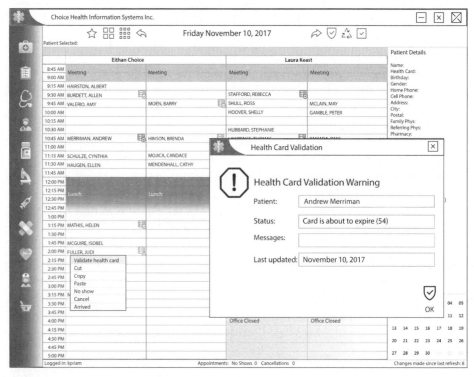

Figure 11.1 Batch card validation screen

Used by permission of Choice Learning, Inc.

Figure 11.2 Batch card validation screen showing invalid health card assessments
Used by permission of Choice Learning, Inc.

3. A prerecorded, coded response will notify you whether the card is valid.

4. You can also access bulletins posted by the ministry for help.

This system has several advantages. It is inexpensive, does not have to be integrated into the office's software system, and allows you to enter a fee schedule code to determine whether a patient is eligible for a service that is covered only once in a given period, such as a routine check-up or a vision examination. For example, suppose your province allows check-ups every two years. Sally has booked a routine check-up on September 12, but her two years will not be up until January 18. You will be given this date and can offer Sally the option of rescheduling or, under certain circumstances, paying for the service herself if she does not want to wait.

IVR does have its disadvantages: It ties up the telephone line and is more time consuming because the process is manual.

> **TIP**
>
> You cannot use a cellphone for IVR validation, because the line is not secure and confidential information may be intercepted by others.

Health Card Reader/Point-of-Service Device   This option includes a range of devices, called magnetic card readers or point-of-service (POS) devices. They are used in jurisdictions with plasticized health cards. Some stand alone; others are integrated into the office's software (see Figure 11.3).

Stand-Alone Devices   The stand-alone POS device uses a dedicated phone line and is much like those used in stores and restaurants for processing credit card purchases. You swipe the health card, the device reads the information on the card's magnetic strip, and then transmits the information to the ministry's computer. The validity of the health card is assessed and a response sent back.

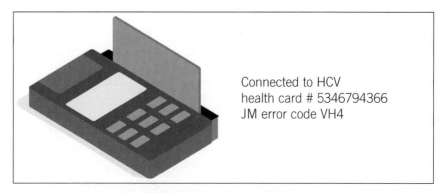

Connected to HCV
health card # 5346794366
JM error code VH4

Figure 11.3   Magnetic card reader and response

PC POS Device   The PC point-of-service device uses a standard PC with a modem and special software. A card is swiped in a wedge device (Figure 11.3) that attaches to the computer keyboard. If the health card is not available, the number can be entered using the keyboard. This process can be integrated within a patient registration system or run in a Windows environment in conjunction with other applications. The software enables the PC to submit the card data and receive a response from the ministry's health card validation service. A patient's health card status is also updated as billings are accepted using the stored health card information. This ensures that a patient's health card status is always up to date.

Checking Patient Information

Validating and updating card information at every visit helps keep your patient records current and valid. When a patient comes into the office and you swipe his or her card, you have an opportunity to review the information. "Your address here is 123 Anywhere Street. Has this changed? Same telephone number, 905-123-3486?" If you are dealing with a patient you do not know, look to see if the face matches the photo on the card, if your jurisdiction uses photo ID cards. Asking for the information can also help prove that the card truly belongs to the patient. "Mrs. Oakley [using the name on the card], can you give me your address, please? Your telephone number?" Someone who had stolen a card may not know this information.

At the same time, look at the expiry date, if applicable. If it is coming up, remind the patient to get the card renewed. (Many people never look at the expiry date on their cards.) It is helpful to offer patients a handout containing a list of locations where cards can be renewed or updated and the identification documents they will need to bring. Many software systems will alert you when you swipe a card that is about to expire.

Invalid Cards

A common reason for claims rejection is an invalid health card, often due to an invalid health number or version code (in Ontario), accounting number, or an expired card. Each time a card is reported lost or stolen anywhere in Canada, the ministry immediately invalidates the card to prevent fraudulent use. Within four to six weeks, the patient receives a new health card with a different number or other changed identifier. In Ontario, the version code would change; in other jurisdictions, the accounting number would change. If a patient finds the old card and tries to use it while waiting for the new one to arrive, it will be rejected when you do a health card validation or submit a claim. Likewise, when a patient's card expires (in those jurisdictions where a card has an expiry date), it is automatically invalidated. Just as you cannot make a purchase with an expired credit card, you cannot obtain health care with an expired health card. Yet many people never look at the expiry date on their cards. Moving or changing your name can also cause a health card to become invalid. Some jurisdictions cross-check driver's licence addresses with those registered to a patient's health card. A mismatch may result in the ministry invalidating a person's health card.

Patients may be issued a temporary card or a new number to use until their new health card arrives. In some provinces, the issuing office may puncture the expired card, indicating that its expiry date has been extended until a new card arrives.

In some provinces, you can use a health number release form to obtain the patient's health card number. If a patient with an invalid card or no card is in the office, you can have him or her sign the health number release form; fax it to the appropriate ministry office and they will provide you with the required information.

If this process does not produce a valid health number, or if a patient repeatedly fails to correct a problem with his or her card, charge him or her for the visit. (You must inform patients *before* they go in for the visit that they will be charged.) The patient can pay by cash, cheque, or credit card. (If the patient pays cash, provide a receipt.) Many offices hold cheques or credit card slips for 7 to 10 days to give the patient time to present a valid card. If the patient presents a valid health card number within that time, do not process the charge and return the cash or cheque. If the patient does not present a valid number within that period, process the charge. If the patient later produces a valid health card, he or she can seek reimbursement from the ministry directly.

Alberta has a "good faith" claim policy. If a resident, whom the physician believes is covered by the Alberta Health Care Insurance Plan (AHCIP), cannot produce his or her personal health care card, the claim can be submitted using a "Y" indicator. The administrative health professional should ask the patient for proof of Alberta residency and personal ID. Individuals covered by other resources (e.g., someone who has moved recently from another province/territory) are not eligible for this consideration. In this case the province of origin is responsible for health payments until the three-month waiting period has expired.

Fraudulent Cards

You may be presented with two types of fraudulent cards. The first is a real health card that appears to be stolen. You may suspect this either because the version code does not match the code on record or because the person presenting the card does not know the address and telephone number. The second type is a counterfeit card. These cards are usually of poor quality and will differ from real cards in weight and colour or may lack the magnetic strip. There is no legitimate reason for anyone to have such a card, as real health cards are supplied free of charge in most parts of the country and replaced for free if lost. You and your employer are permitted to take possession of a health card that is fraudulent or fraudulently used, if it is voluntarily surrendered. You are also required by the Health Disciplines Act to report fraudulent use of a health card. If you are presented with a fraudulent card:

- collect the card, if the patient will give it to you;
- try to determine where and when the card was obtained; and
- report the incident to your ministry's fraud hotline (if available) or to your district office.

A Note on Confidentiality

In submitting a claim, you must provide relevant information to the ministry about the patient and the treatment. In receiving insured services, patients are understood to be authorizing the release of this information. You do not need specific permission to release this information and have no legal liability for doing so.

(L02) COMMONLY USED SERVICES

In all jurisdictions physicians submit claims to the ministry for services they perform. If a physician is practising on a fee-for-service basis, the amount charged depends on several factors:

- The type of visit (which often defines the amount of time the physician spends with the patient)
- Where the service took place
- What is wrong with the patient (the diagnosis)
- Special considerations associated with the service (e.g., a procedure, use of equipment, extra time spent with the patient)

Services that physicians provide for patients have distinct definitions, guidelines, and parameters. The definitions of many services are similar across Canada. Detailed descriptions of most services can be found in the general preamble of the fee schedule in your jurisdiction—see the appropriate website at the end of this chapter. Brief descriptions of the more commonly used services are given later.

Consultation

A consultation is a service provided in response to a written request (called a referral, which is most often faxed) from a physician—often, but not always, a general practitioner/family physician. (A referral can also be made by a chiropractor, midwife, or nurse practitioner.) The referring practitioner must decide that the patient needs the services of a specialist, someone with specialized knowledge in a particular field. For example, a pregnant woman who develops diabetes might be referred to an internist, an obstetrician, or both. A person complaining of chest pain might be sent to a cardiologist. A child diagnosed with leukemia by the primary care physician would be referred to an oncologist or a pediatrician.

> **TIP**
>
> As a general rule, physicians are not allowed to claim for any service (care) provided to their relatives: spouse, children, siblings, parents, grandparents, or any dependents. It is considered unethical for physicians to treat relatives except in an emergency, so this is a situation you are unlikely to encounter.

Primary care physicians sometimes provide consultations themselves, especially if they have advanced training or experience in a field, such as sports medicine or tropical medicine. Generally, however, a primary care physician seeks a consultation with a specialist. A specialist may request a consult from another specialist as well. For example, suppose Frank went to see his primary care physician because of stomach problems. Frank's doctor requested a consultation from Dr. Abdul, an internist. Dr. Abdul conducted an assessment, decided the problem required investigation from a surgeon, and sent Frank to see Dr. van Dyck, a general surgeon. In Ontario, the definition of a consultation was amended in 2015 to include nurse practitioners who may refer a patient for a consult. The consulting physician is required to provide a full report back to the nurse practitioner (and the primary care physician, if appropriate).

TABLE 11.1 Useful Terms and Definitions

Year:	A calendar year beginning January 1
Month:	A calendar month
Sole reason for visit:	Applies when the patient sees the physician with a specific complaint and the physician assesses and treats that complaint only
Most responsible physician (MRP):	The attending physician who is primarily responsible for the day-to-day care of a patient in hospital; this may change depending on the patient's condition and progress
Concurrent care:	A physician other than the MRP who directs care for a hospitalized patient; in some jurisdictions (e.g., Saskatchewan), the physicians must prove that the patient needs care by more than one physician before the provincial or territorial plan will pay for services rendered by the second physician
Transfer of care:	Exchange of information when the responsibility for a patient's care is transferred from one provider to another, for example, if the original provider goes on vacation; note that any consultations involved cannot be billed

A specialist must perform a general or specific assessment, depending on the nature of the referral, and submit findings and recommendations in writing to the referring physician. In some jurisdictions (e.g., British Columbia), a written report must be generated by the specialist within two weeks of the consultation, although some exceptions are made. A specialist may continue to care for the patient if this care is deemed necessary by both the referring practitioner and the specialist. Periodic written reports must be submitted to the referring provider. Patient care would be transferred back to the provider as soon as appropriate.

A specialist may generally bill for only one consultation for a patient in a 12-month period. In some regions, this time frame is six months. However, a second consultation is allowed for an entirely different complaint. For example, Su-Mei was referred to Dr. Hugh, a gastroenterologist, for chronic indigestion. Later in the year, she was again referred to him for unrelenting diarrhea, considered to be unrelated. Table 11.1 contains useful definitions used in physician–patient care, transfer of care, and related timelines.

A consultation (with a specialist) is not payable by most provincial or territorial plans in the following situations:

- The patient makes an appointment without a referral from the primary care physician (most often, you must have a referral from a primary care physician to make an appointment).

- The patient does not ask the primary care physician for professional advice but simply wants to see a specialist for personal reasons.

- The patient arrives for a consultation more than six to nine months after the referral (usually the referring physician would make a new referral).

- The referral is made at the request of a third party.

In these cases, the patient or third party would have to pay.

Repeat Consultation   A repeat consultation includes the same elements as a full consultation and involves periodic assessments of the patient and a repeat referral by the primary care physician. In most jurisdictions, a specialist cannot charge for a full consultation until at least six months after the initial visit for the same problem. For example, suppose Su-Mei's primary care physician sent her to Dr. Hugh for a consultation about her indigestion. She then continued to see the primary care physician, who monitored the problem. Su-Mei did not improve; in fact, the physician thought the problem got a bit worse. He referred her to Dr. Hugh again for the same complaint. This would be noted as a repeat consultation. In Saskatchewan, a repeat consultation is a formal consultation for the same or a related condition repeated within 90 days by the same physician.

It is not a repeat consultation if the specialist asks the patient to return for a repeat visit. The specialist would be paid the accepted provincial or territorial rate for an intermediate assessment.

Limited Consultation A limited consultation involves all the elements of a full consultation but takes much less of the physician's time. In some jurisdictions (e.g., Ontario), it applies to a noncertified specialist asked to investigate a specific problem. For example, Don's primary care physician sends him to Dr. Lemaich, a primary care physician with expertise in sports medicine, because of a knee problem. Dr. Lemaich need only examine Don's knee. In most jurisdictions, the fees charged would be the same as those for a regular visit to another primary care physician.

In most provinces and territories, a limited consultation would be claimed for a reexamination of a patient for the same condition within six months of the original visit.

General Assessment/Complete Examination

A general assessment can be in response to the investigation of a health concern or for an annual health examination (AHE), either as a preventive measure or for a third party (e.g., an employer). In Alberta, Saskatchewan, Manitoba, Ontario, Quebec, Prince Edward Island, and Yukon, annual examinations are covered by the public plan as preventive assessments; there are varying conditions for each jurisdiction:

- Alberta will pay for a full examination every 180 days. If the patient has complex needs, the physician can bill for an extra 30 minutes.

- Ontario has replaced the AHE with a service called a periodic review. This assessment is less extensive than a full physical examination (it is similar to an intermediate assessment). The patient can present with no particular complaint. This assessment must focus on risks associated with age, gender, or personal, family, and social histories.

- Saskatchewan will cover annual health exams, although most primary care physicians no longer do them routinely. Instead, they gauge the necessity based on the patient's individual health circumstances (age, gender, pre-existing disease, family history, and other risk factors).

- In New Brunswick, Newfoundland and Labrador, Nova Scotia, Nunavut, and British Columbia, comprehensive physical examinations must be complaint driven (e.g., in British Columbia, if a patient with no complaints wants a complete assessment, he or she must pay for the assessment as well as any diagnostic or laboratory tests unless significant pathology is found). In most of these jurisdictions, a complete examination would be covered if the patient was going to have major surgery (a preoperative history and physical) or, as mentioned, if the patient had a complaint necessitating a comprehensive history and examination.

- In Nunavut and the Northwest Territories, there are no formal guidelines because physicians practising in those areas are on salaries.

Most jurisdictions will pay for a second general assessment within the same period if a patient presents with clinical signs and complaints that result in a diagnosis unrelated to the diagnosis made during the first general assessment. For example, Ryan, who is 33 years old, had his annual physical examination done in March. He returned nine months later with complaints of fatigue, insomnia, and weight loss. Because these complaints were new and were nonspecific enough to warrant a full investigation, a second check-up would be insured. A second check-up would also be insured if it is done in hospital as an admission assessment, assuming at least 90 days have passed since the patient's general assessment.

General Reassessment

A general reassessment is the same as a general assessment except that only a limited history is needed. This category of assessment does not apply in all jurisdictions. It may be called a partial or regional examination. Usually a general reassessment is a follow-up. For example, Aimee had a general assessment for vague symptoms of abdominal cramping, fatigue, and anorexia. If she returned four months later reporting her symptoms were a little worse, the physician would repeat a thorough physical examination because the physical findings may have changed; however, instead of taking a detailed history, the doctor would merely focus on any changes.

Preoperative/Pre-dental General Assessment

This category applies in most jurisdictions in Canada. Any patient who undergoes general anesthesia for surgery must have a general assessment to determine whether the anesthesia and surgery present risks. In most provinces and territories, a preop assessment for **elective surgery** is done by the primary care physician unless the patient has had a comprehensive assessment within a given time frame (usually a month) prior to the surgery. In this case, the physician may claim only a partial assessment. In cases of emergency surgery, the assessment would be done in the hospital. If the preoperative assessment is for a dental procedure, a diagnosis is not required when submitting this claim. In most jurisdictions there is a limit to the number of preop assessments that can be done in a year. In Ontario, for example, the number is two.

elective surgery surgery that is necessary but not an emergency and can therefore be booked in advance. Examples of elective surgery include removal of a tumour, a hip replacement, or a hysterectomy.

Telehealth Services/Videoconferencing

Telehealth offers a variety of services to people living in remote places. Most recently, it has broadened patient access to specialists and other health care providers who would be otherwise inaccessible unless the patient was transported to a health centre outside of his or her community. Newer technology transmits live images and sound using the internet, other devices, and advanced technology.

The service(s) rendered must be on an approved list. If a specialist at the receiving site requires a primary care physician to be with the patient to assist with the distance examination, he or she can fill in the referral field that a request was made for another physician to assist. Specific rules may apply in various jurisdictions.

House-Call Assessments

In most regions, house-call assessments are considered a primary care service and are usually done by primary care physicians or nurse practitioners. This can be an elective or an urgent home visit, initiated by the physician or generated by a patient request. If elective, the visit is planned at a time that is convenient to both the physician and the patient. If the visit is more urgent in nature, the physician will go as soon as possible, sometimes having to cancel office appointments. Alternatively, he or she may have the patient go to the emergency department. The physician may charge a premium (discussed later in this chapter) because of the travel involved and often the time of day. A home visit is almost always billed as an intermediate (limited or regional) assessment. In most jurisdictions, if someone else in the household is seen during that visit, it is billable at a lower rate. For example, Dr. Morley visits Molly, who is 84 and having some shortness of breath. While the physician is there, Molly's husband, John, complains of a sore back. Dr. Morley can bill for Molly at the full rate for a house call and for John at a lower rate. In Manitoba, this visit is referred to as a *special call*.

Intermediate or Regional Assessment/Limited Visit

An intermediate assessment is considered a primary care assessment and is probably the most frequently used code in a primary care physician's office. It is less extensive than a general assessment but more extensive than a minor assessment (discussed later). It usually entails the following:

- A history of the presenting complaint
- Current information related to the complaint and body parts/systems examined
- An examination of one or more body parts (the affected body part[s], system[s], or mental or emotional disorder, as needed to establish a diagnosis) or direct further tests to establish a diagnosis

In British Columbia, a similar service is called a *partial/regional examination*. Consider two examples of intermediate/regional assessments:

> Arlene comes into Dr. Tran's office complaining of vague gastrointestinal symptoms, including diarrhea and epigastric burning (a burning sensation below the sternum, or breastbone). Dr. Tran does a related history about her eating and bowel habits. He asks some questions related to the cardiovascular system. He does an abdominal examination, perhaps a rectal examination as well, and listens to the heart and chest. This would constitute an intermediate assessment because the physician took a detailed history of the complaint, made inquiries regarding the cardiovascular system and the respiratory system, and examined the gastrointestinal, cardiovascular, and respiratory systems.

> Paul arrives complaining of an earache and a sore throat. Dr. Lyons examines his ears, throat, and lymph nodes, and probably listens to his chest and takes vital signs. She takes a related history. This would also be an intermediate assessment because the physician examined more than one system (ears, throat, lymph glands, and the respiratory system) and asked questions related to each system.

Well-Baby Visits   In most provinces and territories, a well-baby visit is similar in time and complexity to an intermediate or limited assessment. It involves routine periodic assessment during the first one to two years of life. It includes a complete examination, with weight and measurements, and instructions to the parent(s) or caregiver regarding related health care and health teaching and appropriate immunizations covered routinely by the provincial or territorial plan.

Minor/Brief Assessment

A minor or brief assessment is also considered a primary care assessment and is used in many jurisdictions for an office visit. A minor assessment involves a brief history, examination of the affected part or region or mental or emotional disorder, and brief advice or information regarding health maintenance, diagnosis, treatment, or prognosis.

Here are some examples of a minor assessment:

> Trudy had been diagnosed with pneumonia and was treated with an antibiotic for 10 days. She comes back in so that Dr. Dumont can quickly assess her recovery. He asks her how she is feeling, if she has any shortness of breath, fever, and so on. He listens to her chest and, finding nothing, concludes the assessment.

> Victor is going abroad and comes in to see Dr. Dumont to ask what immunizations he will need.

> Mei-Lin has been having trouble with a skin rash, and Dr. Dumont prescribed some new medication for it. She comes in so that he can assess her progress. He checks her rash, asks a couple of questions, and concludes the assessment.

Mini-Assessment In some jurisdictions, a mini-assessment is applied if the physician has to examine the patient for a completely unrelated problem during the same office visit for an examination of a workers' compensation board (WCB) assessment. It can be claimed only in conjunction with a WCB claim, for which the WCB will pay only for a minor assessment during the same visit. It cannot be claimed if the WCB claim is complex or requires a comprehensive examination.

Prenatal Visit—Initial Assessment This is the initial assessment once a diagnosis of pregnancy has been established. This visit is more detailed than subsequent visits and should entail a comprehensive history and physical assessment of the mother-to-be and related health teaching. In most jurisdictions, this visit may only be claimed once per patient per pregnancy.

Routine Prenatal Office Visits These visits for a routine pregnancy are specific and do not involve an in-depth assessment. They equate to a regional or limited assessment in depth and complexity. The assessment primarily includes testing a urine sample for protein, glucose, and acetone; taking the woman's weight and vital signs; taking fetal heart rate (once audible); measuring the height of the **fundus**; asking a range of related questions; and answering any concerns the woman might have.

> **fundus** the top of the uterus. Measuring how high the fundus is in the abdomen provides valuable information about the size of the uterus and the progression of fetal growth.

Antenatal Preventive Health Assessment An **antenatal** visit option, offered in some jurisdictions, is for a patient who is considering becoming pregnant. The physician conducts an examination, reviews the patient's history, and assesses genetic, psychosocial, and medical risks. There may be some restrictions on this visit.

> **antenatal** before birth.

Counselling This is a visit to discuss a patient's problems and help him or her develop an awareness of them and consider solutions. Counselling can be individual or group (two or more people). Counselling sessions are usually provided in half-hour intervals.

L03 PHYSICIAN REGISTRATION/BILLING NUMBER

The billing process can be initiated only if the physician has a valid **physician registration number or billing number**. Physicians must first register with the College of Physicians and Surgeons in the province or territory where they are practising and then apply for a billing number. In many jurisdictions, the physician must also have a practice address. The physician is then issued a unique billing number that must appear on every claim he or she submits. Usually this number is added automatically as a function of the electronic billing process. The process is the same for dentists and other providers eligible to bill a provincial or territorial plan. In Alberta, an osteopath is also included in the definition of *physician*. As noted in Chapter 10, some jurisdictions will allow one physician to bill under another physician's registration/billing number (e.g., as a locum), and others will not. The provider whose number appears on the claim assumes full responsibility for the service provided to the patient. A physician who moves to another province or territory must apply for registration in the new jurisdiction. Numbers differ in structure from one jurisdiction to another but usually cover similar information.

> **physician registration number or billing number** a unique number assigned by the Ministry of Health to every provider eligible to bill a provincial or territorial health plan; it is required for billing.

In British Columbia and Alberta, for example, the physician billing number consists of two parts. One is the unique practitioner number that identifies the provider rendering the service; the second is a payment number, which identifies the person or group (e.g., clinic, hospital) to which payment is to be made. Most of the time, however, these numbers are the same. They differ if the provider rendering the service assigns another physician (e.g., a locum), clinic, hospital, or diagnostic facility to receive payment for fee-for-service services he or she has claimed. This is called *assignment of payment*.

In Ontario, the number consists of three segments:

1. The first four numbers represent the physician's group registration number (if applicable).

2. The next six numbers represent the physician's unique registration number.

3. The last two numbers reflect a specialty code, identifying the physician's field of specialty.

Review the following example for Dr. Simpson, who is a primary care physician in private practice. She might have the following number:

0000-543993-00

Analysis:

0000 = the group identification number (she is billing independently)

543993 = the unique physician registration number

00 = the specialty identification number (family medicine)

Specialty Codes

specialist a physician who holds a certificate from the Royal College of Physicians and Surgeons and who has completed postgraduate studies in a particular specialty field.

Each physician is a **specialist** in a particular area, such as family medicine, general surgery, or obstetrics. This specialty is represented by the specialty identification number, or specialty code. Since 00 represents family practice, in the previous example, Dr. Simpson's specialty number is 00 (family medicine). Table 11.2 shows common specialty codes. These codes are approved by the Royal College of Physicians and Surgeons of Canada.

TABLE 11.2 Specialty codes from the Royal College of Physicians and Surgeons of Canada

00	Family Practice, General Practice	The practice of a primary care physician, also called a family physician, general practitioner, or family doctor. These physicians complete postgraduate studies in family medicine and are generalists; they are usually the first contact when someone seeks medical care.
01	Anesthesia	Pain management and the use of anesthetics, and patient monitoring for surgical/diagnostic procedures. An anesthesiologist (or anesthetist) may give regional or general medications to achieve complete or partial loss of sensation during procedures. An example of a regional anesthetic is an epidural, which is often given to women for pain control during labour and delivery. A general anesthetic is one that renders the patient unconscious and is used during major surgeries. The anesthetist is primarily hospital based and does not usually have a private practice.
02	Dermatology	Practised by a physician who has completed postgraduate studies in diseases/conditions of the integumentary system, or the skin. These conditions include rashes, injuries, allergic reactions, and diseases of the skin, nails, and hair. A dermatologist also removes moles, cysts, warts, and malignant growths; addresses cosmetic problems; and is involved in skin grafting for such conditions as burns.
03	General Surgery	Performed by a specialist in general surgical procedures. These procedures can relate to curative, preventive, or palliative treatment of diseases/conditions. Does not usually include more specialized surgical procedures, such as neurosurgery or vascular surgery.
04	Neurosurgery	The operative intervention of conditions of the central nervous system and the brain.
05	Community Medicine	A specialist in community medicine does not usually deal directly with individuals, but with groups or populations. He or she assesses and evaluates the health needs of sectors of a population or specific groups of people, considering, among other things, social, environmental, biological, and behavioural factors. He or she then develops, implements, and evaluates programs and treatments to address these needs based on the occupational, social, and economic needs and the political climate affecting the designated population or group.
06	Orthopedic Surgery	Surgical procedures of the musculoskeletal system. Treatment and procedures may be restorative, preventive, or supportive. An orthopedic surgeon (sometimes called an orthoped) will do procedures such as hip and joint replacements, back surgery, and repair of complex fractures.

the diagnostic 650 (normal pregnancy) could be used for the urinalysis. Each procedure (diagnostic or therapeutic) will have a unique billing code, either numeric or alphanumeric. For example, in British Columbia the first three digits of the codes for lab procedures done in a physician's office are usually 151, and minor procedures are usually 136. If preceded by a B in the schedule, it indicates the procedure is part of the visit. In Ontario, the prefix G or Z is often used in conjunction with a numeric component.

Technical and Professional Components

The addition of a suffix can have a specific meaning in codes for diagnostic and therapeutic procedures:

- A—Technical and Professional Components
- B—Technical
- C—Professional

In all provinces and territories, diagnostic tests can be billed as one or two components. In some circumstances, a diagnostic test has two insurable components that are claimed separately. (In the Ontario fee schedule, codes marked with # can be delivered and billed in two components.) This is common in such specialties as nuclear medicine and diagnostic radiology. For example, if a physician ordered an X-ray for a patient, the physician would bill for his or her services, and the diagnostic facility would bill for its services. In many jurisdictions, these two components are referred to as technical and professional.

The technical element can include preparing the patient for the test, performing the test, making arrangements for follow-up care, completing records resulting from the test, providing health teaching or advice, or preparing and transmitting a written report to a referring physician.

The professional component can involve supervising and monitoring a test, performing any associated clinical procedure that is not separately billable (this may include monitoring the patient after the procedure is complete), or interpreting the results of a diagnostic procedure. (To claim the professional component, the physician must interpret the test results.) Another example is an electrocardiogram. Juanita had an ECG in Dr. Moore's office. Dr. Moore was also able to read or interpret the tracing. In this case, Dr. Moore would claim both components. In Saskatchewan the claim would be 03.52A for the technical portion of the test (doing the test) and 03.52B for the interpretation of the test (the professional component).

When the physician orders a test from a separate facility, the physician's billing would use a C suffix for the professional component. The diagnostic facility would use a B suffix for the technical component. Diagnostic and therapeutic procedures in a primary care physician's office are generally submitted as one claim using the A suffix. For example, if a physician in Ontario completed a urinalysis in the office, the claim would be submitted as G010A.

Special Service Code Notifiers

Some jurisdictions use a special service code notifier to point out parts of a service that are included in the visit and thus must not be billed separately. (An example would be doing a Pap smear as part of an annual health exam.)

Use Visit Code (UVC)   The UVC code is an example of a special service code notifier. Beside some items in the Schedule of Benefits in Ontario, the UVC code appears instead of a specific procedural code. Do not claim for these items separately; they are considered part of a visit. For example, removing a Shirodkar suture (a stitch put into a woman's cervix to prevent spontaneous abortion) is marked UVC in the schedule. You would not submit a claim for this procedure but would simply bill the appropriate code for the office visit during which the stitch was removed.

Two other variations of notifiers are independent consideration and manual review, both of which are discussed in Chapter 12.

Codes and Primary Care Groups

As mentioned in Chapter 4, the billing for primary care groups is complex. As well, the billing format and the codes used are constantly changing. What is current in 2016 may well be outdated in 2019.

Services claimed in these groups have unique codes, some common and others specific to each primary care reform model. These codes apply to the following:

- After hours, holidays, and weekend services (including working in the clinic)
- Patient enrollment (which includes several categories)
- Diabetic management
- Smoking cessation (simple discussion and counselling are separate codes)
- Primary mental health services

Ontario has made more headway than many other jurisdictions in implementing patient enrollment models and in developing a related billing format. Most PEMs (primary care enrollment models) are paid for each patient they enroll. In Ontario, the code for this is Q200A, and the Ontario Health Insurance Plan pays about $5 per patient for the first year only. New physicians get more for enrolling patients and use the code Q033A. This is called the New Physician–New Patient Agreement. In addition, all physicians can claim for taking on a new patient who has no physician and has been discharged from a hospital; that person must enroll with the physician within three months of being discharged from the hospital. Q023A, the unattached patient acquisition code, would be used. Diabetic management is Q040A. Discussing smoking cessation is Q141A, and counselling about smoking cessation is Q142A. Q016 can be added to existing visit codes for patients seen on weekends and after hours (e.g., intermediate assessments).

As mentioned in Chapter 4, most jurisdictions use numerous tracking codes. Use of the codes is voluntary and intended to make it easier for the administrative staff to monitor and calculate cumulative bonus payments for preventive-services goals achieved. These codes include exception codes as well. For example, the tracking code for a Pap smear is Q11A (for women between 35 and 70 years of age). The exception code is Q140A (women who have had a hysterectomy). Any woman who has had a hysterectomy obviously would be excluded from the list of eligible women for whom the ministry expects the physician to complete Pap smears, unless the cervix has been retained.

Time Units

Time units are used for some services rendered by a primary care physician (e.g., counselling). They are, however, most often used for specialists, such as surgeons and anesthetists. For example, 15 minutes might be one time unit; an hour would be four time units. Sometimes a hardship benefit may apply after a certain point. For example, suppose the time unit is 15 minutes and the cutoff point is 2 hours; the hardship point allows doubling the units. For example, a physician assisting with a surgical procedure is allowed 3 hours. The total number of units should actually be 12 (3 hours × 4 time units). However, you would count the first 2 hours as 8 units, then double the units in the last hour to count as another 8 units, producing a total of 16 units. In most jurisdictions, there is also a preset number of base units. If 4 base units are allowed for this procedure, you would bill for 20 units (16 time units + 4 base units).

Counselling, for example, is usually based on time units, with a minimum of 20–30 minutes. If it is less than 20 minutes, the practitioner should only charge for an intermediate or limited visit. In Saskatchewan, for example, the first unit of time is 15 minutes (40-B), and the second 15 minutes or major portion is 41-B. Most jurisdictions will pay for a specific number of counselling sessions in a calendar year. There are sometimes different codes for counselling based on specific medical problems and general counselling for healthy lifestyles.

Premium Codes

A premium code is a code that, under special circumstances, may be claimed *in addition to* service codes listed under "consultations and visits" and "diagnostic and therapeutic procedures." It is payment to a provider for services over and above the routine—for example, services provided after hours, away from the office (to the patient's home or a long-term care facility), or at the expense of office hours (having to leave the office) for emergency work and added responsibilities. A visit to a patient's home or a long-term care facility is sometimes referred to as a special premium visit. Certain premium codes are based on time units.

Diagnostic and Therapeutic Procedures   Most provinces and territories allow a premium code as an "add on" for certain procedures. This involves more complex procedures for which the basic procedural fee is deemed inadequate. A premium code may also apply to a "tray fee," which is compensation for the use of equipment that is disposable or that must be cleaned or sterilized. A tray fee could apply to a service claimed for doing a complex dressing or removing sutures, or a Pap smear, for example. The procedures that the extra premium code applies to will be clearly marked in your province's or territory's fee schedule. For example, taking blood from a baby is considered more complex in most jurisdictions. If this is the case, the procedural code for this service would be identified with a marker indicating that you can also claim a premium code (sometimes called a basic fee-for-visit premium).

Care of Older Adults   Premium codes also apply to some assessments done for older patients because they often have more complex medical problems and take more time to assess. In many jurisdictions, premium codes for care of complex, time-consuming patients have been eliminated and remuneration for services for designated age groups has been increased. In Alberta, for example, the special code 03.03Z is used for a limited visit with a patient over the age of 75.

In Ontario, G700 is the basic fee-for-visit premium related to certain procedures marked (+) in the Schedule of Benefits. The procedural code for performing venipuncture on an infant is G480. In the schedule it appears as +G480. That means that you can also submit a claim using the code G700 in addition to G480 for the procedure. These codes apply only to visits where an applicable therapeutic or diagnostic procedure was completed.

Surgical Assist Premium Codes   A premium code also applies if a physician assists a surgeon with an operative procedure after hours or at the cost of office hours. For emergency surgery, in particular, a surgeon will often call in one or more other physicians to assist. In smaller communities, this is often a primary care physician. As with special visit premiums, there is recognition given for the time of day or night the physician must work and how long the physician must work. The assistant's fee is calculated by a formula including a basic rate and time units. Premium payments are usually determined as a percentage of a calculated or predetermined fee.

Premiums and Detention   "Detention" occurs when a physician must spend longer than the usual amount of time with a patient. The physician may claim a premium for the extra time, usually calculated by time unit.

Special Visit Premium Code/Call-Out Premiums

A special visit premium code may be claimed in addition to specified services when, for medically necessary reasons, a physician must travel to render a service. This includes visits to a patient at home, in a hotel, in a vehicle at the side of the road, or in a health care facility. This premium can be claimed only when the patient cannot realistically visit the physician's office. Usually there is one code for the first patient seen during a special visit and another one (with a lesser premium) for any other patients seen at the same facility on the same visit. Moreover, the physician may claim only one premium code for a single visit to a patient. For example, if Dr. Paquette saw George to suture his laceration and he complained of a sore throat that had to be examined, Dr. Paquette could charge only one premium code related to that visit.

Special visit premium codes also reflect the time of the service: during the day (7:00 a.m.–6:00 p.m.), evening (6:00 p.m.–12:00 a.m.), and night (12:00 a.m.–7:00 a.m.). The evening code is often the same one used for weekends and holidays. Hours may vary. In British Columbia, 8:00 a.m.–6:00 p.m. and 6:00 p.m.–11:00 p.m. define the day and evening premiums; 11:00 p.m.–8:00 a.m. the night premium; and another premium rate applies for services rendered on weekends and statutory holidays between 8:00 a.m. and 6:00 p.m.

In British Columbia, premiums paid for home visits are called *call-out charges*. The codes used are 01200, 01201, and 01202 in addition to the service code for out-of-office visits.

When a physician goes into a home to pronounce a patient dead, this is billed as a home visit in some jurisdictions with no extra remuneration for filling out a death certificate. In Ontario, however, a special code (A902) can be used. This visit includes counselling for those involved with the patient. A premium may apply depending on the time of day. If a physician does a pronouncement of death in a place other than a patient's home, it is considered an intermediate assessment, which pays a lower value than an A902—but the doctor can still charge a premium code related to the time of day the visit occurred

Hospital and Long-Term Care Visits and Assessments

In all provinces and territories, physicians attend to patients within the hospital setting. Most often the most responsible physician is a specialist, but the primary care physician may still visit the patient in hospital, providing some element of care. This concurrent visit is billed to the provincial or territorial plan. The physician provides the information on how many visits he or she has made and when. Each province and territory will have unique codes for services provided to patients in hospital, both inpatients and outpatients. If you are working for a primary care physician, it is your responsibility to ensure that all claims for hospital visits and procedures are submitted. The types of visits you can bill for may include the following:

- *Admission assessment.* If necessary, the primary care physician can complete and claim for a complete physical assessment.

- *Subsequent hospital care* (usually limited to one visit per patient per day).

- *Concurrent or supportive care.* The primary care physician provides services in collaboration with the specialist.

- *Long stay in hospital.* The number of visits allowed is reduced compared to those allowed in acute care settings unless acute episodes are related to the admission or another illness arises.

- *Attendance in labour and delivery.* Many primary care physicians assist with deliveries, particularly Caesarean sections. Codes used may be time based or have a premium code, depending on the delivery's time of day.

- *Newborn hospital care.* Usually a specialist delivers a baby in hospital but does not care for the baby. The primary care physician often assumes immediate newborn care. He or she can claim for the newborn assessment and daily visits as required up to a maximum number of days, usually 10. (Note: If a midwife delivers the baby, she will provide care for both the mother and the newborn.)

- *Operative assist.* Some primary care physicians assist in surgery for their own patients. These claims may be calculated on units of time and would likely have a premium code depending on the surgery's time of day.

- *Palliative care in hospital or another place.* Palliative care visits are made to a patient suffering from a terminal disease (e.g., cancer, AIDS) who is not being actively treated. Visits can be made daily. Usually these visits are billed after the patient has died.

- *In long-term care facilities.* Physicians can claim a facility visit for seeing patients in long-term care facilities, such as nursing homes. The permitted frequency of these visits may vary but ranges from a visit every two weeks to once a month. If required, more frequent visits can be claimed with supporting documentation.

BILLING EXAMPLES

This section includes examples to which you can apply the various codes relevant in your province or territory. Work in class with your instructor to complete the sample blank billing screens. Use the links listed at the end of the chapter to look up the fee and diagnostic codes.

Submit the appropriate claim information as requested by each of the following examples, using your medical software program or a hard copy of a claims form designed by your instructor.

Intermediate Assessment in the Office

Example #1: Scratchy Throat   Helen, 52, comes in to Dr. Cardinal's office complaining of a scratchy throat and chest tightness. The physician takes a history related to her cardiovascular and respiratory systems. He listens to her heart, checks for swelling in her feet and ankles, and listens for bruits (sounds) in the neck region. He listens to her chest. He looks at her throat and palpates for swollen glands.

To reach a diagnosis, the physician

- took a history of the presenting complaint and related systems, and
- examined one or more body systems.

This is an intermediate or a regional/limited assessment. The diagnosis is acute bronchitis (use that diagnostic code).

Example #2: A Sore Knee   Jack, 25, comes in to see Dr. Connelly about a sore knee. It is swollen, and he has been having difficulty bearing weight. The physician does a thorough investigation into the history, asking about recent injury, onset of clinical signs, and so on. He does a thorough examination of the knee, compares it with the other knee, and checks Jack's ability to walk and bear weight. Dr. Connelly makes a diagnosis of bursitis (inflammation of the bursa). Use the diagnostic code for bursitis.

This is an intermediate or partial/limited assessment because the physician

- took a detailed history relating to the complaint, and
- did a thorough examination of the knee, joint, and leg.

Minor or Brief Assessment in the Office

Example: Itchy Skin   Asha is 80 years old. She saw Dr. Connelly on April 28. Her complaint was itchy skin on her right forearm.

Dr. Connelly looked at the area but did not see anything significant. He prescribed a cream. The visit was quick. No in-depth examination was done. He questioned her briefly about possible causes. This fits the criteria for a minor or a brief assessment. The diagnosis is pruritis (use that diagnostic code).

Office Visit for a Procedure

Example #1: Procedure with Assessment   Leslie is 32 years old. She comes in to see Dr. Simanek for an allergy shot. She also sees the physician about a brief assessment of her allergies. Here you have a brief visit to discuss allergies and a procedure (allergy shot). Use the diagnostic code for rhinitis.

Example #2: Procedure without Assessment   The following week, Leslie comes in for her second allergy shot. The nurse gives her the injection, and she does *not* need to see the physician. Will the value of this procedure be more than the value of the same injection by a physician who could also charge for a minor assessment? This visit is only for a procedure. Use the diagnostic code for rhinitis unless otherwise directed.

Example #3: Procedure with Unrelated Intermediate Assessment   Ian is seven years old. He arrives at the office with his mom for an immunization and a visit to have his asthma medication adjusted. Use the diagnostic code for asthma. You would bill for the intermediate assessment. You would also submit a procedural code for the immunization.

Example #4: Intermediate Assessment with Related Urinalysis   Marco is 32 years old. He comes in complaining of low back pain and a burning sensation on urination. The physician completes an intermediate assessment and does a urinalysis in the office. Use the diagnostic code for urinary tract infection. You would also claim a procedural code for a dipstick urine test. Is a diagnostic code required?

Premium Codes

Example #1: House Call after Office Hours   Margaret calls Dr. Baird and requests she come to see her at home outside of normal office hours for complaints of generalized weakness. Dr. Baird goes to see Margaret at 5:30 p.m., just after the office closed. What is the service code for a home visit? Select the premium code for a visit between 7:00 a.m. and 6:00 p.m.

Example #2: House Call during Office Hours   Margaret asks Dr. Baird to come during office hours. She has fallen down and cannot get up. Use the same service code for a house call. Select the premium code for a house call at the sacrifice of office hours.

Example #3: House Call on a Weekend Evening   Dr. Baird makes a house call to see Margaret at 10:00 p.m. on Saturday because she complains of abdominal pain. Use the same service code for a house call. Select the premium code for visiting a patient during the evening on a weekend or holiday.

Example #4: Visit to a Long-Term Care Facility (LTC) after Office Hours Dr. Baird goes to see Tomas at a nursing home at 5:00 p.m., after office hours, for complaints of generalized weakness. Find the service code for a visit to an LTC facility. Select the premium code for a daytime visit that is not at the expense of office hours.

Example #5: Visit to an LTC during Office Hours   Dr. Baird goes to see Tomas at the nursing home because he has fallen down. It is an emergency during office hours. Use the same service code for a visit to an LTC facility. Select the premium code for a visit at the expense of office hours.

Example #6: Visit to an LTC Late at Night   Dr. Baird is asked to come and see Tomas at the nursing home at 3:00 a.m. Use the same visit code for the nursing home. Select the appropriate premium code for a 3:00 a.m. visit. Format a claim for this visit.

Example #7: Late-Night Normal Delivery   Sarah delivered a healthy baby boy at 3:30 Wednesday morning. Select your provincial or territorial visit code for a vaginal delivery with no complications. Because the delivery occurred between 12:00 a.m. and 7:00 a.m. on a weekday, a premium code can also be claimed—select the appropriate code.

Example #8: Pronouncement of Death with Premium for Sacrifice of Office Hours   Dr. Hoffman is called to Elena's home during office hours. She pronounces Elena dead, the underlying cause of death being COPD. Use the diagnostic code for COPD. Format a claim for the appropriate service code for pronouncement of death at home and a premium code for sacrifice of office hours. The same diagnostic code is applied to both items.

L06 COMMON FORMS USED IN CLAIMS SUBMISSION

Reciprocal Claim Form

Although reciprocal claims are usually submitted electronically, a reciprocal claim form is used occasionally by a provider who renders care to an individual from another province or territory. (Remember that Quebec does not usually take part in the Reciprocal Medical Billing System.)

Out-of-Province/Territory Claim Form

An out-of-province/territory claim form is used by a provider who provides services to someone from out of the province or territory if the patient's home province or territory does not participate in the Reciprocal Medical Billing System or if the services are excluded from the billing system (see Figure 11.4). The claim may be sent directly to the patient's home province or territory. The provider may also bill the patient directly; the patient can then apply to his or her Ministry of Health for reimbursement.

Request for Approval of Payment for a Proposed Dental Procedure

This form is used by a dental provider seeking coverage for a service not routinely covered by the provincial or territorial health plan. The provider must present a good

Ontario

Ministry of Health and Long-Term Care

Out-of-Province/Country Claim Submission

- Do not submit receipts for prescription drugs as they are not an insured Ontario Health Insurance Plan (OHIP) benefit.
- Complete, sign and return this form with your *original* detailed statement that gives a complete breakdown of all charges to a Ministry of Health and Long-Term Care office. Keep copies for your records.
- If the *original* statement is not in English or French, for accounts:
  - Under $1000 Canadian, a non-certified translation with a signed statement is acceptable.
  - $1000 and over, a certified translation is required.
- If the other criteria for payment set out in the *Health Insurance Act* and Regulations are met, the ministry will pay the amount payable under the Act to an eligible hospital or health facility *directly* upon receipt of an itemized invoice and the signed authorization and direction (see below). The ministry will not make payment directly to an out-of-country physician.
- If the other criteria for payment set out in the *Health Insurance Act* and Regulations are met, the ministry will pay the amount payable under the Act to the client *directly* for **hospital** or **physician** charges upon receipt of an itemized invoice and *original proof of payment*.
- Accounts must be submitted within 12 months from date of service. Please allow 6–8 weeks for payment. All payments will be in Canadian funds.

Patient Information

Health Number	Version	Patient's Last Name	First Name

Date of Birth (year month day)	Sex ☐ Male ☐ Female	Telephone No. (home) ( )	Telephone No. (business) ( )

Mailing Address Street Name	City	Province	Postal Code

Residence Address Street Name	City	Province	Postal Code

Date of Departure from Ontario (year month day)	Date of Return to Ontario (year month day)	Country/Province Where Treatment Provided	Type of currency paid

In the previous 12 month period, have you been absent from Ontario for a period of more than 212 days?   ☐ No ☐ Yes   If yes, provide details.

Are you covered by any travel/supplementary insurance?   ☐ No ☐ Yes   If yes, name of insurance company   Policy Number

Treatment Information *(Complete this section in full)*

Was this treatment required due to a condition which arose outside Ontario, was acute and unexpected, and required immediate treatment?
☐ Yes ☐ No

Reason for Visit/Diagnosis *(nature of illness)*	Type of Treatment Received

Place of Treatment ☐ Office ☐ Home ☐ Hospital ☐ Other *(specify)*_____	Treatment Date (year month day)	Time of Treatment :	☐ A.M. ☐ P.M.

Hospital Information

Hospital Name	Admission Date (year month day)	Discharge Date (year month day)

Hospital Address	Please Check (✔) One ☐ inpatient ☐ outpatient

Knowingly providing false information is an offence punishable by fine and/or imprisonment. The information given on this form is true and accurate.

Signature of Patient/Guardian   Date

X

Authorization and Direction *(The ministry will pay the amount payable by OHIP directly to an eligible hospital or health facility upon receipt of an itemized invoice and the signed authorization.)*

I, _____ authorize and direct the Ministry of Health and Long-Term Care to pay the
      Name of Patient *(print)*

amount of my hospital / health facility bills that are payable by OHIP directly to _____
                                                                          Name of Hospital/Health facility *(print)*

Signature of Patient/Guardian   Date

X

By submitting this form to the Ministry, you are consenting to the Ministry's use of the information contained in this form for the purpose of assessing, verifying and monitoring eligibility for payment for OHIP insured services and for the proper administration of the *Health Insurance Act* and other Acts/programs administered by the Ministry. For information about collection practices, call 1 800 268–1154, in Toronto (416) 314–5518, or by mail to your local Ministry of Health and Long-Term Care Office.

For more information, contact a claims processing office (collect calls accepted) or visit our web site at: www.health.gov.on.ca

London 217 York St. 5th floor, N6A 5P9 519 675–6800	**Oshawa** 419 King St. W., L1H 8L4 905 576–2870	**Ottawa** 75 Albert St., 7th Floor, K1P 5Y9 613 237–9100	**Thunder Bay** 435 James St. S., Suite 113, P7E 6T1 807 475–1353

0951–84 (2010/09)   ©Queen's Printer for Ontario, 2010   ©Imprimeur de la Reine pour l'Ontario, 2010   7530–4568

Figure 11.4   Out-of-province/country claims submission form
© Queen's Printer for Ontario, 2010. Reproduced with permission.

Ministère de la Santé
et des Soins de longue durée

Demande de remboursement en cas de traitement hors de la province ou du pays

- N'envoyez pas de reçu pour les médicaments sur ordonnance, car ils ne sont pas couverts par l'Assurance-santé de l'Ontario.
- Vous devez remplir, signer et envoyer le présent formulaire avec votre déclaration *originale* détaillée donnant une ventilation complète des honoraires à un bureau du ministère de la Santé et des Soins de longue durée. Conservez-en une copie pour vos dossiers.
- Si la déclaration *originale* n'est ni en français ni en anglais, il faut y joindre une traduction.
  - Pour les demandes de moins de 1 000 $CAN, une traduction non certifiée est acceptable si elle est accompagnée d'une déclaration signée.
  - Pour les demandes de 1 000 $CAN et plus, une traduction certifiée est nécessaire.
- Si les autres critères de paiement énoncés dans la *Loi sur l'assurance-santé* et les règlements ont été satisfaits, le ministère versera le montant payable en vertu de la Loi directement à l'hôpital ou à l'établissement de santé admissible sur réception d'une facture détaillée et de l'autorisation et de la demande ci-dessous dûment signées. Le ministère ne paiera directement aucune somme à un médecin pratiquant à l'étranger.
- Si les autres critères de paiement énoncés dans la *Loi sur l'assurance-santé* et les règlements ont été satisfaits, le ministère versera le montant payable en vertu de la Loi au client ou à la cliente pour les frais d'hospitalisation ou les honoraires de médecin sur réception d'une facture détaillée et d'un *reçu original comme preuve de paiement.*
- Les demandes de remboursement doivent être transmises dans les 12 mois suivant la date de traitement. Veuillez prévoir de six à huit semaines avant de recevoir les paiements. Tous les paiements sont effectués en dollars canadiens.

Renseignements sur le patient ou la patiente

N° de carte Santé	Version	Nom de famille	Prénom

Date de naissance (année mois jour)	Sexe ☐ homme ☐ femme	Téléphone (domicile) ( )	Téléphone (travail) ( )

Adresse postale Rue	Ville	Province	Code postal

Adresse personnelle Rue	Ville	Province	Code postal

Date de départ de l'Ontario (année mois jour)	Date de retour en Ontario (année mois jour)	Pays/Province où le traitement a été reçu	Devise utilisée pour le paiement

Au cours des 12 derniers mois, avez-vous été à l'extérieur de l'Ontario pendant une période de plus de 212 jours?   ☐ Non   ☐ Oui ▷   Dans l'affirmative, veuillez fournir des détails.

Avez-vous une assurance de voyage/supplémentaire?   ☐ Non   ☐ Oui ▷   Dans l'affirmative, veuillez indiquer le nom de la compagnie d'assurance.   Numéro de la police

Renseignements sur le traitement *(Remplir cette section en entier)*

Le traitement a-t-il été nécessaire en raison d'un état grave et imprévu qui s'est déclaré à l'extérieur de l'Ontario et qui a exigé un traitement immédiat?   ☐ Oui   ☐ Non

Raison de la consultation/du diagnostic *(nature de la maladie)*	Genre de traitement reçu

Lieu du traitement   ☐ bureau   ☐ domicile   ☐ hôpital   ☐ autre *(précisez)* _____ | Date du traitement (année mois jour) | Heure du traitement :   ☐ A.M. ☐ P.M.

Renseignements sur l'hôpital

Nom de l'hôpital	Date d'admission (année mois jour)	Date de sortie (année mois jour)

Adresse de l'hôpital | Veuillez cocher (✓) une case   ☐ hospitalisation   ☐ clinique externe

Le fait de fournir sciemment de faux renseignements constitue une infraction passible d'une amende ou d'une peine d'emprisonnement, ou les deux. Les renseignements donnés dans ce formulaire sont justes et précis. | Signature du (de la) patient(e)/tuteur(tutrice)   X | Date

Autorisation et demande *(Le ministère versera le montant payable par l'Assurance-santé de l'Ontario directement à un hôpital ou un établissement de santé admissible sur réception d'une facture détaillée et de l'autorisation signée.)*

Je, _____ autorise le ministère de la Santé et des Soins de longue durée à verser le montant de mes frais
Nom du (de la) patient(e) *(en lettres moulées)*

d'hospitalisation ou de séjour dans un établissement de santé payable par l'Assurance-santé de l'Ontario directement à

_____ et lui demande d'effectuer le paiement.
Nom de l'hôpital ou de l'établissement de santé *(en lettres moulées)*

Signature du (de la) patient(e)/tuteur(tutrice) X	Date

En présentant ce formulaire, vous permettez au ministère d'utiliser les renseignements qu'il contient pour évaluer et vérifier les services couverts par l'Assurance-santé de l'Ontario, pour déterminer leur admissibilité au paiement et pour assurer l'application adéquate de la Loi sur l'assurance-santé ainsi que d'autres lois et programmes dont le ministère est chargé. Pour obtenir des renseignements sur la collecte de renseignements, veuillez composer le 1 800 268-1154 ou le 416 314-5518 à Toronto, ou encore écrire au bureau du ministère de la Santé et des Soins de longue durée de votre localité.

Pour obtenir plus de renseignements, communiquez avec l'un des bureaux chargés du traitement des demandes de remboursement (Nous acceptons les appels à frais virés) ou consultez notre site Web à l'adresse : www.health.gov.on.ca

London	Oshawa	Ottawa	Thunder Bay
217, rue York, 5e étage	419, rue King Ouest	75, rue Albert, 7e étage	435, rue James Sud Bureau 113
N6A 5P9	L1H 8L4	K1P 5Y9	P7E 6T1
519 675–6800	905 576–2870	613 237–9100	807 475–1353

0951–84 (2010/09)   ©Queen's Printer for Ontario, 2010   ©Imprimeur de la Reine pour l'Ontario, 2010   7530–4568

Figure 11.4 *(Continued)*

argument as to why the ministry should cover the costs of the proposed procedure. The request will be reviewed and the provider notified. Normally, the dentist would wait for approval before proceeding. If the request is turned down, the patient would have to pay if he or she still wants the service.

Request for Approval for Proposed Surgery

Similarly, a physician may request coverage for a surgical procedure not normally covered. An example might be a breast reduction surgery or reversal of a sterilization procedure. Again, the physician must argue why the procedure should be covered in this case and should wait for approval before proceeding. If the proposed claim is rejected, the patient can decide whether to pay for the surgery him or herself.

Request for Prior Approval for Out-of-Country Health Services

This form is completed by a physician on behalf of a patient for a procedure to be rendered out of the country, usually for a medically necessary service that is not available in Canada.

Health Card Number Release Form

These forms are used in every province and territory (see Figure 11.5). They allow legal access to the patient's health card number and version code. This would allow you to process a claim if the patient forgot to bring his or her health card or if it was lost or stolen. The patient will likely not know the health card number and version code; even if he or she does, you will likely want to check that the information is correct. If you do not know the patient, perhaps because he or she is a walk-in or from out of town, it is important to check whether he or she is eligible for coverage.

Consent is necessary because, under the Freedom of Information and Protection of Privacy Act, the health card number and version code are confidential information that belongs to the patient. When the patient presents you with his or her health card, the act of presenting it indicates consent. However, if the patient does not have the card to give you, written consent is needed.

Copies of these forms are supplied by the designated office. Most jurisdictions also have them available on the internet. The form must be completed and signed by the patient at the point of service. You may *not* charge patients a fee for completing this form. Often specialists' offices seeking health card information will request it from the patient's primary care physician, which may also necessitate accessing the information from the provincial or territorial ministry.

L07 CLAIMS MONITORING AND CONTROL

All provinces and territories use similar methods to monitor fee-for-service claims submitted. The monitoring body (usually the Ministry of Health) must ensure that claims are made properly and honestly and that payments are for health services authorized by provincial or territorial guidelines. The monitoring process helps identify irregularities and fraud.

Inappropriate billing by organizations and physicians and the fraudulent use of health cards are ongoing problems that cost the provincial and territorial plans dearly. All claims submitted are routinely subjected to computer checks, and if they do not meet health plan requirements, they may be rejected or only partially paid. Selected

Figure 11.5 Health number release form, Ontario

© Queen's Printer for Ontario, 2005. Reproduced with permission.

claims may be forwarded to a medical review committee to determine whether the claim is valid and should be paid. Periodically, physicians will be asked for copies of their records or be audited. As well, British Columbia produces an annual profile report for each practitioner who receives fee-for-service payment. Physicians are divided into peer groups, and a profile of each group is created and compared for billing practices.

Ministries investigate reports of inappropriate billing promptly and thoroughly. Both the medical associations and the ministries may take disciplinary action.

Ministries also try to reduce invalid claims by educating and supporting physicians and their administrative staff. Most jurisdictions have a regional information service to answer questions about claims and provide clarification. Contact this service if you are not sure whether a service is insured or how to submit a particular claim.

Prior Approval

Each province and territory also has a list of health services that must be individually reviewed and approved in advance. Breast reduction is one example. If the proposal is rejected and the patient still wants the service, she must pay for it or appeal the decision. A physician who fails to seek approval for an otherwise unapproved service risks not being paid for it.

Patients also need prior approval to seek some treatments outside their own province or territory—usually major services such as surgery. Claims for minor ailments (sore throat, earache, etc.) are submitted at point of service and paid for by the patient's province or territory of origin under the reciprocal agreement (except in Quebec).

Verification Letters/Service Verification Audits

Some jurisdictions send computer-generated letters to randomly selected patients who are asked to verify that the physician actually provided the service he or she billed for. (Letters will not be sent about services that patients may regard as especially private, such as abortion; treatment of sexually transmitted diseases, AIDS, or dementia; assessment of genitalia; or organ retrieval after death.) Moreover, individually prepared letters may also be sent to the patients of physicians who are under review or are suspected of inappropriate or fraudulent billing.

›› WHAT TO WATCH FOR

- Continuing changes in how primary care physicians are funded.
- How physicians providing services in acute care hospitals evolve, including the greater use of "hospitalists" and less involvement of the primary care physician.

- Ongoing revision of premium or incentive codes related to preventive care.

SUMMARY

1. Health card validation is accomplished through web-based validation methods or by using interactive voice response options. It is important to validate all patients' health cards to reduce related errors in claims submission and the fraudulent use of health cards. It is also a convenient way to update the patient's information at each visit. Validating the patient's health card can be the beginning of the claims process since it ensures that the patient is eligible for health care.

2. The categorization of health care services is fairly similar across the country. They range from a full physical assessment and an intermediate visit to a minor visit, which requires the least amount of a physician's time. Visit types are closely aligned with the type of service or item code used, which, in turn, determines how much the provider can charge for the service.

3. To submit a claim to the ministry, all providers must have a billing number. Assignment of this number ensures that the provider is eligible to bill for services in his or her designated jurisdiction. The last two digits of the number indicate the provider's specialty.

4. Diagnostic codes represent the reason for the patient's visit (e.g., hypertension, cold, skin rash). The service or item code is the type of assessment (and determines the length/complexity of the visit). Other codes include premium codes, diagnostic and therapeutic procedural codes that relate to tests and procedures performed during a visit (e.g., a Pap smear, immunization). They must be included in claims submitted for each visit.

5. Premium codes are also called incentive codes. These codes relate to preventive care measures taken by physicians to ensure their patients are offered and reminded of steps they can take to maximize their health outcomes. Some examples include reminding patients when immunizations are due (e.g., the flu vaccine) and periodic monitoring of chronic conditions such as diabetes.

6. A number of forms are used in claims submission. These forms will, of course, vary with each jurisdiction. These include the reciprocal claims form (used when a Canadian resident is claiming for services outside of their province of origin) and the out-of-country claims form. You should be able to properly use these forms as required by your patients.

7. It is important to understand the health claims review process. The submission, processing, and payment of a health claim is similar to one submitted to an insurance company, for example a claim for damage to your car. The payment agency (the provincial/territorial ministry) examines all claims to ensure they are legitimate and properly submitted.

KEY TERMS

antenatal 317
elective surgery 315
fundus 317

physician registration
number or billing
number 317

service code, billing code, fee
code, or item code 322
specialist 318

REVIEW QUESTIONS

1. Compare and contrast the advantages and disadvantages of the three methods of health card validation noted in this chapter. If you are in British Columbia and have a Services Card, what if any changes are there to the validation process?

2. How do Ministries of Health monitor claims in your jurisdiction to ensure they are valid?

3. Is a complete physical examination publicly funded in your jurisdiction? What are some common eligibility criteria and restrictions?

4. Explain the structure of a physician's billing number.

5. Discuss the format of billing codes for a limited visit, intermediate visit, and complete assessment in your province or territory.

6. What are the criteria for a house-call assessment in your jurisdiction?

7. List the various premium codes used for out-of-office visits to a home and to a long-term care facility in your jurisdiction.

8. What is meant by *concurrent hospital care*?

9. What are diagnostic and therapeutic procedural codes used for?

10. Explain reciprocal billing.

APPLICATION EXERCISES

1. Independently or with a peer, think of effective ways to encourage patients to present their health cards. Consider a creative sign for the reception area. Plan two responses to patients who repeatedly do not update their health card information or who leave their cards at home.

2. Marty is 70 years old and lives in Spruce Lodge, a nursing home. The nurses call Dr. Thompson at 0200 to say that Marty is short of breath and complaining of feeling weak. Dr. Thompson arrives at 0230. Use the applicable codes in your jurisdiction to answer the following:

   a. What service/visit code would you use?

   b. What premium (or equivalent) code would you use?

3. For each of the following scenarios, use your medical billing software program to fill in the service/visit code, procedural code (if applicable), diagnostic code (if applicable), and premium code (if applicable). Use the sites listed under Websites of Interest or the tables in this chapter.

   a. Leigh came to see the physician complaining of an earache in her left ear. She was also having difficulty swallowing. The physician examined her ears, looked at her throat, and listened to her chest. He took a detailed history relating to her complaint and asked questions about her respiratory system. He diagnosed otitis media and tonsillitis and sent her home with a seven-day prescription of antibiotics.

   b. Ivan came in because he was experiencing lower back pain. The physician obtained a detailed history related to the complaint and noted on the chart that Ivan also had dysuria and was febrile. A urine sample was tested in the office. The physician diagnosed cystitis and prescribed antibiotics.

   c. Bill came to the physician and complained of a skin rash on his forearm. The physician looked at it and asked some questions related to the complaint. She quickly diagnosed contact dermatitis.

   d. Kirsti came in complaining of a sore stomach and diarrhea. The physician completed a history about the complaint and related system. He examined her abdomen. He concluded that she had the flu.

   e. Ardelle came in with her one-year-old son, Zachary, for a well-baby check-up.

   f. Ravi is 50 years old and comes in for a physical examination (in Ontario this would be a periodic health visit). What are the billing implications if this was for a pre-employment physical exam?

   g. Latoya came in for an allergy shot. The nurse gave it to her. Latoya did not see the physician.

   h. Mrs. Purves came in for her annual physical examination. Mrs. Purves is 90 years old.

   i. Gregory came in complaining of dysuria (pain on voiding), low back pain, and some hematuria (blood in the urine). The physician diagnosed pyelonephritis and started Gregory on an antibiotic. She also had the nurse complete a dipstick urinalysis in the office.

   j. Agnes Morrow called the office and asked if the physician could come visit her after office hours. She was bedridden and had noted some increased shortness of breath. The physician made the house call at 10:00 p.m.

WEBSITES OF INTEREST

Provincial Health Care in Canada

http://canadanews.about.com/cs/provhealthcare

This is a "one stop" link to all the Ministries of Health. About the Following Websites

Each province and territory has a comprehensive manual outlining billing procedures, rules, regulations, and fee codes. Although they are complex, it is essential that you understand the manual in your jurisdiction. This manual will become your major resource for billing purposes if you are working for a physician. Each begins with an introduction, general preamble, or something similar. It is important to read this section thoroughly as well as the sections on definitions, if it is separate. These sections explain, among other things, the various types of visits (e.g., a consultation, limited visit, comprehensive visit), what they entail, and billing exceptions. The manual will have an index, either on the side of the screen or at the beginning of the site. The sections on therapeutic and procedural codes and explanatory codes are ones you will probably use. If your course focus is on general billing procedures (versus for a specialist), you will use the section on general practice. There you will find the visit types, codes, and rules applying to those visits and codes.

Some jurisdictions have a site for diagnostic codes, while others do not. The diagnostic codes are the same across Canada. For an excellent resource (if you do not have one in your own province or territory or access to them on your computer software), use the *Ontario Resource Manual for Physicians*. These codes are the same in your jurisdiction.

Ontario Resource Manual for Physicians

www.health.gov.on.ca/english/providers/pub/ohip/physmanual/physmanual_mn.html

Go to section 4, page 34. The codes are clear and in alphabetical order.

ICD-9 Diagnosis Codes

http://icd9cm.chrisendres.com

Alternatively, try this website. These diagnostic codes are the same but are broken down into detail. To test this guide for accuracy in your region, try a few to see if they match the diagnostic codes used for various conditions in your jurisdiction. For example, compare acne rosacea and vulgaris, amenorrhea, dysuria, and vomiting. Consider vomiting—it can have several codes: 787 is under symptoms of the digestive system, but 586 can also be used for persistent or habitual vomiting.

British Columbia
British Columbia Medical Services Plan—Information for Physicians

www2.gov.bc.ca/gov/content/health/health-drug-coverage/msp

Access this page for fee schedules and billing information. You can choose areas applicable to your learning. The preamble (important to read) describes various services as well as outlining policies and guidelines. General practice includes the office fee codes that you will use for provincial or territorial billing.

British Columbia MSC Payment Schedule

www2.gov.bc.ca/gov/content/health/practitioner-professional-resources/msp/physicians/payment-schedules/msc-payment-schedule

Explanatory Codes for BC

www2.gov.bc.ca/gov/content/health/practitioner-professional-resources/msp/claim-submission-payment/explanatory-codes

Diagnostic Codes Used for Billing in BC

www2.gov.bc.ca/gov/content/health/practitioner-professional-resources/msp/physicians/diagnostic-code-descriptions-icd-9

Alberta
Alberta Health

www.health.alberta.ca

Schedule of Medical Benefits—Alberta

www.health.alberta.ca/professionals/somb.html

"Medical Governing Rules" gives you an overview of how to use the rest of the schedule; click on "Medical Benefits Procedure List" for service codes. You will need to familiarize yourself with services performed by a primary care physician, for example, immunizations (13.42); comprehensive office visit (03.04A). You can do a search in the box at the top to quickly find what you are looking for—by code, word, or phrase.

Alberta NetCare

www.albertanetcare.ca

This website will provide you with current information on the technical and practical applications of electronic health records in Alberta.

Alberta Medical Association

www.albertadoctors.org

The *Alberta Doctor's Digest* (under "Member Services," "Publications") is a terrific resource for general information regarding what is happening in primary care and other medical topics.

Alberta Diagnostic Codes

www.health.alberta.ca/documents/Diagnostic-Code-ICD-9.pdf

This webpage is useful for finding diagnostic codes for billing purposes.

Alberta Health and Wellness: Physicians' Resource Guide

www.health.alberta.ca/documents/Physician-Resource-Guide-2015.pdf

Resource manual for physicians (and health professionals) on how to handle Alberta fee-for-service claims.

Saskatchewan
Saskatchewan Health

www.saskatchewan.ca/government/health-care-administration-and-provider-resources

Under "Resources for Health Care Businesses and Career Development," click on "Physician: Health Care Resources" to find links to Saskatchewan's payment schedule. Read through the introduction and definitions, which gives you insight into the rest of the manual. Under the list of insured services, you will see general practice in section B.

Manitoba
Manitoba Health—Physicians Manual

www.gov.mb.ca/health/documents/physmanual.pdf

Contains descriptions of visits, fees, codes, and more.

Ontario
Online Resource Manual for Physicians

http://health.gov.on.ca/english/providers/pub/ohip/physmanual/physmanual_mn.html

This is an excellent resource for essential information for the primary care physician's office. It has been extracted from the Schedule of Benefits. It includes explanation of various visits, billing procedures, fee codes, diagnostic codes, and more. (Section 4 has diagnostic codes.)

Ontario Schedule of Benefits

www.health.gov.on.ca/english/providers/program/ohip/sob/physserv/physserv_mn.html

Read the "General Preamble" carefully. Page 12 of the preamble begins explanations about the various types of visits. Of note: Page 15 has a table of diagnostic codes that OHIP requires you to submit with the related fee code; page 19 discusses E080 code for hospital discharge; page 42 discusses delegated procedures; page 44 covers special visit premiums; page 54 discusses data on time units. Section A covers family medicine.

Quebec
Manuel de Facturation (Billing Manual)

www.ramq.gouv.qc.ca/fr/professionnels/medecins-omnipraticiens/manuels/Pages/facturation.aspx

New Brunswick
New Brunswick Physicians' Manual

www.gnb.ca/0394/pdf/2015/physician_manual-e.pdf

The General Preamble begins on page 49. On page 94 (General Practice) the manual states that the fees cannot be interpreted without knowledge of the preamble—read that section carefully. The definitions for various types of visits begin on page 50. Note also Chapter 4 (Items Common to All Practitioners) and Chapter 5 (Specialties, which covers General Practice in Section 1). Page 100 covers visits to vessels in harbour and at wharf.

Nova Scotia
Physician's Manual

www.medavie.bluecross.ca/static/MSI/PhysicianManual.pdf

Prince Edward Island
Schedule of Benefits

www.gov.pe.ca/photos/original/doh_masteragree.pdf

Newfoundland and Labrador
Medical Care Plan

www.health.gov.nl.ca/health/index.html

This is the main site for all information related to the medical care plan in Newfoundland and Labrador. General information that patients may ask for, as well as links to information for health professionals, is contained here.

Physician's Information Section

www.health.gov.nl.ca/health/mcp/providers/phys.html

This webpage provides links to the *Physician's Information Manual* (a valuable resource for anyone working in a physician's office), the Physician On-Call Payment Program, the Medical Care Plan Medical Payment Schedule, Physician Registration, Claim Submission, Claim Payment, and Provider Audits.

Medical Payment Schedule

www.health.gov.nl.ca/health/mcp/providers/mcpmedpymt.html

This is a direct link to the payment schedule. The site contains almost all the relevant information required for billing for medical services. The preamble is particularly important.

Chapter 12

Billing

torsakarin/Fotolia

LEARNING OBJECTIVES

On completing this chapter, you will be able to:

1. Explain the principles and process of web-based claims submission.

2. Understand the steps of the billing cycle.

3. Apply information gathered during patient registration to the claims process.

4. Describe the components of a claim.

5. Define your role in the claims submission process.

6. Submit rejected claims identified by error codes.

7. Discuss your responsibilities related to reports returned from the ministry.

8. Manage the various components of third-party billing.

Chapter 10 outlined the provincial and territorial health care plans; Chapter 11 introduced the elements of billing. This chapter discusses the actual process of claims submission, the technologies available to facilitate it, and approaches to billing payers other than the provincial or territorial health plans. While the processes and elements of billing are described here in generic terms, the preamble to your jurisdiction's fee schedule of benefits will give you more detail. It is important to know your schedule and use it when in doubt. All provincial schedules are online (see the links at the end of this chapter).

LO1 WEB-BASED CLAIMS SUBMISSION

electronic transfer (ET) a vehicle for the electronic transmission of medical claims from the source computer to the ministry's mainframe computer. ET is used generically to refer to various names for electronic transfer across Canada.

In the not-to-distant past, claims were submitted by tape cassette, magnetic tape cartridge, or disk. Today, **electronic transfer (ET)** is the only way claims can be submitted in most jurisdictions. In Ontario, the process is called Medical Claims Electronic Data Transfer (MCEDT) and uses a secure provincial network called GoNet. In British Columbia, providers submit claims to the Medical Services Plan through the Teleplan system. In Alberta, billing is done through an accredited submitter using H-Link (an electronic communication system that connects the provider's computer to the Alberta Health mainframe). Saskatchewan uses a system called Complete Billing Systems.

ET is a secure method of sending and receiving information. To be functional, it requires special billing software to be installed on the provider's computer. This allows claims, information, and other reports to be sent to and received from the ministry. Billing software used to interface with electronic transmission must facilitate the exchange of information as **machine-readable input/output (MRI or MRO)**. Most of the time billing software can be integrated into the provider's existing system.

machine-readable input/output (MRI/MRO) any information that can be read by a computer, whether it is sent or received.

Software that facilitates the ET process is different from billing modules that are used to prepare claims in a health office or clinic (discussed later in this chapter). The software is written specifically for your province or territory and reflects your own jurisdiction's coding and billing format, including diagnostic codes, service codes and their value, and other coding systems used in your province/territory. More recent requirements may also necessitate that the software be able to compress files if the ministry sends designated files in a compressed format.

Support

It is important to be aware of the support the software vendor provides to the physician and administrative staff for times when you have problems with the software or simply have questions about it. For example, is the support available onsite or by phone (if so, have the number handy), and when is support available?

Likewise, the ministry will have support available to answer questions you may have about the billing process, such as what code to use for a specific encounter, or why a claim was paid at a reduced rate or rejected completely. Keep the ministry's support number handy as well.

Security

Only designated users are given a dedicated password providing them access to the ET system. This password allows the user to log on, upload files, and download (receive) files and reports sent back from the ministry. Other administrative staff in the office may be involved in adding codes to patient encounters, but they will not be involved in batching and submitting them to the ministry. Files must be downloaded before they are readable. Each staff member using the computers in the office will have a password that is different from the one(s) used to access the ET system.

Advantages of Electronic Transfer

The following outlines some of the benefits of using an ET system:

- In most provinces and territories, claims can be submitted any time except on Sundays.
- Security is enhanced for both sending and receiving information because only authorized individuals have access.

- There is no paperwork to send; you save courier costs and packaging time.

- Claims are transmitted and received much more quickly.

- You receive timely confirmation that your file has been received.

- If one of your files is rejected, you get a File Reject message within hours, allowing you to correct the problem and resubmit the file promptly.

- An error report is returned to you, usually within 24 hours, notifying you of acceptance or rejection of claims batches.

- Remittance advice reports are available earlier, allowing for reconciliation of accounts.

- Error reports in most jurisdictions can be sent in a machine-readable format so that your software can be programmed to reconcile the accounts automatically.

- You can use electronic health card validation through a web-based system (described in Chapter 11), thus reducing claims rejections.

  - Most jurisdictions have a website offering access to online forms, interactive billing tutorials, electronic versions of your jurisdiction's payment schedule and ICD-9 coding manual, and related ministry bulletins.
  - Many physicians, particularly those starting out, work as locums for multiple clinics and various fractional practices. The result is a demand for a "virtual office." Web-based claims submission offers the same services to new physicians as physicians in established practices and clinics. All the provider needs is a computer equipped with the required software and an internet connection.

Electronic Transfer and Claims Deadlines

Claims deadlines have always been a reality. ET provides greater latitude with respect to these deadlines. Claims must be submitted by a specific date (determined by the payment agency) to guarantee reimbursement within the next billing cycle—which is monthly in most jurisdictions. This date is usually the eighteenth to twentieth of the month. (Some jurisdictions, including Newfoundland and Labrador and British Columbia, have a two-week cycle.) In Alberta, claims submitted by Thursday of one week are processed for payment on Friday of the following week. Payments are made via electronic funds transfer. The ministry makes every effort to ensure that the monthly payment includes all correctly submitted claims received by the designated deadline. In British Columbia, a payment for claims submitted electronically using Teleplan includes all correct claims received at least seven days prior to the next payment date.

ET users are encouraged to submit claims daily or several times a week. More frequent submission has two benefits. First, the earlier in the cycle the ministry receives your claims file, the sooner you will get your error report and other files back. Thus, you will often have time to correct and resubmit rejected claims by the guaranteed payment date. Second, you are more likely to receive payment within the billing cycle for claims sent late in the month. Although the ministry guarantees payment only for claims received by the stated date, if time and volume permit, it will continue processing claims, sometimes up until the month-end computer cut-off date. Thus, some months you may receive payment for claims sent as late as the twenty-eighth of the previous month.

L02 THE BILLING CYCLE: A SUMMARY

The process of the billing cycle itself is relatively simple, with minor variations among jurisdictions. Using electronic submission requires that you follow a relatively predictable schedule if you want the process to work efficiently and to take advantage of one of the major benefits of ET: the prompt payment of claims. You must be cognizant of submission deadlines and protocols for sending and receiving reports, especially those returned early in the billing cycle identifying claims rejected because of submission or coding errors. Early return of this type of report gives you an opportunity to correct the mistakes and resubmit the claims for payment within the same billing cycle.

The following is a summary of the basic steps of the billing cycle related to the use of ET systems. Details of the billing process, claims submission, and reports returned from the ministry are discussed in detail later in the chapter.

Your Role

If is your job to do the following:

- Ensure all information collected when the patient registers for an appointment is correct.
- Check that all codes added to a claim after each encounter are correct.
- At the end of each day (this is the recommended timeline), batch your claims, upload them, and send them to the ministry.
- Check daily for notification of rejected files or batches of claims.
- Review the claims error report, and correct and resubmit claims within the billing cycle (usually around the eighteenth of the month).
- Respond to other reports and ensure that payment is received as per the schedule in your jurisdiction.

The Ministry

Here are the responsibilities of the ministry:

- Receives the files and accepts or rejects all or parts of your file submissions prior to processing them
- Reviews the claims, rejecting those that are incorrect; some jurisdictions send back an error report in time for you to correct and resubmit claims within the same billing cycle
- Provides a reconciliation statement detailing all claims and payment decisions
- Sends out payment to the provider

L03 PATIENT REGISTRATION AND CLAIMS INFORMATION

Registering patients (or checking them in) occurs when a patient arrives in the office. The information gathered is part of the information used to complete a claim for submission to the ministry. This includes reviewing and validating the patient's health card, because the ministry will reject a claim before it is even reviewed if the health card information is incorrect. In many jurisdictions, even a change of address that is not reported to the ministry will result in an invalid health card. Correcting this problem before the claim is submitted will avoid a claims rejection notice for that encounter.

Figure 12.1 shows a long and a short patient registration screen. Once the information is entered, the system will store the required data until you choose to change or remove any. Some software programs have the capability of storing a photo of the patient as well, which is helpful in preventing health card fraud. It is also convenient if your software allows you to paste selected information, such as the patient's name and address, to documents in other applications (e.g., letters and insurance forms).

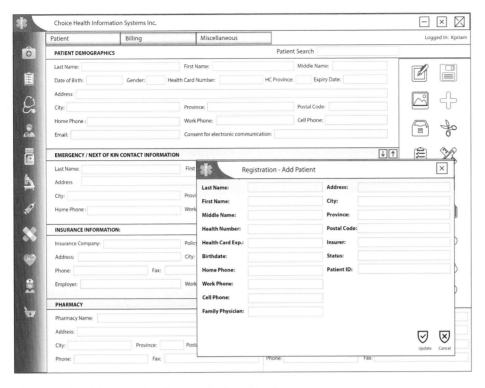

Figure 12.1 A long and a short patient registration screen

Used by permission of Choice Learning, Inc.

Basic registration information includes the following:

- First and last names, initial or middle name
- Title (Mr., Mrs., Ms., Dr.)
- Date of birth
- Gender
- Address
- Phone number (home, work, cell)
- Email
- Greeting (this field is not standard on all medical software programs; it is meant to indicate how the patient prefers to be addressed, e.g., Mrs. Smith or Suzanne; Catherine or Katie)

You can search for a patient's record on the system by entering any part of the registration information:

- First or last name, in part or in full
- Date of birth
- Telephone number
- Chart number
- Address

If you use a point-of-service device that requires the patient's health card to be swiped, run it through your card scanner at a steady speed, being careful to keep the card level. The health card information appears automatically on the screen; check to make sure it is current and correct. Figure 12.1 shows the information that will be displayed when a card is swiped. If the patient is already in the registry, other information will also appear, such as the default provider (the patient's usual physician) and the patient's address, phone numbers, and billing defaults. If the patient has not been registered before in your office or if information is missing, you will see empty fields. Once you have filled them in, you can save the updated patient information to your registry.

What to Do if the Card Will Not Swipe

Occasionally, the health card will not register on your screen when you swipe it. This often happens with a bent or worn card or, in Ontario, with the older red-and-white cards. Try to swipe the card two or three times. Sometimes, putting a thin paper over the magnetic strip will help it be swiped properly. If this does not work, you can enter the information manually. Suggest that the patient get the card replaced.

L04 BILLING: THE COMPONENTS

After the valid health card and patient information has been updated and the patient's encounter with the physician has been completed, the claims process can move forward. You must become familiar with the billing features your computer system offers and how to both process and submit claims efficiently.

Software Billing Options

The method of processing claims varies with each computer system: how codes are accessed, which interfaces are most efficient for adding the required codes and processing the claims, and how to access the patient's billing history.

Day Sheet/Calendar Billing   When you register a patient, you will collect much of the information you will need to submit a claim. The scheduling module automatically creates a list of patients whom you need to bill for. Day sheet or calendar billing uses the information the system already contains (see Figure 12.2). When you select a billing

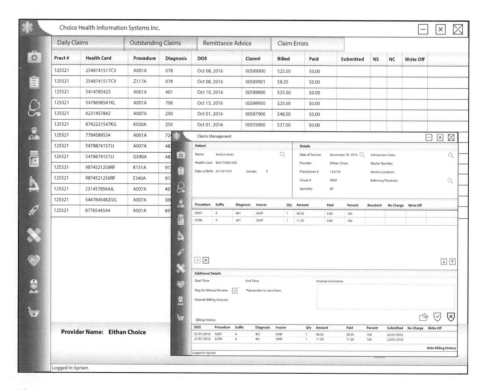

Figure 12.2   A billing/calendar day sheet from which you can enter claim codes
Used by permission of Choice Learning, Inc.

provider and a date, the day's list of appointments is presented on a spreadsheet. You can go through the list and enter service and diagnostic codes for each appointment. Identify no-shows and delete them from the billing record. Once you are satisfied with the billing record, you can file all of the claims simultaneously, submitting them to the ministry with your next cumulative submission. Day sheet billing works well if you have high volume and mostly straightforward billing.

Information Components of a Claim

Most claims contain standard information. Note that provincial and territorial billing software systems need certain data (e.g., numbers, dates) in a specific format. However, your computer screen may not show information in this format. Some programs display data in a reader-friendly format, and on submission it automatically converts the data to the required format. You can find the various components of a claim in Figures 12.3 and 12.4 later in this chapter.

Physician Registration Number This number is shown on some billing screens; others show the provider's name or may show neither. This number must be on every submission to the ministry, whether the physician bills individually or as part of a group. Software programs that do not show it on the billing screen will add it when claims are batched.

Date of Birth For cards and older systems, the ministry requires the date of birth for each patient to be entered with two digits each for year, month, and day, with no punctuation or spaces. For example, November 9, 1950, would be 501109. Your software program may have a specific format for dates.

Accounting/Claims Number Automated systems will have a computer-generated number (generally up to eight alphanumeric characters) used for accounting and claims reconciliation.

Chart Number This item is not needed for claims submission but is used internally if your office assigns a number to each patient's chart for filing purposes. Some filing systems are organized by name or colour-coded charts instead.

The Payment Program The software will offer three choices:

- HCP—health care plan
- RMB—reciprocal medical billing
- WCB—workers' compensation board (or your jurisdiction's equivalent, for example, WSIB in Ontario)

Most often, the payment plan is HCP, and most software programs select this choice by default. If the encounter is related to a workplace incident covered by workers' compensation, select WCB/WSIB. If the service was provided to an out-of-province/territory patient (assuming neither you nor the patient is from Quebec), select RMB. Some programs will automatically change the setting to RMB if you swipe an out-of-province/territory health card. Computerized billing can handle reciprocal billing electronically in the same way as claims to your own jurisdiction. If you have a patient with a WCB claim and an unrelated medical claim on the same visit, the claims must be submitted separately by using the appropriate codes for your province or territory.

RCMP Billing Formerly, health coverage for members of the Royal Canadian Mounted Police was the responsibility of the federal government. In 2013, the Canada Health Act was amended, shifting responsibility for health care for the RCMP to the jurisdiction in which they live. However, claims for services provided to RCMP members for work-related injuries/illnesses should be directed to the RCMP and not to the provincial/territorial plan.

The Payee   The payee is the party paid for the encounter or service. It rarely changes from "P," meaning the submitting provider. ("S" means pay the patient.) In fact, the payee is not shown on newer billing modules. If you are using an older computer program or billing cards, enter "P." Even with workers' compensation claims in provinces or territories where the Ministry of Health acts as the payment agency, the payee is still "P" because the provincial or territorial plan pays the provider.

Referring Physician   If the patient has been sent to a specialist for a consultation, the ministry will want to know who made the referral—usually the primary care physician. Insert the referring physician's registration number.

Facility Number   This is a number assigned to a facility, such as a nursing home or hospital. It is added when claiming for services rendered at the facility for inpatients or outpatients.

Inpatient Admission Date   This field, which may appear as "Admin Date" on the computer screen, represents the date a person is admitted to a hospital or other facility. Include two digits each for year, month, and day. As with birth dates, the claim uses no punctuation; however, your screen may show a specific format.

Manual Review Field   In all jurisdictions, some claims will require clarification—an explanation or supporting documentation, such as an operative report. The manual review field is used to flag or identify claims that deviate in some way from programmed billing criteria and require an explanation of the circumstances. With this box checked, someone at the ministry will review the claim individually. Any claim marked for manual review must have supporting documentation, which should be sent (usually faxed) the same day the claim is submitted. (Instead of faxed documentation, the physician can fill out a form intended specifically for that purpose.) Some programs have a manual review feature that will support the entry of review comments for printing at the time of submission. In Ontario, it is called a Claims Flagged for Manual Review Form.

For example, in some jurisdictions, circumcision is no longer covered unless deemed medically necessary. If a physician performs a circumcision for medical reasons, you would check the box and submit an explanation as to why the physician considered the procedure medically necessary. Similarly, if you billed for two services for the same patient on the same day or submitted a premium claim for a surgical procedure that took longer than usual, you would need to explain the circumstances. Figure 12.3 shows a screen with a space for such an explanation. Some programs have a manual review feature that will support the entry of review comments for printing at the time of submission.

Likewise, a request for approval for a proposed procedure, such as the aforementioned circumcision, requires a manual review. The request should, however, be submitted before the surgery, if possible. If the procedure is urgent, the supporting documentation would be sent along with the flagged claim.

Independent Consideration (IC)   Some services are marked as IC on the fee schedule. (Some jurisdictions may use a different symbol.) This means "independent consideration," and such claims are also reviewed manually. This is sometimes referred to as being marked with a "Y" indicator. If you submit claims electronically, remember that you must fax the supporting documentation when you submit that claim. If your claims are submitted on disk or tape, send the supporting documentation the same time that you send the tape or disk.

Shadow Billing   Shadow billing (or similar billing format) is used in practices that have entered into primary care agreements. It enables a direct comparison of the capitation fee or other alternative payment plan the ministry is paying the provider with

Figure 12.3 Billing screen with claims details, including a request for a manual review of the claim

Used by permission of Choice Learning, Inc.

the costs that would be incurred if the provider were billing fee-for-service. The format of this billing may vary. There may be a special code used for rostered patients and a shadow billing option on the computer software system. For rostered patients, you will enter other information as usual but click the "shadow" tab. A zero balance is submitted. Not all software programs have this option. In some jurisdictions, billings are done for rostered patients as if they were fee-for-service, and the ministry's computer identifies them and separates them from fee-for-service patients.

Example: Dr. Chen is working in a primary care group. In one calendar year, she was paid $300 000 under the capitation formula to take care of 2000 patients while providing extended hours and other health care services to her patients. The shadow billing for her practice year showed that, under the fee-for-service system, she would have billed the Ministry of Health $350 000. In this case, capitation saved the ministry $50 000.

Service Date   This is the date the service was provided. Make sure it is accurate—an incorrect date could result in the claim being rejected. Generally, it is best to process claims every day so that the service date will be the current date—which your software program will show automatically. However, there may be days when you just do not have time to complete the claims. If you are doing claims for the previous business day or if, for any other reason, you are claiming for a service provided earlier, be sure to change the service date manually. You can usually select a calendar and simply click on the date you want.

Service Code   As described in Chapter 11, this code identifies the type of service or encounter that is claimed and generates the amount charged for the claim (see Figure 12.4).

Diagnostic Code   As discussed in Chapter 11, this is usually a three- or four-character code that indicates the diagnosis made at the time the service was rendered.

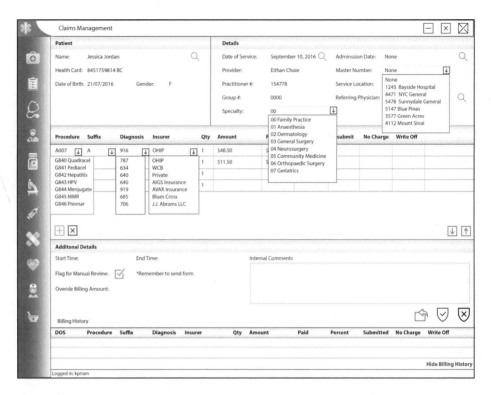

Figure 12.4 Billing screen showing more detailed components of coding
Used by permission of Choice Learning, Inc.

If there is more than one diagnosis, use the primary code. In Figure 12.4, the diagnostic code is 460, which refers to a cold or acute nasopharyngitis. Diagnostic codes are discussed in more detail later in the chapter.

Number of Services   Number of services refers to the number of encounters the patient has had with the physician. Usually the number of services is one. For example, Chad visits the physician in the office because of an earache. The physician assesses and treats Chad. That is one service or encounter. If Chad also mentions that his knee is troubling him, the physician cannot bill for two assessments. If Chad left and returned on the same day with the complaint of a sore knee, and the physician submitted a claim for another intermediate assessment, the ministry would either disallow the claim altogether or pay it as a minor assessment. If the physician performs both an intermediate and a minor assessment, bill for the intermediate assessment. However, as noted in Chapter 11, you may claim for a number of services if they are on consecutive days for inpatients in health care facilities. For example, if Helga was in hospital for five days, the most responsible physician (MRP) might visit her daily. You would submit a single claim for five services. However, you would submit separate claims for visits that are not on consecutive days (e.g., you would submit separate claims for a visit on November 9 and one on November 11).

Some software systems require that the number of services consist of two digits. If there are fewer than 10, use a zero followed by the number (thus, the most common entry is 01). For other software systems, you may enter the number of services as they appear (e.g., 1). Provincial or territorial billing software will customize the format as required.

Price per Unit (PPU)   For most services, a "unit" is the service and the PPU is the amount allowed in the fee schedule for that service. For time-based services, a unit is the amount of time designated in the fee schedule; for example, a unit of time might be designated as 15 minutes. Each 15-minute period spent with a patient would be worth a certain value. Extra units sometimes have a different code than that for the base unit. For example, in Figure 12.3, the service is A007A, an intermediate assessment. The fee for this assessment is $33.70; this is the PPU.

Fee Submitted The fee submitted is the amount allowed for the service provided, and it relates directly to the service code submitted for a particular encounter (each service code has a predetermined fee attached to it). These amounts are listed in the fee schedule. Your software program will automatically insert the fee when you enter the service code.

For most services, the fee submitted will be the same as the PPU. However, if more than one service is claimed (as in consecutive hospital visits), or if the service is time based and the provider spent more than one unit of time, the fee will be the PPU times the number of services.

The input required for the health plan's (or ministry's) computer does not use dollar signs or decimals. Thus, $27.05 would be simply 2705. However, as with birth date formats, your program may show prices in a more reader-friendly format but will convert them to the required format before submitting.

Claims Categories

Three types of claims are submitted to the provincial or territorial plan, which correspond to the payment programs (insurer) discussed earlier in this chapter. The majority of claims apply to the health care plan (HCP) itself (for instance, in Figure 12.4 the insurer is listed as OHIP, which is the HCP in Ontario); the others are reciprocal billing (RMB) and workers' compensation (WCB) claims. Most systems default to the HCP option.

Reciprocal Claims The reciprocal billing format is the same across Canada. If your office is computerized, you will claim for out-of-province/territory patients just as if you were billing your own health care plan, except that you need to make sure that RMB is selected as the payment program. Also check that the patient's province or territory of origin appears in the appropriate field. Usually, the software will automatically insert the province or territory code when you swipe the card; if it does not, insert it manually. (See Table 10.2 for a list of two-letter province and territory codes.)

If you bill manually, use a reciprocal claims form. Double-check the form to be sure that you have included the following:

- The code of the province or territory
- The patient's health card number or the equivalent
- The patient's name, gender, and date of birth
- The patient's home address
- Payment program (RMB)
- Payee (P)

Always validate the patient's health card, as discussed in Chapter 11. If the card is not valid, charge the patient and let him or her know how to seek reimbursement from the home province or territory when his or her eligibility is re-established. Most plans will not accept reciprocal claims submitted after 90 days.

Services Excluded from RMB Check to see that the service in question is covered under RMB. Some services, even though they may be covered by your jurisdiction, are excluded from RMB. If the patient is not willing to wait to have the service done in his or her home province or territory, bill the patient directly. Some of the more common excluded services are as follows:

- Cosmetic surgery
- Sex reassignment surgery
- Therapeutic abortion
- Annual health exams or physicals and periodic ocular assessments
- In-vitro fertilization and artificial insemination
- Lithotripsy for gallstones
- Acupuncture, acupressure, hypnotherapy services to individuals covered by other agencies, such as a workers' compensation board or Veterans Affairs
- Genetic screening

WCB Claims   Workers' compensation claims, as discussed in Chapter 10, relate to on-the-job injuries. In most jurisdictions, the Ministry of Health acts as a payment agency for the worker's compensation board. Physicians submit workers' compensation claims directly to the Ministry of Health, as long as the patient has valid provincial/territorial health coverage. In some jurisdictions, the billing is the same as for provincial/territorial claims except that you must make sure the payment program selected is WCB/WSIB. In other jurisdictions, you would submit the claim to the WCB using preferred codes. In British Columbia, for example, the code 19930 is used for telephone consultation between a WorkSafeBC medical advisor and a community physician within 24 hours of being initiated by the medical advisor; an office consultation would be coded as 19919 (this is time based for up to 15 minutes); a return-to-work consultation is 19950; if a physician reviews a return-to-work plan, you would use the code 19976. (The visit, conversation, or consult has more detailed parameters attached to the billing criteria; see the WorkSafeBC Physician Reference Guide, available at the website listed at the end of the chapter.)

If a patient cannot produce a valid health card, the provider would bill the workers' compensation board directly. Physicians must bill the WCB directly for services not covered by the health care plan, such as medical–legal reports, office interviews with WCB representatives, and selected services noted in the fee schedule. In most jurisdictions, providers other than physicians, such as chiropractors, chiropodists, osteopaths, optometrists, private physiotherapists, private occupational therapists, dentists, audiologists, and pharmacists, bill the WCB directly for claims. Out-of-province/territory physicians, opted-out physicians, and private laboratories also bill directly.

When a physician assesses a patient for a workers' compensation matter and also provides a service for an unrelated problem at the same visit, you must submit the unrelated claim separately to the provincial or territorial health plan. There may be restrictions on the type of service you can submit to the public plan. For example, in Ontario the other service is claimed using the service code A008 for a mini assessment, provided that the WSIB claim is for a minor assessment. It is important to be aware of services the WCB does not cover in your jurisdiction.

L05 COMPLETING A CLAIM: YOUR ROLE AND RESPONSIBILITIES

Claims submission is the last step in the billing cycle and must be completed in an organized manner. Claims submission also involves being attentive to messages, files, and notifications sent back from the ministry and responding accordingly. For example, not correcting and resubmitting rejected claims can amount to considerable financial loss for your employer.

Assigning Responsibilities

When you start a new job, if claim submission and billing is your responsibility—or if it becomes your responsibility at a later date—an orientation period is essential. The billing process is complicated and, for many, it is often not a favourite responsibility.

For claim submission and billing, a provider may

- hire an outside person or billing agency,
- assign the responsibilities to you or another staff member,
- prefer to add the codes him or herself, relying on you to complete the process, or
- divide the responsibilities, having one person prepare the claims and another submit them to the ministry.

If billing is your responsibility, use the method that works best for you and maximizes the options offered on your computer system. For example, you can enter claims into the computer after each encounter, at the end of the morning, and again at the end of the day. Using the billing day sheet simplifies the process.

It is impossible to remember all of the codes, although you will become familiar with the commonly used ones. Know where to find the coding information you need. Most software supplies basic coding information on a drop-down menu on your computer (see Figure 12.4); you will find this feature a tremendous time saver. If the code you are looking for is not on your software, check your provincial fee schedule or contact your local claims support office. As well, many software vendors will supply a summarized list of the codes commonly used in your province or territory—a type of quick reference guide.

Accuracy and attention to detail are vital in the claims submission process. Omissions or coding mistakes can result in extra work for you and a significant loss of revenue for the physician. With time, you will become familiar with the codes and know when to use them, as well as the exceptions. When you are starting out, go slowly and focus on accuracy.

It is important to work as a team, no matter how your provider prefers to bill, since you will likely share the responsibilities. For example, if the physician relies on you to add codes to the claims, he or she should provide the information you need as soon as possible. Try to process it according to a regular schedule. If the provider tends to enter the codes him or herself (usually after each encounter), the days' encounters would be filed, but you would be expected to prepare (batch) the claims for submission to the ministry.

Uploading Claims

Claims generated from patient encounters are stored on your computer until you send them to the ministry. At that time you gather up, or "batch," the claims to upload and send to the ministry (once uploaded, that batch of claims is referred to as a file). Once a batch of claims has been prepared for submission, your computer will notify you that the files are ready (see Figure 12.5). You then log on using your dedicated password and activate the electronic file transfer process.

After claims files are submitted, the ministry will send back a variety of reports, including those that contain rejected claims (discussed later). This process involves several categories of codes not yet discussed, which are broadly called *rejection codes*.

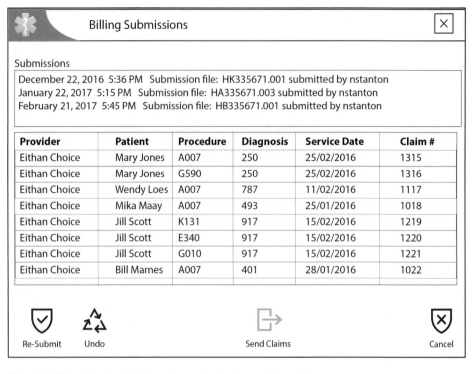

Figure 12.5 Batch of claims for submission to the ministry

Used by permission of Choice Learning, Inc.

L06 CODES FOR REJECTED CLAIMS

In the claims process, there are a number of codes that have not been discussed elsewhere in detail, but that you will need to know—these are contained in reports sent back by the ministry (discussed later). They identify claims that have been rejected for numerous reasons. *Explanatory codes* are used in most jurisdictions. In addition, all provinces/territories will have a variety of other codes used to categorize or simplify the identification of claims errors. For example, *error codes* are used in Ontario, and *action codes* in Alberta.

Explanatory Codes

An explanatory code is assigned to a claim when a problem has been identified after the claim has been processed. The claim is reviewed and a decision is made either to pay the claim as submitted, pay it at a reduced amount, or not to pay it at all. If the claim is not paid as submitted, the claim is sent back to the provider with an explanatory code assigned to it. This explanatory code will identify the reason the claim was rejected. You must review each rejected claim, correct the problem, and resubmit the claim to the ministry, ideally within the same billing cycle. If the problem takes more time to correct, remember that the claim must be resubmitted before it is stale-dated in accordance with the cut-off time in your province.

The explanatory codes assigned to returned claims include the following:

- Eligibility rejections (the service date was not within the eligible period, the claim was stale-dated, or patient coverage has lapsed)
- General reasons (the service is not an insured benefit, it was claimed by another physician within the group, or the claim is under review)
- Problems related to diagnostic and therapeutic code claims (the service is not

allowed as a repeat procedure, payment has been reduced, the limit of payment for this procedure has been reached, the service is not allowed in addition to a visit fee)

Note that you may also have overpayments if the fee has increased since your software billing program was updated.

The structure of explanatory codes differs among jurisdictions, but the principles for claim rejection are the same. For example, in British Columbia, explanatory code AA indicates the patient's PHN (personal health number) is missing or invalid. In Ontario, VH1 means the patient's health number is invalid, and VH2 means the health number is missing. Remember the good faith policy Alberta has for patients who cannot present their valid health card number, discussed in Chapter 11? The explanatory code 01C indicates a claim rejection if a good faith claim was previously paid for that patient or the patient was covered by another plan.

Error Codes (Ontario)

In Ontario, when a mistake is detected in a claim before it has been processed, an error code is assigned to that claim. It is removed from the ministry's system and returned to the provider; the code indicates the type of error to the provider. As with explanatory codes, the claim can be corrected and resubmitted to the ministry.

Error codes identify the following types of problems:

- Assessment rejects (wrong gender for service, no such service code, duplicate claim)
- Reciprocal medical billing rejects (missing province or territory code, service excluded from RMB)
- Validity rejects (error in claim number, expired card, missing payee address, invalid surname)

Action Codes (Alberta)

In Alberta, error claims submitted must have an action code, which indicates if the claim is a new or a resubmission of a previously processed claim. There are four valid action codes. An A (for access) would accompany a new claim or a claim that was paid at a zero value and resubmitted; C (for change) is used when you change data, such as the claim number on the statement of assessment; R (for response) is used when resubmitting a previous partially paid or unpaid claim; and D (for delete) is used to delete a claim that was paid previously.

L07 FEEDBACK FROM THE MINISTRY

Once the ministry has processed or adjudicated your claims, it will send out reports that advise you of the status of your claims. These reports are returned electronically and must be downloaded so that your billing software can convert them into a readable format. They are the only notification that you will receive of files, batches, or individual claims that have been rejected. *All downloaded files are kept for a designated time frame, usually five to eight days.*

Unless they are marked for manual review, claims are generally validated electronically. Information related to the manual review process may be faxed. The information submitted will be automatically compared with the guidelines for coverage of service. For example, in jurisdictions where physical examinations are covered once per year, a second examination will be rejected unless the claim is flagged for manual review and supported with documented reasons for the repeat examination.

Electronic submission of claims in most jurisdictions contains the following steps or a combination of them:

- Receipt of a claims file or batch
- Notification if the entire file or components of the file were rejected
- One or more preliminary checks of the file (e.g., may include a pre-edit and an eligibility edit, each checking different components of the claim)
- Return of rejected claims so that they can be corrected and resubmitted in the same billing cycle
- Acceptance of corrected claims
- Adjudication—final check on claims—where explanatory codes are assigned
- Remittance and payment (a remittance advice report, see Figure 12.7, lists those claims accepted, partially paid, or ultimately rejected within one billing cycle)

File Reject Message

Systems in all provinces and territories will send a message if all of your files have been rejected. Such messages are uncommon and are usually caused by technical difficulties. You would receive this report a few hours after your claims submission has been received by the ministry. If an entire file sent on tape or disk is rejected, your local ministry office will phone you.

Batch Edit Report

This report, offered by some electronic processes, lets you know whether your *claims batch* (or parts of it) have been accepted or rejected. You should get this report within 24 hours of receipt. If your claims are sent on a weekend or holiday, or at the end of the month, the ministry will send you this report on the next business day. If you are submitting your claims on disk or magnetic tape and a batch has been rejected, you will be notified by telephone on the next business day.

Claims Error Report

A claims error report (see Figure 12.6) lists all the rejected claims from a particular file and gives an error code for each rejection (which, as previously mentioned, will identify the reason for the rejection), usually within 48–72 hours. It is not unusual to receive several claims error reports in a month. Rejections (claims errors) occur for a variety of reasons.

Resubmitting Corrected Claims and Adjudication   You must correct problems noted in error messages and resubmit corrected claims immediately. This process may be referred to as a re-routing claim. (As noted earlier, a huge advantage of ET is that you get your claims error reports more frequently and can respond faster, increasing your chances of being paid within the current billing cycle.) If you work in British Columbia and discover errors in claims, you can notify Teleplan. They will delete the entire submission, and you can resubmit the corrected claims batch. This is referred to as "zapping" the claim.

Payment and Remittance Advice

remittance advice (RA) a monthly statement of approved claims from the ministry.

A **remittance advice (RA)** report is a file returned to you once a month from the ministry listing all submitted claims from the previous billing cycle (see Figure 12.7). It is sometimes also referred to as a *reconciliation advice*. You will receive it on tape, disk, or electronically, depending on how you submitted the claims. Generally, the RA is sent out at the same time as payments; in Ontario, this will usually be about the seventh or

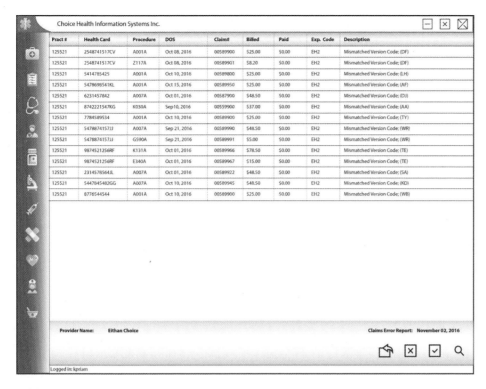

Choice Health Information Systems Inc.

Pract #	Health Card	Procedure	DOS	Claim#	Billed	Paid	Exp. Code	Description
125521	2548741517CV	A001A	Oct 08, 2016	00589900	$25.00	$0.00	EH2	Mismatched Version Code; (DF)
125521	2548741517CV	Z117A	Oct 08, 2016	00589901	$8.20	$0.00	EH2	Mismatched Version Code; (DF)
125521	5414785425	A001A	Oct 10, 2016	00589800	$25.00	$0.00	EH2	Mismatched Version Code; (LH)
125521	5478698541KL	A001A	Oct 15, 2016	00589950	$25.00	$0.00	EH2	Mismatched Version Code; (AF)
125521	6231457842	A007A	Oct 01, 2016	00587900	$48.50	$0.00	EH2	Mismatched Version Code; (DJ)
125521	8742221547KG	K030A	Sep 10, 2016	00559900	$37.00	$0.00	EH2	Mismatched Version Code; (AA)
125521	7784589534	A001A	Oct 10, 2016	00589900	$25.00	$0.00	EH2	Mismatched Version Code; (TY)
125521	5478874157JJ	A007A	Sep 21, 2016	00589990	$48.50	$0.00	EH2	Mismatched Version Code; (WR)
125521	5478874157JJ	G590A	Sep 21, 2016	00589991	$5.00	$0.00	EH2	Mismatched Version Code; (WR)
125521	9874521256RF	K131A	Oct 01, 2016	00589966	$78.50	$0.00	EH2	Mismatched Version Code; (TE)
125521	9874521256RF	E340A	Oct 01, 2016	00589967	$15.00	$0.00	EH2	Mismatched Version Code; (TE)
125521	2314578564JL	A007A	Oct 01, 2016	00589922	$48.50	$0.00	EH2	Mismatched Version Code; (SA)
125521	5447845482GG	A007A	Oct 10, 2016	00589945	$48.50	$0.00	EH2	Mismatched Version Code; (KD)
125521	8776544544	A001A	Oct 10, 2016	00589900	$25.00	$0.00	EH2	Mismatched Version Code; (WB)

Provider Name: **Eithan Choice**   Claims Error Report: **November 02, 2016**

Logged in: kpriam

Figure 12.6   Claims error report

Used by permission of Choice Learning, Inc.

eighth of the month if you submit electronically, and between the twelfth and eigh-teenth if you submit on tape or disk. The RA may be issued to a single provider or to a group that has submitted billings jointly.

The RA is analogous to a bank statement because it includes records of transactions for the previous month. Just as many people reconcile their bank statement by comparing

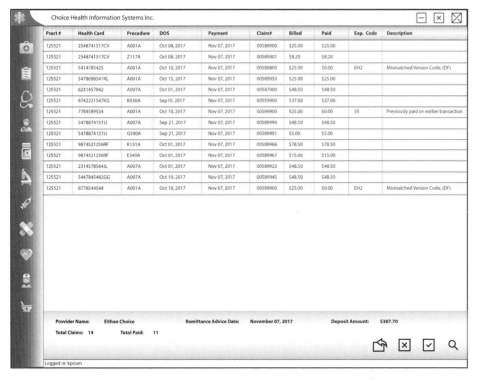

Choice Health Information Systems Inc.

Pract #	Health Card	Procedure	DOS	Payment	Claim#	Billed	Paid	Exp. Code	Description
125521	2548741517CV	A001A	Oct 08, 2017	Nov 07, 2017	00589900	$25.00	$25.00		
125521	2548741517CV	Z117A	Oct 08, 2017	Nov 07, 2017	00589901	$8.20	$8.20		
125521	5414785425	A001A	Oct 10, 2017	Nov 07, 2017	00589800	$25.00	$0.00	EH2	Mismatched Version Code; (DF)
125521	5478698541KL	A001A	Oct 15, 2017	Nov 07, 2017	00589950	$25.00	$25.00		
125521	6231457842	A007A	Oct 01, 2017	Nov 07, 2017	00587900	$48.50	$48.50		
125521	8742221547KG	K030A	Sep 10, 2017	Nov 07, 2017	00559900	$37.00	$37.00		
125521	7784589534	A001A	Oct 10, 2017	Nov 07, 2017	00589900	$25.00	$0.00	35	Previously paid on earlier transaction
125521	5478874157JJ	A007A	Sep 21, 2017	Nov 07, 2017	00589990	$48.50	$48.50		
125521	5478874157JJ	G590A	Sep 21, 2017	Nov 07, 2017	00589991	$5.00	$5.00		
125521	9874521256RF	K131A	Oct 01, 2017	Nov 07, 2017	00589966	$78.50	$78.50		
125521	9874521256RF	E340A	Oct 01, 2017	Nov 07, 2017	00589967	$15.00	$15.00		
125521	2314578564JL	A007A	Oct 01, 2017	Nov 07, 2017	00589922	$48.50	$48.50		
125521	5447845482GG	A007A	Oct 10, 2017	Nov 07, 2017	00589945	$48.50	$48.50		
125521	8776544544	A001A	Oct 10, 2017	Nov 07, 2017	00589900	$25.00	$0.00	EH2	Mismatched Version Code; (DF)

Provider Name: **Eithan Choice**   Remittance Advice Date: **November 07, 2017**   Deposit Amount: **$387.70**

Total Claims: **14**   Total Paid: **11**

Logged in: kpriam

Figure 12.7   Remittance advice report

Used by permission of Choice Learning, Inc.

it with entries in their cheque book, you should reconcile the RA by comparing it with your own claim records and investigate any apparent discrepancies. Every claim you submit should correspond with either a line on the RA or a line on a claims error report. Review each one individually (many offices keep a hard copy of both submitted claims and RAs). If there are any **partial claims payments**, you should understand why the amount paid differs from the amount you claimed.

The RA includes a summary that categorizes the contents of the report and enables you to determine whether you received what you billed for. Rejected claims may be listed as exceptions at the end of the RA. Some software programs will extract rejected claims lines and shift them to another file. This list will include the account number (internal use), the patient's name, health card number, date of service, service code, and a code indicating why the service was underpaid or not paid. (This information is similar to the claims error report, except that the latter shows only irregularities.) Payments for WCB-related services will appear on the RA with "WCB/WSIB" in the payment column.

Items Paid in Full The majority of the items will (hopefully) be claims paid in full (i.e., the amount you billed).

Underpayments Some items may be *underpayments*; that is, the ministry has not rejected the claim but has paid less than you claimed. Payment reductions are based on the ministry's computer analysis, which in turn is based on claims policies and regulations. There may be a number of reasons for the reduction, which will be explained by the appropriate codes on the RA. For example, if you claimed a service as an intermediate assessment (on the basis of the diagnostic code) but it should be a minor assessment, you would receive the fee for a minor assessment with an error code explaining the difference. If you are in British Columbia and submitted a service code used for a patient over 70 years old, but the patient's health information indicated that he was 60 years old, you would likewise be paid a reduced amount and see an error code on your RA. You must review these claims, and you have the option of resubmitting them with an explanation.

Rejected Claims There may be some rejected claims on the RA report if the error was not picked up during the preliminary batch edit. (Some types of errors can be picked up right away; others are picked up only at the RA level.) Unpaid and partially paid claims that have not been previously corrected and resubmitted after a claims error report will be included, along with a code indicating why the claim was rejected or underpaid. Review each rejection individually. Correct errors and resubmit promptly. Sometimes, you may have to submit supporting documentation or a more detailed explanation. If you do not understand or accept the reason for a rejection or underpayment, use a remittance advice inquiry form. All inquiries should be submitted within one month and no later than four to six months after the original claim was submitted or the date on which the service was rendered. Submit all inquires relating to the same RA at one time.

If the claim is rejected again and your provider still believes he or she is entitled to payment, you can appeal. All jurisdictions have a medical eligibility committee (or equivalent) that examines the facts, interviews the provider, and decides on disputed claims.

Note: The date for claims to be resubmitted is variable. Ontario, British Columbia, Saskatchewan, Yukon, Nunavut, and Manitoba allow six months before a claim is stale-dated. The other provinces/territories have a three-month time allowance. Only the Northwest Territories allows a full year.

Computer-Generated Reports

Computer programs will generate various summaries and highlights of ministry reports. An example is the rejected billing line report. This report, offered by some software, provides you with rejection details on a line-by-line basis within a reconciliation. At the end of the report is a summary of the number of claim lines rejected, how much was billed, and how much was paid.

Payment of Claims

The most important return from the ministry is the monthly payment itself. The provider may receive the payment by cheque or by direct deposit. Arrangements for direct deposit may be made through the providers' registry section at the ministry office.

Alternative Payment Plans—Primary Care Groups Every jurisdiction has different alternative payment plans that, for the most part, are combined with fee-for-service remuneration. Capitation-based funding is the most widely used. The ministry pays the physician based on certain demographic and health information specific to each patient. You are not required to submit any claims for this payment plan.

In most primary care models, physicians are paid bonuses or incentive payments for achieving certain service goals. Again, you are not responsible for billing the ministry for these. You may, however, be responsible for tracking certain patient groups regarding services they have received if the physician is renumerated for that service. As mentioned in Chapter 11, these services are primarily preventive in nature, including immunizations, mammograms, flu shots, and Pap smears. You must also be knowledgeable about other new services for which the physician can claim, such as smoking cessation and diabetic management.

Figure 12.8 shows a diagram of the billing cycle, using Ontario as an example.

OHIP Submission

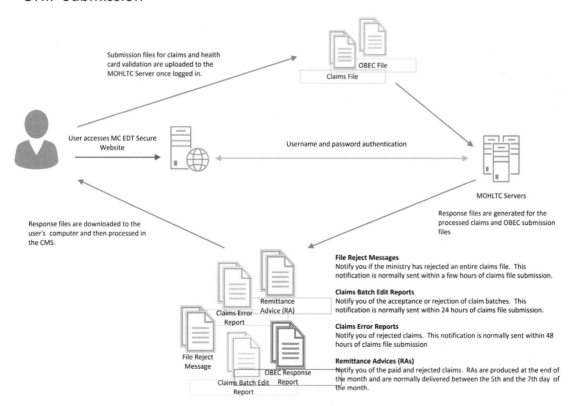

Figure 12.8 Diagram of the billing cycle

L08 BILLING FOR SERVICES NOT PUBLICLY INSURED

The majority of a physician's billings will be to some form of public insurance, most often the provincial or territorial health plan. However, when services are not covered you will have to collect payment either directly from the patient or from a third party.

Services Charged to the Patient

A range of services that a patient might need or want (listed in Chapter 10) are not covered by provincial and territorial health care plans. Moreover, sometimes patients will have to pay for services that would normally be insured because they are not eligible for coverage, perhaps because they are recent immigrants, are residents of Quebec visiting your province or territory, or do not have a valid health card. In such cases, you need to collect payment directly from the patient.

This will probably be a fairly infrequent, but significant, part of your total billing if you work for a physician. For other providers, such as chiropractors and optometrists, it can be a major part of total revenue. For example, oculo-visual examinations will be covered under certain circumstances, depending on the jurisdiction, but the patient will normally pay for the glasses him- or herself. Most companies that offer employee benefits cover eyeglasses, but most optometrists want direct payment, so the patient pays and seeks reimbursement from the insurance company.

In most jurisdictions, the physician must inform the patient or the person responsible for financing the service of the cost of the service *prior* to rendering the service. This may be accomplished by means of a notice prominently placed in the reception area of the provider's office or a patient handout listing all uninsured services the provider offers. However, you should never assume people have read this information. In addition to written notices, always discuss payment directly with the patient. Be clear. Make sure the patient understands what, when, and how he or she will be paying. This is really the physician's responsibility, but you can provide reinforcement. Also let the patient know if there is a way he or she could get the service covered—for example, if an examination would be covered if he or she waited a couple of months or if the service is offered free to patients at a hospital.

Note: Recall from Chapter 4 that extra-billing (billing the patient more for an insured service than the provincial or territorial plan pays) is illegal. (This does not apply to certain enhanced services for which a co-payment may be made.) You may be held liable for knowingly participating in extra-billing. Be careful not to inadvertently bill a patient for any insured service. If you suspect that your provider is extra-billing, speak to your provider to clarify the issue or seek legal counsel.

Block Fees Some physicians offer an arrangement in which a patient pays a single block fee, for an individual or a family, for a range of uninsured services over a period of time—not less than 3 months and not more than 12 months. Some patients feel more comfortable with a block fee than having to pay separately for uninsured services. Block fees are particularly appealing to older patients who often need telephone advice or who take numerous medications that are frequently renewed.

The College of Physicians and Surgeons in each province and territory has set out rules for the block-fee model. If your provider offers block fees, post these guidelines prominently. Note that block fees are subject to GST or HST (depending on your province/territory).

Transfer of Medical Records   When patients request that their medical records be transferred, they are responsible for the cost. It's surprising how many patients think that a transfer of records involves simply packaging up their original chart. The process should be carefully explained. As well, the patient must be *clearly notified in advance that this is an uninsured service* and what the cost will be. A good way to do this is to include the cost of transfer in the consent form that patients must sign. Most physicians base the cost on the number of pages involved. Some will charge a set rate for the first 5 or 10 pages and an additional per-page rate after that. One province recommends a charge of $37.00 for pages 1–5 and $1.50 for each subsequent page. If the physician spends a considerable amount of time arranging or summarizing the patient's chart prior to transfer, he or she may also charge for the time. If the patient's chart is large, it may cost the patient less to have the physician review and summarize it, transferring only relevant information, than to pay for photocopying everything.

Preparing the chart of a psychiatric patient is more detailed. The physician must be careful about the nature of the information transferred; charges for transfer of this type of information are sometimes higher.

Accepting Payment

Most physicians find that asking for payment at the time the service is rendered is most effective. Many offices keep a petty cash supply on hand and accept only cash. Some offices will also accept personal cheques, certified cheques, debit cards, or credit cards, such as Visa or MasterCard. To accept debit or credit cards, you need prior arrangement with a bank (which involves a fee) and a card-swiping device (manual or tied into your computer system and modem). Always record the transaction in a ledger and issue a dated receipt. Some physicians will agree to bill patients under certain circumstances. Your physician may also be willing to set aside normal policies for financially disadvantaged patients who cannot afford to pay.

It is important to stick to office policies whatever they may be. If you make exceptions for patients because "I don't have the correct change" or "I forgot my wallet at home," you will often spend considerable time asking for payment, and in some cases you will never be paid. Consider this approach: A patient comes into the office to pick up completed insurance forms, which she has been told she would have to pay for. When you ask for $20, the woman looks surprised, hesitates, and says, "I don't have my purse. I can pay you later." She clearly expects to be handed the forms, but you respond brightly, "That's fine, Mrs. Christie. When you have the money, come back and the forms will be waiting." The woman comes back less than an hour later with the money.

The more closely you follow a policy of payment at point of service and the more firmly you deal with patients, the fewer outstanding accounts you will have. It may seem harsh, but patients will soon learn that payment is expected. Think about picking up a bag of chips at the local convenience store. Would the clerk let you walk out and come back later to pay?

Tips for Direct Billing

- Always discuss uninsured services with a patient before the service is rendered (when the patient is booking an appointment, and then again when he or she arrives at the office).

- Have an office policy either posted or in a handout—it must be detailed and clear.
- Keep your accounts up to date.
- Be consistent with account follow-up, and be organized.

Insurance Coverage

As discussed in Chapter 10, private insurance (often, but not always, as part of an employee benefits package) pays for many services not covered by provincial or territorial plans. Arrangements for payment differ. Most often the patient will pay the provider and then submit receipts to the insurance company for reimbursement. Beyond providing a suitably detailed receipt, you have no involvement with the insurer.

In other cases, the patient signs an assignment of benefits, which allows the insurance company to pay the provider directly. In this case, you will need to invoice the insurance company, which will send a cheque directly to the office. Alternatively, the patient may ask you to bill the insurance company on his or her behalf; the insurance company will send a cheque to the patient, who endorses it to the provider. These arrangements can be negotiated between the provider and the patient and also depend on the policies of the insurance company. Make sure you know your employer's policies. Many providers prefer to bill an insurance company, which will usually pay reliably (if not necessarily quickly). If you are billing on behalf of a patient, there is always the risk that the patient will forget to endorse and send on the cheque.

Collection

If you send bills, it is inevitable that you will sometimes have outstanding accounts. It is important to have a follow-up policy. Most offices will telephone or mail a bill twice. (Some providers charge interest on outstanding accounts; if so, the rate must be noted on all notices for payment.) After two notices, the account goes either to small claims court or to a collection agency. Before taking that step, it is important to ensure that the patient actually received the notices. Sometimes patients simply forget they owe money, move, and do not receive any reminder until they are contacted by a collection agency. The most reliable approach is to remind patients when they come into the office or to phone and get a patient to confirm that he or she is aware of the debt.

Small claims court is an option when attempts to collect directly are unsuccessful. However, most jurisdictions require that someone from the office attend court, which is time consuming and may not be cost effective. More physicians are resorting to collection agencies, which charge only if they are successful in collecting.

Third-Party Services

third-party service a service carried out at the request of someone other than the patient or for the explicit use of someone other than the patient.

A **third-party service** is generally considered any service carried out at the request of someone other than the patient or for the use of someone other than the patient. For example, an employer, a camp, or a school may require a physical examination. A health certificate may be a requirement for a pilot's licence or a commercial driver's licence or may be required before entering into a contract for life insurance. An insurance company may need an assessment to settle a claim, or a lawyer may need an assessment to take to court. Services may involve filling out forms or transmitting medical information to the third party and may include a complete physical

TABLE 12.1 Common types of insurance forms

Attending Physician's Request Statement	Sent out after an applicant for life insurance has completed preliminary information forms. Requests information from the patient's chart, including medical history, progress notes, and findings about any noteworthy medical problems.
System of Disease Questionnaire	Requests information about a patient's treatment and progress regarding a specific—often a chronic—disease. Usually sent directly from the insurance company.
Insurance Medical Examination	Requires the physician to complete a general physical examination and related functional inquiry for insurance purposes. The patient may bring in this form, or it may be sent by the company.
System-Specific Examination	Asks the physician to assess a specific system, such as the respiratory or the cardiovascular system, including a functional inquiry. This would be similar to an intermediate medical assessment.
Clarification Report	Usually sent directly to the physician, this form may be used to settle an insurance claim. Asks for clarification and perhaps an update on previously submitted information and does not usually require the physician to see the patient.
Comprehensive Narrative Report	A more detailed form than the clarification report that is used in complicated disability claims. Requests information about specific medical interventions, patient progress, and diagnostic test results.
Disability Certificates	May be required by an insurance company or a government agency to certify that a patient is injured and cannot work. Requires a physical examination and related functional inquiry. May be sent to the physician or brought in by the patient.

examination, a system-specific examination, or diagnostic tests. All these services would be billed to the third party or sometimes to the patient, depending on payment arrangements. Just as with claims to health plans, a bill may include fees for more than one component; for example, for an assessment, a diagnostic test, and a report. Where a third party requires ongoing or subsequent assessments, the physician may bill for additional services. In some circumstances, a service may be covered by a provincial or territorial plan but the related documentation is not. For example, if a physician feels that, for the patient's health and safety, he or she should be assessed before returning to work, the health plan would cover the assessment because it is considered medically necessary. However, if the patient's employer requires a return-to-work note, that would not be covered; either the employer or, more likely, the patient would be responsible for the cost.

Following are some of the common types of third-party services.

Government Forms   The federal government pays for physicians to complete a number of types of forms, including medical reports on applicants for immigration, applicants to the Armed Forces, and reports on disability to qualify for disability payments under the Canada Pension Plan, the Disability Tax Credit, and similar benefits.

Insurance Forms   Insurance companies generate a variety of forms and related services for physicians. Table 12.1 lists some of the more common types; names and specifics may vary. Always make sure you have the patient's permission to release any information. This is usually obtained by the insurance company and sent to the physician along with the requested forms. Figures 12.9 and 12.10 show a sample consent form and cover letter.

```
SLI STABILITY LIFE INSURANCE COMPANY
                                                        P.O Box 12345
                                                        Edmonton, AB
                                                        T3G 5N6
                                                        780-564-2929

February 25, 2017

Dear Dr. Linh:

Re: John Doe Contract 2344          Claim 12344—Member ID 456789

I am writing about John Doe's claim for long-term disability benefits.
    To evaluate Mr. Doe's claim fully, we require his consultation reports from
September 30 to December 31, 2016.
    We also need you to complete the enclosed Physical Capacities Evaluation form.
    I have enclosed an authorization form for the release of Mr. Doe's medical
information.
    I would appreciate receiving the consultation reports and the completed
evaluation form no later than April 15, 2017. Please include your correspondence fee
with your reply.

Thank you for your assistance in this matter.

Yours truly

JR Benesh

JR Benesh
Disability Adjudications
Stability Life Insurance Company

/jb
encl
```

Figure 12.9   Cover letter from insurance company requesting medical records and form completion

Medical–Legal Issues   Physicians may become involved in court cases in several ways. A physician may be served with a subpoena to appear in court to testify in a case involving a regular patient or one he saw in an emergency department. A physician may also be asked to appear as an "expert witness" in a case involving a patient he or she has never met; the physician may be asked to further assess the person's medical condition or to give a general opinion. Physician payment in such circumstances is managed by the courts or privately at preset or prearranged amounts. It may be your responsibility to bill for such services. You must be very careful to ensure that proper protocol is followed before releasing any patient information. The patient must give written consent for the release or discussion of any medical information, explicitly specifying to whom it may be released, unless a court order for the release of the information is presented.

Payment   Most third-party services paid for by agencies and insurance companies are paid by cheque or direct deposit. Usually, you do not have to invoice; the company will send a cheque on receipt of the report. Always issue receipts and record transactions in a ledger. In some jurisdictions, a physician may enter into an annual contractual arrangement, similar to a block-fee system, with third parties such as insurance companies. These payments are subject to GST.

Table 12.2 summarizes the process of billing health care plans.

SLI STABILITY LIFE INSURANCE COMPANY

PO Box 12345
Edmonton, AB
T3G 5N6
780-564-2929

Consent for Release of Information

I authorize the Stability Life Insurance Company to conduct a thorough medical assessment for my condition and:

1. to be allowed to receive, review, and obtain copies of all hospital, medical, X-ray, laboratory, psychological, vocational, and other related records related to my medical condition that will assist in completing this assessment, and

2. to discuss any relevant information, including test results or identifying information, with the appropriate health professionals, employer, or related insurance personnel involved in my assessment, disability, and/or rehabilitation process.

I agree to the appropriate photocopying of this information as deemed necessary by those involved in my assessment.

I understand that the main purpose of this referral and gathering of information is to assess my medical condition and determine my entitlement to the appropriate benefits and/or rehabilitation.

DATED THIS 2ND DAY OF JANUARY 2017

At Edmonton, Alberta

SIGNATURE *John Doe*

WITNESS *JR Benesh*

Figure 12.10 Consent form for release of information to insurance company

TABLE 12.2 Summary of health care plan billing	
Method Timelines	• Electronic transfer (ET) • Claims must be in by the eighteenth of every month to be guaranteed payment within that cycle. • If you use ET, you can send in claims up to the end of the month and they will be paid, providing the claims office is not too busy. • Payment is made by the eighteenth of the next month.
Information Components	Many of these data are entered automatically on some software programs but must be entered manually on cards.
Patient's Demographic Data	• Full name • Address • Date of birth • Sex • Province or territory
Additional Card Information	• Health card number • Version code, if applicable • Expiry date (on some systems)
Provider Number	
Payment Program	Most computers default to HCP

(continued)

TABLE12.2   *(continued)*

Payee	Indicates who is getting the money: P for provider and S for patient
Accounting Number	Usually computer generated; optional
Date of Service	
Service Code and/or Procedural Code	
PPU	Price per unit (PPU)/service
Number of Services	May appear on screen as units
Diagnostic Code Fee	Same as PPU unless the service is time based or more than one service is claimed
Facility Number	Used only if the patient has been admitted to a hospital or other facility
Referring Number	Used only if the claim is made by a specialist; the referring physician's registration number
Admission Date	Used only for a patient in hospital

▶▶▶ WHAT TO WATCH FOR

- Variations in the way physicians are remunerated as the manner in which primary health care is delivered continues to evolve.

- Claims submission becoming more efficient, with providers assuming greater responsibility for completing their own claims.

- Continued changes in the technology used for electronic transfer, with more jurisdictions using compressed files.

SUMMARY

1. Web-based claims submission (electronic transfer) is used in all jurisdictions. This secure process requires special billing software to be added to the provider's computer system; some can be integrated with the software currently used. Dedicated users are provided with a secure password they must use to log into the system.

2. Understanding the steps of the billing cycle is important. Your responsibilities begin with claims preparation and completion, uploading the claims, and transmitting them to the ministry. In return, the ministry sends back a variety of reports that you must respond to.

3. Patient registration provides information that must be used to submit claims. This includes a valid health card and basic patient information, such as their name and address. It is important to ensure that this information is correct and the health number submitted is valid—outdated health card numbers result in a claims rejection.

4. A health claim contains numerous components, all of which must be properly entered. A physician's number is automatically entered in most software systems. Be careful to ensure that the correct payee is checked off before submitting a claim—most of the time this is HCP (the health care plan). RMB (reciprocal medical billing) involves all provinces/territories except Quebec.

5. Claims submission can be divided into two parts: preparing the claims and batching/uploading them to send to the ministry. Providers may have an outside person/agency do the billing or assign the responsibility to administrative staff. Some physicians do most of their own code entry. Knowing your role and working as a team with the provider allows you to develop a routine for submitting claims, thus reducing errors and improving efficiency.

6. Claims rejections are part of every claims submission cycle. Errors in applying service, diagnostic, or procedural codes are common. The ministry uses explanatory codes on a claims error report to identify why claims are rejected. Most jurisdictions use explanatory codes in addition to other categories of rejection codes specific to the region. Correcting and returning claims within the same billing cycle will ensure that payment is received within that cycle.

7. A variety of reports are returned to you from the ministry in addition to the claims error report. You must watch for these reports and download them to read. Initial reports include notice if an entire file has been rejected or if batches of claims have been rejected. A remittance advice (RA) report is a file returned to you once a month from the ministry listing all submitted claims from the previous billing cycle.

8. Third-party billing will take up a significant amount of your time. Any services that the provider charges for must be posted and visible to patients. Payment policies will vary with office procedure; many accept cash or cheques. For services covered by an insurance company, the patient commonly pays the provider and then seeks reimbursement from the insurance company. You will also have to invoice government agencies and insurance companies for the completion of forms and other services.

KEY TERMS

electronic transfer (ET)   342
machine-readable input/
    output (MRI/MRO)   342
partial claims payment   358
remittance advice (RA)   356
third-party service   362

REVIEW QUESTIONS

1. What are the advantages of electronic transfer (ET)?
2. What is the significance of claims deadlines related to ET claims submission?
3. Outline, in sequence, the steps of the patient registration process.
4. How is the day sheet used in the claims submission process?
5. What is the purpose of the accounting number used in claims submission?
6. List and explain the payment programs used in claims submission.
7. What is the purpose of the manual review field on a billing screen?
8. Describe the intent and content of a remittance advice report.
9. What should you do when you receive a claims error report?
10. State the difference between a batch edit report and a file reject message.
11. Before you charge for an uninsured service, what information must the patient have?
12. What is meant by a *third-party service*?
13. Explain each of the headings in the following screen sample:

Item Code	PPU	Units	Type	Date	Diag. Code	MR	Amount	Status

APPLICATION EXERCISES

1. Compare the advantages and disadvantages of electronic claims submission versus submission on disk or tape.

2. Research electronic claims submission in your province or territory. Identify the files generated by this electronic billing system. Compare them with those described in this chapter, considering name, purpose, and content. Are claims submission deadlines the same as those discussed in this chapter?

3. Create a form on your computer similar to the one shown later, or use your software billing program to fill in all appropriate codes for each situation. If not shown by default on your billing program, current amounts can be obtained from your jurisdiction's fee schedule website.

   a. Ivy comes in to have her ears syringed. She is on warfarin and requires a dose adjustment based on her last INR of 5.

   b. Mia comes in for some family planning advice. She is worried about the risks of becoming pregnant. The physician spends time counselling Mia about genetic risk factors. Mia also has a Pap smear while she is there.

   c. Craig comes in complaining of vague symptoms of diarrhea and epigastric discomfort. The physician does a urinalysis in the office and a fairly thorough examination but cannot reach a conclusive diagnosis.

   d. Dr. Shymloski has seen Peter several times for a complaint of chest tightness. He sends Peter to Dr. Jamison, an internist, for a consultation. First he does an ECG in the office. You work for Dr. Shymloski.

   e. Complete the chart for the scenario in part (d). This time you work for Dr. Jamison.

   f. Dr. Oran made a house call for Mrs. Erickson at 9:30 p.m. Her diagnosis was congestive heart failure.

   g. Regina was assessed for complications of her diabetes, and her insulin regimen was regulated. Home care was ordered to assess and apply a dressing to her foot.

   h. 1:00 a.m., the physician delivered Tina Smalley's baby. It was a spontaneous delivery with no complications.

   i. The physician is unable to make a diagnosis for Mark and has put on the chart that he has a collection of vague symptoms.

   j. Lana's diagnosis was a plantar wart. The physician removed the wart using a chemical substance.

   k. Harnek is in hospital. Dr. Yu visits him as the MRP on day 1, day 2, and day 3.

   l. Hassan visits the office with a form that is required to be completed by the physician for admission to a long-term care facility.

   m. Cole, who is six months old, requires routine vaccinations.

Item Code	PPU	Units	Type	Date	Diag. Code	MR	Amount	Status Acct#	Err.
a.									
b.									
c.									
d.									
e.									
f.									
g.									
h.									
i.									
j.									
k.									
l.									
m.									

4. Dr. Hui is a busy primary care physician. You discover that he sometimes adds codes for procedures he has not performed and bills for special calls/house calls when you know he has not made these visits. You owe your employer faithfulness according to ethical principles. What would you do? What are your options?

WEBSITES OF INTEREST

British Columbia

1. Medical Services Plan Schedule:
   www2.gov.bc.ca/gov/content/health/practitioner-profes-sional-resources/msp/physicians/payment-schedules/msc-payment-schedule

2. WorkSafeBC Physician Reference Guide:
   www.worksafebc.com/en/resources/health-care-providers/guides/physician-reference-guide?lang=en

3. Medical Office Assistant Billing Guide:
   www2.gov.bc.ca/gov/content/health/practitioner-professional-resources/msp/physicians/medical-office-assistant-billing-guide

Alberta

1. Schedule of Benefits:
   www.health.alberta.ca/professionals/SOMB.html

2. Explanatory Code List:
   www.health.alberta.ca/documents/SOMB-Explanatory-Codes-2016-04.pdf

3. Billing Tips:
   www.albertadoctors.org/services/physicians/compensation-billing/billing-help/billing-tips

Saskatchewan

1. Medical Billing Instruction Manual:
   www.saskcbs.com/Manual/Billing_V4_3f.pdf

2. Physician Payment Schedule:
   www.sma.sk.ca/99/physician-payment-schedule.html

3. Caregiver Explanatory Codes:
   www.wcbsask.com/care-providers/caregiver-explanatory-codes

4. WCB Physician Service Rates:
   www.wcbsask.com/wp-content/uploads/2013/11/physician-fees.pdf

Manitoba: Physician's Manual

www.gov.mb.ca/health/documents/physmanual.pdf

Ontario

1. Schedule of Benefits for Physician Services:
   www.health.gov.on.ca/english/providers/program/ohip/sob/sob_mn.htm

2. Online Resource Manual for Physicians:
   www.health.gov.on.ca/english/providers/pub/ohip/physmanual/physmanual_mn.html

Quebec: Resource and Billing Manual

www.ramq.gouv.qc.ca/en/Pages/home.aspx

New Brunswick: Physicians' Manual and Fee Schedule

www.gnb.ca/0394/pdf/2015/physician_manual-e.pdf

Nova Scotia: Physician's Manual and Fee Schedule

www.medavie.bluecross.ca/static/MSI/PhysicianManual.pdf

Prince Edward Island: Physician Resource Manual

www.gov.pe.ca/photos/original/doh_masteragree.pdf

Newfoundland and Labrador: Medical Payment Schedule

www.health.gov.nl.ca/health/mcp/providers/mcpmedpymt.html

ICD-9 Diagnostic Codes

http://icd9.chrisendres.com/index.php

This site allows you to enter a diagnosis and find the code, or enter a code and find the diagnosis.

Chapter 13
Health Information Management

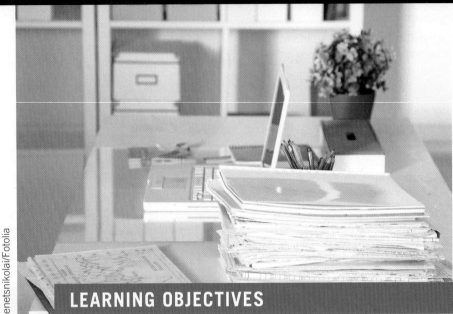

lenetsnikolai/Fotolia

LEARNING OBJECTIVES

On completing this chapter, you will be able to:

1. Apply the general principles of health information management to medical charts.

2. Differentiate between the electronic medical record and the electronic health record.

3. Explain the advantages of computerized record keeping.

4. Explain the concept, acquisition, and use of an electronic medical records system.

5. List the components of a patient's chart.

6. Summarize the phases of the health record life cycle.

7. Choose the most appropriate filing method for a particular health office environment.

8. Discuss the importance of security, privacy, and confidentiality of health records and explain how to preserve them.

Health information management is a field in its own right. Many colleges and universities across Canada offer undergraduate and graduate diplomas and degrees in health information management and health informatics. A national organization, the Canadian Health Information Management Association (CHIMA), has nearly 5000 members who are largely responsible for patient records at both micro and macro levels in private offices, clinics, and all health care facilities across the country. CHIMA members have the designation Canadian Health Information Manager. They manage health records from the time the information is retrieved until the point at which the information is disposed of, whether in paper or electronic format. Of equal importance is the security of the health information under their management—these individuals are acutely aware of provincial, federal, and agency confidentiality guidelines and ensure they are adhered to. These professionals, with their extensive knowledge of health information, are key players in the continued transition from paper-based record keeping to an electronic format.

This chapter will focus on the management of health information primarily in an electronic format in a doctor's office—a task less onerous than managing health information in a large facility, but one requiring specialized knowledge nonetheless. Most health facilities, medical offices, and clinics across Canada are still in transition to an electronic environment, particularly with the electronic medical chart.

LO1 GENERAL PRINCIPLES OF HEALTH INFORMATION MANAGEMENT

Scanning and uploading all of the data from paper charts (often called *pCharts*) into the patient's electronic medical record is time consuming. Most practices are long past this phase, with all their patients charts now in electronic format. Some doctors still like to keep selected documents in the patient's pChart for a variety of reasons, such as for reference or for legal purposes. These pCharts may be stored on- or offsite.

Despite the transition to electronic medical records, pCharts, at least in part, will be around for a number of years. If nothing else, they will act as a reservoir for health information not uploaded into an electronic format. As well, in many cases pCharts must be kept for a certain time period for legal purposes.

The Terms

First it is necessary to clarify the meaning of some of the terms and phrases associated with handling health information and identify key players involved in the creation, use, and storage of electronic health information.

eHealth is a general term used to describe electronic health information—its creation, use, and management. The electronic health record is a significant part of eHealth initiatives supported by the federal government.

The Canada Health Infoway is a federally funded organization with a mandate to facilitate the national implementation of electronic health records. The organization works collaboratively with all levels of government, regional authorities, health facilities, and a variety of health professionals. The Canada Health Infoway provides a forum where stakeholders can share ideas, information, and successes about implementing and using health records systems. Good ideas can provide a foundation for moving forward with some initiatives; unsuccessful projects can be shelved or modified.

Under the Canada Health Infoway, electronic health information systems and electronic health records projects are approved, funded, and implemented. Examples of these include electronic access to diagnostic imaging and drug and laboratory information. The electronic medical record and the electronic health record are part of this process.

Health information is defined as any information pertaining to someone's physical or mental health, condition, or infirmity, whether given orally or recorded in any manner, that is created or received directly or indirectly by a health professional or health organization. It includes services rendered, treatments and treatment plans, health teaching and education, and payment for services. Personal information and

health information any information pertaining to someone's physical or mental health, condition, or infirmity, whether given orally or recorded in any manner that is created or received directly or indirectly by a health professional or health organization.

demographic data gathered to provide medical services are also considered health information. Although this definition of health information is widely accepted and comprehensive, the definition varies and is interpreted differently by individuals and organizations.

The definition of health information management is equally diverse, meaning different things to different people. Responsibilities related to health information management include the physical management of information systems, ranging from computers to modems and printers. It includes the design and programming of related software. Any person or organization responsible for managing health information is a **health information custodian**.

health information custodian a person or organization who has the responsibility for safeguarding and controlling personal health information in connection with the powers and duties performed.

L02 L03 THE HEALTH RECORD

health record any documentation relating to a health care patient. The term *record* is used for a single document, such as a doctor's note on an assessment or a lab report; it also refers to a collection of documents, such as a patient's chart.

In general terms, a **health record** is any documentation relating to a health care patient. The term *record* is used for a single document, such as a doctor's note on an assessment or a lab report; it also refers to a collection of documents, such as a patient's chart. Records may be paper based or electronic. Whether in a private practice or in a hospital, a record must be kept of every aspect of the patient's interaction with a health professional or a health facility. This includes the patient's presenting problem, assessment, treatment, and outcome. Health care providers usually create health records, although other professional staff may also capture clinical and nonclinical information. Traditionally, we view a health record as a paper-based collection of information, and a chart as a file folder containing this information.

The current trend is managing this information electronically. Electronic management of health records has produced the terms *electronic medical record* and *electronic health record*, each with different characteristics.

A physician in private practice is ultimately responsible for health records; in a hospital, the administration is legally responsible and delegates this responsibility to health information services—which is the more current title for what was previously called the medical records department. Standards for documentation are set by professional colleges, legislation, and health organizations. This includes *all* activities relating to the care and treatment of a patient as well as the names of those rendering the care.

Detailed, accurate health records are essential to high-quality health care. A large component of this is continuity of care—knowing the patient's medical history, problems, medications, and treatments. If 75-year-old Freda, who lives in Vancouver, was seen by a doctor in Calgary or in the emergency department in a hospital in Burnaby, her medical records would be available to the treating physician, enabling the physician to make informed decisions based on Freda's medical history.

The health record is also used

- for medical–legal purposes,
- as the source information for billing,
- for funding initiatives,
- for mandatory reporting to various governmental bodies,
- as a quality monitoring tool,
- as a program evaluation tool,
- for teaching,
- for research, and
- for hospital, regional, and provincial or territorial health services planning.

The Electronic Medical Record (EMR)

An **electronic medical record (EMR)** is a legal health record in digital format. It contains the patient's health information collected by one or a group of providers in one location—a medical practice, hospital, or clinic. *It is a subset of the electronic health record (EHR)—in other words, part of a larger record.*

electronic medical record (EMR) a legal health record in digital format. It contains the patient's health information collected by one or a group of providers in one location. It is a subset of the electronic health record (EHR).

The Electronic Health Record (EHR)

An **electronic health record (EHR)** is an accumulation of essential information from an individual's electronic medical records that is accessed electronically at different points of service for purposes of patient care. The EHR follows the patient and is available whenever and wherever he or she needs care. *The EHR is a compilation of EMRs.*

electronic health record (EHR) an accumulation of essential information from an individual's electronic medical records that is accessed electronically at different points of service for purposes of patient care.

In the office setting, software that creates, maintains, and stores electronic medical records information is different from software that supports the electronic health record. The EHR system is much broader, and the software supports connectivity to a variety of caregivers to allow sharing of a patient's medical information. It may include demographic information, a cumulative profile, progress notes, pharmacy records, laboratory information, and diagnostic reports. Probably the greatest electronic challenge facing health care is how to effectively network various health facilities within a community, let alone on a national level, so that the EHR is both viable and useful.

Electronic Medical Records Systems

An **electronic medical records system** is a total medical office system—hardware and software—with the capabilities of replacing all components of a paper chart and supporting its use in an electronic format.

electronic medical records system a total medical office system, including both hardware and software, with the capability of replacing all components of a paper chart (health record) electronically.

Because EMR programs are new and complex, most still have their share of glitches. This is frustrating and expensive for offices that have converted to EMR systems. I have seen medical groups buy and discard entire systems because they did not meet their expectations or had too many operational glitches or inadequate vendor support.

A software program that supports EMR is, in most cases, an extension of the scheduling and billing software. In other words, the software components are created, integrated, and sold as one system. Some vendors do have separate EMR systems and scheduling/billing systems that are able to connect and work together. For example, you could purchase an office scheduling system from The Scheduling Expert and buy an EMR system from Records to Go, thus running two separate systems together. Currently, it is recommended that a provider purchase a system that has both scheduling and EMR units built into one system. A single system seems to have fewer problems.

In terms of storing information, vendors will offer two options. A *local solution* stores the health information onsite in your office or clinic. With a local solution, it is the responsibility of the staff or the physician to back up the health information and keep it secure.

The other option is a *central solution*, where information is hosted remotely by an application service provider (ASP). The provider retrieves and stores all of the health information for patients in an offsite location. The vendor ensures that the information is backed up regularly and kept secure. It is also the vendor's responsibility to archive electronic files that are no longer of use.

All EMR systems must offer the following functions:

- An audit trail[1]
- The ability to allow providers to sign off on entries and prescriptions using electronic signatures
- The means to regularly save and back up data
- Effective protocols for information recovery

Creating an EMR System

The health record, regardless of its storage medium, has a predictable cycle: retrieval of information, storage and management of the information, and archiving the information when it is no longer useful. Components of a paper medical chart, as well as its life cycle, are discussed in more detail later in this chapter.

To create a complete EMR system in a doctor's office, the basic information required includes a patient's demographic information, medical history (PH), social and family history, functional inquiry (FI), history of present illness (HPI), diagnosis (Dx), and problem list, medication list, and allergies, if any.

To demonstrate this, consider Mr. Smith and his first appointment with Dr. Ryder, a family physician. Mr. Smith calls Sarah, the receptionist, at the office one Monday morning to make his initial appointment. Sarah asks Mr. Smith the reason he wants to see the doctor. It is for an annual physical, but he also states he has a sore back. With this information, Sarah is able to determine the urgency of the visit as well as the length of time Mr. Smith will need to spend with the doctor. Sarah asks Mr. Smith to bring a summary of his medical history from his previous doctor when he arrives for his appointment the following Tuesday. Sarah records the appointment information in Dr. Ryder's electronic scheduler; this action marks the initial retrieval and documentation of Mr. Smith's health information.

When Mr. Smith arrives next Tuesday, Sarah obtains his demographic information to initiate a computer database. As well, she needs his health number and other insurance information for billing purposes. The demographic portion of Mr. Smith's EMR is now complete.

The next step is to obtain Mr. Smith's health history. In a health office, this may be your responsibility or the nurse's—probably by interviewing the patient. Alternatively, the questionnaire may be completed by Mr. Smith himself, then scanned and attached to his EMR. In this example, the nurse, Alia, retrieves the information from Mr. Smith by direct questioning and enters it into the computer as he answers the questions. This information is filed in his EMR under patient or patient history and becomes part of his health information documents.

On her software, Dr. Ryder has chosen a template specifically designed for physical examinations. The template contains fields for all required elements of a complete physical examination (CPX). The doctor completes a thorough investigation of Mr. Smith's problems and a physical examination, addressing all of the elements discussed earlier. She specifically asks Mr. Smith about the sore back (HPI). Dr. Ryder determines that Mr. Smith has muscle strain but prescribes no treatment. Mr. Smith's physical reveals some osteoarthritis of his lower limbs and mild hypertension. This information is added to Mr. Smith's EMR. His vital signs are taken and become part of a *flow sheet* that will track and graph future vital signs. His past medical records show

---

[1]An audit trail is necessary to track all activity within the EMR computer system. Unauthorized entry attempts can be tracked, as can the activities of all users, holding them accountable for any irresponsible/illegal breach of security policies. As well, all data entered can be tracked and retrieved. A computer system can have several types of audit trails.

that he is borderline diabetic but controls it through diet. The visit itself becomes part of Mr. Smith's *encounter record*. Medications Mr. Smith takes are added to his *medication profile*—in this case, "calcium 500 mg tid" and "Actonel 5 mg od."

His *problem list* now contains the diagnosis of back strain, essential hypertension, osteoarthritis, and type II diabetes. Mr. Smith is allergic to penicillin. This is added to the *allergy alert* portion of his EMR. The doctor orders a CBC, FBS, cholesterol and triglyceride levels, and electrolytes. He also orders an X-ray of Mr. Smith's lumbar spine and lower extremities. When the lab sends back these test results, you will add them to the *lab and diagnostic tests* portion of his EMR. They may be sent electronically or as hard copy.

In the coming week, Alia loads all of the essential information from Mr. Smith's transferred health information, thus completing his EMR. You now have a basic electronic chart with the first physician encounter documented and entered directly into the computer.

Managing an EMR System

The paperless office is a myth. However, properly managed, there can be a significant reduction in paper use. The freed-up space available after paper charts are destroyed or removed from the office is, in itself, an advantage.

Rapid Access to Information   Accessing information in electronic format is easy and efficient. Dr. Ryder's office calls requesting the reports from Mr. Smith's recent diagnostic imaging. It takes seconds to load the chart, locate the images, and send them electronically to Dr. Ryder's office (provided the office has the connectivity capabilities to exchange with other providers). Consider a patient calling your office to find out about lab results. Instead of first locating and then shuffling through a paper chart to find the lab section, you simply key in the patient's name, electronically open the chart, click on the lab section, and view the latest results.

Documenting Patient Information   When Mr. Smith arrives for his next appointment, the administrative health professional (AHP) or the nurse can obtain his vital signs and chief complaint and enter them into the appropriate field in the encounter window in his chart. You can also add alert notes or highlight recently returned lab tests that you want to bring to the doctor's attention. This can all be done from any workstation, including the computer in the front office. The doctor can immediately view this entry from a wireless tablet or a computer and be prepared with the required information before entering the examination room.

Follow-Up Tests and Appointments   After completing her assessments, the doctor can enter any lab or diagnostic requests and transfer them to you. You can follow up and be ready with any required information by the time the patient is dressed and out of the examination room. The doctor can also send a message requesting any follow-up appointments, which you can immediately schedule.

In most regions, at least some labs provide their results electronically, eliminating the necessity for you to scan the results into the system and store them on the patient's EMR.

L04 ELECTRONIC HEALTH INFORMATION IN THE DOCTOR'S OFFICE

Conversion to EMR is expensive and time consuming. As well, many doctors are not fully comfortable with the use of this technology. They find security in the paper chart—the ability to see it, hold it, and record on it. The information is there and always retrievable, even if the computer system is down. Slowly but surely, however, medical offices are converting to EMRs. Because you are part of this progression, it is helpful to understand the process.

Data Entry in the EMR

Clinical records are usually classified as either *open text* or *fully structured*. Open text allows the provider to document much as he or she did on the paper chart. The provider records findings on a blank page and can use templates to keep the charting orderly and reduce repetitive entries; for example, there is a template for SOAP charting (subjective, objective, assessment, and plan). One disadvantage of open text is that it holds information as it is entered and does not lend itself to summarizing patient health information into categories. For example, you could not pull all a patient's blood work together, or send blood pressures into separate flow sheets or summary databases.

Fully structured is the other extreme and is highly regimented. It requires that patient information be entered into defined data fields. It is, perhaps, more time consuming in terms of determining what to put where and in entering infinite detail that many doctors feel is unnecessary. However, this design does lend itself to effortlessly assimilating material into easily accessible summaries.

Most users prefer a mix of the open text and the fully structured format. For example, it may be more effective to use open text to record the patient's chief complaint and history of present illness and related documentation, and use the structured format to record lab data, medications, and vital signs.

Every software system will be somewhat different. For example, the names of the parts of the EMR may vary, available templates will be different, and the appearance of the screens will be different.

Security and the EMR

Each medical practice must identify in writing the level of access by any authorized person using the EMR system. The usual rules for protecting any computerized information apply: protecting the screen from unauthorized viewers, using and updating passwords regularly, and never allowing anyone else to use your password. Passwords should be hard to guess and should contain a combination of alphanumeric characters. Some practices also incorporate **fobs,** or authentication tokens, thus implementing a two-step ID process. As well, it is necessary to have audit logging to record the actions of all users.

fob a small security device that can be added to a computer for access purposes. It displays a randomly generated access code that changes every few seconds.

If a provider has computers in an examination room or other areas where a patient (or anyone else) has access, it must be electronically "locked down" to prevent unauthorized access.

Because offices using EMR and EHR systems are connected to the internet, it is essential to have an effective firewall. This will provide protection against illegal attempts to access your computer system. Antivirus software is also a must. Moreover, strategies to deal with system failures and lost data are imperative. As previously mentioned, with a local solution you are responsible for backing up and securing system data. Imagine having to reconstruct all of your patients' medical records! You would have to rescan all of the data from the old paper charts and (somehow) try to find sources for information you have lost. Much of it would be irretrievable.

Backup systems store encrypted copies of medical records; backups should be performed daily. The information should be stored on a disk or portable hard drive off the premises in case of a fire, theft, or other disaster.

Use of Portable Computers and Devices

Many offices have a combination of desktop and laptop or other portable devices. If the office has a wireless system, ensure that the system is appropriately encrypted. If the office staff or physicians use laptops containing health information at home, it is essential to follow through with security procedures. Never leave the computer unattended unless it is locked down or turned off. It's easy to be a little more relaxed in the home environment. However, it's better to be safe than sorry. Following security protocol is also a sensible habit to develop—with no exceptions.

Acquisition of New Computers

When a health office acquires new computers, the information on the existing computer must be professionally destroyed to ensure that the information is permanently removed. Most vendors will provide this service. Moreover, physician groups usually have a team of IT experts capable of removing this information.

Implications for the Staff

Training Any vendor who sells an EMR system should be responsible for training the users. If you are involved in starting up an EMR system, this training is essential and usually requires several sessions. It is expensive and frequently not included in the purchase price of the system. Your employer will cover the cost.

The sessions can be conducted onsite (in the office) or offsite. If the vendor is selling the system to a group of doctors (e.g., a primary care reform group), there will be a significant number of individuals to train—staff and providers. An offsite venue allows the vendor to rent a facility where trainers can set up multiple computer stations to accommodate everyone. Usually once training is completed, the trainers will make appointments for further onsite and hands-on instruction.

Transition from Paper Charts to EMR Format Medical offices that convert to EMR must make a decision about what process they will use to move information from paper charts to electronic format. Special attention must be made to address the security of the information to ensure its safety and confidentiality. The office may decide to scan all or parts of the paper chart as PDFs, or start entering health information from the first day of their EMR implementation. Rules governing how long paper charts must be kept depend on the conversion process. If a patient's entire chart is uploaded, the paper version is redundant. However, most Colleges of Physicians and Surgeons across Canada recommend keeping the paper version for at least six months. If chart content is summarized and scanned or preloaded, the patient's paper chart must be kept in accordance with provincial or territorial regulations. This is indefinitely if the person remains an active patient. Doctors must ensure that all clinical information is available (electronic, paper, or a combination) for the duration of the legal chart retention period. Charts that can be destroyed should be shredded. Companies that specialize in paper shredding will come onsite to do this. It is advisable that office staff supervise the process.

Converting Paper Charts to EMRs and Purging The process of converting pCharts to EMRs is time consuming and tedious and requires that informed decisions be made about what to keep and what to eliminate. The process requires someone (usually the doctor) to go through each page in the chart and extract all essential information for uploading to the patient's "new" EMR. In a general practice, some charts will be several centimetres thick, particularly if they have not been regularly **purged**. It is both unnecessary and impractical to consider scanning an entire chart. Most pCharts contain duplicate, old, and superfluous information. Usually, only vital information from a patient's chart is scanned (e.g., important elements of the patient's history, lab and diagnostic reports, medications, latest medical profile). Elements of the patient's chart that are lengthy can be reviewed and summarized by the

purge (of file) review and reorganize to remove outdated information that is no longer actively needed to provide care to the patient.

physician and uploaded into the EMR (e.g., operating room and consultation reports, interviews/discussions, old histories).

As an AHP, your responsibilities will likely include preloading the chart—that is, entering demographic information and creating the basic EMR. Once the EMR has been created, you can begin scanning the patient's medical information (as provided by the physician) into the chart and filing it in the appropriate locations within the chart. There may be situations wherein an AHP is asked to assume more responsibilities with respect to purging a pChart, for example, reviewing lab reports and discarding older ones, or updating a medication list. Purging a chart also involves getting rid of information in the chart deemed no longer needed. These records are confidential and must be destroyed according to protocol (shredding is the usual method).

Once the EMR system itself is functional, some doctors and AHPs find it easiest to start uploading a patient's new electronic chart when he or she comes into the office. At that point, the old chart is summarized and either scanned or preloaded. The process of converting a practice of perhaps 2000 patients takes an enormous amount of time. On average, the task takes a year or more, depending on the resources and time assigned to the process.

L05 THE PATIENT'S CHART

Although a single document is sometimes called a chart, generally a chart refers to a folder containing all the records relating to a patient's care with a provider or facility. As previously mentioned, the electronic counterpart of this is the electronic medical record.

A patient's paper chart, like the EMR, originates when the patient first seeks care with the provider. The creation of an EMR was outlined in the example of Mr. Smith's encounter with Dr. Ryder. In terms of creating a paper chart, it can be prepared in advance of the first appointment. The appropriate folder may be selected and the patient's name (or numeric identifier) added. As well, a blank form for recording patient encounters, a blank cumulative patient profile, and a history and physical form can be added. Having some generic charts made up ahead saves time. The minute the patient has his or her first contact with the health care provider, the provider must begin keeping records and the empty folder becomes a patient chart. The paper chart will continue as long as the patient comes to the provider or until the provider converts the chart to EMR format.

Components of a Chart

The format, design, and organization of a patient's medical chart will differ with each provider and each agency, but there are common elements. In the electronic setting, the format of the EMR will vary with the type and design of the software.

1. The chart must contain the patient's name, address, birth date, and health card number. In the electronic environment, this is part of the patient's database and can be electronically transferred to any electronic documents.

2. The chart must be kept neat, accurate, and complete. With a pChart, keeping it neat entails purging the chart regularly—discarding duplicate information (e.g., lab results) and irrelevant documents. With the EMR, this is done by deleting extraneous information. (Make sure none of the information is legally required for audit purposes.) An advantage to the EMR is legibility of entries. As well, documentation is entered into required fields; thus, good organization is a product of the software.

3. Each encounter and service rendered must be entered into the chart with the appropriate date.

4. Each recorded encounter must contain the relevant history obtained, details of the medical examination rendered, documentation of any investigations ordered by the doctor, and results of those investigations, when available. All advice given to a patient and the particulars of any referral must also be entered on the encounter record.

5. The chart must be safely and properly stored.

6. The charts must be kept confidential in accordance with provincial or territorial legal guidelines. Governing bodies of health care providers also have guidelines.

pCharts and electronic charts (the EMR) contain the same basic information. The appearance and order of the information will vary. In the EMR you simply scroll to access different parts of the EMR or enter various parts of the chart using pneumonics. The patient's chart in a doctor's office will vary, but most charts contain the same or similar records,

History (Interview) Sheet   This is a questionnaire that the patient is asked to fill out, usually on the first visit to the provider's office (see Chapter 9). Usually, someone (the doctor, the nurse, or the AHP) will help the patient fill out the sheet or review it with him or her. In some offices the questionnaire is filled out using a tablet. If the questionnaire is paper based you would (as with all relevant paper documents) scan it into the patient's EMR.

Cumulative Patient Profile (CPP)   The paper chart version of a cumulative profile, shown in Figure 13.1, starts with the answers to the history questionnaire and is updated periodically to provide a cumulative view of the patient's history and current health status. It is often kept at the very front or back of the chart. The CPP may require special attention from a nonphysician provider who likely sees the patient less frequently. Figure 13.2 is an example of an electronic CPP for Melissa Sweet. It profiles almost every component of her health history, including her health problems over the previous five visits and her drug allergies/reactions profile.

List of Allergies   The patient's allergies will appear on the history sheet but should also be listed in a prominent place at the front of the chart, either on the outside or the inside cover. It is helpful to note allergies in red. Some practices list allergies on each progress sheet as well. With the EMR, these allergies can be noted as an "Alert" on the computer system, popping up as soon as you swipe the patient's health card or access the EMR. Depending on the database, some systems will automatically notify the provider if he or she writes a prescription electronically that the patient is allergic to.

Encounter Record   This documentation occurs each time the patient has an encounter with the health care provider. With paper charts, the doctor must either take time between seeing patients to complete documentation, or trust his or her memory and document later in the day. Charting encounters at the end of the day can result in errors or lapses in memory: "Let's see—was Mr. Smith here about a sore back, or was that Mr. Slithers?" In the EMR environment, the physician can document as he or she completes a patient's assessment, using a computer in the examination room or a portable device, often as he or she is interacting with the patient. However, some patients complain that the doctor spends more time entering data than talking with them.

In a doctor's office, the physician is the primary user of an encounter record. Nurses and other staff members (if trained to do so) may make entries related to telephone calls, test results telephoned to the office, and appointments (e.g., repetitive broken appointments or no-shows). If you notice that documentation is absent from the encounter record of a patient the provider has seen, flag it, leave a note, or ask the doctor personally.

In a paper chart, the most current progress sheets should be at the front of the stack. Add a blank sheet to the chart when the current one is approximately two-thirds full. In an EMR setting, the order of encounter entry is up to the provider's preference.

History and Cumulative Profile

Home Phone

ID # or File #

Health Card Number   Version

Present Marital Status   Sex   Date of Birth
S M Sep. D W Other   M   F   D   M   Y

| | | | | | | | | | | | | | | | |

2. PERSONAL AND FAMILY
(e.g., occupation, life events, habits) | Dates

3. PAST HISTORY (e.g., past serious illnesses, operations)
RISK FACTORS (e.g., genetics/familial diseases) | Dates

4. ALLERGIES/DRUG REACTIONS | Dates

5. DATES OF: ↓
Initial Visit | General Assessment → | |
| Summarized Record on CPP → |

| Codes/ Nos. | 6. ONGOING HEALTH CONDITIONS (e.g., problems, diagnoses, dates of onset) | Date Recorded | Date Co |

| Codes/ Nos. | 7. LONG-TERM TREATMENT REG. (e.g., medications, dosage/frequency) | Date Started | Date Discont. |

8. CONSULTANTS

Figure 13.1 Patient cumulative profile, paper chart

In EMR format, the encounter screen is entered by clicking on an icon—sometimes simply called "patient visit." Once on the screen, you can choose among several preset templates, such as one for a complete physical examination, another for a prenatal visit, or one for a regular encounter. You can also select a documentation template; for example, SOAP charting is commonly used for patient visits:

- **S** means subjective and refers to anything the patient says to describe the problem: "I feel weak and tired. I have a headache."

- **O** stands for objective and is what the examiner sees. Perhaps the patient is flushed, or bent over with pain, or has a swollen hand.

- **A** refers to the examiner's assessment. It is what he or she elicits from the examination, and his or her diagnosis.

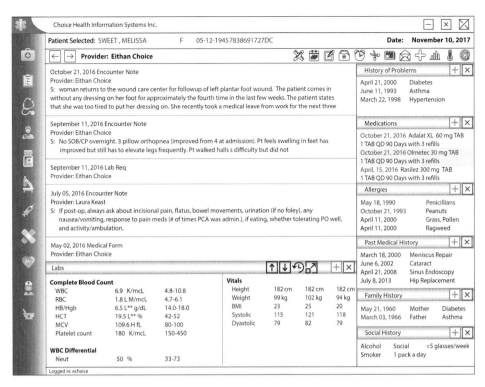

Figure 13.2 Cumulative profile and health history in an EMR

Used by permission of Choice Learning, Inc.

- **P** is the examiner's plan for the patient. He or she might put the patient on an antibiotic or pain medication, or send the patient to a dietitian, for example.

Figure 13.3 and Figure 13.4 illustrate an EMR template using SOAP charting. Figure 13.3 is a blank template; Figure 13.4 is the same template illustrated as it relates to a well-baby visit.

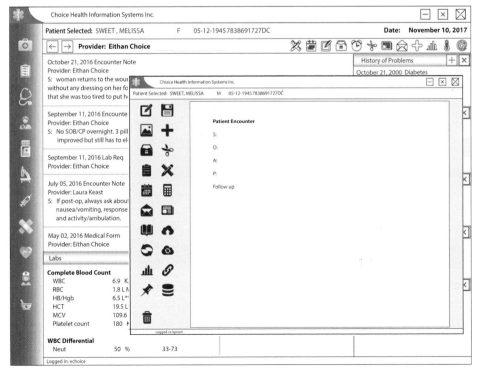

Figure 13.3 A blank EMR SOAP template, with health information on the right

Used by permission of Choice Learning, Inc.

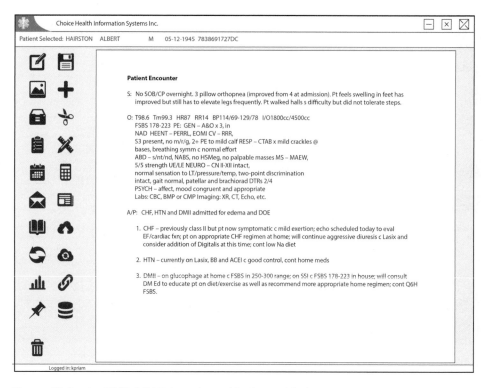

Figure 13.4 An EMR SOAP template with data added

Used by permission of Choice Learning, Inc.

Physical Assessment   The physical assessment sheet may be formally prepared, as shown in Figure 13.5, or just noted on the progress notes. The doctor should take full notes every time the patient has a complete examination, whether annual or symptom-driven. Figure 13.6a and Figure 13.6b show a complete physical assessment using an EMR.

Lab and Diagnostic Tests   As discussed in Chapter 6, you will get reports from patients' diagnostic tests, as well as hematology, microbiology, and biopsy results. Some lab requisitions are used for several types of lab tests, which reduces the number of reports on a chart. If you receive results online, print out a hard copy to keep in the file. Some lab reports are cumulative, including earlier test results. If so, discard earlier reports that merely duplicate the same test results. Keep test results together, with the most current on top.

Some labs have the capability to send results electronically; others still fax or send reports by courier. In some jurisdictions, electronic results are sometimes received piecemeal at different times. This makes them time consuming to read and summarize for the EMR. If results come in paper format, you have the option of scanning the reports for electronic storage, or simply adding them to the computer. If the latter, be very sure that you accurately transcribe the results. When you are rushed, mistakes are easy to make—an incorrectly placed decimal point or transposed numbers can result in serious errors.

Operative Reports   Any surgical procedure will generate a report. Keep these and related reports together, the most current on top.

Consultation Reports/Letters   Consultation reports include initial contact letters, reports on assessment, and progress or follow-up reports. Keep these in the chart along with a copy of any letters sent to the patient. Many of these reports are faxed and may have to be scanned into an EMR for electronic storage.

DR. D THOMPSON
FAMILY MEDICINE
IMMUNIZATION & PHYSICAL EXAMINATION RECORD

Name: _____   Date of Birth: _____

PHYSICAL EXAMINATION

N-Normal   / Please state defects

Height Weight	Vision	O.D. 20/	O.S. 20/
Eyes	W/ Correction:	O.D. 20/	O.S. 20/
E	Right		Left
Abdomen			
Extremities			
Cardiovascular			
Gastrointestinal	Genitals		
Respiratory			
Nervous System			
Genitourinary	Reproductive		
Nutrition	Skin		
Posture			
Thyroid	Other Glands		
Tonsils	Adenoids		
Allergies Specify:			

Comments

Examination Date: _____   **Physician's Signature:** _____

Figure 13.5 Physical assessment form—paper

| Patient Name: **Jamie Sweet** | D.O.B.: **21/10/1975** | Sex: **F** | Age: **30** |

Patient Name: **Jamie Sweet** D.O.B.: **21/10/1975** Sex: **F** Age: **30**
Ht.: 174 cm Wt.: 59 kg BMI: 19.5 Temp.: 36.1 C Resp.:

System	Notes
☐ **SKIN** Mark and describe lesions if present	

☐ **HEAD, NECK** inspect, palpate (symmetry, lumps, tenderness)
☐ hair, scalp (loss, texture, lesions)
☐ palpate frontal, maxillary sinuses (transilluminate if tender)
☐ TMJ (click, deviation)
☐ thyroid (palpate), swallow (CN 9,10)
    nodes (submental, submandib, tonsilar, preauric, post.auric,
    occipital superficial c, deep c, post c, supraclavic, infraclavic)
☐ light touch temples, cheeks, chin (CN 5)
☐ clench (palpate muscles) (CN 5)
☐ facial expression (show teeth, frown, puff cheeks, squint) (CN 7)
☐ shrug, turn head (CN 11)	

☐ **EYES** inspect (level, brows, lashes, discharge, colour, edema ☐ inspect sclera, cornea (with light) pupils, conjunctivae ☐ acuity (with corrective lenses) (CN 2) ☐ visual fields (CN 2) ☐ eye movements (including nystagmus, convergence, accommodation reaction) (CN 3,4,6) ☐ pupillary reflex (direct and consensual) (CN 3) ☐ fundoscopy (ed reflex, retina, vessels, macula, optic disc)(CN 4)	
☐ **NOSE** general inspect and palpate (symmetry, lumps, tenderness) ☐ mucosa (with light)(colour, vessels, hair, septum, polyps) ☐ patency ☐ acuity (CN 1)	
☐ **MOUTH** general inspect (lips, gums, teeth, mucosa, glands) ☐ inspect tonsils, pharynx ☐ inspect tongue (extend) (CN 12) ☐ TCM (below) "Ahh" gag reflex (uvula deviation) (CN 9, 10)	
☐ **EARS** general inspect (dryness, eczema, creases) ☐ palpate (including pulling, tragus) ☐ acuity(finger rub, Weber, (lateralization), Rinne (AC vs.BC)(CN8) ☐ otoscopy (pull up, back out) (canal, disch, wax, TM COL (ant- infer)	
☐ **THORAX, LUNGS** general inspect (symmetry, skin, colour) ☐ fremitus ("99")(3 medial, 1 lateral) ☐ expansion (at lower ribs) ☐ percussion (5 medial, 2 lateral) ☐ excursion (diaphragm level change) ☐ auscultation (breathe through mouth) (5 med, 2 lat, include mid. lobe) ☐ kidney punch	

Figure 13.6a   Physical assessment form (page 1)—EMR

☐ **CHEST, ABDOMEN**
☐ percuss lungs (4 medial, 2 lateral)
☐ auscultate lungs (4 medial, 2 lateral)
☐ popliteal, dorsalis pedis, posterior tibial pulses
☐ general inspection (edema lower limbs, symmetry, skin colour)
☐ auscultate carotids, thyroid
☐ auscultate heart (bell and diaphragm)(aortic 2R, pulmonic 2L, tricuspid 4L, mitral 5L, MCL, Erb's 3L)
☐ auscultate arteries (arota, renals, iliacs, femorals)
☐ auscultate quadrants, liver
☐ percuss abdomen, liver borders, spleen borders
☐ palpate axillary nodes (central, lat, pectoral subscap, infraclavic)
☐ palpate (light and deep)(general, rebound, LV, KI, SP); inguinal nodes
☐ abdominal reflex (V sup (T 8,9,10), inf(T 10, 11, 12) umbilicus
☐ breast exam (below)
☐ orthostatic BP

☐ **MUSCULOSKELETAL, NEUROLOGICAL**
☐ nails, skin on hands (including capillary refill)
☐ ROM neck (flex, extend, lateral flex, rotate), shoulder (flex, extend, abduct, adduct, rotate)
☐ elbow (flex, extend, rotate), knee (flex, extend), ankle (dorsiflex, plantarflex) hand strength (grip) hip strength (flex)
☐ DTR's (biceps C5, triceps C7, brachioradialis C6, patellar L4, achilles L 3,4 plantar L5, S1)
☐ toe proprioception (identify up, down) (peripheral nerve)
☐ graphesthesia (sensory cortex)
☐ pain (sharp / dull) (forearm, shin)(increased, decreased, absent)
☐ vibration (thumb, great toe), (peripheral neuropathy)
☐ coordination (thumb, to fingers), (touch finger/ touch nose) (Standing)
☐ walking (gait, pattern, balance)
☐ walk heel to toe (ataxia)
☐ walk on heels, toes (UMN)
☐ shallow knee bend (weakness)

BREAST   general inspect arms at side, over head, hands pressed against hips, leaning forward (colour, size, symmetry, contour, dimpling)
☐ light , medium, deep, palpation (including tail)
☐ nipple (flattening, retraction, discharge)

☐ **PROSTATE**   palpate (tenderness, sulcus, size, symmetry, texture, masses

Figure 13.6b   Physical assessment form (page 2)—EMR

Miscellaneous All children's charts should include growth charts. These, along with prenatal or antenatal records and labour and delivery records, are frequently filed after the progress notes. Electronically, the data appear on a flow sheet as well as on the encounter record. In most provinces and territories, the EMR contains flow sheets that focus on a specific condition, perhaps related lab values and treatments. An example of a diabetic flow sheet from an EMR is illustrated in Figure 13.7. This diabetic management flow sheet tracks the patient's diabetic education, glucose self-monitoring, diet, physical activity, and blood work. This sheet would likely become part of the patient's EHR as well. For example, if the patient was in an emergency department hundreds of kilometres from home in a diabetic coma, the doctors could electronically access this sheet and make informed treatment choices for him or her.

Type of diabetes: ☐ Type 1 ☐ Type 2 ☐ Gestation			Patient Information		
Risk factors, Co-morbidities ☐ CAD ☐ Neuropathy ☐ Mental health ☐ PAD ☐ ED ☐ PCOS ☐ CVD ☐ Hypertension ☐ HIV ☐ CKD ☐ Dyslipidemia ☐ 2° cause ☐ Retinopathy ☐ Smoking (Date stopped: _____)		**Vaccinations** Flu (annual): _____ (date) Pneumococcus (once, repeat if age >65): _____ (date)	Name: _____ DOB: _____ HCN: _____		
Date of Diagnosis:		Date	Date		Date
GLYCEMIA					
A1C: Target ≤7% or _____					
Hypoglycemia					
Driving counselling					
SMBG (if applicable): Pre-prandial: 4-7 • 2-hr post-prandial: 5-10		B L D	B L D		B L D
Glucose meter/lab comparison (annual)					
BP (target <130/80)					
CHOLESTEROL					
LDL-C					
HDL-C					
TG					
Non-HDL-C					
ApoB					
NEPHROPATHY					
ACR					
eGFR					
RETINOPATHY					
NEUROPATHY					
Foot exam (annual; each visit if abnormal)	☐ sensation ☐ pulses ☐ lesions	☐ sensation ☐ pulses ☐ lesions	☐ sensation ☐ pulses ☐ lesions		☐ sensation ☐ pulses ☐ lesions
Other (ED, GI)	☐ no symptoms ☐ symptoms:	☐ no symptoms ☐ symptoms:	☐ no symptoms ☐ symptoms:		☐ no symptoms ☐ symptoms:
CAD/PAD/CVD					
Symptoms	☐ no symptoms ☐ symptoms:	☐ no symptoms ☐ symptoms:	☐ no symptoms ☐ symptoms:		☐ no symptoms ☐ symptoms:
ECG: baseline & q2 years if indicated	Date:	Result:			
Statin	☐ if ≥40 yrs; ☐ >30 yrs and >15 yrs duration; or ☐ end organ damage	☐ yes Date assessed: ☐ not indicated ☐ declined			
ACEi/ARB	☐ if >55 yrs; ☐ end organ damage; or ☐ ACR >2.0 (even in the absence of hypertension)	☐ yes Date assessed: ☐ not indicated ☐ declined			
OTHER					
SELF-MANAGEMENT					
Patient Goals					
Barriers to Self-management					
Self-management Education					
Physical activity: Aerobic 150 min/wk • Resistance 2-3 times/wk					
Pre-conception counselling					
Weight/WC					
PLAN					
Medication Changes					
Follow-up					

Figure 13.7 Diabetes flow sheet from an EMR

LO6 LIFE CYCLE OF A RECORD

The life cycle of a health record is the same in both the hospital and the office/clinic environment. In the hospital setting, the various components of the records cycle are more complex and are included in this discussion.

Creation

A patient's record originates when he or she registers for health services from a particular provider. Much like the case of Mr. Smith discussed earlier, the initial retrieval of information marks the initiation of the health record. Specific data include the name, address, telephone number, date of birth, health insurance number, next of kin, insurance information, and employer information. (See Chapters 11 and 12.) Besides generating a paper chart or EMR, the registration process creates a record in the master patient index (MPI), a database of all patients registered with the practice or facility. The creation of a record includes assigning an identifier, which may be the patient's name or a number. Though hospitals create a new chart (electronic or paper) each time the patient is admitted, a doctor's office keeps a cumulative chart (electronic or paper), starting with the first encounter. Hospitals across Canada are at various levels of computerization; thus, charts are, for the most part, a combination of electronic and paper data. In many hospitals, the medication administration records and doctors' orders remain as hard copies.

Maintenance

Records are maintained on the basis of their value, which may be historical, operational, legal, or fiscal. Although the health record is a legal document, its value is primarily operational and historical as it relates to the individual patient. Maintenance includes organizing records through some kind of filing or indexing system so that they are accessible.

Provision

Because of the sensitive nature of health records, distribution of and access to the information are strictly controlled. Policies will generally dictate who may access a patient record, for what purpose, and for how long.

Although the hospital is responsible for protecting patient information, there are situations where health information may be shared or released. A patient, by virtue of his or her admission to the facility, gives implied consent for use of personal health information for a variety of purposes. The hospital can use or disclose patient information for the following reasons:

- Provision of necessary health care for the patient
- Risk management purposes aimed at improving the quality of patient care
- Financial purposes (payment for services, submitting claims to the provincial or territorial health plan)
- Research purposes
- Marketing purposes (this usually requires express consent)
- Teaching and education (particularly in a teaching or university hospital)
- Supplying a religious organization with the patient's name unless specifically requested not to do so by the patient

Individuals who have the right to access the patient's personal information include the following:

- Anyone within the patient's circle of care (at the hospital to which the patient was admitted) and other organizations providing care to the patient
- The Ministry of Health, if such information is required
- The related chief public health officer or a similar designated authority as established under federal law

Unlawful Access   In the computerized environment, particularly in hospitals, individuals with access to EMR systems sometimes purposely and inappropriately view health information belonging to others. In other words, they are not part of a patient's circle of care and have no business looking at his or her chart. Hospital IT systems can track such occurrences, and perpetrators may be suspended or fired. Unlawful access is a serious offence because it violates the law as well as the moral and ethical principles of the health professions.

Paper charts, likewise, are vulnerable to someone walking in and looking at the information. I have seen individuals working for insurance companies or law firms attempt to access a patient's chart. Question anyone you do not recognize who is doing this.

Lock Boxes   In a physician's office, the term *lock box* refers to segments of information within a patient's chart that the patient has specifically asked the doctor to keep confidential—between the patient and the physician. That means that others involved in the patient's circle of care are denied access to this information. If, during the course of the patient's care, the physician feels that this information should be revealed, he or she must first seek the patient's permission. The patient has the right to refuse. However, if the physician determines that not sharing this information may result in harm to the patient, he or she can refuse to continue treating the patient (unless the situation is an emergency). The only exception is information that must be disclosed according to provincial or territorial law.

outguiding a system for keeping track of paper health records taken from their normal location.

Outguiding   Outguiding applies primarily to paper records. In a manual environment, it is frustrating not to find a file when you need it. Patients' charts are more likely to go missing in a hospital, but it can happen in a busy group practice or a doctor's office. Paper charts should never be removed from the premises, and only authorized persons should be allowed access to them.

If you work in an environment where more than one or two individuals may be using a file, make sure that you keep track of who has it and where it is. In a small private practice, this can be done informally; there are only so many places a file could be, and it is easy to check the appointment schedule or look on the physician's desk.

With computerized records, this is not a problem. In larger facilities, the greatest frustration related to accessing electronic chart information is finding a free computer.

Delivery   In private practices, records are kept in a secure location and generally do not move out of the office. In a hospital, records are usually released from health information services only to other areas within the hospital for patient-care purposes; all other requests for access to the record require the authorized requestor to view the record in health information services.

In a paper-based environment, records are generally delivered in hard copy to the intended individual. In an electronic environment, physical control of the *paper* record is replaced by controlling access to the *electronic* record through the use of user names and passwords or some biometric mechanism to uniquely identify the user. In large facilities, users have different levels of access or privileges; for example, patient accounting may display only insurance and billing information. Because electronic records remove the gatekeeper function associated with accessing paper records, access to the EHR must be monitored through the use of audit trails that show what was viewed, by whom, and when.

Disposition

In the hospital environment, as long as a patient is alive and has the potential to seek treatment, a health record remains active and therefore should not be destroyed. However, it is not possible to maintain comprehensive health records from birth to death, especially if the record is paper based. Large physical files simply become too unwieldy, and even large facilities have limited space.

Files must periodically be purged to remove extraneous and duplicate information. Even in an electronic environment, making all components of a patient record immediately available at all times is not an efficient use of resources. At some point, electronic records should be transferred to archival media (see the section later in this chapter on archiving).

Transferring Medical Records   It is the patient's responsibility, not the doctor's, to seek transfer of copies of his or her chart. If a patient requests that you transfer his or her medical records, keep the originals and transfer a copy of the records to the requested destination. Even when the transfer is at the patient's request, you or the physician must receive a signed consent from the patient before the information is transferred. The provider may charge for the costs involved. (See Chapter 12.) The patient must be made aware of any costs involved. Take special care to ensure confidentiality of the information when photocopying or downloading. Keep the pages in order, and count them to ensure that you do not misplace any. With a paper chart, return the pages to the original chart and file the chart appropriately. If the patient has left the practice, file it with your inactive charts. In the case of an EMR, the electronic file can be added to an inactive file vault on an alternative hard drive or other storage device. Give the material for transfer to the patient in a sealed envelope or send it directly to the new provider by a secure method.

Physician Moves and Retirement   If a doctor moves, dies, or retires, charts must be stored properly and kept accessible to patients. If a doctor relocates or retires but maintains his licence, he is responsible for the records for a minimum of 10 years and must ensure patient access, often through a designated custodian. This might be a company whose business it is to store medical charts. If a doctor dies, retires, or gives up her medical licence, she (or her estate) is obligated to keep the charts for only two to six years. The records may be transferred to another provider at the same address and phone number, or patients may be notified that they must, within a specified period (two to six years) collect their medical records or request that they be transferred to another doctor. A physician who is unsure about his or her obligations in a particular situation should contact the Physician Advisory Service of the College of Physicians and Surgeons or the Canadian Medical Protective Association (CMPA). Likewise, most provincial and territorial Colleges of Physicians and Surgeons have an information line for patients concerned about their medical information.

Computerized versus Traditional Systems in a Doctor's Office

Although most physicians' offices and clinics are now computerized and keep electronic patient records, many still maintain traditional filing systems (in addition to EMRs). Those who do have paper charts usually only have older patient records contained therein. It is likely that once computerized, all patient information moving forward is in EMR format. This is primarily because converting to an electronic system takes time, and many doctors do not intend to include everything in a patient's chart in an EMR. For that reason, traditional charts must be kept until they can legally be disposed of. One of the major disadvantages to storing files the traditional way is lack of space. Many physicians' offices in Canada are faced with increased patient loads without a corresponding increase in space to keep their files.

L07 FILING SYSTEMS

If you keep paper health records, you will need some way to identify and locate them.

Identification Systems

Whether records are paper or electronic, each patient is assigned a unique identifier, which may simply be his or her name or may be a number assigned by a person or computer system. In any case, it acts as a reference and differentiates that patient from others in the system. Usually, the identifier is assigned when a patient first seeks services from a provider or facility, is associated with the chart, and remains the same as long as the patient continues with the provider or facility. A small practice may choose to use the patient's name (last name, first initial, second initial) as the identifier. In a family practice, where more than one member of a family may carry the same last and first names, another variable, such as date of birth, may be incorporated into the identifier.

Larger offices and hospitals generally use a numbering system. The numbering system may be based on some piece of patient-specific data, such as birth date. Or it may be a serial number assigned to the next new patient, either from a manual log, known as the *master number control*, or computer generated. In a family practice, often the identification system ties the family members to the same number; the whole family's records may be filed as a unit or may be kept next to each other.

Organization of Files   In physical filing systems, files are usually organized on the basis of the identifier. Most practices that use traditional paper-based charts use fairly straightforward filing systems. To those familiar with a highly sophisticated health information environment, some of these methods may seem somewhat archaic. However, they do work, and they are relatively commonplace. The methods used for chart identification and retrieval reflect those choices discussed earlier.

Alphabetical   Alphabetical filing is one of the oldest and most straightforward systems. Alphabetical filing systems do not require an index. They are considered direct access systems because you need only have the patient's name to file or find the record. However, they require the user to be a reasonably good speller.

Using this system, last names are used first, followed by the first name and then the second name, if applicable. Names are filed by the first different letter. For example, Reid comes before Sachs; Sachs comes before Smith; Smith comes before Smyth; Smyth comes before Smythe. Use legal names, not nicknames or short forms; thus, Robert Smith would come after Richard Smith even if Robert is usually called Bob.

Alphabetical order works well if there is no opportunity of misspelling a patient's name. However, even if the patient has been registered with the correct spelling and the record is correctly filed, looking for the name under a misspelling may make it hard to find the record.

To overcome problems with misspelling, some organizations use a filing technique known as *phonetic* or *soundex* filing. This method groups similar-sounding consonants together and removes all vowels. Although this has largely gone out of vogue in paper-based systems because it is complex and not easily learned, computer-based registration systems use algorithms to search for names phonetically. Some systems group all names beginning with Mc and Mac together at the beginning (or at the end) of the M section.

In a family practice, if members of a family have different surnames, charts may be cross-referenced.

Numeric   Numeric filing systems are effective with records that are filed and retrieved by number. Unfortunately, filing systems that are organized by a strict numeric sequence almost always require an index or pointer to the record location. If patient records are asked for by name, you would need an index that would give the number for each name. For this reason, numeric systems that require an index are sometimes called *indirect access systems*.

There are two methods of filing numbered records: consecutive numeric and terminal digit.

Consecutive Numeric   This system files consecutively numbered files or documents in a strict sequential order (i.e., 101, 102, 103, etc.). As an example, medical records 123455, 123456, and 123457 would all be filed side by side. This system is normally used for records that are prenumbered, such as cheques, invoices, vouchers, and purchase orders. This method of filing requires very little training.

Terminal Digit   Terminal-digit filing is a variation of consecutive numeric and was developed to overcome congestion in large filing systems when the most active records are being filed in consecutive order. (This is not usually a concern in an office; these systems are mostly used in large facilities.) Basing the filing sequence on the last few digits of the number disperses the files throughout the system, thus allowing easier access. Terminal digit is particularly valuable when dealing with a long number string. This system segments a number into component parts. As an example, number 123456 could be broken into three segments: 12-34-56. Reading the segments right to left, 56 is the terminal digit, 34 is the secondary digit, and 12 is the primary digit. In this example, the total filing area would be partitioned into 100 filing sections (00–99). Each section would be partitioned into 100 areas, and each area would have room for 100 records. Record 12-34-56 would be filed in section 56, area 34, and would be record 12. Records 11-34-55 and 13-34-57 would be filed immediately before and after record 12-34-56. Middle-digit and primary-digit filing are variations of the terminal-digit sequencing.

Colour Coding   Some practices combine either the alphabetical or numeric method of filing with colour coding. The file folders themselves can be different colours, or you can buy coloured tabs to add to neutral-coloured file folders. Each letter in the alphabet, or each number, may have a specific colour. In a busy office with a large number of charts, colour coding can prevent misfiling (because a misplaced file will stand out) and make it faster to find a chart.

Centralized versus Decentralized Storage

Record storage may be centralized or decentralized. Private practices use a centralized system: All records are stored in one location until they are purged. Hospitals may use centralized, decentralized, or a combination thereof, depending on the facility's policies, size, geographic proximity to treatment areas, record sensitivity, and staff availability.

Centralized   Centralized filing systems designate one location in which to house all records. In a hospital, this is usually health information services. All health information on a particular patient is stored in one physical chart and is located in one department.

Decentralized   Decentralized filing systems allow parts of the patient record to reside in areas outside health information services, although the locations of these parts of the record are available through the MPI. Records that would not be needed for all visits may be stored in specific clinics, such as ophthalmology, audiology, and dental clinics. This can be convenient if the hospital is spread over more than one site. Particularly sensitive records, such as those relating to therapeutic abortion or AIDS, may also be kept in the treatment areas to keep them out of general circulation.

Filing Paper Charts

Regardless of the method of organizing files, most agencies and providers place patients' health information in charts or individual file folders. These are cardboard folders that come in a variety of colours, thicknesses, and finishes. The two most popular sizes are standard and legal. Most facilities use shelves or filing cabinets to store patient files. You are unlikely to be asked to create and manage a new paper filing system, so learning to access, file, and manage existing systems will be required. In most offices, essential components of the patient's chart are scanned into a computer and stored electronically. For new documents (consultation letters, laboratory and diagnostic reports) received in paper format, you would scan them into the computer, ensuring they are filed accurately with the right patient's electronic chart. Paper charts are still kept by many providers and only referred to if information not contained in the electronic chart is required.

Filing Office Forms

Even offices that keep patient records on computer will have some papers to file. For example, every office has a number of blank forms and documents, some of which are used more frequently than others. The most efficient method of filing these is by subject. Variations on this method exist, some of which are very creative. Some systems incorporate alphabetical or alphanumeric sorting and colour coding. For subject filing, it is a good idea to have a broad subject category followed by more specific categories. For example: insurance forms, workers' compensation forms, and government-related insurance forms (e.g., disability forms). Familiarize yourself with the ones commonly used in your office. Many lab forms will be online. Common ones you may be required to complete are for ultrasound, MRI, stools for occult blood, hematology, and biochemistry.

COMPUTERIZED RECORD KEEPING

Computer record-keeping systems must meet certain criteria:

- The system must provide a visual display of the recorded information.
- The system must provide a means of accessing the record of each patient by the patient's name and, if applicable, the health number.
- The system must be capable of printing recorded information promptly.
- The system must be able to visually display and print the recorded information for each patient in chronological order.
- The system must have an audit trail that records the date and time of each entry of data for each patient, it must indicate any changes made in the recorded information, and it must preserve the original content of the recorded information when changed or updated and be capable of being printed separately from the recorded information of each patient.
- The system must provide for security by including a password that provides reasonable protection against unauthorized access.

- The system must automatically back up files and allow the recovery of backed-up files or otherwise provide reasonable protection against loss of, damage to, and inaccessibility of information.[2]

You will usually be responsible for maintaining the files accurately and ensuring that the information is relevant and current. As with paper-based charts, this involves periodically reviewing and deleting obsolete, repetitive, or outdated information.

ARCHIVING

For a number of reasons, files or charts may be **archived**, or removed from current or active use to an inactive status. Charts are *closed* when patients leave the practice for any reason or die. When a patient leaves the practice with your knowledge, you would send a copy of the patient's files to the new doctor. Charts are considered *inactive* when a provider has not seen a patient for a certain period of time but is not sure whether the patient has actually left the practice. The length of this period depends on the type of practice. Some specialists may see a patient only once a year, or only once in a lifetime. Some consider a patient who has not returned within one to three years inactive.

archive removing a file from active status and storing it in a secondary location or on a secondary medium.

Some providers use inactive files to revitalize their patient base. A chiropractor or a dentist, for example, might have the office staff call patients from the inactive list to ask how they are doing; if they are having problems, the staff may suggest that they come in for a reassessment.

All these charts must be stored for a designated length of time. In Ontario, legislation requires that hospitals maintain patient records for 10 years after the date of last contact or, in the case of a child, 10 years after the patient turns 18. Generally, hospitals view this as a minimum requirement and set their own retention schedules.

In Canada, no provincial/territorial or federal privacy legislation states how long health information must be kept. However, the federal government's Personal Information Protection and Electronic Documents Act (PIPEDA) does state that organizations must develop their own minimum and maximum retention periods. Legislation at provincial/territorial and federal levels does hold that personal information is to be destroyed when it is no longer required for functional or legal reasons. Keeping personal and health information longer than required can be done legally only if there is justifiable cause.

Physicians across Canada must turn to their provincial or territorial colleges and medical associations for retention guidelines. The CMPA also has retention recommendations. It is important to note that keeping medical records must also be in compliance with provincial and territorial statutory requirements. Guidelines on the retention of health information are only guidelines and are not legally binding. Some jurisdictions do have legislation for physicians relating to retention. From the date of the last entry, physicians in Quebec must keep the information for a minimum of five years (data relating to genetic testing must be kept for 10 years); in Ontario, 10 years; and in British Columbia, 6 years. Other jurisdictions do not specify.

Provincial or territorial college guidelines and the CMPA recommend keeping a patient's health information for at least 10 years for all jurisdictions. The CMPA also recommends keeping telephone logs, appointment books, and scheduling files for 10 years. The statute of limitations in each jurisdiction affects how long records are kept. In Ontario, the limit is 15 years; thus most practitioners and health organizations keep health information for at least that long.

Records of minors must be kept for 10 years after they reach the age of majority. For patients who have disabilities, or when there is an untoward outcome, it may be prudent to keep records for even longer and, in some cases, indefinitely.

---

[2]Adapted from *The Law and Electronic Medical Records—Ontario Regulation 114/94*, Sections 20 and 21. Copyright © Queen's Printer for Ontario, 2000.

Paper Charts

Health offices using manual filing systems usually store files in their original forms in designated storage areas. Inactive and closed files must be stored securely and kept in proper condition. In the case of paper files, space can be a problem. Paper files are sometimes stored offsite in a secondary location. This may be a specialized company or simply a room in the basement. Depending on the location of the storage area, it may be inconvenient to retrieve data. But for an office with paper records, limited space, and no microfilm reader, there may be no other choice. The archive space should be locked and distribution of keys controlled. Properly stored paper files should stay in excellent physical condition for many years. They must be filed in such a way that they can be retrieved quickly, if needed. They may be filed by the same system used for active files. Some practices store files by year or by range of years (e.g., 1997–2001).

Electronic Health Information

Electronic charts are usually moved to another medium for archiving. For example, you might copy files onto a backup disk and then remove them from your computer's hard drive. Regardless of the medium on which the record is stored, its integrity must be maintained; that is, it must be possible to produce a copy of the original record with all the information intact.

Hospitals and other large facilities will have very old chart information stored on microfiche, microfilm, or CD-ROM. You would likely be involved in retrieving information from those formats only if you work in health information services in a hospital.

L08 PRIVACY, SECURITY, AND CONFIDENTIALITY

The patient health record is a highly sensitive file containing intimate personal information. Anyone handling health records must take care to keep them secure so that unauthorized individuals do not gain access to them. Unlike most records, health records have dual ownership: The provider or facility owns the records themselves, but the patient owns the information. This includes everything contained within the file except correspondence of a medical–legal nature and third-party/independent health examinations. Property owners must develop policies and procedures to ensure that the capture, use, and disclosure of personal health information follow standards of practice and that patients are informed about how their information is being handled.

⟫⟫ POINTS TO PONDER

For the most part, individuals involved in a patient's circle of care are entitled to access information in a patient's chart without the express consent of the patient. A patient can, however, request that his or her health information (or parts of it) be kept strictly confidential (only the primary physician or stated health professional(s) can view it). Some jurisdictions use the term *lock box* to refer to information that is to be kept confidential. Some hospitals may require the patient to fill out a special form to keep information private.

You must be aware of such patient requests in either the hospital or the office setting to ensure the patient's wishes are honoured. Note that there are some legal exceptions to this, for example if the missing information is deemed important to the patient's care.

Charts in a Group Practice

In most group practices, a patient usually sees the same physician, who may be considered the most responsible physician (MRP) for that patient. Usually, the group agrees that the patient's health information belongs to the MRP. If it is not clear who the primary physician is, the group must come to an agreement about chart ownership. It is best to ask the patient whom he or she wishes to be designated as the primary physician.

Transfer of Medical Information

In most cases information may not be disclosed to others without the patient's express consent. The major exception is exchange of information between a referring physician and a consultant or between a physician and a hospital. It is important that all providers have current, relevant information. This eliminates subjecting patients to repeat testing and often allows treatment plans to be formulated more quickly. These exchanges are usually based on implied rather than informed consent. For other transfers of information, the patient must sign a medical records release form first.

One exception is that the Ministry of Health may inspect a physician's medical records. A qualified person designated by the ministry who shows authorization must be allowed access to the charts.

Mandatory Reporting

There are certain circumstances in which medical information must be reported. In Ontario, some statutes that require mandatory reporting are the Highway Traffic Act, the Child and Family Services Act, the Health Protection and Promotion Act, and the Aeronautics Act. Physicians must, for example, report certain communicable diseases that are considered a threat to public health, such as sexually transmitted infections (STIs) and severe acute respiratory syndrome (SARS). Physicians must also report suspected physical or sexual abuse of children. In these cases, patient permission is not required. The Regulated Health Professions Act (RHPA) requires reporting of any misconduct on the part of a health care provider. It is permissible to give medical information to other professionals involved directly in that patient's care.

Minor Patients

There is no minimum age for consent to the disclosure of health information, which can create difficulties for health care providers. In Ontario, the Health Care Consent Act of 1996 recommends that a physician determine the ability of the minor to understand the consequences of the disclosure of health information. If the child is not capable of such understanding, the physician may not disclose without consent of the parent or guardian. There is also no clear statement of the age at which physicians should no longer reveal health information to parents. Physicians must make similar judgments of the minor's ability to understand the health information and its consequences. In practice, once a minor is old enough to visit the doctor alone, most doctors will not share information with parents without the minor's permission.

Patient Access to Charts

Patients have a right to access all information contained in their medical charts. If a patient wishes to view his or her chart, he or she should be supervised to ensure that no information is changed or extracted, which in some situations could have legal consequences. Alternatively, you can give the patient a photocopy, for which you can charge a reasonable fee. A patient may be refused permission to view his or her chart only if the physician deems that the information would be detrimental to the patient's physical, mental, or emotional health or to that of a third party. The physician must be able to defend this decision. Some patients who have no family doctor keep a photocopy of their medical chart from the last provider, presenting it at the emergency department, for example, when they seek health care. This is quite legal, since the information is theirs.

Charts from Hospitals

An individual can get copies of his or her hospital records as well. Most hospitals have clear directions about how to do this online. You must submit a written request accompanied by a signed consent for disclosure of health information form for release of information. However, a family physician, if his or her name is listed on the patient's chart, can request a copy of the patient's records without consent. If the name is not on the chart, then the consent for disclosure form must be completed by the patient. Most facilities charge a fee for chart acquisition; this covers the work and materials involved in preparing the chart (e.g., printing or photocopying from an electronic or paper chart). In many hospitals, some departments keep their own records, such as clinics, physicians' offices that are located in that facility, and sometimes medical imaging. If a person is unable to sign for a chart, an authorization must be issued by the patient's power of attorney for personal care or legal next of kin to request records.

Privacy of Information in Canada

There are currently two privacy laws in Canada: the Privacy Act (implemented in July 1983) and the PIPEDA. The latter was initiated in January 2001 and implemented in three stages, the final of which became law in January 2004.

The Privacy Act concerns departments and agencies within the federal government in terms of outlining obligations, rules, and policies related to the collection, disclosure, and use of personal information. It also gives all Canadians the right to both access and control any personal information the government may have about them.

In addition to national legislation, three provinces, Quebec, Alberta, and British Columbia, have their own private-sector privacy legislation that technically replaces PIPEDA. However, if any information issues cross over the borders of any of these provinces, PIPEDA legislation takes precedence. Thus it is vital that anyone or any organizations involved with the cross-border exchange of information in these provinces are thoroughly familiar with both acts. The flow of information across provincial borders is commonplace given the internet, the national EHR system, and the establishment of businesses in other provinces. Just what privacy legislation applies can sometimes be confusing.

Four provinces have health-specific legislation: Saskatchewan's Health and Information Protection Act (HIPA), Alberta's Health Information Act (HIA), Manitoba's Personal Health Information Act (PHIA), and Ontario's Personal Health Information Protection Act (PHIPA). All of these acts are similar to PIPEDA. They deal specifically with the collection, use, and disclosure of personal *health* information by provincial health care organizations and other approved individuals and agencies.

PIPEDA

PIPEDA outlines how organizations and businesses within the private sector (including all health care agencies, offices, and organizations) can collect, use, or disclose personal information.

Note that the federal government retains the power to provide an exemption to any organization that has its own privacy laws if those laws are deemed equivalent to the federal law.

Rights Afforded to Patients under PIPEDA

■ To know how and why an organization collects, uses, and discloses their personal information

■ To expect the organization to collect, use, and disclose their information reasonably and appropriately and not to use it for any purpose other than that for which it was intended and for which consent was given

■ To have their information protected by security measures

■ To expect the information that is held to be accurate, complete, and current

■ To obtain access to their personal information and ask for corrections, as needed

■ To hold the organization accountable to the Privacy Commissioner of Canada through a formal complaints process for the rights mentioned earlier

See the websites listed at the end of the chapter for more details about these rights.

Ten Principles of PIPEDA

1. *Accountability.* Each office/facility should have a privacy information officer who is ultimately responsible for the compliance of the organization with the standards spelled out in the act.

2. *Identifying Purposes.* You must inform the patients of the purpose for the collection of their information either before or at the time of collection.

3. *Consent.* Consent must be obtained to collect the information.

4. *Limiting Collection of Personal Information.* A clear link must be established between the information that is collected and the reason for doing so.

5. *Limiting Use, Disclosure, and Retention.* You cannot use or disclose any information for purposes other than those for which it was collected; information must be kept only as long as it serves its intended purpose; information must be appropriately stored and destroyed.

6. *Accuracy.* Information should be accurate and complete in terms of how it is recorded to facilitate its proper use.

7. *Safeguards.* The organization must take appropriate and practical measures to protect the information from unauthorized access, use, or tampering.

8. *Openness.* Information about policies relating to the management of personal information must be readily available to the patients.

9. *Individual Access.* With written request to the privacy information officer, patients shall be given access to their personal information. Patients have the right to review and correct any information the organization has about them. When required, the organization must provide the patient with a copy of any personal information requested; if this is not done, the patient must be provided with the reasons why access is denied, subject to the exception set out in Section 9 of the act.

10. *Challenging Compliance.* Each organization must have a process in place to handle complaints with respect to the way personal information is collected, used, or disclosed or the manner in which the organization complies with the legislation.

Personal Information Defined

Personal information includes information that may be considered factual or subjective. The information may be recorded data or data that are orally exchanged about a person who is identified by virtue of the information disclosed.

This includes the following information (in any form):

- *Personal Descriptors.* Includes name, age, place and date of birth, gender, weight, height, eye colour, hair colour, fingerprints

- *Identification Numbers.* Includes health card numbers, social insurance numbers, any personal passwords/numbers, and credit card numbers

- *Ethnicity and Race.* Includes colour and national or ethnic origin

- *Health Information.* Includes medical records and any physical or mental disabilities—essentially anything relating to health status, practices, or history

- *Financial Information.* Includes credit status, loans, purchases, and expenses

- *Employment.* Includes employee files, employment history, evaluations, reference interviews, and disciplinary actions

- *Legal Information.* Includes any recorded interactions with the law, charges, or criminal convictions

- *General Data.* Includes perceived reputation, social or marital status, affiliation with political parties, and educational history

Personal information does not include the name, title, business address, or telephone number of an employee of an organization.

Complaints Process

It is imperative that your organization understand, abide by, and implement the rules and regulations set out by PIPEDA. Any patient who is concerned that his or her right to privacy has been violated may submit a complaint to the Privacy Commissioner of Canada, whose responsibility it is to investigate and resolve complaints. Your organization may be subject to review, reprimand, a fine, or other legal action.

The Consent Form

Each organization must prepare a consent form for all patients to sign. This consent should clearly outline who the privacy information officer is and establish that all health professionals within the organization are cognizant of and will abide by the policies and rules outlined in the act. The consent form should contain detailed, pertinent, clearly stated information regarding what the organization is doing to comply with the act, the reasons why personal information is collected, and how it will be used.

For example, an organization might state that the information is used for the following reasons:

- To competently assess the patient's health care needs

- To establish a diagnosis

- To devise a plan of treatment and care for the patient

- To deliver high-quality, comprehensive care to the patient

- To articulate appropriately to other health professionals the diagnosis and implementation of treatment

- To ensure high-quality, comprehensive follow-up care as necessary

- To initiate and maintain communication with the patient, as required, for direct medical and medically related purposes

- To complete all related third-party insurance forms and related information as designated by law or the patient's needs

I have read and understand the information contained herein. I have no unanswered questions about this information. I understand the purpose for collecting my personal information, the manner in which this information will be used, and the steps this organization is taking to protect and store my information appropriately.

I agree that _____ can collect, use, and disclose personal information about _____ (patient's name, or me) in keeping with the policies of this organization in compliance with the Personal Information Protection and Electronic Documents Act.

_____

Signature of Patient

_____

Printed Name

_____

Date

_____

Witness

We are obliged and will inform you if new purposes arise for the use and disclosure of your personal information, and will seek your approval before such information is disclosed.

- To comply with legal and regulatory requirements involving the patient's chart and health information contained therein in a timely manner according to the provisions set out by the provincial Ministry of Health, the College of Physicians and Surgeons, and the Regulated Health Professions Act
- To process credit card payments
- To collect unpaid accounts
- To comply in general with the law

The patient must also be advised of the implications of signing a consent form. Text such as the following should be included:

By signing this consent form, you have agreed that you understand the information contained herein. You give permission for the collection, use, and, when appropriate, disclosure of your personal information for the purposes outlined in this document. Your information may be assessed by the Ministry of Health and our regulatory body [for example, the College of Physicians and Surgeons of British Columbia, or the Royal College of Dental Surgeons of Ontario], fulfilling its mandate under the RHPA and for the analysis and/or defence of any legal issue. If any unusual requests are received, we will contact you (the patient) for permission to release any information; we will advise you if we feel that the release is inappropriate. At any time you may withdraw your consent for use or disclosure of any and all personal information collected by this organization.

Provincial Health-Related Privacy Acts

As mentioned earlier, four provinces have their own privacy acts related specifically to health care. The shared perception was that PIPEDA was never designed to address the specifics of Canadian's personal health information. Health information is considered by most to be more sensitive, personal, and sacred in terms of who has access to it. According to most health-related acts, health information can only be disclosed by and shared with a health custodian (health providers, health facilities, and others authorized by a health facility). Implied consent is considered and is often valid for the provision of certain types of health care. It is important to note that if there are any conflicts between these provincial acts and PIPEDA, the federal legislation will supersede the provincial legislation unless the provincial act has been deemed similar enough to PIPEDA. In that case, provincial legislation would apply.

Privacy by Design

Another valuable privacy model, entitled Privacy by Design, was developed by Ontario's Information and Privacy Commissioner, Dr. Ann Cavoukian, in the 1990s and is currently recognized as a global standard for privacy. Privacy by Design advocates that privacy policies should be an integral part of anything people use, build, or advocate. How many times have you overheard conversations that you were uncomfortable with, in an insurance office or a lawyer's office, or while waiting for your car to be repaired? Or perhaps worse, have you ever sat in a doctor's office or a diagnostic facility and overheard someone's mammogram results? An exercise at the end of this chapter can provide you with an entirely new perspective on how this concept works. It may well make you think twice about sharing personal information—how and with whom—as well as whether you should publicly discuss something intensely private to another person. Application Exercise 5 in this chapter provides a link to a Privacy by Design exercise as well as its curriculum. This includes PowerPoint presentations that provoke thought and ideas as to what privacy means and how to take steps toward achieving privacy for yourself, others, and your organization.

Forms Management

You will deal with many forms in your work that are used to collect and transmit data. Most of these will come to you preprinted, and you will only need to file them, send them out, and sometimes help patients fill them out. You always need to be aware of what forms you have and when they must be used. A list of forms is helpful.

Sometimes, you may be asked to help develop or revise a form. For example, the physician may want to develop his or her own history questionnaire. Good form design helps you collect the information you need. Poorly designed forms can result in missing or erroneous information and can be time consuming and frustrating to deal with. Clarity is paramount. Make sure questions can be easily understood by the intended user and that they are worded to elicit unambiguous answers. Test the form before printing and using it.

⧉⧉ WHAT TO WATCH FOR

- Continued progress made by the Canada Health Infoway in their efforts to achieve a fully integrated, secure national health records system with the following main operative components:
  a. Point-of-care systems where data can be retrieved
  b. Repositories for storing data
  c. The ability for all systems to work together
- Progressive digitalization of medication profiles, lab tests, and diagnostic imaging.
- Continued growth of EMR usage with triple the number of physicians using EMR in the last seven years.
- Continuous advancement and use of the Panorama public health surveillance module, which now covers 75 percent of the population and provides health practitioners with support and information on immunizations, inventory, and case and outbreak management.

- Progress in providing Canadians with access to online laboratory and diagnostic test results (e.g., LifeLabs in some jurisdictions will give an individual an access code that can be used to log on and view test results). This service is not available in all jurisdictions but is improving quickly. British Columbia has moved ahead of other jurisdictions in providing access to online tests and lab results.
- Development of InfoCentral by the Canada Health Infoway—a new community-based platform that will allow individuals and groups to connect to a variety of stakeholders, allowing them to access information, virtually attend educational seminars, connect with experts, and host meetings.
- Continued solutions to problems with community, provincial/territorial, and national health databases (EHR). Clinicians in most communities still face communication barriers mediated by siloed EMR systems that often do not talk to each other.

SUMMARY

1. Record keeping is a vital component of excellent ongoing health care. Responsibilities related to health information management include the physical management of information systems, ranging from computers to modems and printers. It includes the design and programming of related software. Any person or organization responsible for managing health information is a health information custodian.

2. An electronic medical record (EMR) is a legal health record in digital format. An electronic health record (EHR) is an accumulation of essential information from an individual's electronic medical records that is accessed electronically at different points of service for purposes of patient care. The EHR follows the patient and is available whenever and wherever he or she needs care. The EHR is a compilation of EMRs.

3. Electronic filing offers many benefits. All of a patient's information can be instantly accessible from your desk or the examining room and can be easily integrated with billing software.

4. An electronic medical records system is a total medical office system—hardware and software—with the capabilities of replacing all components of a paper chart and supporting its use in an electronic format. Physicians are able to enter patient information into the EMR system at every encounter, and AHPs and nurses are able to add supplementary information, such as diagnostic test results. Training is required to learn how to use these systems properly.

5. The health record, or patient chart, documents a patient's medical history, treatment, and progress and serves both as a reminder to the provider and as communication with other providers. A patient's chart typically includes a number of forms, such as a history sheet, progress notes, lab reports, reports of assessments, and a summary. The chart must be kept current and accurate. All treatments, tests, and diagnoses must be recorded. Check the chart to make sure the doctor has added the necessary information. Purge duplicate copies.

6. Every record goes through a life cycle, including creation, maintenance, provision, and disposition. A medical chart begins with registration when the patient first comes to the office or facility and becomes inactive when the patient dies or stops coming.

7. Files may be paper based, electronic, or a combination. Charts are commonly identified either by the patient's name or numerically. The identification forms the basis for the filing system. Whatever system is used, absolute accuracy is essential to prevent loss of information. Shelves, vertical or lateral filing cabinets, and rotary cabinets are options for storing paper files. A small storage space for currently pulled files helps prevent them from going missing.

   The disposal of health records is a complex activity bound by legislation. In Ontario, health records must be kept for at least 10 years or, for minors, 10 years after the age of majority. Inactive records may be put in offsite storage (for paper) or on alternative media (for electronic records) but must be secure and retrievable.

8. A patient's record contains personal information and must be kept confidential. Only qualified professionals involved in the patient's care should access or add to a patient's medical record. A patient's health information cannot be released to anyone not directly involved in the patient's care (e.g., a consulting physician) unless the patient signs an authorization for transfer of information or there is an official, legal request for access. The principles and policies outlined in PIPEDA governing patient information must be adhered to. Note that physicians are required to report certain types of information, such as that relating to reportable diseases or suspected child abuse. Paper files should be locked up; computer files should require a password for access.

KEY TERMS

archive   393
electronic health
    record (EHR)   373
electronic medical
    record (EMR)   373

electronic medical records
    systems   373
fob   376
health information   371

health information
    custodian   372
health record   372
outguiding   387
purge   377

REVIEW QUESTIONS

1. Explain the role of the Canada Health Infoway with respect to electronic medical and electronic health records.

2. List 10 uses of the health record, and describe each.

3. What is a unique identifier, and why is it important?

4. Outline the life cycle of a record, defining each stage.

5. Name and describe three methods of filing paper records.

6. When and how may a health record be destroyed?

7. Describe three methods of archiving records.

8. Discuss the ownership of the health record.

9. Define security, privacy, and confidentiality in relation to the patient health record.

10. Who should be given patient information and under what circumstances?

APPLICATION EXERCISES

1. Identify at least six sources where you would find standards for the creation and maintenance of health records. Discuss the impact these guidelines have on the creation and management of health records.

2. Identify five privacy statements published by any facility, organization, or company. Compare those statements with those of the Canadian Standards Association.

3. Develop sample medical records for a private practice. Obtain samples of blank forms from a practice, if possible, and include a description of each component.

4. Four provinces have health-specific privacy legislation: Saskatchewan's Health and Information Protection Act (HIPA), Alberta's Health Information Act (HIA), Manitoba's Personal Health Information Act (PHIA), and Ontario's Personal Health Information Protection Act (PHIPA). Divide the class into small groups. Each group will review one of the four province's health privacy acts and compare the fundamental principles to PIPEDA. Discuss your findings in class. Consider these questions: Are these various acts comparable to PIPEDA? If so how? Where do they differ?

5. a. This activity is meant to stimulate thoughts about how to incorporate privacy into the things you do, your environment, and even your workplace. This Privacy by Design activity should be done in small groups to promote discussion and ideas and facilitate understanding. Before attempting this exercise, review the concepts of what privacy is in this chapter. Privacy by Design is an initiative produced by Ontario's Information and Privacy Commissioner. Access the following website: www.ipc.on.ca/english/Privacy/Introduction-to-PbD. Under Resources—Educational Material, click on Privacy by Design Lesson. Complete the activity provided.

   b. You work in a doctor's office. Your office area is not well protected from the reception area with respect to sound. Conversations you have on the telephone and with patients can be heard by everyone waiting to see the doctor. Discuss what steps you could take to change this, or at the very least minimize having conversations overheard and potentially sensitive information revealed to others.

WEBSITES OF INTEREST

ARMA—The Association of Records Managers and Administrators

www.arma.org

CHIMA—Canadian Health Information Management Association

www.echima.ca

Office of the Privacy Commissioner of Canada

www.priv.gc.ca/index_e.ASP

Rights under PIPEDA Legislation

www.privacysense.net/privacy-rights-pipeda

Privacy Legislation across Canada

www.priv.gc.ca/resource/fs-fi/02_05_d_15_e.asp

Hospital Procedures

Part V of this textbook has been written specifically for programs that include hospital unit administration.

Most hospitals across Canada use a blend of electronic and manual tools to manage the patient-care units. The majority of acute-care hospitals have electronic patient charts (eCharts) and electronically prepared medication records (eMARs), and process orders on the computer. Doctors' orders are still handwritten in many hospitals, while in a growing number of facilities the orders are entered (and for the most part processed) electronically. Computerized physician order entry (CPOE) is among the latest technologies that hospitals are adopting. In the CPOE environment, the emphasis of the responsibilities of the clinical secretary have shifted from order entry to other administrative tasks—no less hectic, just different. Almost all hospitals still have a physical chart for patients—in this text referred to as a paper chart (pChart), including those who have transitioned to CPOE. Patient-care units claiming to be paperless are not entirely so. Thus, it is helpful to know how to manage selected pChart forms and other documents as well as how to integrate components if the eChart with a pChart as required by facility practices and procedures.

Chapter 14 explains the structure and function of various hospital departments and units and the roles and responsibilities of the clinical secretary. Chapter 15 examines the purpose and structure of documents that are common to most hospitals. You will also learn the administrative responsibilities involved with respect to admissions, patient flow initiatives, discharges, and transfers. Chapters 16 to 21 deal with the responsible and complex task called order entry, as well as addressing the variations you will find in the CPOE environment. You will also understand the relevance of each physician order as it pertains to the nurses and the patient (e.g., medications, lab and diagnostic tests, assessments, interventions, patient care). This knowledge is important to have if you want to work as an effective, informed member of the health care team, set priorities, and efficiently organize your administrative responsibilities. In the CPOE environment, although order entry responsibilities are substantially reduced, this knowledge base will prove invaluable as your role expands with respect to communication-related and administrative responsibilities. These chapters will also provide you with an understanding of how a patient-care unit functions within the context of the hospital setting, and how various departments and health professionals (including the clinical secretary) collaborate to maximize patient outcomes.

Chapter 14   The Hospital Setting

Chapter 15   Hospital Documents and Procedures

Chapter 16   Order Entry

Chapter 17   Understanding Intravenous Therapy and Related Orders

Chapter 18   Orders Related to Nutrition

Chapter 19   Orders Related to Digestion and Excretion

Chapter 20   Orders Related to Respiration and Circulation

Chapter 21   Orders Related to Rest and Activity

Chapter 14
The Hospital Setting

Black Star/Alamy Stock Photo

LEARNING OBJECTIVES

On completing this chapter, you will be able to:

1. Discuss health care facilities found across Canada, considering types, organization, and accreditation and restructuring initiatives.

2. Describe the departments found in hospitals, and discuss the purpose of each.

3. Explain the responsibilities of health professionals who work in the hospital setting.

4. Identify the responsibilities of the clinical secretary.

5. Recognize the components of a patient-care unit.

6. Summarize the functions of computers in hospitals.

7. Apply the principles of confidentiality in the hospital environment.

8. Outline your responsibilities when dealing with hospital security policies.

Health care facilities across Canada offer different types and levels of care, from long-term care to acute-care hospitals. A hospital is a health care facility that is licensed by the province or territory to provide a range of health care services on both inpatient and outpatient bases. A hospital's basic functions include the following:

- Providing expert medical, surgical, or psychiatric diagnosis and care
- Preventing disease and promoting health

- Meeting the needs of communities (with input from district/regional health organizations)
- Conducting health-related research and education

This chapter outlines the structure and functions of a hospital, the various hospital departments, and the responsibilities of a clinical secretary. Administrative health professionals in hospitals and clinics may be called *ward clerks* or *health/nursing unit coordinators*, but *clinical secretary* is one of the more common terms, and it will be used throughout this part of the book.

The responsibilities are tremendous, the pace in most areas is fast, and stress is part of the job, yet working in the hospital environment is both exciting and rewarding.

L01 TYPES OF HEALTH CARE FACILITIES

Most health care facilities in Canada are publicly operated and funded by the provincial/territorial or federal government, although some private, for-profit facilities do exist. "Private" does not necessarily mean that patients pay for services. The province or territory may pay private facilities a fee to provide medically necessary services. Patients receiving insured services present their health cards, and doctors performing these services bill the provincial/territorial plan, just as they would in a public hospital. These facilities may also offer uninsured or enhanced services, which patients would pay for (as discussed in Chapter 10).

Most provinces and territories have delegated funding and funding decisions for hospitals to regional health authorities. Decisions made are more reflective of the needs of the hospital and the community together.

Many new hospitals have been built, others have been renovated or have undergone expansion. This work has been done using a "P3" approach. This refers to a public–private partnership—a contractual arrangement wherein a blend of private and public money is used to both build and manage hospitals. The private provider is obliged to deliver a specified level of services under specified terms in exchange for public financing. In British Columbia, for example, an acute-care hospital in Abbotsford (under the Fraser Health Authority) is a P3 arrangement, as is the Academic Ambulatory Care Centre at Vancouver General Hospital. The Alberta government has allowed the construction of private surgical facilities through the passing of Bill 11, the Health Protection Act. These facilities provide selected services that include overnight stays. This is managed through regional health authorities. It is important to emphasize that the clinical functions of *all* Canadian P3 hospitals operate within the public health care system.

There are several classifications of health care facilities, some of which are province or territory specific. The most common are as follows:

- General or acute-care hospitals (may include specialty hospitals, such as the Hospital for Sick Children in Toronto)
- Convalescent hospitals
- Chronic care hospitals
- Nursing homes
- Active treatment/teaching psychiatric hospitals
- Active treatment facilities for alcohol and drug addiction (rehabilitation hospitals, federal hospitals)

General Hospitals

A general hospital provides the community with a variety of services, 24 hours day, seven days a week, ranging from medical/surgical to obstetric and psychiatric services, both on inpatient and outpatient bases. This type of hospital may also be referred to as an acute-care hospital because the majority of hospital beds are designated for those with who require **acute care** (illnesses and conditions that are serious but expected to run a short course). However, they may also have beds designated for chronic care, rehabilitation, palliative care, and respite care. Chronic care beds are usually for short terms, and patients needing long-term care are transferred to a chronic care facility. The kinds and levels of care available vary. Teaching hospitals also provide learning opportunities for medical students.

Hospice

Palliative care can be delivered in a number of different locations or settings, including the hospital, home, long-term care facility, or hospice—the latter becoming a more desirable choice. The purpose of palliative care is to relieve suffering and improve the quality of life for individuals suffering from a life-limiting disease. Palliative care provides the individual with pain relief as well as physical, emotional, and spiritual support delivered by a team of highly trained health professionals. The Canadian Hospice Palliative Care Association estimates that less than 30 percent of Canadians have access to palliative care in a hospice. Across Canada, hospices are only partially funded by government bodies, leaving much of the expense to the community and individuals requiring such services.[1]

> ### ▶▶▶ POINTS TO PONDER
>
> Often patients in hospital or long-term care reach a point when their medical condition is considered life threatening or terminal. Many may not be aware of the services a hospice offers, or where in their community these services are offered. Others may consider a hospice as a place where you go to die, not realizing that the services offered can greatly improve the quality of the patient's life through support and pain control as well as support for the family and loved ones. Be aware of such services in your community and the procedures for referring patients, and have information about services offered on hand for the nurses to give to patients as needed.

Convalescent Hospitals

A convalescent hospital provides recuperative care to individuals who are expected to recover and return to their own homes or to other community placements. A physician and skilled nursing staff are available around the clock.

Chronic Care Facilities

A **chronic care** facility is also referred to as a *continuing care hospital* or *hospital unit* (e.g., chronic complex continuing care, extended care, or auxiliary hospital). It provides continuing, medically complex, or specialized services to those who, because of chronic illness or marked functional disability, require hospitalization but not acute-care services. Services can be provided for extended periods of time or on a short-term basis (e.g., respite care needs).

---

[1]Canadian Hospice Palliative Care Association, "Fact Sheet: Hospice Palliative Care in Canada." www. chpca.net/media/400075/fact_sheet_hpc_in_canada_march_2015_final.pdf.

Nursing Homes

Collectively, nursing homes are also called *long-term care homes*, *residential care facilities*, or, in Manitoba, *personal care homes*. Nursing homes provide continuous nursing and medical care for individuals who cannot be maintained at home and who are chronically ill or incapacitated. They do not, however, have all the facilities of an acute-care hospital. Residents in a nursing home may depend on the staff for such activities as dressing, walking, bathing, and sometimes feeding. (In contrast, retirement homes are essentially housing choices for individuals capable of living independently or in a reasonably independent manner but that may provide a range of supportive services that either are included in the fee or purchased separately.)

Nursing homes may be either publicly or privately funded. Patients at a private facility pay the full cost; for public facilities, government subsidies are available to patients who need them. Some provinces and territories offer an income tax break for patients paying for retirement accommodation. Residents in publicly funded nursing homes can request a private room, but they must pay the difference between standard accommodation (often a four-bed room) and a private room. Many newer nursing homes are offering only semi-private rooms, preferred semi-private rooms (a two-bed room with a partial wall separating the two areas), or private accommodation.

Rehabilitation Hospitals

Rehabilitation hospitals care for people needing professional assistance to restore physical functioning following an illness, injury, or surgery.

Psychiatric Hospitals

A psychiatric hospital provides diagnosis, and intensive and continued clinical therapy for those with a mental illness or who require mental rehabilitation. (Many general hospitals also offer psychiatric inpatient and outpatient services.)

Drug Addiction/Alcoholic Treatment Centres

These facilities can be publicly or privately funded and offer rehabilitative care for those suffering from drug or alcohol addiction. Most facilities have follow-up programs that offer treatment, guidance, and support to patients after discharge.

Federal Hospitals

Federal hospitals are operated throughout Canada by departments of the federal government for the care of special groups of patients, such as the military, veterans, and Indigenous peoples.

Other Types of Facilities

Hospitals may also be categorized by size and type of service offered. A *primary care* hospital offers basic care, including health promotion and prevention of illness. It is mainly community based. A *secondary care* hospital offers specialist services. A *tertiary care* hospital offers highly specialized skills, technology, and support services for patients with acute and chronic illnesses. This type of hospital is usually found in big cities and often takes patients referred from smaller hospitals.

Accreditation of Health Care Facilities

Accreditation is the process by which facilities are granted recognition for meeting certain (preset) standards. For hospitals and other health care facilities, these standards relate to patient care and services. Standards for excellence in health care facilities across Canada are maintained by a periodic assessment of each facility by Accreditation Canada. This organization sets standards of services and care for health establishments as well as providing a system of external peer reviews for these facilities. Accreditation Canada provides benchmark standards that are recognized nationally and internationally (Accreditation Canada itself is accredited by the International Society for Quality in Healthcare). All aspects of health care are scrutinized, from patient care to safety and ethical practices. Although obtaining accreditation is voluntary, most organizations opt for it because it enhances their status and improves the services and care they provide. Formal accreditation assessments occur about every three years and give the organization an overview of its strengths and the areas where it can improve. The Canadian Council on Health Services Accreditation looks at how the organization compares with national standards in the following areas:

- Quality of care
- Community accessibility
- Appropriateness of care (does the intervention meet the patient's needs?)
- Effectiveness of care
- Timeliness
- Continuity of care (Are patients followed up? Is care modified, if needed? For example, if a patient comes to a diabetic clinic for teaching, does the facility follow through until the patient has met the learning goals?)
- Safety

If the organization meets all of the standards, it becomes an accredited organization, usually for another three years. If a facility falls short, it may be accredited for a year, during which time it is expected to correct the areas in which it was deficient. Losing accreditation not only undermines the facility's reputation but may result in a loss of funding.

The period leading up to accreditation is hectic and stressful in any organization. Most organizations conduct their own review to prepare for the formal assessment. Every component of every service and procedure, both clinical and administrative, is put under a microscope. The goal is to maintain and improve adherence to all standards at all times. This is not entirely realistic. As a clinical secretary, you will be heavily involved in the administrative components of review and evaluation. The work can be overwhelming, but the process can be made bearable if everyone involved is organized and efficient and works as a team.

THE ORGANIZATIONAL STRUCTURE OF A HOSPITAL

Except for the few that are privately run, hospitals are not-for-profit corporations that operate under a special section of each province/territory's Corporations Act. Rules, regulations, and corporate structures vary by province or territory. Most of these hospitals have formed partnerships with other hospitals/organizations, resulting in centralized management.

As corporations, hospitals are headed by a board of directors. The board is either appointed or elected by its membership. The board of directors for Vancouver Coastal Health, for example, are appointed for two-year terms by British Columbia's Board

Resourcing and Development Office. The makeup of a hospital membership varies across Canada. Members may include donors and interested community members. Board members are elected for specific terms, and they may be reelected. Each board will have a nominating committee that accepts nominations of community members or invites members to consider standing for election.

The board of directors appoints a chief executive officer (CEO) for their hospital or partnership of hospitals. The CEO, a salaried position, is accountable to the board of directors and is ultimately responsible for the management of the organization, including such things as hiring and operating within a budget set by the board of directors.

The remaining organizational structure of each hospital will be different but will follow similar guidelines. There may be several vice-presidents or vice-chairs reporting to the CEO, chair, or president; in some structures, vice-presidents may report to an executive vice-president. A hospital involved in a **collaborative partnership** usually has a site administrator or a clinical administrator who oversees the daily operation of the hospital. Most hospitals also have a chief of staff who represents the hospital's medical staff. There will be someone who is responsible for each department or group of departments within the organization, such as chief of medicine, chief of surgery, manager of information technology, and director of acute-care services. Titles and exact responsibilities of positions vary among hospitals and may shift rapidly within a hospital. Generally, the position of clinical leader or clinical manager has replaced that of the head nurse. This person may be responsible for several nursing units but would have a charge nurse or clinical resource nurse (or several) who takes responsibility for each patient-care unit on each shift. As clinical secretary, you would typically report to the charge nurse or clinical resource nurse. The next person in the chain of command would be the clinical leader or manager.

One of the websites at the end of this chapter provides a couple of examples of hospital organizational charts.

collaborative partnership the relationship among hospitals that have entered into an agreement to form a partnership, sharing clinical and administrative responsibilities.

Restructuring of Hospitals and Hospital Services

Over the past number of years, communities across Canada have had to evaluate what kind of care hospitals provide, where and how they provide it, and how they are managed. Hospitals have been restructured in an attempt to make the best use of limited resources without sacrificing the quality of medical care—although debate continues on whether this has been achieved or is even possible. Hospital restructuring will continue as ministries struggle to find a balance between cost cutting and providing high-quality care. More recently, regional health authorities in many jurisdictions have been given the responsibility to oversee governance of health care issues (including health care facilities). This is in accordance with the continuing belief in most jurisdictions that local health authorities/councils can more effectively determine the needs of their own regions.

In most provinces and territories, health care restructuring resulted from government efficiency studies. Because community-based recommendations were considered, changes have varied from one region to the next. However, across the country most hospitals have had beds eliminated, and others have been closed outright. In search of efficiency, some hospitals have joined collaborative partnerships or alliances with a single central administration. **Rationalization of services** has been instituted to avoid duplication of services. For example, in Kitchener, Ontario, one hospital treats serious cardiac conditions while another treats cancer. The London Health Sciences Centre now sends pediatric cardiology cases to the Hospital for Sick Children in Toronto. (Hospitals offering specialized services to a wide area are sometimes referred to as *regional centres*.) Some hospitals have active emergency departments that operate 24 hours a day, while others offer only limited care for certain hours. In rural communities, several hospitals partnering under an alliance or other agreement may offer routine services at different

rationalization of services centralizing certain services, particularly those that require specialized care, to one hospital in a region.

sites (e.g., cataract surgery in one community hospital and rehabilitation services at another). Although rationalization of services may allow small hospitals to remain viable, it may be difficult for patients to travel from one town to another for care.

Restructuring has also included a plan to meet the needs of an aging population. Although the number of acute-care beds across the country has been reduced, many new beds have been opened in long-term care facilities. Some regions have opened more beds for patients who need a lesser degree of nursing or medical care, called **subacute, transitional, or step-down care** (because it is a "step down" from acute hospital care). Ultimately the goal is to care for older Canadians in their homes.

subacute, transitional, or step-down care medical and nursing care that is less intensive than traditional acute-care hospital treatment.

Despite the attempts to cut costs, most regions have had to spend money to modernize aging hospital equipment. Partly to avoid readmissions, some hospitals have introduced help lines, staffed by a registered nurse, to answer questions from newly discharged patients. Patients are also encouraged to use government-run telephone advice services, such as Ontario's Telehealth or British Columbia's HealthLink.

Hospitalization versus Home Care

Across Canada, the demand for community-based or home care has greatly increased—partly because of an aging population, an increase in chronic diseases (because of improved medical intervention and people living longer, many with more than one chronic disease), more procedures done on an outpatient basis, day surgery, and shorter hospital stays. With **day surgery**, a patient is admitted in the morning, operated on, and discharged by the end of the day, if stable. This is made possible by a change in attitude and by advances in surgical techniques. Laparoscopic and keyhole surgical techniques are constantly expanding the types of procedures that can be done on an outpatient basis. For example, a few years ago gallbladders were removed by an open cholecystectomy ("open chole," pronounced *collie*), which required a large incision under the right rib cage. Now surgeons use a visualizing instrument called a **laparoscope** to perform a "lap or closed chole" through a much smaller incision, and patients go home the same day (unless there are complications). Cataract surgery is almost always done on an outpatient basis. Even hysterectomies and some cancer surgeries, under the proper conditions, are done as outpatient surgery. Hospitals are offering more outpatient and ambulatory care services, creating a "hospital without walls" that keeps more patients at home with the support of community care services or often overburdened family members.

day surgery surgery conducted with a hospital stay of less than 24 hours.

laparoscope a type of endoscope (a visualizing instrument with a tube and lens) that allows surgeons to visualize internal structures. Using this tool, surgery can be done through incisions often 5 centimetres in length or smaller.

Home care services in Canada are delivered by both the public and private sectors. Accreditation Canada and the Canadian Home Care Association, through their respective mandates, influence policy development, best practices guidelines, and the delivery of quality care. Providing proper home care greatly reduces the need for in-hospital stays as well as the number of people admitted to long-term care. As with other sectors of the health care system, home care services are stretched to the limit, with increasing demand for services, limited funds, and a shortage of human health resources. In many cases, individuals depending on publicly funded home care services are unable to get the number of hours of care they require; the alternatives are to hire a private organization to provide the care, depend on family members, go without, or move into a facility that can provide the needed care.

The Victorian Order of Nurses, a not-for-profit organization that has provided home care for Canadians since 1897, closed programs in 2015 in Alberta, Saskatchewan, Manitoba, New Brunswick, Prince Edward Island, and Newfoundland and Labrador because of funding shortfalls. Ontario- and Quebec-based operations have not yet been affected. Many home care organizations are under contract with their respective provincial/territorial government, and funding is often dependent on available finances.

Cost-Saving Initiatives within Hospitals

Finding ways to deliver hospital services in a more cost-effective manner is an ongoing process. As budgets tighten, efficiency studies have become popular. An outside company is hired to evaluate how hospitals and their services operate and to recommend a plan to cut costs. Such initiatives are often met with fear and apprehension by hospital staff, particularly if job losses are likely to occur.

In an effort to enhance efficiency and reduce costs while improving patient outcomes, a number of Canadian hospitals have embraced *lean* methodologies. Saskatchewan, for example, has made a commitment to implement lean across its health care system. The lean concept originated in Japan and has been applied to business and manufacturing. The basic philosophy behind lean is to maximize customer value while minimizing waste. In health care, the customer is the patient, value refers to the patient's experience and care received, and waste refers to inefficient use of both products, time, and services.

Hospitals that have implemented lean methodologies have experienced a reduction in emergency department wait times, more efficient use of operating rooms, decreased patient length of stay, better use of diagnostic services, and lower rates of nosocomial infections. Moreover, few if any jobs have been lost, and job satisfaction improved, as did the patient experience.

Adopting lean into a facility requires extensive training, patience, and team work. If you become a part of this or any other initiative to deliver health services more efficiently, be a positive team member and do your personal and professional best to help things improve.

L02 HOSPITAL DEPARTMENTS AND SERVICES

The internet and social media have contributed greatly to helping the average Canadian become more informed about the services that hospitals offer to their communities. Most hospitals post their services, the location of available services, and operational hours online—either on their own websites or on social media sites such as Facebook. Individuals can scroll through the programs and services offered, access their own health records, pay bills, submit complaints, and survey job opportunities. General services are usually listed, with specific services as a subcategory. These services may include community-based residential and home health care services, mental health and addiction services, public health services programs, research, and in-hospital care. In addition to inpatient services, larger hospitals offer a variety of outpatient clinics, including a mental health and addiction clinic, ambulatory clinic laboratory, cancer clinic, fracture clinic, pediatric outpatient clinic, healthy living clinic, dialysis clinic, and surgical prescreening unit/clinic. Other programs may be dedicated to preventive care, health, and wellness.

Hospital Departments

Hospital departments are divided according to the services they offer: administrative, informational, therapeutic, diagnostic, or supportive. The numbers, functions, and names of hospital departments vary. Larger general hospitals have more services and departments than smaller general hospitals. In a smaller hospital, for example, the department of medicine may be responsible for cardiology and internal medicine; in a larger hospital, these would be managed as separate departments. Chronic care and rehabilitation facilities do not offer the same range of services as a general hospital. The following descriptions cover the departments typically found in a general hospital.

Admitting/Patient Flow Department The admitting department is usually the first point of contact for patients coming to the hospital for either inpatient or outpatient services. Emergency admissions arrive through the emergency department but, if admitted to hospital, are processed through admitting. Information is gathered and noted on the admission sheet. The patient is given an identification bracelet in admitting, emergency, or upon arrival at the floor. The admitting department tracks all admissions and discharges and directs patient admissions, notifying physicians of bed availability. If beds are limited, admitting will try to juggle admissions to find suitable accommodation for the patient. Often a patient is admitted to accommodation for which he or she does not have coverage. The admitting department tracks such admissions, moving the patient to the appropriate or insured accommodation as soon as possible.

Some hospital departments and patient-care units handle components of the admission process but, ultimately, everyone who receives hospital services will be processed in some manner by the admitting department. The admitting department takes a daily census, checking with all units to record admissions, transfers, and discharges.

Patient flow (which is discussed in detail in Chapter 15) may be a separate department or part of the admitting department (may also be called *patient registration*). Patient flow is usually staffed according to the size of the region and the number of health facilities serviced by the hospital. Registered nurses and clinical secretaries most often assume responsibility for patient flow activities, working with a complex communication network to ensure that patients have access to the bed and services they require (see Chapter 15).

The Business Office   This department manages the hospital's business activities, from billing provincial/territorial plans and private insurance companies to collecting payment from patients for services they must pay for. Patients are usually asked to go to the business office upon discharge to pay any outstanding accounts. The business office tracks all financial information for the finance department.

Public Relations   The public relations department is responsible for community liaison. It may also be responsible for authorizing any newspaper or magazine articles related to hospital activities. This department tries to generate publicity and community support for fundraising initiatives, which are important to most hospitals.

Human Resources/Employee Services   This department is responsible for recruiting and interviewing new employees and preparing termination agreements for those who leave, voluntarily or otherwise. Human resources advertises vacant positions internally and externally. Human resources also manages transfers within the facility and all employee services, such as benefits, leaves of absence, and retirement.

Medical Records/Health Information Services   Health information services manages medical transcription and is responsible for all charts and documents generated or used within the hospital. Upon discharge, all patient charts go to this department, where they are reviewed and collated for storage. If parts of the chart are incomplete or missing, someone will contact the appropriate department. When a patient is admitted to hospital, the clinical secretary calls health information services for the patient's previous records. Anyone wanting to view the chart of a discharged patient must present appropriate authorization.

Purchasing Department   The purchasing department is responsible for taking inventory and ensuring that all necessary supplies and equipment are purchased in a timely manner.

Information Services   Information services is responsible for communication systems within the hospital. This includes computer services. Responsibilities may involve in-service education for new and continuing staff on new technologies, computer procedures, and policies.

Auxiliary/Volunteer Services   Volunteers are vital to most hospitals. They range from students in a health care field assisting professionals (see Chapter 1) and high school students who visit patients, to people who play key roles in running shops and other fundraising ventures. This department may be headed by a paid manager or coordinator. It is his or her responsibility to recruit and interview volunteers and check references. Some facilities also require potential volunteers to go through a police background check.

Employee Health Services   This department is responsible for employees' work-related medical needs, including pre-employment medical certificates and immunizations. It also deals with work-related injuries, including needle-stick injuries and exposure to body fluids, and workers' compensation referrals. This department may employ a physician and one or more nurses. In most facilities, the physician is available at designated times throughout the week.

Risk Management/Infection Control   This department oversees infection control policies and procedures within the facility. If there are any infectious outbreaks within the hospital setting, they are investigated by this department for possible breaks in procedure, sources of the infection, and containment solutions. In some facilities, this department oversees any isolation needed.

Pharmacy   All acute-care hospitals have a pharmacy department staffed with pharmacists and pharmacy technicians or assistants. This department is responsible for all medication used in the hospital. In hospitals with automated medication administration systems, the pharmacy department codes all medication loaded into medication dispensing units and tracks all patient medication. They upload all medication orders to the patient's electronic chart (eChart) and create/amend electronically prepared medication records (eMARs). In addition, the pharmacy will stock medications and dispense and track controlled drugs.

Nutritional/Dietary Services   This department provides all patient meals and fills orders for special diets as well as other forms of nutrition. (See Chapters 18 and 19.) It also provides counselling to both inpatients and outpatients upon referral.

Sterile Processing Department (SPD)/Central Supply/Materials Management Department   This department is responsible for sterilizing and distributing sterile equipment, ranging from suture removal trays to operative instruments. In some, but not all, facilities, equipment received from this department has to be requisitioned.

Stores/Materials Management   In some facilities, this department is under the same umbrella as the central supply department or SPD. All equipment and supplies, other than those that must be sterilized, are obtained here. This is the department you would call to get most of the equipment needed on the patient-care unit, ranging from prepackaged sterile dressing trays, catheters, and flashlight batteries to nasogastric suction machines, **emesis basins**, and intravenous supplies.

Environmental Services/Housekeeping   This department is responsible for the cleanliness of the facility, including **terminal cleaning** of rooms.

Laundry   This may be a separate department or part of environmental services. The laundry department is responsible for supplying patient-care units with clean laundry. They have special procedures for dealing with laundry that has been used for patients in isolation or is otherwise contaminated. In many facilities, a certain amount of clean

emesis basin a small basin, usually kidney shaped, used for patients to vomit into or cough up sputum or phlegm into. It is also used to hold solutions for a variety of purposes. It may be ordered sterile or just clean.

terminal cleaning a thorough wash with a disinfectant solution of all equipment (bed, bedside unit, etc.) used by a patient upon his or her discharge.

laundry (towels, blankets, sheets, pillowcases, pillows, etc.) is allocated to each patient-care unit, and it may be difficult to get more. Some nurses "hide" clean supplies for the oncoming shift or borrow from other units. The laundry cart may be kept in the clean utility room. Some carts have hamper bags, often colour coded, each for a certain item (fitted sheets, top sheets, gowns, etc.). Individuals from housekeeping collect soiled linen as necessary or at routine intervals; some departments have laundry chutes. Increasingly, hospitals are sending their laundry to offsite services and independent businesses.

Maintenance/Environmental Engineering   The maintenance department ensures that equipment is safe and operational and keeps up with daily repairs to the physical structure of the building, from changing lightbulbs to painting. The clinical secretary is often responsible for passing on messages regarding maintenance issues on the floor. For example, he or she would call maintenance for any repairs on the patient-care unit. This could be a malfunctioning call bell in a patient's room or an electrical outlet at the nurses' station. In some facilities, this department will check any electrical appliances brought in by patients to ensure that they meet the facility's safety standards.

Patient-Care Units

A patient-care unit is a dedicated area for inpatient accommodation, usually an entire floor where services of a similar type are rendered. Each patient-care unit functions both independently and interdependently. It has its own staff and its own nurses' station and looks after its own patient care, communication, and administrative needs. However, the unit also collaborates with other services both inside and outside the hospital.

Medicine   Patients are admitted to medical units for diagnosis, nonsurgical treatment, and recovery from an array of diseases and conditions. The range of medical units reflects a hospital's designation and size. Small to mid-size hospitals may have a single *general medical unit* serving patients with conditions ranging from heart disease (e.g., a telemetry unit, which monitors patients with arrhythmias and who have been transferred from **CICU** to the floor) to diabetes. A large regional hospital includes specialized patient-care units.

> **CICU** stands for *coronary intensive care unit*, which is an intensive care unit that specifically looks after patients who have had heart attacks and cardiac surgery, including heart transplants.

Nephrology   This unit cares for patients with diseases and disorders relating to the kidney. Often, patients with such conditions are admitted to general medicine or, if surgical intervention is required, to the urology or general surgery unit.

Cardiology and Telemetry   This unit treats medical conditions relating to the heart and vascular system. Telemetry, which involves cardiac monitoring, may be a separate unit or may be part of the cardiology unit. It is explained in more detail in Chapter 20.

Neurology   This unit provides any nonsurgical treatment of diseases relating specifically to the neurological system, such as Parkinson's disease or multiple sclerosis.

Palliative Care   A **palliative care** unit looks after patients who have terminal illnesses. They may be admitted for stabilization or pain management during more acute episodes of their illness. They may be admitted when they are dying. The staff on these units are trained not only to look after the patient's emotional and physical needs, but also to provide guidance and support to the patient's family and loved ones.

> **palliative care** care for a person with a terminal illness who is in hospital to die, to have a condition stabilized, or for pain control.

Psychiatry/Mental Health Services   This unit, sometimes simply called "psych," involves the care of individuals with mental or emotional conditions. Many facilities have both inpatient and outpatient psychiatry units, which may constitute a separate hospital department. Outpatient units offer care, treatment, and support for those who live in the community. Patients who are unable to manage in the community are treated in the inpatient units.

Oncology/Systemic Therapy   This unit treats individuals with cancer. Some communities have specialized hospitals dealing only with cancer. Some patients undergo surgery to remove cancerous tumours, and many receive postoperative treatment, including medication (chemotherapy) or radiation. Chemotherapy may be intravenous, oral, or a combination of both. Depending on the type of cancer, the treatment, and the response, therapy may be inpatient or outpatient. Intensive chemotherapy, such as that given for some types of leukemia, may make the patient sick and weak and impair the immune system. Such patients are kept in the hospital until they have recovered some strength. They may be kept in reverse isolation, meaning that extra precautions are taken to protect them from infection.

Rehabilitation   Patients are transferred to "rehab" to recover function after a stroke, trauma, or surgery. They are often discharged to continue rehabilitation as outpatients.

Pediatrics   This unit treats children, typically up to age 16 years, although the age limit may vary. Some hospitals, such as the Hospital for Sick Children in Toronto, care only for children. A children's hospital will have units specialized for the type of illness, intensity of care needed, and the age of the child.

Gynecology   This unit looks after patients (sometimes surgical as well as medical) with complaints related to the female reproductive system. Some gynecology units offer pre- and post-abortion counselling and support groups and have community services related to infertility.

Integrated Mother/Child Services   Many facilities now have integrated services combining labour, delivery, and recovery from childbirth. This unit is often grouped together and called "mat–child." The mother would be admitted to one room, called the LDR (labour, delivery, recovery) room, where she would labour, have the baby, and recover. Often, there is accommodation for family members or significant others who wish to stay and support the mother. The baby stays with the mother unless there are complications necessitating specialized care. The unit may offer parenting classes and breastfeeding clinics.

If the mother requires an abdominal delivery (Caesarean section), she may have to be transferred to the "section room," which is usually on the same floor.

Some hospitals are designated as regional obstetrical or pediatric centres, offering different levels of newborn/infant care. A centre offering full intensive care services is designated a level II care centre.

Surgical Patient-Care Units

Surgical units are also patient-care units, like medical units, but they look after patients preparing for or recovering from surgery. In a large hospital, units are specialized by type of surgery. These units do not include operating rooms where the actual surgery is done.

General Surgery   General surgery would be a unit more likely found in a small or mid-size hospital. Patients come to recover from a variety of relatively simple operations on different organs and systems: gallbladder, gastrointestinal, appendix, bladder, and so on.

Cardiac Surgery   Cardiac surgery units deal with surgery to the heart and vascular system, such as bypass surgery.

Orthopedic Surgery   This unit cares for patients who have had surgical procedures related to the musculoskeletal system, such as hip or knee replacements or spinal surgery.

Thoracic Surgery   This unit deals with surgery of the chest and the respiratory system, such as the removal of a lung section, a lung transplantation, or treatment for a collapsed lung (pneumothorax).

Neurosurgery   This unit cares for patients who have had surgery on the brain, spinal cord, and other parts of the nervous system. For example, individuals with brain tumours or **subdural hematomas** would be cared for here.

Gynecological Surgery   This unit cares for patients who undergo surgical procedures relating to the female reproductive system. It may be combined with the medical gynecology unit. Patients who have had a stillbirth or spontaneous abortion are often transferred to this unit if they must remain in hospital to spare them the agony of watching mothers with newborn babies.

GI/Endoscopy   This unit cares for patients who have had gastrointestinal (GI) surgery (anything to do with the digestive tract), such as bowel resection, stomach surgery for ulcers, or a colostomy. **Endoscopy** is often an outpatient procedure. Some hospitals designate one large room or a ward to which patients for endoscopy procedures are admitted and discharged. The ward may be a section of the GI unit.

Ophthalmology   This unit specializes in procedures related to the eye. Some surgery may be done on an outpatient basis.

Pediatric Surgery   This unit is for children who have had surgical procedures. Larger hospitals may have more specialized units, such as pediatric neurosurgery, although more specialized procedures may be performed at designated children's hospitals.

Plastic Surgery   Plastic surgery is usually managed on an outpatient basis. Unless the surgery is medically necessary, the cost is borne by the patient. Some procedures, such as breast reduction, involve an overnight stay, while reconstructive surgery after a car accident or burns usually involves a longer stay.

Vascular Surgery   This unit serves patients who have had surgery for an aneurysm or reconstructive vascular surgery.

Urology   This unit deals with the care and recovery of patients who have had any surgery done on the urinary system.

Intensive Care Units

Patients who are **critically ill** (whether or not they have received surgery) and require specialized, intensive treatment and nursing care are placed in an intensive care unit (ICU). These units can also be specialized, for example, a *neonatal intensive care unit* (NICU), which cares for newborns, or a *coronary intensive care unit* (CICU), which cares for those with cardiovascular problems. CCU is sometimes used to refer to a constant care unit, which mimics the ICU, for the most part.

Emergency Departments

Emergency departments, in theory, are for individuals who need urgent care for serious conditions, such as victims of motor vehicle accidents and other traumas or those experiencing uncontrolled bleeding or symptoms of stroke or heart attack.

— Outpatient Clinics

Hospitals often have outpatient clinics in such areas as diabetes, psychiatry, orthopedics, and oncology.

Diagnostic and Therapeutic Services

Some departments offer diagnostic services alone, and others offer both diagnostic and treatment services. Most of these departments offer services to both inpatients and outpatients and to the community at large. Physicians order inpatient services and refer outpatients to the clinic.

Renal Dialysis   This unit has a special machine that filters waste from the blood of patients who have advanced kidney disease or whose kidneys are nonfunctional. Large and mid-size hospitals may offer renal dialysis, but it is unlikely at smaller facilities. Many patients have dialysis units in their home, but they must be connected to a hospital offering renal dialysis for periodic assessments.

Cardiology Services   Health professionals, such as cardiologists and cardiology technologists, provide a range of diagnostic testing to diagnose structural abnormalities of the heart and other factors that may impair its function.

Respiratory Services   Medical staff, along with respiratory technologists and technicians, provide diagnostic procedures, including pulmonary function tests, and therapeutic interventions. Cardiology services and respiratory services may be combined in a single cardiopulmonary services unit.

Diagnostic Imaging   In this department, radiologists, medical radiation and nuclear technologists, and **ultrasonographers** offer imaging services, such as ultrasonography, magnetic resonance imaging (MRI), computed tomography (CT), nuclear medicine, fluoroscopy, mammography, and vascular/interventional radiology.

ultrasonographer a technician who operates an ultrasound machine.

Laboratory Services   In this department, pathologists and other physician specialists, medical laboratory technologists, microbiologists, and phlebotomists deliver a range of laboratory services to inpatients and outpatients in such areas as chemistry (or biochemistry), hematology and blood bank, microbiology (which may include bacteriology, virology, and mycology), and pathology (which may include histology and cytology).

Physiotherapy   The physiotherapy department works with patients after illness, surgery, or trauma to facilitate rehabilitation and recovery. Patients may have functional disabilities, such as back and joint problems, cancer, heart attacks, or stroke, or they may require postoperative rehabilitation.

Speech Therapy   The speech therapist works with patients needing corrective or rehabilitative treatment for speech disorders. These include speech impediments, such as stuttering and lisps. Other patients include people who are deaf or hearing impaired and stroke victims.

Occupational Therapy   Therapists here will identify the patient's interests and skills and try to get them involved in recreational activities. Often they work with physiotherapy to recommend activities that will be physically therapeutic as well as recreational.

Social Services

This department works with patients to help them reestablish themselves or a family member in the community after an illness or surgery. This service may be ordered by the physician or requested by the nurse, patient, or family members. The social worker draws on community resources to meet the patient's needs. If the patient cannot return home, a social worker will work with the patient and family to find an alternative solution, such as placement in a long-term care facility. Social workers also provide patients with support and counselling.

> ## ▶▶ POINTS TO PONDER
>
> When applying to work as a clinical secretary in a hospital, as previously mentioned, there is a wide selection of areas in which to work. If you find that the area you are initially hired to work in is not what you expected, or you feel you are not suited to, do not make any snap decisions. Give yourself time to become familiar with the responsibilities in your department, the professional staff, and the technology before you decide the position is not for you. Often feeling "in control" of what you are doing, and confident of what you are doing, makes a difference. If you remain unhappy with where you are working after you give it a fair chance, (e.g. the emergency department, or in palliative care) watch for internal postings that appeal to you.

L03 THE PROFESSIONAL STAFF

(See Chapter 4 for more detail on some of the professions listed later.)

If you work in a hospital, you will interact with many different health care professionals. Each type of facility will have a somewhat different mix. For example, a nursing home will have proportionally fewer registered nurses (RNs) than a hospital and more registered practical nurses (RPNs) and personal support workers (PSWs).

It is important to know who these professionals are and how they contribute to the health team. While reading the following section, keep in mind that titles and job descriptions vary with facility and location and are constantly shifting as facilities try to improve efficiency while following trends in political correctness.

Physicians

emergentologist a physician specializing in emergency medicine.

As discussed in Chapter 4, some physicians are salaried and on staff full time at hospitals, especially teaching hospitals. **Emergentologists** may work only at a hospital; they may be salaried or bill fee-for-service. Many doctors, including general practitioners and specialists, such as internists and cardiologists, have private practices outside the hospital; they attend their own patients in hospital. Surgeons may be salaried to work in a hospital but also have private practices. Anesthetists work almost exclusively in hospitals but usually bill fee-for-service.

credentialling a process whereby a peer group judges an individual's qualifications to perform certain services.

Health care providers, such as physicians and midwives, must apply to a hospital for admitting privileges before they can admit patients to that facility and actively participate in the patient's treatment. In a process called **credentialling**, their qualifications are first carefully examined by a committee composed of members of the medical staff and perhaps someone from the hospital administration. The provider must then follow the facility's policies and regulations and may have admitting privileges revoked if he or she fails to meet standards of conduct, practice, and care.

Unit Manager or Clinical Leader

In the traditional hospital structure, each hospital unit was typically managed by a head nurse. The head nurse almost always worked on the day shift. She did not routinely provide patient care but oversaw all activities that took place on the floor and acted as the primary contact for physicians. She would accompany doctors on their rounds to visit patients, often writing down the physicians' orders. She was a fount of information on each patient's condition and treatment plan. She also reviewed all patients' medications for the day and checked the charts for any missed orders. Unless absent from the patient-care unit, the head nurse transcribed all doctors' orders. She completed a staffing schedule for each day and assigned a charge nurse for each shift. Other nurses on the floor would take direction from the charge nurse.

Today, a nurse does not usually accompany the physician on rounds. Instead of instructing a nurse, the doctor writes down the orders or enters them directly into the computer at the bedside using a portable device (discussed in Chapter 16) and informs the patient's nurse about any critical issues. Each patient-care unit still has a person who is ultimately responsible for the unit, as well as someone on each shift who takes a lead role. Nursing staff and the clinical secretary first turn to this shift leader if they have problems and then to the unit manager.

The person responsible for the unit may be called a *manager* or *clinical leader*. This person may or may not be a nurse. He or she may be responsible for several floors or units, usually related ones; for example, he or she may be manager of surgical and emergency services or inpatient medical services. Typically this person remains the ultimate reporting authority for the clinical secretary.

The Clinical Resource Nurse

The person who coordinates and manages a unit for a shift may still be called a *charge nurse* but is more often called a *clinical resource nurse*; other titles also exist. This person is always a nurse but may be hired on a full-time or part-time basis. One person may be permanently assigned to a shift, or several people with the same title may rotate through shifts. This is the person you will work most closely with, who will check your processed doctors' orders, and to whom you will take any problems that arise during the course of your shift.

Professional Nurses

There are a number of categories of nursing professionals: the RN/BScN and RPN/LPN, each with their own scope of practice. Each unit will have different nursing requirements. Some units, such as the ICU, use only RNs. Some hospitals hire only RNs for specific units. However, the majority of hospital units are staffed by RPNs/LPNs and sometimes health care aides or PSWs. Some units use team nursing. A team may consist of any blend of professional nurses.

Registered Nurses   The College of Nurses in each province and territory clearly outlines nursing responsibilities of each level of nurse. An RN may be a graduate of a diploma or a degree program, usually of three or four years. (Ontario, as have most jurisdictions, has phased out diploma programs in favour of BScN [Bachelor of Science in Nursing] degrees.) Some provinces have accelerated degree programs graduating students with BScN in less than the usual four years. After graduation and before writing provincial or territorial examinations, the nurse is known as a *graduate nurse*. Upon successful completion of provincial or territorial examinations, he or she becomes an RN. Qualifications are specific to the province or territory; an RN who moves from Ontario to British Columbia or Newfoundland and Labrador will have to recertify by taking that province's exams. In some facilities, RNs are the only nurses who can dispense medications; they maintain responsibility for the drug cart. RNs are also the only nurses who can carry out highly complex delegated responsibilities, such as giving intravenous medications, looking after acutely ill patients, monitoring patient-controlled analgesic pumps, doing complex dressings, and inserting nasogastric tubes. The role of the RPN/LPN is expanding at a rapid rate as it assumes more and more of the responsibilities formerly done by the RN.

Registered psychiatric nurses provide professional nursing and mental health nursing services in mental health care facilities and in the community. Educated predominately in British Columbia, Alberta, Saskatchewan, and Manitoba, registered psychiatric nurses receive postsecondary education at either the baccalaureate or diploma level.

Registered/Licensed Practical Nurses   The RPN/LPN is a graduate of a college program that varies from one-and-a-half to two years in length. RPN/LPNs form the second-largest body of regulated nursing professionals in the country. The scope of practice of the RPN/LPNs is more limited than that of the RN, although it has expanded greatly in recent years. For example, RPNs/LPNs now assume charge positions in some health care facilities, give medications, manage intravenous therapy, and administer a wide range of prescribed treatments to patients.

Nurse practitioners (NPs) are assuming increasingly complex roles within and outside of hospitals (see Chapter 4 for more detail). In most jurisdictions, NPs can write orders on inpatients. They function as part of a medical or surgical team and work closely with the attending physician(s). NPs are also employed in many emergency departments in hospitals, doing primary assessments and triaging patients. In most provinces only midwives, dentists, and physicians may admit or discharge patients from a hospital, but that policy is changing—some jurisdictions are approving legislation allowing NPs to admit and discharge patients as well. Such a law was passed in Ontario in 2012.

Personal Support Workers

This position used to be called a health care aide, but the term *personal support worker* is becoming more popular in some regions. Some agencies still train PSWs on the job, but most are graduates of a three- to six-month certificate program at a community college or equivalent. Although some PSWs work as team members with nurses in hospitals, they are more likely to work in nursing homes, long-term care facilities, and community agencies.

Paramedics

Paramedics are first responders often based out of hospital emergency departments. Levels of training vary with jurisdictions. For example, education requirements to become an advanced care paramedic can be up to two years in addition to qualifications already held. In Canada, the National Occupational Competency Profile for paramedics in conjunction with the Paramedic Association of Canada outlines the scope of practice of paramedics. Depending on training and the region in which they practice, paramedics may initiate intravenous therapy, administer selected drugs, intubate patients, and provide frontline emergency treatment in other emergency situations. Paramedics also work in emergency departments along with NPs, physicians, and other primary care providers.

Orderlies

Some hospitals employ orderlies (usually male) to carry out such duties as transporting patients. They may be trained to bathe patients and perform such tasks as male catheterization, especially when there is no male nurse available and a patient is uncomfortable with being treated by a woman. Orderlies may be trained on the job.

Housekeeping Staff

Housekeeping staff are often assigned to specific units, although they may rotate. Their duties include cleaning and disinfecting vacated beds and bedside accessories. You may be responsible for notifying housekeeping (often electronically) when a patient has been discharged so that they can clean the room. It is important to communicate clearly with the housekeeping staff to ensure efficient use of hospital beds. Some clinical secretaries keep an updated list of discharges on the floor for housekeeping staff (often a book kept at the desk in the nurses' station). There may be times when a bed is urgently needed, but a discharged patient is still occupying it. If the patient is able, he or she may be asked to wait in the reception area so that the bed can be prepared for the new admission.

Most hospitals request that discharged patients leave by a certain time, often 11:00 a.m. Do your best to encourage the patient to leave on time to allow the room to be prepared. Often, elective (nonemergency) admissions are asked to come in around 3:00 p.m.

Pharmacists

Many patient-care units have an assigned pharmacist or pharmacy assistant. Pharmacists are university graduates, often entering into pharmacy with an undergraduate degree in the sciences (see Chapter 7). Among other things, the pharmacist manages the stocking of medications, often for more than one unit. This is largely done in conjunction with modernized electronic innovations wherein replenishing medications is mediated by a pharmacy robot or other centralized mechanisms.

Physiotherapists

Physiotherapists are university graduates, often with an undergraduate degree in kinesiology and a master's degree in physiotherapy. If you process an order for physiotherapy, you would phone or email the physiotherapy department. If a patient is ambulatory, he or she will probably go to the physiotherapy department; if not, the physiotherapist will come to the patient. Note the appointment time on the patient intervention screen. Keep a list of the patient's activities to avoid scheduling conflicts and ensure that the patient is ready. For example, if Jovana (who relies on the nurses to help her get bathed and up in the morning) has an 8:30 a.m. appointment with the physiotherapist, make a note so that the nurse can plan to get her ready on time. Many physiotherapists work in hospitals but also practice independently in most jurisdictions.

Respiratory Therapists

A respiratory therapist (RT) may be a graduate of a three- or four-year college program or may have a master's degree. Some universities provide students with the option to receive a Bachelor of Health Sciences in conjunction with an RT diploma. These health professionals may be found in neonatal nurseries, operating rooms, intensive care units, general wards, and emergency departments. They work with patients of all ages and with a variety of conditions, including those with breathing issues and heart/lung problems. RTs provide inhalation treatments, set up and monitor oxygen therapy, manage patients on respirators or using spirometers, obtain blood gases, and monitor patients' respiratory progress. There is usually an RT on every shift, and one will respond to a cardiac or a respiratory arrest. Nurses will initiate oxygen therapy if an RT is unavailable.

Laboratory Technologists and Technicians

Medical laboratory technologists, as discussed in Chapter 6, are graduates of a postsecondary program and perform a vast array of laboratory tests ordered by the doctor, with the help of laboratory technicians and sometimes phlebotomists.

Registered Dietitians

Registered dietitians are university graduates, usually from a four-year program. They may be helped by dietary assistants. You will work with dietitians and dietary assistants when arranging dietary counselling, processing nutritional orders, or cancelling or delaying a patient's meal because of tests.

L04 THE CLINICAL SECRETARY

clinical secretary an administrative health professional working in a hospital who assumes responsibilities for the secretarial, clerical, communication, and other designated needs of a hospital unit or department.

The **clinical secretary** is often described as the hub in the wheel that keeps the patient-care unit operational. Consider the following comments by nurses:

"If our clinical secretary calls in sick, I get a sinking feeling in my stomach. We can't really manage without her."

"Our clinical secretary holds our floor together."

"The clinical secretary on our unit is the best thing that ever happened to us. She is competent, organized, and keeps everything on track and running smoothly."

"We simply would not be able to manage without our clinical secretary. I sometimes wonder how she keeps up with the doctors' orders and also keeps our unit so organized."

The scope of responsibilities and duties discussed here is general. Exactly how you carry out these duties will depend on the type of patient-care unit, the facility's policies and organization, and how computerized the hospital is.

Clerical/Secretarial Responsibilities

If you work on a patient-care unit, you will likely perform the following tasks:

- Manage the administrative components of admission, discharge, and transfer.
- Greet patients and visitors and answer questions, which may include a brief orientation to the unit (e.g., location of the reception area, meal times, general policies).
- Work with team members on bed flow procedures and policies, reporting admissions, discharges, and transfers to the bed flow manager or equivalent.
- Schedule, book, and coordinate patient appointments by receiving appointment requests, making/adjusting arrangements as directed, and notifying required personnel.
- Maintain appointment diaries by arranging and confirming appointments.
- Arrange and coordinate transportation for patient appointments, transfers, repatriation, and discharges with the appropriate escort service; ensure all chart forms/reports are prepared as indicated.
- Process physicians' orders according to the facilities protocols and complete follow-up responsibilities (see Chapter 16).
- Notify nurses of stat orders and changes in patients' care (as directed by the physician).
- Process diet changes for patients (you may have to verbally notify the dietary department of short notice changes in diets, admissions, or discharges).

- Assemble and maintain eCharts and pCharts by performing duties such as receiving admissions documentation, adding appropriate forms/attachments, inputting patient data, and transcribing information into relevant systems.

- Label pCharts with patient information and the doctor's name, ensuring that new orders are flagged in the chart (handwritten).

- Access, upload, and download patient files and reports (medical record publishing).

- Integrate the patient's eChart and pChart as per hospital/unit policies and procedures.

- Manage requests for professional consultations for patients.

- Coordinate pickup and delivery of lab specimens as required.

- Accept calls from nursing staff regarding illnesses and absences from work and communicate the information received to the appropriate personnel; call in relief nursing staff according to predetermined guidelines and refer problems to a supervisor.

- Maintain timekeeping records for staff and submit/enter this information into payroll systems as required; receive and process requests for vacation or leaves of absence, and prepare necessary documentation for terminations and forward it to the appropriate authority.

- Keep notices and posted schedules current.

- Orient new staff to the unit's communication systems.

- Communicate work requests to volunteers.

- Perform related clerical duties such as data entry; word-processing; setting up and maintaining filing systems; and compiling, preparing, and maintaining statistics, such as daily census, and producing related reports.

- Receive incoming/outgoing material by sorting, directing, and prioritizing reports/letters for the attention of the manager or staff; respond to routine enquiries by drafting correspondence for signature as indicated.

- Manage inventory and order supplies.

- Manage requests to deal with broken equipment (e.g., sending requisitions to maintenance).

- Clean and organize the desk area.

- Check that equipment in the nursing station is in working order.

Communication Responsibilities

In any hospital unit, you will play a vital role as the central point for incoming and outgoing communication. On a patient-care unit, you are likely to perform the following tasks:

- Communicate with visitors, answering questions, providing direction, and putting them in touch with nurses/doctors as required.

- Screen and direct visitors and health professionals.

- Act as an information and education resource for patients.

- Respond to and direct intercom calls from patients as indicated by the facility's internal communication system (e.g., call bells).

- Answer the telephone, direct calls, and take messages.

- Communicate with health team members, including physicians, responding to their questions and providing direction and assistance as indicated.

- Locate physicians and other members of the health care team.

- Notify staff and physicians of admissions, transfers, discharges, and deaths.

- Make calls to physicians, other hospital departments, and community agencies.

Communicating effectively in the hospital requires the same skills as those for a health office (see Chapter 8). Interacting with patients and families can be a special challenge. Hospital patients may have altered communication patterns because of illness, recent surgery, or medications, or be at various stages of accepting their illness and are missing the familiarity of their homes. Family and friends, too, may be worried and stressed by altered role functions. You need to apply your knowledge of altered role function and sick role behaviour (discussed in Chapter 2) to interact adaptively.

You will also need to deal effectively with physicians, nurses, and many other health care professionals. This can be challenging, too, especially when you are new. You will be working with every type of personality and with people who are often under stress. An overworked nurse or a surgeon about to perform difficult or critical surgery after the end of his or her normal shift may be too distracted or tense to remember courtesy. This is when you especially need to call on the communication and interpersonal skillsdiscussed in Chapter 1. Physicians can be your best friends or your worst enemies, depending on how their day is going. You may also feel the brunt of negativism or frustration from the nursing staff. In a hospital, there are (wrongly or rightly) hierarchies. Each profession guards its scope of practice, and power struggles are frequent; sometimes you may be caught in the middle.

Some will treat you as a "gofer," although this attitude is much less prevalent than a few years ago. You have a demanding and responsible position. Be polite but firm when you need to be. There is always a way to respond courteously while maintaining control of your own activities. For example:

> Dr. Green: "Mary, get me Mr. Reynolds's file. I don't see it on the desk."
>
> (Mary, on the phone taking lab results, holds up her hand and nods to Dr. Green.)
>
> "I'll be a minute, Dr. Green. It might be by the computer over there."

Mary is polite. She acknowledges that she has heard Dr. Green. At the same time, she is going to finish the task at hand. She lets Dr. Green know that she will help when she can but offers a suggestion, which might prompt Dr. Green to look a little further herself. Review Chapter 8 for more tips on communicating effectively.

Computer Responsibilities in the CPOE Environment

Many of the responsibilities listed earlier also apply to the computerized physician order entry (CPOE) environment. The major difference is that you will have little to do with transcribing orders—although there are some responsibilities in this area. You will be required to check all eCharts for new orders each shift, ensuring that nothing has been missed. You will work mainly from a screen called the *patient access list*. This is the main screen where you can see and open patient charts to check orders and carry out required tasks. At times you will be required to amend orders (e.g., pending lab orders), ensure that old diet orders are removed and the latest diet order is active, update the name of the most responsible physician as needed, enter a patient's height and weight if forgotten by the nurses, and manage professional consultations.

Cross-Coverage

cross-coverage moving from one area to another, or covering two units.

In many hospitals, you may be expected to manage two or three patient-care units at different times, each involving different administrative tasks. This is called **cross-coverage** and is one of the reasons your job is so challenging. For example, if another clinical secretary calls in sick, or if another unit is busy and yours is not, you may be asked to move to another unit for part of the day. Because each unit involves different tasks and requires different areas of knowledge, you must be flexible and able to take in a large body of information. You may even be asked to cover both units at once. This double responsibility calls on you to hold many threads in your mind and to set priorities. You need to draw on all your organizational skills. Because hospital staff are dealing with ill patients, you may have to respond to instructions given quickly and in stressful situations. This can be especially difficult if you are on a unit you are *not* entirely familiar with. Try to keep yourself focused on the task at hand, and set priorities.

Scope of Practice

Scope of practice (discussed in Chapter 1) refers to the boundaries of a person's responsibilities. All professionals have a scope of practice—determined by regulation, by a professional governing body, or by the facility—and it is important to stay within these boundaries. An RPN would not take out someone's appendix, a PSW would not add medication to an IV, and a chiropractor would not excise a skin lesion. These limits assure the public that the person looking after them is qualified.

A clinical secretary does not render direct patient care of any type. You are not qualified to give patient care. If a patient asks you to help him get up to the bathroom or to get her a medication, you must refuse because this is not within your scope of practice. You would, however, find the appropriate person to carry out the task. At no time should you ever be left alone on a patient-care unit—even just a minute. For example, on an evening shift, there could be four nurses on the unit, two of whom are at supper, and the third off the floor to get something. If the fourth nurse has to go to the washroom, you are left alone—a situation that is unfair and unacceptable to both you and the patients.

In most facilities, the clinical secretary is not permitted to take telephone orders from a physician but can take the results of lab tests. A physician may initially become irritated if you refuse to take a phone order unless he or she understands you are not a nurse. Answering the phone by stating your name and position will help (e.g., "Fourth floor, Nancy, clinical secretary/unit clerk.") This may seem like a mouthful, but it often eliminates unnecessary explanations that can save time in the long run. When a doctor does call in with orders, find a nurse soon as possible. If the nurse caring for the patient in question is unavailable, another nurse can take the orders.

When you are new, be aware of your learning curve. Do not attempt to do something unless you are certain you will do it correctly. If you are in a training position, ask the nursing staff or your preceptor. Be positive and confident, but do not be afraid to clearly state your limitations.

Choosing Your Job Setting

One advantage of working in a hospital is the wide selection of areas in which you can work. Your job description will vary somewhat from one department to another, and the required skills and temperament vary even more. To work in the emergency department, you must enjoy a fast, demanding pace and be very organized and able to multitask. The emergency department is a stressful environment, but what is stress to one person is a challenge to another. The work in a palliative care unit is usually less fast paced but requires compassion and the ability to deal with grief and death. If you thrive on patient contact and interpersonal communication, you may find working in health information services unsatisfying. However, if you prefer administrative responsibilities, enjoy detail, and pride yourself on your unwavering accuracy, health information services might be your ideal job. Medical and surgical units, particularly in large teaching hospitals, are challenging environments and, like the emergency department, require a clinical secretary who can multitask, works well under pressure, and has excellent communication skills.

Adapted for a submission by Heather Jeanes, Clinical Secretary on the Telemetry Unit, North York General Hospital, CPOE Environment

The following reflects a typical day for a clinical secretary—bearing in mind that no two days are ever quite the same, nor can times be assigned to these activities. Things happen randomly—sometimes seemingly all at once, sometimes spaced out a little. There is rarely a quiet time. For the most part, on top of administrative responsibilities, phones are ringing, nurses and doctors are asking questions and wanting things, and visitors are needing information. To manage effectively, sometimes just to get through each hour, being organized, staying focused on task while being continually interrupted, staying calm when you are really feeling pressured, knowing your job (and where to get answers when you don't have them), and maintaining a high level of professionalism will see you through. *Remember, these activities do not include processing physician orders, which is a major responsibility on units that do not have CPOE and can number up to 20–25 different order sets in the course of a day.*

Coming on a day shift:

The first task is to assess issues that have arisen during the night that require immediate attention. This can take a couple of hours, and related responsibilities can persist throughout the day. Here are some examples:

- A patient was scheduled for an angiogram at another hospital at 9:00 a.m. that day. His condition deteriorated during the night, so the doctor cancelled the procedure earlier that morning. I had to call the other hospital to cancel the angiogram. Next I called to cancel the ambulance scheduled to transport the patient to and from the hospital where the procedure was to be done.

- A cardiac patient had been scheduled for a pacemaker insertion later in the week. He developed a serious arrhythmia during the night, necessitating an urgent (same-day) appointment for the procedure. I prepared and faxed a referral package to several regional hospitals to see who had space for the patient. One hospital had space; the nurse and I worked together to complete the transfer package, including other reports and copies of the patients eMARs. Next I called to secure a medical transport number required to schedule an ambulance for pickup (and return).

These calls and queries came in continuously through the day (phones are ringing, and every call is a new task):

- Diagnostic imaging called confirming appointments and related preparations with the nurse (information had to be relayed).

- Nuclear medicine called confirming the patient list (for tests) and wanted to be sure if patients have remained NPO (which stands for "nothing by mouth"). I have to check information with the nurse or go directly to the patients for this information and relay the information back to nuclear medicine (any instructions related to tests are entered into the computer—NPO, clear fluids).

- The lab called with abnormal test results: One patient has tested positive for an infectious virus. My job is to notify the charge nurse, the bedside nurse, then infection prevention and control. I have to make arrangements to have the patient transferred to an isolation bed. I have to call patient flow and request an isolation bed, plus do all the administrative work involved in the transfer. After the patient was transferred, I had to activate isolation protocol. Protocol requires me to put a sign on the patient's chart and on the room door. Next I have to message housekeeping to clean the patient's now vacated unit. When the bed has been cleaned, I must place another call to patient flow to tell them the bed is ready for a new patient; the bed is added to the electronic bed board.

- The lab called questioning an order; when this happens I have to review the order and patient history to clarify. (If I am unsure, I have to check with the nurse or call the physician).

- I am responsible for reporting/requisitioning repairs for all broken equipment. A nurse came to me stating a bed was broken. In such cases I have to submit an online maintenance request for a broken bed. Another nurse reports a broken glucometer. Here I have to arrange to send it to the lab. Another person reports the back of a chair is broken; I have to arrange for the chair to be taken to the maintenance department. Other equipment needing attention includes anything from burned out lightbulbs to leaky faucets.

- A nurse reported that she needs some supplies asp that are not on the unit. These have to be ordered electronically (using the online ordering system). The item the nurse needed has a 24-hour turnaround time; I had to track this order to ensure it arrives on time.

Other daily duties:

- Maintain both paper and eCharts (e.g., filing paper reports, updating the eChart, removing obsolete treatment orders); check each patient's eChart for new or outstanding orders at least once per shift.

- Obtain numerous patient records from other hospitals, long-term care facilities, or doctors' offices. Once received, I must view the reports and add an appropriate barcode sticker to the report stating the type of report. This enables medical records (also called health information management) to scan and file the reports correctly.

- Prepare packages for patients returning to long-term care or going to rehab; the eMARS are faxed to the receiving facility's pharmacy either the day before or the same day the patient is discharged. Transportation is arranged accordingly.

- Obtain patients' insurance information and send it to patient accounts as required (e.g., if a patient requests a room accommodation change). I must also deal with insurance companies for patients who have supplemental room coverage.

- Check office supplies and order appropriately. Supplies must be submitted according to a schedule; late ordering results in supplies not being delivered.

- Refrigerate certain medications that are brought up by porters throughout the day.

- Call codes and provide required assistance during the code (usually making phone calls and directing respondents to the location or patient). After a code I must call the porter to get the supplies needed to restock the crash cart.

- Find time between all of this to calculate and enter the nurses' hours for payroll.

L05 ANATOMY OF A PATIENT-CARE UNIT

Although the layout may vary, the nurses' station is the focus or hub of a patient-care unit, and the patient rooms and service rooms revolve around it. A common floor layout is a rectangle with the nurses' station in the middle and rooms up and down each side and at both ends. The central nurses' station keeps nurses as close as possible to all patients, saving steps and allowing them to respond to patient needs quickly in an emergency.

The Nurses' Station

The nurses' station (also called the *nursing station*) is the "head office" and communication hub of the unit; administration and communication are managed here. The patients' charts (even skeleton charts that usually still present in the computerized environment), computers, telephones, fax, intercom controls, and stationery are all found here. Although not your private office, this is where you will do most of your work. A wide variety of other staff will also be using the station, so it is important to keep it organized and uncluttered. One clinical secretary says, "If you have a messy area, then you don't know where things are in case of an emergency. I feel overwhelmed if my area is not organized." The nurses' station also functions as a reception area. Visitors will stop here seeking direction or wanting to speak to a health care professional.

Equipment and Materials at the Nurses' Station   Generally, you keep track of the equipment at the nurses' station and make arrangements for needed repairs and replacements. Doctors and nurses will often ask you where to find various items.

Mobile Phones   It has become common practice for nurses on a patient-care unit to carry mobile phones, often using Wi-Fi connections. It may be your responsibility to keep them charged and organized and distribute them to staff. It is important to know who has which phone.

Stethoscopes   **Stethoscopes** are used to listen to the heart and take blood pressure and are usually found hanging on a hook or in a drawer. They are used not only by physicians but also by nurses, respiratory therapists, and physiotherapists. Though many health professionals have their own stethoscopes, some still rely on the supply at the nurses' station. Label stethoscopes clearly (e.g., "3 south") because they are expensive and may easily be taken by mistake and end up in another unit or a doctor's office.

stethoscope a device that amplifies sound and is used by doctors and other health care professionals to listen to the heart and to take blood pressure.

Blood Pressure Cuffs and Sphygmomanometers   Each floor will have a designated number of blood pressure cuffs and **sphygmomanometers**, which are usually kept at the nurses' station. They are used mostly by nurses but also by doctors. They may be the portable type, kept in a soft zippered case, or a larger unit with the

sphygmomanometer a device used to take blood pressure.

sphygmomanometer on wheels. Many units have wall sphygmomanometers beside the beds but will also keep a few portable kits. Keep them in a specific place so they are accessible but unlikely to be dropped or bumped. These kits do not disappear as readily as stethoscopes, but they should still be labelled, especially the smaller ones in cases. Some units account for their blood pressure equipment at the end of each shift. It is the nurses' responsibility to let you know if one is broken. You would then fill out a repair requisition and send the item to maintenance.

ophthalmoscope a device used to examine the eyes.

otoscope a device used to examine the ears.

Ophthalmoscope/Otoscope Kit   **Ophthalmoscopes** and **otoscopes** are used primarily by doctors for eye and ear examinations, respectively. Typically, both devices come together in a small hard case. They have batteries, which are usually rechargeable. You may be responsible for charging the batteries at night or when the devices are not in use and making sure that extra batteries and bulbs are available. This equipment should be checked at the beginning of each shift. There is nothing more frustrating for a physician than having to interrupt an examination to look for working equipment.

Flashlights   There are usually several flashlights kept in the unit. Because corridor lights are kept low and many patients would be disturbed by a room light, nurses use flashlights to make their rounds at night. (They usually make rounds at least every half-hour to check on patients and make sure that, for example, an IV is in place and flowing). Nurses also use a flashlight for patients with head injuries—the light is shone into the eye to assess the pupil's response to light. An abnormal response may indicate increased pressure in the skull. Doctors may use the flashlights to examine a patient's eyes or throat. You may be responsible for making sure the flashlights are in good working order and that spare batteries are available.

Percussion Hammer/Tuning Fork   Doctors and sometimes nurses use these devices in physical examinations. The percussion hammer is used to check reflexes (such as the knee-jerk) as a check of neurological functioning, and the tuning fork is used to check hearing.

Tongue Depressors   These are disposable items. They may be kept on the supply cart in the clean utility or treatment room, but it is a good idea to also keep a small supply at the nurses' station, within easy reach when a physician wants one.

Stationery Supplies   You will be responsible for keeping the nurses' station stocked with basic office supplies, such as pens and pencils, paperclips, staplers, highlighters, erasers, and rulers. You will have to order these items and may have to work within a budget. Keep supplies that you use daily in an organized manner in a convenient spot. Keep a notepad by each telephone. With pens and pencils, you have to find a balance between having too few and too many. Doctors and nurses will often have their own pens but will sometimes need one from the nurses' station. However, if you have plenty lying around, they will disappear. You may want to keep a few on the desk and some tucked away. Many units refuse to order pens, keeping only a few for administrative staff.

The Treatment Room

This is a room where physicians, nurses, and other health professionals perform examinations and minor procedures without having to take the patient out of the unit. In a pediatric unit, the treatment room might be used to start an IV or do a biopsy. In gynecology, it might be used to do pelvic examinations or Pap smears. Not all floors have a treatment room, and not all units have a treatment room.

Equipment frequently used for examinations in your unit should be kept available in this room. If you know that a particular examination is going to take place, check to be sure that the equipment needed is on hand. You may find it in the clean utility room. For example, if a doctor is going to do a Pap smear, make sure a range of speculums is available in the treatment room. It is disruptive for the patient and the doctor to have to stop and call for equipment.

The Clean Utility Room

This is a room for storing frequently used supplies, such as **dressing trays**, various types of bandages and dressing supplies, catheters, intravenous bags and tubing, nasogastric tubes, and emesis basins (also called kidney basins or K-basins). The list varies with the type of unit; a surgical unit, for example, would need more dressing trays and **suture removal trays** than would a medical unit. You may be responsible for taking inventory, checking supplies against a master list, and reordering. These supplies are usually kept on a large cart with several shelves, covered over with a zippered plastic sheet. In some facilities, supply staff exchange the cart at night for a fully stocked one. The clean utility room may also be used by the nurses to set up trays for nursing procedures, such as suture removal or insertion of a catheter or nasogastric tube.

dressing tray a specially prepared sterile tray containing the basic equipment to change a dressing on a wound or surgical incision. It contains a K-basin, 4 × 4 gauze dressings, a galley cup (a small metal or glass cup about the size of a shot glass used for cleansing solutions), and usually two sets of disposable forceps.

suture removal tray a specially prepared sterile tray similar to the dressing tray, but containing suture removal scissors or clip removers. Some facilities use a dressing tray and nurses simply add a disposable suture removal blade or prepackaged clip removers.

The Dirty Utility Room

This is an area for used equipment and supplies, such as dressing trays, bedpans, and basins. Reusable equipment, such as a nasogastric suction machine, may be rinsed or cleaned here and prepared for return to central supply or the sterile processing department. Disposable equipment, such as soiled catheters, nasogastric tubes, IV bags and tubing, and items soiled with body fluids, are disposed of according to Standard Precautions (see Chapter 5) and agency guidelines. Dirty linen may be kept here until picked up for laundry. It is not uncommon to find extra IV poles, wheelchairs, and so on in this room. This room may also contain a bedpan hopper: an automatic unit for disposal of waste and sanitization of bedpans. (Bedpans will still need to be sterilized before they are given to other patients.) Many patient-care units, however, have two or three separate hopper rooms.

Medication Room and Medication Management

Usually the medication room is near the nurses' station. This is an area where medicines are kept as well as (in most cases) automatic medication dispensing units (ADUs). In addition, you will find supplies of stock medications and commonly used IV solutions and IV solutions to which medicines have been added by the pharmacy. Most medication rooms also have a refrigerator for storing certain medications. Medication rooms are kept locked, with keypad access. You would have the code, as well as the nurses and pharmacist. You may be required to put medications sent up from pharmacy into the refrigerator.

An ADU is a computerized unit that stores and dispenses medications; it may also be called an automated dispensing cabinet, or ADC (see Figure 14.1). Managed by the pharmacy department, ADUs are used in almost all acute-care hospitals as well as other facilities. The units are preprogrammed to dispense a patient's medications according to a designated schedule. ADUs come in a variety of shapes and sizes; protocols for use may vary. Larger, stationary units resemble a large cabinet with numerous compartments that contain patient and/or stock medications. ADUs require nurses to dispense the patients' medications where the unit is situated and transport them to the bedside. Smaller mobile units can be brought to the bedside, allowing medications to be dispensed near the point of care while still controlling and tracking drug distribution.

Figure 14.1 An automatic medication dispensing unit (ADU)

The medications for smaller, mobile ADUs dispensed from the pharmacy are placed in drawers assigned to each patient (this is done according to medications ordered by the physician). Some drawers may contain carefully labelled stock (commonly used) medications. As with all units, the nurses log in, input their password and/or fingerprint, and proceed by looking up the patient's name to retrieve the required medication. If a nurse tries to retrieve a medication for a patient at the wrong time, or retrieve the wrong medication, the system will disallow entry. In some situations, the nurse can override the automated system. Omnicell is a popular unit used across Canada. Some facilities may still use a manually operated mobile medication cart (referred to as the med cart). These medication carts are under double lock.

Workstation on Wheels The workstation on wheels (WOW) is a mobile workstation used in many facilities (see Figure 14.2). The WOW facilitates real-time access to patients' charts, including medication profiles, lab work, patient history, vital signs graphs, and so on. Nurses can enter notes and access, process, or amend doctors' orders at point of care. Larger facilities may have a WOW for each patient. Some units have a feature that enables a nurse to scan the bar code on a patient's ID bracelet for identification purposes when giving the patient a medication. It also provides a surface for the nurse to work on, as well as storage drawers, reducing trips back to the nursing station.

Storage Room

Not all units have a storage room; some use the dirty utility room for this purpose. When there is a storage room, it is frequently larger than the utility rooms and serves to store such items as wheelchairs, IV poles, gurneys (stretchers), and a larger cart containing a more comprehensive array of supplies than what is found in the clean utility room. You might find sterilized bedpans, commodes, and basin sets here as well. If the

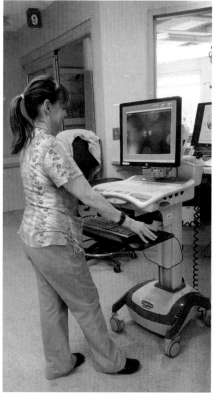

Figure 14.2 Mobile workstation allowing nurses access to patients' electronic charts, including their medication profiles.

unit does not have a storage room, these items would be kept in the clean and dirty utility rooms. Sometimes, you will find wheelchairs and gurneys lining the hallways. This obstructs the movement of patients and staff and poses a hazard when people need to move quickly, as in a fire or responding to a cardiac arrest. Try to clear the hall; if no other space is available, put the equipment in an alcove.

Conference/Communication Room

Some facilities have a conference room for team conferences, meetings, and patient interviews. Some units would consider this a luxury. If you have such a room, it is an ideal place for interprofessional meetings such as patient-care conferences or bed management/flow conferences. This room may also be used for nurses who still give and take **shift reports**, which often contain highly confidential information. For the most part, nurses coming on shift get the information they require from a summary in the patient's eChart. However, nurses on many patient-care units still have a brief verbal exchange on each patient they are turning over at the shift's end. If you overhear confidential information at any time, politely try to take corrective action. For example, if a door is ajar, quietly go over and close it. If the nurses are taking reports in the nurses' station, ensure that the doors of the rooms around the station are closed. Sound carries, as anyone who has had a bed near the nurses' station can testify.

shift report when essential patient information is passed on to the next shift of nurses.

Kitchen

Some floors will have a small separate kitchen, or one may be shared by two or more floors. This room usually contains a refrigerator, kettle, dishes (often disposable), and a few food items. Sandwiches, fruit, milk, tea, coffee, and juice may be kept here for patient use, although budget cutbacks often limit the food available. Sometimes the nurses will put extra sandwiches that have been delivered to the floor in this fridge.

The dietary department may send up special snacks that have been ordered for patients (such as a mid-morning, afternoon, or bedtime snack for a diabetic) and store them, labelled, in the fridge. Other units might store such special orders in the refrigerator in the medication room.

Computer/Dictation Room

Most often adjacent to the nursing station, this room provides a confidential environment for doctors to dictate progress notes, admission and discharge notes, consultation notes, and operative reports. Nurses may use it to complete charting. It contains dictation equipment and often one or more computer stations. Many doctors dictate notes from home or elsewhere in the hospital. Most have internet access to the hospital's computer system. Most physicians use voice recognition software (not voice recorders).

Waiting/Reception Room

Most units have a waiting room or reception area. Ambulatory patients may visit friends and relatives in this room. Visitors will wait here for a patient who has not yet returned from surgery or a test. Sometimes patients like to sit in the reception area for a change of scenery or to watch television.

Most facilities have limits on visiting hours and on the number of visitors a patient may have at a time. Although most patient-care units are somewhat flexible, there are times when these rules must be enforced. If visitors are disturbing the patient in the next bed, you can politely ask them to visit in the reception area. If the patient is not ambulatory, suggest that only two visitors remain in the room at one time and the others wait in the reception area. Many facilities announce the end of visiting hours over the PA system. If visitors ignore this announcement, you might have it repeated. If that fails, you may have to politely remind visitors that visiting hours are over.

Patient Teaching Room

Large hospitals may have a special room for patient teaching, often on an outpatient basis. For example, people scheduled for elective surgery may be asked to come in beforehand to get detailed information about what to expect, including discussions of pain control, diet, and ambulation. You may be responsible for booking these sessions.

Housekeeping Supply Room

This is a smaller area where the housekeeping staff store pails, mops, other cleaning supplies, and sometimes toilet paper and tissues.

Dumbwaiter

A dumbwaiter, or lift, is a mini-elevator for small objects and is still present in some hospitals. It is often found in the kitchen or in a location central to the units using it. It consists of a large box, sometimes with a shelf, accessed through doors that open vertically. There are two buttons: one to summon the lift and one to send an object away. You cannot send the dumbwaiter to a particular location. If a department is sending something to you, they will notify you that the item is on the lift. You then go to the lift door, press "come," and the lift will appear shortly with the item on it. There may be several articles for other departments; make sure you take only what is meant for your floor. Everything placed on the lift should be clearly labelled. For example, the dietary department may call to notify you that the ginger ale you ordered for Mr. Samuels is on the lift. There may be other bottles of ginger ale for patients on other floors; Mr. Samuels's bottle should have his name on it. When you are finished, close the doors or the lift will remain where it is and other departments will not be able to use it.

L06 COMMUNICATION TOOLS

Communication systems in a hospital are complex, varied, and vital. Communication is discussed in more detail in Chapter 15. You will likely use most of the following tools daily.

Telephones

Most nurses' stations have several telephones, each with a different extension. The style and model of telephone will vary; some are more complex than others. Since you will be on the telephone a great deal, you should have one close to your computer.

Mobile phones (wireless phones) are used by the nurses in most health care facilities. Nurses use this mobile unit to communicate with you, other nurses, and the patients. For example, if a patient activates a call bell, it will go to his or her nurse's mobile. If that nurse is unable to respond, by default the call will go to another nurse's phone, and then if not answered it will go to you at the desk. The use of these phones provides patients with a faster response time. As well, the system also reduces the need for audible alerts, leading to quieter floors. This provides patients with a more restful environment and serves to lower stress levels for patients and nurses alike.

Paging Systems

Paging by PA The hospital switchboard is your link to the internal communication system. You contact the switchboard by telephone, usually by dialling 0. If you want to page someone within the hospital, call the switchboard operator and ask him or her to do so, giving your unit number. Usually, the operator will announce something like, "Would Dr. Majid please call 3 South," or "Dr. Majid, 345 please." Many facilities avoid loudspeaker messages to decrease noise and disturbance. Instead, they use pagers.

Pagers Some facilities supply designated health professionals with pagers (also called beepers). You should have a list of all relevant pager numbers and use them to contact any of these people. In this case, the PA would be used more discriminately or perhaps only for emergencies, such as a cardiac arrest or fire. Many hospitals provide pagers to individuals waiting for someone in the operating room or undergoing testing. For example, the parents of a child having a surgical or diagnostic procedure performed maybe given a pager; instead of having to wait in a designated area, they can move about the hospital, go for coffee perhaps, and be sure that the moment they are needed they will be paged.

Locating Systems Some hospitals have a locating system that flashes codes. For example, Dr. Thompson's code might be 234, or Dr. Green's 232. If you wanted Dr. Thompson, the number 234 would flash over the system and he would call the locating department to find out who was calling him.

Mobile Devices and the Patient

At this point the use of mobile devices by patients varies across the country. Policies range from unrestricted but responsible use to use in specific areas of the hospital, such as the cafeteria, lounges, and private offices (where there is no potential for the device to interfere with medical equipment) to no use at all. Patient confidentiality is an issue (because of the camera/video option on these phones), as is the lack of privacy related to personal conversations.

Wi-Fi

Almost all facilities have Wi-Fi, which is used by the nurses for internal communication using cellphones. It also enables patients to access the internet with their iPads, netbooks, or laptop computers. This may be restricted to certain patient-care units or other areas of the hospital. The Ottawa Hospital makes internet access available throughout the main hospital building, including patient rooms, waiting rooms, the cafeteria, and the main lobby. However, Wi-Fi creates security issues, confidentiality issues (e.g., email), and patient behaviour issues (e.g., whether they are getting enough rest or spending too much time on the computer). The use of Wi-Fi in hospitals varies greatly, and policies are constantly changing. What is certain, though, is that Wi-Fi will be available on some scale in most facilities in the near future.

Unit Intercom System Controls

The unit intercom is a system of communicating with patients. There is an intercom beside each bed or on the wall beside each bed. The patient can call by pulling a cord attached to a switch. Usually, a light will go on over the patient's room door and a signal on the intercom control panel at the nurses' station will activate. Even in hospitals that have upgraded to other patient-to-staff contact systems, activation points (such as those in bathrooms) remain and have a sustained ring and flashing light indicating a possible emergency. If a nurse attends to the patient, he or she will deactivate the signal at the bedside.

If you respond to a patient call and the patient needs a nurse, determine what the patient wants and relay the message to his or her nurse or member of the nursing team immediately. Obviously, if it is an emergency you must let the nurses know that. Otherwise try to give the patient a time frame: "The nurse will be in to see you in about five minutes." If you simply say that a nurse is coming and he or she does not appear immediately, the patient is likely to keep calling. Nurses do their best, but with staffing shortages waits are often unavoidable. If the request is something that you can handle—for example, the patient simply wants someone to turn out the light, close the door, or put the telephone back on the hook—do so, or ask anyone available to do so. If no one is available, at least you know that the matter is not urgent, even if it seems so to the patient.

Hospital Information Systems

Some hospitals create their own software; most purchase commercial software designed for hospitals. There are several commercial computer applications used in hospitals across Canada. They may be referred to as hospital information systems (HIS) or patient-care information (PCI) systems. Meditec and Cerner are the most commonly used HIS in Canada.

Using a commercial software platform may require that hospitals create their own database, customize and test the system, and train staff. This is a complex, time-consuming process. Staff will need several training sessions, practice time, and a chance to apply and integrate their skills. The unavoidable and continual improvements to IT platforms and software updates are challenging to staff members, who often feel that they have just mastered a program or module when it changes. Physicians are no exception; some find the use of CPOE an onerous task; many find it easier for you or a nurse to do it for them.

Most facilities are computerized with the exception of CPOE, although it is slowly being integrated into acute-care facilities. The cost of implementing CPOE is sometimes a determining factor in how fast a hospital can accomplish this. That said, few hospitals are truly paperless. In addition to an eChart, many facilities still have a binder that contains printed components of the eChart. The binder is referred to as the patient's paper chart (pChart). A number of hospitals keep a hard copy of the patient's admission sheet, signature sheet, and certain reports. If doctors' orders are still handwritten, these orders will also be in the pChart. Whatever system you are introduced to, you will use the patient registration and order entry modules frequently. Through the process of order entry, you will interface with almost all of the other components of the eChart. You will have the ability to make changes if you make a mistake or the doctor changes an order. You can update information, modify problem lists, and "clean up" the main patient-care screen (called the patient intervention screen; see Chapter 15).

HIS are used for the following purposes:

- Order entry (e.g., admissions, discharges, transfers)
- Ordering lab and diagnostic tests and viewing results
- Clinical documentation (assessments, flow sheets, medication administration, plans of care, clinical notes)
- Communicating with other departments
- Billing
- Tracking, distributing, and monitoring the use of medications
- Scheduling treatments, procedures, and diagnostic services
- Tracking admissions and discharges, and keeping the hospital census
- Accounting
- Ordering supplies
- Calculating a hospital's operational expenses
- Tracking human resources
- Handling payroll

The scope of a clinical secretary's job depends on the level of computerization at the hospital (especially in hospitals using a fully integrated CPOE system); you need to be highly skilled with computers and adaptable to ongoing technological change. Most of your work will be on the computer, ranging from processing, monitoring, and checking doctors' orders to accessing other departments to data entry. Usually you will have a designated computer of your own and, of course, your own password. There may also be one or more additional computers at the nurses' station for other staff (this is in addition to the computers set aside for physicians and other members of the health care team). In most facilities there are also computers at each patient's bedside for use by health professionals to enter data (e.g., vital signs) or look up patient information.

All hospitals have a specialized information technology department, which provides orientation, staff education, and support. A help line is usually also available, but you can ease the struggle by helping familiarize staff with the functions they need to know.

Pneumatic Tube System

Some hospitals also have a pneumatic tube system that is used for communication—a series of interconnecting tunnels nestled between the walls that connect all units and departments. A small cylindrical container, large enough to hold files and forms, travels along this system to a preset destination. An apparatus somewhat resembling a miniature launching pad is located in the nurses' station. There is an "out" channel or port into which you place a tube, and an "in" channel or port where tubes are received. Each floor has a code; you dial the appropriate code on the top side of the cylinder to determine its destination. Although convenient, the pneumatic tube system is notorious for getting plugged. Most agencies allow only paper items in the tubes.

(L07) CONFIDENTIALITY

Security is essential in hospitals. All information should be treated as confidential unless you are authorized to share it.

Computers

Confidentiality is increasingly an issue as hospitals shift to computerized patient records. You will have your own password and, in some hospitals, encrypted digital signatures. Guard these closely. Here are some important safeguards for maintaining confidentiality:

- Never share your password with anyone.
- Make sure you know who is authorized to access and retrieve information and what information they should have access to.
- Never allow an unauthorized person to view a patient's health information.
- Question anyone you do not know who attempts to access the computer system. Physical access to computer terminals should be limited.
- Position your computer screens and keyboards so that others cannot see them.
- Program screensavers to come on if the computer is left idle for any period of time, such as more than a minute.
- Always log out when you leave your computer terminal.
- Store disks and printed information out of sight; if the information is redundant, erase disks and shred paper.
- Ensure that all files are properly and securely backed up.
- Make sure you know hospital guidelines outlining what information is confidential.
- Encrypt all files you send by email that contain confidential information.
- Release medical information only in accordance with legal guidelines and agency policies.

Release of Information

Since you will handle most incoming calls, you will get calls from individuals inquiring about a patient's health status or progress. As discussed in Chapter 2, you must be very careful about giving out such information. Make sure you know your unit's guidelines. You may be allowed to give a basic status update to family members or to a designated family member. You may recognize family members' voices and know what kind of information they are privy to. If only specified individuals are allowed information on a patient, the designated caller can use a code to identify him or herself. If in any doubt, do not give information, even if it seems harmless. Instead, pass the call on to the patient's nurse.

The same rules apply to in-person conversations. Any medical information about a patient must remain confidential. Some people may think that sharing good news is harmless, but that is no excuse to breach confidentiality. Consider the following situation:

> A student we will call Jane was working in labour and delivery when a family friend came in and delivered a baby girl. The student went across to the residence to get a

book and then went back to the delivery room. As she passed the hall telephone, Rebecca, another student nurse and a mutual friend, shouted out, "Jane, I hear Elisabeth had her baby. What did she have?" "A girl," replied Jane breathlessly as she rushed back to the hospital. Rebecca made a few phone calls. By the time Elisabeth's husband got out of the delivery room and phoned her parents to announce the new arrival, they already knew. He felt robbed of the opportunity of sharing the news firsthand. This was a blatant breach of confidentiality on the part of both student nurses.

Be mindful of confidentiality at all times, and do not release any information without the patient's express consent.

L08 SECURITY

Security is a concern in any hospital and becomes more complex in a larger and busier environment. Since the devastating events of September 11, 2001, and the subsequent anthrax attacks in the United States, facilities across the continent have begun to review their emergency planning. Very few facilities would be truly prepared to cope with a bioterrorist attack. Yet hospitals now consider themselves potential targets and are upgrading disaster plans to deal with types of attacks that still seem unthinkable. They should be able to respond promptly and effectively to an internal threat and to meet the needs of the community in the event of a widespread threat or disaster. This includes being adequately stocked with antibiotics, antitoxins, antidotes, and other emergency equipment needed to treat and sustain potential victims. Hospital laboratories in many larger hospitals are improving their technology for prompt identification of potentially infectious substances. Response to potential bioterrorist attacks should be incorporated into the training and drills for hospital staff.

Although the risk of a terrorist attack is low in most Canadian communities, natural disasters, such as flood, fire, or violence, can strike without warning. Consider the effects of the forest fire that ravaged Fort McMurray, Alberta, in 2016. Most communities see hospitals as a critical resource for medical management of any external disaster. Links with other health facilities and community emergency resources are essential if a hospital is to respond efficiently. Every staff member must have a role and be prepared to perform it efficiently. You may be asked to assist in organizing patient evacuation, triaging patients, recording events, or managing the communication centre. You may be on a reserve list to be called in if such a disaster occurs. You may be calling others in should the need arise. You can prepare to do your share in the event of a disaster by knowing your role, attending in-service seminars, and participating in any mock disaster drills.

Security and Emergency Codes

Even without terrorist attacks or community-wide disasters, hospitals by their nature are subject to a daily risk of smaller-scale emergencies. All hospitals use a set of universal codes to alert staff to a variety of emergencies. The codes in Table 14.1 are those recommended by the Ontario Hospital Association; other provinces and territories may use different codes, although these are fairly standard. Be sure to become familiar with the emergency code system in any hospital you may work in.

It may be your responsibility to give the emergency signal. Here are some tips to keep in mind should you ever be in such a situation:

- Know the protocol. Know your role.
- Stay calm; getting upset will only impede your ability to respond.
- Get all the information needed (including the location of the emergency), and make sure it is accurate.
- Promptly notify the appropriate people.

TABLE 14.1 Universal emergency codes (Ontario and British Columbia)

Code	Emergency
Red	Fire
White	Violent/aggressive patient or physical danger
Green	Evacuation
Orange	External disaster/lockdown, limited access
Brown	Hazardous chemical spill
Blue	Cardiac arrest/adult medical emergency
Pink	Pediatric cardiac arrest or medical emergency
Yellow	Missing patient
Black	Bomb threat/suspicious object
Grey	Critical infrastructure failure/combative person

In many hospitals, you would notify switchboard or the central communications operator. For example, in the event of a cardiac arrest, you may be required to dial switchboard and say, "Code blue in room 342, west three south."

Missing Patients

Sometimes a patient will go missing—most often a confused or disoriented patient. Such a patient is at risk, particularly if he or she requires urgent or continuous medical care. There are also times when patients will simply walk out for personal reasons, for example, if they are dissatisfied with the medical care they are receiving (or not receiving). As soon as you hear that a patient seems to be missing, initiate a search. If you learn that the patient has left the unit, announce the appropriate code to notify staff. Internal guidelines will spell out how staff are given further information, such as a description of the patient. Security will participate in the search inside the hospital and on hospital grounds. If the patient cannot be located promptly, the police will be notified to assist with a broader search.

If a patient threatens to walk out of the hospital, try to locate a nurse or physician to reason with him or her. If the patient is upset enough to try leaving, there may be no reasoning. If the patient refuses to wait or to discuss any concerns, ask him or her to sign a waiver stating that he or she has left the hospital without permission of the provider and assumes full responsibility for his or her own health status. Some will sign, and some will refuse. If the patient refuses, make a note of that fact and record the time of departure.

Identification Tags

Most facilities require all personnel to wear photo ID tags. If someone you do not know comes to your unit without proper identification, introduce yourself, ask if you can help, and ask for his or her name and professional designation. For all you know, the person you're speaking to may be the hospital's chief of staff—but err on the side of caution. If the person seems suspicious, aggressive, or argumentative or refuses to identify him or herself, get help. Do not confront anyone alone if you feel the situation is potentially volatile or dangerous.

Secure Units

Some areas may be designated as secure units, such as the psychiatric unit or the maternal–child unit. Just how secure these units are and the type of security they have will vary. Often, these units have a camera to show anyone who is approaching. Some units may be locked, and designated staff will have keys. There will be a bell or signal at the door, which the approaching individual will activate. It may be your responsibility to open the door. If you do not recognize the person, ask for identification and the purpose for visiting the unit. There may be individuals who are not welcome in the unit. For example, a new mother may have told staff that she does not want to see her estranged partner. Follow agency protocol when handling such situations. Many units now apply an electronic band to the baby that will sound an alarm if that child is brought close to an exit. See Chapter 15 for more details about newborn security. Intensive care units, although not usually designated secure, will also have restrictions on who may visit and when. Visitors are often required to ring a bell; a nurse or the clinical secretary will answer and determine whether it is in the patient's best interest to have a visitor at that moment.

>>> **WHAT TO WATCH FOR**

- The continued growth in the use of computerization in health care facilities and the widespread integration of CPOE.
- Measures to ensure that computerized health records and the exchange of other health information is secure.
- Continued research and implementation of infection control measures in hospitals and other health care facilities to identify, control, and contain infectious outbreaks (including better reporting and related communication with such facilities as the World Health Organization). Current concerns include the Zika virus.
- Improved measures for meeting the needs of a culturally diverse society, for example, the thousands of Syrian and other refugees who have come to Canada from war-ravaged countries (e.g., some hospitals now offer unrestricted visiting hours, with exceptions and limits on the numbers of visitors if another patient's well-being is compromised, such as a roommate).

SUMMARY

1. Health care facilities include general (primarily acute-care) hospitals, convalescent hospitals, chronic care facilities, nursing homes, rehabilitation hospitals, psychiatric hospitals, and drug addiction/alcohol treatment centres. Accreditation, while not mandatory, enhances a facility's status and funding opportunities. Preparing for accreditation is a hectic process.

   Hospital restructuring has included rationalizing services, discharging patients earlier, and replacing acute care with chronic care and "step-down" beds. There is a concerted effort across Canada to develop strategies to enable older Canadians (and others) with multiple and chronic health problems to live at home for as long as possible.

2. Almost all departments are interdependent in some manner. Patient-care units, which house the patients, are central. They are usually specialized, in that care is rendered to patients with similar problems—for example, medical, surgical, obstetrical, or pediatric. Other departments provide administrative, technical, diagnostic, and other types of support.

3. Nurses make up the largest portion of health professionals working in the hospital setting. Depending on the facility, registered nurses or registered/licensed practical nurses usually assumes leadership roles. In an acute-care hospital, an RN is likely to assume the leadership roles. The health care team includes physicians, pharmacists, physiotherapists, social workers, and occupational therapists—most of whom are involved in decision making related to the patient's ongoing care.

4. As clinical secretary, you will be instrumental in managing the communication and administrative functions of a patient-care unit. You will have clerical responsibilities

(such as maintaining charts and schedules, ordering supplies, and transcribing orders) and communication responsibilities (such as answering the telephone and keeping co-workers informed). You will coordinate the unit's administrative functions and liaise with other departments. Never disregard the boundaries that define your scope of practice. If a patient needs care, find a nurse.

5. The nurses' station is the communication and administrative hub of a patient-care unit. Other components include the reception area for patients and visitors, treatment rooms, utility rooms, a kitchen, the medication room, and conference areas. You may be required to give visitors or patients a brief orientation of your unit.

6. Most hospitals are completely computerized—almost all administrative functions depend on an electronic environment. Everything from patient registration, the use of eCharts, and medication administration is done electronically. You must be absolutely comfortable with the computer systems used in your hospital and keep abreast of changes and software updates. Very little is done manually, but you must maintain a solid knowledge base of how to manage and integrate components of a pChart and eChart, how to complete requisitions manually, and how to download and prepare reports as required.

7. Keep al health information confidential. Never allow an unauthorized person access to patient charts. Never reveal information on the telephone or in-person without authorization. Guard your computer screen from unauthorized viewing, change your passwords regularly, and log out or lock your screen if you will be away from your computer from any length of time.

8. Become familiar with your facility's security policies and emergency procedures. Learn the universal codes (or those used in your facility). Do not hesitate to ask for identification if someone you do not know is seeking access to a closed area or to patient records. Most hospitals require photo ID tags. Some units are "secure" and require that visitors and staff identify themselves before entering.

KEY TERMS

acute care   406
chronic care   406
CICU   414
clinical secretary   422
collaborative
    partnership   409
credentialling   418
critically ill   416
cross-coverage   424
day surgery   410

dressing tray   429
emergentologist   418
emesis basin   413
endoscopy   416
laparoscope   410
ophthalmoscope   428
otoscope   428
palliative care   414
rationalization of
    services   409

shift report   431
sphygmomanometer   427
stethoscope   427
subacute, transitional, or
    step-down care   410
subdural hematoma   416
suture removal tray   429
terminal cleaning   413
ultrasonographer   417

REVIEW QUESTIONS

1. Differentiate between an acute-care or general hospital and a nursing home.

2. What is meant by a partnership agreement among hospitals?

3. What are the implications of hospital restructuring in Canada for health office professionals?

4. List the clerical and communication duties of the clinical secretary.

5. What is meant by the phrase *scope of practice?*

6. List the various parts of the patient-care unit and their functions.

7. What are a clinical secretary's responsibilities in regard to equipment kept at the nurses' station?

8. Identify three actions you could take to keep eCharts confidential.

9. What would you do if a patient threatened to leave the hospital without permission?

10. What would you do if a patient had a cardiac arrest?

APPLICATION EXERCISES

1. Using the internet, research the job description of a registered nurse, a registered practical nurse, and a personal support worker. List specific activities that each is qualified to carry out. Interview a family member or friend and ask him what he thinks these professionals do. Interview someone in one of these professions. Compare her answers with those other students have collected and with the internet job descriptions.

2. Interview a clinical secretary (or ward clerk). Ask her to describe her responsibilities. Compare them with those discussed in this chapter.

3. Research the community resources in your community that are available to provide support and services to discharged patients requiring home care. Include long-term facilities, admission policies, and the approximate wait time for a bed.

4. With another student, create a set of guidelines for maintaining confidentiality of electronic medical information on a patient-care unit. Draw on research from your school or municipal library or the internet.

5. With two or three other students, investigate the use of cellphones in hospitals within your region. Include the facilities' policies on bringing computers to the hospital and the implementation of Wi-Fi.

6. With another student, investigate the accreditation process in facilities within your region: What hospitals are accredited? Hhow often is the review process conducted? What impact does a review have on hospital staff—including the clinical secretary? This will require interviewing some staff members or clinical secretaries.

7. Choose two hospitals in your area. Compare their emergency code systems to each other, as well as to Table 14.1 in this chapter. Detail the implications of and actions required for each.

WEBSITES OF INTEREST

Sample Organizational Charts

www.sickkids.ca/AboutSickKids/who-we-are/Organizational-Charts/index.html

Hospital Trends in Canada

https://secure.cihi.ca/free_products/Hospital_Trends_in_Canada_e.pdf

This report from the Canadian Institute for Health Information provides a historical analysis of statistical and financial data on hospitals in Canada.

Accreditation Canada

www.accreditation.ca

This site provides complete information on the accreditation of health care facilities in Canada.

Nursing Homes

www.retirementhomes.com/homes/Nursing_Care/Canada/index.html

This site provides links to nursing homes across Canada. Search by name, city, or province.

www.nursinghomeratings.ca/nursing-homes

This site lists nursing homes and also provides ratings.

Chapter 15
Hospital Documents and Procedures

Pearson Education

LEARNING OBJECTIVES

On completing this chapter, you will be able to:

1. Understand the initiatives and strategies related to patient flow.

2. Discuss how to admit a patient to hospital considering patient flow procedures, and describe four types of hospital admission.

3. Describe how to generate and manage a medical and surgical chart.

4. Identify the components of a surgical chart.

5. Discuss the clinical secretary's responsibilities related to preparing a patient for surgery.

6. Differentiate between the responsibilities related to transferring a patient within the hospital and discharging, and describe how to arrange transportation for a patient.

7. Identify general files and resources found in the hospital.

The procedures and forms discussed in this chapter will provide you with an overview of hospital document usage, content, and format as well as applications to an environment using predominantly computerized practices (while still interfacing with manual components). The most highly computerized hospitals use computerized physician order entry (CPOE), while others still have handwritten doctors' orders, and a few still process medication administration records manually. Specific features of the electronic order entry systems and the patient's electronic chart (eChart) will be discussed throughout Chapters 16–21.

This chapter assumes you will be working as a clinical secretary in a hospital environment integrating computerized and manual administrative practices. Responsibilities you would have in a CPOE environment are also introduced. Regardless of what department you are working in, you will be handling many of the same documents, as well as some that are unit specific (e.g., surgical verses medical). How things are done in different hospitals will vary (in terms of procedures and protocols), and hospital information systems (HIS) differ as will the terms used to describe various modules within the system. Hospitals build their own modules within an HIS, access them using different commands, and assign them different names. A good example is the patient-care summary screen, which all hospitals have. This is where a summary of the care patients receive is found, including the treatments and interventions ordered, health teaching required, discharge planning, and sometimes pending lab and diagnostic tests. Names for this summary include the *patient intervention (PI) screen*, *eKardex*, or *worklist*. Although the terms used in these chapters may differ, in general the information related to these terms is fairly generic. Patient flow is another important aspect of hospital work, which some hospitals now call the admitting department patient flow because it is more descriptive of bed management initiatives (discussed later).

L01 BED MANAGEMENT: PATIENT FLOW

Efficient bed management is a priority for health care facilities across Canada because of chronic bed shortages, particularly in acute-care hospitals. The process of bed management and the names given to it vary: Patient flow, patient access and flow, electronic bed management, or patient navigation are common titles. Note that a bed refers not only to the physical bed but all the services that go with that bed—for example, medical, surgical, rehab, or long-term care.

Patient flow refers to policies and procedures generated by health care facilities to coordinate efforts that will facilitate patient access to *the right care* in the *right place* at the *right time*. Typically, patient flow addresses the need for timely admission to and discharge from an acute-care hospital to the appropriate discharge destination. This could be to a facility with a rehabilitation bed, a long-term care facility, or home—with or without community support (how patient flow policies and procedures impact discharging a patient is discussed later in the chapter). Patient flow also includes the discharge of a patient requiring a higher level of care to the appropriate facility, and **repatriation** back to a community hospital as soon as clinically appropriate. The required care may be available within or outside of the patient's own community—in some cases the patient may be sent out of the province/territory or to the United States (e.g., premature twins requiring neonatal intensive care beds when none are available in the province). Provincial patient flow initiatives extend to Canada's remote northern communities as well; for Indigenous people on reservations, there is a federal component to organizing access to the required care.

patient flow the process of maximizing efficiency for moving patients through their health care experience; mainly associated with hospitals and other health care facilities. It is ensuring patient access to the *right care* in the *right place* at the *right time* in the most efficient way possible.

repatriation returning a patient who has been discharged to another facility back to the original hospital. For example, if a patient requires a higher level of care and is sent to another hospital, returning the patient to the original hospital is called repatriation.

Communication Networks

The success of patient flow depends largely on a streamlined communication and information sharing network that connects facilities within any given community, across the province or territory, and beyond. The structure of the network will vary with each jurisdiction, particularly at the local level. However, most jurisdictions provide a dedicated number (e.g., CritiCall in Ontario) that is accessible 24 hours a day to physicians, providing consultation and advice regarding patient situations, access to trauma or critical response teams at available locations, and access to a "bed board" that monitors available beds within the jurisdiction.

Emergency transport teams, such as STARS (Shock Trauma Air Rescue Society) in Western Canada, can be contacted to transport critical patients. At a regional level there will be a central number that provides physicians and other health professionals with similar information for one or a group of hospitals. For example, Bedline is the contact point for physicians wanting to admit a patient to hospital in southern Saskatchewan.

Successful patient flow policies have the following results:

- Improved patient outcomes
- Reduced wait times for both emergency and elective admissions
- The ability to admit patients to the type of bed they require
- Moving patients to discharge destinations that meet their needs both within and outside of their immediate community
- Reduced costs for the hospital because patient stays are shorter and they occupy the bed they need (i.e., alternative level of care patients are not occupying acute-care beds)

Working in Patient Flow

Acute-care hospitals will have a patient flow program that is managed 24 hours a day, 7 days a week. The training and background of staff members working in patient flow departments varies greatly. Individuals in these positions assume a significant amount of responsibility; some jurisdictions use only registered nurses (RNs), others use RNs with a team of individuals who have a medical office administration diploma or previous experience working in a hospital. These positions have a variety of titles, including *bed allocator*, *bed operator*, or *patient flow coordinator*.

To work in patient flow, excellent communication skills and the ability to stay calm when responding to calls in an often hectic environment are essential. You may be managing one call when another phone is ringing while having to keep an eye on the electronic bed board on the computer. Other responsibilities may include tracking and updating the status of all beds within one or a group of facilities using an electronic bed board (or equivalent), interacting with patient-care units to open beds and assigning these beds according to protocol, providing a communication link with referring departments, and managing all incoming and outgoing calls for repatriation requests. Working in patient flow involves extensive computer work, so the ability to concentrate is important, as are break periods.

How Patient Flow Affects the Admission Process

new admission a patient recently admitted to hospital.

A referring doctor seeking a hospital bed (a **new admission**) for a patient would call the designated patient flow number within the community; this typically involves an urgent admission from the doctor's office or elsewhere in the community or for someone in the emergency department (ED). Depending on the situation, the physician may or may not require or want a telephone consultation with another physician (e.g., an emergentologist or specialist). In many jurisdictions the patient flow department would arrange this conversation. The consultation could involve the referring physician seeking direction or advice regarding the kind of care the patient needs and which hospital can provide the required care, or the referring physician may want to consult with a specialist at a designated hospital to transfer the patient's care to that specialist and give him or her a summary of the patient's condition. Once the decision has been made to admit a patient, the physician contacts patient flow requesting a specific bed for the

✓	Room Bed	Unit	Serv	Req Accm	ISO	Patient Name	EDD	Comment	Resv
	E3.622-01	1SRG	GS	SP	N	SURG,ONE		HOYER LIFT REQUIRED	
	E3.622-02	1SRG	GS	SP		SURG,TWO			
	E3.622-03	1SRG	GS	SP	N	ELF,TWO		FOR TELEMETRY	
	E3.622-04	1SRG	GS	SP		ELF,ONE			
	E3.626-01	1SRG	GS	SP		DWARF,JONATHAN JAMES	03/06/16		
	E3.626-02	1SRG	GS	SP		ELF,THREE			
	E3.626-03	1SRG	GS	W	N	ELF,FOUR		PT WANDERS	
	E3.626-04	1SRG	GS	SP	N	ELF,FIVE			
	E3.632-01	1SRG	GS	SP	N	ELF,SIX		VRE+ FOR LTC	
	E3.632-02	1SRG	GS	SP	N	ELF,SEVEN			
	E3.634-01	1SRG	GS	W	N	DWARF,COL			
	E3.634-02	1SRG	GS	SP		IMAGING,ONE			
	E3.636-01	1SRG	GS	SP		ELF,EIGHT			
	E3.636-02	1SRG	GS	SP	N	ELF,NINE	06/06/16		
	E3.638-01	1SRG	GS	SP	N	ELF,TEN			
	E3.638-02	1SRG	GS	SP	N	ELF,ELEVEN			
	E3.646-01	1SRG	GS	SP	N	ELF,TWELVE	03/06/16		
	E3.646-02	1SRG	GS	SP	N	ELF,THIRTEEN		OFF SERVICE-STROKE	
	E3.646-03	1SRG	GS	SP	N	ELF,FOURTEEN			
	E3.646-04	1SRG	GS	SP	N	ELF,FIFTEEN			
	E3.648-01	1SRG	GS	SP	N	ELF,SIXTEEN		ALC CCC-CONF TRANSFE	
	E3.650-01	1SRG	GS	SP		ELF,SEVENTEEN			
	E3.662-01	1SRG	GS	SP		ELF,EIGHTEEN			
	E3.664-01	1SRG	GS	SP		ELF,NINETEEN			
	E3.666-01	1SRG	GS	SP		ELF,TWENTY			
	E3.668-01	1SRG	GS	SP		MARX,GROUCHO			

Figure 15.1   Example of an electronic bed board
Huron Perth Healthcare Alliance

patient. Patient flow would search for and assign that patient to the appropriate bed (e.g., surgical, telemetry, medical) at the preferred location (if possible).

Patient flow monitors all beds available in all hospitals within their catchment area using a bed board. The bed board is updated regularly and presents a reasonably current picture of available beds. Shown in Figure 15.1 is the bed availability for each unit in an acute-care hospital. Listed is the total bed capacity of the unit, the number of beds occupied, the number of beds available, the occupancy rate (percentage) for each unit, and the number of confirmed as well as pending discharges. Especially noted are the number of isolation beds and alternative level of care beds.

If the required bed is not readily available, patient flow will call nursing units to see if a bed can be "freed up"—for example, if there are pending discharges that, upon review, can be discharged early. The staff member in patient flow will also know when beds currently occupied will come available, called *confirmed discharges* (e.g., Mrs. Czekaj, who is occupying a medical bed, is leaving at 11:00 a.m.). If there is no suitable bed available within a reasonable time frame, the bed allocator will call around to see if there is a bed that can be opened up. Alternatively, the bed allocator may find the type of bed required at another hospital or at another campus connected to the same hospital. Most hospitals have a time limit (e.g., three hours) within which they must find accommodation for the patient.

Tracking Bed Availability on the Unit

Each patient-care unit is responsible for managing patient flow in their designated area(s), ensuring that the patient flow department is kept up to date on the unit's bed status (e.g., reporting all interfacility transfers as well as confirmed and pending discharges). Although hospitals will have regular (e.g., daily or twice daily) group meetings to assess their admissions and discharges, there are always unexpected discharges, transfers, and admissions that must be reported as they occur. As the clinical secretary on the unit, this would likely be your responsibility.

L02 TYPES OF ADMISSIONS

Elective Admissions

Most elective admissions are primarily for booked surgical procedures (e.g., cardiac bypass surgery, hernia, hip replacement). Elective admissions for medical purposes are less common than they were even a few years ago, unless acute medical problems are managed by an interdisciplinary team of health professionals in clinics, elsewhere in the community, or at home. For example, advances in information technology have led to sophisticated home-monitoring systems that, when combined with connectivity to a team of health professionals, allow individuals with complex medical problems to be managed at home. If their condition becomes acute, the patient would likely be admitted to hospital through patient flow as high priority or as an emergency.

Prebooked elective admissions for surgery are almost always admitted the same day as the surgery (admit same day, or ASD). In some hospitals, prebooking a bed is left to the operating room (OR) or surgical services. They would advise patient flow how many and what type of surgical beds are needed anywhere from several weeks to one or two weeks in advance. Patient flow, in turn, would factor those prescheduled beds into their bed count, probably close to the day the surgery is booked. OR time is often booked weeks to months in advance; for example, a person requiring hip surgery may have a six-month wait for OR time and surgeon availability, not a hospital bed. Surgeons are allotted a certain amount of operating time. Often the surgeon is available, but cost constraints limit the availability of the operating room.

Patients being admitted electively usually have their admission procedures completed in advance at a pre-admit clinic, which may involve viewing videos preparing them for what to expect before, during, and after surgery, and to complete a variety of questionnaires and an admission sheet (also called a face sheet). Some hospitals have all of this information online for the patient to complete and submit either electronically or to download and bring to the hospital. Patients go to patient registration or directly to the surgical pre-admit unit, where the remaining paperwork and admission process are completed. Their ID band will be applied, vital signs taken, and, if required, an IV started. Depending on the surgery, a nurse may insert a Foley catheter (discussed in Chapter 19).

Emergency Admissions

If an individual presenting in the emergency department (ED) is seriously ill or hurt, chances are he or she will be admitted to hospital. When the physician decides to admit someone, the clinical secretary in the ED (or sometimes the team leader) must call patient flow to request an appropriate bed (e.g., medical, surgical, pediatric, or obstetrical). Patient flow assigns a bed and calls the appropriate patient-care unit to let them know they are receiving an admission. The clinical secretary on the receiving unit notifies the nurses that they are receiving an admission. Once the patient arrives on the unit, the clinical secretary will initiate the patient's eChart (adding the appropriate data sheets for the receiving unit) and probably generate a physical chart. A paper copy of the ED admission sheet (there may or may not be a hospital card or ID stickers) will be sent to the unit with the patient. The patient should have an ID band on. There will likely also be a written set of admission orders completed by the emergentologist, possibly on the ED admission sheet (see Figure 15.2). The ED admission sheet will outline the reason for the admission, a patient assessment, and any procedures or treatments the patient has received. There may be a separate doctor's order sheet. If there are separate doctor's orders, they have probably been written by a specialist (usually an emergentologist) who saw the patient in the ED and who may temporarily be the most responsible physician (MRP).

<table>
<tr><td></td><td>CTAS</td><td colspan="2">Patient Name</td><td>H #</td></tr>
</table>

STRATFORD GENERAL HOSPITAL
EMERGENCY DEPARTMENT
46 General Hospital Drive,
Stratford, ON N5A 2Y6
Phone: 519.272.8200 Fax: 519.272.8243

HPHA
HURON PERTH
HEALTHCARE
ALLIANCE

	DOB	Age Gender Visit #
ARRIVAL MODE	Address	
AMB.ARRIVAL TIME	City	Postal Code
REFERRED BY	Phone	
HISTORY BY	Health Card #	Attending Physician
RECEPT.DATE	Emergency Contact & Relationship	Emerge Contact #
RECEPT. TIME	Family Physician	WSIB ☐ Employer Name & Address

CHIEF COMPLAINT

TRIAGE NOTE

TRIAGE DATE	
TRIAGE TIME	
TRIAGE RN	
REG. DATE	

ALLERGIES

MEDICATIONS
☐ Meds   ☐ Pt has meds
☐ See attached list/MRF   ☐ Meds Unknown
☐ Please call Pharmacy _____

T	P	R	BP	/	SpO2	WT

TRIAGE REASSESS NOTES

SECONDARY NURSE ASSESSMENT

ROOM	TIME	PRIMARY RN

Appearance: Alert Well Drowsy Ill
Colour: WNL Pale Flushed Cyanotic Jaundiced
Behaviour: WNL Anxious Aggressive Withdrawn
Pain: ___/10 _____

Distress: ___/10 _____

_____
_____
_____
_____
_____
_____

PHx: _____
_____
_____

Safety/Confort: Bed Rails Call Bell Warm Blanket
Medical Directive: _____

DIAGNOSTIC TESTS

Hematology	Order Sets	Urine
☐ CBC	☐ ABD	☐ Urine Preg
☐ TB7R(BUN, CREAT, LYTES, GLUC.)	☐ CARDIAC	☐ Urine Dip
☐ LFTs	☐ OD	☐ Urine R&M
☐ AMY	☐ STROKE	☐ Urine C&S
☐ EKG	☐ TRAUMA	
☐ INR		
☐ PTT		**Imaging**
☐ BHCG		
☐ TROPONIN		
☐ BC x _____		
☐ Ca⁺⁺, Albumin		
☐ Mg⁺⁺, PO4		
☐ _____		
☐ _____		
☐ OLD CHARTS		

ORDERS

Ordered At	Ordered By	Order	Admin'd At	Admin'd By

☐ MD Order Sheet Attached

FORM#FR0004M4 12 10 ISBO1A

MD Signature: _____

Figure 15.2 Emergency department sheet
Courtesy of Stratford General Hospital

STRATFORD GENERAL HOSPITAL
EMERGENCY DEPARTMENT
46 General Hospital Drive, Stratford, ON N5A 2Y6
Phone: 519.272.8200 Fax: 519.272.8243

HP HA
HURON PERTH
HEALTHCARE
ALLIANCE

Patient Name					H #
DOB		Age	Gender	Visit #	
Address					
City			Postal Code		
Phone					
Health Card #			Attending Physician		
Emergency Contact & Relationship			Emerge Contact #		

FLUID BALANCE

INTAKE				OUTPUT				INTERVENTIONS		
Time	Oral	IV		Urine	Stool	Emesis		Time		Initials
Total										

☐ Fluid Balance Record Attached

VITAL SIGNS

Time	Temp	Pulse	RR	BP	SpO$_2$	Initials	Time	Temp	Pulse	RR	BP	SpO$_2$	Initials

☐ Vital Signs Record Attachd

Clinical Notes

Time		Initials

☐ Clinical Notes Attached

DEPARTURE

Care Completed/Left ER Time : ____ / ____ by: ____ / ____ Home LWBS LAMA OR Admitted Transferred
Transferred to: _____ Transfer of Accountability given to: _____
Discharge Vital Signs: T:____ P:____ BP: ____ / ____ SpO$_2$:____ Teaching: _____ Initials:____
Workload (Date/Time/Shift): _____

Name	Signature	Initials	Name	Signature	Initials

ER0004M3

Figure 15.2 *(Continued)*

When the patient arrives on the floor, it is important that you look carefully to see if there are any stat or urgent orders to implement since these are common with ED admissions. Also be alert for any returning test results from procedures that may have been ordered while the patient was still in the ED. In hospitals with CPOE, orders will have been processed electronically, but you still need to review them to ensure the information has been properly added to the patient's eChart (e.g., lab work, level of activity, nursing interventions/assessments).

Note that in most emergency departments the admitting physician is an emergentologist who works at a number of hospitals. He or she may be unfamiliar with your hospital's computerized system (especially in CPOE environments), thus the ED admission report may be computer generated with the patient's demographic information, but then downloaded and completed manually by the emergentologist.

> ### ⟫⟫ POINTS TO PONDER
>
> The ED is a fast-paced, sometimes stressful environment to work in. You must be organized, detail oriented, and able to work well under stress. The ability to multitask is also essential, as is the ability to anticipate the needs of a variety of people—from the health professionals to the patient and the patient's family. Do not forget the patient's family. Situations will differ, but for the most part they are anxious, wanting as much information as possible, and perhaps feeling helpless. Answer their questions as completely as you can, appropriately refer them to the correct health care professional to have other questions answered, and offer them a kind smile, a soothing word, and encouragement. Many families tell stories of how the clinical secretary made their ED experience so much better than it could have been.

Obstetrical Admissions

Patient flow monitors admissions and discharges from obstetrical units and will assign beds as required. Most obstetrical (or maternal–child) units admit a woman once she is in established labour. Nurses triage based on the woman's status; she may be admitted, sent home, or kept for a while to see if labour becomes clearly established, at which point she will be admitted. If a woman is in early labour, she may be asked to come back when labour has become more active. The actual admission process is the same as any admission except that additional forms are needed for the chart, such as labour assessments forms, delivery records, postpartum assessment sheets, and an obstetrical flow sheet. In the computerized environment, an obstetrical care plan will be added to the eChart. The woman must sign a consent form for delivery (which may cover the necessary use of interventions, such as forceps). If a Caesarean section is planned, she may need to sign another form. Often the forms needed for frequent documentation in labour and delivery are paper based—even in highly computerized environments.

Admitting the Baby   The baby is considered present for admission after it is born. The clinical secretary on the unit must notify the admitting department to "admit" the baby, providing such information as the baby's name, sex, date/time of delivery, type of delivery, weight, mom's full name, room and bed number, and the name of the baby's doctor. This can be accomplished with a computer or by telephone. Admitting will send up a hospital ID bracelet for the baby, generate an admission sheet, and a matrix for ID stickers.

Outpatient Admissions

Patients who are *not* admitted to hospital overnight, including day surgery patients, are considered in some facilities to be outpatient admissions. They may be admitted to a medical day unit or a surgical day unit. The patient is issued an ID band, and the basic information required is similar to that required for an inpatient admission. However, the patient's chart (electronic or paper) will contain only forms related to the treatment, service, or procedure the patient is to receive. Most facilities have an outpatient admission sheet.

Insurance and Type of Accommodation

Patients admitted under urgent or emergency conditions will be assigned the bed for which they have coverage, if available; otherwise they will take the bed that is offered. In an ideal situation, there is a choice of accommodation on admission. You must confirm the type of accommodation the patient has coverage for, or if the patient has a specific request. A patient who requests accommodation not covered by private or supplemental insurance (noted on the admission sheet) must sign a form assuming financial responsibility for the cost difference between the requested accommodation and provincial/territorial or private coverage. All provincial and territorial health plans provide standard, or ward, coverage—usually four beds to a room. Suppose James lives in Newfoundland and requests a private room. He has no insurance other than the Newfoundland and Labrador health plan. You would ask James to sign a statement saying that he will pay the difference between ward accommodation (covered by the province) and private accommodation. Now suppose that James has a Blue Cross policy covering semi-private accommodation. He must then assume financial responsibility for the difference between the semi-private room and the private room. Here is a breakdown of the cost coverage for James's stay:

■ The provincial plan covers standard accommodation.

■ Blue Cross pays the difference between semi-private and standard accommodation.

■ James pays the difference between semi-private and private accommodation.

Patients are not responsible for the cost of upgraded accommodation if they were not offered the choice. For example, Janet has only standard accommodation coverage and is admitted to a semi-private room because that is the only room available. Janet is *not* charged for the cost of the semi-private room. As soon as a standard bed becomes available, Janet should be offered the choice of moving or paying for the added cost of the room from that point on. If she is not offered the choice, she continues to get the semi-private room at no charge.

Make the choices clear to the patient. Suppose that when Janet was admitted the clinical secretary asked her if she wanted a semi-private room. If she said yes, she would be responsible for the cost of the semi-private room even if there were no standard beds available. The ethics of doing this are questionable because she was not given full information. She would probably not realize that if she had said no she could have had the semi-private room free of charge until a standard bed became available.

Admission Procedures

The hospital department where patients are registered or admitted has typically been called *patient registration* or admitting. Since the adoption of patient flow initiatives, a growing number of hospitals refer to these departments as patient flow. The basic function is the same: Patients are admitted to the facility, but patient flow brings with it the added responsibility of bed management, as discussed earlier. You will see the term patient registration used in most clinics and outpatient facilities.

An individual being admitted to the hospital will usually first go to patient flow (or admitting or patient registration) or directly to the patient-care unit if it admits its own patients. The ED, maternal–child, and outpatient units are examples of areas that may handle their own admissions.

The clinical secretary admitting the patient would fill out the patient's admission sheet (or update the information if the patient is already in the database), prepare a hospital **identification (ID) band**, and prepare and print two or three sheets of ID labels. In some hospitals the admission sheet remains online; in others, it is printed and sent along with ID stickers and will follow the patient until he or she is at her designated inpatient unit (e.g., ED to the floor, to the same day admit clinic, to the OR, to recovery, to the floor).

To admit a person (from any department) you would use the patient registration module. Select the patient from a central databank that contains a list of all patients who have ever had an encounter with the hospital; if the patient is new, you will enter the information. Most systems will allow you to search for the patient by name, health card number, or hospital number.

For example, suppose Matthew Smith arrives at your unit. You access the registration module and the central name bank and start by entering the patient's last name and perhaps the first initial. This would bring up all patients within that name range:

> Smith, Malachi
> Smith, Martha
> Smith, Matthew
> Smith, Matthew
> Smith, Michael
> Smith, Moira
> Smith, Murray

There are *two* Matthew Smiths. Look at the initials, if any, or date of birth. Then, look at the health numbers of both to see which Matthew Smith's chart you need to access.

Most computer programs colour code the status of each patient. For example, all active inpatients might be blue; discharged patients, yellow; and outpatients, red. Matthew Smith is an inpatient, so under this system his name would be highlighted in blue.

TIP

Be sure to ask the patient if he or she has any allergies and follow agency policy with respect to highlighting what they are. This is essential information that could result in a serious adverse event if the information is inaccurate or not recorded properly.

Select the correct "Matthew Smith," and press Enter. You can then begin to create a new chart, access the patient's current chart, or access charts from any previous admissions. Each admission or other hospital encounter would be in the databank with a different account number, but in most cases the same hospital number will be used.

Completing the Admission/Face Sheet   An admission sheet is completed for all individuals who are admitted to hospital. In many hospitals the admission sheet is still completed when the patient arrives at the hospital, not in advance. You can populate the admission sheet with the required demographic details obtained from the database for previously admitted individuals, but make sure to validate all information. You may be required to print a copy of the admission sheet to be sent to the floor with the patient. Often a hard copy of this document is kept in the patient's chart.

On admission, the patient is assigned a computer-generated medical records number (MRN) that appears on the admission sheet, an ID band, and ID labels. The printed admission sheet and set of ID labels go to the floor with the patient. The bed/unit will have been assigned by patient flow. It is important to note the patient will have only one MRN (**hospital number**) that remains the same for all admissions. The admission sheet will also contain an account file number that is unique

identification (ID) band a plastic bracelet bearing the patient's name, hospital number, and a bar code that can be scanned to validate patient identification (e.g., for medication administration). The bracelet is removed upon discharge.

hospital number (also called a medical records number, or MRN) a unique number assigned to each patient admitted to hospital.

to that patient for *that* admission. This number is used by the finance department for billing purposes.

Preparing the ID Band

Issuing an ID band on every admission is important for basic patient safety. Most hospitals issue ID bracelets that are encoded with the required patient information retrieved from the hospital information system. This information can be scanned for patient identification purposes (e.g., at the bedside when a nurse is giving the patient his or her medication). Radio frequency ID (RFID) is an emerging technology that involves implanting a chip on the patient's ID band. The information it contains is more detailed and is read with a transponder (see Figure 15.3).

> **TIP**
>
> If you populate the admission sheet electronically with the demographics already recorded in the patient's electronic database, remember to review the pertinent information to ensure it is current and accurate.

Usually the clinical secretary who is actually admitting the patient applies the appropriate ID bands to the patient's wrist (plus an additional colour-coded band if the patient has allergies). If the patient is not wearing an ID band when he or she arrives on the floor, or if it comes off at any time, call admitting and have it replaced.

Preparing ID Labels The majority of hospitals have replaced the plastic "hospital card" with ID labels. ID labels are preprinted with essential patient information, have bar codes (similar to the ID bracelet), and have adhesive backs so they can be easily applied to all patient documents.

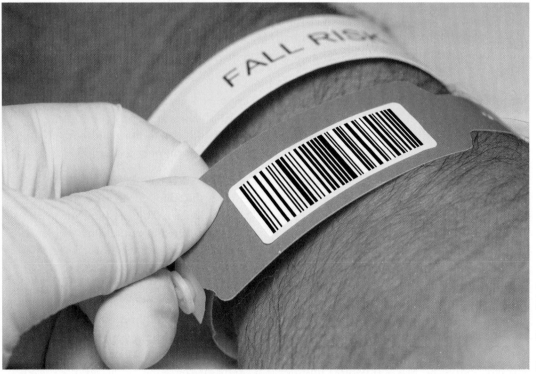

Sherry Young/Fotolia

Figure 15.3 Hospital ID band with bar code

Identifying Patient Documents   ID labels are only relevant in facilities/units where printed chart forms/records are used. ID labels must be affixed to any printed patient documents. If a patient goes to another hospital department (for tests, treatments, or surgery) where hard copies of the eChart components are needed or likely to be generated, an extra supply of these ID labels should be kept in the chart that accompanies the patient.

Any printed reports or forms that are kept in the patient's pChart/binder must have patient labels on them unless printed with the patient information present. *Never* let anyone enter information on a printed chart form that is not labelled. Documents are easily mixed up and could end up in the wrong patient's chart. As well, medications could be given to the wrong person or tests conducted on someone for whom they are not intended.

L03 GENERATING AND MANAGING A CHART

A patient's eChart is generated on admission, regardless of the type of admission or which hospital department admitted the patient. Once the admission sheet has been completed, a relevant care plan must be attached to the patient's eChart (e.g., medical, surgical, neurology). How this is done varies. Initially, a patient's eChart contains all of the basic chart fields, but they are empty. Once attached, the care plan populates the various fields of the patient's chart with a comprehensive list of assessments and interventions related to the patient's condition. For example, an attached medical care plan would not list assessments and interventions concerning a surgical incision or mobilizing a patient after major surgery. This list will be amended and individualized to the patient's needs when the doctor writes the orders.

In a CPOE environment, *everything* is done electronically. After the patient is admitted (admission sheet completed), the physician enters an order set that will include investigations, treatments, patient care, medications, and interprofessional consults. The nurse completes an admission assessment, which includes a head-to-toe assessment, clinical history, allergies, height/weight, social history, activities of daily living, and some best practice assessment.

> ### ▶▶▶ POINTS TO PONDER
>
> Clinical secretaries who do not work in a CPOE environment are unsure of how their job description will change if CPOE is implemented in their hospital, especially if they are not directly involved in order entry. However, clinical secretaries working in CPOE facilities state that they are as busy, sometimes more so. They remain the hub of communication, and their time is directed to more administrative duties, organizing consults, admissions, transfers and discharges, and payroll, and entering stats into the computer. However, they are still responsible for monitoring electronic orders (and are still involved in some components of order entry), as well as maintaining the integrity of both paper and eCharts.

Any printed components of the patient's information are kept in a binder that is referred to either as the patient's chart, the pChart, or the binder. A patient-care unit will have a specific place to keep charts. It may be a "wheel" or large circular structure (like a lazy Susan) that has slots into which the charts fit, or it may be shelves with narrow slots. The charts are labelled and sequenced according to room number. A patient admitted to room 301, bed 1, would have a chart labelled 301-1. Most charts have a sleeve for identifying information: the patient's room (and bed number if not in a private room), first and last names and initial, and the physician's name. Do not write the patient's diagnosis on the chart label. This would be a breach of confidentiality since anyone going by could read it. Patients still have pCharts in CPOE environments with selected records still printed and kept there.

When a patient is admitted, take the appropriate binder, label it, and put the chart forms in their appropriate places in the chart. In some hospitals, the various doctors are assigned colours. If Dr. deMarco has red, any patients admitted under her services would have their names written on a red chart insert with Dr. deMarco's name underneath. If a patient has more than one doctor, use the MRP's name and label colour. For example, suppose Dr. deMarco admitted Lorne West to 301 with a diagnosis of pneumonia on Sunday. On Monday, Dr. deMarco requested a consultation by Dr. Talbot, an internist. If Dr. Talbot assumes care for Lorne for the duration of his hospital stay, Dr. Talbot would become the MRP, and you would have to redo the label. Some patient-care units put the names of both doctors on the label with the MRP's name first. If two specialists are caring for a patient, one still assumes the role of the MRP. Sometimes you have to find out which one is the MRP. This information is important to record so that nurses know which doctor to contact if there are concerns.

Old Charts

If a patient is readmitted to hospital, the doctor may request to see his or her old charts. pCharts are retrieved from health information services (often still called medical records). Retrieved charts are identified using the patient's name and either the date of birth or the MRN. Most hospitals have scanned old charts—at least back to a designated past date. The scanned charts as well as past eCharts are part of the newly created eChart, which is usually accessible through the patient intervention screen (or stored separately under "history").

This information can be separated into segments: for example, admission demographics, all previous order sets, flow sheets, medications, and a variety of laboratory and radiology reports.

Framework of a Chart

Most eCharts will contain similar fields or categories of information. If pCharts (or components of pCharts) are used, the forms will likewise be comparable. The reason for a patient's admission determines what other documents are required (e.g., whether the admission was for a medical condition such as diabetes, congestive heart failure, a hip replacement, abdominal surgery, or to have a baby). The medical chart is probably the most basic. Documents in pCharts are usually in a specific order: admission sheet, signature sheet, doctor's orders, vital sign sheet, fluid balance sheet (if used), multidisciplinary notes, lab and diagnostic test results, consultation reports, and progress notes. Surgical charts would have documents relating to the surgery at the back of the chart. The same documents are found in the eChart. Depending on the system used, you would either click on an identifier or scroll through the various components.

The Basic Medical Chart

Admission Sheet The admission sheet, as illustrated in Figure 15.4, contains a collection of information gathered from the patient upon admission to hospital. As previously mentioned, it may also be referred to as a face sheet and, generally, a hard copy is kept as the first sheet in the patient's chart (if pCharts are kept). Any patient admitted to hospital, regardless of the length of stay, has an admission sheet. This includes outpatients and patients admitted to the ED who are treated and released. The patient's general information, including name, gender, address, telephone number, date of birth, family doctor, and next of kin, is found here. Note that the admission record is also used for information collected on discharge.

Patient ID # _____ Registration Clerk Initials _____	CONESTOGA GENERAL HOSPITAL MOUNT FOREST ON N5A 2Y6	
Surname: Previous Name:	First Name:	Birth Date: _____ YYYY MM DD
Age: Sex: Marital Status:	Previous Admission Date:	Street Address:
City/Town/Village:	Postal Code:	Tel No. Home: Business:
In case of emergency notify:	Relation:	Tel No. Home: Business:
Health Number:	Other Health Insurance: Information (Semi-Private & Private):	
Company Group Name and Address:	Certificate Number:	Group No.
Attending Physician:	Attending Physician:	Family Doctor:
Admitting Diagnosis:	Surgery/Procedure:	
LOS:	Admitted & Surgery Same Day (ASD): Inpatient: Day Surgery: DS - Short Stay Unit:	
Discharge Diagnosis:	Surgical Ambulatory Care: Accommodation: Ward: Semi-Private: Private:	

Figure 15.4 Routine admission sheet

Admitting and Discharge Diagnosis   The admission sheet records the patient's admitting (or provisional) diagnosis—the reason for coming to the hospital. This may differ from the diagnosis the patient leaves the hospital with. There is usually a space on the admission sheet for the discharge diagnosis, which may be written in by the physician. For example, suppose a patient was admitted with a **provisional diagnosis** of abdominal pain not yet diagnosed. After investigation, the doctor determined that the patient had ulcerative colitis, which becomes the patient's definitive or actual diagnosis, and entered this as the discharge diagnosis. Alternatively, consider Clair, who was admitted with a provisional diagnosis of ovarian cyst. After investigation, it was determined she had an ectopic pregnancy. The discharge diagnosis would be ectopic pregnancy.

provisional diagnosis a diagnosis subject to change after an actual diagnosis has been established.

Surgical Procedures   Any surgeries the patient has had in hospital will be listed on the admission sheet upon discharge. If there has been more than one surgery, they would be listed in order of occurrence.

Discharge Information   The date and time of the patient's discharge and the length of stay (LOS) are usually noted on the admission sheet. You or a nurse may be responsible for this. Ensure that someone has entered this information before the chart is sent to health information services.

Insurance Information   Private insurance companies cover services not included under provincial or territorial plans. It is important for you to know what type of coverage the patient has, particularly if he or she requests a room other than standard or ward accommodation.

Religion   This is important information if the patient wants contact with someone of his or her own faith. When patients are asked about religion, they are usually also asked if they want a clergy visit. If a patient later asks to see a member of the clergy (perhaps when he or she is in critical condition and not communicating clearly), you can look up this information on the chart and know whom to call.

Next of Kin   The next of kin is the person you would contact in case of an emergency. Strictly speaking, the next of kin refers to the closest relative, but the term has fallen out of favour given the modern blend of families and diverse relationships. It is usually, but does not have to be, a spouse, common-law spouse, parent, or other relative. If you need to contact someone on the patient's behalf for any reason, the next of kin is the person to call. If you need to contact someone to make a decision about the patient's medical care when the patient is unable to do so, you must contact the person who has the power of personal care (the aspect of power of attorney relating to health care decisions) or who has been legally granted the responsibility to do so. This may not be the person listed as next of kin. Ask if it is the same person. If no one has been granted the power of personal care, the decision would rest with the person's closest relative.

Admission Interview/Assessment Form   In most hospitals, nurses complete an interview assessment with each patient. The form is often in questionnaire format. It includes questions about a range of things, from the person's nutritional, rest, and activity habits to roles and relationships and how the patient copes with stress. The nurse will also review current medications and ask again about allergies. The purpose of the interview is to provide caregivers with a holistic overview of the patient so that care can be individualized and the patient's hospital stay made more comfortable. Another important aspect of the interview is to determine any cultural needs of the patient.

The information may be entered electronically or be handwritten. In some facilities the patient is given the questionnaire to complete, after which the nurse will review it with the patient. This form is kept either at the front or the back of the chart. In CPOE and other electronic environments, the patient interview and assessment is done by the nurse and entered directly into the patient's eChart. The nurse will include the patient's height and weight. If the nurse does not do this for some reason (e.g., because of the patient's condition), you will be flagged to remind the nurse to get this information when possible. It is important information that is sometimes used to determine the dose of medications.

The Care Pathway

After the admission sheet is completed and a care plan added, a care pathway, if pertinent, is attached to the chart. This may be done electronically or in paper format. Most hospitals have care pathways for more common conditions (e.g., congestive heart failure, pneumonia, COPD, stroke, or for a patient who has had surgery). It outlines *generalized* goals and expectations for patient recovery, complications notwithstanding. Care pathways also recommend guidelines for standard diagnostic and lab tests, frequency of related nursing assessments and related goals, as well as patient education. In some hospitals, nurses add the specific components that define the patient's care pathway to the patient's eChart.

Patient Information Access Screen

This pertains to eCharts only. Most hospital computer systems have a screen or field that lists all of the patients in a unit, allowing the viewer to point and click on any patient, opening up their eChart. Once into the patient's eChart, there may be another screen listing the various parts of the patient's eChart.

Patient Intervention Screen

The patient intervention (PI) screen (sometimes called an eKardex) contains a broad range of information about the patient. This includes information about such things as patient education, tests, respiratory therapy, nursing interventions, nursing assessments, treatments, and discharge planning. Every nursing intervention will have a corresponding nursing assessment. Some PI screens contain information about vital signs, intake and output, and pain control. The PI screen is updated as needed, with interventions added, deleted, or amended in accordance with orders written by the health care team.

Signature Sheet   Most facilities keep a signature sheet in each patient's chart or in the medication binder if used. If stored in the chart, the signature sheet is often found behind the admission sheet and in front of the doctor's orders, or at the very back. Any health professionals providing care to a patient must first write the date, print then sign their full name, and provide a sample of their initials on that patient's signature sheet. From then on, they can simply initial the sheet. This provides a method of identifying who has given medications or provided other patient care. In the electronic document, a PIN or password identifies the person entering data.

Doctors' Orders   The doctor's orders give specific directions regarding almost all aspects of patient care and are written by the primary physician responsible for the patient (the MRP). Doctors' orders are either handwritten and kept in the patient's pChart or electronically added to the eChart. The types of doctors' orders are discussed in Chapter 16.

Vital Signs Flow Sheet   The vital signs flow sheet is used in manual environments, often for patients who are very ill and have vital signs taken frequently. Vital signs are assessed at designated intervals, either according to facility protocol or ordered at specific times by the physician.

Vital signs in the electronic environment are entered into the computer by the health professional (usually the nurse) at the point of assessment using a handheld device or the patient's bedside computer. They are automatically graphed onto a flow sheet under "clinical parameters." (See Figure 15.5.)

Multidisciplinary Note/Interdisciplinary Notes   Sometimes also called nurses notes, *multidisciplinary notes* are usually electronic, although you may see them kept as a hard copy in the patient's pChart. They may also be referred to as *clinical notes*. These notes are kept mostly by nurses, who usually input data every shift or as

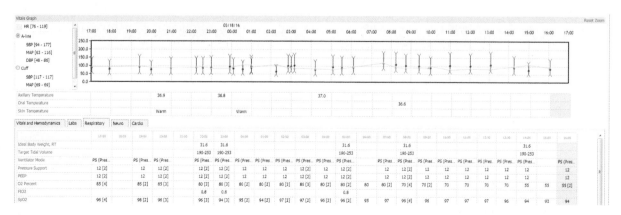

Figure 15.5   Vital signs
Courtesy of North York General Hospital

needed, about the patient's care and progress. If they are called *nurses' notes*, only nurses (strictly speaking) are allowed to make entries. Other professionals, such as physiotherapists, respiratory therapists, or social workers, may keep their own notes or may use the progress notes (see "Progress Notes"). If the sheet is called multidisciplinary notes, any health professional involved in the patient's circle of care may make entries. Comments on the patient's progress as it relates to care pathways can be charted here or in a separate area. Flow sheets are used for documentation as well. Electronic formats differ, but they will be contained in the patient's eChart and must be dated and signed.

Progress Notes   Progress notes are primarily used by physicians, nurse practitioners, and perhaps physician assistants. Typically they contain documentation of the physician's assessment of the patient, including general well-being and response to treatment while in hospital. The practitioner usually records progress notes each time he or she sees the patient. There may be more than one physician who records in these notes. Each entry must be dated and signed. In a computerized environment, doctors can add notes electronically from any computer linked to the hospital system or remotely from an offsite location (e.g., the provider's office or home).

Other health professionals who participate in the patient's care may use the progress notes or include their own progress notes and other assessment tools in this part of the chart (e.g., a respiratory therapist or a physiotherapist).

Reports   Reports of any kind in the electronic environment are prepared and attached to the patient's eChart. A number of hospitals still keep hard copies of lab and diagnostic test results in the patient's binder. Consultation and diagnostic reports must be dictated, almost always using voice recognition software. Once these reports have been edited, they will be electronically added to the patient's chart. Some hospitals prefer to keep a hard copy of consultation reports in the patient's binder as well.

A *consultation report* is generated when one physician asks another physician to assess a patient. For example, an internist may ask a cardiologist to see a patient who is having chest pain. The information contained in the consultation report is a result of the specialist's findings.

Diagnostic Reports   A diagnostic report is a summary of results done on the patient (such as X-rays, bone scans, mammograms, or an MRI). Diagnostic reports are almost always produced by a radiologist. Diagnostic images are usually available for online viewing by the physician. A pathology report is the analysis of a tissue sample/biopsy as interpreted by a pathologist and would also be filed with reports.

Laboratory reports (which were discussed extensively in Chapter 6) are customarily generated by the lab department that processed the test, but each lab handles reports differently. The results of all lab tests, including pathology reports from surgery and biopsies, will be sent electronically to the patient's eChart (see Figure 15.6) or occasionally also in paper format. If a paper copy is printed, file it in the appropriate section of the patient's chart. The lab will call the floor if the results are abnormal and need prompt attention and physician notification. Most labs will notify the physician directly if there is a concerning result.

Medication Administration Records   In most hospitals, medication administration records are entirely electronic (eMARs); they are generated by the pharmacy and attached to the patient's eChart. The process of obtaining the medication from an automated dispensing cabinet, scanning the patient's ID bracelet for identification and medication verification, and signing for the medication is all computerized. Medication administration records may be downloaded in some circumstances (e.g., if a patient is going for surgery).

Aurora Systems Ltd.

RUN DATE 02/03/17				PAGE 1
RUN TIME 1700H	STAT Y	URGENT	ROUTINE	
USER THOMDOUG				

NAME Joe Black	AGE 87	SEX M	MRP Dr. Brown
HOSP # 434543	UNIT 3S	ROOM 302	UNIT # 1234
DOA 02/01/17	STATUS Inpatient		

SPECIMEN # 21243	COLLECTED ON	02/03/17	REQ # 543455
	RECEIVED ON	02/03/17	MRP. Dr. Brown
			FAMILY DR. R Fleming OTHER

TEST ORDERED: PTT   Y   N
RELATED DATA: CLIENT ON ANTICOAGULANTS: heparin drip
                    PLEASE DETAIL

TEST	RESULT	FLAG	REFERENCE RANGE
PTT > PTT		> 150	29-40 SECONDS
	RESULTS CALLED TO UNIT AND TO DR. BROWN The APTT therapeutic range for clients receiving unfractonated heparin is 52-83 sec Critical value when not on therapy is > 100 s Critical value when on heparin is > 150 s **		

Figure 15.6   Electronic lab report (APTT)

In the partially manual environment, the pharmacy department will generate the medication administration records (MAR; discussed in Chapter 16). Paper MARs are kept in a binder, usually located on a medication cart. One patient may have several paper MARs, depending on the number of medications he or she is on or the type of medication (e.g., standing/regularly administered medications on one MAR, and PRN [as needed] medications on another). Paper MARs must be signed by the nurse each time a medication is given. If you ever notice that a medication has not been signed for, let the nurse involved know.

There may be more than one medication binder depending on the size of the unit. For example, rooms 301–312 may have one binder and one med cart, while rooms 314–328 have another binder and another med cart.

L04 THE SURGICAL CHART

Preparing a patient for surgery can be done either on the surgical pre-admission unit (same-day admit) or on the surgical floor. The surgical chart is prepared for any patient coming into hospital for an operative procedure or an invasive diagnostic procedure requiring anesthetic. In the electronic environment, a surgical care plan would be attached to the patient's eChart on admission and may contain the required pre-surgical forms—some may be completed electronically, while others may have to be downloaded to be filled out and perhaps signed. In many facilities pre-surgical forms (e.g., consent, anesthetic questionnaire, preop checklist) are paper based. As well, you may be required to print out a copy of the patient's current MARs to send with the patient. When the surgery is over and the patient has "recovered," the recovery room will notify you that the patient is ready to be transferred to your floor. All pre-surgical chart forms in printed format will be sent to your unit with the patient; you should place them safely in the patient's clinical binder/chart. The following forms are those that you would most often add to the patient's chart.

Consent Form   A consent form may have been filled out prior to the patient's admission if the surgery is elective, but must be in the patient's chart if it was signed electronically. Check to be sure it is part of the eChart. If you cannot find the consent form (paper or electronic) or if it is not signed, notify the nurse immediately. If a paper-based consent form has not been completed, put the patient's ID label on the form and fill out as much as you can—usually the type of surgery and the date. This information can be obtained from the doctor's orders or admission sheet. Give it to the nurse to review with the patient and complete. The nurse must have the patient sign it and sign it him or herself as witness.

Pre-anesthetic Questionnaire   The patient should always fill out and sign this questionnaire before undergoing any operation or procedure involving anesthetic. It typically questions patients about factors that may affect the safety of anesthetic use, including heart, lung, and kidney disease; blood pressure; diabetes; fluid retention; use of tobacco and alcohol; prior experience with anesthetics; allergies; and current medications. The nurse should review this form with the patient. If there are any dubious answers, the anesthetist may review the information with the patient. The anesthetist usually visits the patient briefly prior to surgery to review the questionnaire and ensure that the patient's questions related to the anesthetic have been properly answered. The anesthetist will often write preoperative orders at that time. Electronic completion of this or any form would likely be done on a tablet.

History and Physical Assessment   To ensure the patient is fit for surgery or to identify any current risk factors, the patient must have a history and physical done prior to surgery—usually within two weeks. The report needs to be on the patient's OR chart. If the assessment has not been done or the report is not on the chart, surgery may be delayed or cancelled. This assessment may have been done by the patient's family doctor or by an intern or resident in the hospital. If you can't find the report, there are two actions you can take: (1) Call the family doctor's office to see if it is there; if so, have them fax a copy to you; (2) if the assessment was done in the hospital, the report might have been dictated but not edited or transcribed, and thus is sitting in medical records. Call them; if it is there, they can prepare the document and send it to the floor.

Preop Checklist   The preop checklist is an inventory of all essential tasks that must be completed before the patient goes to the operating room. This checklist is kept in the front of the chart. Check off and initial checks you have made or all the tasks you have completed. If an item is not applicable, do not leave it blank; enter N/A and add your initials. If the item is left blank, it may be assumed that a needed step has been missed (see Figure 15.7).

Anesthetic Record   This form is used by the anesthetist during the surgery and may be in electronic or paper format (in CPOE environments it is electronic). You may be required to add the date, patient's age, height and weight (must be actual and not stated weight), the presence of any allergies, and any preop medication that has been ordered (include the name of the drug and the dose). The nurse will add the time it was given and sign after he or she gives it.

| | 2016-Mar-18 |
	13:45
⊿ **Measurements**	
Height/Length (cm) cm	
◈ Weight (kg) kg	
▦ Body Mass Index Measured (m2) m2	
⊿ **Special Conditions**	
Special Conditions	
⊿ **Pre-Procedure Checklist**	
Procedure Name	
Pt Questionnaire-Anaesthesia Completed	
Patient ID Band on and Verified	
MRN/FIN Verified	
Allergy Band on and Verified	
Procedure Consent Signed	
Blood Consent Signed	
Procedure Identical All Places in Chart	
Previous Patient Chart Accessible	
Preparation Complete	
Pre-Procedure Preparation (MH Only)	
Bladder Emptied by	
Last Void	
Saline Lock in Situ and Patent	
Dentures	
Contact Lenses/Glasses	
Prosthesis Removed	
Other Items Removed	
Pre-op Medication Administered	
Anticoagulant Held	
Pre-Op Blood	
POC Glucose mmol/L	
Review of Labs	
ECG (Current) in Medical Record	
H&P (Current) in Medical Record	
Tests Completed, Resulted in Chart	
Pre-Procedure Consultations	
Last Fluid Intake	
Last Food Intake	
Reports Not on Chart	
Orientation	
Affect/Behaviour	
Pre-Procedure Checklist Completed By	
Patient and Chart Accepted	
Checklist Incomplete Items	

Figure 15.7 Electronically generated preoperative checklist
Courtesy of North York General Hospital.

Fluid Balance Record   Some patients will have a postoperative order written for intake and output (I&O). In many cases it is automatically assessed. This means that the nurses must keep track of everything that goes into the patient—whether through drinking or by intravenous (IV)—and everything that comes out, including urine, vomitus, and drainage from any tube inserted (e.g., a drainage called a *hemovac* is sometimes inserted into a wound after surgery; this would be emptied every shift and the amount of fluid in the tube noted as output). Patients getting IV solutions (discussed further in

Chapters 17 and 19) are almost always put on I&O. For example, postoperative patients often have an IV until they are drinking well on their own and voiding without difficulty. Even patients without an IV will have their fluid balance assessed until they are voiding properly postop. In a mixed manual/electronic environment, you would therefore add an I&O record to most postoperative charts. Other patients may be on output only. This usually means that urine output must be recorded, but intake does not need to be.

In computerized settings, fluid balance information is entered into the patient's eChart and tracked/tallied electronically. Most systems will generate a flow sheet that graphs the patient's intake and output. This is visually much easier for physicians to follow.

Chart Forms for the Operating Room

Before the patient goes to the operating room, you may be required to add the following additional records to accompany the patient (in addition to the pre-surgical reports/forms):

- eMARs printed or transferred from the medication binder (unless electronically sent). Nurses may have transferred these already, but do not rely on them to do so; check that they are there. The anesthetist must have these sheets to review the patient's most current medication profile.
- Additional patient ID stickers

When you must add operative sheets in hard copy format, add the patient's ID sticker to each sheet. In many facilities, these records are added to the front of the chart, ahead of the doctor's orders.

L05 RELATED RESPONSIBILITIES OF THE CLINICAL SECRETARY

It is important to be organized, to know which forms and reports are required (e.g., consent, recent history and physical, ECG report), which are electronic, and which (if any) are to be printed and put into the patient's clinical binder/pChart (e.g., hard copies of the eMARs). You may also need to ensure that everything is in order prior to the patient leaving the unit for surgery (a last minute check of the chart).

When an inpatient is going to the operating room, you may be responsible for posting an NPO sign in the patient's room or writing NPO on the white board beside the patient's bed (precise procedures will vary). Make sure that dietary services cancels the patient's meal trays until further notice. Usually NPO begins at 10:00 the night before, although for a surgery late in the day it may begin at 6:00 or 8:00 a.m. after a light or fluid breakfast. You would change the patient's dietary status to NPO for the morning of the surgery, and change it again when the patient returns to the unit (to whatever is ordered postoperatively). Sometimes a doctor will allow the patient to take a specific medication orally with a sip of water.

For same-day admit patients, they will have been instructed to refrain from eating or drinking at approximately the same time—10:00 p.m. the night before the surgery or, in some cases, it may be 8:00 p.m. Upon arrival at the pre-surgical unit, you or the nurse (depending on the distribution of responsibilities) must confirm that patients have followed instructions. If a patient "forgot" and had something to eat or drink within a few hours of the surgery, surgery will likely be cancelled or postponed because the patient is at high risk for vomiting and aspirating when intubated and given an anesthetic.

Current Orders

When a patient goes to the operating room, all existing orders are usually considered void until reordered. Generally, medications are put on hold until they are reordered. In an electronic environment it will likely be the nurse who makes note of this. If the medications remain the same, the only thing you may need to change is the reorder date for paper MARs. In a computerized environment, pharmacy usually generates new eMARs when medications are reordered.

Orders for Preoperative Preparation   *Chapter – 10 (Fundamentals)*

For an inpatient, the doctor will not likely write preoperative orders until the day before the surgery. Process any preoperative orders promptly, especially if some of them involve time-sensitive medications, tests, and assessments, such as blood work or an ECG. Some preparations are routine, such as the NPO status.

Premedication   The anesthetist may order a preoperative medication, such as a mild sedative, a muscle relaxant, or an anti-nauseant. Some physicians also order ranitidine (Zantac) or metoclopramide preoperatively to deal with gastric reflux problems often associated with surgery (particularly when related to the gastrointestinal system). The latter may be ordered to be taken orally with sips of water despite the fact that the patient is NPO. For some surgeries (e.g., gastrointestinal or orthopedic surgeries), IV antibiotics may also be ordered preoperatively. In most cases this is all handled electronically. If not, be aware that preop medications are due and add them to the appropriate MAR or anesthetic sheet, depending on facility protocol.

Scheduled Operating Room Time

Patients booked for surgery, particularly **elective surgery**, will have a designated time for the surgery assigned by the operating room.

A surgical schedule (also called the OR list) is sent to the floor electronically, outlining the surgeries booked for the following day. You will receive a list of all same-day surgical admissions coming to your unit postoperatively in addition to any surgeries booked for inpatients. There may be a master list sent to all surgical units. Because the list is widely circulated, to ensure confidentiality it does not give the patient's name; only the floor, room, bed number, procedure, and time are noted. Some facilities will add patient names to the list for specific units. For example, the list sent to 3 West will display the names of the patients on that unit going to the operating room; names of patients going from other floors will not be listed. Review the list, highlight any surgeries that pertain to your unit, and post the list in the designated place, usually a bulletin board. You can then prepare the surgical charts on the basis of this list.

Surgical schedules are usually fairly accurate, but there is no guarantee that surgery will take place exactly as scheduled. Emergency surgery or complications with an operation can cause delays. That is why preoperative medication orders are written to be given one hour or half an hour before surgery. Either you or the nurse can call the OR to see if they are on schedule. In some hospitals, the policy is to assume the OR is on time unless they call the floor to let you know they are running late.

On a day surgery/**preadmission** unit, patients are admitted on the day of the surgery, usually one to two hours before they are booked for surgery. The OR will notify you if their surgery is delayed.

Valuables   Prior to surgery, the nurses will often collect the patient's valuables, such as a wedding ring or a small amount of money, and put them in a sealed envelope to be

elective surgery surgery that is necessary but not an emergency and can therefore be booked in advance. Examples of elective surgery include removal of a tumour, a hip replacement, or a hysterectomy.

preadmission a process wherein patients who are booked for surgery receive preoperative and postoperative teaching and fill in documents ahead of time.

kept in a locked cupboard in the nurses' station. You may be asked (prior to surgery) to add the patient's ID sticker to the envelope. The nurse and the patient often sign over the sealed envelope. The envelope is recorded in the nurses' notes. After the surgery, nurses should return the valuables. It is helpful to mention this to the nurse as an extra check. For example, you could ask the nurse if he or she would like you to return the valuables.

Postop Bed   The patient is usually brought to the operating room on a stretcher. Occasionally, the OR will want to transfer the patient directly to his or her own bed from the OR table, in which case the prepared bed must be brought to the operating room. The nurses make what they call a "postop bed," raised to the height of the gurney and with the linen arranged in a particular way to ease the transfer. The nurses will also set up the room with such things as an IV pole, emesis basin, and oxygen. If the OR calls for the bed to be brought to the OR, make sure it is done promptly.

The Patient's Family   Surgery is a trying time for the patient's significant other, family, and friends. Often, they are at a loss as to where to wait, how long to wait, and how to find out about their loved one. You may be their primary contact and source of information. Some facilities provide family members with a pager that allows them to leave for coffee or a bite to eat or to engage in other activities. When the patient returns to the floor and is ready to be seen, you would page the family. Otherwise, all facilities provide lounges where family members can wait.

Generally, surgeons tell their patients the anticipated length of the surgery. Still, family members get worried and restless if they feel that the process is taking too long. Delays in the start time of the surgery, unforeseen complications, and time in the recovery room can add to the wait time. You can call the OR or the recovery room to get information on the status of the patient and a timeline as to when he or she is expected back on the floor. In some cases, a family member or loved one will be given permission to go into the recovery room briefly.

Confidentiality, Security, and Patients' Charts

Health care professionals should look only at their own patients' charts. If a physiotherapist or even a doctor comes in and proceeds to look at the pChart or eChart of a patient he or she is not taking care of, that is considered unauthorized access unless the patient has given permission. Though you may find it difficult to challenge a doctor, you must question anyone who seems to be seeking unauthorized access. You could approach the person and say something like "I see you are viewing Mrs. Smith's information. Dr. Morgan was in just a few minutes ago. Is there something I can help you with?" The person will usually either explain or stop what he or she is doing.

All facilities have tracking protocols so that anyone logging into a computer and viewing a patient's health information can be traced. Keeping your computer screen secure and logging out or locking your screen when you are away from your work area is essential. If someone accesses your computer under your password and views any patient's chart, you will be identified, not the unauthorized individual.

These days most hospitals keep only selected information in a pChart, which is not often accessed. That said, if a doctor's orders are handwritten, encourage the doctor to return the chart to its proper location when the orders have been completed. There may be a designated spot for active orders (which should be flagged). When a patient is required to leave the floor for a test or an assessment and the pChart must go with him or her, be sure it returns when the patient does.

Security on the Maternal–Child Unit

The maternal–child unit is one of the most secure units in a hospital. Parents must have all aspects of unit security explained to them upon admission (this may have been discussed during a pre-admit program, but should still be reviewed). Security is achieved with an intercom (and sometimes video) system. Individuals visiting must announce their arrival using an intercom placed outside the unit's locked door. The clinical secretary or nurse answers and, if appropriate, remotely unlocks the door to allow the person in.

Many facilities also apply an electronic band to the baby's ankle for added security against potential abduction. The bracelet has a unique ID number and every exit point in the unit is electronically monitored to detect the bracelet. This bracelet will cause an alarm to sound if the baby is brought outside of the secure unit (and even sometimes if the baby is carried too close to an exit) and if someone tries to remove or tamper with the bracelet (other than a member of the health care team).

L06 TRANSFER AND DISCHARGE PROCEDURES

Transfers within a Hospital

Sometimes patients are transferred from one unit to another *within* the facility, usually on a doctor's order, either for medical/surgical reasons, such as to receive surgery that the original unit cannot offer, or to provide appropriate accommodation. The patient may keep the same hospital number but may be assigned a different account number depending on where he or she is moved within the facility. Check that the patient is being moved as a **transfer**. Some facilities require that the patient must be discharged if moving to another service within the same hospital; for example, if a patient is moving from a medical unit to a mental health unit, the move could be considered a discharge and not a transfer. However, a patient moving from surgery to intensive care is a transfer, and the same account number would be used.

transfer the act of moving a patient from one place to another within the same health care facility.

Patients will also be transferred if they are occupying a bed they no longer need—most commonly if a patient is in an acute-care bed but no longer needs acute-care services. That patient, if unable to be discharged, would move to an ALC (alternative level of care) bed when available. Depending on the hospital's funding formula, it can be expensive having patients in a bed they do not require. The province may not fund that bed, meaning that the hospital would be charged for the cost of the bed the patient is occupying. (Remember that the term *bed* means the bed and all of the services that come with that bed—medical, surgical, intensive care, etc.).

The patient's eChart will be the responsibility of the receiving unit. As the clinical secretary on the receiving unit, you would access the eChart through the hospital information system. You may have to remove the previous care plan and add your own (e.g., if you are on a surgery unit receiving a patient from a medical unit, you would remove the medical care plan and attach the surgical care plan). You may have to review the patient's PI screen and adjust/amend, delete, or add assessments and interventions to the care plan. Follow your facility's procedures, completing all information and updating the patient's eChart as quickly as possible.

When transferring a patient with a pChart, remove all reports/forms from the binder, put them in a labelled envelope, and send them with the patient. Make sure all the patient's belongings, medications, and MARs (if in paper format) go with him or her. Notify patient flow of the transfer so they can adjust their bed board. All the relevant hospital departments (e.g., laboratory and diagnostic services, dietary services, pharmacy) will be electronically notified of the patient's new location so they can act accordingly.

The term *transfer* is sometimes mistakenly used when a patient is being discharged to another facility. For example, a nurse may tell you, "Mr. Bastone is being transferred from Calgary General to Happy Meadows Nursing Home by ambulance." In actual fact, Mr. Bastone was admitted for dehydration and treated and is now being discharged back to his nursing home residence.

Interhospital Transfers

You must also keep a list of transportation services for patients who require assistance moving to another facility, such as a patient going somewhere upon discharge from the hospital, or a patient being sent to another facility for a test and returning to the hospital of origin within a few hours. In some jurisdictions, patients transported between facilities require a special transportation tracking number. The number is generated by a provincially regulated agency; for example, in Ontario the agency is the Provincial Transfer Authorization Centre. A medical authorization transfer number is obtained for the patient prior to transfer with any transport organization. This tracking number applies to any patient leaving or going to any facility within and outside of the jurisdiction (e.g., repatriation). This system is in place to track patients in the case of an infectious disease.

As previously noted, tracking patients' transfers and discharges are usually done electronically using a tracking system that interfaces with the hospital communication system. Suppose you receive confirmation that a patient is being discharged by ambulance to a long-term care facility. Here is what you would need to do:

■ Check for any restrictions on the time the patient can go.

■ Call the receiving facility to see when they are prepared to receive the patient.

■ Call for a medical authorization transport number, if applicable.

■ Call the transport/transfer company and arrange the pickup time for the patient (give them the transport authorization number, if applicable).

■ Notify family members of the date/time/destination if no one is with the patient.

■ Fill out and download any forms related to patient transport.

■ Print all relevant medical information and place it in a sealed envelope (depending on the patient's destination).

■ Check that all patient belongings/personal medications are transported with the patient.

■ If the transportation is more than a half-hour late, call to see why there is a delay and to get their expected time of arrival.

■ Proceed with routine discharge procedures; notify patient flow that the patient has left.

If booking online:

■ Use your required facility login to access the transport site (if you have problems, there should be a help line to call).

■ Fill in the required transport form.

■ Wait for an email confirmation of your request (for most online bookings, all of the submitted information is manually reviewed to ensure it is clear and accurate). During usual working hours you will likely get confirmation within an hour.

Be aware of the hours of operation of transport organizations: how long you should call ahead to book a transfer (some companies require you to book at least four to six hours in advance), what happens if you book during the evening/weekend, and any other policies and procedures specific to the organization. Most hospitals use selected companies, so there should be no surprises as long as you familiarize yourself with the company's protocol.

Discharges

The term **discharge** applies to any patient who is permanently leaving the hospital, whether for home, a nursing home, a retirement home, or another health care facility. This is different from a transfer. Remember, a **transfer** occurs only when a patient is moved from one place to another within the *same* health care facility.

discharge any release from a health care facility by doctor's orders.

Discharge Planning   Discharge planning is an integral part of patient flow initiatives; this discussion is a continuation of the patient flow procedures discussed at the beginning of the chapter.

As mentioned earlier, the goal of a hospital is to get the patient back to the appropriate discharge destination as soon as the patient is able. With that in mind, plans to discharge a patient begin the moment he or she is admitted. Discharge planning is based on the patient's assessment, previous situation (e.g., functional abilities), diagnosis, and plan of care.

As previously discussed, on admission a care pathway is attached to the patient's eChart, if appropriate. For example, when Irene was admitted, a care pathway for COPD would have been attached to her eChart (see Figure 15.8). Irene's EDD (estimated date of discharge), as estimated by the COPD care pathway, would typically be five days from the date of admission. Plans for discharge consider the patient's probable discharge destination (e.g., home, whether there is a need for home care or other community resources, a rehab or step-down facility, or a long-term care facility). Discharge planning may involve contacting external resources, such as a social worker, community placement worker, or physiotherapist. Discharge planning becomes more tangible as the patient's condition evolves. Let's assume that Irene is able to go home on day five, but she needs oxygen and a home care assessment. In addition, Irene smokes and wants help to quit. Discharge planning might include anticipating some or all of the following actions:

- Arranging an assessment with a case manager to determine what kind of home care support she needs

- Making an appointment with a smoking cessation clinic (perhaps offered by her primary health care team)

- Making a follow-up appointment with her family doctor

- Ensuring she has any prescriptions the physician has left for her (or having her prescription medications sent to her residence by her pharmacy of choice)

- Arranging transportation if she is unable to provide her own

Discharging a patient is more complicated than simply following a care pathway to determine when the patient can go home. Discharge planning involves the entire team of health professionals within the patient's circle of care.

Assessing a Patient for Discharge   Patient care in most hospitals is delivered by an interprofessional team, not just doctors and nurses. All health professionals involved in the patient's circle of care work together to facilitate the patient's recovery, discharge from hospital, and ongoing care and support. Discharge rounds are held daily on most inpatient floors. The interdisciplinary health care team meets and reviews all patients on a particular unit and discusses who is ready for discharge. Team members

SAMPLE OF SELECTED COMPONENTS OF A PATIENT CARE MAP/PATHWAY FOR A PATIENT ADMITTED WITH COPD				
COPD clinical pathway	Admission Phase (avg 1–2 days)	Transition Phase (Avg 1–2 days)	Pre-discharge Phase (1–2 days)	Discharge (Avg LOS 5 days
	DATE	DATE	DATE	DATE
Clinical Assessment and Monitoring	O2 sats & q2h X2 if acute otherwise q4hX2 (report Temp ↑38 Resp ↑28 Chest Assess QID &PRN colour/consistency of sputum IV as ordered Notify for chest physio as needed Dyspnea -at rest? Complete admission questionnaires, determine level of health teaching needed	O2 sats VS TID or as ordered by MRP -within normal parameters? Chest Assessment q6h colour of sputum improved? IV d/c or as ordered Dyspnea -at rest, light or moderate exertion?	O2 sats and VSq12H or as ordered Chess Assessment Q12h Colour of sputum clear? No dyspnea with lite to moderate exertion? (relate to patients normal status)	O2 sats &VS 0800 ok if normal Ok if Chest Assessment improving to patients normal status O2 needed at home? Home support? Team Assess for discharge OK
Standing Orders for lab and diagnostic tests	CXR pa and latera; EKG if ordered -do if angina present CBC, lytes, CR, BUN on admission and day 1 INR, PT if ordered; ABGs if dyspneic; sputum C&S Theophylline levels if on drug	Repeat CXR if no improvement Blood cultures x3 if temp ↑38.5 ABGs if sats ↓90% on room air	Assess need for home O2 and order if not in place Lung assessment if ≤ one year	O2 @ home arranged Next INR date noted if indicated
Consultations	RRT; physiotherapy, Registered dietician social worker Community care	OT Pharmacy (if on IV meds)	RT for directions r/t home oxygen if needed and home O2 sats -arrange follow-up with family doctor + team for monitoring Arrange for VS monitoring at home	Patient has all necessary contact information, directions, phone numbers.
Nutrition	Consult with RD as required Monitor food and fluid intake Push fluids	Tolerating diet	Intake adequate, following recommendations	No questions Diet and fluid intake satisfactory
Activity	AAT based on patients functional ability Up in chair QID Short walks chair to door or father if tolerated TID Assess ability for self-hygiene, up to BR or commode	Up in chair QID and PRN, short walks with/ without assistance 5-6 meters +/- To BR with assistance or assistive device; hygiene partial or no assistance (reflecting previous level of functionality)	Up ad lib with little of no dyspnea, able to walk 9+ meters Can mobilize independently according to usual function; self care unless has not done prior to admission Assess need for community support	Community support ordered as needed Appoint for home care confirmed with patient/home care agency

Figure 15.8 Partial care pathway for a patient with COPD

Discharge Planning	Discuss discharge plans and EDD with patient Discharge destination discussed Patient and family understand/communicate needs upon discharge Preliminary arrangements for home care arranged if needed	Patient care assessment meeging arranged with health team and family if necessary Assess need for in-patient rehab (in-patient and at home) Assessment for home care with case worker/ social worker if needed Referral to family doctor ahd his health care team -VS and oximetry monitering at home Smoking cessation support if requested	Act specific concerns Assess patient at discharge rounds Make appropriate arrangements Make final arrangements Ensure equipment and linkage in place Arrange as needed	Discharge order written & Arrange discharge time/ transportation if needed; Give patient any locked belongings Review all educational material and medications and instructions (steroids, antibiotics) Ensure all scripts and appointment dates given to patient/family member

Figure 15.8 (*Continued*)

include the MRP and sometimes consultants, nurses (perhaps the team leader, an RN, or an RPN/LPN), a personal support worker, a social worker, a respiratory therapist, a speech and language pathologist, an occupational therapist, and the unit manager, depending on the structure of the unit. Each team member involved in a given patient's circle of care gives his or her assessment of the patient's readiness to leave the hospital and voices any concerns that may result in pushing back the patient's discharge date. Consider Alan, who had a stroke. From the doctor's perspective, he is medically stable, but the nurses have some concerns about his ability to bath and dress himself. The physiotherapist and the occupational therapist agree. In addition, the physiotherapist reports that Alan has not met his goal to ambulate the length of the hall with a walker and climb four stairs. For these reasons, Alan's discharge is delayed. Instead, a decision was made to move Alan to a rehabilitation facility until such time as he could be discharged home, perhaps with home care.

Discharge rounds would classify Alan as a pending discharge (meaning a planned discharge), and this would be noted by patient flow. Once the doctor writes the order for discharge, the pending status would be changed to confirmed. You would then begin the discharge process, beginning with the search for a rehab bed. Once found, and once Alan has been physically discharged, you would notify patient flow. They in turn will mark his now empty acute-care bed as available on the bed board.

The Discharge Order A patient must have a written doctor's order to be discharged. These orders may be written on the day of discharge or in advance. Frequently, the decision to discharge a patient is made at discharge rounds. Alternatively (or if the hospital does not have discharge rounds), a physician may come in to do rounds in the morning, decide which patients can go home that day, and write the orders. A discharge order may also be obtained by telephone, but the nurse taking the order must write it on the doctor's orders sheet and sign and date it. The usual discharge time is around 11:00 a.m. In most jurisdictions, the provincial or territorial plan is charged for another day of hospital stay if the patient is not discharged by noon.

It is not uncommon for a doctor to tell a patient that he or she can go home but forget to tell the nurses or to write the order. The patient may make arrangements to be picked up and arrive at the nurses' station to say goodbye only to discover that there is no written order. Sometimes a doctor writes an order for a new mother to leave but forgets to write the order for her baby. The baby will have his or her own chart and cannot be discharged until an order is received. If a patient tells you that he or she is going home, check the doctor's order; if there isn't one, let the nurses know. Depending on protocol, you may have to track down the doctor to confirm that the patient is being discharged and to ask the doctor to prepare an order. Technically, the patient must remain in the hospital until a formal order is received. In practice, it is uncommon for a patient to wait for an extended length of time, but delays in discharge do occur as a result. The doctor or the person covering for the doctor's practice will usually write the order. Sometimes the doctor may not have told the patient he or she could leave; it may have been the patient's own idea. If you cannot locate the doctor, ask the nurses to deal with the situation (see "Unauthorized Departures").

Discharge Procedures   Most health care facilities will have a discharge protocol detailing your responsibilities. Discharging a patient requires teamwork. Doing this efficiently and in a timely manner contributes to effective bed management. Here are some of your responsibilities:

- Confirm that there is a written discharge for the patient.

- Check immediately with the patient about when he or she expects to go home and, if necessary, advise the patient of the hospital's policies. The sooner this is done, the better. The patient can make plans, and you can activate discharge procedures in a timely manner. The patient may ask you to call someone to come and pick them up. If the patient requires an ambulance or the use of medical transport services, plan this well in advance and write down the time they expect to arrive. There will be a protocol to follow for this.

- Assemble any routine discharge information for the patient. This may include follow-up medical appointments, a list of current medications, and discharge teaching material. You should also check to see whether the patient has any medications or valuables in safekeeping; if so, remind the nurses to return them.

- Notify dietary services. In a computerized environment, as soon as the patient's discharge order is processed, dietary services receives notification of the discharge and will automatically cancel the patient's dietary orders. Otherwise, call dietary services as soon as a discharge order is confirmed. If a patient is unable to leave before noon, you can have his or her lunch tray delivered to the floor. If the patient is able to vacate the bed, he or she can have lunch sitting in a chair or in the lounge. If a tray for a discharged patient does come to the floor, the usual policy is to send it back to the kitchen. The nurses may use items on the tray for other patients (e.g., a piece of bread or a cup of coffee). They may even store a sandwich in the unit refrigerator in case someone gets hungry and wants a snack. Under no circumstances should staff members help themselves to the tray. Staff have been reprimanded and even fired for doing this. In some hospitals, the food is delivered in heated carts, and each plate prepared individually. There will be no "wasted" prepared tray, but the individuals distributing the food still need to know if the patient is no longer there.

- A terminal cleaning of the bed and other furniture used by the patient is done upon discharge. Items are thoroughly cleaned with a disinfectant solution. For certain rooms (e.g., isolation) the cleaning protocol may be specifically designed. Be sure that housekeeping staff are immediately aware of pending and actual discharges so they can plan their schedules. Although physical resources is notified when a discharge is entered into the computer, the process is expedited by verbally communicating with or calling housekeeping staff, since most carry a cellphone. There will be housekeeping staff assigned to your floor—and they usually check frequently for discharge information. You may want to keep an up-to-date list of discharges on the counter of the nurses' station as a resource for the housekeeping staff. Each unit may have its own internal procedures for notifying housekeeping.

Discharge Procedures for Patient Records   When a patient is discharged, all documents in the pChart must be dealt with according to facility policies; eCharts are stored electronically and archived if inactive for a certain time frame.

■ Remove the components of the pChart (if used) from the binder, and place them in a specific order according to hospital protocol. If you are dealing with only a few reports/items, there may be no need to organize the sheets in any special manner. The items (unless they are duplicates of information already contained in the eChart) will be scanned into the eChart by health information services.

■ If the hospital uses paper MARs, you are required to remove them from the medication binder and add them to the disassembled chart. Check to be sure the nurses have initialled for all medications.

■ Make sure the time of discharge has been added to the admission sheet, whether it is paper based or electronic.

■ When the patient has left and all charting is completed, send the chart to health information services. eCharts are also filed or stored in health information services, and you must do a similar check for completeness.

■ There is a space on the admission sheet, usually marked LOS, for length of stay. You would enter the number of hospital days in that area or field.

■ The patient's discharge diagnosis and any surgical procedures are also listed on the admission sheet. Often, the doctor will fill these areas in when he or she signs the discharge order. If you are not allowed to do this, ask the nurses to complete it. The information is usually on the patient's progress notes. You may be asked to fax or electronically transmit the admission sheet and any prescriptions given to the patient to the family physician. Alternatively, the MRP may include this information in the discharge summary, which would be faxed or otherwise transmitted to the family physician. This process contributes to continuity of care by keeping the family physician informed of where the patient has gone and what medications he or she has been taking.

Unauthorized Departures

If a patient insists on leaving the hospital without a physician's order, ask him or her to sign a release form stating that he or she is leaving without permission. This action ensures that the patient is assuming responsibility for his or her own health. This type of departure is referred to as an **AMA**, or leaving *against medical advice*. A patient who insists on leaving is often upset or angry and may refuse to sign the form. Ask a nurse to deal with this situation. If the nurse is not readily available, be polite and try to keep the patient calm. Often giving these patients undivided attention and just listening to them helps. If the patient leaves before the nurse arrives, you may be asked to chart what occurred. Be clear and concise. Quote directly what you can remember of the conversation. Likewise, the nurses will make the appropriate documentation on the patient's chart. Notify the doctor as soon as possible.

AMA an acronym that means "against medical advice." This refers to a patient leaving the hospital without the physician's approval.

Death of a Patient

The death of a patient in the hospital affects everyone in one way or another—including you and members of the health care team, especially if the patient is familiar to you. The nature of the death as well as the context in which it occurs (peaceful and expected, or sudden and traumatic) affect staff and family alike, as well as the level of support required for the patient's family and loved ones. Be aware of cultural issues, lifestyle choices, and sexual orientation (e.g., if the deceased has a same-sex partner or is transgender). Regardless of your personal beliefs, you must be absolutely objective and supportive in all of your interactions with those close the deceased person. This includes how to best interact with and approach others regarding necessary administrative details concerning the death.

As the clinical secretary, who knows hospital protocol and where to find the necessary forms, it is essential to maintain a calm, caring, and respectful attitude. Although you may be asked questions by family members/loved ones, it is the responsibility of the physician and the nurses to have any necessary forms completed and to discuss related matters. If spiritual support is requested, you may be asked to call the appropriate person. In most hospitals, a patient with religious affiliations will have the name and contact information of his or her clergy recorded on the admission sheet. Otherwise, family members may give you the required contact information.

> ## >>> POINTS TO PONDER
>
> The legalization of physician-assisted death in Canada (in 2016) will, at some point, impact health professionals as well as patients and their families. You may be exposed to a patient seeking this option in the hospital setting, and you may or may not agree with the patient's decision, especially if the patient is known to you. You may think the person has more quality life yet to live. Remember, though, it is *the patient's decision*, and usually one that the family agrees with (although not always). If you have deep personal feelings and ethical beliefs about physician-assisted death, especially if you believe it is wrong, you must come to terms with the fact that it is *the patient's decision*. Whether you have developed a relationship with the patient or not (e.g., in a palliative care unit where the individual has been a patient for a considerable length of time), it will be easier if you accept that it is the *patient's right to choose*.

When a patient dies, a doctor—or sometimes a nurse—confirms that the patient is deceased. A death certificate is a legally required document that must be filled out and signed by a doctor. You would put it in an envelope and give it to the responsible family member or as directed by facility protocol. Deaths must be registered in the province/territory in the same manner as births are registered. You may be asked to call the morgue when the body is ready to be removed from the floor. There will be special procedures for health professionals to follow if the deceased person has a known or suspected infection, and there will likely be related forms to be completed. Cultural practices around death (e.g., moving the body) will vary. Most hospitals will accommodate specific requests, particularly if the family has discussed their needs in advance.

Other forms may include those required for organ or tissue donation (e.g., the cornea). If organ donation is a possibility, the physician (or sometimes a nurse) will approach the family to discuss the matter. The family may not be aware of the wishes of the deceased, and these discussions can become contentious. Some or all family members may disagree even when the wishes of the deceased are known. Varying philosophies and the relationship family members had with the deceased—and with each other—influence how they react, particularly when coping with loss and grief. If a decision is made to donate the corneas of the deceased, you may be asked to call a designated physician to remove the patient's eyes. This procedure also requires the consent of the family member/person who has power of attorney for personal care if prior consent by the deceased was not given.

When a patient dies, the physician (MRP) should be notified first, as he or she may want to contact the family (in cases where no family member is with the patient at the time of death). In some situations, notifying family when a death is imminent or has occurred may be left to you, particularly if the patient has been on the unit for a while and you know the family. In the case of sudden death, the physician would assume that responsibility.

The grieving family will likely want to spend time at the bedside with their loved one. If the deceased is not in a private room, providing this opportunity is a little more complicated. If there are other patients in the room and they are able, the nurse will ask them to leave for a while. You may be asked to find a temporary place for them to go. Often, if a death is anticipated, the patient will be moved to a private room in advance. Usually there is no charge to the patient/family for this accommodation if it is ordered by the physician. You would notify patient flow of this move; it is not considered a transfer, just a room change. If there are several family members or they wish to go elsewhere, you can also direct them to the hospital chapel (if your facility has one) or an empty conference or meeting room. Extended family and close friends may arrive asking for directions. Be aware of the family's wishes regarding visitors at this time. They may want their privacy, or they may simply not feel up to seeing individuals outside of their immediate circle. Some facilities also post an identifier on the patient's door, such as a butterfly. This indicates that there has been a death and staff knows not to randomly enter (e.g., dietary services, housekeeping). In the event of the death of a baby, the mother may be moved off the parent/maternal–child unit. In most cases, the mother is discharged as soon as she is able.

If you receive calls from people asking if their friend/relative has passed away be sure to know hospital/unit policies about responding in the absence of directions from the family. It may be best to ask the nurse involved with the patient and family to take the call. Or simply say, "I am sorry, but I cannot give you any information." The rules of strict patient confidentiality still apply.

Comfort Measures   For patients who are dying with no hope of recovery (e.g., they may be in the last stages of cancer, heart disease, or multiple conditions), there are a variety of comfort measures that can be implemented to make the patient as comfortable as possible. In these cases, active intervention only prolongs the patient's life, so active treatment measures are often withdrawn, such as intravenous therapy (an IV port may be left in place to administer pain medication), administering antibiotics, or sometimes (but not always) limiting the use of oxygen. Taking the patient's vital signs is also often discontinued. Every case is unique.

Comfort measures, which are different from do-not-resuscitate orders, address the physical, psychological, and spiritual needs of the patient. Comfort measures include controlling the patient's pain (with the goal of keeping the patient pain free), administering medication as required to reduce restlessness, turning the patient at appropriate intervals for positions of comfort (or activity as tolerated by the patient), using a low-flow air mattress (see Chapter 21), keeping the patient's mouth moist, applying lip balm to sooth cracked lips, and sometimes applying eye drops. The patient's environment should be calm and soothing. Comfort measures required for each patient are individualized.

It is not uncommon for the family of a patient who is unconscious and declining to want everything possible done for their loved one, even against impossible odds. Sometimes this course of action can cause the patient to endure more pain. A physician can gently explain the rationale for "letting the patient go." It is the family's decision, but being fully informed helps them make the decision that is right for them.

In such cases the doctor must write a clear order (e.g., "Hydromorphine 2 mg q3h and prn IV as needed for pain" or "Ativan 2 mg IV for restlessness and adjuration"), not just "comfort measures only." He or she must be specific: Discontinue the IV, remove nasal prongs, discontinue the antibiotic (naming the antibiotic), and implement comfort measures. The nurses, along with the family, will determine how to best do this. The prn order for hydromorphine allows the nurses to give more pain medication if the patient needs it outside of the three-hour window.

If the patient is not in a private room, the physician may order that he or she be transferred to one. Some facilities offer the families the option to play music in the room: opera, soft classical, or hymns.

In cases where active treatment is withdrawn, the death of the patient usually occurs sooner. It does not change the grief reactions loved ones experience when the person dies, but the family is usually at peace with the decision(s) they have made.

Most long-term care facilities do not keep patients who require intravenous therapy. In these facilities, if the patient has requested level 1 (no intervention) treatment when they become very ill the patient is kept comfortable. What level of intervention the patient wants is determined when a patient enters a long-term care facility. For example, the patient may want to be transferred to hospital if he or she needs an IV or antibiotic therapy, but the patient may not want CPR. Sometimes the wishes of the patient conflict with the wishes of the family in that the patient wants no intervention but the family does. This makes for an uncomfortable situation most of the time.

L07 OTHER STANDARD FILES AND RESOURCES

In almost any hospital environment, even those that are considered paperless, there will be the occasional need for paper forms, reports, requisitions, community agency forms, teaching materials, and blank copies of schedule/assignment sheets used in the patient-care unit. The required forms may be available electronically (and downloaded as they are needed) or kept available as hard copies. Organize a filing system that is easily accessible and easy to use. Keep your filing system up to date, reviewing documents and purging at regular intervals.

Requisitions

A requisition is simply an order form. Chapter 6 discussed requisitions for laboratory and diagnostic tests. In a computerized environment, requisitions are electronic, unless they must be signed by a physician (e.g., an MRI). You would send a request for a CBC to the lab electronically where it would be filed in their system until processed. The lab would print out a label for the technician to use when obtaining the specimen. Once available, results would be sent back electronically.

For both pCharts and eCharts, you would call diagnostic services to schedule an appointment (if required) or the clinical secretary in the lab would book it and notify the patient-care unit. For stat orders, you would enter the order into your system and call the lab to ensure that they know. Sometimes lab technicians are away from their computer and may not check in for a while. If they carry cellphones you would call them; otherwise use the paging system. A stat order usually requires a prompt response—it could be for blood work or a diagnostic test (e.g., portable chest X-ray,

ECG). If a label is required, the label can be printed on the unit. The lab technician would retrieve the label when he or she comes to the floor. Orders for specimens collected by nurses (e.g., urine, sputum, stool) also require requisitions. In computerized facilities, they may be computer generated and printed right in the nursing unit.

Paper-based requisitions, if used, are often in duplicate, and a copy is kept in the chart. When ordering a test or service electronically, some systems automatically note the order and the date results are expected in the lab section of the PI screen.

Community Agency Forms

For many patients, discharge planning involves support from a community agency, which may require referral and assessment forms that are often completed and signed by the patient and given to the social worker /community support liaison person or faxed to the related community agency. In a paper system, file the blank forms alphabetically by agency. In a computerized environment, the forms would be completed online or downloaded.

Teaching Material

Many patient-care units keep preprinted health teaching information (e.g., what to expect and how to care for yourself following surgery, diabetic teaching, stroke management at home, recommendations for health management after a heart attack). This information can sometimes be downloaded from the hospital intranet. If the patient is comfortable with a computer (some older Canadians are not), the patient can be given a website where he or she can access the information at home. You may be responsible for giving the teaching information to the patient at the request of the nurse, during the hospital stay, or upon discharge.

Daily Assignment Schedule

Every facility will have its own method of posting staff assignment schedules, either by the unit manager or the team leader. It may be completed on the computer and printed off, available on the desktop, or written on a white board (in a private area like the nurses' station). Staff assignments indicate which nurses are looking after which patients, assigned lunch and coffee breaks, and any other specific duties assigned to staff members (e.g., one nurse may be responsible for giving all the medications or doing all the treatments). With recent cutbacks in many hospitals, more registered/licensed practical (RPN/LPN) nurses are being hired, as well as personal support workers. In an environment with a mix of nursing skills, team nursing is popular; for example, a registered nurse may work with two or three RPN/LPNs and two personal support workers. Be aware of which nurses to contact if someone (including the physician) wants information about a patient or if you need to direct a call to a nurse about a patient.

If a nurse calls in sick, it may be your responsibility to find a replacement from a staffing list. Be sure to follow proper protocol when calling the nurses. Contacting someone to come in when another nurse is "next" on the list and should have been offered the opportunity can cause problems. This responsibility can actually take a significant portion of your time, and it is difficult to do in the middle of a busy day. There is rarely extended periods of time when you can make these calls.

Transportation Services Records

You must also keep a list of transportation services for patients who require assistance moving to another facility. It could be a patient going somewhere upon discharge from the hospital, a patient being repatriated, or a patient being sent to another facility for a test. This is usually done electronically and would include selected patient information and the tracking/transportation number, in jurisdictions that use them.

The Hospital Intranet

The hospital intranet is a web communication system used within a specific facility. It is made up of an array of resources, infrastructure, and software and is password protected. The intranet contains a wide range of features, such as web-based and intranet-enabled medical knowledge resources: the CPS (a drug manual), the Merck Manual (a diagnostic reference), hospital-directed staff education documents, manuals on hospital policies and procedures (also referred to as a standard operational procedures manual), nursing procedures, nutritional and infection prevention and control manuals, teaching information for patients, online forms, order sets, and clinical practice guidelines. It can also provide nurses, physicians, and pharmacists with access to online and current pharmaceutical resources. Most intranet systems also contain staffing schedules for nurses and physicians as well as physician on-call schedules. A newer method of scheduling nurses is called self-scheduling. The nurse logs onto the appropriate place on the intranet and enters his or her desired schedule. Internal job postings would also be contained here. For new employees, the intranet may provide forms needed to access and complete certain courses prior to their hospital orientation.

Hospital Policy Manual   A hospital policy manual (which is more often than not found online) contains a detailed account of facility policies, from response to a disaster to those related to visiting hours, the work environment, and the use of electrical equipment.

Nursing Procedure Maunal   The nursing manual (usually electronic) is a resource providing nurses with detailed instructions on procedures such as inserting a nasogastric tube, inserting an indwelling Foley catheter, or monitoring a patient on **head injury routine**.

Infection Prevention and Control Resource Guide   One of the most important resources in a hospital details policies and procedures relating to the prevention and control of infections within the hospital. Measures for everyone—from visitors and patients to hospital staff—are detailed in this manual. Isolation policies and procedures outline what types of isolation are appropriate and in what circumstances, how to initiate isolation procedures, and what steps to follow.

head injury routine a special assessment for a patient who has had head trauma or surgery, including checks on neurological functioning, such as verbal response and pupil dilation.

>>> **WHAT TO WATCH FOR**

- Changes in the roles and responsibilities of the clinical secretary/unit clerk with the integration of more technology into hospitals, such as computerized physician order entry.

- A continuing shift toward community-based care (e.g., home care) and how provinces/territories fund and regulate provider organizations.

- Changes to hospitals as renewed budget restrictions force them to revisit staffing and the delivery of patient care (e.g., using more personal support workers and practical nurses to replace registered nurses).

- Continuing efforts to maximize the appropriate use of hospital beds using patient flow initiatives.

SUMMARY

1. Patient flow initiatives are active in most acute-care hospitals across Canada. The goal is to maximize the use of hospital beds so that hospitals provide the right service to the right patient at the right time. Patient flow success depends on a complex communication network, staff members with excellent communication and computer skills, and coordinated efforts of patient-care units in the hospital.

2. There are four general types of hospital admissions: emergency, elective, outpatient, and obstetrical. The process of admission has changed with the application of patient flow procedures, although the basic steps are similar. Some units admit the patient directly on the unit (e.g., maternal–child; the baby must be admitted once he or she is born).

3. Your responsibilities will include generating eCharts for admissions to the unit you work on. You must attach a care plan to the chart upon admission that reflects the service for which the patient is admitted. This care plan populates the eChart with the fields related to the patient's assessments and interventions. In most hospitals, you will be required to integrate portions of the patient's eChart with the pChart.

4. Surgical charts contain documents related to pre- and postoperative assessment and care; for example, a preoperative questionnaire, a preoperative checklist, and an anesthetic record. In many hospitals, procedures call for medication administration records to be printed and sent up to the OR as hard copies.

5. Your responsibilities regarding preparing a patient for surgery will vary depending on if the patient is admitted the day of surgery to the pre-admit unit or as an inpatient. An inpatient must be NPO the night before surgery, requiring an NPO notification be added to the patient's white board. You must ensure that all chart components are present; for example, a recent history and physical report, any required lab tests (e.g., an ECG), or the preoperative checklist). You may have to remind the nurses to have a postoperative bed ready for the patient.

6. Transferring a patient within the hospital is different from and less complicated than a patient discharge. Discharging a patient requires organization and planning to ensure that all discharge details are in place, including the time of departure, that the patient has the required forms (e.g., prescriptions, teaching materials, follow-up appointment times), and that transportation is arranged, as required. You must enter the discharge into the computer, notifying various departments that the patient has left (e.g., housekeeping so they can clean the bed unit, and patient flow so they can note that the bed is available on the electronic bed board).

7. Hospital units have an array of resources (usually online) for staff members to use. These may be in paper format or downloaded as needed. Important information can be found in the hospital intranet, including policies and procedures of the hospital, procedures for carrying out certain nursing tasks (e.g., isolation protocol, inserting a catheter, admitting and discharge), and teaching materials.

KEY TERMS

AMA   471
discharge   467
elective surgery   463
head injury routine   476

hospital number   451
identification (ID) band   450
new admission   444
patient flow   443

pre-admission   463
provisional diagnosis   455
repatriation   443
transfer   465

REVIEW QUESTIONS

1. What is the goal of patient flow initiatives?

2. How does patient flow affect the manner in which patients are admitted to hospital?

3. Differentiate between an elective and an emergency admission.

4. What special steps are involved in an obstetrical admission?

5. What is the first step in charting for a new admission in an electronic environment, as outlined in this book and in a hospital in your community?

6. What types of information can be found on the admission sheet? State the purpose of each.

7. Compare and contrast the forms contained in the medical and surgical charts in a hospital in your community.

8. What general responsibilities does a clinical secretary have when a patient goes to the OR?

9. Differentiate between a transfer and a discharge, and list the steps you would take to book an interhospital transfer.

10. What are the clinical secretary's primary responsibilities related to a patient discharge?

11. What is the purpose of a requisition?

12. Mrs. Jasper comes to the desk. She has been in a standard room with three loud patients. They are up late at night, talk loudly, and have visitors who disturb her. She angrily demands another room or threatens to go home. She is unwilling to pay for alternative accommodation and no other standard room is available. In a small group discuss how you would handle this, and what your alternatives are.

APPLICATION EXERCISES

1. Using documents supplied by your professor, assemble (a) a medical chart and (b) a surgical chart. Describe the purpose of each chart form.

2. Suppose the cost of ward accommodation is $150 per day. The cost of a semi-private room is $240 per day. The cost of a private room is $320 per day. State the amount of money that Ted would have to pay for the following:

   • Three days' accommodation in a semi-private room if he has no supplemental insurance

   • Three days' accommodation in a private room if he has no supplemental insurance

   • Three days' accommodation in a private room if he has semi-private coverage through Blue Cross

3. Sheila is a patient in your unit. She is upset because she feels that she is not getting the care and attention she deserves. After repeated attempts to contact her doctor, Sheila comes to the nurses' station dressed, with her belongings, and crying. She says she is leaving. In small groups, discuss strategies to handle this situation. If Sheila insists on leaving, what steps would you take?

4. Karl has been discharged. He tells you that he cannot possibly leave until mid-afternoon, at which time his daughter can come directly from work to pick him up. Discuss how you might handle this situation.

5. In groups of four or five, visit hospitals in your area and interview a clinical secretary/unit coordinator to assess the use of computers in his or her unit. Include the components of the chart (if any) that are paper based, requisitions that are used in paper format, and what type of patient-care summary is used. Summarize your findings and present them in class. You may choose to have a group visit different areas within one hospital, such as a medical unit, a maternal–child unit, or the ICU.

WEBSITES OF INTEREST

CritiCall Ontario

http://criticall.org/webconcepteur/web/criticall

Institute for Health Care Improvement: Optimizing Patient Flow

www.ihi.org/resources/pages/ihiwhitepapers/optimizingpatient-flowmovingpatientssmoothlythroughacutecaresettings.aspx

Hospital Admissions

www.emedicinehealth.com/hospital_admissions/article_em.htm#hospital_admissions_introduction

Chapter 16
Order Entry

Juanmonino/E+/Getty Images

LEARNING OBJECTIVES

On completing this chapter, you will be able to:

1. Recognize changes in order entry responsibilities as hospitals embrace improved technologies such as computerized physician order entry.

2. Realize the importance of a sound knowledge base and accuracy in order transcription.

3. Identify the tools/equipment required for order entry procedures.

4. Differentiate between individualized doctors' orders and order sets.

5. Identify categories of information on the patient intervention screen.

6. Describe nine basic steps for processing orders.

7. Apply the principles of order entry to processing medication orders.

LO1 LO2 THE IMPORTANCE OF ACCURATE ORDER ENTRY

When a person is admitted to hospital, a physician will provide directions to the nursing staff about the person's care and activities. Doctors do this by writing **doctors' orders**.

In many hospitals, the clinical secretary is no longer responsible for entering medication orders. This function (or variations of it) has largely been assumed by hospital

doctors' orders written or oral directions given by a physician to the nursing staff and other health professionals regarding the care, medications, treatment, and laboratory and diagnostic tests that a patient is to receive while in hospital.

pharmacies, as detailed later in this chapter. Knowing how to transcribe medication orders, however, may still come in handy. In hospitals not using computerized physician order entry (CPOE), the clinical secretary is responsible for processing orders for laboratory and diagnostic tests, and nursing assessments and interventions. In such hospitals a solid knowledge of medications, diagnostic tests, and other components of treatment will serve you well, enabling you to understand and process selected orders, identify errors, and prioritize work in a competent and informed manner.

order entry the process of interpreting, recording, and generating the administrative steps required for doctors' orders to be implemented.

The administrative steps toward putting those orders into action are called **order entry**. You will also hear staff refer to the process as *transcribing* or *processing* the doctor's orders. This process may take place in a patient-care unit, the emergency department, or any area of the hospital where doctors or other qualified health professionals (e.g., a nurse practitioner) write orders. (Note that although orders are sometimes generically referred to as *doctors' orders*, there is a difference, depending on the health professional writing them.) Order entry is largely the responsibility of the clinical secretary and will be one of your most important responsibilities.

Order entry demands absolute accuracy. Recognize your own limitations; if in any doubt, ask for clarification. The same principles apply to manual and computerized order entry. Although most facilities use computerized order entry, the ability to process orders manually will remain a necessary skill; there will be times when it is necessary, even in the most highly computerized environments.

Accuracy and knowledge of order entry procedures are only the beginning. To enter orders effectively, you will also need a strong theoretical base in almost all areas of diagnosis, disease, care and treatment, and pharmacology. You must be able to prioritize orders, recognize possible errors, and know the times at which these medications should be administered. You must know how to assign stop dates, which medications require frequent lab assessment (e.g., if a patient is on heparin, you would order a daily [OD] CBC, and aPTT. If the patient is on warfarin, you would order daily INR), and when received, results must be reported immediately. Orders involving nutrition and elimination require a general knowledge of various types of diets and how diet relates to diagnostic tests and procedures. For example, a patient having fasting triglyceride and cholesterol levels done in the morning must not have anything to drink after midnight the night before—although sometimes they are allowed to take medications with sips of water. You need to understand the reasons for parenteral therapy, the medication delivery methods, the equipment needed for particular procedures, and where to obtain it. You must know your hospital's policy on how often to change an intravenous (IV) site and tubing. Orders relating to rest and activity require a knowledge of progressive ambulatory procedures. You need to understand the purpose, procedure, and policies related to diagnostic and laboratory tests to ensure proper booking, patient preparation, and documentation.

You must also interact effectively with other hospital departments and know the roles of fellow staff members. For example, if you have an order for stat IV medication, you would tell the nurse who is responsible for that patient's care. Becoming expert in this important role will take time and experience; however, solid theoretical knowledge will give you an excellent foundation. This knowledge will make you more accountable, able to assume more responsibilities, and will increase your scope of practice within the profession.

ORDER ENTRY: TOOLS OF THE TRADE

The initial doctor's orders, whether handwritten or computer generated, represent the beginning of the order entry process. In a completely computerized environment, the computer and telephone are your primary tools. The eChart contains numerous fields you will use, beginning with the patient intervention (PI) screen. You will be exposed to doctors' orders in various formats (electronic and handwritten), the PI screen, and other modules in the hospital information system (e.g., nutritional services, lab, diagnostic imaging, respiratory services). In partly computerized facilities, you may need other tools, such as the medication administration record (MAR), community agency reports, and at times paper requisitions.

Doctors' Orders

Doctors' orders (electronic or handwritten) cover such things as

- type of care,
- tests,
- medications,
- level of activity,
- diet, and
- nursing and therapeutic interventions.

Who Writes Orders?   Orders are typically written on admission and throughout the patient's hospitalization by the most responsible physician (MRP), or perhaps a hospitalist. A patient cannot receive any care in the hospital without a doctor's order. It is important to note that a doctor may, at any time, cancel, change, or write new orders on the patient, which is usually dictated by the patient's ongoing condition or test results. New orders must be processed immediately according to hospital protocol. Strictly speaking, not even a tray of food can be given to a patient unless the doctor has ordered a specific diet.

In many hospitals, family physicians have relinquished admitting privileges. If a family physician feels that a patient needs hospital care, he or she refers the patient to the appropriate specialist (also called a consultant); if the patient is admitted to hospital, usually the specialist becomes the patient's MRP if that specialist is providing most of that patient's care. The family physician usually assumes care for the patient again when he or she is discharged from hospital. When family physicians do admit patients to hospital, they may or may not write orders for the patient. If they do, and the patient is also under the care of a specialist, they are giving concurrent care.

In some jurisdictions other health professionals, including nurse practitioners, pharmacists, and dietitians, are also allowed to write certain orders. Nurse practitioners who work in the hospital setting work collaboratively with physicians; they assess certain components of the patient's care and write related orders. When signing the order, the person's designation must be clearly noted.

When more than one practitioner is writing orders for a patient, duplicate or contradictory orders may be written. For example, an activity order written by one doctor may state the patient is to remain on strict bed rest, while another may state that the patient can have bathroom privileges. Always clarify such discrepancies. Generally, the MRP's orders will be followed. However, before disregarding or overriding any orders, check with the patient's nurse. If he or she doesn't know, then check with the MRP or the physician who wrote the order as he or she may be able to clarify the situation as well. For example, suppose you have a patient who has been under the care of a specialist, but you have a discharge order from the family physician. You might question the validity of that order. But it might turn out that the specialist has verbally discharged the care of the patient back to the family physician, who can then write the discharge order. Checking with the appropriate doctor will make this clear. When two or more specialists are caring for a patient, they may have to coordinate plans together.

Orders: Format, Types, and Management

Orders may be handwritten or electronic; they may be patient specific, or generated from online or printed order sets. A growing number of hospitals use electronic doctor's orders, as shown in Figure 16.4 later in the chapter. There are two types of electronic orders: those a physician enters with a computer using existing software (almost like handwriting orders, but entering them electronically) and CPOE, which requires special software embedded into the hospital information system. CPOE capabilities are discussed later. If doctors' orders are handwritten or if order sets are printed, they are usually found in the front of the pChart, just behind the admission sheet. Blank order sheets are sometimes coloured, varying with the hospital. Typical colours are pale blue, green, or pink if the patient has a drug allergy.

Before you process a doctor's order, ensure that the order sheet contains the patient's identifying information, usually with a computerized sticker/ID label. If you are unable to do this, write the patient's first and last names and hospital number on the order form. The order must also be signed by the physician. If it was a phone order, the nurse must sign it "per" the physician (e.g., Janet Sumpty RN/Dr. A. Mahood). All orders must be dated and signed by the physician (or the nurse if it is a phone order).

TIP

Never transcribe an order that has not been signed by the physician, nurse practitioner, or other authorized health professional. If the order is unsigned, or the doctor verbalizes an order but forgets to write it down, contact the patient's nurse—he or she may be able to write a verbal order or sign off on it.

Handwritten Orders

Doctors are notorious for poor handwriting. With practice, you will get used to various handwriting styles and be able to decipher most orders. But even an experienced clinical secretary or nurse can be stumped by illegible scrawl. Remember that accuracy must be absolute. If in doubt, seek clarification. One incorrect letter in the name of a drug or one misplaced decimal in the dosage could result in a serious (and potentially fatal) medication error. Ask the nurses for help; if they cannot make out the order either, or if they are not certain, call the physician who wrote it. It is better to deal with a grumpy physician than with an inaccurate order.

Not only do many doctors have poor handwriting, they may also have different short forms to represent a particular test they are ordering. If you don't know what the test is and cannot find the mnemonic in order entry, ask the nurses in your area if they can interpret the order. They may know the doctor's "short form" habits. If the nurses cannot help, another unit to which the physician admits patients might be able to. Even the lab might know. Minimize the calls you make to the doctor; on the other hand, if calling the doctor is the only way to clear something up, you may have to call.

Figure 16.1 shows a doctor's order sheet with three sections for writing orders. The doctor can record three different sets of orders or, if the order is lengthy, simply take as much space as necessary. The physician must sign and date orders each time he or she makes a new entry—even if the new entry is just a few hours after the previous one. The doctor cannot add to that set later because it will have been processed. Physicians may also add the time at which the order was written. Some hospital information systems automatically date the orders at the time they are written; the physician must add his or her electronic signature.

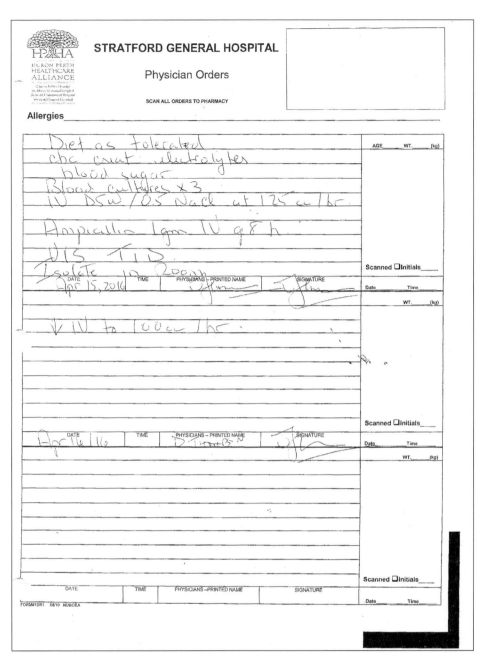

Figure 16.1 Doctor's order form with handwritten admission orders for a patient with pneumonia

Huron Perth Healthcare Alliance

Faxing Orders to the Pharmacy As soon as a doctor's order is written, it is sent to the pharmacy. This can be accomplished in one of two ways: by faxing the order directly to the pharmacy or by scanning the written order into the computer. Once attached electronically to the patient's eChart, the pharmacy has access to it and then has a record of all medications and relevant IV solutions (those that contain medications), which they use to dispense medications appropriately to the floor (or to the medication cabinet) or to list the patient's medications on the patient's chart. In hospitals using paper MARs, the pharmacy prepares the MARs during hours of operation. This is done every 24 hours. Each 24-hour cycle will reflect new or altered orders ordered by the doctor the previous day. If a doctor changes an order during the day, the pharmacy may immediately generate a new MAR; if they cannot, you or the nurse will manually transcribe the orders onto the MAR.

Order Sets

Order sets are groupings of medical orders based on pre-established clinical guidelines. They are aimed at standardizing a patient's treatment options based on the diagnosis or procedures ordered. Examples of diagnoses include congestive heart failure, chronic obstructive pulmonary disease, stroke, or pneumonia. Examples of procedures include cardiac cauterization as well as pre- and postoperative orders for major surgery. Order sets comprise orders listed with adjacent boxes so that the physician checks off the orders he or she wants. Orders within an order set are generally listed in categories: lab and diagnostic tests, IV therapy, patient assessments and interventions, and medications. Some order sets have a space at the bottom where the physician can write additional orders. Figure 16.2 shows an electronic order set generated on a CPOE system for a patient with pneumonia. Figure 16.3 is an example of a computer-store, printed order set for major bowel surgery.

Order sets are primarily in digital format. Some are accessed and implemented electronically (there is no paper component, such as Figure 16.2), others, particularly in facilities where orders are handwritten, are stored on the computer, but printed as they are needed (e.g., Figure 16.3). In hospitals that have CPOE capabilities, order sets are embedded

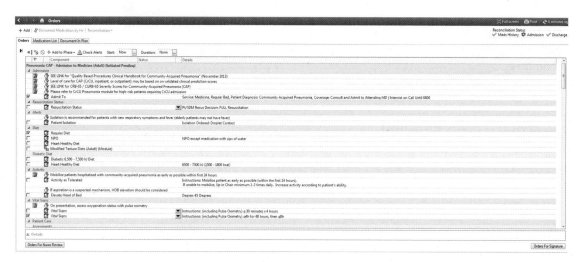

Figure 16.2 Electronic order set for a medical admission with a diagnosis of pneumonia
Courtesy of North York General Hospital

CONESTOGA GENERAL HOSPITAL

Diagnosis   **Client ID**

Allergies (IF NONE INDICATE THIS)

PREOPERATIVE DOCTORS ORDERS: COLON RESECTION
Cross out orders not indicated; Check appropriate box for active orders

Lab and Diagnostic Tests
- ☐ CBC, electrolytes, serum albumin
- ☐ FBS, HbAlc (if client diabetic)
- ☐ Cross and Type for 4 units of packed cells
- ☐ ECG if client over 45 or has pre-existing heart condition
- ☐ Chest Xray PA & Lateral if patient over 40
- ☐ Abdominal CT

Hydration

- ☐ Start IV NS @ 100cc/hr on the morning of surgery.
- ☐ 5%D.W @ 100cc/hr the morning of surgery
- ☐ Give 300cc bolus when OR calls for client.

Activity
- ☐ As previously ordered
- ☐ Other

Preparation
- ☐ Routine Bowel prep 8 hours prior to surgery
- ☐ Bowel prep hs day before surgery

Nutrition
- ☐ DAT until bowel prep
- ☐ FF
- ☐ CF
- ☐ NPO 8 hrs prior to surgery

Other
- ☐ Actual height and weight on Anesthetic sheet (not stated)

Physician Signature_____   Printed Name _____

Figure 16.3 Preprinted preoperative orders for a colon resection; may be also referred to as standard orders

into the software and include physician access to databases containing the latest information regarding diagnosis and treatment options. The layout of order sets varies depending on the user interface design, offering different features for the provider. Order sets are created by groups of specialists, are reviewed regularly, and are based on best practice clinical guidelines. One hospital system may contain up to 300 different order sets.

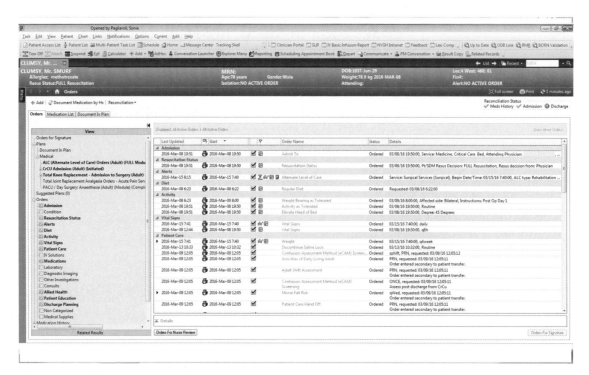

Figure 16.4 Screen showing active orders for Mr. Smurf

Courtesy of North York General Hospital

In hospitals where physicians enter their orders electronically, they choose their order set themselves, adding it to the patient's eChart. They do the same for individualized orders. In hospitals where orders are handwritten, the physician may ask you for a specific order set or, if you know what one the doctor will use (you get to know the doctors' preferences and routines), you would add it to the pChart. Order sets that are used in paper format can be stored on the computer and printed as required. Alternatively, some patient-care units keep selected order sets printed and in a file.

It is important to note that new orders for patients are written, changed, discontinued or renewed frequently—sometimes several times a day. In any environment you will likely be required to check the eChart or pChart for new orders at least once per shift. It is important to ensure that only active orders are implemented (i.e., old orders have been properly discontinued or modified accordingly). Figure 16.4 shows active orders for a patient (Mr. Smurf).

Postoperative Order Sets   Figure 16.5 shows preprinted *postoperative* (after surgery) orders for major surgery. Note that options are arranged into a few basic groupings based on the patient's typical needs: a choice of analgesics and routes for the immediate postoperative pain; orders for a PCA pump, followed by a less potent analgesic; something for nausea (numerous routes), which is common postoperatively; a laxative or an enema to stimulate the peristaltic action of the bowels following surgery; a diet graduated according to the needs of the patient; and the option of a catheter inserted into the bladder in case the patient has problems urinating after the surgery. There is also provision for ordering IV therapy to sustain the patient until he or she can drink adequately and to provide a route for IV medication, if needed. In each category, the physician chooses the option he or she considers most appropriate. There is space allotted for any additional orders the physician might deem necessary.

Pre-admission Orders and Preparation   Pre-admission orders are those completed prior to the patient's admission to hospital (see Chapter 15 for more on patient admission). They apply to patients who are admitted and discharged the same day (day

CONESTOGA GENERAL HOSPITAL

MAJOR SURGERY: Client ID

ALLERGIES _____ None ____

Analgesics

___Acetaminophen 325 (Tylenol, plain) tab 1-2 q 3-4 h prn po max 4 g/day

___Naproxen (Naprosyn) 250 mg po tid with food

___Meperidine (Demerol) ____mg I.M. q ___h prn x ____ post-op days.

___Tylenol #3 tab 1-2 po q 4-6 h prn x _____ post-op days

_____

PCA OPIOD

__Morphine 2 mg/ml

__Hydromorphine 0.4 mg/mL

__Fentanyl 25 mcg/mL

PCA dose: _____mg/mcg (circle one)

PCS dose/Bolus dose: range 0-____mg/mcg (circle one)

Delay Interval: _____minutes

If pain still not controlled, increase PCA dose by ____ mg/mcg increments q1h until pain is controlled or maximum dose specified in PCA dose range is reached.

_____

Antiemetic:

___Dimenhydrinate inj 50 mg/mL 25-50mg (0.5 – 1mL) IV q6h prn (for IV dilute in 50mL IV fluid and give over 30 minutes).

___Dimenhydrinate (Gravol) 50-100 mg I.M. or po. q _____h prn

___Prochlorperazine (Stemetil) 10 mg I.M. q ___h prn if Gravol ineffective

Other: _____

Laxative:

___Magnolax 30 mL po bid 2nd post -op day prn

___Fleet enema 3rd post op day prn

___Other: _____

Lab:

___CBC first post op day

Diet

___if n/g tube present, CF to DAT after removed.

___Transitional diet starting when bowel sounds present.

Catheter: Parenteral Therapy

___Foley ____remove 1st post-op day   2/3 & 1/3 @_____cc/hr

    ____Other   N/S @_____cc /hr

                                                     D/C when drinking well

                                                     Other _____

If patient unable to void in 6 hrs post surgery or after catheter removal insert Foley. If output *greater* than 350 cc leave catheter in to straight drainage until further notice

Activity

____ ambulate post op night as able

____ ambulate first post op day.

Other

___Family doctor notified

Additional Orders

Physician's Signature_____

Date _____

Figure 16.5 Printed order set with postoperative orders for major surgery

surgery) and to patients admitted the morning of their surgery but who will be staying one night or more (admit same day, or ASD patients).

Your role is to ensure that the orders have been carried out. These orders typically include blood work, urine testing, and perhaps an ECG. A preoperative examination would have to be completed, and the patient may or may not have had a consultation with a specialist. All reports must be on the patient's chart (eChart or pChart). As well, the patient may have been asked to carry out certain procedures at home. These may include a fleet enema or a laxative and remaining NPO (nothing by mouth) after a certain time, usually 10:00 p.m. This is important because an anesthetic may cause the patient to vomit any food in the stomach and aspirate.

Requisitions

You may or may not be exposed to paper requisitions for lab and diagnostic tests when processing doctors' orders. If the order requires a physician's signature on a hard copy, you would fax it to the appropriate destination and scan the requisition into the patient's eChart. Orders for lab and diagnostic tests are submitted electronically for the most part (see Chapters 6 and 15). Using the computer, you would select the appropriate laboratory department, enter the type of test, the date and time the test is to be done, the urgency, who will obtain the test, and any necessary clinical information. Figure 16.6 illustrates an electronic requisition for an abdominal ultrasound. You would file or send the request, which will be received electronically in the appropriate department. When entering requests for lab or diagnostic tests, you will not always need to free text.

Let the nurse know if you have an order for blood for a patient. This requires a written consent from the patient.

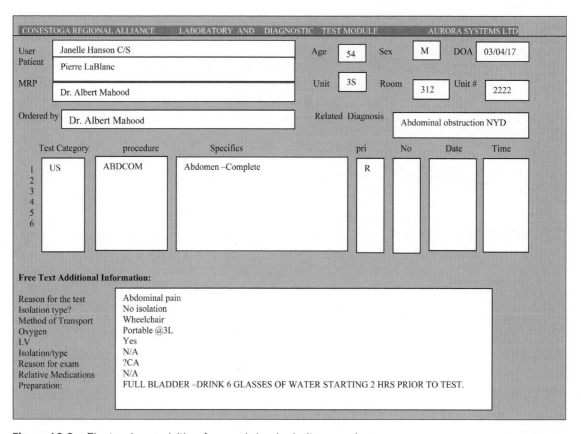

Figure 16.6 Electronic requisition for an abdominal ultrasound

Central Patient Database

Almost all of your responsibilities will require you to use the computer, not the least of which are tasks related to order entry. This holds true, to a certain extent, in the CPOE environment as well. You will interface with almost all components of the patient's eChart and with most hospital departments. A hospital information system will have a central database providing access to the eCharts of all patients on your unit. The configuration of this screen and what information it contains will vary with the hospital's computer system. At North York General Hospital in Toronto, Ontario, which uses CPOE, the patient access list offers a number of features, from point-and-click access to the patient's eChart, to alerts as to when new orders are written for a patient, to alerts indicating if there are outstanding orders. It is a handy interface to use when processing orders or addressing any necessary changes in the chart. Remember that this central database will allow you (and any other authorized user) to look up any recent or past patient data that has been put in place. You can view medications the patient has or is currently on (Figure 16.7 shows a medication profile), lab and diagnostic tests ordered, and the results. You can find out if blood products ordered are ready for the patient (e.g., whole blood, packed cells, platelets). As well, you will find radiology reports, ultrasound summaries, patient history, consultations, and discharge summaries—essentially everything concerning that patient.

Patient Access List

Figure 16.8 shows a patient access list used in electronic environments (such as CPOE) that lists all patients on a particular unit. This list facilitates access to all parts of any patient's eChart. Information on each patient can be easily accessed.

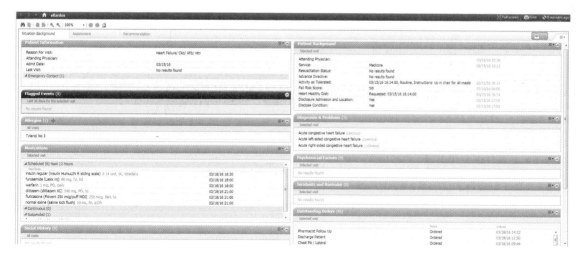

Figure 16.7 Example of a PI screen showing a patient's medications
Reprinted by permission from Health Metrix.

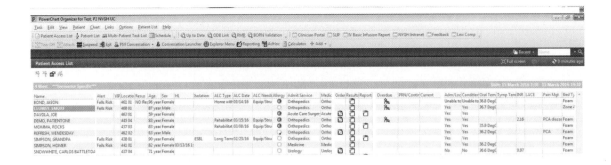

Figure 16.8 Patient access list used in CPOE environments showing all patients in a patient-care unit
Courtesy of North York General Hospital

When new orders are entered by a provider, a *clipboard* will appear at the top of the screen. If you click on the clipboard, a screen will open revealing the new orders or outstanding orders that require attention on your part (e.g., arranging a consultation, ensuring the patient's height and weight are appropriately entered, or a request to obtain a patient's old health records). Clicking on the patient's name will open the patient's chart, allowing you to navigate through the chart viewing new orders and related results. Next to the clipboard is a *phone icon*. Clicking on that will reveal any orders that are outstanding—orders that require you to do something or follow up on something (e.g., arranging a consultation, ensuring the patient's height and weight are entered, or a request to obtain old health records on a patient). This screen also has a *Resus column*. This refers to the patient's code status (e.g., full code or do not resuscitate). The *VIP column* is checked if you are not to release any information on the patient. This is flagged in admitting/patient flow if the patient so chooses. If someone called inquiring about a patient, you would check here to see if you can even acknowledge that the patient is in the hospital. This screen also includes if the patient is a fall risk or in isolation, discharge information, as well as specific information about patient care (e.g., pain management, vital signs, INR values).

Patient Intervention Screen

patient intervention (PI) screen a computer-based patient-care document listing a patient's information, including the code status, health education/teaching requirements, discharge planning, and patient assessments and interventions that have been ordered. It will identify the status of the order.

Many orders—especially those related to assessments, treatments, and direct patient care—are recorded on a patient data profile commonly called the **patient intervention (PI) screen**, or sometimes an electronic Kardex (eKardex) (see Chapter 15 for more details). Figure 16.9 illustrates an example of a PI screen. The status column is activated by the clinical secretary. "A" means that the intervention is active, and "C" indicates the intervention is complete or no longer monitored. Note that there are many variations to how this screen might look.

As noted in Chapter 15, the PI screen is a centralized source of information that begins with admission and addresses almost every component of the patient's treatment and care while in hospital. A large portion of the orders processed are recorded on the PI screen. Nurses may print parts of it at the beginning of their shift and carry it as a guide to treatment. Keep in mind that your facility may call this summary document by a different name. Many examples in this part of the textbook are illustrated with a generic electronic format. You will likely be using some electronic equivalent. The important thing to note is the *information* captured. Information that is added to the PI screen depends on facility guidelines. In electronic environments, the PI screen is usually populated with lists of options for each intervention category. You simply highlight or activate the intervention option the physician has

Interventions

Clinical Parameters	Status	Freq
Vital Signs, monitor	A	QS
* ward routine		
I&O, monitor	A	Q4H
Oxygen Saturation, monitor	A	Q8H
* O2 to keep O2S > 92%		
Weight, daily	A	QD
* weight before breakfast		

Treatments	Status	Freq
Oxygen Therapy	A	PRN
* to keep O2S > 92%		
Catheter, foley	A	PRN
Catheter, removal	A	PRN
Catheter, reinsert	A	PRN
Catheter, in&out	A	PRN

Specimens	Status	Freq
Urine, to be obtained	A	
* C&S and R&M		
Sputum, to be obtained	A	
* C&S		
Stool, specimen	C	
* for Occult Blood X 3		

Activity	Status	Freq
Activity, as tolerated	A	
Up, with one assist	C	
Up, with no assist	A	
Shower, independent	A	QD
Hygiene, independent	A	QD
Diet, as at home	A	
* Regular		
Feed, self	A	

Assessments	Status	Freq
Gastrointestinal assess	A	QD
Cardiovascular assess	A	QD
Respiratory assess	A	QD
Physiotherapy assess	A	QD
Occupational Therapy assess	A	QD
Social Work assess	A	once
Nutritional assess	A	once
*poor appetite		
Wound, site 1	A	QD
*left leg ulcer		
Wound, site 2	A	BID
*left heel ulcer		

Medications	Status	Freq
Medications, IV	A	QS
Medications, IM/SC	A	QS
IV Heparin	A	QS
IV Vancomycin	C	

Discharge	Status	Freq
Discharge, home	A	
Discharge, respite care	A	
Discharge, teaching	A	

Figure 16.9 Example of PI Screen

ordered so that the specific order is noted as relevant or active on the PI screen (e.g., bed rest, IV orders, or a dressing change). (Note the "A"—indicating the option is active—under the status column in Figure 16.9.) Computerized systems have vast databases and lookup files from which to choose—ranging from IV solutions and medications to diets.

The following is a brief explanation of patient care and assessment categories you will be working with; most of this information will be kept on the PI screen.

Diagnosis   The patient's admitting diagnosis is noted here. It may change during the hospital stay as investigations are completed. The diagnosis might include a primary diagnosis—the reason the patient was admitted—and a secondary diagnosis—a condition that was present but not the main reason for admission.

A differential diagnosis is an inclusion of other possibilities. For example, Alice might be admitted with a provisional diagnosis of possible appendicitis, meaning the doctor thinks she probably has appendicitis. However, ectopic pregnancy and a ruptured ovarian cyst present with some similar clinical signs, and until further investigations have been completed the doctor cannot rule these out; they are differential diagnoses. If Alice also had a bladder infection on admission, her secondary diagnosis would be cystitis.

Teaching/Education and Emotional Support   This is activated for most patients as almost all require some degree of health education. Teaching needs vary with the patient and the situation. It may relate to various areas of self-care related to the patient's diagnosis. Surgical patients would require detailed information about their recovery at home (e.g., ambulation, diet, pain control, follow-up care). If the patient comes in on the morning of the surgery, preop teaching will likely have been done. When you are admitting the person, it is a good idea to ask the patient if this teaching has occurred. If not, be sure to tell the nurse. Patient education may involve conferencing and interviews as well as family-centred teaching.

Emotional support is highlighted or noted only if the patient needs extra emotional support. The nursing staff often fills out this area, as they are best able to assess emotional needs. Extra emotional support would be needed, for example, if the patient is facing a limited recovery or a terminal illness; sometimes family tragedy coincides with the person's hospitalization; sometimes the person's coping mechanisms are such that increased emotional support is required in what others consider to be routine situations.

Clinical Pathways   If a clinical pathways is added to the patient's chart it will be noted, sometimes under a section called "Nursing Interventions." It may have sections for the nurses to enter dates when a particular phase of the pathway has been completed and to add any notes.

Nutrition   A diet is ordered, at least initially, by the doctor but may change with tests, surgery, and the patient's condition. In CPOE environments, the order would automatically be sent to dietary services. Otherwise, you are responsible for the initial and subsequent orders as well as for making routine changes, such as cancelling breakfast or ordering a special diet in preparation for a test. Many facilities mention NPO status under this heading, as well as alternative feeding methods, such as tubes. Often patients who are NPO also have a nasogastric tube connected to a machine called a

Gomco suction machine, which may or may not be listed here. In some hospitals, the diet may be ordered or altered by a dietitian (e.g., for a diabetic patient).

Activities of Daily Living   Some PI screens list activities of daily living (ADL); others do not. When the heading is present, it calls for a statement about whether the patient needs help with ADL, such as bathing, eating, and elimination. This may affect the amount of teaching and emotional support the patient requires. In CPOE environments the ADL statement may be activated when the physician enters the initial order or it may be left to you or the nurses.

Activity   This is most often ordered by the doctor and reveals the level or type of activity the patient is allowed or capable of, and the amount of help the person needs (e.g., activity as tolerated [AAT], complete bed rest [CBR]). A patient weighing 115 kg (250 pounds) with limited weight-bearing capacity would likely require two nurses to get him or her up to a chair, whereas the same person who could bear weight may only need one nurse. In both situations, if the person were to walk the length of the hall, two nurses might be advisable until it became apparent the patient was strong enough to manage independently or for one nurse to handle the patient. In CPOE environments, you would check to be sure the order has been entered properly.

Clinical Parameters   Many computerized facilities group anything that has values attached to it under a heading called "Clinical Parameters." This can be confusing, since some of the interventions may also appear in other sections of the PI screen. An example would be a procedure or an intervention that also has a value (e.g., finger-prick glucose or a drain where the output is measured). Both of these have values but also involve nursing interventions and are procedures. Typically included under clinical parameters are vital signs, lab values, parenteral therapy, intake and output, and the patient's height/weight.

Vital Signs   Vital signs usually include temperature, pulse, respiration, and blood pressure. Most hospital units will have a standard protocol for how often to take vital signs; for example, surgical units take vital signs frequently during the immediate postoperative period, reducing to *q* shift (once every shift) once the patient is stable. The doctor may order more or less frequent assessment. If a patient's condition worsens, the nurses may also decide to take vital signs more often. This would be a nursing order; it would not be written on the doctor's orders but would be entered on the PI screen. Sometimes the patient's temperature is taken only once or twice a day despite the fact that the pulse, respiration, and blood pressure are done more frequently.

Intake and Output   Intake and output are automatically activated for any patient on parenteral therapy, but a doctor may order it for others as well. The nurses enter the values directly into the computer. The values are then automatically tallied or graphed onto a computerized flow sheet. If the environment is manual, the nurses usually take care of entering the values, which are typically totalled every eight hours even if the nurses are doing 12-hour shifts. This is to facilitate closer monitoring of the patient's intake and output status. In the manual environment you must ensure that a paper intake and output sheet is on the patient's chart.

Lab Values   Any lab values relating to tests done on a regular basis are kept on the PI screen. This usually includes blood sugar results and INR or aPTT results. INR results are used for patients on warfarin, and aPTT values for patients on heparin (see Chapter 6 for details). Newer drugs called *low-molecular-weight heparins* (discussed later) do not require routine blood work.

Parenteral/IV Therapy   Monitoring of parenteral therapy or IVs is carefully followed and is the nurse's responsibility. You may be required to keep track of dates when the IV site is to be changed, as well as the IV tubing. Facilities will differ in how often this is to be done. PRN adaptors (also called saline locks) are noted here also—and the times the site is to be flushed. If the adaptors are not flushed at least q shift, they could become clogged.

Procedures, Treatments, and Direct Care   This section lists any entities involving nursing assessment or care. Some interventions and assessments may also appear under clinical parameters, if a value is involved (e.g., doing routine finger-prick blood sugar). The nurse does the procedure and reports the value. Tubes and drains appear here because they require assessment as well as measurement and other nursing actions; for example, monitoring and removal.

Safety Management   Safety management entails recording those things the nurses must do to ensure the patient's safety during the hospital stay. This includes the use of side rails (some patients may be confused and require the side rails to be up), the call bell (some patients may be unable to use the call bell because of a disability or their condition, necessitating another means for the patient to call the nurse), and night rounds (routine checks, but which may be needed more frequently for some patients).

Safety management sometimes includes the use of either physical or chemical restraints—but only in extreme situations. The doctor must order such restraints. It has been proven in many cases that the use of physical restraints increases a patient's anxiety and restlessness and can lead to profound injury. Chemical restraints reduce a patient's cognition and level of both consciousness and awareness, which carries its own set of consequences.

Hygiene   Hygiene identifies specific needs of the patient. Some may be allowed to shower, others to take a bath; some may need special mouth care, others foot care (e.g., a diabetic person). Patients unable to ambulate require a bath at the bedside. Patients who are incapable of self-care require the nurse to attend to their bath and other hygiene needs. Hygiene also appears under levels of activity, notifying the nurse how much help the patient needs.

Elimination   This section clarifies the needs of the patient regarding use of the bathroom or, alternatively, the commode or bedpan. Advising the nurse if the patient has an ostomy will allow the nurse to prepare for this type of care. You would also note if the patient is to have an enema or not and add the date if one is given (e.g., third day postoperatively). In this section, you would identify whether the patient has a catheter or not, what type, when it is to be removed, and any other related orders.

Rest and Activity   This section is where you would note the order for the specifics of ambulation (e.g., up as tolerated) or particulars for patients with unique needs for ambulation, skin care, and related treatments.

Isolation   The process of keeping the patient away from the rest of the hospital population is called *isolation*. The is done either to prevent the spread of an infection the patient has or to keep him or her from acquiring an infection from someone else (called reverse isolation). You would also note here if the patient is VRSA-, MRSA-, VRE-, or *C. difficile*-positive and whether infection control has been notified. In most hospitals, all new admissions must be tested for some or all of these infectious diseases. If positive, patients are either separated by closed curtains or put into a private room or into isolation.

Respiratory Care   All assessments and treatments related to respiration are usually grouped together, including nursing assessments, treatments rendered by the respiratory therapist, and physiotherapy. These might also be summarized under Treatments, Assessments, or Procedures. Suctioning orders would also be noted.

Postoperative Assessments/Care   Any specific needs related to the patient after surgery are contained in the PI screen—for example, if the patient has a surgical wound that needs to be assessed and how often or when clips or sutures must be removed. Some facilities also record issues related to pain management. CMS stands for *circulation, sensation, and movement.* This assessment is required for a person with compromised circulation. This may be due to a vascular condition, the presence of restrictive bandaging, or a cast.

Transfer/Discharge Planning   Discharge planning (as discussed in Chapter 15) would be noted here. Add to this section any formal plans regarding the patient's transfer or discharge, including estimated discharge dates and any community support that the patient might need. Much of this information will come from the health care team after their discharge planning meetings (which are part of patient flow initiatives). You would note here if the patient were transferred *within* the hospital (e.g., from intensive care to telemetry or an asurgical unit).

A well-planned and well-managed discharge plan not only shortens the patient's hospital stay but also eases the patient's transition to home or another facility.

Lab and Diagnostic Tests   Some facilities also record specific lab tests that have been ordered for the patient on the PI screen (those ordered stat, those repeated at specific intervals, and atypical ones). They would be tracked on the computer under the heading of "Lab Tests" or "Laboratory and Diagnostic Tests," and they are listed by the date they were ordered. As well, results are entered into the computer by the lab or diagnostic imaging and are thus available to the physician. It may be that only tests routinely ordered are added (e.g., FBS and 2h p.c. BS q2 days), tests that take a while to collect (e.g., sputum for C&S [culture and sensitivity] or stool for OB [occult blood]). In CPOE environments, lab tests are entered by the physician and processed automatically. As previously mentioned, you would be required to monitor such orders and results.

Consultations   Various consultations may be requested for the hospitalized person. This may relate to assessment and care during the patient's hospital stay or to ongoing care upon discharge. *Physician consultations* occur when the MRP determines that further investigation is needed by someone from another specialty. *Pastoral care* provides spiritual support in the face of grave illness or simply at the request of the patient. A *home care liaison nurse* in some jurisdictions plans the patient's care after discharge from hospital. A *social worker* may be needed to help the patient and his or her family cope with hospitalization or make plans after discharge, particularly if it involves a move to another facility, such as a nursing home. If *physiotherapy* has been ordered, it would be noted on the PI screen. A patient recovering from knee replacement surgery would have physiotherapy ordered to maximize knee function and help with walking. *Occupational therapy* may also be required to help the person achieve maximum psychosocial and physical function. *Dietary* consultations may be ordered for the hospitalized patient or upon discharge to ensure the patient is able to cope with changes that may have occurred in his or her dietary needs.

In CPOE environments it will likely be your job to notify the appropriate person when a physician or nonphysician consult is requested. You would be notified on a task screen of an ordered consultation and would respond accordingly. Once you have notified the person that there is a consult request for them, you would mark the task as complete.

Level of Nursing Care   Facilities that track patient-care hours use this information to assist with collating care hours required by the patient. This is done electronically and may or may not be document driven. Hospitals that are financed according to other principles do not concern themselves with this.

Advance Directives/Level of Intervention   If the patient has advance directives, they are noted here. It is vital that *all staff* are aware of the patient's wishes regarding resuscitation and which life-saving measures are to be implemented or withheld.

Surgery   If the patient has surgery, add the type and date here postoperatively.

L06 ORDER ENTRY: THE PROCESS

In CPOE environments, the provider enters the orders and most are automatically processed. Your role is to monitor orders, notify nurses of new orders as required, and complete certain tasks related to the order process. This will vary with different hospitals. You will have a task screen and be notified when there is a task to complete. When you have completed a task, you mark it as complete. Knowing how to process orders is still a valuable skill, as it will be a few years yet until CPOE is in all major hospitals.

Although order entry follows a fairly straightforward process, each order will be dealt with somewhat differently.

1. Identify Orders to Be Processed

The first step is to be aware of a newly written order. This is fairly easy when you expect orders, such as when a patient has just been admitted to hospital or just returned from the operating room. It is harder, at times, to catch unexpected orders. Make sure also to check for any diet changes or any new daily blood work that has been added. You would want to write the latter on your daily blood work board (if your unit keeps one) and add the next day's blood work in order entry; for example, T + 1 = today plus 1 = tomorrow.

At any point during a patient's hospital stay, a physician may write a new order, amend an order, or discontinue orders, such as treatments and medication. Doctors usually write orders when they come to the floor to see the patient. This occurs most often during rounds, in the morning or late afternoon, but may be at any time—particularly when there are interns and residents as well as the specialist caring for the patient. To notify the staff that an order has been written, hospitals usually ask doctors to **flag** charts containing new orders. Facilities have different flagging systems; one of the more common is to stick a coloured marker in the chart (see Figure 16.10). Some facilities use an indicator, often red, on the back of the chart. In CPOE environments, you will be notified on your task screen when new orders have been written.

Check the charts frequently for flags. However, do not count on physicians to flag their orders; sometimes they forget. Routinely check doctors' order sheets in all charts

flag (of a chart) to draw attention to a new entry by sticking a coloured marker in the chart, placing a coloured sticker on the back of the chart, or using some other device to visually draw attention.

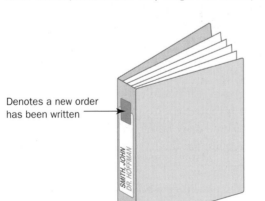

Denotes a new order has been written

SMITH, JOHN
DR. HOFFMAN

201

Figure 16.10   Chart flagged for new order

for newly written orders. A good time to do this is at the start of each shift and again around the middle of the shift or after a group of doctors has left the unit. If it gets busy, for example, a physician will sometimes put a chart back in the wrong slot—or put it back without signing off on an order. Every chart must be checked at least once per shift, preferably more frequently to ensure that orders are signed and processed.

When you review a newly written order, make sure that the order sheet is identified, dated, and signed by the doctor or, if taken by telephone, by the nurse per the physician (e.g., Nancy Yang/Dr. P. Rosenberg).

2. Review the Orders for Anything Urgent

Next, look over the order for anything that is urgent or stat. If you have more than one set that needs to be processed, quickly review each set, and prioritize and complete all of the stat orders in each set of orders in an organized manner. In a CPOE environment, you would review the newly written orders and notify the nurse of any urgent orders to ensure that he or she is aware of them.

Stat orders may include medications, IV therapy, blood work, and diagnostic tests. Identify or highlight these orders and process them immediately, or place a mark beside the order (not through it). (Note that some facilities do not recommend using a highlighter because it interferes with legibility when they are copied or faxed.) Because stat orders are frequently medication orders, it is helpful to highlight all of the medication orders (perhaps in yellow, or put a yellow mark beside the medication) after you first look over the sheet. This clearly displays any medication orders and ensures that they have been given the appropriate attention. If the orders involve a change to a medication the patient is already on, go back and highlight the earlier orders in blue (or make a blue mark beside the order) so that a physician or nurse can quickly see the connection if they want to check back. (Do that for all changes in medication orders—stat or otherwise.) In some electronic environments, MARs printed by the pharmacy will have an order number on them that you can use for identification purposes.

Follow through with all necessary steps connected to a stat order promptly. For example, if you have a stat medication or IV order, you would notify the nurse immediately so that she can implement the order. If it is a stat X-ray, you would have to call diagnostic imaging to arrange to have it done (if the request is for a portable X-ray, the technician would come to the patient's room; let the nurses know). If it is stat blood work, depending on your system, you would have to call the lab or call or page the technician to come and take the blood (e.g., "This is 7 south calling. We have a stat CBC for Mr. Reaves in room 703").

The lab may have the capabilities to print their own requisition, or you may have to print it on the unit to be ready for the technician when he or she arrives. Electronic orders offer the option of printing a label for the blood work or a requisition on the patient-care unit; then, when the technician comes to take the blood, the tube label and requisition are already available. For nonurgent orders that option is not chosen; the technician would print the label and requisition in the lab when the orders are downloads and bring it to the floor with him or her.

3. Process the Orders

After you have dealt with anything urgent, organize your time to enter the rest of the orders. Again, if you have several sets of orders to process, deal with the highest priorities first (stat orders aside). For example, if a patient is soon going to the operating room, those orders would need prompt attention. If a patient is waiting to go home and the discharge order has just been written, you should attend to the patient's discharge order; if a patient is in pain and the nurse is waiting for you to process an analgesic order, that would also require immediate attention. An order for routine blood work or a change in a patient's activity order would not be an immediate priority. Your responsibilities to some orders (e.g., patient discharge) remains the same in CPOE environments.

If all orders are equal in terms or priority, draw up your own plan. Some clinical secretaries prefer to deal with shorter orders first, others like to get the longer ones, such as new admissions and postop orders, out of the way first. If you work in a hospital and are processing medications, it is a good idea to complete your medication orders, if any, first. It is essential to be organized and focused. There will rarely be a time when you are not disturbed by the telephone, intercom, or questions from staff or visitors. Many new graduates say this is one of the greatest hurdles to overcome—multitasking, remaining organized, and completing tasks. It will take patience and concentration to remain focused on what you are doing as well as carrying out your other responsibilities. Even seasoned clinical secretaries find this part of the job challenging.

Process each order individually, and *think each order through methodically*. Simply entering it into an electronic database or physically processing it is only one step. For each order, ask yourself what else needs to be done. Is there someone to call? Should I tell the nurse? Are there implications for the patient? Is there something about this order that doesn't seem correct—perhaps a medication dose or the patient has an allergy to that family of medications?

After you finish the medication orders or fax the order sheet to the pharmacy, you might then proceed to IV orders, lab and diagnostic tests, and then to orders relating to nursing care. The actual steps of processing are similar, but naturally each type of order processed will have variations. For example:

- Copy medication orders to the MAR or fax the order sheet to the pharmacy.

- Enter nursing-related orders, such as assessments, activity and rest, nutrition, elimination, and comfort measures, to the PI screen.

- If you are in an electronic environment, lab orders are entered electronically. Fill out the required information electronically and send it to the appropriate department in the lab. If it is a stat order, call the lab and print the requisition on the unit. In a manual environment, fill out a paper requisition and send it to the lab per facility protocol (by fax, pneumatic tube, or manual transport). If a person picks up and delivers requisitions (which is done at designated intervals), the facility will have an "outbox" where completed requisitions are kept. As with electronically filed orders, follow up stat orders with a phone call.

- Take the necessary steps to implement referral orders for after-care discharge (e.g., home care, community nursing, outpatient physiotherapy). You will usually have to phone, fax, or email and may also need to prepare a written requisition.

4. Identify the Orders as Completed

On the doctor's order form, note each order when you finish processing it to keep track and avoid duplication or omission. Remember that each facility, and sometimes each person, has a *unique set of symbols* that are used to indicate an order has been entered and is thus complete, but the following codes are used in this book:

- MAR or MS (med sheet) indicates that a medication order has been copied to the MAR—the same as in the electronic environment. (Keep in mind that few environments have manually completed MARs anymore.)

- R indicates that a computerized requisition has been completed and sent. You may or may not have to note this on the PI screen.
- PI means nursing-related orders or direct patient-care orders (e.g., ambulation, insert a catheter, start oxygen) have been activated on the PI screen.

> **TIP**
>
> Every facility will have a commonly used code or identifier to identify when an order has been completed. The type of identifier is irrelevant; the fact that you must use one is not. Be methodical, thorough, and accurate when processing orders. Using this identifier will go a long way to keeping you organized and help prevent errors.

5. Check Your Work

Recheck your orders sequentially, carefully, and thoroughly.

6. Have Your Orders Checked by the Nurse

Unless you have been authorized to complete the orders on your own, have the designated person, usually the charge nurse, check your orders before you sign off. This step takes a bit more time but is well worth it for your peace of mind and, ultimately, the patient's safety. If an error occurs and you did not have the orders validated, you may be held legally responsible. For example, in most facilities, if there is a proper communication system in place between the nurse and the clinical secretary, the clinical secretary can be held accountable for the **transcription** component of the job. If there is a med error because the nurse didn't verify the order, the clinical secretary will be considered responsible for the transcription error. In other words, it is the clinical secretary's responsibility to ensure that all the proper checks are completed.

transcription creating a written copy of a dictated or recorded message.

> **TIP**
>
> Always have a nurse check your orders. If you are not certain this has been done in a detailed manner, ask the nurse to check them more thoroughly and to sign off on the entered orders. Failing to do so can result in harm to a patient if errors are missed.

7. Sign Off

Before signing off, check once more to ensure that the patient's name on the orders and the name on the MAR match. Mark the orders as complete, as per facility guidelines, usually by signing your name or initialling with the date and time of completion. You must also have the designated nurse check your orders and initial or sign as well to indicate the orders have been reviewed. Some hospitals use a stamp with an imprint detailing the date, signature of the nurse (who checked the order with you), and your own signature. If you are working from an electronic order (which is different than CPOE), you would electronically note each order as it is processed. The process is the same for orders entered electronically. In the CPOE environment, you only acknowledge orders requiring you to complete a task.

8. Fax or Scan the Order to the Pharmacy

Fax the order to the pharmacy and note on the order that it has been faxed or scanned into the chart and sent. *Note that in some facilities the policy is to fax the orders to the pharmacy before they are completed and signed off on*—this facilitates prompt preparation of the medications ordered; there may be a little box to check off beside the order indicating that you have faxed it or scanned the order. If the pharmacy department is appropriately computerized, scanned orders will appear on their "smart screen." They show the patient's name and room number and are prioritized on the screen (which is constantly monitored in that department).

9. Return the Chart to Its Proper Place

Once an order has been completed, it is important to return the chart to its proper place. This keeps the desk area tidy and prevents charts from being misplaced or lost. If the chart was flagged for order identification, remove the flag.

L07 TRANSCRIBING MEDICATION ORDERS

The attending physician, nurse practitioner, or consultant must order all medications given in hospital. Even medications that a person takes routinely at home must be ordered if they are to be continued while in hospital. *No* medication—not even Aspirin—should be given to a patient or taken by a patient if it is not ordered. If patients come with medications, they are asked to send them home with someone. Failing that, the nurse should take the medications and store them until the patient is discharged. It's a good idea to mark somewhere on the patient's chart that there are meds in safekeeping to ensure they are returned to the patient upon transfer or discharge. Keeping the medications prevents, at least in part, unauthorized self-medication. The physician must have an accurate record of what medications the patient is taking. If a patient self-medicates, there is always a potential for adverse drug interactions with prescribed medications, overdose, or interference with lab tests. For example, Raja was getting Tylenol 3 from the nurses for arthritic pain but found it was not keeping it under control. She had some Percocet in her purse. She took two, resulting in an overdose. Salimu was on anti-coagulants; he had a headache and, not wanting to bother the nurses, took four Aspirins from the bottle tucked away in his bedside drawer. This affected his blood test results because Aspirin has anti-coagulant properties and potentiates the action of anti-coagulants.

Any medication that is ordered in the hospital must be copied onto the appropriate form, usually the MAR. This is done by the clinical secretary, nurse, or pharmacy, depending on the circumstances. A profile of the patient's current, amended, and discontinued medications is usually kept in the patient's eChart. If a medication is changed or discontinued, the clinical secretary draws a neat line through the medication, but never erases it.

Medication Administration Records

The format of MARs varies with each facility. The design may depend on facility preference, whether the MARs are computer generated, or their purpose (e.g., stat and single-dose medications, scheduled or PRN medications, which are discussed in detail subsequently). They may even differ in design from one floor to another—surgical, medical, or obstetrical services.

In the computerized environment, MARs are typically prepared by the pharmacy department. These are often called *eMARs*. In most hospitals, eMARs are generated every 24 hours. Completed eMARs are either kept in the MAR binder on the med cart or returned to the patient's chart. There is an eMAR for scheduled (regularly taken) medications and another for PRN meds. Some facilities also have separate eMARs for recording anti-coagulants and hypoglycemics. Figure 16.11 is an example of a single-day eMAR for scheduled medications.

In facilities where MARs are manually prepared, the MAR will have enough spaces for five to seven days. See Figure 16.12 for an illustration. The nurses just sign beside the hour they give the medication under the appropriate date. For example, if the nurse, Amy, gives psyllium to a patient at 8:00 a.m. on January 20, she would initial the space beside 0800.

Categories of Medication

For purposes of recording, most facilities divide medications into categories.

Routine or Scheduled Medication Orders   These usually must be taken at specific times every day: od, bid, tid, qid, or qhs (see Chapter 7, Table 7.2 for an explanation

CONESTOGA GENERAL HOSPITAL
SCHEDULED MEDICATION ADMINISTRATION RECORD

From Mon 20 April/xx 0700h   to Tues 21 April/xx @ 0659h

Allergies: GENTAMYCIN

Diagnosis

Severne Aubert
23 Capilano Dr
Vancouver B.C.
#123432333 Dr. G. O'Neal

Medication and Directions		07 08 09 10 11 12 13 14 15 16 17 18 19 20 21 22 23 24	01 02 03 04 05 06
	Hours		
Psyllium Cap 1 cap po tid Swallow one cap at a time 0800 1400 2200	Initial	Start Jan 20/xx	
Metronidazole Tab 250 mg 500 mg (2 tabs) po tid with food 0900 1300 1800	Initial	Start Jan 20/xx	
Ramipril Cap 10 mg I cap po od (hold if **SBP** < 110)* 1000	Initial	Start Jan 20/xx	
Amitriptyline Tab 25 mg take 1 tab po qhs 2200	Initial	Start Jan 20/xx	
	Initial		
	Initial		

Room # 302 Bed# 2   MAR Checked by *BT*   Page # 1

Figure 16.11   Single-day eMAR for scheduled medications

CONESTOGA GENERAL HOSPITAL

Severne Aubert
23 Capilano Rd.,
Vancouver B.C.
#123432333 Dr. G. O'Neal

Check here if more than one page □

Scheduled Medication Administration Record

Start /reorder	Stop date	Medication dose, route, frequency	Hour Due	Jan 20	21	22	23	24	25	26
Jan 20/xx		Psyllium 1 cap po tid	0800							
			1400							
			2200							
Jan 20/xx		Metronidazole 250 mg. —	0800							
		Caps 11 tid with food.	1200							
			1700							
Jan 20/xx		Ramipril 10 mg po od	1000							
		Hold if sbp < 110								
Jan 20/xx		Amitriptyline 25 mg po qhs	2200							

Figure 16.12 Scheduled MAR for a manual environment

of these abbreviations). A medication taken every other day or once a week would also be in this category as long as it is taken on a regular schedule. Some scheduled medications are taken for a designated time, others indefinitely. Antibiotics, for example, are usually taken for 7 to 10 days. Some medications, such as thyroid, heart, or blood pressure medication (anti-hypertensives), may be taken throughout the hospital stay since the patient may be on them for life. Others, such as anti-inflammatories, are taken until a patient's condition has stabilized or reversed itself.

PRN Medications This category of medications includes any taken only as needed, usually to relieve a symptom (also called a clinical sign). For example, Genna may take acetaminophen or Aspirin when she has a headache, dimenhydrinate or dramamine (Gravol) when she experiences nausea, or lorazepam (Ativan) when she feels anxious. In the hospital setting, the decision that the medication is needed is usually made by the patient or collaboratively by the nurse and the patient. A maximum frequency will be given; for example, q4h PRN means that the drug may be taken as needed, every four hours. See Figure 16.16 for an example of PRN orders.

Stat Medication Orders Stat medication orders may include anti-seizure medications, analgesics, antibiotics, steroids, or anxiolytics, among others. The common element is that the need for the medication is urgent. For example, if a patient suddenly developed very high blood pressure, the doctor would order an anti-hypertensive or a diuretic stat, perhaps by injection or IV to speed up the effect. In response to a migraine headache, a doctor will sometimes order an analgesic stat. In response to an epileptic seizure, a doctor might order an anti-convulsant stat. If Gertrude has a bladder infection, once a urine specimen is obtained the doctor often orders an antibiotic with the first dose given stat. Stat medications are either recorded on a specific form or on the scheduled MAR and clearly identified as stat. This can be done by underlining it, highlighting it, or writing it in red. You must always notify the patient's nurse of a stat order.

Single-Dose Medications   For a variety of reasons, the doctor may order only one dose of a medication. Often preoperative medications are single-dose medications. RhoGAM for an Rh-negative mom who had an Rh-positive baby is also a single dose. As with stat medications, single-dose medications are either recorded on a specific form or on the scheduled MAR and identified as one dose only. As with stat meds, this can be done by underlining it, highlighting it, or writing it in red.

A doctor will sometimes write an order for a scheduled medication late in the day that would normally start the next morning. If the doctor wants one dose given that evening, he or she will write instructions to that effect. This is not considered a single-dose medication. (See Figure 16.13, Lasix and enalapril, for an example.)

The Process of Transcribing Medication Orders

In many hospitals, the pharmacy will generate MARs as required, so dealing with medication orders of any kind will not be your responsibility. A growing number of hospitals are fully automated with respect to medication administration: Pharmacy prepares the eMARs as required, and prepares and dispenses all patient medications using automated medication dispensing cabinets from which the nurse gives out patient

	CONESTOGA GENERAL HOSPITAL DOCTORS ORDER SHEET	
Please fax to Pharmacy & note date/time		
	cbc	Dietz, Henry 123 Duncan St. Vancouver B.C. DOB 22 09 47 071608 Dr. G. Hanson
	Electrolytes	
	Urine for C&S	
	Valium 5 mg po hs	
	Lasix 20 mg od Give first dose tonight	
	Demerol 100 mg IM stat	
	HCT 12.5 mg od	
	Enalapril 5 mg BID Give first dose tonight	
	Eltroxin 0.1 mg od	
	Demerol 50-75 mg IM q4h PRN	
	Gravol 50 mg q4h PRN	
date *Jan 2/XX*	time *2000*	Physician's printed name Dr. G. Hanson	Signature *Dr. G. Hanson*	

Figure 16.13   Initial doctor's orders for Mr. Dietz

medications. The nurse electronically identifies the right patient by scanning the patient's ID bracket. In CPOE environments, the process is similar.

The following section on medications and order entry is relevant only for environments in which paper MARs are used (either entirely prepared by hand or generated by the pharmacy and downloaded for the nurses to use when giving medications to patients). eMARs discussed in this section refer to MARs that were computer generated by the pharmacy and downloaded into paper format. Fully computerized MARs are not downloaded for order processing.

This section will work through an example of a straightforward set of doctor's orders. You will follow Mary, a clinical secretary, as she processes orders for Mr. Dietz.

The Protocol In this scenario (at Conestoga General Hospital), eMARs are generated every 24 hours, arriving on the patient-care unit each morning at 0700 hours and used until 0659 the next morning, at which time a MAR for the next day is produced. eMARs for new admissions are generated until 1900 hours, after which they are prepared manually by the nurse or clinical secretary. Changes to existing MARs of inpatients are done manually but will be incorporated into the eMARs generated the next morning. In this hospital, stat orders are transcribed onto the scheduled MAR. Note that the level of computerization in hospitals regarding medication administration is continually evolving.

For this explanatory exercise, all of the medications are to start on the day on which the orders are written, January 2/XX. Note that in this section we will deal only with orders related to medication.

Mr. Dietz has been admitted to Mary's medical patient-care unit from the emergency department with a provisional diagnosis of abdominal pain NYD (not yet diagnosed). Because he comes to Mary's floor after 1900 hours (and the pharmacy is closed), Mary manually processes the medication orders that are required for Mr. Dietz between admission and 0659 the next morning. Mr. Dietz has been asking for something for his pain.

Step 1: Check Orders The nurse who brought Mr. Dietz to the unit hands orders to Mary that were written by Dr. Hanson in emergency, who is Mr. Dietz's MRP (see Figure 16.13). Mary quickly checks for the date and the doctor's signature. She notes that there are no allergies.

Step 2: Identifying and Prioritizing Medication Orders

- Mary glances over the order sheet looking for any stat orders (see Figure 16.14). She places a checkmark beside the medication orders to make them stand out; finding a stat order for Demerol (which Dr. Hanson has written in response to Mr. Dietz's requests for something immediate for pain), she highlights that with an asterisk and processes that order first.

- Mary notifies the registered nurse of the stat order.

- Mary prints out a blank MAR for scheduled medications and adds Mr. Dietz's ID label (as shown in Figure 16.15a). She then writes in the order for Demerol (including the dose and route and the fact that it is a stat order) and underlines it. Mary has also added "stat order given at" so the nurse has to enter the time and initial it once she has given the medication. Mary gives the MAR directly to the nurse.

- The nurse takes the MAR, prepares the medication, gives Mr. Dietz Demerol, initials the MAR, and gives it back to Mary. In some hospitals, as further verification, a nurse who gives a stat medication also initials or signs the doctor's written order for the medication, along with the date and the word "given." The nurse must have the MAR with her to prepare the medication—she uses it as a guide, ensuring she

<table>
<tr><td colspan="3" align="center">**CONESTOGA GENERAL HOSPITAL**
DOCTORS ORDER SHEET</td></tr>
<tr><td colspan="3">*Please fax to Pharmacy & note date/time*</td></tr>
<tr>
<td></td>
<td>*cbc*</td>
<td rowspan="3">Dietz, Henry
123 Duncan St.
Vancouver B.C.
DOB 22 09 47   071608
Dr. G. Hanson</td>
</tr>
<tr>
<td></td>
<td>*Electrolytes*</td>
</tr>
<tr>
<td></td>
<td>*Urine for C&S*</td>
</tr>
<tr>
<td>*MAR*</td>
<td>*Valium 5 mg po hs prn* √</td>
<td rowspan="9">**Note that Mary has identified the meds using checkmarks—for the stat med she has chosen to use an asterisk to set it apart as needing to be attended to immediately.**
As Mary later writes the meds onto the MARs, she symbolized the process by writing MAR in the left column. This is a double check to remind Mary that that medication has been processed. Some facilities use a highlighter, but it has been found to cause visibility problems when the sheet is faxed.</td>
</tr>
<tr>
<td>*MAR*</td>
<td>*Lasix 20 mg od*   *Give first dose tonight* √</td>
</tr>
<tr>
<td>*MAR*</td>
<td>*Demerol 100 mg IM stat*   ✳ ✳ ✳ *Nurse notified @ 2010*</td>
</tr>
<tr>
<td></td>
<td>*HCT 12.5 mg od*   √</td>
</tr>
<tr>
<td>*MAR*</td>
<td>*Enalapril 5 mg BID*   *Give first dose tonight* √</td>
</tr>
<tr>
<td></td>
<td>*Eltroxin 0.1 mg od* √</td>
</tr>
<tr>
<td>*MAR*</td>
<td>*Demerol 50-75 mg IM q4h prn*   √</td>
</tr>
<tr>
<td>*MAR*</td>
<td>*Gravol 50 mg q4h prn* √</td>
</tr>
<tr>
<td>:</td>
<td>**Because only the Valium, Lasix, Demerol, Enalapril and Gravol are required that evening, she leaves the other drugs for pharmacy to print off on the eMAR the next morning.**</td>
</tr>
<tr>
<td>date
Jan 2 / XX</td>
<td>time
2000</td>
<td>Physician's printed name
Dr. G. Hanson

Signature
Dr. G. Hanson</td>
</tr>
</table>

Figure 16.14 The same doctor's orders for Mr. Dietz, with medications highlighted and transcription symbols added, signifying that the medications have been processed

has followed the five rights for giving medications: the right patient, the right drug, the right dose, the right route, and the right time.

■ As her next step, on the doctor's order (see Figure 16.14), Mary writes that the nurse has been notified and the time. Mary also writes "MAR" on the order form beside Demerol, meaning it has been transcribed to the med sheet. Mary has now completed the steps for dealing with a stat medication.

Step 3: Completing the Medication Orders Having completed the stat order, Mary finishes processing the remaining medication orders.

Processing Scheduled Medications

Mary has already added Mr. Dietz's ID label to the scheduled MAR. The scheduled meds that must be given that evening are the Lasix and the enalapril (Figure 16.13 shows that the doctor ordered a dose for both of those medications to be given that evening).

■ Mary carefully copies the medications onto the scheduled MAR she has printed off under the stat order for Demerol. She includes the start date for each medication.

■ She enters the dose, route, and frequency, making sure the information is transcribed accurately.

CONESTOGA GENERAL HOSPITAL
SCHEDULED MEDICATION ADMINISTRATION RECORD

From *Jan 2/XX 2000 to: Jan 3/XX @ 0659h*

Allergies: No Allergies *None*
Adverse Reactions
Diagnosis
Circle time med given and initial below.

Dietz, Henry
124 Duncan St.
Vancouver B.C.
DOB 22/09/47
#123432333
Dr. G. Hanson

Medication and Directions																									
Hours	07	08	09	10	11	12	13	14	15	16	17	18	19	20	21	22	23	24		01	02	03	04	05	06
Demerol 75 mg. IM stat	*Stat order given at:*																								
Initial																									
	07	08	09	10	11	12	13	14	15	16	17	18	19	20	21	22	23	24		01	02	03	04	05	06
Initial																									
	07	08	09	10	11	12	13	14	15	16	17	18	19	20	21	22	23	24		01	02	03	04	05	06
Initial																									

Figure 16.15a   Mary has transcribed the stat order for Demerol onto a MAR (the same format is used by the pharmacy for eMARs)

CONESTOGA GENERAL HOSPITAL
SCHEDULED MEDICATION ADMINISTRATION RECORD

From *Jan 2/XX 2000 to: Jan 3 /XX @ 0659h*
Allergies: No Allergies *None*
Adverse Reactions
Diagnosis
Circle time med given and initial below.

Dietz, Henry
124 Duncan St.
Vancouver B.C.
DOB 22/09/47
#123432333
Dr. G. Hanson

Medication and Directions																									
Hours	07	08	09	10	11	12	13	14	15	16	17	18	19	20	21	22	23	24		01	02	03	04	05	06
Demerol 75 mg. IM stat	*Stat order given at: 2115 RM* Note: the nurse has given the Demerol and added the time and her initials, and given the MAR back to Mary to complete the med orders you see below																								
Initial																									
Lasix 20 mg po bid *0800 1800*	*Start date: Jan 2/XX* *Give first dose tonight* Note: The nurse will give the Lasix and the enalapril that evening as per the doctor's order. The next day, the nurses will resume giving the meds at the times outlined on this MAR																			The orders for these 2 meds are not considered stat or one dose only					
Initial																									
Enalapril 5 mg po bid *1000 1800*	*Start date: Jan 2/XX* *Give first dose tonight*																								
Initial																									
	07	08	09	10	11	12	13	14	15	16	17	18	19	20	21	22	23	24		01	02	03	04	05	06
Initial																									
	07	08	09	10	11	12	13	14	15	16	17	18	19	20	21	22	23	24		01	02	03	04	05	06
Initial																									

Room # Bed#	MAR Checked by *VT*	Page #

Figure 16.15b   Scheduled med orders to be given that evening are manually prepared by Mary

■   She adds the times at which the medications should be given (most hospitals have a list of the most common medications and when they should be given—for example, with meals, without meals, first thing in the morning).

■   She does not include a stop date as none was indicated and these medications are not subject to automatic stop dates. Mary has also written in the doctor's instructions—all medications must be transcribed exactly as the doctor writes them,

TABLE 16.1 Components of transcribed medication orders (as shown in Figures 16.13 and 16.14)

Name	The name of the drug as the physician ordered it.
Dose	The amount of the drug the patient is to receive (e.g., Lasix 20 mg).
Frequency	How often the medication is to be given (e.g., Lasix od or daily).
Route	How the medication is to be given. Mostly ordered po here. Demerol and Gravol were ordered IM.
Times	Mary adds the times at which the medications must be given. (There is usually a hospital protocol outlining the times each medication or group of medications is to be given.) On eMARs you will note that the pharmacy adds the times, as shown in Figure 16.17.
Start Order	The start date is the date on which the order should be implemented. If the doctor does not specify otherwise, the start date is the same as the date on which the order was written (January 2, in this case). The start date is written out for each medication. Some MAR formats have two columns for written medication—one for the start date and one for the stop date.
Stop Date	Automatic stop order policies are meant as a safeguard for patients to prevent prolonged use of specified medications. The stop date is not always filled out. All controlled drugs have automatic stop dates. The controlled drugs, such as Demerol and morphine, will have automatic stop date hours. This will vary with each facility, but the automatic date usually ranges from 48 to 72 hours. As well, doctors can order a specific stop date—for example, if the automatic stop date for morphine is 72 hours, the doctor can extend that time frame: "hydromorphine 0.5—1 mg po q2h prn 7 days for pain." Antibiotics often have automatic stop dates of seven days unless otherwise stated. Most facilities review all medications each month. Patients rarely stay that long in an acute-care hospital, but long-term care or nursing facilities often use a standard one-month stop date. Computerized systems have posed some problems with automatic stop dates in that some medications have been automatically stopped when the physician wanted them continued.

including explanations or specific instructions. (See Table 16.1 for a detailed explanation of the components of a MAR.) Figure 16.15b shows those orders added to the MAR.

Processing PRN Medications

Mary must now transcribe the PRN orders. She prints off a PRN MAR. They all must be processed manually because Mr. Dietz may want one of them during the remainder of the evening or night. His Valium can be given at bedtime, and it is likely he will need more Demerol. Gravol is often given with Demerol to counteract nausea, which can be a side effect of Demerol. Remember that an eMAR will be sent to the floor at 0700 the next morning. In manual environments, the PRN MAR will likely be designed for use over several days.

- As with the scheduled medications, Mary carefully copies the PRN medications onto Mr. Dietz's MAR. She includes the date on which the medication is started.

- She enters the dose, route, and frequency, making sure to enter numbers accurately.

- Mary also adds the automatic stop date beside Demerol (at this hospital all narcotic medications have an automatic stop date of 72 hours). Valium and Gravol do not have automatic stop dates. (In some hospitals, Valium would have an automatic stop date of 30 days, but it is highly unlikely that Mr. Dietz will be in the hospital that long, so the stop date is left blank.)

- Mary adds the transcription symbol "MAR" beside each medication on the doctor's order as she processes it, signifying that she has copied the medication to the MAR. This is illustrated in Figure 16.14.

See Figure 16.16 for Mary's completed PRN MAR.

All narcotic analgesics have automatic stop dates unless otherwise specified by the doctor. Mary's hospital uses a stop date of 72 hours for Demerol, so Mary counts

CONESTOGA GENERAL HOSPITAL
PRN MEDICATION ADMINISTRATION RECORD

From *Jan 2/XX 2000h to: Jan 3/XX @ 0659h*
Allergies:　　**No Allergies**　*None*
Adverse Reactions
Diagnosis
Circle time med given　and initial below.

Dietz, Henry
124 Duncan St.
Vancouver B.C.
DOB 22/09/47
#123432333
Dr. G. Hanson

PRN Medication and Directions		07	08	09	10	11	12	13	14	15	16	17	18	19	20	21	22	23	24	01	02	03	04	05	06
Hours																									
Valium 5mg. po hs prn		*Start January 2/XX*																							
	Initial																								
Demerol 50 – 100 mg IM *Q3 – 4 h prn*		*Start January 2/XX* *d/c January 5/XX @ 2000h*																							
	Initial																								
Gravol 50 mg IM or po *q3 – 4 h prn* *Disc/renewal January 5/xx*	Initial	*Start January 2/XX*																							
	Initial																								
	Initial																								

Room #　Bed#　　　　　　　　　　　　　MAR Checked by　*VT*　　　　　Page # 1

Figure 16.16　The PRN MAR Mary prepared from orders shown in Figure 16.14

forward three days from the start date and puts a stop date of January 5. If a patient still needs the drug after the stop date, the nurses will request that the clinical secretary ask the doctor for a renewal or reorder. In a noncomputerized environment, you could leave a note on the patient's chart or call the doctor. In a computerized environment, there is usually a "bulletin board" or "message board" somewhere in the patient's eChart where you would write the request. The physician should check this message board regularly. As with the scheduled medications, an eMAR would be prepared by the pharmacy and sent to the floor before 0700 the next morning. It will be for the next 24–hour period, Jan 3/XX 0700–Jan 4/XX 0659, at which time a new eMAR would be generated for the next 24 hours.

Dose Range for PRN Medications　Some PRN medication orders are written with a dose range. In this case, the doctor ordered a range of 50–75 mg of Demerol, meaning the nurse may give the patient either 50 or 75 mg, depending on how severe the patient's pain is. The nurse may make this decision in consultation with the patient. A *pain scale* is a helpful assessment tool. The patient is asked to assign a number (usually between 0 and 10) to the pain he is currently experiencing, with 0 as no pain and 10 as the worst pain he has ever experienced. If the patient rates his pain at 3, for example, the discomfort probably doesn't warrant 75 mg of Demerol, but if the patient rates it as a 10 it would.

Frequencies for PRN medications are maximums and provide safety parameters. Q4h means that the medication may be given no more often than every four hours. Some doctors order a range, such as q3–4 hours. Demerol, for example, could be given every three hours if needed. Often, nurses will give it as much as a half-hour earlier, but no sooner. This is considered appropriate by most facilities.

These orders are now complete. Mary rechecks her orders, has the nurse check her orders, and signs off. She either tears off the back copy and sends it to the pharmacy or

SCHEDULED MEDICATION ADMINISTRATION RECORD

Dietz, Henry
124 Duncan St.
Vancouver B.C.
DOB 22/09/47
#123432333
Dr. G. Hanson

From <u>Jan 3/xx 0700 to: Jan 4/xx @ 0659</u>
Allergies: No Allergies *None*
Adverse Reactions
Diagnosis   Abd pain NYD
Circle time med given and initial below.

Medication and Directions		07	08	09	10	11	12	13	14	15	16	17	18	19	20	21	22	23	24		01	02	03	04	05	06
	Hours																									
Lasix (furosemide) 20 mg po bid **take on empty stomach** 1000 1600 (ward stock)		Start date: Jan 03/xx Stop date: none given																								
	Initial																									
		07	08	09	10	11	12	13	14	15	16	17	18	19	20	21	22	23	24		01	02	03	04	05	06
Enalapril (Vasotec) 5 mg po bid **take with or without food** 1000 1800		Start date: Jan 03/xx Stop date: none given																								
	Initial																									
		07	08	09	10	11	12	13	14	15	16	17	18	19	20	21	22	23	24		01	02	03	04	05	06
Hydrochlorothiazide (HCT) 12.5 mg po od (HydroDIURAL) **take with or without food** 1000		Start date: Jan 03/xx Stop date: none given																								
	Initial																									
		07	08	09	10	11	12	13	14	15	16	17	18	19	20	21	22	23	24		01	02	03	04	05	06
Eltroxin 0.1 mg po od (levothyroxin) 1000 (ward stock)		Start date: Jan 03/xx Stop date: none given																								
	Initial																									
		07	08	09	10	11	12	13	14	15	16	17	18	19	20	21	22	23	24		01	02	03	04	05	06
	Initial																									

Figure 16.17   eMAR showing medications from Dr. Hanson's orders (Figure 16.13) printed for a 24-hour period starting January 3

faxes the order to the pharmacy (depending on hospital routine). She returns the chart to the appropriate place. The eMAR the pharmacy creates for January 3 is shown in Figure 16.17.

Discontinuing Existing Orders

Usually only a physician (or a nurse practitioner) can discontinue an order. Orders are discontinued if there is an automatic stop date and the doctor doesn't renew it (e.g., for narcotics), after the last dose when a designated time frame is identified (e.g., pen G 500 units po qid 7 days), or because the doctor is changing a dose of a medication or discontinuing the medication altogether, as shown subsequently. The clinical secretary or nurse must go to the appropriate MAR and write "d/c" beside the medication and, if appropriate, a time. For example, Dr. Hanson comes to the unit on the morning of January 3 to reassess Mr. Dietz. He decides that Mr. Dietz doesn't need HCT as a diuretic. (He is also on Lasix, a diuretic sometimes used in combination with HCT.) He also finds that Mr. Dietz has become increasingly anxious and feels that prescribing Valium throughout the day as well as at night may help. Mary finds Mr. Dietz's chart on her desk, flagged to notify her that there is a new order (Figure 16.18a).

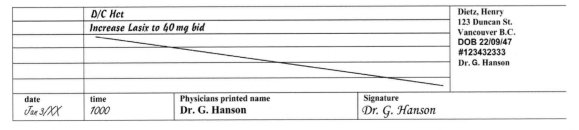

		Dietz, Henry 123 Duncan St. Vancouver B.C. DOB 22/09/47 #123432333 Dr. G. Hanson
	D/C Hct	
	Increase Lasix to 40 mg bid	
date *Jan 3/XX*	time *1000*	Physicians printed name **Dr. G. Hanson**	Signature *Dr. G. Hanson*

Figure 16.18a   Doctor's order sheet showing new orders

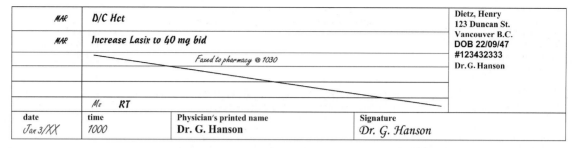

MAR	**D/C Hct**	Dietz, Henry 123 Duncan St. Vancouver B.C. **DOB 22/09/47** **#123432333** Dr. G. Hanson
MAR	**Increase Lasix to 40 mg bid**	
	Faxed to pharmacy @ 1030	
	Ms **RT**	

date *Jan 3/XX*	time *1000*	Physician's printed name **Dr. G. Hanson**	Signature *Dr. G. Hanson*

Figure 16.18b Doctor's order sheet showing new orders with transcription codes added by Mary as she processed the orders: HCT has been discontinued and the Lasix has been increased

- Mary checks the new order to be sure Mr. Dietz's ID sticker is on it. She ensures that the order is dated and signed by Dr. Hanson. She notes again there are no allergies.

- The medication orders must be transcribed to Mr. Dietz's scheduled MAR, so she gets them out of the medication binder, which is on the medication cart. The MAR she uses is the eMAR that was sent to the floor at 0700 that morning. This replaces the one that Mary manually prepared on the evening of January 2, when Mr. Dietz was admitted.

- Mary scans the order, noting medication changes. She immediately notifies Mr. Dietz's medication nurse that his HCT has been discontinued and the dose of his Lasix changed. She also tells her that a new medication, Valium, has been ordered, which the nurse can start immediately.

- Mary then begins to process the new orders. The first order is to discontinue or stop Mr. Dietz's HCT. To do this, Mary clearly marks d/c on the eMAR record and draws a line across the MAR beside it (see Figure 16.19). She also writes in the time the HCT was discontinued, which would be effective immediately. If the nurse had already given the 1000 dose of the HCT, the order would, in reality, be effected the next morning. In this case she had not, because Mary had notified the nurse of the medication changes immediately. Mary now repeats her actions for the Lasix, which must be discontinued as well. She adds the new order for Lasix underneath the Eltroxin. Because the nurse had not given the 1000 dose of the Lasix, the new order can be started at 1000. If the nurse had given the 1000 dose, the new order would start when the next does was due—at 1600 hours. A new eMAR will be sent from the pharmacy the next morning at 0700 that will incorporate the changes Mary manually added to the January 3 eMAR.

- Mary adds the transcription symbols as she processes the orders (Figure 16.18b), reviews her orders once transcribed, and has them checked by the nurse. Both Mary and the nurse sign off on the order. Mary then faxes the order to the pharmacy, marks the order as faxed, and returns the chart to the holder. She removes the flag from the chart.

Loading Medication Doses

loading dose a medication ordered as a single-order stat medication with a dose that is higher than the usual or routine dose.

bolus the usually rapid infusion of additional IV fluids in addition to the base amount ordered for the patient.

A **loading dose** is a higher-than-usual dose of a medication given to rapidly increase the level of the medication in the patient's bloodstream. It can be ordered by any route—orally, intramuscularly, subcutaneously, or intravenously. If a doctor orders a rapid infusion of an IV fluid—without a medication—it is referred to as a **bolus**. There are numerous types of conditions under which a doctor will order a loading dose of a medication—for example, an antibiotic for a severe infection, a diuretic for congestive heart failure, or a sedative for someone who is extremely agitated.

CONESTOGA GENERAL HOSPITAL
SCHEDULED MEDICATION ADMINISTRATION RECORD

From Jan 3/xx 0700 to: Jan 4/xx @ 0659h
Allergies: No Allergies *None*
Adverse Reactions
Diagnosis Abd pain NYD
Circle time med given and initial below.

Dietz, Henry
124 Duncan St.
Vancouver B.C.
DOB 22/09/47
#123432333
Dr. G. Hanson

Medication and Directions		
Hours	07 08 09 (10) 11 12 13 14 15 16 17 18 19 20 21 22 23 24	01 02 03 04 05 06
Lasix (furosemide) 20 mg po bid **take on empty stomach** 1000 1600 (ward stock)	Start date: Jan 03/xx Stop date: none given *D/C effective 1010 Jan 3/xx*	
Initial		
Enalapril (Vasotec) 5 mg po bid **take with or without food** 1000 1800	07 08 09 10 11 12 13 14 15 16 17 18 19 20 21 22 23 24 Start date: Jan 03/xx Stop date: none given	01 02 03 04 05 06
Initial		
Hydrochlorothiazide (HCT) 12.5 mg po od (HydroDIURAL) **take with or without food** 1000	07 08 09 (10) 11 12 13 14 15 16 17 18 19 20 21 22 23 24 Start date: Jan 03/xx Stop date: none given *D/C effective 1010 Jan 3/xx*	01 02 03 04 05 06
Initial		
Eltroxin 0.1 mg po od (levothyroxin) 1000 (ward stock)	07 08 09 10 11 12 13 14 15 16 17 18 19 20 21 22 23 24 Start date: Jan 03/xx Stop date: none given	01 02 03 04 05 06
Initial		
Lasix 40 mg po bid *** new medication*	07 08 09 10 11 12 13 14 15 16 17 18 19 20 21 22 23 24 *Start Jan 3/xx 1000 Hours. Stop date: none noted*	01 02 03 04 05 06
Initial		
Valium 5 mg. po tid *1000 1400 1800* ***New medication*	07 08 09 10 11 12 13 14 15 16 17 18 19 20 21 22 23 24 *Start Jan 3 @ 1000* *Stop date: none noted*	01 02 03 04 05 06
Initial		

Figure 16.19 eMAR incorporating new orders

For an acute infection, such as cystitis or pneumonia, a doctor may order a loading dose of antibiotics (perhaps twice the regular dose) to quickly raise blood levels of the medication and hasten therapeutic effects. For example, Ruby Parsons was an inpatient who suddenly developed a high fever because of a newly developed left lower lobe pneumonia. Her MRP, Dr. Pinder, ordered 1 g of penicillin stat (a loading dose) and 500 mg four times a day for 10 days (the routine part of the order). See Figure 16.20, where this order is activated and transcribed noting the requested discontinue date.

CONESTOGA GENERAL HOSPITAL
SCHEDULED MEDICATION ADMINISTRATION RECORD

From *Jan 4 xx 0700 h to: 5 Jan/xx 0659h*
Allergies: No Allergies *None noted*
Adverse Reactions
Diagnosis
Circle time med given and initial below.

Ruby Parsons
65 Second St.
Vancouver, B.C.
DOB 19/12/53
#123432348
Dr. H. Pinder

Medication and Directions		
Hours	07 08 09 10 11 12 13 14 15 16 17 18 19 20 21 22 23 24	01 02 03 04 05 06
Penicillin 1 g stat	*Stat order given @* Note: The nurse will add the time at which she gives the medication, and initial it. The next dose will be given at 1100 as indicated below	
Initial		
Penicillin 500mg po qid *0600 1130 1630 2200*	07 08 09 10 11 12 13 14 15 16 17 18 19 20 21 22 23 24 *Start Jan 4/xx @ 11.30* *Stop Jan 10/xx after 0600 dose*	01 02 03 04 05 06 Note: The nurses will give the 1130, 1630, and 2200 dose using this MAR. The preprinted one will be sent up from the pharmacy the next morning (Jan. 5 @ 0700). Alternatively, in some facilities, if the order is faxed to the pharmacy, they could send up a preprinted MAR to be used for the remainder of that day.
Initial		

Figure 16.20 Order handwritten on an MAR showing a loading dose of penicillin and, underneath, the routine order with a d/c date as noted on the doctor's order sheet

The stat dose would be recorded either on the MAR under single-dose medications or directly on the scheduled eMAR (depending on the facility's protocol). Stat meds are almost always entered into the MAR manually because they must be given immediately and there isn't time to have them preprinted in the pharmacy. In this case, Mary recorded the routine order for penicillin on the existing eMAR. In some facilities, if the order was faxed to the pharmacy, they could send up an eMAR that would be used for the 1130, 1630, and 2200 doses.

Medications with Special Directions

The doctor may write a medication order with specific directions regarding dose or time of administration (e.g., to be given alternate days or every three days). The eMAR will clearly reflect these orders. If the medication is to be given every two days, it simplifies the process to write on the MAR "q2days (even days)" or "q2days (odd days)," whichever fits the date on which the medication was started.

Anti-Coagulant Orders

Anti-coagulants are medications that prevent blood clots from forming and existing clots from progressing. They may be used to prevent clot formation in the hearts of people with atrial fibrillation or certain types of mechanical heart valves. They are also used **prophylactically** to prevent blood clot formation in some postoperative patients.

prophylactic a measure taken to prevent a problem from developing.

The three anti-coagulant medications most commonly used are low-molecular-weight heparin, heparin, and warfarin (Coumadin). Low-molecular-weight heparin is given subcutaneously and is a newer product used in the primary treatment of such conditions as deep vein thrombosis. Although an expensive drug, its advantages over heparin include predictable blood levels and a lower chance of untoward bleeding. As well, it interacts less with platelets, eliminating the need to monitor a person's aPTT or INR. Heparin is given intravenously or subcutaneously and is a fast-acting anti-coagulant; examples include Fragmin and Lovenox. Warfarin is taken orally. Sometimes patients may be on both heparin and warfarin when they are changing from heparin to an oral anti-coagulant; usually, the heparin will be continued only until the warfarin reaches therapeutic blood levels. A patient who is on any kind of anti-coagulant therapy must be carefully monitored by the physician. Partial thromboplastin time (PTT or aPTT) is used to monitor heparin, and the international normalized ratio (INR) is used to monitor warfarin (see Chapter 6).

Note the difference between anti-coagulants and clot-dissolving agents, such as streptokinase and tPA. The latter are used to limit or reverse damage caused by a clot in an artery to the heart or brain. These must be given soon after the damaging event, such as a stroke, and carry the risk of severe bleeding. They are usually stat orders given in the emergency department or the intensive care unit.

The medication order in Figure 16.21 involves special instructions. Some facilities use a regular scheduled MAR to record anti-coagulants; others use a specially designed MAR. This MAR is used for either heparin or warfarin. It has space for the nurse or the clinical secretary to write in the aPTT or the INR as soon as the results are sent to the floor from the lab. In most cases, the nurse will not give an anti-coagulant until the related lab test is known. If the INR or aPTT results are too high, the anti-coagulant will be held until the doctor reviews the situation.

In a manual environment using a multiday MAR, transcribing this warfarin order would entail *clearly* marking off the days on which the medication was to be given. This is illustrated in Figure 16.22, which is a MAR for the following order that Dr. Merion has written for Rick Day: warfarin 2.5 mg q2days. Hold if INR > 3. Figure 16.23 shows the same order on a single-day eMAR.

CONESTOGA GENERAL HOSPITAL
MEDICATION ADMINISTRATION RECORD FOR ANTICOAGULANT PROTOCOLS

From 0700 _____ to 0659 _____

New Order _____   Replaces Order _____   Order Verified (initials) _____

Heparin protocol (indicate) Check APTT and titrate as per protocol Heparin S.C or I.M. Dose_____ APTT____	IV Heparin Time_____ IV Heparin Bolus _____units mL Rate mL/h____ Rate units/h_____ Initials_____	Time_____ IV Heparin Bolus _____units mL Rate mL/h____ Rate units/h_____ Initials_____	Time_____ IV Heparin Bolus _____units mL Rate mL/h____ Rate units/h_____ Initials_____	Time_____ IV Heparin Bolus _____units mL Rate mL/h____ Rate units/h_____ Initials_____
Initials	07 08 09 (10) 11 12 13 14 15 16 17 18 19 20 21 22 23 24			01 02 03 04 05 06
INR _____ Wafarin po od as ordered daily (Coumadin) Dose_____ ordered on_____ By_____ Dose routine_____ Withhold if INR > ___3___ Notify doctor.	Instructions: Call doctor with INR by 1300hrs for daily orders. WATCH FOR ANY SIGNS OF BLEEDING Transiton period: Warfarin _____ Heparin_____			Client Information

Figure 16.21 MAR designed only for anti-coagulants

STRATFORD GENERAL HOSPITAL

STRATFORD GENERAL HOSPITAL
Check here if more than one page ☐

Scheduled Medication Administration Record

Start /reorder	Stop date	Medication dose, route, frequency	Hour Due	Jan 23	24	25	26	27	28	29	30
Jan 23		Warfarin 2.5 mg po od q 2 days			✕		✕		✕		✕
		Hold if INR > 3	1400	✕		✕		✕		✕	
		GIVE ON EVEN DAYS									

Figure 16.22 Warfarin order transcribed on a unit where eMARs are not used

CONESTOGA GENERAL HOSPITAL
SCHEDULED MEDICATION ADMINISTRATION RECORD

Rick Day

From **Jan 23 /xx** 0700 to: Jan 24 /xx @ 0659h
Allergies: Sulpha Drugs   No Allergies
Adverse Reactions
Diagnosis
Circle time med given and initial below.

2944 Blake St.
Calgary, Alberta
DOB 22/09/47
#123432333
Dr. G. Merion

Medication and Directions	
Hours	07 08 09 10 11 12 13 **14** 15 16 17 18 19 20 21 22 23 24 01 02 03 04 05 06
Warfarin (Coumadin) 2.5 mg po od Give odd days only @ 1400hours <u>Watch for any signs of bleeding.</u> <u>Do not give if INR is above 3.</u> Initial	
Hours	07 08 09 10 11 12 13 14 15 16 17 18 19 20 21 22 23 24 01 02 03 04 05 06
   Initial	

Figure 16.23 Warfarin transcribed on an eMAR

	Blood sugars 24h during the day			Dietz, Henry
	Regular insulin 3 u if bs > 15 and 10 u if > 20			123 Duncan St.
	Novolin 30/70 u qam and 5 u ac supper			Vancouver B.C.
				DOB 22/09/47
				#123432333
				Dr. D. Sung
date	**time**	**Physician's printed name**	**Signature**	
Jan 3/XX	1000	**Dr. D. Sung**	Dr. D. Sung	

Figure 16.24 Doctor's order for insulin on a sliding scale

Warfarin and other anti-coagulants are often given at 1400 hours because it allows time for the INR test to be done and the results to be called back to the patient-care unit.

Sliding Scale Orders

Sometimes a doctor orders a drug with a dosage on a sliding scale; that is, to be adjusted on the basis of test results. Insulin is the most common example. The nurses would take a finger-prick blood sugar reading and adjust the dose of insulin accordingly.

When transcribing this order for Mrs. Carrier, Mary would use the scheduled MAR or a special MAR used for hypoglycemics. She would copy the order exactly as it appears. Either Mary or the nurse is responsible for receiving, reporting, and writing the blood sugar results from the lab on the MAR. It is up to the nurse to give the appropriate amount of insulin each time it is administered. An order for insulin on a sliding scale for Mrs. Carrier might look like this:

Give Humulin R 2 units if bs between 10.1 and 12; 4 units if bs between 12.1 and 14, and 6 units if bs between 14.1 and 16. Call if bs is higher than 16.

Another example of a sliding scale order is seen in Figure 16.24. Some facilities put insulin orders—either regular or sliding scale orders—on a special anti-coagulant MAR. Almost every facility has a differently designed eMAR or MAR for recording hypoglycemic medications.

Medication Orders Related to Lab Values

Instead of writing a sliding scale order, the doctor might, if the patient has been reasonably well stabilized on a medication, write the order with a static value of insulin to be given (e.g., regular insulin 5 U qam). However, the doctor may ask to be called with lab test results and alter the order, if needed, on the basis of the results. Similarly, when patients receive certain medications, such as digoxin and gentamicin, serum levels of the drug must be monitored to ensure they stay within the therapeutic range.

Often the lab will telephone the doctor directly with abnormal results or call the floor and ask you to notify the doctor—particularly if the results are very abnormal. Whether the lab results are available online or are paper based, abnormal results will be highlighted or otherwise identified. However, do not rely on someone else to identify problems. Look at lab results yourself, do your best to be aware of abnormal results, and report them promptly to the nurse or doctor.

Alternatively, in the electronic environment, the lab may just send the critical or abnormal lab results to the unit electronically and have them printed on the unit.

Computerized Physician Order Entry

Facilities that use CPOE are virtually paperless (when it comes to orders). The doctor enters orders directly into the computer, and they are processed on the computer. The clinical secretary is still responsible for ensuring that the orders have been transferred to the department responsible and for notifying the appropriate person or department of orders requiring immediate attention.

Such systems are programmed to immediately check all medication orders against the patient's current information to identify potential mistakes or problems, such as allergies. Some hospitals have mobile computerized medication carts. The nurses can access the patient's medication profile and retrieve the required medication using an individualized patient code. Using a handheld computer, they then enter onto the patient's MAR the time and date the medication was given.

Although facilities using electronic orders find them satisfactory and much easier to read, such systems are still not common in many parts of the country. Some physicians and facilities are uncomfortable with computer-generated orders, perhaps fearing they might be tampered with without the safeguard of handwritten, signed orders. However, hospitals that use electronic orders have security measures in place, including an electronic signature.

Medication Orders Related to Surgery

As discussed previously, preoperative, or "preop," medication orders, if any, are usually written by anesthetists.

Preoperative medication orders must be dealt with in a timely and organized manner. With so many patients coming in on the day of the surgery, things can get rushed. If you are prepared, things will be less hectic. If you have preoperative patients on your unit, make it a routine to carefully check the charts of any patients going for surgery for orders; make sure none has been left in an unflagged chart. Do this well before the booked operating room time; it is fairly common for the operating room to call for the patient ahead of time. If you work on a pre-admit unit, you would anticipate that all patients have preop orders to be processed.

Postoperative Medication Orders   When a patient goes for surgery, all previous doctors' orders for inpatients are automatically discontinued or put on hold. After the surgery, orders must be reordered or renewed. Often, doctors write the orders out again, particularly if different from the preoperative orders. Sometimes the doctor will simply order all the orders that were in effect before the surgery. This type of order would simply read "Resume all preop orders." In a computerized environment, the eMAR generated would reflect the previous orders reactivated. If new orders are written, the eMAR would contain the new medication orders. Surgeons will either use preprinted standard postop order sheets (see Figure 16.3 for a preprinted postoperative order for a colon resection) or write the postop orders out entirely by hand on a doctor's order sheet.

Individualized Postoperative Medication Orders   A physician not using a standard order sheet has to write postoperative orders on the routine doctor's order sheet. Each area of care and treatment must be addressed. Figure 16.25 is an individualized postoperative order sheet for Mr. Dietz.

Standard Orders for Major Surgery   Figure 16.3 shows a standard doctor's order form filled out. As previously noted, the doctor selects the specific orders he or she wants activated for a particular patient. All immediate areas of patient care must be addressed. In these orders you will see an order for patient-controlled analgesia (a PCA or "pain pump"). Alternatively, the doctor could simply order a major analgesic to be given IM or IV; this will be followed by an oral painkiller when the patient is able to take oral meds and when the pain is less severe. Anti-emetics are almost always ordered; nausea and vomiting are common postoperatively, particularly if the surgery involved

CONESTOGA GENERAL HOSPITAL
DOCTORS ORDER SHEET

Please fax to Pharmacy & note date/time

		Dietz, Henry 123 Duncan St. Vancouver B.C DOB 22 09 47 071608 Dr. G. Hanson
	IV 2.3 and 1.3 at 100cc/hr, Add 20 meq of KCL to alternate bags	
	Demerol 50–75 mg IM q2–3h prn	
	Gravol 50–100 mg IM q3–4h prn	
	Dangle tonight–up in the am	
	Shorten penrose drain daily starting day 3	
	Foley catheter to straight drainage: remove in the am. May recatheterize if unable to avoid within 8 hours	
	Vital signs as per post op routine	
	N/G tube to low Gomco sucetion. Remove when bowel sounds active	
	CBC and lites in am.	

date *Jan 2/XX*	time *2000*	Physician's printed name Dr. G. Hanson	Signature *Dr. G. Hanson*

Figure 16.25 Individualized postoperative orders

manipulation of the bowel. As well, many of the narcotic analgesics have the nasty side effect of nausea and vomiting. Laxatives are ordered to stimulate bowel evacuation, which is also compromised postoperatively by bowel manipulation or the effects of the general anesthetic. Codeine, which is often ordered as a postop analgesic, also causes constipation, necessitating a laxative. If a laxative is ineffective, a backup order for an enema is usually included.

Resumption of diet depends on the type of surgery and the postop recovery pattern of the patient. If the patient has a gastric tube, resumption of anything orally occurs only after the tube has been removed and there are bowel sounds present. This is much like hearing your own stomach grumbling when you are hungry, and it indicates that the bowel is active and able to process food. Many postoperative patients have a catheter inserted into the bladder following surgery. It is frequently removed on the first postop day, depending on the type and extent of the surgery. If the patient cannot pass urine (void) within several hours after the catheter is removed, the catheter is reinserted. If the patient can't void, the bladder will continue to fill and become distended and possibly atonic. Activity is encouraged as soon as possible after most operations. Despite the lack of enthusiasm on the part of the patient, early ambulation has many benefits and facilitates an earlier recovery.

Patients who are on a variety of medications preoperatively will need them postoperatively as well. If the patient is NPO or has a nasogastric tube, the doctor will order these medications by another route.

Overlapping Orders   Occasionally, an anesthetist and a surgeon will both write orders for postoperative analgesics for the same patient. Do not implement both sets of orders. Check agency policy on how to handle this situation; in most facilities, the orders written last (usually by the surgeon) apply.

SUMMARY

1. Order entry responsibilities for the clinical secretary are changing as hospitals adopt more advanced software programs. Transcribing medications is not a required task in hospitals where the pharmacy department processes medication orders and creates eMARs. In hospitals that have adopted CPOE, you will still be required to monitor doctors' orders, identify errors, ensure orders are processed properly, and follow through with selected orders.

2. Order entry means processing doctors' instructions so they can be implemented. Order entry is one of the clinical secretary's most complex responsibilities, requiring familiarity with agency policies and computer systems and a knowledge of medications, diagnostic tests, and other components of treatment. Equally important are organizational skills, alertness, the ability to set priorities, and attention to detail. Absolute accuracy is essential. Even a misplaced decimal can have serious consequences.

3. Very little can be done for a patient in hospital without a doctor's order—right down to the level of activity and what the patient can have to eat. Orders are always written on admission and new orders are added, amended, or cancelled in response to the patient's progress and condition. You will be primarily using your computer when transcribing orders, and sometimes the telephone and the fax machine. You must be familiar with the patient's eChart, what goes where, and how to toggle between various components of the chart.

4. Doctors' orders may be written as individualized orders or on order sets. Order sets are groups of orders pertinent to a specific diagnosis or for a particular situation, such as pre-admission or following surgery. For the most part, order sets are computerized, but they may be downloaded and used in paper format. CPOE systems have order sets embedded into them along with physician access to current modes of treatment. Order sets are designed by clinicians and reviewed frequently. Individualized orders are widely used.

5. The majority of doctors' orders are noted on the PI screen. It is divided into several categories, such as patient education, activities of daily living, parenteral (IV) therapy, assessments (e.g., vital signs, dressings), and sometimes laboratory and diagnostic tests. Occasionally one assessment or procedure will appear in more

than one place (e.g., clinical parameters containing anything with a value, such as blood pressure or temperature; thus, vital signs may appear under assessments as well as clinical parameters).

6. There are nine general steps to follow when processing any type of order. Develop a routine for transcribing medication orders that works for you as long as you follow hospital procedures (e.g., some hospitals require you to fax the doctor's order sheet to the pharmacy first). You must be watchful for new orders. In an electronic environment an order alert will appear on your task screen. When orders are handwritten, a chart will be flagged. Prioritize orders, processing stat or urgent orders first—and notifying the nurse of any stat orders. Never rush. Always be sure that you are transcribing onto the right patient's chart or electronic file. Be especially careful when there are patients with similar names. Have all orders checked by a nurse; both you and the nurse must sign off on them.

7. Processing medication orders requires concentration and accuracy. Electronic order entry and pharmacy-prepared MARs have gone a long way to reducing medication errors related to order processing. Pay attention to the start and stop dates as well as to the dose, route, and frequency. Always transcribe the order the way it was written. If you are discontinuing a medication, mark it clearly on the appropriate MAR. If a new medication is started, clearly identify the start date. Medications ordered for a specific time frame likewise must have the start and stop dates clearly marked on the MAR. Always notify the nurse of changes in medication orders.

KEY TERMS

bolus   510
doctors' orders   479
flag   496
loading dose   510

order entry   480
patient intervention
    (PI) screen   490

prophylactic   512
transcription   499

REVIEW QUESTIONS

1. How would your responsibilities change in a CPOE environment?

2. What are the basic tools necessary to begin transcribing doctors' orders?

3. Where does the process of order entry begin?

4. What elements must be present on the doctor's order sheet before you can begin transcribing the orders?

5. What are standard doctors' orders, and when are they used?

6. Summarize the information recorded in a PI screen.

7. Why are physicians asked to flag charts? What are the clinical secretary's related responsibilities?

8. What must you do when you have finished transcribing a patient's orders?

9. Differentiate among routine or standing, PRN, stat, and sliding scale medication orders.

10. Why is it important for you to add a patient's MAR to his or her preoperative chart?

APPLICATION EXERCISES

1. Research a hospital or other health care facility near you. Interview a clinical secretary or someone in health information services. Find out what his or her responsibilities are regarding order entry. Questions you might ask include the following: How has information technology affected your role? What process for transcribing orders do you follow? If the facility does not yet have CPOE, is its implementation planned? What hospital information system does the hospital use? Find out how it differs from what is described in this chapter. Are there any specific policies about entry that are not described in this chapter?

2. Using the MAR format used by a local hospital or one supplied by your instructor, transcribe the following orders written by Dr. Smith for Alison Chambers:

    Demerol 75–100 mg IM q3–4h PRN

    Gravol 50 mg IM or PO q4h PRN for nausea

Magnolax 30 cc bid start day 3 PRN

Tylenol 3 po q4h PRN

3. Using the same MAR format as in Question 2, transcribe the following orders written by Dr. Martello for Alia Hondo. Alia is diabetic and has a urinary tract infection.

Insulin Novolin 30/70 20 units qam and 7 units ac supper

Insulin Novolin R 10 units stat

Insulin by reaction Novolin R 5 units if BS greater than 15 qam

Finger-prick blood sugar readings qid

Lasix 20 mg q2days

Septra DS I tab bid 7 days

4. Working from the postoperative orders in Figure 16.5, check off medications you think your patient, Mr. Vrede-veldt, will need postoperatively. Review each category and each order. Choose a major narcotic analgesic and a less potent one. Pick an anti-emetic and a laxative. Process these orders onto the appropriate MARs used in a facility in your area.

WEBSITES OF INTEREST

Confused Drug Names

www.ismp.org/tools/confuseddrugnames.pdf

Chapter 17

Understanding Intravenous Therapy and Related Orders

Monkey Business Images/Shutterstock

LEARNING OBJECTIVES

On completing this chapter, you will be able to:

1. Explain the elements responsible for fluid and electrolyte balance in the body.

2. Discuss the indications for and goals of intravenous therapy.

3. Understand the equipment involved in intravenous therapy.

4. Explain the advantages of patient-controlled analgesia.

5. Transcribe intravenous medication orders.

6. Discuss the use of blood and blood products and related protocols for intravenous infusions.

intravenous (IV) administered directly into the circulatory system via a vein.

Intravenous (IV) therapy is a common hospital treatment and is often critical to the hospitalized patient's recovery. With the current emphasis on home-based care, patients can also be discharged and maintained on parenteral therapy in the home under the supervision of community nurses. Intravenous means "into the vein," and it means that fluids are introduced directly into the body's circulatory system. IV therapy is prescribed for people requiring electrolyte replacement, fluids, calories, vitamins, or other nutritional substances. It is also a route for administering medications, including chemotherapy, and is used for transfusions of blood and blood products.

To accurately transcribe IV orders, you need to understand the purposes and goals of IV therapy, the equipment involved, and the types of solutions ordered by physicians. This chapter will briefly discuss the more common types of IV solutions, IV medications, and blood products.

Although IV solutions themselves are not, strictly speaking, medications, in some facilities they are treated and recorded in much the same manner because they involve introducing something external into the body system. In most facilities, however, IV solutions are tracked and recorded electronically and are not part of the medication administration record (MAR). When a medication is delivered by way of an IV solution, the medication, dose, or dilution are recorded on the MAR and signed for accordingly by the nurse responsible for the medication's delivery.

L01 FLUIDS AND ELECTROLYTES

To fully understand the purpose and goals of IV therapy, you need a basic understanding of the roles that fluids and electrolytes play in maintaining the body's equilibrium.

Electrolyte is a term for salts or ions that dissolve in water and have electrical charges. Salt or sodium (Na), potassium (K), and chloride (Cl) are the three major electrolytes our bodies need to function properly. Imbalances in sodium may be caused by inappropriate fluid loss or retention. Potassium imbalances can cause muscle twitching and an irregular heartbeat. Other electrolytes present are magnesium (Mg), calcium (Ca), zinc (Zn), bicarbonate (HCO_3), phosphate (PO_3), sulphate (SO_2), as well as minute amounts of other substances, often referred to as trace elements. The human body is mostly water—an estimated 60 percent of an adult's weight comprises fluids—so these electrolytes can be found everywhere. Approximately two-thirds of our body fluids are found within body cells (**intracellular**), and the remaining one-third is found inside the blood vessels (**intravascular**) and in the spaces between cells (**interstitial** spaces). Because they are electronically charged, these electrolytes assist in transporting nutrients to and from the cells within the body and play a role in muscle and nerve functions.

Our body depends on a balance, or **homeostasis**, of fluids and electrolytes for normal function and good health.

The body's fluid balance and electrolyte composition are primarily maintained by the respiratory system, the gastrointestinal system, the circulatory and renal systems, and the integumentary system. For example, the kidneys help keep the electrolyte concentrations in the blood properly balanced by decreasing urine output when we are dehydrated. The loss and replacement of body fluids occurs almost continuously. Normally, people lose fluids during the course of the day through breathing and perspiration and through the gastrointestinal system and the kidneys. Generally, we take in fluids at meals and drink when we are thirsty. If the weather is hot or we exercise, we usually take in extra fluids. The feeling of thirst is a compensatory mechanism triggered when the body feels the need for fluid. Hydration occurs without a thought, and for most of us, our body's fluids and electrolytes remain balanced. When someone is ill, maintaining his or her body's homeostasis can become more difficult. With illness, our metabolism is altered; dietary and fluid intake may be compromised by nausea and vomiting, we may not feel like eating or drinking, and normal bowel function may be complicated by diarrhea. All of these changes stress our body's ability to maintain homeostasis. Many illnesses can cause an imbalance in the body's fluids and electrolytes. In many cases, these disturbances must be treated promptly, often with IV therapy.

intracellular within the cells of the body.
intravascular within blood vessels.
interstitial in between the body's cells.

homeostasis a balance between the body's internal conditions and the environment.

L02 INDICATIONS FOR IV THERAPY

Any condition or circumstance that prevents a person from eating or drinking or from properly absorbing food and fluids or that causes excessive fluid loss will result in the need for fluid and nutritional replacement. If the person is ill and cannot eat or drink adequately, this replacement may be required by alternative methods. Doctors will order IV fluid in the following situations:

- The patient is unable to take fluids by mouth (injury or trauma to the mouth, throat, or esophagus; tumours; stroke).
- The patient has had an abnormal loss of body fluids, such as from severe vomiting or diarrhea.
- The patient is injured or has a life-threatening condition, such as **hemorrhage**, and requires immediate life-saving solutions, such as blood or medications (e.g., after a heart attack, medications may be given by IV for faster effect).
- The patient has had major surgery (an IV line usually provides hydration, nourishment, and sometimes medication until the person can resume intake of food and fluids by mouth).
- The patient requires medications that can be given only intravenously.
- The patient requires prophylactic antibiotics while undergoing surgical or invasive diagnostic procedures. Note that some medications can be given intravenously through a PRN adaptor (discussed later), thus the patient doesn't need a continuous IV.

The goals of intravenous therapy reflect the reason the IV therapy is needed:

- To restore the body's acid/base balance
- To restore blood loss caused by hemorrhage
- To stabilize a patient with a bleeding disorder, such as hemophilia
- To correct dehydration by restoring the body's water, electrolytes, and so on
- To provide nutrition when the patient's gastrointestinal tract is resting

hemorrhage loss of a large amount of blood (greater than 500 cc for an average adult).

L03 IV EQUIPMENT
L04

A doctor's order is necessary to start an IV. First, the order is received and the required solution selected. Next, the nurse will select the type of IV tubing required, the appropriate device for inserting the IV into the patient's vein, and the site, or spot, on the patient to start the IV.

IV Bag

The IV bag contains the solution itself and is usually a soft, pliable container, as illustrated in Figure 17.1. (Glass bottles were used for IV solutions until plastic bags were introduced in the early 1970s. Occasionally, glass bottles are still used for medications or solutions that are adversely affected by plastic.) IV bags come in a variety of sizes. The largest routinely used contains 1000 **cc** or mL of fluid. There are 500 cc bags as well. Smaller volumes are also available, from 50 to 250 cc, and are used primarily for medications. IV bags have numbers along the side that indicate the volume of fluid.

cc cubic centimetre; 1 cc equals 1 millilitre (1 mL). In hospitals, cc is used more often than mL.

Nurses reading these markers can see how much solution is remaining in the bag and, therefore, how much has been infused or absorbed into the patient. Nurses will chart the number of cc remaining in the bag as fluid to be absorbed.

IV Access Devices

To start an IV, a needle or IV catheter must be inserted into a patient's vein. Various types are available. The generic name for a catheter is an "intracatheter" or "intracath." Plastic IV catheters have several components. A needle with a bevelled tip is used to enter the patient's vein. The catheter itself is made of a synthetic material and can slide over the needle. The needle is withdrawn, leaving the pliable catheter in the vein. When the needle is properly situated in the vein, a small chamber called a flash chamber (located behind the needle) fills with blood. An **Angiocatheter** (a patented name) is a common type of IV catheter used, often just called an *Angiocath* in the hospital (see Figure 17.2). The **distal** end of the catheter has an adaptor (also called a connector) to which IV tubing is attached. The IV tubing is attached to the IV bag or solution. The site of insertion is known as the IV site. To stabilize the catheter, the site is usually covered with a pliable transparent film, such as Tegaderm. The transparent film also allows the nurses to assess the IV site for problems. The nurse will write the date of insertion of the IV catheter on the tape.

Butterfly   A butterfly (Figure 17.3) is a device used to start an IV in smaller peripheral veins for short-term IVs and when fragile veins make insertion of a larger intracatheter difficult. The butterfly has two wing-like projections on either side of a small needle. The flaps are used as handles to guide and insert the needle. The butterfly is easy to insert and can be successfully started in small veins. The disadvantage is that it can easily slip out of a vein and allow the IV solution to seep into the surrounding interstitial tissues.

Central Venous IV   There are a number of devices used to deliver long-term IV therapy, ranging from weeks to years. They are used for chemotherapy, medication, blood or blood products, hyperalimentation, and monitoring central venous pressure. They are also used for patients with poor veins to reduce the trauma of repeated IV starts. Central venous lines increase patient comfort and help reduce anxiety in patients who must have frequent venous access.

Central Venous Access Device/Catheter CVD or CVC   A CVD (also referred to as a central line) is a small, flexible, plastic tube, the tip of which is placed in the superior or inferior vena cava or the right atrium. It is inserted through a central vein—that is, one that lies in the chest cavity or that is linked directly to the right atrium (the right upper chamber of the heart). The main access veins used are the internal and external

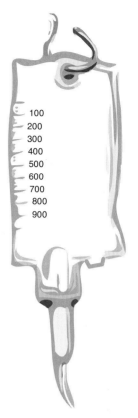

Figure 17.1   The IV bag

Angiocatheter a plastic tube, usually attached to the puncturing needle, inserted into a blood vessel for infusion, injection, or pressure monitoring. Usually just called an *Angiocath*.

distal the part farthest from the body.

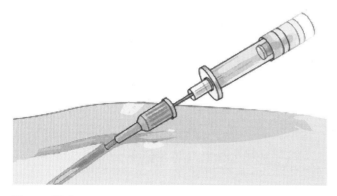

Figure 17.2   An angiocatheter

Figure 17.3   A butterfly

jugular and the subclavian veins. Occasionally the femoral vein (found in the leg) is used. A type of central line called a PICC line (pronounced "pick") is often inserted into the brachial or cephalic vein or others in the arm above the elbow. Although peripheral, these veins are larger and deeper than the ones below the elbow.

Indications and Complications Inserting a CVD into a patient is more invasive than inserting a peripheral line, and the decision to use one is not taken lightly. It is usually done in conjunction with ultrasound by an experienced practitioner. Indications include situations where a peripheral line cannot be established, for delivering solutions that are unsafe to deliver using a peripheral line (e.g., TPN, which is discussed later in the chapter, some medications used for cardiovascular purposes, chemotherapeutic agents, or blood products over a long time frame). They are used to place pulmonary artery catheters and heart pacers and provide access for physicians if frequent blood sampling is required.

Complications that can arise from the insertion of a central line include the development of an air embolism, an arrhythmia, an infection, and perforation of a vessel. Informed consent is required for this procedure, so as the clinical secretary you would need to prepare this document and fill out as much as you can. The nurse or doctor will obtain and witness the consent.

TIP

If you receive an order for a central line, you may have added responsibilities other than simple order entry. These include preparing a consent form for the patient—ensure it is properly labelled, dated, and the procedure filled out. Give it to the appropriate nurse. You may have to order a special tray from the sterile processing department (where items are sterilized for use and where you would call for most equipment used for treatments and patient care) and have it ready on the unit if the line is going to be inserted on the floor. If the patient must go somewhere else (e.g., diagnostic imaging, if the procedure is being done with ultrasound), you will have to arrange that appointment.

Types of Central Line Catheters

Peripherally Inserted Central Catheter (PICC Line) This specialized device is a long, thin, flexible tube that is inserted in a vein in the arm and then goes through the subclavian vein to the vena cava, a large vein that enters the heart (see Figure 17.4). A chest X-ray is usually taken after the line is inserted to confirm that it is in the right place. A registered nurse can draw blood from the PICC to avoid puncturing a peripheral vein. Many PICC lines have two or more lumina (spaces inside the catheter tube), enabling concurrent treatments. PICC lines are usually held in place by sutures but may sometimes be carefully taped to the skin. The site of insertion is covered with a dressing that must be changed periodically. This may or may not be ordered by the doctor. Some facilities consider changing the dressing a routine part of nursing care.

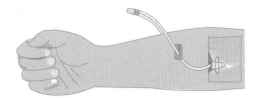

Figure 17.4 An inserted PICC line

It should, however, be recorded on the patient intervention (PI) screen or the care plan.

Tunnelled Catheters Tunnelled catheters, such as the Hickman and Broviac catheters, are inserted under the skin and "tunnel" some distance before entering the vein. These devices must be inserted surgically and are, therefore, more invasive. The surgeon often inserts this line with the assistance of a type of X-ray called fluoroscopy. As with the PICC line, patients with a tunnelled catheter will have a dressing that must be assessed and changed regularly. Most lines require flushing with a heparin solution at specified intervals. These activities must be appropriately noted on the PI screen. There are also implantable devices that provide this type of intravenous access.

Implanted Ports An implanted port has similar characteristics to a tunnelled catheter. It is left entirely under the skin. Required medication is injected *through the skin* into the catheter. Some implanted ports are designed with a small, refillable reservoir to which medications can be added, which are then slowly released into the patient's bloodstream. The advantage of an implanted port is that it is less restrictive to the patient, out of sight, and requires much less care (as opposed to a daily dressing). Chances of infection are smaller.

The Intravenous Site

The choice of site (the point of insertion) depends on the condition of the patient's veins, how long the IV is needed, and the type of solution ordered. The IV site must be carefully checked by the nurses several times during a shift. They watch for infection or inflammation of the vein and make sure that the solution is infusing properly. Occasionally, the IV goes "interstitial"—that is, the needle or catheter is dislodged from the vein, and the solution begins to seep into the interstitial tissues around the site. If this happens, the IV must be stopped and, if necessary, restarted somewhere else. In most hospitals, the IV site is routinely changed every so often. For example, a hospital may have a policy of changing both the tubing and the site every 72 hours. This policy may be set aside for a patient with poor veins, when finding a new site may be painful and difficult. Any time you transcribe an IV order, you must specify site checks. On a paper record, write down that the site is to be checked. On a computer, the instruction may be added to the electronic record by default; if not, add it manually.

Tubing/Infusion Sets

General Characteristics The IV solution is attached to the IV catheter by way of IV tubing—commonly called a drip set or an infusion set. Common components of a drip set include a spiked end that inserts into the IV bag, a drip chamber through which you can see the solution dripping as it drains from the bag, a pinch clamp that the nurses can squeeze to stop the flow, and a regulating clamp that is used to adjust the speed of the infusion (when not connected to an infusion pump). This clamp freely slides up and down the tubing for better flow control if required. In addition, there are two or three access ports that are used to administer IV medications or add a second IV line. There may also be a lock adaptor that can attach to the IV catheter, keeping the vein open but allowing the IV tubing to be removed. One common name for this device is a Luer lock.

Mainline IV Administration Set A mainline IV set (Figure 17.5) includes a length of tubing (about 2 metres) with a spiked end used to pierce the IV bag port. This allows the solution in the bag to drip into the tubing and upper chamber, located

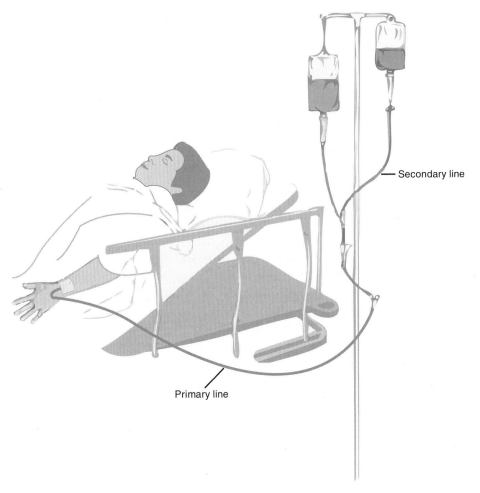

Figure 17.5 Mainline IV set

about 15 centimetres below the insertion port. The IV drops can be visualized in this chamber. These drops are used to calculate the rate of the IV infusion, calculated in **drops per minute (gtt/min)**. A tubing set may be described as a macro drip (which typically delivers about 1 cc of fluid for every 10 drops as visualized in the chamber) or a mini-drip (which delivers 1 cc for every 60 drops), depending on the number of drops per minute. Macro chambers are used to deliver larger volumes of fluid faster. Mini-drips are used when fluid is such that smaller volumes of fluids or medications are required. The drip chamber is designed to deliver a designated volume/drop. The other end of the tubing has a protected sterile tip that is inserted into the distal port on the intracatheter in the patient's vein. This creates a closed, sterile system for the delivery of the fluid into the vein. Even if the IV is regulated by an electronic pump, the nurses monitor the drops as a safeguard.

Along the length of the tubing are one or two roller clamps, which are used to control the rate of the IV infusion. One roller clamp is usually located higher up on the tubing near the IV bag. The other, if present, is found at the end of the tubing near the intracatheter.

There are also one or two ports (access points) where intravenous medications can be added to the IV, usually found about 5 centimetres above the site of insertion and about halfway up the length of tubing. This port is made of rubber. A needle or connector can be inserted; when it is withdrawn, the port will seal itself, maintaining the closed sterile system.

drops per minute (gtt/min) a measure of the rate of an IV infusion.

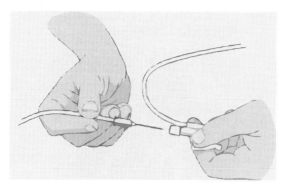

Figure 17.6 Adding a secondary line

"Y" Tubing Set and Blood Infusion Set

Y tubing has two ports and thus can accommodate two IV bags that allow the infusion of two separate solutions simultaneously. Special Y tubing sets used specifically for blood transfusions have a filter in the drip chamber that filters the infusing blood. Typically one bag is saline and the other the blood or blood product. Y tubing may also be used to deliver medications. Sometimes blood is run with two mainline IV sets that are piggy backed at the level of the Angiocatheter. Blood and blood products must *always* be run with normal saline—a good point to remember. Other IV solutions cause the blood to clot.

Medication Administration Sets

When a separate or secondary infusion line is needed, the most popular setup is a medication administration set, or "add-a-line." This is a separate IV tubing set, shorter than a main line set, that is plugged into the main IV line via a port. Using this system may also be referred to as hanging a minibag because the amount of IV solution is usually 250 cc or less (see Figure 17.6). Sometimes a doctor will order a medication to be given by IV, and the nurses will automatically deliver it in a minibag. Occasionally, the doctor will specify that it is to be delivered by an add-a-line or minibag. Special add-a-lines can also be used to deliver blood. As with the Y tubing, this set has a special "blood" filter.

Delivery Systems

Electronic Flow Regulators

Controller   This device controls the intravenous infusion rate by monitoring either the drops per minute (gtt/min) the IV set delivers or the volume of fluid (cc/min or mL/min) delivered. Devices that monitor volume are more popular because the calculations are not affected by the size or viscosity of the drop.

Electronic Infusion Pump   A number of electronic pumps are available, operating on different principles, to deliver IV solutions conveniently and accurately. Some units comprise more than one pump, allowing for the delivery of multiple IV solutions for one patient concurrently. Each pump shown in Figure 17.7 can be calibrated to deliver solutions at different infusion rates. These devices exert pressure on the IV tubing, providing accurate delivery of a programmed volume. They offer readouts of how much solution has infused and how much remains to be absorbed. These pumps will sound an alarm if something obstructs the infusion or if the IV bag runs dry. They increase accuracy and decrease the number of times the nurse must check on the infusion.

Electronic pumps can be used to deliver several different IV solutions, each at a specific rate. The pump in Figure 17.7 is controlling three different IV infusions, each with its own readout and controls. If you hear an IV pump alarm, do not panic. If the

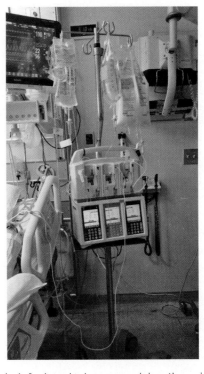

Figure 17.7 An electronic infusion device comprising three infusion pumps capable of managing three IV lines at one time (for one patient)

Valerie D Thompson

Figure 17.8 A buritrol

nurse is not around, find one to check it immediately. Alarms can be sensitive and will sometimes go off if a patient merely bends his or her arm or lies on the tubing. It will also go off if the bag is empty, but the patient is not in any danger—the bag just needs to be replaced or removed. IV pumps may be kept on the floor or you may need to order them from central supply or the stores.

The Buritrol A buritrol (shown in Figure 17.8) is a chamber added to an IV line between the bag and the line to control volumes more closely. It is used to ensure safety when the volume of fluid delivered must be carefully monitored, often with children. Some hospitals require buritrols when an IV line is used for a child under a given age or weight.

Gravity-Based Systems

No devices are needed when gravity is used to deliver IV solutions. The bag is on an IV pole and is held higher than the IV site. The solution drips into the tubing and into the patient's vein by gravity. The nurses regulate the infusion rate by manually adjusting the roller clamp on the IV tubing to the required gtt/min.

Patient-Controlled Analgesia (PCA) Patient-controlled analgesia (PCA) machines have become the standard of care on postoperative units and elsewhere if significant pain control is required. The pumps are complicated. Nurses are responsible for adding medications, setting the frequency these medications are delivered, and monitoring their overall function. They are rarely used in emergency situations.

PCA allows the patient to control his or her own pain by self-administering IV pain medication. It is widely used for postoperative pain. The order may read, "PCA pump for postoperative pain." The pump is attached to the patient's main IV line, sometimes on a portable device such as an IV pole. It contains a syringe prefilled with a designated amount/dose of medication ordered by the physician.

patient-controlled analgesia (PCA) a mechanism by which a patient can self-administer analgesic intravenously with the assistance of a computerized pump. It allows for the introduction of specific doses at preset intervals into the IV line.

Suppose Dr. Hanson had ordered morphine PCA for Mr. Black. The nurse would program the pump to deliver a specific dose over a specific time frame (e.g., 2 mg every five minutes). Mr. Black would have an activation device that looks much like a call bell. Every time he felt uncomfortable, he would press a button on the activation device and receive a small amount of morphine intravenously. With this device, Mr. Black does not have to call the nurse when he is in pain and does not have to wait for him or her to find time to give him an injection. He can get relief almost continuously. Moreover, he is participating in his own care and has a sense of control over his pain.

Studies have shown that getting small amounts of analgesic at regular intervals gives better pain control than doses every few hours. In addition, PCA makes patients less anxious, which can itself reduce pain. It is thought that patients require less medication overall by this method than with conventional medications. A patient with a higher tolerance for pain may choose to use even less. The patient cannot exceed the prescribed maximum dose because the pump is programmed to lock out at a certain level. However, a patient who keeps pressing the button after this point has been reached may still experience pain relief through a **placebo effect**. As well, the use of the PCA pump reduces the number of injections a patient receives and saves the nurses time. It has also been proven to reduce medication errors resulting from nurses administering analgesics every time a patient needs one. Use of this device also provides useful information on an individual patient's pain scale and how much analgesic he or she needs to control pain.

There are disadvantages to PCA pumps, but they are few. The pumps can malfunction, although this is infrequent. Malfunction is often related to human error: connecting the pump improperly, incorrect dose programming (e.g., dose too low, lockout period too long), or an improperly maintained battery. Pumps may not be suitable for some patients with disabilities, resulting in the patient being unable to activate the device to deliver the required analgesic, although pumps are available with alternate delivery modes (other than pressing a button). If a patient falls asleep and is unable to activate delivery of the analgesic, the pain may intensify. This can be overcome by continuous infusion of analgesic in the background—with the bolus being delivered by the patient to curb breakthrough pain.

placebo effect an improvement in symptoms without active treatment that occurs for psychological reasons when a person thinks he or she is getting treatment.

Continuous Medication Pumps   A number of pumps are designed to deliver continuous medication. They are usually used for pain control, often for chronically or terminally ill patients who may be receiving palliative care. Patients may use these devices in hospital, but they are especially useful in allowing effective pain control that enables some people to remain at home. These pumps deliver specified doses of medications, sometimes from a syringe attached to a port or opening that infuses the medication into the patient. A subcutaneous route is often used.

One such device is a computer-assisted dispatch pump. This portable pump is designed for infusions of fewer than 10 cc per day. It can be programmed to provide continuous infusion, to be patient activated, or to deliver doses at specified times. The dose can be altered by the nurse or physician but usually not by the patient.

Heparin/Saline Lock/PRN Adaptor   A **heparin (hep) lock** (also called a **saline lock or PRN adapter**) is an IV connection device that provides IV access (a port) without requiring continuous infusion (or an IV bag of any kind). It sits in the vein and must be flushed at regular intervals to keep it from getting plugged. Some doctors order that it be flushed with a solution containing heparin (Hepalean) to prevent the blood from clotting; this would be called a heparin or hep lock. More commonly,

heparin (hep) lock (saline lock, PRN adapter) a device that provides intravenous access when needed, without continuous infusion. It sits in the vein and must be flushed at specific intervals with saline solution or heparin solution.

physicians order flushing with normal saline (discussed later); the device is then called a saline lock. Flushing frequency varies; the doctor may write an order to "flush saline lock q4h or q shift." Often, this action is implied and is done automatically, as per agency policy (almost always once every eight-hour shift, although this may not be the case if the lock is regularly used for IV infusion). Otherwise, the clinical secretary must ensure that all related instructions for site change and flushing are added accordingly to the appropriate location on the PI screen/eKardex (e.g., under IV therapy or clinical parameters). If the patient is receiving regular IV medication via a PRN adaptor, it may not need flushing. However, if the adaptor is in place and used infrequently, flushing is a must to keep the port patent. On a PI screen, the instructions for flushing would be marked as "A" for activated.

> ### TIP
>
> When a "hep" or saline lock is ordered, be sure you follow hospital protocol to alert the nurses when the device must be flushed. This information is usually recorded appropriately on the nursing care plan (PI screen). There may be a component to add to the MAR, depending on agency policy.

Indications for ordering a saline lock are mainly to provide IV access to the patient—for example, someone who must have frequent IV medications or someone who is undergoing a procedure or has a condition where immediate IV access might be required urgently.

Usually, the doctor does not specifically order flushing because it is considered part of the related routine.

There are several types of these devices on the market. Figure 17.9 illustrates one form of lock. This device can be inserted initially, or an existing IV route can be changed to a heparin or saline lock with the use of an adapter. The doctor might order "Reduce IV to saline lock" or "Reduce IV to hep lock." To implement this order, the nurses would take down the IV tubing and bag and connect an adapter or "lock" to the Angiocatheter that sits in the patient's vein.

When transcribing an order for a hep or saline lock, you may be required to record it on the same sheet as other IV medications or just on the PI screen. Some facilities put the order to flush a hep lock on the standard MAR, noting the route as IV. On an electronic chart, if the instructions to flush with a specific solution at specific times are not in the lookup table, add the instructions as per order or unit policy.

Intravenous Push (IV Push)   Some medications are administered directly into the vein or into an ongoing IV infusion using a syringe and needle. This is known as an **IV push (IVP)** or IV bolus. Be careful with the abbreviation IVP, which is also used for intravenous pyelogram, a radiograph of the renal pelvis and ureter done with contrast medium administered intravenously. (Radiograph IVPs are not done as frequently as in

IV push (IVP) a medication given into the vein or into an ongoing IV infusion using a syringe and needle.

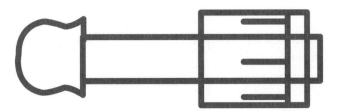

Figure 17.9   A heparin or saline lock

the past, giving way to ultrasound.) The context should make clear which is meant. Medications delivered by IV push can be delivered directly into the vein or through a port in the IV tubing.

Suppose Dr. Hanson issues an order for Mr. Black: "Lasix 20 mg IV push stat." Mary records this on the single-dose MAR, noting the route as "IV push." Dr. Hanson then issues another order: "Give morphine 2.5 mg IV push now. Repeat in 20 min 2 PRN." This means that Mr. Black is to receive 2.5 mg of morphine through his IV immediately and that the dose can be repeated twice, if needed; each repeat must be 20 minutes apart. You may question the frequency of this order, having seen orders for narcotic analgesics given q3–4h by subcutaneous or intramuscular injection. With the IV route, much smaller doses are administered more frequently. The dose takes effect much more quickly, but it also wears off more quickly. You may see IV orders for morphine or MS Contin to be given every 10 to 15 minutes.

L05 COMPONENTS OF AN IV ORDER

When transcribing an IV order, ensure that the following components are included:

- Rate of infusion or flow rate
- Start date
- How long the IV is to be continued
- Solution ordered

Flow Rate

The rate of flow is how fast the doctor wants the fluid to be infused into the patient's vein. The rate ordered depends on the patient's condition and the purpose of the IV. If the patient is dehydrated, the rate may be fairly fast (e.g., 150 cc/h). If the patient is receiving IV fluid to maintain electrolyte balance and hydration, the rate will be moderate (75 cc to 125 cc/h). If the patient is receiving the IV only for medication infusion, the rate may be quite slow (approximately 50 cc/h), noted as "to keep the vein open," or TKVO. Rates must be carefully monitored; too much fluid too quickly can strain the cardiovascular system and compromise a patient, particularly an older adult or a young child.

The rate of flow is regulated by the use of electronic devices (IV pumps) or manually by the nurses using a roller clamp on a gravity-fed IV tubing set. The rate is usually ordered as cc/hour. The nurses will convert cc/hour into drops/minute (gtt/min) using a specific formula for the type or manufacturer of the IV administration set being used. For example, using a Baxter set, 125 cc/h is approximately 21 gtt/min; 100 cc/h converts to approximately 17 gtt/min.

Start Date

This is noted because the nurses will use the start date to determine when the IV or the IV tubing has to be changed. The tubing is changed every so often, as is the site for peripheral IVs, with the exception of most central lines. If it is difficult to start an IV on a patient, it may be left in longer than the routine time, sometimes a week or more if no problems occur. The tubing is changed to decrease the chances of infection, and the site is changed to minimize trauma to the vein resulting from prolonged use. The start date should be added to the appropriate places when the order is transcribed, usually on the patient's eChart or pChart.

When an IV Is Discontinued An IV may be ordered for a specific period or to deliver a specific amount of solution; in other cases, discontinuation may depend on

TABLE 17.1	Common abbreviations for identifying IV solutions
Abbreviation	**Name**
RL	Ringer's lactate
2/3 & 1/3	3.3% dextrose in 0.3% NaCL
D5W	5% dextrose in water
D5NS	5% dextrose in normal saline
N/S	Normal saline or 0.9% NaCL
D5 1/2NS or .45NS/D5W	5% dextrose in half-strength normal saline

the patient's condition. For example, the doctor may order an IV until the patient is able to drink sufficiently to provide him or herself with adequate fluids and nutrition. Orders might be written as follows:

D/C when drinking well

D/C after current bag is absorbed

D/C if IV goes interstitial

D/C when last dose of the medication is through

Carefully note any such instructions on the patient's chart or PI screen.

Types of Intravenous Solutions

There are many IV solutions from which a physician can choose to suit the patient's need and condition. They must be transcribed accurately and legibly. The wrong IV solution can harm or even kill a patient. The more common intravenous fluids are discussed later. In choosing what solution to order for a particular patient the doctor will consider the tonicity of the solution as well as any additives, such as potassium or dextrose. Table 17.1 shows some common abbreviations.

Ringer's Lactate Solution   Ringer's lactate (RL) is sometimes called lactated Ringer's (LR). It contains water and electrolytes (sodium, potassium, calcium, and chloride). Lactate is used for milder cases of metabolic acidosis, for dehydration, and for shock states, such as for burn patients who have lost a lot of extracellular fluid. An order for Ringer's lactate may be written in any of the following ways:

IV lactated Ringer's @ 100 cc/h

Ringer's lactate @ 100 cc/h

RL @ 100 cc/h

LR @ 100 cc/h

2/3 and 1/3   This solution, one of the most frequently ordered, contains 3.3% glucose and 0.3% sodium chloride. The main purpose of this solution is maintaining adequate hydration and normal fluid balance. (It is used for maintenance purposes versus restorative or resuscitative purposes.) It may also be written as "3.3% dextrose and 0.3% NaCl," but you will see it most commonly as "2/3 and 1/3 @ 100 cc/h," for example.

D5W   D5W is also written as 5% D/W (or 5% DW) and means 5% dextrose in water. This solution is used primarily to replace water loss, such as in a dehydrated patient, and to provide some nutrition (about 200 calories per litre). It does not provide electrolytes.

This solution is frequently used to keep the vein open when the physician wants access to the vein through an IV line but has not ordered a saline lock. To keep the vein open, sometimes the physician will order a certain amount of solution per hour and sometimes not. For example, the doctor might write any of the following:

D5W TKVO

5% DW @ 75 cc/h

DW 5% @ 75 cc/h

Normal Saline   Normal saline, which may also be written as 0.9% NaCl, is a solution of pure ordinary salt (made up of sodium and chloride in water). It is referred to as *physiological* or *isotonic* because it will not alter normal electrolyte balance. It is used to treat patients who have lost a lot of body fluids, such as from hemorrhage. This solution restores electrolyte balance but does not contain any calories and, unlike dextrose solutions, will not interfere with a diabetic's sugar levels. Normal saline is the only intravenous fluid that may be run with blood. The moment the blood stops flowing, the normal saline will kick in; it is also used to flush the tubing. In most facilities, all IV meds are mixed in normal saline, and normal saline is used for TKVO unless the patient is severely compromised with some such condition as congestive heart failure and should not have saline. In that case, the internist may order IV meds in D5W. Aside from being used intravenously, it is also used to flush wounds and eyes because it is not irritating. An order for normal saline might be written in any of the following forms:

0.9% NaCl @ 125 cc/h

N/S @ 125 cc/h

Normal saline @ 125 cc/h

5% Dextrose and 0.9 NaCl   This solution is also known as D5NS. It is used to treat dehydration and as fluid for daily maintenance of body fluids and nutrition. It is similar to normal saline.

0.45% NaCl   A 0.45% NaCl solution, also ordered as 1/2 NS, has equal proportions of sodium and chloride but has half the sodium chloride of normal saline. It is often used to dilute acid in the blood when a patient is experiencing metabolic acidosis, a condition in which the body is too acidic. It may be a better maintenance fluid if larger amounts have to be administered.

THE PROCESS OF IV ORDER TRANSCRIPTION

Transcribing IV orders follows the same principles as for medications. IV medications are usually delivered in a minibag (a small IV bag containing 100 cc or less of solution) that is piggybacked on the main line through a port. Medication can also be added straight to the larger bag of IV solution itself. In most hospitals the pharmacy will premix medications in IV bags as ordered and also stock certain more commonly used mixtures of medications with solutions. The pharmacy can also prepare a drug in a much smaller vial that can be connected to an IV port, mixed with a solution, and directly infused into the IV line. A doctor may order more than one solution for a patient and alternate them or otherwise specify just how they are to be infused. Figure 17.10 shows an order for more than one solution and a solution with a medication in it.

This order translates to starting an IV of 2/3 and 1/3 solution using a 1000 cc bag to run at 100 cc/h. When this bag is finished, the nurses are to hang a bag of 1000 cc

CONESTOGA GENERAL HOSPITAL
DOCTOR'S ORDER SHEET

Please fax to Pharmacy & note date/time

		Mr. Black
	100 cc 2,3 & 1/3 @ 125 cc/h alternate with 1000cc RL with 20 meq KCl	
	@ 125 cc/h	

date	time	Physician's printed name	Signature
April 24		Dr. G. Hanson	*Dr. G. Hanson*

Figure 17.10   Doctor's order showing alternating IV solutions

Ringer's lactate with 20 mEq of potassium chloride added. This is to run at 125 cc/h. When the RL is done, the nurses would put up the 2/3 and 1/3, and keep repeating the pattern.

Processing the Order

IV orders are entered onto the PI screen, often onto a section called Clinical Parameters, Clinical Interventions, or Intravenous Therapy. *If medications are involved, the pharmacy would add the medication to the eMAR and the clinical secretary would not be responsible for processing the medication order.* If paper MARs are used, the clinical secretary would transcribe the medication to the pMAR

Let's look at an example. On April 21, Mary, the clinical secretary, receives the doctor's order for IV therapy (see Figure 17.11) for Mr. Black, an inpatient. She applies the steps outlined in Chapter 16. First, she ensures that the order has been dated, signed, and properly labelled with Mr. Black's identifying information. She notes that

CONESTOGA GENERAL HOSPITAL
SCHEDULED SINGLE DAY MEDICATION ADMINISTRATION RECORD   **Mr. Black**

From Mon 21 April/xx 0700h to: Tues 22 April/xx @ 0659h
Allergies:
Adverse Reactions
Diagnosis

Medication and Directions				
Hours	07 08 09 10 11 12 13 14 15 16 17 18 19 20 21 22 23 24		01 02 03 04 05 06	
20 meq of KCl/litre of RL +++initial when new bag is started+++ Initial	Start date: April 21/xx Stop date: None specified IV to run at 125 cc/h.This IV is alternated with 2/3 and 1/3 running at 100 cc/h			
Initial				
Initial				

Figure 17.11   eMAR showing how IV medications in solution are charted

Mr. Black has no recorded allergies. She also checks and finds that there is nothing urgent or stat on the order. She prepares to process the order.

- Mary gets Mr. Black's MAR and opens Mr. Black's eChart.

- She selects "IV therapy" from a lookup menu and accesses the lookup table for IV solutions. A selection of choices appears on the screen.

- Mary selects the first solution ordered—2/3 and 1/3—and transfers this selection to the appropriate place on Mr. Black's PI screen.

- She repeats the preceding step, selecting a 1000 cc bag of Ringer's lactate from the drop-down menu.

- A prompt appears asking Mary to include any related comments or interventions. If "RL with 20 mEq KCl" appears in the drop-down table, she selects it. Otherwise, she manually adds the 20 mEq of KCl that are to be mixed with each litre of RL. In almost all facilities medications ordered for larger IV bags (like KCl) are to be given in minibags or smaller, IV-adaptable vials are prepared in pharmacy and sent to the unit—so nurses are not actually adding medication to IV bags. There may be exceptional circumstances where this is not the case. Mary also adds the related nursing care if it is not included by default. It should include a prompt for nursing assessment of the IV site and the frequency with which the IV tubing and the IV catheter should be changed. Mary enters on the PI screen the dates on which these interventions should occur, as well as the specific instructions for alternating bags. Mary completes the order, signs off with the registered nurse, and faxes the order to the pharmacy.

- Because the Ringer's lactate contains a medication (20 mEq of KCl), Mary must add the medication to a MAR, or wait for the eMAR to be sent to the floor from the pharmacy. Figure 17.11 shows the KCl added to a scheduled eMAR. (Remember, if the pharmacy is completing the MAR, she would not be responsible for this.)

- The 2/3 and 1/3 would not go on the eMAR because it doesn't contain a medication. It would be recorded electronically.

Computerized Recording of IV Solutions

Most facilities now record IV solutions electronically. The clinical secretary would choose the appropriate options for IV management to add to the PI screen. This may appear on the screen as a default under the heading of IV Management. The nurses would note on the clinical record, under IV Therapy, the amount of IV solution infused and when new bags were hung. The only thing recorded on the hard copy of the MAR would be the medication. As far as other charting is concerned, the nurses would note any irregularities related to the IV on the electronic or paper multidisciplinary/nurses' notes.

When ordering IV medications, the doctor may not specify the solution in which the nurses or pharmacy should dilute the medication or the volume of solution. There are guidelines that clearly outline what medications may be mixed in what solutions and in what volume. Often, the choice will be normal saline or the same solution as the person is getting in the main line, if there is one. If the patient has a saline or heparin lock and is getting only IV infusion with the medication, normal saline or 5% D/W is the usual choice. The nurses would record the solution they infused it in, and the volume would be added to the fluid balance tracking sheet.

CONESTOGA GENERAL HOSPITAL																								
SCHEDULED SINGLE DAY MEDICATION ADMINISTRATION RECORD																						**Mrs. Hiu**		
From Mon 21 April/xx 0700h to: Tues 22 April/xx @ 0659h																								
Allergies:																								
Adverse Reactions																								
Diagnosis																								

Medication and Directions																								
Hours	07	08	09	10	11	12	13	14	15	16	17	18	19	20	21	22	23	24	01	02	03	04	05	06
Ancef 1 g in 100 cc n/s IV q6h × 5 days Start Apr 21 @ 1200 D/C Apr 26 @ 0600 _____ Initial																								
Initial																								

Figure 17.12   eMAR recording Ancef for Mrs. Hiu

Suppose that on April 21, Dr. Hanson also wrote the following order for another patient, Mrs. Hiu: "Ancef 1 g IV q6h 5 days." Note that the doctor has specified only the medication, route, dose, and frequency. In this case, Mrs. Hiu does not have an actual IV. It is understood, then, that this medication will be delivered in a minibag using an add-a-line through a PRN adaptor. In the computerized environment where the pharmacy prepares the eMARs, they may specify the solution in which the medication is prepared as well as the volume in the information that is printed on the eMAR (see Figure 17.12). On this eMAR, the pharmacy has specified the type of solution (normal saline) and the volume (100 cc) that the Ancef is mixed in. They have also noted the discontinuation date. For the most part, the pharmacy premixes such medications. There are occasions when the nurse mixes the medications in a minibag on the floor in a solution, following facility/pharmacy guidelines.

An IV medication added to a minibag is considered a scheduled medication and is recorded on the scheduled MAR (shown in Figure 17.12). In the electronic environment, the Ancef in the minibag (also called a secondary line) would be added under the appropriate heading on the PI screen. Mary has noted the dates for routine changing of the PRN adaptor. Although the Ancef is to be given for five days, there is no specific order to discontinue the PRN adaptor; hence, Mary has left that part blank.

Note that doctors often prescribe IV antibiotics because this route can overcome many of the drawbacks involving oral agents. The concentration of the antibiotic is more stable and predictable because the medication is not affected by variables in the gastrointestinal tract affecting absorption. As well, IV antibiotics are used for more serious infections that need immediate and aggressive treatment. Some of the more powerful antibiotics are not available as oral agents.

L06 BLOOD TRANSFUSIONS

A physician who wants to order blood replacement for a patient can choose from several blood products, depending on the patient's needs and diagnosis and sometimes on the patient's wishes. The patient may refuse to have a blood transfusion for personal or religious reasons. Jehovah's Witnesses, for example, usually refuse to receive any blood or blood products because they believe the Bible prohibits them from doing so. For the most part, their right to refuse treatment is respected, although there have been cases where the province or territory has overridden the parents' wishes when a physician believes the transfusion is necessary for a child's survival.

Reasons for Blood Transfusion

Doctors most commonly order blood transfusion as prophylaxis for a patient undergoing major surgery, to treat anemia, or to treat blood loss from hemorrhage. Other blood products are administered for various reasons. For example, factor VIII is given to hemophiliacs for clotting, often with other components in the form of a solution called cryoprecipitate.

Prophylaxis Most surgeons will order blood, usually packed cells (see explanation that follows) to be available for patients having major surgery in case of excessive blood loss during surgery. Blood will be cross-matched for a patient and held in the lab for him or her. If the patient does not need the blood, it will be released and available for another suitable recipient.

Anemia Anemia is characterized by too few red blood cells in a person's blood. There are a number of causes for this. Severe anemia is usually treated with the infusion of packed cells.

Acute Blood Loss Any situation in which a person loses an excessive amount of blood (usually over 750 cc) is called a hemorrhage. This causes the body to go into shock. The most effective way to treat massive hemorrhage is by blood replacement.

Preparation

Before receiving a blood transfusion, a patient must be cross-matched and typed (i.e., his or her blood type and Rh factor among other things must be determined) to ensure that he or she receives compatible blood. Otherwise a serious reaction could occur. The physician will order the type of blood or blood product the patient is to receive.

Types of Blood Products

Whole Blood If a doctor orders whole blood, it will be ordered as a unit of blood: approximately 520 cc of donated blood. It may be used to treat excessive blood loss resulting from trauma, surgery, or burns. Whole blood is not frequently ordered.

Platelets Platelets are extracted from whole blood and ordered for someone with thrombocytopenia, or a low blood platelet count. Anyone with low platelets is at risk for bleeding disorders, in particular disseminated intravascular coagulopathy (DIC), a potentially fatal condition characterized by widespread bleeding. Platelets, too, are ordered by the unit.

Fresh Frozen Plasma Plasma, derived from whole blood, contains all coagulation, or clotting, factors and is given to patients with coagulation defects. One unit is usually approximately 225 cc.

Packed Cells The most commonly ordered blood product is packed cells: red blood cells separated from whole blood by a process called centrifugation. Packed blood cells may be used to correct anemia when extra volume is not desirable for a patient (e.g., in the case of congestive heart failure). Because it does not contain white blood cells, it poses less risk of minor reactions. A doctor might order "Cross and type for two units of packed cells" or "CT for 2 units of packed cells on cross-match for two units of packed cells."

Albumin   This is a protein extracted from the blood and is often used to expand fluid volume within the blood vessels.

Cryoprecipitate   Cryoprecipitate is part of the fresh frozen plasma that contains a clotting factor called factor VIII. It is most commonly given to hemophiliacs to help control bleeding.

The Blood Transfusion Process and the Clinical Secretary's Responsibilities

Though procedures vary from one hospital to another, the following section outlines the typical process. If the blood is ordered (in case it is needed) for someone who is going in for major surgery, the person will be cross-matched and typed. The selection and amount of blood product ordered will be prepared for the patient and held in the blood bank until used, or until it is clear that the patient will not need it. The blood bank will send a list of the units prepared for the patient. Each unit of blood product will be assigned an identification number. Always note it on the PI screen if blood is being held for a patient.

Whether manually or electronically, a requisition is sent to the blood bank, and the blood bank notifies the floor when the blood product is ready. If it is to be given as soon as available, someone from the patient-care unit will go to the lab to pick it up. You may occasionally be asked to do this. If so, you must complete a series of checks with the lab technologist to ensure that you are getting precisely what has been ordered for the patient. Bring the floor's copy of the blood requisition or the patient's identifying information (e.g., ID stickers); in entirely electronic environments, follow facility protocol. Check this information against the unit of blood product being sent to the floor and against the ledger in which the same information is recorded. Check the blood product again with the nurses, confirming the patient's name, hospital number, room number, blood type, and the number assigned to the unit of blood product.

In a manual environment, you may need to create a special vital signs graph used for patients receiving transfusions. The nurses check the patient's vital signs frequently to detect any reaction, especially in the first hour, when reactions are most likely. In a computerized environment, the nurses would enter the vital signs electronically. Even in computerized environments, vital signs taken frequently are sometimes documented on paper as well.

HYPERALIMENTATION OR TOTAL PARENTERAL NUTRITION

Hyperalimentation or total parenteral nutrition (TPN) is the intravenous administration of nutrients to patients who cannot absorb food through their gastrointestinal tract. This is discussed in Chapter 18.

⟫⟫ WHAT TO WATCH FOR

The sale of blood plasma in Canada: Canada is embarking on an initiative to sell blood plasma. Only a few provinces have actually opened clinics for this purpose; donors are given gift cards for reimbursement, since paying someone for blood is illegal. The plasma is used for blood products and is in short supply; Canada buys plasma abroad.

SUMMARY

1. Our health depends on a balance of fluids and electrolytes, known as homeostasis. Healthy people take this balance for granted and maintain it naturally. Our bodies correct imbalances; for example, thirst prompts us to maintain fluid levels. The most common elements in maintaining homeostasis are sodium, potassium, and chloride. These electronically charged ions assist with the transport of nutrients within the body and contribute to muscle and nerve functions. Sick people are especially at risk for fluid and electrolyte imbalances.

2. Intravenous therapy is used to correct electrolyte imbalances, maintain homeostasis, deliver medications, and supply blood products, when needed. It is used to rehydrate patients or maintain hydration and fluid balance in patients who cannot eat or drink because of disease, trauma, or surgery.

3. IV Infusion can be started with an IV catheter, a butterfly needle, or a central line. A central line is more invasive but is required when a stable line is needed for long-term therapy and patient treatment is more complex. A PICC line is one of three types of central lines commonly used. Various types of tubing are available, depending on the patient's needs. A variety of IV solutions are used and are carefully selected by the physician based on the patient's needs. IV medications, such as antibiotics, are often delivered into the mainline IV using minibags.

4. IV solutions may be delivered by gravity, with the rate controlled by roller clamps, or, more commonly, by various types of pumps. Patient-controlled analgesia (PCA) pumps allow patients to administer their own pain relief as needed (within strict parameters). Their use is associated with a faster recovery rate and effective pain control. Small portable pumps, some of which are computer assisted, allow patients with terminal or chronic illnesses to manage pain at home.

5. Transcribing IV orders follows the basic steps outlined in Chapter 16. The IV order must include the solution, the rate, and the start date. You would note any related nursing responsibilities or specific criteria, including site assessment and changing the IV and tubing. Orders for the same solution may sometimes be written in several ways. Be sure you understand the order that you are transcribing. Always check the rate carefully as well. Too much fluid, or the incorrect fluid, can be harmful, even fatal. Any medications given are recorded on a MAR, but only in facilities using paper MARs. Otherwise you are not responsible for recording IV medications, just the solutions appropriately on the PI screen.

6. Blood and blood products are ordered for anemia or excessive loss of blood and as a precaution for surgery. The most commonly ordered product is packed cells. A patient's blood type and Rh factor must be checked carefully against donor blood to find a match and prevent potentially fatal reactions. Special infusion sets are used for blood transfusions, and normal saline is the only IV solution that should be used.

KEY TERMS

Angiocatheter 523
cc 522
distal 523
drops per minute
   (gtt/min) 526
hemorrhage 522

heparin (hep) lock
   (saline lock, PRN
   adapter) 529
homeostasis 521
interstitial 521
intracellular 521

intravascular 521
intravenous (IV) 520
IV push 530
patient-controlled
   analgesia (PCA) 528
placebo effect 529

REVIEW QUESTIONS

1. List the common elements that control our body's fluid and electrolyte balance, and briefly describe their functions.

2. What are four indications for intravenous therapy?

3. Briefly describe the goals for intravenous therapy outlined in this chapter.

4. What is a medication administration set?

5. Where would you locate an electronic pump, if required?

6. What would you do if you walked into a room and the alarm on an electronic pump was sounding?

7. What is the purpose of patient-controlled analgesia, and how does it work?

8. Where are medications added to a minibag usually transcribed?

9. Why is it important to include the flow rate when transcribing IV infusion orders?

10. What information should be transcribed onto the PI screen along with the actual IV order?

APPLICATION EXERCISES

1. Interpret the following IV orders, and transcribe them onto the format advised by your professor:

   a. 4000 cc 5% DW over 24 hours

   b. 1000 cc 0.45% NaCl 3 @ 100 cc/h

   c. 1000 cc 2/3 and 1/3 2 then reduce to TKVO if drinking well

   d. Infuse 1 unit of packed cells, then reduce IV to saline lock

2. a. Transcribe the following order onto the format advised by your professor:

				Long, Tom
	Insert PICC line stat			978 Victoria St.
	IV normal saline @125cc/hr			Stratford ON
	Gentamicin 80 mg IV qh with gentamicin levels in 2 days			N5A 2G3
Date Apr 07/xx	Time	Physician's Name Printed Dr. McManus	Physician's signature Dr. N McManus	M 29 06 42 099342 744210088 McManus, Dr. N.

   b. Answer the following questions:

   i. Differentiate among a PICC line, a central line, and an intracatheter.

   ii. What is meant by a bolus, and why might it be given in this case?

   iii. Look up the drug gentamicin online. Why is this drug ordered IV, and why did the doctor order gentamicin levels be done in two days' time?

   iv. What are some advantages of giving antibiotics intravenously?

3. Jim, who is about to be hospitalized, asks you to describe what an IV is and what he can expect. Draft a brief response. Ask friends or family members who have had an IV; incorporate any helpful information into your draft explanation.

4. Marina is worried about having a central line inserted and asks you whether it is the same as having a small IV started in her arm. With a partner, draft a brief summary of what a central line is and briefly explain its benefits. Discuss the responsibilities of the clinical secretary related to an order for a central line.

WEBSITES OF INTEREST

Canadian Blood Services

www.blood.ca

Chapter 18
Orders Related to Nutrition

Monkey Business Images/Shutterstock

LEARNING OBJECTIVES

On completing this chapter, you will be able to:

1. Outline six factors affecting an individual's nutritional needs.

2. Discuss patient nutrition, considering the role of a registered dietician, patient preferences, and food distribution, and the implications for the clinical secretary.

3. Explain the various types of diets that may be ordered in the hospital and their purpose.

4. Discuss dietary changes related to laboratory and diagnostic tests and hospital procedures.

5. Describe the purpose and types of tube feedings and total parenteral nutrition.

Every person admitted to hospital must have an order for some type of diet. Nutrition is an essential element in the treatment and recovery of all patients. A number of variables affect our dietary intake and nutritional status. These needs are sometimes heightened when we are ill or undergo a surgical procedure and thus must be considered when meeting the nutritional needs of the hospitalized patient. An example is a patient recovering from major surgery—a diet high in protein is essential for tissue repair.

[LO1] FACTORS AFFECTING NUTRITIONAL NEEDS

Genetics

metabolic rate the amount of energy expended in a given period, or the physical changes that occur in the body that result in heat production.

Our basic body structure is predetermined by genetics and affects our basal **metabolic rate**. Thyroid gland function is also genetically influenced. Low thyroid function slows a person's basal metabolic rate, and increased thyroid function increases it.

Age

Metabolic rate usually slows with age, and fewer calories are required. Children, on the other hand, have a much higher metabolic rate and therefore need more calories in proportion to body weight than do adults for ideal growth and development. This is especially so during growth periods, such as during the first two years of life and in adolescence. It is thought that a person's basal metabolic rate starts to slow between the ages of 20 and 22 years.

In hospital, older patients often complain of being served too much, while younger patients ask for more. Dietitians consider a patient's age and weight as well as health status when making up nutritional supplements and special diets.

Gender

Men tend to need more calories than do women, partly because they are, on average, larger and have more muscle mass. Hormones may also play a role in increasing metabolic rate. A diabetic man would usually be prescribed more calories than would a diabetic women. Male hospital patients often eat more than female patients.

Pregnancy

metabolism the physiological and biochemical processes that promote growth and sustain life.

During pregnancy, women must adjust their daily caloric intake to ensure a healthy, well-nourished baby. The woman's **metabolism** increases to meet the energy demands of supporting a pregnancy. Currently, a woman who delivers a baby in hospital spends very little time in the facility. However, when she is there, a diet high in protein and appropriate calories is important. This is especially true if the woman is breastfeeding.

Activity

The more active a person is, the more calories he or she expends—as those trying to lose weight are usually told. Not only does exercise use energy directly (anywhere from 14 to 40 percent of our total energy is used in activity), but it increases metabolic rates as well. People who are unable to be active because of illness or physical limitations require fewer calories than they otherwise would. Individuals in the hospital are typically inactive and may require fewer calories. Having said that, illness itself and the process of healing (e.g., from surgery) will increase the body's caloric use.

Illness

As previously mentioned, illness will alter a person's caloric needs in various ways. Fever raises the basal metabolic rate, as does trauma, such as surgery. Extra calories, and sometimes extra protein, are also needed to promote tissue repair and recovery.

L02 NUTRITION IN THE HOSPITAL

Many Canadian hospitals are becoming more conscious about the need to provide patients with food that is not only nutritious but that offers more variety and tastes good. As with most things, the problem is balancing a budget, shifting expenses, and coming up with innovative ways to accomplish this. A move to using local produce is in motion in many Canadian cities.

Canada's Food Guide remains the guiding principle for hospitals; its website is provided at the end of this chapter. It includes a link where you can request a free print copy or download a PDF version. It is also available in 10 other languages in addition to English and French. This might be valuable for patients requesting information about nutritious eating.

The hospital provides all meals and snacks that are ordered by the physician for inpatients, and the cost is covered under the provincial or territorial plan. Hospital schedules reflect traditional meal times. Typically, breakfast arrives between 7:00 and 8:00 a.m., lunch between 11:30 a.m. and 12:30 p.m., and supper between 4:00 and 5:00 p.m. Many of a patient's activities, from tests and appointments to medications, revolve around meal times.

Serving Hospital Meals

Patient meals are an integral part of treatment, hence the provision and consumption of a balanced diet, which is essential to aid recovery. A number of food service systems are used to provide meals for patients in the hospital. Many are prepared offsite and brought in at the appropriate times. Special diets, however, are overseen by a team of dieticians.

In some hospitals meals are prepared onsite; in others, food services are contracted out, prepared elsewhere, and brought in. They arrive in two ways: individual trays prepared for each patient, or in cafeteria-style carts and served on the patient-care unit. The heated carts keep the food hotter, and patients have more food choices (e.g., rice or potatoes, peas or beans). The dietary staff and sometimes the nursing staff assist with meal distribution. You may sometimes be asked to help when the unit is short staffed. If you are free, the nurses will always appreciate it if you offer to help distribute trays. Bringing in meal trays sometimes involves "setting up" the patient. The over-bed table may have to be cleared to make room for the tray. Patients may need the head of their bed rolled up and the over-bed table repositioned so they can reach their food. Some may need to be helped into position. Sometimes a patient will ask you to arrange the food, cut the meat, pour the tea or coffee, open the milk cartons, or add salt and pepper. More incapacitated patients need to be fed. Feeding patients is not your job; leave it to nurses or family members.

Just after the trays are delivered, be prepared for complaints from patients about incorrect diets, missing trays, or missing items on trays. Nurses will also let you know if a particular diet has not been changed to match new orders. To save time, check with all the nurses, make a list of required changes, and make a single phone call to nutritional services (calling is usually faster than contacting them electronically). If you get an answering machine, leave a message. Nutritional services will need the patient's name, room number, the type of diet, and then the request. They usually respond promptly. Omitted items and additional food orders may be delivered to the floor or put on the lift if there is one (see Chapter 14). Someone will call to tell you about items on the lift.

In most facilities, dietary staff will come to the patient-care unit, collect the trays, and take the carts back to the kitchen.

The Patient's Diet

All hospitals and other health care facilities employ a registered dietitian and often dietary assistants. The registered dietitian is a knowledgeable and valuable resource for the health care team.

The diet a provider orders for a patient may not be entirely suitable, requiring adjustments for a variety of reasons. Diet orders are sent to nutritional services electronically. You will frequently interact with the department with information about changes to diet orders that may occur because of changes in the patient's condition or because of scheduled tests. For example, a surgical patient may require clear fluids for a day or two, and then progress to a soft diet; if a test such as a colonoscopy is ordered for a patient, you must notify nutritional services that the patient is NPO until further notice. You may also notify nutritional services if someone orders consultation (e.g., for a newly diagnosed diabetic or a heart patient who is placed on a cardiac diet). Individuals on a diabetic diet often have snacks ordered. Sometimes they appear on the counter at the nurses, station; let the nurse know the snack is there or deliver it yourself if it has been there more than 15–20 minutes. It is important for diabetics to have snacks as ordered to keep their blood sugar from dropping, especially if they are on insulin.

Patients who are hospitalized may lose their appetite because they are ill or because the food is different from what they are used to. To many people hospital food is simply unappealing for a variety of reasons. What people like to eat is affected not only by personal taste but also by cultural factors. Registered dietitians take on the challenge of designing a diet that takes into account the patient's physical ability to ingest food and nutritional needs, including any special needs caused by illness, while trying to adapt the institutional diet to the person's lifestyle, religion, culture, and personal preferences. They make an effort to accommodate individual needs and wishes within the constraints of the doctors' orders, staff time, and availability of supplies.

You may encounter families that want a specific order requested for the patient (e.g., the patient would like cereal for breakfast instead of oatmeal). This can usually be done without a doctor's order. If you are uncertain, ask the nurse. A dietary consult can be ordered to review the existing diet options so that food more palatable to the patient's needs and tastes can be included. Sometimes, family will request something simple—for example, the patient would like apple juice instead of orange juice. Or they or the patient may request a morning or an afternoon snack, which can be arranged unless contraindicated by the patient's condition. You can enter it as a DSN (dietary special needs) for nutritional services to keep a note in the patient's file.

LO3 TYPES OF DIETS ORDERED AND PROCESSING DIETARY ORDERS

Therapeutic Diets

A therapeutic diet is one ordered by a physician as part of a treatment for a disease or clinical condition. It responds to the person's health state and physical ability to tolerate

TABLE 18.1 Short forms for typical diet orders

Usual Order	Explanation	Usual Order	Explanation
NPO	Nothing by mouth; place a sign by the patient's bed	Low sodium or low salt	Limits sodium intake to less than 3000 mg/day
DAT	Diet as tolerated; that is, regular diet: no restriction	Very low sodium	Limits sodium intake to 2000 mg/day or less
CF	Clear fluids (with no residue)	Soft/surgical soft	Low in fibre; some fruits and vegetables are not allowed
FF	Full fluids		
CF–DAT	Start with clear fluids and progress to diet as tolerated	CDA diet 1200 cal	(Number of calories may vary) diabetic diet; carbohydrates controlled or
FF–DAT	Start with full fluids and progress to diet as tolerated		1200 cal CDA sugary and fatty foods restricted
NAS	No added salt; limits sodium intake to about 3000–4000 mg/day	Cardiac diet	Restricts fat, cholesterol, and sometimes salt and calories
		d/c or dc	Discontinue

certain foods. Some therapeutic diets are short term; others are long term or for life. Typical diet orders are summarized in Table 18.1.

Cardiac   This diet is usually ordered for patients who are admitted with or have pre-existing heart disease (e.g., someone who has had a heart attack). There are variations, but the diet is generally low in fat and cholesterol and may restrict sodium (salt) and calories.

No Added Salt/Na Restricted   This diet may be written as NAS, meaning no added salt. Salt should not be added at the table, and unless otherwise stated, salt should not be added during the preparation/cooking process. Processed cheeses and cured or smoked meats are avoided, as well as sports drinks, such as Gatorade, and other commercially prepared products with a high sodium content. Desserts, such as sherbet, ice cream, ice milk, yogurt, puddings, and custards, are allowed. It is ordered for patients who have problems with **fluid retention** or congestive heart failure (a condition in which the heart does not pump efficiently).

fluid retention an accumulation of fluid in body tissues or body cavities.

Diabetic   Diabetes mellitus is a **metabolic disorder** characterized by the inability to properly use glucose. A hormone called insulin, produced by the pancreas, facilitates the entry of glucose from the blood into cells where it can be used. If insulin is absent or insufficient or is inefficiently used, the body cannot properly use glucose, so it builds up in the bloodstream. Constant high blood sugar levels in the body damage the organs and the vascular system.

metabolic disorder a condition characterized by the body's inability to synthesize or process food into forms the body can use for energy, growth, and development.

Dietary intake is an important part of controlling a diabetic's blood sugar. Diet control is important for people taking insulin because the dosage needed is affected by diet and exercise. The dietitian plays an important role, especially with a newly diagnosed patient, in education and in establishing and monitoring a diet. Support is important for newly diagnosed diabetics, who usually experience considerable stress; not only have they learned that they have a serious disease, but they must also cope with taking medicine and changing their eating patterns and lifestyle.

A diabetic diet is prepared individually after consultation with the patient and the physician, and it contains a wide range of food choices. It contains a prescribed number of calories and certain proportions of fats, carbohydrates, and proteins. It may be called "1200 cal CDA" or "1400 cal CDA." CDA refers to the Canadian Diabetes Association. Sugary foods should be avoided because they cause the blood sugar to rise very quickly. Excessively fatty foods should also be avoided to reduce heart risk.

Diabetic patients, particularly those with type 1 diabetes (also known as insulin-dependent diabetes mellitus, or IDDM) may receive snacks throughout the day, usually brought by the dietary staff mid-morning, mid-afternoon, and at bedtime. They may be placed on a counter in the nurses' station or in the refrigerator in the kitchen. Make sure you know which patients receive snacks and when. Although distributing snacks is not your responsibility, if you see a snack sitting on the counter that you know should be given to a patient, let the nurses know. These snacks are important to maintain safe blood sugar levels. When insulin is not balanced by food intake, blood sugar drops, and a potentially dangerous insulin reaction can occur. Know the warning sings: irritability, confusion, sleepiness or headaches, shaking, pallor, and sweating. If you suspect a patient is having such a reaction, call the nurse immediately. If the nurse is not available, encourage the patient to eat or drink something containing sugar. Most established diabetics will recognize these signs and know what to do. Newly diagnosed diabetics may not.

Gluten Free   Celiac disease involves an atrophy of the mucosa (lining) of the upper small intestine. People with this disease cannot properly absorb gluten, a protein found in wheat, rye, barley, oats, triticale, and spelt. If they eat an ordinary diet, they may suffer severe diarrhea and vitamin deficiencies. Individuals diagnosed as celiac must be on a gluten-free diet for the rest of their lives.

Gluten-free versions of common foods, such as bread, pastries, and pasta, are now available in many stores. They are often made with rice flour, which has a short shelf life, so baked goods are usually sold frozen. Gluten-free all-purpose flour is now available, which can be substituted in some recipes quite successfully. As rice flour tends to be very fine and dry, recipes usually work best if they contain vegetable oil, butter, or eggs.

TIP

Individuals (celiacs) on gluten-free diets find purchasing gluten-free products expensive. Many do not realize that if they keep all food receipts they can submit them on their income tax returns as a medical expense. This is worth letting any such patients you may have know in case they do not already.

High Fibre   Large quantities of fibre stimulate peristaltic action and bowel movements. A high-fibre diet is ordered for patients who have sluggish bowels or constipation. Foods include lean meat, potatoes, vegetables such as spinach or cabbage, stewed fruit, whole grains, and bran.

High Protein   This diet may be ordered for a patient who needs to gain weight or to repair tissue, such as in the case of someone recovering from major surgery. It emphasizes high-protein foods, such as meat, fish, milk, eggs, legumes, and nuts.

High Calorie   High-calorie diets are ordered for patients who have had excessive weight loss resulting from illness or who, for other reasons, cannot reach or maintain a healthy weight. As well as ordinary foods high in calories (butter, ice cream, fried foods, etc.), these diets often include special supplements, such as fortified milkshakes (e.g., a product called Ensure).

If someone on your unit is on supplemental feeds, make sure the supplements are refrigerated when they come to the floor and notify the nurses. Although giving the supplements is the nurses' responsibility, you can help by keeping them informed.

Low Residue/Surgical Soft   This type of diet, which decreases fibre and cellulose to reduce bowel motility, may be ordered for someone who has had gastrointestinal surgery, who has a partial bowel obstruction, or who has a colostomy or an ileostomy. This diet includes some cheeses, yogurt, eggs, plain pastas, white bread, boiled chicken and turkey, well-cooked beef, and broiled fish. Fruits that are canned, baked, or stewed without skins or seeds (bananas, apple sauce) as well as cream of wheat, cornflakes, and rice cereal would be allowed.

Bland   A bland diet may be ordered for someone with long-term or chronic gastritis, peptic ulcers, dyspepsia (upset stomach), or a **hiatus hernia**. This diet contains foods that are easily digested, such as lean tender meats, pasta, potatoes, and canned fruits and vegetables; fried and highly spiced foods are avoided.

hiatus hernia a condition in which the upper part of the stomach, which is joined to the esophagus or feeding tube, moves up into the chest through a hole (called a hiatus) in the diaphragm.

Regular   A "regular diet" means that the doctor is placing no restrictions on what the patient can eat. It is also ordered as DAT, for "diet as tolerated." With this order, nurses have some flexibility to alter patients' meals and can avoid foods the patients cannot tolerate. Doctors may rely on nurses to alter the diet to suit the patients' needs. A nurse may ask you to order a different diet for a patient on the basis of nursing assessments.

Ice Chips or Sips Only   This is the first part of a progressive diet and is ordered primarily for patients who have had major surgery. The patient is allowed to suck ice chips or take very small occasional sips of water to moisten the mouth and lips. There is nothing to order for this. Ice is available on most patient-care units, as is cold water.

Clear Fluids   A liquid diet minimizes residue and is easier on the digestive system. "Clear fluid" is usually one you can see through; this includes some soups and juices, ginger ale (often given flat), coffee, tea, and plain Jell-O. A clear fluid diet may be ordered for preoperative and postoperative patients or for those who are acutely ill or have acute diarrhea or vomiting. It is also ordered prior to certain investigative tests, such as a colonoscopy. A clear fluid diet is not nutritionally adequate in the long run but will keep the patient hydrated until he or she can tolerate a full-fluid or soft diet. Usually, foods are introduced slowly and as tolerated.

Full Fluids   A full-fluid diet offers more choice than a clear fluid diet but is still relatively restrictive. It is ordered for pre- and postoperative patients, patients with stomach problems, and those who cannot tolerate or chew solid foods. If often follows a clear fluid diet and is therefore considered transitional or temporary.

This diet includes all the foods in the clear fluid diet, with the addition of strained soups, milk, and milk products, such as yogurt and ice cream. Fruit and vegetable juices may be taken, as well as eggnog mixtures and custard puddings.

Soft/Mechanical Soft Diet   The mechanical soft diet consists of foods soft in texture, moderately low in fibre, and processed by chopping, grinding, or puréeing to be easier to chew. Most milk products, tender meats, mashed potatoes, tender vegetables, and fruits and their juices are included in the diet. However, most raw fruits and vegetables, seeds, nuts, and dried fruits are excluded.

A soft diet is one that involves little or no chewing and is ordered for patients who have problems chewing or digesting. It may also follow the full-fluid diet as a surgical patient begins to tolerate more foods. It includes liquids, puréed foods, strained cereals, and puddings. Some facilities include eggs and toast.

Puréed   A puréed diet is ordered for patients who cannot chew or who have **dysphagia** (difficulty swallowing). Someone who has had a stroke would be an example. All food is ground to a soft, silky texture. Sometimes thickeners are added to hot or cold fluids until they are of the desired consistency. Most patients resist a puréed diet; it looks unappealing, and the taste is usually not much better.

dysphagia difficulty swallowing.

Minced   A minced diet is one in which all food is ground to a fine texture but not as fine as a puréed diet. This diet is used for individuals who can swallow a little but who cannot tolerate larger chunks of food.

Progressive   A progressive diet is a sequence of diets that introduces foods in stages as the patient can tolerate them. It is usually used following major surgery or an illness involving the gastrointestinal tract. It may be ordered as a progressive diet, or the stages may be ordered separately. A progressive diet can start anywhere along the continuum, ranging from sips only through clear fluid, full fluid, and soft, and finally to a regular diet. This diet is discussed in more detail later.

Transitional Diet   A transitional diet is a temporary, limited diet used as an alternative to the progressive diet before and after surgery. This diet may be used for patients before and after abdominal and other types of surgery. Instead of beginning with clear fluids, the patient is immediately introduced to selected solid foods. To reduce indigestible carbohydrates to a minimum, all fruits and vegetables are omitted except strained fruit juice and tomato juice; milk as a beverage is not allowed. Eggs and tender meat are used. Studies have shown that patients tolerate this diet fairly well and receive more nutrients than on a fluid diet. However, some physicians prefer the progressive diet.

Transcribing Diet Orders

When processing a diet order, access nutritional services in the computer and click on the icon that reveals a list of diets (see Figure 18.1). Select the required diet. Once

NPO	Fluid Restricted 500ml (200mL ontray)
NPO after Midnight	Low Fat Diet
Clear Fluid Diet	Low Iodine Diet
Full Fluid Diet	Low Residue (Fibre Restricted)
Regular Diet	NAS Diet
Dental Soft Diet	MAOI Diet (Tyramine Restricted)
Minced Diet	Paediatric Clear Fluid Gastro
Pureed Diet	Paediatric Baby 4 to 6 months
Heart Healthy Diet	Paediatric Baby 7 to 8 months
Eating Disorder Diet	Paediatric Baby 9 to 11 months
Gluten Free Diet	Paediatric Toddler 1 to 2 years
Lactose Restricted Diet	Paediatric Child 3 to 5 years
Anti Reflux Diet	Paediatric Child 6 to 12 years
Diabetic 4,000 - 6,000 kJ Diet	Paediatric Adolescent 13 to 18 years
Diabetic 6,500 - 7,500 kJ Diet	Post Gastrectomy Diet
Diabetic 8,000 - 10,000 kJ Diet	Renal Diet
Diabetic 10,500 - 12,500 kJ Diet	Sodium 87 mmoL REstricted Diet
High Fibre Diet	Thickened Fluid Diet
Hight Protein/High Energy Diet	TPN + NPO
Hyperemesis Diet	TPN + Clear Fluids
Fluid Restricted 1500mL (1200mL on tray)	TPN + Full Fluids
Fluid Restricted 1200mL (1000mL on tray)	TPN + Diet
Fluid Restricted 900mL (600mL on tray)	Wired Jaw Diet
Fluid Restricted 700mL (400mL on tray)	

Figure 18.1   List of available diets to choose from

Courtesy of North York General Hospital

Figure 18.2 eChart showing two active diets

selected, the diet appears in another field, along with the patient's identifying information and a field asking for additional information (e.g., food allergies). Enter any relevant information, and file the order. Nutritional services will receive the order and add that diet to the patient's profile. Some systems will automatically add the diet to the patient's chart, usually in the PI screen. If changes are needed for the next meal, for example lunch, *call nutritional services* to ensure they have processed the change in time for lunch. Otherwise, lunch may reflect the previous diet the patient was on or not be sent at all if the patient is a new admission.

In a computerized physician order entry (CPOE) environment, although you may not directly responsible for processing the diet order you are responsible for ensuring that only the active order (which is usually the most recent order) is displayed or otherwise identified as active (i.e., with an "A" beside it). Figure 18.2 shows two diets as they might appear in an eChart (NAS and a regular diet). If the latest order was NAS, you would delete the regular diet. Other environments may display the diets with an Active or Inactive notification beside them, "A" or "I."

In all environments (whether you do order entry or CPOE), you will be responsible for ensuring that diet orders are adjusted for patients undergoing tests and surgical procedures (e.g., ensuring that the NPO status of a patient is properly implemented) and that the proper diet is activated when the patient can resume eating. In the CPOE environment, you will need a "resume diet" order from the physician, but then you will implement the changes yourself. In addition, in all environments you may change the status of a progressive order upon the nurse's assessment of the patient's condition (e.g., changing a full-fluid diet to a soft diet). In the CPOE environment, you will be required to add the name of the nurse who gave you the order and identify how the order was communicated (e.g., verbal, written).

New Admissions   In most circumstances, a patient just admitted to hospital must have a diet order before you can order him or her something to eat. Frequently, new admissions either do not have a diet order, nutritional services has the order but fails to send a tray for the patient, or the doctor has not yet written an order. Stay on top of this. When a new patient arrives, check to see if there is a diet order—this is especially important if the patient arrives shortly before a meal (e.g., noon or supper time). If there is an order, call nutritional services to tell them the patient is on the floor and needs lunch or supper. If there is no order, let the nurses know. Sometimes they will evaluate the patient and ask you to order him or her something to eat.

Orders for Discharged Patients   You need to cancel meals for discharged patients. Find out when the patient plans to leave. As discussed in Chapter 14, patients are encouraged to leave mid-morning, so you need to notify nutritional services to cancel lunch, using your facility's normal procedure. Once a patient discharge has been entered into the computer, all pertinent departments will automatically receive that information (including nutritional services). However, if the discharge order comes through late, you need to call nutritional services to let them know. Also, if a patient has arranged to stay through lunch, you have to call nutritional services and ask them to send up the patient's lunch.

104 DIAGNOSTIC TESTS AND HOSPITAL PROCEDURES

If the patient is scheduled for a diagnostic test, you often need to ensure that his or her diet has been appropriately altered. The diet preparation will not usually be spelled out in the order for the test; you will be expected to know what tests require diet restrictions and to make sure they are implemented. Before any test requiring an anesthetic, the patient must remain NPO, usually for 8 to 10 hours. The same holds true for any test that involves visualizing parts of the gastrointestinal tract and for certain blood tests. Other dietary preparations may also apply. Consult the procedure or laboratory manual for clarification. Refer to Chapter 6 for preparatory details regarding the following tests for the hospitalized patient: barium enema, barium swallow, oral glucose tolerance tests, vanillylmandelic acid test (VMA).

Remember that for fasting blood tests for the inpatient, you must post an NPO sign. If a patient is to have a fasting blood sugar or a blood test for cholesterol and triglycerides, he or she must remain NPO for 8 to 12 hours, except possibly for sips of water with certain medications. Post an NPO sign by the patient's bed the night before. Usually, the blood will be drawn early in the morning just before breakfast arrives, so you may have to hold breakfast briefly but will not usually need to cancel it. Patients who are aware that they are not to eat and are cognitively normal can be trusted to wait but should be reminded. If there is any doubt, the patient should not be given the breakfast tray until after the blood is drawn.

Postoperative Diets

What and how soon the patient is able to eat after surgery will depend on the type and extent of the surgery and the patient's response to the anesthetic. General anesthetics cause the gastrointestinal tract to be sluggish and unable to digest food properly; some people recover intestinal motility faster than others. In addition, some people experience nausea and vomiting. Physicians will consider the patient's response in ordering postoperative diets. Patients who have had surgery on the gastrointestinal tract itself may be NPO for a period of time after the operation and often have nasogastric or **gastric suction**, which is commonly referred to as Gomco suction (see Chapter 19). Patients who have had minor surgery or local anesthetic are more likely to be able to eat later on the day of surgery but may still require a lighter than normal diet.

When a patient comes back from the operating room, the physician typically orders "CF to DAT" (meaning a progressive diet starting with clear fluids and progressing to a regular diet as tolerated) or "Sips to DAT" (meaning starting with ice chips or sips only and progressing to a regular diet). Occasionally a doctor will just write "as tolerated," leaving the progression of the diet up to the nurses. The nurses will let you know what type of diet to order for the patient or will order it themselves.

Usually, a patient who has just returned from the OR will be given only ice chips or sips of water. If the patient has had major bowel surgery even ice chips may not be allowed until **bowel sounds are present (BSP)**. The postoperative diet would advance then to clear fluids, full fluids, soft, and finally a regular diet. Table 18.2 shows the typical progression. However, the rate of return to a normal diet depends on the patient and the surgery. Some patients may be able to omit certain steps. A patient who has had a minor operation may have clear fluids for the first few hours and then move right on to a soft or regular diet. Some will take longer, especially if the surgery involves the gastrointestinal tract.

gastric suction also called Gomco suction, this is gentle suction applied to a tube placed in the stomach to remove excessive secretions, such as saliva and gastric juices, that tend to accumulate in the stomach after surgery or trauma because the intestine is sluggish. This can prevent or relieve nausea and vomiting.

bowel sounds present (BSP) the audible return of gastrointestinal movement or function, also called peristalsis, often charted as BS X4, meaning it sounds audible in all four abdominal quadrants.

TABLE 18.2 Typical progressive diet after major surgery (not involving the GI tract)

Surgical day	NPO or ice chips or "sips" of water
Day one	Clear fluids … maybe full fluids at suppertime
Day two	Full fluids … maybe a soft diet at suppertime
Day three	Soft diet to a regular diet

Postoperative Orders for Same-Day Admissions   You need to notify nutritional services about postoperative diets, but you cannot do so until the patient comes to the patient-care unit and the doctor writes the orders. Some hospitals have a standard protocol. If the patient stays overnight but the surgery is minor, a soft diet might be ordered. For other surgeries, the diet could be clear fluids. If you get orders well ahead of time, you can simply send an electronic requisition, but if you are processing orders close to a meal time and the patient needs a tray, call nutritional services. They may not check their computer for diet notices in time.

Postoperative Orders for Patients Already in Hospital   Sometimes surgery is booked for a patient already in hospital. Suppose Mr. Black had been admitted for investigation of abdominal pain. Three days later, his doctor discovered a tumour and decided to operate. As soon as you receive the operative orders and have a confirmed surgery date, cancel the patient's diet, effective after dinner the day before surgery (or otherwise, as ordered). Otherwise, breakfast will appear the next morning for Mr. Black, who is perhaps already in the operating room, and the tray will be wasted. (Most facilities have strict rules that unused trays are to be returned untouched. They are not meant to provide snacks for hospital employees or visitors.) If the order comes in just before it needs to be implemented, call nutritional services. In the two hours before a meal, they are too busy to check their computers or requisition forms.

TUBE FEEDINGS/ENTERAL FEEDS

An **enteral feed** is one that is administered directly by a tube into the gastrointestinal system. Tube feedings bypass a person's swallowing mechanism and carry food directly into the stomach or bowel. They are used for individuals who cannot swallow, such as some stroke victims or people who have had part of their upper gastrointestinal tract removed because of cancer or trauma, and for people who cannot digest food (sometimes called malabsorption syndrome). Tubes may be inserted temporarily or permanently.

enteral feed feeding by tube directly into the gastrointestinal system.

Tube feedings are also used to reintroduce food for patients who have been unable to take food orally for prolonged periods of time and whose nutrition has been maintained by other methods such as total parental nutrition (discussed subsequently). Gastric feeds called "trickle" feeds are begun; this means that the gastric pump is set to deliver the nutritional supplement very slowly, perhaps at 10 drops per minute (see Figure 18.4 for an example). Note that the pump used is different from the pump used to deliver and monitor intravenous fluids and total parenteral nutrition feeds. Order implications for tube and enteral feedings are discussed in Chapter 19.

Sites of Insertion

Tubes are usually referred to and ordered by site of insertion. Physicians often have preferences.

- A **nasogastric tube (N/G tube or Levine tube)** (see Figure 18.3) is put through the nose into the stomach. A tube can also be inserted through the mouth into the

nasogastric tube (N/G tube or Levine tube) a feeding tube put through the nose into the stomach.

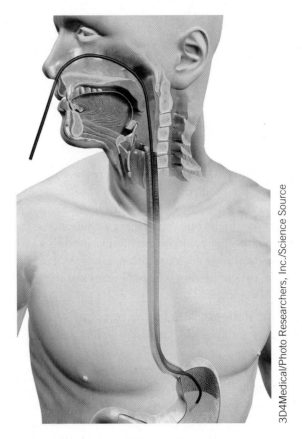

Figure 18.3 Levine tube (also called a nasogastric tube)

stomach. Mouth tubes are rarely used in adults because they are uncomfortable and stimulate the gag reflex. They may be used with young infants, who have weak gag reflexes and initially breathe only through the nose. N/G tubes are also used to decompress the stomach, irrigate the stomach, and treat bleeding.

gastrostomy tube (G-tube) a feeding tube inserted through an incision in the abdomen into the stomach.

jejunostomy tube (J-tube) a feeding tube placed through the abdominal wall into the small bowel.

percutaneous endoscopic gastrostomy tube (PEG tube or PEG catheter) a feeding tube inserted via endoscopy into the stomach or jejunum.

Bard button (MIC device) a feeding device placed permanently in the stomach to facilitate supplemental feedings.

- **Gastrostomy tubes (G-tubes)** are inserted through an incision in the abdomen into the stomach.

- **Jejunostomy tubes (J-tubes)** are placed through the abdominal wall into the jejunum, or small bowel. This site is chosen when the stomach cannot tolerate food because of such conditions as gastritis (inflammation of the stomach), pancreatitis (inflammation of the pancreas), or gastroesophageal reflux.

- Tubes can be inserted into the duodenum, but this is not common.

- A **percutaneous endoscopic gastrostomy tube (PEG tube or catheter)** is inserted through a puncture through the skin and subcutaneous tissues of the abdomen and stomach using an endoscope (a flexible instrument used to visualize organs). This catheter or tube has a bulb that is inflated once inside the stomach or jejunum and keeps the tube from falling out.

- There are a number of skin-level devices available to facilitate gastric feedings. The **Bard button** is one of the most common. These buttons are surgically placed into the stomach through the abdominal wall. The Bard button is made of pliable silicone with a mushroom-shaped dome at one end and a flat rectangular flap with a safety plug on the abdominal side. Only the flap with the safety plug attached is visible on the skin surface of the abdomen. An anti-reflux valve helps prevent gastric leakage through the tube. Special feeding tubes are necessary to connect the button to a feeding bag or syringe.

Tube Sizes

Feeding tubes are measured by *bore*, or diameter, in units called French (Fr.), after the inventor of the feeding tube. A small-bore tube might be 6 to 8 Fr.; a large-bore tube might 10 to 14 Fr. The smaller tubes are more difficult to insert and tend to become clogged easily.

Orders might read as follows:

- Insert a 10 Fr. nasogastric tube
- Insert a #14 Levine tube

Types of Feeds Ordered

Enteral feeds can be given in two ways: continuous or periodic intervals.

Continuous Feeds If these are ordered, usually the nurses will infuse the solution in small quantities measured every hour. To control volume, an electronic pump is sometimes used to administer the feed. Continuous feeds are usually better tolerated but are somewhat restrictive: The patient cannot easily move around because there is always solution dripping through the tube. A trickle feed is considered a continuous feed (see Figure 18.4)

Periodic Feeds The nurse will administer a certain volume of the prescribed solution every few hours, following a schedule usually drawn up by the dietitian: for example, 100 cc of Ensure @ 0730, 1130, 1630, and 1800.

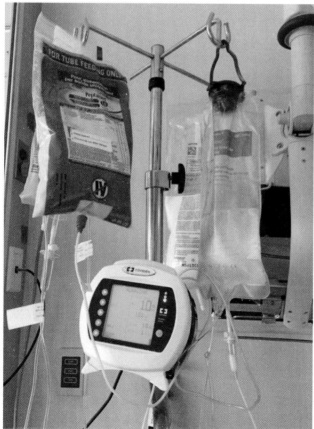

Valerie D. Thompson

Figure 18.4 A gastric feed set up delivering 10 gtt/minute

Enteral Solutions

In many facilities, formulas will be made up for the patient on the basis of standard recipes. These might include blended mixtures of meats, vegetables, and fruits with added nutrients. Therapeutic diets can be accommodated: The formula can be made lactose free, gluten free, or salt free and can be tailored to the appropriate number of calories, carbohydrates, and fat. Even a vegetarian diet can be formulated for tube feeding.

Premixed commercial formulations tailored to different needs are also available. Doctors may order them specifically, or hospitals may use them to save time. Common ones include the following:

- Osmolite
- Jevity
- Ensure
- Compleat
- Enrich
- Travasorb
- Ensure Plus

Medication may also be crushed and added to the feeding tube. Continuous feeds often help diabetics achieve better blood sugar control because both carbohydrates and insulin can be supplied at a constant rate. Diabetics will need adjustments to their insulin.

TOTAL PARENTERAL NUTRITION FEEDS

Total parenteral nutrition (TPN) is a complete form of nutrition, containing protein, sugar, fat, and added vitamins and minerals combined to meet the patient's individual nutritional needs. TPN is often delivered through a central line or a PICC line as these sites are most suitable for long-term feeding. TPN is indicated for patients who

- are severely malnourished and being prepared for surgery (a malnourished person will not recover as quickly from surgery);
- are receiving radiation therapy or chemotherapy and are malnourished or unable to eat;
- have had major surgery, severe burns, or multiple fractures and are unable to take or absorb nutrients with oral or enteral feeding;
- are in a prolonged coma;
- have severe anorexia;
- have severe inflammation of the bowel, such as ulcerative colitis; or
- are terminally ill and unable to eat.

Accompanying Blood Work

TPN orders are interpreted and handled by nutritional services. Most hospitals have a standard order form for TPN. When a TPN diet is ordered, blood work will be ordered at the same time to provide the physician and dietitian with baseline values from which to monitor the patient's state and determine nutritional needs. The doctor might order specific blood work or, in some facilities, you would automatically order a standard set of tests by a blanket term, such as "TPN baseline." This blood work might include the tests shown in Table 18.3.

TABLE 18.3 Blood tests typically ordered with TPN

Glucose	Albumin, INR
BUN	Triglyceride, PTT
Creatinine	Bilirubin total
Electrolytes	AST
Calcium	Phosphorus

Progressive or Transitional Diet and TPN

A physician may order a progressive feeding schedule for a patient that starts with TPN, moves to enteral feeds, and finally to oral food intake. As with any progressive diet, the rate of progress depends on the patient's condition; patients may sometimes have to take a step back to an earlier stage.

SUMMARY

1. A number of factors affect our nutritional needs, including gender, age, activity, and illness. Individuals who are ill or who have undergone surgery require carefully planned diets high in protein to aid in the healing process. Containing costs while providing patients with nutritious, appealing meals following Canada's Food Guide is a challenge. A move to using local produce is in motion in many hospitals.

2. A registered dietician oversees hospital meals and special diets ordered for patients. He or she must consider the patient's allergies (if any), culture, likes and dislikes, and construct the diet in accordance with special orders (e.g., low sodium, gluten free). Sometimes families make special requests as well. A dietary consult can be ordered to help a patient learn about a new diet as well as simply to discuss diet options if the patient does not like the food being served.

3. Physicians can order a variety of special (or therapeutic) diets for their patients— for example, a diabetic or low-sodium diet. Patients returning from surgery may have a diet order reading clear fluids to DAT. You must be aware of any diet changes and communicate with the nurses regarding these changes. Be sure to amend/change orders in the patient-care summary as soon as an order changes, and delete or inactivate old diet orders.

4. Diets must be adapted before many diagnostic tests. Make sure to order the adjustments needed. Some tests require restrictions or supplements up to two days in advance. Many tests require an NPO period; cancel or delay the patient's breakfast the day of the test, and put an NPO note at the patient's bedside. Patients who have had surgery are usually ordered a progressive or transitional diet, or one that reads "clear fluids to DAT." This means the diet order changes as the patient recovers and can tolerate incremental changes in his or her diet (e.g., clear fluids to full fluids to a soft diet).

5. Alternative methods of providing nutrition are used for individuals who are unable to eat. Tube feedings, also known as enteral feeds, administer nutrients through a tube that is placed into the patient's stomach or intestine. This is done when a patient cannot swallow or digest food. Solutions may be premixed commercial blends or prepared by the hospital and can include a full range of foods or

be adapted for therapeutic purposes. These feeds can be delivered at set intervals or continuously.

Another method of providing nutrition is called total parenteral nutrition (TPN). This involves the infusion of amino acids, glucose, fats, vitamins, minerals, and trace elements through an IV line. TPN is used for severely malnourished patients or those who cannot receive nutrition through the gastrointestinal route. TPN orders will be accompanied by a routine set of blood tests.

KEY TERMS

Bard button 552
bowel sounds present
    (BSP) 550
dysphagia 547
enteral feed 551
fluid retention 545
gastric suction 550

gastrostomy tube
    (G-tube) 552
hiatus hernia 547
jejunostomy tube
    (J-tube) 552
metabolic disorder 545
metabolic rate 542

metabolism 542
nasogastric (N/G tube or
    Levine tube) 551
percutaneous endoscopic
    gastrostomy tube (PEG
    tube or PEG
    catheter) 552

REVIEW QUESTIONS

1. What factors alter a person's basal metabolic rate?

2. What is a responsibility of the clinical secretary after trays have been given out to patients?

3. In point form, list the responsibilities of a hospital dietitian.

4. State the difference between a regular diet and a therapeutic diet.

5. Why are diabetic patients given snacks?

6. List the stages of the progressive diet, and describe each.

7. Differentiate between a progressive diet and a transitional diet.

8. What is an enteral feed?

9. Identify five types of feeding tubes, and give an example of how each might be ordered.

10. What is the purpose of total parenteral nutrition?

APPLICATION EXERCISES

1. Choose one of the diets listed in this chapter. Research the conditions for which the diet is ordered and the rationale for the diet. Write up your findings in an essay two to three pages long, and share your findings with the class.

2. Compare and contrast the advantages, disadvantages, and indications for enteral feeds and TPN.

3. With one of two classmates and using information from Canada's Food Guide (link provided subsequently), create meals for yourself for a period of one week. Consider

individual food preferences as well as affordability, local food, and good nutrition.

4. In small groups, choose a special diet and follow it for a week—for example, a celiac or a diabetic diet, or a restricted-calorie or low-fat diet, or a heart-healthy diet. Prepare your meals in accordance to diet requirements. Record how it feels to be restricted to the diet you choose and the frustrations you experience. At the end of the week, discuss your experience in class.

WEBSITES OF INTEREST

Canadian Celiac Association

www.celiac.ca

Canada's Food Guide

www.hc-sc.gc.ca/fn-an/food-guide-aliment/index-eng.php

Canadian Diabetes Association

www.diabetes.ca

Chapter 19
Orders Related to Digestion and Excretion

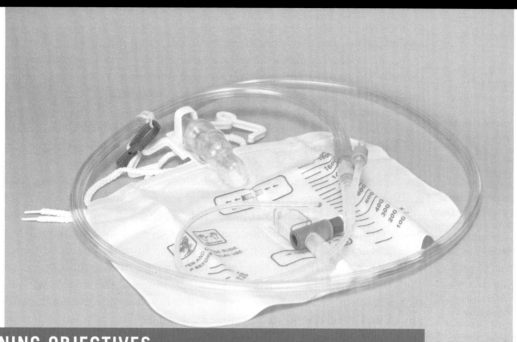

Sherry Young/Fotolia

LEARNING OBJECTIVES

On completing this chapter, you will be able to:

1. Summarize the digestive tract, considering function, disruptions, and common diagnostic tests.

2. Understand gastrointestinal assessments and interventions and your related responsibilities.

3. Explain the indications for a bowel resection and related complications.

4. Describe nasogastric suction, considering its purpose and related procedures.

5. Determine time frames when transcribing postsurgical dressing treatments.

6. Discuss genitourinary assessments, treatments, and procedures.

7. Explain indications for the use of urinary catheters.

LO1 THE GASTROINTESTINAL TRACT

Digestion and excretion concerns the function, assessment, interventions, and treatments related to the digestive system (the urinary system, also involved in the excretion of waste, is discussed separately). Review the anatomy and physiology of the gastrointestinal system and the urinary system covered in your anatomy and physiology courses as well as the related terminology in your medical terminology courses to better understand the content discussed in this chapter. Knowing about the gastrointestinal system will help you carry out the general tasks you would assume in the role of a clinical secretary, whether you are directly involved in order entry or working in a computerized physician order entry (CPOE) environment where order entry tasks are modified.

Altered GI function often indicates the onset of an illness. A variety of laboratory and diagnostic tests, a physical examination, and patient history are used to diagnose related diseases, which may include issues with associated structures, such as the liver, gallbladder, and pancreas. Surgical procedures, anesthetics, and other traumatic or invasive events, as well as disease processes and infections, alter GI function.

Conditions affecting GI function range from the flu and **gastritis** to **diverticulitis**, Crohn's disease, ulcerative colitis, ulcers, celiac disease, and cancer. Surgery is often necessary when conservative or nonsurgical treatments fail.

Cancer anywhere in the GI system (colorectal cancer is the most common) usually requires surgery, either laparoscopic or through a larger incision. Chemotherapy and radiation may also be recommended and are almost always administered on an outpatient basis. The presence of cancer is confirmed by a biopsy. If a tumour is in the large intestine, the biopsy is obtained during a diagnostic test called a **colonoscopy**. A colonoscopy is also done as a screening test for individuals with a family history of colorectal cancer. Colonoscopies may be done on an outpatient basis, either in an independent clinic or within the hospital. If cancer of the stomach is suspected, the biopsy is obtained during a procedure called an upper endoscopy or **esophagogastroduodenoscopy (EGD)**. This procedure involves passing the scope down the person's throat, allowing for visualization of the lining of the esophagus, stomach, and first part of the small intestine. An **endoscopic retrograde cholangiopancreatography (ERCP)** is a diagnostic test done to diagnose (and treat) disorders of the pancreas and bile ducts.

gastritis inflammation of the stomach.

diverticulitis inflammation of a sac-like bulge that may develop in the wall of the large intestine.

colonoscopy a diagnostic procedure used both as a screening test and to investigate certain GI complaints. Using an endoscope (equipped with a small camera), the physician can view the entire rectum and colon. The physician can also take a biopsy, if needed.

esophagogastroduodenoscopy (EGD) a diagnostic procedure used to investigate complaints of the stomach and upper part of the small intestine. Using an endoscope (equipped with a small camera), the physician can view the throat, stomach, and part of the small intestine. A biopsy can be obtained, if needed.

endoscopic retrograde cholangio-pancreatography (ERCP) a diagnostic test allowing visualization of the pancreas and bile ducts. A biopsy can be obtained, if necessary, during this test.

L02 GASTROINTESTINAL ASSESSMENTS

Assessment of the GI tract is a routine part of a nurse's assessment of a patient. The depth, frequency, and specificity of these assessments will vary with the patient's condition, diagnosis, treatment, and health state. Nurses also carry out a variety if interventions and treatments as ordered by the physician based largely on the assessments they make.

Most hospitalized patients will have assessments carried out daily—some routine and others specific to the disorders they have or are being assessed for. Assessments do not always relate directly to the reason for hospitalization. For example, if a patient is admitted to hospital for a knee replacement and has **ulcerative colitis**, irritable bowel syndrome, or an ulcer, part of the nurses' daily assessments would include the GI tract to monitor these conditions. A person admitted with myocardial infarction who also had a colostomy would be monitored for bowel function.

ulcerative colitis inflammation and ulceration of the innermost lining of the colon (the large intestine).

Bowel Function

Nurses routinely monitor patients' bowel elimination patterns, usually when taking the patients' vital signs (temperature, pulse, and respiration [TPR]; may also include oximetry, which measures O_2 saturation levels) at the beginning of the day. Even people who normally have regular bowel movements may be thrown off schedule by hospitalization. Their normal pattern may be affected by emotional strain, different food, and the loss of normal activity. Having to use a bedpan or a commode may contribute to constipation because of difficult positioning and discomfort, as well as lack of privacy.

The nurses enter assessments for bowel function directly into the patient's eChart. The information may be displayed in close proximity to the vital signs graph or in a separate section on the patient intervention (PI) screen. The nurse doing the morning TPRs usually asks the patient how many bowel movements he or she has had in the past 24 hours. If the patient goes more than a day or two without a bowel movement, he or she would likely be given a laxative.

Auscultation for Bowel Sounds

Nurses and doctors can assess bowel activity by auscultating (listening) for bowel sounds—that is, listening to a patient's abdomen with a stethoscope. Most postoperative patients will have abdominal assessments done every shift until **peristalsis** has returned. A physician's postop order may or may not include abdominal assessment; it is usually included automatically as a routine postop assessment. You would activate abdominal assessments on the patient's PI screen for any patient having surgery, likely under the heading "Assessments" or "Nursing Assessments."

peristalsis wavelike movements of the gastrointestinal tract that propel food and other contents along.

You may see a related order directing when the patient can resume a progressive diet that reads "clear fluids until BSP" (bowel sounds present) or something similar. BSP means the person's diet can progress to the next level when return of peristaltic action is evident.

GASTROINTESTINAL INTERVENTIONS

Enemas

An **enema** is the introduction of fluid to the lower bowel for the purpose of cleansing the bowel or to stimulate bowel function. Many patients have difficulty independently establishing bowel function after an operation. Almost routinely, doctors will order enemas approximately 72 hours postoperatively to stimulate bowel function if the patient is unable to have a bowel movement even with the aid of a laxative. Enemas are also sometimes used instead of or along with a laxative to prepare for bowel surgery and certain diagnostic tests (such as a colonoscopy or barium enema) for which an empty bowel is necessary. Doctors can order several types of enemas.

enema the introduction of liquid into the rectum for cleansing the bowel and for stimulating evacuation of the bowels.

Fleet Enema A Fleet enema contains a balanced solution in a disposable container that is instilled into the lower bowel. Fleet enemas are small, effective, and convenient. A variety of solutions are used, each with a specific action. The solution may contain bisacodyl or sodium phosphate, both of which are bowel stimulants. The solutions are hypertonic and draw water into the bowel, softening fecal material. Many standard postoperative orders contain an order for a Fleet enema. An order might read, "Fleet enema PRN on 3rd postoperative day." PRN means "as needed" and, in this case, would refer to whether or not the patient has had a bowel movement.

Tap Water Enema A tap water enema (TWE), also referred to as a large volume enema, is more "heavy duty" than some of the other enemas. It involves instilling 500 to 1000 cc of tap water into the lower bowel, sometimes higher than the sigmoid colon. Kits used can either be disposable or reusable. A TWE is used as an intervention for constipation and for a bowel prep for diagnostic procedures or bowel surgery. A TWE can be quite uncomfortable for the patient, causing cramping. TWEs are not ordered as much as they were in the past.

Figure 19.1 Fleet enema

Small Volume Enema   This is the same procedure as that used for a TWE, but a smaller volume of fluid is introduced (around 100 cc) see Figure 19.1 Fleet Enema. It is suitable for evacuating the lower bowel and is primarily used for constipation.

If a doctor wants a very thorough cleansing of the bowel, he or she might order enemas until the returns are clear. This means that the nurses would repeat the enema until the liquid expelled from the rectum is clear, with no stool. This is very uncomfortable and can be energy draining, especially for an old or very ill person.

An enema order might be worded in one of the following ways:

Fleet enema 3rd postop day PRN

TWE 2nd postop day

TWE until clear

Oil Retention Enema   This enema instills approximately 100 cc of a mixture with an oil base into the bowel. It is used in constipated patients and is effective in softening hard stool that may be sitting in the lower bowel.

Transcribing Enema Orders   Orders for enemas are added either electronically to the PI screen (or simply activated if already listed) under "Nursing Interventions," "Assessments," or the equivalent.

Layouts for PI screens vary. If the doctor has ordered an enema to be given on a certain day, it is important to add that date beside where you either recorded or activated the intervention. For example, if the doctor ordered, "Fleet enema 3rd postop day PRN," and the surgery took place on February 16, you would add February 19 as the day on which the enema was to be given. This makes it easier for the nurses to keep track of when to give the enema. The day of surgery is always counted as Day 0, so February 17 is Day 1 (the first day postop), and February 19 is Day 3. On a PI screen, this order would be under such a heading as "Procedures" or "Nursing Interventions."

Suppositories

Rectal suppositories may be ordered to facilitate bowel evacuation. They may soften the stool in the rectum, promote rectal distension by releasing gas, or stimulate nerves in the rectal mucosa, thus promoting evacuation of the bowel. Suppositories are also used as a route to administer medication; medications commonly administered this way include Aspirin, dimenhydrinate (Gravol), or Indocid.

Transcribing Suppository Orders   A suppository may be ordered as follows:

Glycerin supp. PRN

or

Gravol suppository 50 mg for nausea q4h PRN (an order for Gravol may include a range of routes: Gravol 50–100 mg PO, IM, or suppository)

If the patient is vomiting, the nurses would consider an injection or a suppository. Sometimes Gravol is mixed in with an analgesic such as Demerol given intramuscularly (if the patient is not on a pain pump, which is also called patient-controlled analgesia).

Transcribe the order exactly as it is written. If the suppository is a medication, a specific dose *must* be noted. In most facilities, suppositories (other than glycerin) are considered a medication and recorded on the appropriate medication administration record (MAR or eMAR).

L03 L04 L05 ORDERS RELATING TO GI SURGERY AND PROCEDURES

If a patient has had GI surgery, the nurses must assess and monitor a number of things closely, ranging from the incision site to the status and progress of GI function, including the return of normal motility and normal elimination patterns. Some of the more common GI surgeries you will deal with if you are working on a surgical unit are outlined below. Any type of surgery resulting in a large incision or clips (or sutures) requires careful assessment by the nurse. Your responsibilities include checking that orders for assessment and intervention are properly transcribed or, in the CPOE environment, that they are correctly transcribed and amended as necessary.

Bowel Resection, Colostomy, and Ileostomy

A **bowel resection** and *anastomosis* (may also be called *end-to-end anastomosis*) involves removing a section of the bowel and connecting the healthy ends together again. This can occur anywhere along the large or small bowel. If the surgery is straightforward, the patient will have an abdominal incision as described previously. If the bowel cannot be reconnected to the rectal portion because it is diseased or because of widespread cancer, a **colostomy** or an **ileostomy** will be created. This is a procedure where the end of the bowel is brought out to the abdomen and a **stoma**, or artificial opening, is created, through which feces are excreted (see Figure 19.2). A colostomy involves the colon or

bowel resection surgery where a section of bowel is removed and the remaining bowel is reconnected.

colostomy a surgical procedure that creates an artificial opening from the colon to the surface of the abdomen through which feces are excreted.

ileostomy a surgical procedure that creates an artificial opening from the ileum to the surface of abdomen through which feces are excreted.

stoma an artificial opening; in this case, one from the bowel through the abdominal wall.

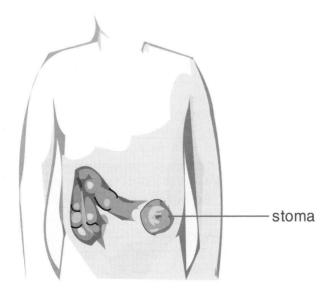

stoma

Figure 19.2 A stoma

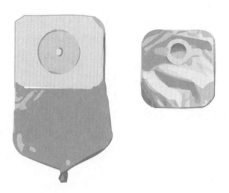

Figure 19.3 Ostomy bag and wafer

large bowel; an ileostomy involves the ileum or distal small bowel. In the case of a colostomy, the fecal matter has been largely processed and a formed stool is produced; in the case of an ileostomy, fluid has not been absorbed, and the result is an almost continuous drainage of loose fecal matter.

Nurses must carefully monitor the stoma as it heals for signs of infection or skin breakdown around the stoma site. A variety of ostomy supplies are used to facilitate healing of the stoma and ongoing management of the colostomy or ileostomy. These include disposable or reusable bags, shown in Figure 19.3, that collect the waste. They are attached with "wafers," devices that fit around the stoma. The wafers have an adhesive back and stick to the abdomen, forming a seal around the stoma. The ostomy bag attaches to the wafer, also forming a seal. Doctor's orders do not usually refer to ostomy supplies, but a nurse may ask you to order them.

Patients who have a colostomy or ileostomy require a tremendous amount of emotional support as well as health teaching to deal with what has happened to them.

Bowel Irrigations   Bowel irrigation may be ordered if a patient with a colostomy is having difficulty passing stool. It is based on the same principle as an enema or an evacuation suppository. Fluid is introduced into the bowel through an irrigation tube placed into the stoma. Bowel irrigation trays or kits are available from central supply.

Nasogastric Suction

Nasogastric (N/G) suction involves inserting a tube through the nose into the stomach. It is often connected to an electric suction device to gently remove solids, liquids, or gases from the stomach. It is usually a short-term measure. An N/G tube may also be inserted to obtain a sample of gastric contents and then removed. Figure 19.4 shows a patient with an N/G tube with a nurse extracting gastric contents.

Following surgery on the GI tract or related organs (e.g., removal of the gallbladder through a large incision [called an open cholecystectomy], a gastrectomy, or bowel resection), N/G suction is frequently necessary to rest the stomach and the bowel and allow it to heal. It may also be ordered to relieve excessive nausea and vomiting. In some instances, N/G suction is initiated to empty the stomach prior to gastric surgery. Suction may also be ordered as a conservative treatment to decompress the stomach or small intestine when a **bowel obstruction** is suspected.

Various suction machines are available, most of which are portable units brought to the patient's room. A popular device is the Gomco machine (illustrated in Figure 19.5), an electric pump that gives intermittent suction by varying the air pressure. Red and green lights flash as the pressure changes, indicating that the suction is working. There

bowel obstruction a blockage in the intestines that prevents their contents from moving forward.

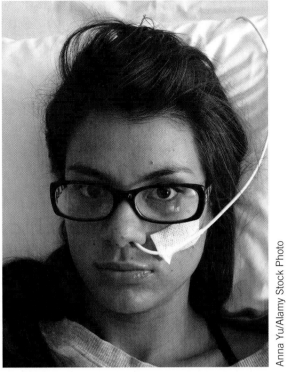

Anna Yu/Alamy Stock Photo

Figure 19.4 Patient with a nasogastric tube

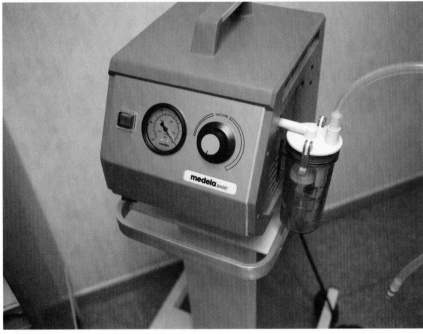

Rob Walls/Alamy Stock Photo

Figure 19.5 Gomco suction machine

is also a switch for high and low suction (the high setting is rarely used). If the doctor's order does not specify, low suction is assumed.

The gastric material is collected in a drainage bottle, which must be monitored and emptied appropriately. Nurses must record all drainages. Some facilities leave space for this at the bottom of the vital signs graph. Others record the data as output under "Tubes and Drains" on a fluid balance sheet. In the electronic environment, nurses usually enter it on an electronic fluid balance document.

If a Gomco suction or any other type of suction unit is required, you may be responsible for ordering it from central supply. Nasogastric (Levine) tubes are usually kept in the clean utility room. If none of the correct size is available, the nurses may ask you to order one from central supply (or the equivalent). If they need it immediately, phone and arrange to pick it up or have it sent up. The lift or dumbwaiter could be used for this purpose. As discussed in Chapter 18, N/G tubes come in a variety of sizes. The most common sizes used for N/G suction in adults are 16 or 19 Fr. The physician may not order a specific size, leaving it up to the nurses' judgment. When you phone central supply, specify the type and size of tube you need.

Another type of tube, a sump tube, may be used for gastric lavage.

Suction Orders   Doctors ordering suction may be specific about the type or may leave the details to be assumed. A doctor may order "Insert N/G tube to Gomco suction." Using suction with an N/G tube is almost always low, intermittent suction, so the doctor may simply order "Gomco suction." Or he or she may not even specify the type, but just order "N/G suction." In this case, you would assume that the doctor wants whatever type of suction is most commonly used in your facility. If the nurses are unclear about the type of suction or pattern of suction wanted, they can ask the doctor for clarification.

As with other intervention orders, suction orders are appropriately transcribed to the PI screen. In the CPOE environment, you may be responsible for ensuring the order is inactivated once it is discontinued.

Most often following surgery, the N/G tube is inserted in the operating room, in which case there may be no related insertion orders. The order may say "N/G suction to straight drainage," indicating that it is already in place. This would be transcribed in the same manner onto the PI screen along with any assessments. Orders to remove an N/G tube are often included in the postop orders (e.g., "Remove N/G tube when drainage less than 100 cc/shift"). This means that when the fluid from the GI tract in the Gomco suction container is less than 100 cc in an eight-hour shift, the nurses can remove the tube and discontinue the suction. Alternatively, the doctor will assess the patient daily and order the suction removed when he or she deems it appropriate.

If an N/G tube becomes plugged, it must be irrigated with normal saline to clear the obstruction. The nurse detaches the N/G tube from the tube leading to the suction machine and, with a large syringe, instills a measured amount of saline or water into the tube leading into the patient's stomach. The nurse either withdraws the fluid with the syringe or simply reconnects the N/G tube to the suction machine; the fluid then drains into the large bottle at the other end of the suction tubing. The nurses may keep a tray at the patient's bedside containing the apparatus needed to irrigate or flush the tubing. *They may ask you to order an irrigation tray.* It is important to specify the type of irrigation tray needed; a bladder irrigation tray, for example, is quite different from an N/G irrigation tray.

The Surgical Incision

Following abdominal surgery, or surgery of any kind where an incision is involved, the nurses must keep a close eye on the dressing and the incision to ensure the wound is healing properly. There is always the potential for bleeding, especially soon after surgery, and for infection to develop as time progresses. The type of dressing placed on the incision when the patient returns from the operating room will depend on the type, extent, and location of the surgery. Larger incision lines usually have a heavier dressing, ranging from layers of gauze bandages and other surgical dressings (sometimes called ABD, or abdominal pads) to a much lighter long strip dressing or a clear overlay (e.g., Tegaderm). Regardless, the physician usually orders the dressing changed at some point after surgery. Larger, bulky dressings are often reduced first, usually on the second or third postop day. The order would read "Reduce dressing in 72 hours" (or 48 hours).

Reducing a dressing means the nurse would remove the bully original dressing and replace it with a smaller dressing. *Be sure to add dates to such orders*; the day of surgery is counted as the surgical day, and the next day is Day 1. For example, if the surgery was on March 1, that is the surgical day. For the order instructing the nurse to reduce the dressing in 72 hours, March 4 would be the date that should appear on the PI screen prompting the nurses to reduce the dressing that day.

All incision sites are assessed, and in many cases they are changed daily. Related order sets should address dressing changes as well as clip/suture removal. Clips are like small staples, and sutures (also called stitches) are made of some type of thread. Both are used to close an incision. Usually sutures or clips are removed within five to seven days of surgery (unless there are complications, such as an infected incision line).

Sometimes a doctor will order that some of the clips or sutures be removed at first to be sure the incision is healing properly. The order might read "Remove alternate clips Day 4, and remaining clips Day 5," or "Remove clips/sutures Day 7." Again, be sure your dates are accurate when processing this order. In the CPOE environment, be sure to check the dates on these processed orders. Although it is also up to the nurses to check the dates before they carry out the procedure, ensuring that the correct dates are on the patient's eChart may prevent an error.

Often, patients are discharged from hospital before their clips or sutures are removed. As part of the patient's discharge planning, you must be sure an appointment is made for the patient to return to see the doctor to have this done, or arrangements are made with a community agency for a nurse to visit the patient for this purpose.

L06 THE GENITOURINARY SYSTEM

The genitourinary system refers to the male and female reproductive systems and the urinary system. The focus in this section of the chapter is on the urinary system. Assessments and interventions related to the reproductive systems are similar to those discussed throughout this chapter. For example, surgery on the reproductive system (e.g., a hysterectomy or Caesarian section) results in an incision with the same assessment, treatments, and interventions as any abdominal incision. Because female reproductive organs (the uterus, ovaries, and fallopian tubes) are in close proximity to the bowel and the bladder, similar routine assessments apply.

Urinary function is monitored, particularly intake and output (I &O), in patients admitted with related conditions such as kidney stones, kidney infections (e.g., pyelonephritis), urinary tract infections, cancer, and in most postop patients, especially those who have had a general anesthetic. Surgery on the uterus or the prostate gland often affects urinary function because of their close proximity (and thus a risk of damage) to the bladder and related structures. Patients who have had surgery on the urinary or reproductive systems will be given closer attention.

Failure to eliminate body waste (fluids) adequately results in a number of problems, including fluid retention. This could affect the heart and cardiovascular system or cause a buildup of toxic wastes in the person's body. It also causes edema—swelling of body parts, such as the legs and ankles, because of retained fluid. Sometimes the bladder itself can be problematic; for example, if the person is unable to urinate (the technical term is *maturate*), the bladder can become too full. A person's bladder can become so overstretched that it becomes *hypotonic*, meaning it loses its tone or strength and the person must be catherized. Conversely, someone who excretes more than he or she takes in will become dehydrated, which leads to a number of different issues.

If there are any concerns regarding fluid balance in any patient, a physician will order monitoring of intake and output. As discussed in Chapter 17, this is usually automatic in most cases when a patient has an IV. The values are entered by the nurse onto the patient's PI screen and the daily totals are automatically calculated. Too little or too much urinary output requires physician intervention.

Urinary Conditions and Related Procedures

The following are some conditions patients will present with in the hospital setting. Knowing a little about these conditions will help you understand the related tests, assessments, and interventions you will be dealing with in your role as clinical secretary.

Urinary Tract Infection (UTI)   Bacterial infections of the urinary tract are common and involve a number of pathogens, including intestinal *Escherichia coli*. Infections can occur anywhere in the urinary tract, including the kidneys, but most occur in the lower tract. Especially common is cystitis, an infection of the bladder. Kidney infections may be treated aggressively with IV antibiotics. For UTIs, a doctor will often order mid-stream urine (MSU) or a clean-catch specimen (see Chapter 6)—usually immediately and, when the results come back, will start the patient on an antibiotic. The order would read "MSU stat."

If the patient is in great discomfort, the doctor may prescribe the antibiotic before getting the results, making an educated guess; when the results come back, he or she will change the medication if the results show that the causative organism is resistant to the antibiotic prescribed for the patient. That order would read "MSU stat, then start … (the doctor will leave instructions for the antibiotic)." As discussed in Chapter 16, the medication order would be processed by the pharmacy, and the drug dispensed accordingly.

You would process the order for the MSU. If the patient is already on an antibiotic, it is important to state which antibiotic on the electronic lab requisition form (usually a window will appear prompting you to enter that information). This is because any antibiotic the patient is on may affect the results of the MSU. The doctor may also order "push fluids" (meaning the patient is encouraged to drink a lot) to flush the kidneys. See Figure 19.6 for typical orders.

It is important to note that you may be asked to take the MSU specimen to the laboratory's microbiology department. The specimen sample must be refrigerated for sterility; if you take a specimen to the lab after hours, leave it in the refrigerator, *not on a counter*. Specimens for routine and micro do not require refrigeration.

Timed urine testing includes 24-hour urine collection, which is used to assess kidney function. The collection must be added to a bottle containing a special solution, an

				Daryl Dark
	MSU stat; then start Amoxil 1 g stat and 500 mg po qid			123 Duncan St. Stratford ON N5A 2G3
	Push fluids			M 22 09 47 071608
	Strain all urine			3238494232
date *Jan 2/xx*	time *1000*	Physician's printed name Dr. G. Hanson	Signature *Dr. G. Hanson*	**Dr. G. Hanson**

Figure 19.6   Doctor's orders for a patient with a UTI and suspected kidney stone

opaque bottle, or refrigerated (or a combination thereof). Call the lab to make sure the correct bottle is on the floor for the patient to begin the collection. Ensure that the bottle(s) are properly labelled and kept according to test requirements.

Kidney Stones

A person may or may not be admitted to hospital with **kidney stones or calculi**. Patients with this condition are more often diagnosed and treated on an outpatient basis. If the person is hospitalized, it may be because of contributing factors or the person is too frail to be treated as an outpatient.

Kidney stones result from the buildup of crystallized salts and minerals, such as calcium, in the urinary tract. Stones, also called *calculi*, can also form after an infection. If large enough to block the kidney or ureter, they can cause severe pain in the middle and lower back, radiating around into the abdomen and groin. Although the process can be quite painful, the stones often pass through the urinary tract on their own. In some cases, they may need to be removed surgically. Patients admitted with a diagnosis of suspected kidney stones may have an order written to strain all of the urine to see if the stones have been passed—which may also be confirmed by X-ray, by ultrasound, or by the pain subsiding. Transcribe this order into the "Interventions" or "Assessments" section of the PI screen. The patient is given a filter to strain all his or her urine for the presence of kidney stones. A commonly used filter resembles a large cone-shaped coffee filter. These filters are obtained from central supply.

kidney stones or calculi hard objects built up from salts and minerals in the urinary tract.

Cancer of the Bladder

Nearly all cancers of the bladder start in the layer of cells that form the lining of the bladder. Different types of cancer can behave in different ways. For example, it may occur as a small, wart-like growth on the inside of the bladder, which can be removed in a simple operation and is unlikely to recur. Sometimes, it can form a large growth in the muscle wall of the bladder, which requires more aggressive treatment. This may include systemic chemotherapy, surgery, or any combination thereof.

Cystectomy

If a tumour is too large to be removed using a **cystoscope**, it may be necessary to remove all or part of the bladder, an operation called a **cystectomy**. A new storage place for urine will need to be created. If part of the bladder is removed, the operation is called a *partial cystectomy*. Patients who have had a partial cystectomy can void as usual, but their bladder will obviously be smaller and thus able to hold less urine than previously.

cystoscope a long, thin, flexible instrument with a light at the end used to examine the bladder. It is inserted through the urethra and threaded up into the bladder.

cystectomy surgical removal of the urinary bladder.

Urostomy

The most common way of providing a new storage place for urine is to form a *urostomy*, or the creation of an artificial opening. This involves using a segment of the small bowel, joining the two ureters to one end of it, and bringing the other end out to the abdomen, creating an artificial opening. An ileal conduit is created when a piece of bowel (ileum) creates a channel to drain the urine from the ureters to the new opening, or stoma, on the abdominal surface. The urine drains into a bag in a process similar to that used for colostomies and ileostomies. Sometimes a sac to store the urine is created using part of the bowel. This sac is drained periodically with a catheter so that the person does not have to wear a drainage bag.

L07 URINARY CATHETERS

Catheterization is one of the most common interventions ordered for the patient who has problems passing or retaining urine. Catheterization is the insertion of a flexible tube into the bladder. This is done under sterile conditions and drains the urine that is in the bladder. It can be put in and left for a designated period of time or inserted and removed as soon as the bladder has been drained. The majority of patients who have a catheter will either have their fluid intake and output measured (ordered as "I&O" or "strict I&O") or just their urinary output measured (ordered as "output only").

Reasons for Catheterization

Catheterization is used to

- empty the bladder in case of urinary retention;
- obtain a sterile urine specimen;
- manage extreme urinary incontinence, as a last resort;
- rest the bladder following surgery on genitourinary structures; or
- manage urinary function postoperatively.

Urinary Retention   A patient may be unable to pass urine for a number of reasons, including disease, trauma resulting from surgery on the bladder or related structures, or lack of sensation and muscle tone from the anesthetic used in surgery.

Obtaining a Sterile Urine Specimen   If a sterile urine specimen cannot be obtained by other means or if it is important that the specimen be absolutely sterile, the physician may order a catheter to obtain a specimen directly from the bladder.

TIP

If you are asked to take a urine specimen for culture and sensitivity to the lab, do so immediately. Or, if you see a specimen sitting at the desk, check to see if someone is looking after transporting it to the lab or put it in the refrigerator. If the specimen is left unrefrigerated, it will grow bacteria and potentially invalidate the results of the culture.

incontinence the inability to control urine elimination (urinary incontinence) or bowel function (referred to as *incontinent of bowel*).

Managing Urinary Incontinence   In some circumstances, **incontinence** is managed by inserting a catheter. Urinary incontinence may result from trauma to the bladder or the urethra, altered states of consciousness, or nerve damage caused by stroke, paralysis, or disease. Some patients can learn to insert a catheter several times a day to empty their own bladders. Infection is always a concern any time a catheter is inserted but seems to be less of an issue when patients self-catheterize at home.

TIP

When a catheter is ordered for a patient, the nurse must insert it under sterile conditions. Know the types of catheters, their sizes, and where they are kept on your unit. If the nurse contaminates the catheter when inserting it, he or she may ask you to bring down another (packaged) catheter.

Postoperative Management   A general anesthetic may suppress the sensation or urge to urinate or affect the tone of the bladder muscle. Postoperative orders generally address bladder function (see Chapter 16). To avoid bladder distension, most physicians want the patient catheterized if he or she is unable to void within eight hours postoperatively. Even if the patient is not taking fluids, he or she may be receiving continuous fluids by IV, which can quickly fill the bladder.

Types of Catheters

There are a variety of catheters on the market, each with a purpose. They come in a range of sizes, rated according to the same French scale used for N/G tubes. The higher the number, the larger is the catheter. Typical adult sizes are 14 or 16 Fr.

Indwelling or Retention Catheter An **indwelling** or retention catheter is one that is inserted and kept in place for a period of time. It is attached to a disposable drainage tube and bag, forming a closed, sterile system. The most commonly used is the Foley catheter (named after the physician who invented the catheter), which has two lumina, or channels. One channel is for urine; the other is used for inflating a small balloon that sits in the bladder and keeps the tube from falling out. Once the catheter is inserted into the bladder, the balloon is inflated by using a syringe to inject air, sterile water, or normal saline through a small resealable port at the distal end of the second channel of the catheter. The collection tube attached to the catheter has a clamp on it that can be closed off to prevent the urine from draining from the bladder into the bag (see Figure 19.7).

indwelling left in place.

Nonretention or Straight Catheter A **nonretention or straight catheter** (also called a *red rubber catheter* to describe a common type) is inserted into the bladder to drain the urine and then removed. It is suitable for specimen collection. It does not have an inflatable bulb.

nonretention or straight catheter one that is inserted to drain urine and then removed.

Suprapubic Catheters Suprapubic catheters are inserted under general or local anesthesia through an incision made in the lower abdominal wall and into the bladder. There is a balloon inflated to keep the catheter in place, as with an indwelling Foley catheter. Suprapubic catheters pose less danger of infection than those inserted through the urethra and allow the patient more mobility.

Three-Way Catheters When bladder irrigation (discussed later) is needed, it is done with a three-way catheter, which has the two channels of a Foley catheter, plus a third channel leading to a sterile irrigation solution.

Cudet Catheter When a nurse cannot insert a Foley catheter, especially in men, the doctor may order a Cudet catheter. This device has a curve on the tip that facilitates passage through the urethra, under the prostate, and into the bladder.

Condom Catheters When inserting a catheter through a man's urethra is contraindicated, a condom catheter may be used. This is an external device much like a condom that fits over the penis. It has a drainage tube attached to a closed urine drainage system.

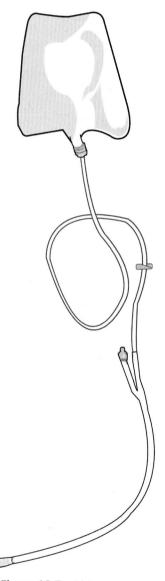

Transcribing Catheter Orders

Orders for catheterization might be worded in any of the following ways:

Catheterize if unable to void 8 h postop

Catheterize PRN postoperatively

Indwelling Foley catheter if unable to void

Indwelling Foley to straight drainage if unable to void

Note that the doctor specifies when to catheterize only in the first example. Often, doctors leave the timing to the nurses. They will assess the patient for bladder distension and discomfort, and also keep in mind the eight-hour norm. The last two examples specify an indwelling Foley catheter. The first two do not specify, but it is assumed that the catheter is indwelling. If the doctor wants a straight catheter, he or she will specify so. "To straight drainage," specified in the final example, means that the drainage system is left attached so that the bladder drains continually. This, too, would be assumed if not specified.

After surgery, trauma, or long-term catheter use, people may have trouble regaining bladder tone and, thus, completely emptying the bladder. To stimulate normal

Figure 19.7 Urine drainage bag and tube attached to the Foley catheter

bladder function and retrain the bladder, the doctor may order that the catheter be clamped for a period and then opened.

Catheter orders are transcribed to the PI screen under "Elimination" or under "Tubes and Drains."

Some patients come back from the operating room with an indwelling catheter already in place, particularly if they have had major surgery or bladder surgery. In this case, the doctor's orders would address when to remove the catheter. Orders might read "Remove catheter on 3rd postop day" or "On 2nd postop day start clamping and unclamping catheter q4h."

Transcribe the order to the PI screen, probably under "Elimination," as it is written. If the order states a particular day for the removal of the catheter, calculate when that would be and insert the date.

Residual Urine

Residual urine is urine left in the bladder after voiding. Sometimes, especially after bladder surgery, the bladder does not empty completely, which can lead to infection. To find out how much urine is left in the bladder, the physician will order catheterization after the patient has voided. If the residual urine exceeds a certain volume (typically 50 or 100 cc), the physician might order the catheter to be reinserted and left in place. A physician becomes concerned if the amount of urine remaining in the bladder is more than 50 to 100 cc. An order might read "On the 4th postop day, catheterize for residual urine. If more than 50 cc, leave catheter in to straight drainage." This order would be transcribed onto the PI screen.

Bladder Irrigation

Postoperative   Following surgery on the bladder, prostate, or urethra, it may be necessary to remove blood and debris by irrigating or flushing the bladder with a sterile solution, usually normal saline. After surgery on the bladder or, for men, on the prostate gland, a certain amount of bleeding occurs in the bladder and related structures. Blood clots often plug the catheter, preventing the urine from draining. Irrigating or flushing the catheter tubing restores drainage. Continuous bladder irrigation may be ordered; this is a closed, sterile system, usually using a three-way catheter. When a three-way catheter is required, it is almost always inserted in the operating room. Irrigation may also be ordered in one of the following ways: "Irrigate bladder PRN to keep free from clots" or "Irrigate bladder PRN." This order would be transcribed onto the PI screen under "Elimination" or "Additional Nursing Care."

For Treatments   Sometimes a physician orders bladder irrigation with a specific solution, such as an antiseptic solution, to treat a bladder infection or a chemotherapeutic medication to treat a bladder tumour. A catheter is inserted into the bladder, and the irrigating solution is introduced through the catheter. For this type of irrigation, a two-way Foley catheter is often used. The doctor's order identifies the frequency of the irrigation and the type, amount, and strength of the solution. This may be done over several hours and the catheter removed until the next treatment, or the catheter may be left in place.

SUMMARY

1. Altered gastrointestinal (GI) function often signals the onset of illness or a disease process, ranging from the flu to ulcers or cancer. Some conditions can be treated conservatively; others require surgical intervention. Some conditions are diagnosed through tests, such as a colonoscopy or an esophagogastroduodenoscopy (EGD). An endoscopic retrograde cholangiopancreatography (ERCP) is used to diagnose and treat conditions of the pancreas or bile ducts. Biopsies can be performed during any of these tests.

2. Anesthetics and manipulation of the GI tract during surgery can immobilize the bowel, necessitating frequent assessments for the return of bowel sounds, which indicate the ability of the GI system to process and eliminate food. The depth, type, and frequency of assessment depend on the patient's condition. Bowel evacuation using suppositories or enemas is an important intervention required prior to bowel surgery. These assessments are recorder appropriately on the PI screen.

3. Patients who have diseases of the GI tract, including advanced inflammatory bowel disease or cancer, may have to have a section of the bowel removed; they may then need a colostomy or an ileostomy, which creates an artificial opening called a stoma through the abdominal wall as an alternative means of evacuating the bowel. Nurses must monitor how the stoma is healing and offer the patient support as well as health teaching, such as how to care for the stoma using a variety of ostomy supplies. A bowel irrigation is sometimes necessary if constipation occurs.

4. Nasogastric (N/G) suction is used for several reasons, including resting the bowel after surgery. This is most often accomplished by inserting a tube through the patient's nose into the stomach. The tube is attached to a drainage system and a suction machine. Orders relating to N/G suction are transcribed to the PI screen.

5. A surgical incision requires nursing assessments to ensure the wound is healing without the presence of infection. Physicians will sometimes order a larger, bulky dressing be reduced on the second or third postop day (the day of surgery does not count). Likewise, the removal of clips or sutures are usually ordered in a similar format (e.g., "Remove alternate clips on Day 5 and remaining clips on Day 7"). Be sure to add the correct date beside the order when you transcribe it to the patient's chart.

6. Urinary function is monitored for patients with urinary tract complaints and patients who have had surgery. Monitoring a patient's fluid balance (intake and output) is one of the most frequently ordered and most valuable assessments. Fluid retention can strain the cardiovascular system, causing edema and heart failure. Excessive loss of fluid can result in dehydration. Urinary infections can occur in any part of the urinary tract; the most common is in the bladder itself. A midstream urine (MSU) sample is ordered when a urinary tract infection is suspected and should be obtained before the patient is started on an antibiotic.

7. Catheterization is often ordered PRN postoperatively; if the patient cannot void within eight hours, the nurses will insert a catheter. Catheters are also ordered to relieve urinary retention, manage incontinence, and obtain a sterile urine sample. A variety of catheters are used, but the most common is an indwelling Foley catheter, which is left in for some time; a straight catheter is inserted to drain the bladder and then removed.

KEY TERMS

bowel obstruction   562

bowel resection   561

colonoscopy   558

colostomy   561

cystectomy   567

cystoscope   567

diverticulitis   558

endoscopic retrograde
   cholangiopancreato-
   graphy (ERCP)   558

enema   559

esophagogastroduoden-
   oscopy (EGD)   558

gastritis   558

ileostomy   561

incontinence   568

indwelling   569

kidney stones or calculi   567

nonretention or straight
   catheter   569

peristalsis   559

stoma   561

ulcerative colitis   558

REVIEW QUESTIONS

1. State the purpose of an abdominal assessment.

2. Under what heading(s) on the PI screen might an abdominal assessment be transcribed?

3. **a.** If a doctor orders a dressing reduced 72 hours post-surgery, how would you calculate the date to add to the PI screen?

   b. In the CPOE environment, what would be your responsibility related to this order?

4. On admission to the preadmit clinic, a patient tells you he has not carried his preoperative bowel routine out at home as requested. Why is this important information to be reported to the nurse?

5. How would you respond if a dietary aid delivering supper trays asks you if patient who is second day postop from a bowel resection can have a full diet tray?

6. Where would you transcribe a suppository ordered as "Gravol supp. 50 mg q4h for nausea"?

7. Why is it important to maintain an NPO sign above the bed of a patient on N/G suction?

8. Mrs. Fras is on strict intake and output. You are in her room talking with her about accommodation coverage, and she asks you to get her a glass of water. What would you do, and why?

9. A nurse is putting in an indwelling catheter; she contaminates the catheter and contacts you at the desk, asking you to bring her another one. Where would you get it, and what information is important to have before doing so?

10. Mr. Willis, who has a diagnosis of kidney stones, has been ordered to strain all urine. Why?

APPLICATION EXERCISES

1. Explain the following orders:

   a. Fleet PRN 3rd day postop

   b. Start N/G Gomco suction

   c. Insert #16 Foley to straight drainage

   d. Remove catheter 2nd postoperative day

   e. Obtain residual urine. Leave Foley in if more than 75 cc.

   f. Irrigate bladder PRN to remove clots

2. Transcribe the orders in Exercise 1 using the format outlined by your professor.

3. Research the etiology and most common diagnostic tests and treatments for colon cancer, Crohn's disease, or ulcerative colitis.

4. With another student, develop a teaching handout suitable for a patient who has just had a colostomy or ileostomy.

5. A patient is admitted for surgery related to cancer of the colon. He has been told that he may have to have a colostomy. With another student or in a small group, research the psychological impact this surgery may have on a patient and his or her partner. This will help you understand the impact such surgery has on a patient as well as their loved ones.

WEBSITES OF INTEREST

Canadian Cancer Society

www.cancer.ca

Crohn's and Colitis Canada

www.crohnsandcolitis.ca

Canadian Association of Gastroenterology

www.cag-acg.org

Chapter 20

Orders Related to Respiration and Circulation

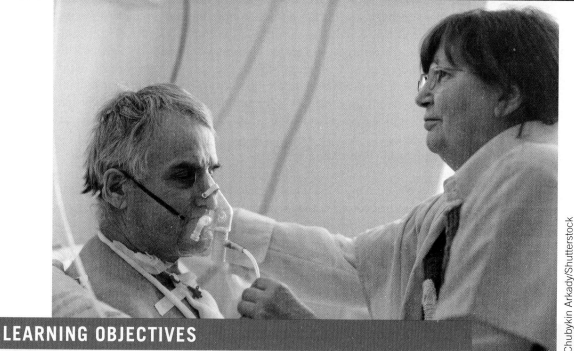

Chubykin Arkady/Shutterstock

LEARNING OBJECTIVES

On completing this chapter, you will be able to:

1. Discuss common cardiorespiratory conditions, considering causes and treatments.

2. Outline the roles and responsibilities of health professionals involved with respiratory problems.

3. Understand the interventions indicated for respiratory problems.

4. Describe diagnostic tests and procedures ordered for oxygen-compromised patients.

5. Discuss assessments and treatments related to the cardiovascular system.

6. Transcribe orders related to cardiorespiratory conditions.

7. Respond as indicated within your scope of practice to a cardiac or respiratory arrest.

Oxygenation is the process of providing the body with adequate amounts of oxygen. Adequate oxygenation depends on proper functioning primarily of the cardiovascular and respiratory systems (often referred to as the cardiorespiratory systems). Problems in any body system may affect oxygenation; conversely, inadequate oxygenation will affect every body system.

This chapter will familiarize you with conditions common to these systems and the related interventions for which you will be processing orders if you work on almost any unit in an acute-care hospital. Larger hospitals have specialized units for cardiac and respiratory problems—particularly for heart conditions. In many communities across Canada, there are designated hospitals specializing in certain categories of treatment such as cancer or cardiac (see Chapter 14). For example, in Kitchener/Waterloo, Ontario, St. Mary's General Hospital is the cardiac centre, but the Grand River Hospital is the cancer centre. That is not to say that other hospitals will not treat patients with heart problems or those who have cancer, but those requiring more specialized diagnosis and care would go to the designated centre.

Cardiac centres will have cardiology patient-care units for patients who have less acute conditions or are recovering from cardiac surgery. A telemetry unit (which monitors, for example, patients who have had a heart attack or who are admitted with a cardiac arrhythmia) may be part of or separate from a cardiac patient-care unit. As well, the facility will have acute-care areas, sometimes called a coronary care unit or CCU (much like an ICU—intensive care unit). Heart transplants are only done in hospitals with highly specialized physicians and care, usually associated with a university. Larger facilities may also have a specialized area for patients with respiratory conditions (e.g., a chest unit). Medium and smaller-sized hospitals will care for patients with cardiorespiratory conditions on a medical or surgical unit. Physicians attending to individuals with these conditions are usually cardiologists, internists, or respirologists.

It is recommended that you review the anatomy and physiology of the respiratory and cardiovascular systems; this will help you more clearly understand the related conditions and interventions you will be involved with during the order entry process, as well as other responsibilities that may fall within your scope of practice.

L01 CARDIORESPIRATORY CONDITIONS

Common cardiorespiratory conditions include arteriosclerosis, hypertension, myocardial infarction, congestive heart failure, stroke, pneumonia, asthma, and chronic obstructive pulmonary disease. The majority of hospitalized patients will present with one or more of these conditions. Understanding these conditions will help you recognize related interventions and prioritize your actions. **Arteriosclerosis** is commonly referred to as hardening of the arteries. Common causes of arteriosclerosis include age, high blood pressure, deposits of calcium, and deposits of fatty plaque in the inner artery walls. Arteriosclerosis causes the vessel walls to become less pliable, causing the heart to work harder to pump blood. **Atherosclerosis** is a narrowing of the arterial walls caused by fatty deposits.

arteriosclerosis hardening of the arteries; reduces blood flow.

atherosclerosis arteriosclerosis because of deposits of fat in arterial walls.

All of these conditions can narrow the arteries, reducing blood flow and leading to a risk of a blockage in the blood flow. Such a blockage may deprive the heart of oxygen, leading to a *myocardial infarct* (heart attack). Or it may cut off blood flow and, thus, oxygen to a part of the brain, leading to a stroke.

Myocardial Infarction

myocardial infarct (MI, heart attack, or coronary) damage to the heart caused by a blockage in one of the coronary arteries, cutting off blood supply to a part of the heart.

A **myocardial infarct** (or heart attack) occurs when part of the heart muscle is damaged or dies because it is not receiving oxygen. The majority of heart attacks are caused by a blockage in the coronary arteries, most often because of atherosclerosis. Signs of an impending heart attack vary widely. They may include complaints of crushing chest pain, which may or may not be accompanied by nausea, vomiting, or sweating. The pain may radiate to the jaw or left shoulder. Conversely, the patient may experience a sensation similar to that of heartburn or a feeling of tightness in the chest and shortness of breath (SOB). All hospital units have a **crash cart**, either on the unit or close by, which contains the essential tools and drugs to treat a heart attack. The cart is checked frequently (each shift in many hospitals) to ensure that it is fully stocked (this may be your responsibility). Someone would be assigned to bring the cart when responding to a call for an arrest.

> **crash cart** a cart carrying the supplies needed for immediate treatment of a heart attack.

Cerebral Vascular Accident

A **cerebral vascular accident (CVA)** is more commonly called a stroke and describes a sudden neurological event caused when a part of the brain is deprived of its blood supply. Strokes can result in temporary or permanent alteration in mental ability, speech, or use of part of the body. They affect the area of the body controlled by the part of the brain where the event occurred.

> **cerebral vascular accident (CVA)** (stroke) damage to the brain that occurs when the blood supply to an area of the brain is diminished or occluded completely.

Hypertension

Hypertension, or high blood pressure, means excessive force of blood against the walls of blood vessels as the heart pumps it through the body. Blood pressure is measured in two numbers: the top number, **systolic pressure**, measures the pressure on the vascular walls when the heart is contracting, and the bottom number, **diastolic pressure**, measures the pressure exerted on the vessels when the heart is relaxing. Optimal blood pressure in a healthy young adult is 120/80 or lower; anything over 140/90 is usually classified as hypertension. Hypertension is common, especially in older people. Obesity, stress, and excessive consumption of salt and fat can be contributing factors, along with genetic predisposition. Hypertension is often called a "silent killer" because the person may have no symptoms for years, until finally the hypertension leads to a heart attack or stroke.

> **hypertension** (high blood pressure) excessive force of the blood against the vessel walls as the heart pumps it through the body.
>
> **systolic pressure** the pressure on the vascular walls when the heart is contracting.
>
> **diastolic pressure** the pressure on the vascular walls when the heart is relaxing.

Congestive Heart Failure

A number of conditions cause **congestive heart failure (CHF)**, or heart failure, including hypertension, coronary heart disease, and a heart attack. In CHF, the heart becomes weakened and loses its ability to pump effectively, compromising the amount of oxygenated blood that circulates throughout the body. As the muscles of the heart continue to weaken, blood pools in the lungs and other parts of the body. Breathing is also compromised. Patients with CHF will often complain of dyspnea (difficulty breathing) when they are lying down; this improves when they elevate their head on two or more pillows, or sit up.

> **congestive heart failure (CHF)** a condition in which a weakened heart is unable to pump all of the blood out of the lungs each time it beats. Blood pools at the bottom of the lungs, interfering with breathing.

Cardiac Arrhythmias

The heart has a conduction system that regulates both the rate and the rhythm of the beat. Normal rhythm is called *sinus rhythm*. An irregular heartbeat is sometimes referred to as an **arrhythmia**. Although many types of arrhythmias cause no problems, others cause cardiopulmonary difficulties. The most common arrhythmia is a condition called **atrial fibrillation** (AF or atrial fib), in which the steady, rhythmic contractions of the atrial muscle are replaced by a rapid, irregular twitching that is not in synchrony with the ventricular contractions. The treatment of choice in most cases are drugs to slow and stabilize the heart, a pacemaker (to regulate the heartbeat), or anticoagulants to prevent stroke.

> **arrhythmia** loss of normal rhythm of the heartbeat.
>
> **atrial fibrillation** an abnormality of heart rhythm in which chambers of the heart no longer beat in synchrony, with the atrium beating much faster than the ventricles. The heart rate is fast and irregular.

Conditions that Affect Oxygenation

pneumonia an acute infection of the tissues of the lung.

Pneumonia is a lung infection that can be caused either by a virus or bacteria (streptococcus). It can be acquired in the hospital or in the community. Bacterial pneumonia is treated with antibiotics, which should only be prescribed after a sputum sample has determined the cause and which drug the bacteria is sensitive to. Viral pneumonia abates on its own, and the patient is treated symptomatically.

asthma a disease that affects the air passages in the lungs, causing wheezing and shortness of breath.

Asthma is a chronic disease of the upper airways that is often characterized by acute episodes. Asthma attacks can be trigged by airborne allergies, pollution, exercise, and respiratory infections. Causes are probably a combination of genetic and environmental factors. Treatment for asthma includes methods to prevent attacks as well as a broad selection of medications for both quick relief and long-term control (e.g., inhaled corticosteroids).

chronic obstructive pulmonary disease (COPD) any chronic lung condition in which the flow of expired air is slowed down.

Chronic obstructive pulmonary disease (COPD) is an umbrella term used to describe a variety of progressive lung diseases, including emphysema and chronic bronchitis. This disease is characterized by increasing breathlessness. Smoking is the leading cause of COPD, although air pollution, chemical fumes, or dust also may contribute.

HEALTH PROFESSIONALS INVOLVED WITH RESPIRATORY PROBLEMS

Respiratory problems are treated and assessed by a team that includes the physician, the respiratory therapist (RT), the nurse, and the physiotherapist. Although their work may overlap, most facilities use a coordinated team approach to carry out doctors' orders and provide feedback on patients' progress.

Registered Respiratory Therapists (RT)

RTs are responsible for the cardiorespiratory care of patients of all ages requiring both acute and chronic intervention in their disease. They may initiate, administer, and supervise treatments ordered by the doctor, respond to cardiac arrests, and supervise oxygen therapy devices, such as inhalation devices and respirators. They work closely with patients, family, and other health providers. Orders for respiratory testing would be sent to respiratory services.

Physiotherapists

Physiotherapists (sometimes referred to simply as "physio," a short form that also describes physiotherapy) provide respiratory assessments and related physiotherapy. When a doctor orders "chest physio," the physiotherapist assesses the patient, devises and helps with deep breathing exercises, and teaches him or her how to cough effectively to keep the lungs clear.

Nurses

Nursing staff provide ongoing assessment and feedback about a patient's oxygenation status. If an RT or physiotherapist is not available, a nurse can initiate and supervise chest physio or administer oxygen and inhalation treatments.

ROUTINE TREATMENTS AND RELATED ORDERS
Chest Physiotherapy

Chest physio is often ordered for patients with a buildup of secretions in the lungs. Techniques vary from routines that patients can do on their own to interventions provided by physiotherapists or nurses.

Deep Breathing and Coughing Exercises   Secretions in the lungs can become thick and difficult for the patient to cough up. If the secretions are left sitting in the lungs, they can become infected or exacerbate an already-present infection, further compromising the patient's breathing. Many patients can cough these secretions up by themselves if they are shown the proper technique. Either a physiotherapist or a nurse can teach the patient deep breathing and coughing exercises (DB&C), which should usually be done every two to three hours while awake. Often a physiotherapist and a nurse work together to ensure that the patient understands the exercises and performs them properly and regularly. A device called a spirometer (discussed later) may help the patient assess how effectively he or she is breathing and performing the exercises. Doctors often order DB&C for patients with respiratory difficulties.

Chest Physio with Postural Drainage   People with large amounts of mucus or thick secretions or who have weak breathing muscles or ineffective coughs may need more than DB&C to loosen and move the secretions out of the lungs. They may be helped by chest physio accompanied by **postural drainage**, that is, positioning the patient with his or her head lower than the body so that gravity can help move the secretions. The physiotherapist may also manually loosen stubborn chest secretions by **clapping or percussion**: using cupped hands to gently but firmly strike affected regions of the chest to move secretions to the bronchi, from where they can be coughed up more easily. The physiotherapist may also stimulate movement of secretions by placing flattened hands over the congested area and using rapid **vibrations**.

postural drainage positioning the patient with the head lower than the body so that gravity can help drain the mucus and secretions.

clapping or percussion using cupped hands to gently but firmly strike affected regions of the chest to move secretions.

vibrations rapid movements of flattened hands over the patient's chest to move secretions.

Orders for Chest Physiotherapy   When doctors order chest physio, orders may be more or less specific, as in the following examples:

Chest physio bid

Encourage DB&C exercises q2h while awake

Postural drainage by physio tid

Routine postop physio by physiotherapist

If the doctor orders simply "chest physio bid," the order implies a request for an assessment and development of an appropriate routine. Send a requisition (paper or electronic) to the physiotherapy department. Transcribe these orders to the PI screen, either under "Respiratory," "Treatments," or "Interventions."

A doctor might make a much more specific order, for example, "Encourage DB&C exercises q2h while awake." This order can be initiated and supervised by the physiotherapist or the nurse and does not require a requisition. On many surgical units, a physiotherapist routinely visits all postoperative patients, with or without an order, to implement these exercises, either routinely or if they are having trouble breathing. The physiotherapist may complete an initial assessment and run through the exercises with the patient once or twice. The nurses encourage the patient to continue with the exercises and complete chest assessments as per protocol. If sustained contact with the physiotherapist is required, usually an order and a requisition are necessary.

If a doctor orders "postural drainage by physio tid," this would require a requisition because it is more than the routine treatment. An order for tid would probably involve a morning–afternoon–evening routine or a morning–early afternoon–late afternoon routine. Add the times to the PI screen; typical times for this order would be 1000, 1400, and 1700; or 1000, 1600, and 2000. Alternatively, the physiotherapist may choose the hours of treatment based on his or her schedule. It is important, as with any treatments the patient is receiving, to ensure that you do not book other tests that would interfere with this treatment regime (or if you do, that you notify the physiotherapy department). If there is no physiotherapist on duty in the evening, the nurses would complete the postural drainage routine.

If the facility does not have physiotherapists to routinely assess postop patients, the nurses would recommend a physio consult if they deemed it necessary. A doctor may also order a consult, perhaps as "Routine postop physio by physiotherapist." The therapist will visit the patient, assess his or her needs, and implement a specific routine. If a formal request is made, send a requisition to the physiotherapy department. Physiotherapy is often part of a patient's discharge planning.

Nursing Assessment

Vital Signs/Respiratory Assessments   Respiratory rate is part of routine vital signs assessment (along with oximetry, temperature, and pulse), which is normally done at least once or twice a day (see Chapter 16). Nurses will also assess other characteristics of the patient's breathing, such as depth and regularity. Vital signs also provide an indication of the cardiac condition. Blood pressure is not always included in routine vital signs in many facilities. For example, vital signs may be ordered qid, and blood pressure only od. Vital signs are usually taken more frequently for postoperative patients until they are stable and for patients with abnormal vital signs, such as an elevated temperature, pulse, or respiratory rate, perhaps accompanied by **dyspnea**. Nurses may increase the frequency of vital signs within policy guidelines if their assessments indicate a problem, or the doctor may order a certain frequency. For example, a doctor may order one of the following:

dyspnea difficulty breathing.

V/S qid

V/S and BP qid

V/S q15 min × 4, q1/2h × 6, q1h × 8, and then qid if stable

In the last example, the doctor wants signs checked every 15 minutes for an hour, then every half-hour for three hours, followed by every hour for eight hours. After that, if the vital signs are stable, the nurses can reduce assessment to four times a day.

If the doctor is concerned about a patient's blood pressure or circulation, he or she may issue more specific orders for blood pressure assessments. For example, "Monitor BP in lying and sitting position in both arms bid." Here the doctor orders blood pressure to be read with the patient in two different positions to see if it changes with position. If so, the patient may be suffering postural hypotension, that is, an abnormally low blood pressure in certain positions. Taking blood pressure in both arms will identify compromised circulation on one side, for example, because of a narrowed artery.

Chest Assessments   In a chest assessment, a doctor, respiratory technician, or more usually a nurse assesses the patient's colour and ease of breathing and auscultates or listens to the patient's lungs through a stethoscope. If breath sounds are diminished or absent, that indicates impeded or diminished air exchange caused by conditions like pneumonia. Adventitious or extra sounds include **crepitation or crackles**, and **rhonchi or wheezes**. Crepitation sounds something like air blown through a straw immersed in fluid and usually indicates the presence of fluid in the small airways. Rhonchi can be high pitched or low pitched and are caused by air moving through airways narrowed by swelling or partial obstruction.

crepitation or crackles sounds produced by air passing over airway secretions.

rhonchi or wheezes musical-pitched sounds produced by air passing through narrowed bronchi, heard on auscultation of the lungs.

Chest assessments are routine for postoperative patients and for those with cardio-respiratory problems. The physician may order a chest assessment at specific intervals or may rely on hospital routines. A respiratory unit might have qid as routine, whereas an orthopedic unit might have bid or od as routine. Postoperative chest assessments range from bid to qid and decrease as the patient recovers. Transcribe the order to the PI screen under "Oxygenation" or "Nursing Assessments/Interventions" and add the times; for assessments od, you would probably record the time as 1000. No requisition is required.

Diagnostic Tests, Procedures, and Related Orders

Pulse Oximetry Pulse oximetry is a method used by nurses and respiratory therapists to determine oxygen levels in red blood cells in the arterial blood. A pulse oximeter, shown in Figure 20.1, is a sensor that can be attached to the patient's finger, toe, or sometimes the earlobe. The measurement is reported as arterial blood oxygen saturation (SaO_2 or O_2 Sat). Normal adult SaO_2 values should be at least 95 percent.

Patients are monitored with pulse oximetry after surgery, during surgical and diagnostic procedures, and when there is a concern about oxygenation. Monitoring may be continuous, or oximetry levels may be read at specific times. In orders, oximetry is abbreviated to "ox," and saturation levels to "sats." Thus, doctors may write an order in any of the following ways (although pulse oximetry is now routinely measured along with vital signs in most acute-care hospitals):

Pulse ox tid

O_2 sats bid

Monitor pulse ox for 8 hours

Oximetry qid

Transcribe the orders to the PI screen. Some facilities want frequency translated into specific times.

Arterial Blood Gases An arterial blood gas assessment is done on a patient to determine the amounts of oxygen and carbon dioxide dissolved in the blood. The test

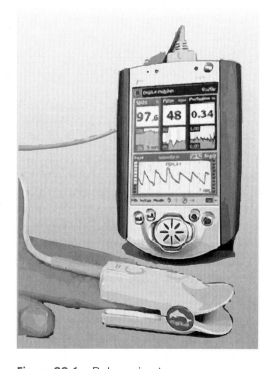

Figure 20.1 Pulse oximeter

TABLE 20.1 Laboratory results for arterial blood gases

Test	Explanation	Normal Values
O$_2$	Saturation percentage of arterial hemoglobin carrying oxygen	95%–98%
PO$_2$	Partial pressure of oxygen in the blood	80–100 mm Hg
PCO$_2$	Partial pressure of carbon dioxide in the blood	38–42 mm Hg
HCO	Related to the pH of the blood	24–18 mEq/L
Ph	Acid/base measurement of the blood	7.35–7.45

also calculates the blood's pH, or acid/base balance. Table 20.1 shows the categories of results and normal ranges. These measures indicate how well the person's blood is being oxygenated and thus the patient's respiratory status. The test helps physicians monitor the effects of oxygen therapy and respirator management.

Blood gases are usually ordered as "ABGs." Usually this is a stat order. The sample must be arterial and is a little more complex to take than a routine blood sample. The physician, respiratory therapist, or specially trained nurse collects the blood. If the order is stat and the patient is on the patient-care unit when the blood is drawn, prepare and keep the requisition on the floor (as with any stat lab order). If using a manual system, label the requisition and set it aside for the nurse, RT, or physician. In a computerized environment, select the option of printing the sample label in the unit instead of in the laboratory. The request will be sent electronically to the lab for their records. Depending on where you are working, you will have to call respiratory services if an RT is going to draw the blood. In a larger teaching hospital, you may have to page the appropriate resident or intern. You may have to call the lab to bring the required equipment to draw and store the blood sample.

The lab usually phones the results to the patient-care unit or faxes the results to the floor. As with any lab test, read back the values to ensure accuracy, and verify the patient's name and hospital number. Report the results to the physician immediately, especially if the physician has asked you to do so, if the order is stat, or if the results are not within normal limits. In most cases, the physician will want you to report the results even if normal.

The first order in Figure 20.2 is for arterial blood gases. The nurses will ask you to organize stat blood gases (as previously mentioned) if the oxygen saturation (also referred to as pulse ox or ox sats) drops below 90 percent. The orders for sputum for cytology and **acid-fast bacilli (AFB)** would be entered appropriately onto the PI screen. There is no one to call because the nurses (or sometimes the physiotherapist) would obtain the specimens when the patient can give them, print a label, and send the specimen to the lab. You would book the **pulmonary function test (PFT)** with respiratory services, ensuring that the patient was not involved in another procedure. A paper requisition may be required in a noncomputerized environment. For the thoracocentesis, you would tell the nurses, ensure that an extra nurse was available the next morning, and order the equipment from central supply or the sterile processing department. You would also check to be sure that the treatment room was free and that a consent for the test was prepared for the patient to sign. Some patient-care units have a schedule for use of the treatment room. If this is the case, mark in the date and time the room will be in use for the procedure.

Spirometry See Chapter 6 for details about this test. Because RTs usually perform this test in the respiratory department, you would electronically remit an order for spirometry to that department. A default window will appear on which you would note how the patient will arrive (e.g., ambulatory, by stretcher, by wheelchair). Note

acid-fast bacilli (AFB) a "rapid" test done to isolate and identify microorganisms such as the one that causes tuberculosis.

pulmonary function test (PFT) a test done on a patient to measure the breathing capacity of his or her lungs.

Please fax to Pharmacy & note date/time

ABGs stat if pulse ox drops below 90	Dietz, Henry 123 Duncan St. Vancouver B.C. DOB 22 09 47 071608 Dr. M. Label
Sputum for cytology X 3	
Sputum for AFB X 3 am spec	
Book for PFT this week	
Thoracocentesis tomorrow @ 1000 in the treatment room—have tray on floor and	
nurse available for assist.	

date *Jan 6/xx*	time	Physician's printed name **Dr. M. Label**	Signature *Dr. M. Label*

Figure 20.2   Order for blood gases and other tests related to respiratory conditions

also if the patient has altered cognition. Spirometry requires patient cooperation and may be ineffective if the patient is too confused. The respiratory department will notify you by telephone or electronically of the date and time of the test. Note this on the patient's eChart.

Sputum Specimens   All sputum specimens should consist of mucous secretions, not saliva, from the airways (bronchi), lungs, or throat. Because of this, the nurse or doctor may request chest physio for the patient to assist him or her to cough up the mucus. The physician may order a test to identify cell types, or "sputum for cytology." For this type of test, usually three specimens must be collected and must be coughed up early in the morning. The doctor may write "sputum for cytology × 3," as shown in Figure 20.2, or may assume that you know that three specimens are needed. When transcribing this order to the PI screen, note that three specimens are to be collected and add "early morning." Write in "1, 2, 3" for the nurses to keep track of the specimens. As they collect each, they cross out the number. The same information can be noted under "Comments" or "Additional Information" on an electronic record. See Figure 20.2 for a typical order.

Lung Scan   You would book a lung scan with nuclear medicine. If the order is stat, call the department for a booking time. As with spirometry, it is important to relay information about the patient's condition, ability to mobilize for the test, and level of cognition. It may be that a nurse has to accompany the patient. Lung CT scans may also be done. Handle the order as described for spirometry.

Thoracocentesis   A thoracocentesis (also called a pleural tap) is a procedure to remove fluid from the space between the lining of the outside of the lungs (pleura) and the wall of the chest. It is done for diagnostic or therapeutic purposes. This procedure may be done in the patient's room or in the treatment room if there is one in the patient-care unit. Usually the physician ordering the test performs it, so he or she may set the date and time.

Thoracocentesis requires the patient's consent. Label a consent form, fill it out as completely as possible, and leave it in the front of the patient's chart for the nurses to have signed. It is the physician's responsibility to ensure that the patient understands the procedure but, as with many surgical consent form, the nurses actually obtain the consent and sign as a witness. If your unit does not stock thoracocentesis trays, the nurses might ask you to order one from central supply. No requisition is required. In the order the physician may have asked for a tray and for a nurse, but they will often omit that part. It is up to you to know what is required and have things ready; you would order the tray and notify the nurses so that someone is available to assist with the procedure.

Inhalation and Oxygen Therapies

Incentive Spirometer   Incentive spirometers, also known as sustained maximal inspiration devices (see Figure 20.3), are often used after surgery to encourage the patient to do deep breathing exercises. (Note that this differs from the spirometry described earlier as an assessment.) The patient breathes through a mouthpiece into a container that has little balls at the bottom; he or she is encouraged to inhale deeply to keep the balls floating as long as possible. This allows assessment of how effectively the patient is breathing. Spirometry may also be ordered to diagnose pulmonary disease or to determine the progression or regression of existing diseases, such as pneumonia and **emphysema**.

> **emphysema** a disease characterized by the gradual destruction of the alveoli, which fuse to form large air spaces. Exchange of oxygen and carbon dioxide through these larger air sacs is inadequate.

Inhalation Therapy   The physician may order selected medications to be delivered by a mask to the patient, often to treat asthma. RTs or sometimes nurses administer this therapy. Commonly used drugs include salbutamol (Ventolin), ipratropium bromide (Atrovent), and budesonide (Pulmicort). The medication is usually diluted in a measured amount of normal saline before it is added to the aerosol chamber in the mask. Sometimes the medication can be given using corrugated tubing instead of a mask, especially to children, who usually do not like the mask. Medications are also given by a metered dose inhaler, as discussed in Chapter 7. Salbutamol inhalation is frequently ordered as a PRN medication, and both budesonide and ipratropium bromide are ordered as scheduled inhalation treatments. For example, a doctor may order "Atrovent inhalation qid." To transcribe these orders, enter the treatment on the scheduled or PRN medication sheet, notify the respiratory department, and add the treatment to the patient's PI screen in the appropriate place (often under "Oxygen Therapy").

Oxygen Therapy   Patients who, for any reason, do not have enough oxygen in their blood require supplemental oxygen. The decision to order oxygen for a patient is based on his or her diagnosis, general condition, cardiopulmonary status, oxygen saturation

Figure 20.3   Incentive spirometer

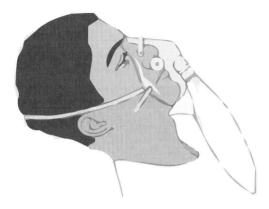

Figure 20.4 Oxygen mask

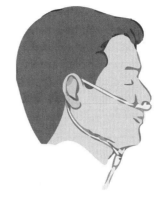

Figure 20.5 Nasal prongs

levels, and blood gases. Patients may also be put on oxygen postoperatively until the anesthetic wears off and an effective respiratory pattern is reestablished.

Oxygen may be dispensed from a cylinder (compressed gas), piped in (wall oxygen), given as liquid oxygen (which uses a small portable tank that must be refilled), or given through an oxygen concentrator. Oxygen may be delivered by face mask or nasal prongs. A face mask fits over the patient's mouth and nose. A variety of masks are available, the simplest of which (shown in Figure 20.4) delivers oxygen concentrations from 40 to 60 percent when set between five and eight litres. When possible, nasal prongs will be used instead. As shown in Figure 20.5, the prongs are small and fit into the nose, connecting to the oxygen tubing fitted around the face. They are less restrictive than an oxygen mask and allow the user to speak and eat comfortably with the oxygen running. They are not suitable, however, for patients who require oxygen concentrations of more than 40 percent or when the patient is a mouth breather. If the oxygen is set at 1 L/min, the patient will get 24 to 25 percent oxygen; if the oxygen is set at 6 L/min, he or she will get approximately 40 percent. Typically, doctors will order nasal prongs with the oxygen delivery level set for 2–3 L/min.

A Venturi mask (also called a high-flow mask) is ordered when the physician is trying to titrate the patient's oxygen levels, when the patient has trouble with nasal prongs, or when more accurate control of the amount of oxygen delivered is required. This mask, usually disposable, contains a mechanism that draws in room air and mixes it with 100 percent oxygen to a predetermined concentration. The oxygen delivered can be set to levels ranging from 24 to 32 percent.

Unless he or she is confined to bed, a patient usually uses a combination of stationary and mobile oxygen systems. At the bedside, oxygen is obtained from a wall unit. A variety of portable oxygen tanks on specially designed transporters are available for use within and away from the hospital. More sophisticated units, containing oxygen-conserving devices, weigh only a few pounds and can provide up to eight hours of oxygen. Electric or battery-operated devices (called oxygen concentrators) that concentrate oxygen from the air are also available. The respiratory department is responsible for maintaining portable oxygen supplies in the patient-care unit. If oxygen tanks are kept on the floor, they must be stored safely in cool places that do not obstruct traffic.

If a patient on oxygen leaves the unit for any reason, make sure the nurses have assessed him or her to determine whether a portable oxygen system is required. In most hospitals, these units are ordered from the respiratory department, although most clinical areas have two or three portable units. Note that if you are asked to move a patient on oxygen in his or her bed, make sure the oxygen tubing has been disconnected from the wall unit. It's surprising how often the nurses forget to do this, particularly in an emergency.

Safety measures must be observed near oxygen. Oxygen facilitates combustion. People must not smoke, light a match, or do anything that might initiate a spark. Often patients or visitors forget or are unaware of this danger. Although most facilities are smoke free, reminders should still be posted.

Oxygen is ordered by the physician, and can be ordered continuously or PRN; if the order does not specify, it is assumed to be continuous. In some situations, other health professionals may initiate oxygen therapy and obtain an order later. In ordering oxygen, the physician specifies the amount or concentration of oxygen, the method of delivery, and the number of litres per minute, often two litres. A typical order would be "O_2 per N/P @ 2L." If the patient required more oxygen, the levels may be set higher. The order might read "O_2 by mask @ 2 litres" or "O_2 by Venturi mask @ 35%."

TIP

If a diabetic patient on metformin tablets is having a CT Angio, the medication must be put on hold 24 hours prior to the procedure and for 48 hours afterward, unless otherwise ordered by the physician.

If the records are manual, complete a requisition when you transcribe the order. In a computerized environment, the respiratory department will be notified electronically. In either case, if the order is stat, phone to notify the respiratory department. Oxygen may be set up by an RT or a nurse depending on the facility's policy and the time of day. (Some facilities do not have an RT available on the late evening or night shift, so the nurse assumes this responsibility.)

Humidifier   A humidifier is often used for a patient who is experiencing respiratory difficulties. A humidifier moistens the air, helps keep mucous membranes moist, and loosens secretions in the upper respiratory tract. Most oxygen delivered to a patient is also humidified.

Artificial Airways

tracheostomy an artificial airway through an incision in the trachea.

Tracheostomy   A **tracheostomy** is the creation of an artificial airway through an incision in the neck into the trachea. A tube is inserted to assist with breathing and to keep the trachea from collapsing.

You may see orders for the maintenance of a tracheostomy, especially if you work on a specialized respiratory unit. The order might read "Trach care q2h" (or "q4h" or "PRN"). Nurses must keep the airway patent (open) and clean. They will often need to suction the airway and change the dressing around the tracheostomy from time to time. This care is considered a sterile procedure. You may be asked to order a tracheostomy tray or kit for the nurses. This would be obtained from central supply or the sterile processing department. A patient who has a permanent tracheostomy eventually learns how to care for it him or herself.

Endotracheal Tube   An endotracheal tube is a device that is inserted into the airway of a patient about to receive a general anesthetic or as an emergency procedure for someone who cannot breathe independently. It is inserted with an instrument called a laryngoscope. One would be kept on the crash cart in every patient-care unit. Doctors will sometimes write an order to *extubate* a patient, that is, to remove the tube. Extubation typically takes place in an intensive care unit, not on a patient-care unit.

Suctioning   In terms of the respiratory system, suctioning or aspiration means applying negative pressure to remove mucus, phlegm, and other secretions from the airways to make it easier for a person to breathe. Suctioning is used to clear airway obstructions, to remove built-up secretions that may lead to infection, and to keep airways clear for patients on mechanical ventilation. It may also be used to obtain a specimen. It is necessary mostly for patients who are unconscious, have altered consciousness, or are too weak to cough up secretions.

Suctioning requires a catheter, attached tubing, a wall-mounted or portable suction machine, and a drainage bottle. Suction catheters and tubing should be kept in the treatment room on your unit.

Simple suctioning can be done through the nose or the mouth. Suctioning through the mouth is called **oropharyngeal suctioning**. It reaches only the mouth, or the mouth and the back of the throat. Suctioning through the nose is called **nasopharyngeal suctioning**, and it reaches the back of the mouth and throat. **Deep suctioning**, such as **endotracheal suctioning**, is more complicated and involves going through an endotracheal tube to reach deeper into the breathing passages. This is a strictly sterile procedure.

Suctioning is always ordered PRN. The physician may write "Suction PRN." Sometimes suctioning is ordered after chest physio to remove the loosened secretions. The doctor may also order "Endotracheal suctioning PRN." If the doctor does not specify the route, suctioning is assumed to be via nose or mouth; the nurse or RT will decide which is more appropriate or convenient. The physician may also indicate the type and size of the suction catheter needed. Add suction orders to the PI screen under "Respiratory" or "Additional Nursing Care."

Ventilator   You will not encounter an order for a ventilator unless you work in a critical care unit or in long-term care where a person has a ventilator for life. A ventilator is a machine used to support breathing (see Figure 20.6). It is used when a patient is

oropharyngeal suctioning suctioning with a catheter through the mouth to reach the mouth only or the mouth and the back of the throat.

nasopharyngeal suctioning suctioning with a catheter through the nose to reach the mouth and throat (pharynx).

deep suctioning introducing the suction catheter into the lower trachea and bronchi.

endotracheal suctioning suctioning through an artificial airway known as a tracheostomy.

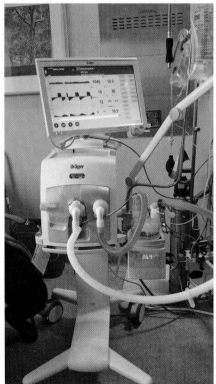

Valerie D. Thompson

Figure 20.6 A ventilator

anesthetized, such as during surgery, or if for some reason the patient is unable to breathe on his or her own. Another situation requiring mechanical ventilation is keeping someone in an induced coma (such as Canadian freestyle skier Sara Burke, who died after a tragic accident in January 2012). To receive mechanical ventilation sufficient for life support, the patient must first be intubated. The doctor would write the order for the desired type of mechanical ventilation, and an RT from respiratory services would be responsible for setting it up and maintaining the patient on the ventilator.

L05 L06 CARDIOVASCULAR ASSESSMENTS AND TREATMENTS

Nursing Assessments

In taking vital signs and checking the respiratory status, nurses are conducting a basic cardiac assessment as well. However, more complex assessments may be ordered.

Peripheral Vascular Assessment   Doctors may order peripheral vascular assessment for patients admitted with peripheral vascular disease, including arteriosclerosis, varicose veins, thrombophlebitis, or general evidence of poor circulation. This assessment may also be called a CSM for *circulation*, *sensation*, and *movement*. Nurses observe the colour and temperature of the skin in the affected area (e.g., the legs), ask about the patient's feeling or sensation in the area, note any edema or other abnormalities, and check for peripheral pulse in the affected area. Transcribe this order onto the PI screen under "Nursing Assessments" or "Vascular Assessments." No requisition is required.

Although the following tests are discussed in Chapter 6, what is detailed here is relevant data for order entry procedures. Relevant data for order entry is detailed subsequently.

Chest X-Ray

For an inpatient, a chest X-ray would be booked with diagnostic services, and the patient would go to that department for the X-ray. A chest X-ray may be ordered as a "portable" for the patient who is unable to leave the floor. This is usual if the patient is very ill and moving him or her would be detrimental. For a portable X-ray, call the X-ray department and keep the requisition on the floor.

Telemetry

Most hospitals have what is called a *telemetry unit*. A patient can be admitted directly to this unit for cardiac monitoring or may be transferred to this unit as a "step down" from the intensive care unit for ongoing assessment. A telemetry monitor—a small box connected to the chest by wires and electrodes, much like a Holter monitor—is used to trace the heart's activity; however, the readout is displayed on a small screen. A nurse continuously monitors the screen for abnormalities. An alarm sounds if the patient's heartbeat slows down or speeds up to preset rates or becomes irregular. When a doctor orders telemetry, arrange for an in-hospital transfer, including transferring any hard copies of the patient's chart, eMAR, and any old charts that may be on the floor.

Pacemakers

A pacemaker is a small electronic device that regulates the heartbeat by sending electrical signals to the heart. Pacemakers are used for patients with abnormal heartbeats, which may be irregular or too slow (**bradycardia**). These abnormal beats affect the

bradycardia extremely slow heartbeat.

patient's circulation and decrease oxygenation. The pacemaker is implanted in the hospital on an inpatient or outpatient basis, with the patient sedated. When a physician orders pacemaker insertion, book the procedure with the cardiologist's office. For an inpatient, prepare an operating room chart and initiate preoperative routines, such as cancelling or delaying meals and ensuring that the nurses know that the patient will be NPO the night before the procedure. A consent is required for this procedure.

Not every facility is equipped to insert a pacemaker. You may have to arrange an appointment for the patient to have this procedure done elsewhere. If so, you must first find a facility that can accommodate the patient (you may have to make several calls), prepare the necessary patient records, and arrange transportation to and back from the facility where the procedure is being carried out.

Cardiac Catheterization

This test is booked with and performed in a special unit referred to as a *cardiac cath lab*. If the hospital does not have this service, the patient will be sent to another facility that does. Book the appointment at the appropriate facility, then implement the preparation for the patient. In many regions, you must obtain a transportation number for a patient requiring any test at another facility. As well, you must send the patient's chart (or printed components of the patient's electronic chart) and any eMARs along with him or her. The patient must be NPO the night before the procedure. The morning of the procedure, a groin prep will be done. A consent is necessary.

Other Tests

The ECG, stress test, Doppler ultrasound, and echocardiogram are all tests that you would book with cardiopulmonary services. With the exception of the ECG, the patient goes to the department for the test. An ECG can be ordered stat or routine— they are usually done at the patient's bedside. If it is stat, as usual print the requisition on the floor and call the lab to have someone come to do it.

Although previously mentioned, remember that when booking any test you need to ensure the appointment does not conflict with another test the patient is having. Be sure to add in the free text field any relevant information regarding the patient's ability to ambulate and whether he or she is on oxygen or has any cognitive impairment. In some cases, a nurse will accompany the patient. If so, be sure that a nurse is available. You may need to call someone in or have someone come from another unit.

Chest CT Scan

A chest computed tomography (CT) scan shows much more detail than a standard X-ray and is used when better visualization of the lungs is required (e.g., to follow up on questionable abnormal findings on a chest X-ray). This test is booked with diagnostic imaging.

Coronary Angiography

Angiograms are performed in the catheterization (cath) lab of a hospital. An angiogram is usually an outpatient procedure. Some facilities ask the patient to avoid solid foods for four hours prior to the test (clear fluids are allowed). This test is done to diagnose narrowing of the major blood vessels. The entry point for the catheter is the femoral artery (in the groin) or, a newer approach, the radial artery (in the arm), which is more convenient and results in a shorter reovery period for the patient.

Often heart patients have to be transferred to another facility to have this procedure done. You will need to arrange an appointment, prepare required patient records, and book transportation to and from the diagnostic facility. A *pulmonary angiography* (where the catheter is directed into the lungs) is used to diagnose a pulmonary embolism (blood clot in the lungs).

L07 CARDIOPULMONARY EMERGENCIES

You will probably have a role to play if a cardiac or respiratory arrest occurs on your floor. Know the hospital procedures and exactly what is expected of you. You will likely be asked to "call the arrest," that is, notify the appropriate people. Be familiar with the procedures and codes for cardiac and respiratory arrests. In some facilities, the same code is used for both; other facilities use two different codes. Act quickly, but remain calm. Collect the required information; this usually includes the patient's room and bed numbers—make sure you have the correct numbers. Most facilities have a special emergency number. Go to the nearest telephone and dial the number. Give the information clearly and concisely to the operator. Response will be swift.

During the course of resuscitation attempts, you may be asked to keep a record of what is happening—drugs that are given and procedures that are implemented, as well as who does what. You would be given this information by health professionals attending the arrest and asked to record it. (You would not be expected to guess what is happening.) In some cases you may be directed to fetch equipment from the crash cart or treatment room (e.g., an IV solution). Stay out of the way, follow directions, and remain calm. If you are recording information, write neatly and clearly, and stay organized. Record in the order that the information is given to you. If possible, include the time you are given the information—for example, "IV hung at 12:32," "Paddles applied at 12:35." As well, you may be asked to record the official time of death if resuscitation efforts are terminated.

Be aware of any family members who are nearby. If they are present, guide them to a place where they can wait during resuscitation procedures. Keep them informed; be empathetic and supportive. Comfort for friends and family members at such a time is extremely important and can go a long way to reducing their stress and assisting them to cope with their loss.

SUMMARY

1. The lungs oxygenate the blood, and the heart pumps the oxygenated blood throughout the body by way of the vascular system (veins and arteries). Problems with any component of these systems can result in insufficient oxygen perfusion to one, several, or all parts of the body. Arteriosclerosis (hardening of the arteries) and atherosclerosis (narrowing of the arteries) can compromise proper oxygenation and tissue perfusion. Sometimes complete occlusion of oxygen to an organ occurs. If that organ is the heart, a heart attack results; it that organ is the brain, a cerebrovascual accident (stroke) may occur. Respiratory conditions, such as COPD, affect not only respiration but also other systems and body parts.

2. Respiratory therapists (RTs), physiotherapists, and nurses provide ongoing assessment and care related to respiratory problems. RTs are highly skilled individuals who initiate, implement, and monitor most respiratory-related treatments. In

addition, as part of the cardiac response team, RTs respond to cardiac emergencies that occur in the hospital. RTs can intubate patients and manage ventilators in the ICU. Nurses also administer inhalation treatments and manage/monitor patients receiving oxygen.

3. Respiratory assessment (rate, rhythm, volume, etc.) is done as part of routine vital signs assessment, which often includes pulse oximetry. Chest assessments, completed by nurses, RTs, and physiotherapists, involve auscultating for abnormal sounds, such as crackles (crepitation) and wheezes (rhonchi). Chest assessment is routine for postoperative patients and may be ordered with specific frequency.

4. Oxygen therapy is commonly ordered postoperatively and for patients who have low oxygen saturation levels (sats) determined by pulse oximetry. Other tests that measure oxygenation and lung function include pulmonary function tests and arterial blood gases (ABGs). You may have to remind the nurse to take the patient off oxygen for a time frame prior to having blood for ABGs drawn, if the order is for blood gases on room air. Suctioning is an intervention used to clear a patient's upper airway if excessive mucus impairs breathing. More aggressive interventions include the use of ventilators and performing a tracheostomy, which is done as a last resort when the upper airway is completely occluded.

5. Treatments and interventions a physician may order for cardiac problems sometimes overlap with those ordered for the respiratory system, such as vital signs, chest assessments, and chest X-rays. An ECG is cardiac specific and is done if the doctor thinks the patient has an abnormal heart rhythm or has had a heart attack. A stress test assesses heart function when the person is exercising. A Holter monitor assesses the person's heart rate and rhythm over a time frame, perhaps several days.

6. Transcribing orders for cardiac and respiratory conditions includes medication orders and a variety of assessments, diagnostic tests, and treatments. Some hospitals have to transfer a patient to another hospital for tests such as an angiogram or for the insertion of a pacemaker. You will need to make an appointment for the patient, prepare pertinent records, and arrange transportation to and back from the appointment. Most assessments and interventions are added to the PI screen.

7. Each facility will have a protocol outlining the appropriate response to a cardiac or respiratory arrest. You may be responsible for calling the arrest and entering verbal orders into the computer (even in CPOE environments). It is important to remain calm and to be organized. When calling an arrest, be sure to have the right information—especially the patient's room number.

KEY TERMS

acid-fast bacilli (AFB) 580
arrhythmia 575
arteriosclerosis 574
asthma 576
atherosclerosis 574
atrial fibrillation 575
bradycardia 586
cerebral vascular accident
    (CVA) 575
chronic obstructive
    pulmonary disease
    (COPD) 576

clapping or percussion 577
congestive heart failure
    (CHF) 575
crash cart 575
crepitation or crackles 578
deep suctioning 585
diastolic pressure 575
dyspnea 578
emphysema 582
endotracheal suctioning 585
hypertension or high blood
    pressure 575

myocardial infarct 574
nasopharyngeal
    suctioning 585
oropharyngeal suctioning 585
pneumonia 576
postural drainage 577
pulmonary function test
    (PFT) 580
rhonchi or wheezes 578
systolic pressure 575
tracheostomy 584
vibrations 577

REVIEW QUESTIONS

1. What is the relationship between the cardiovascular and respiratory systems with respect to oxygenation?

2. List the main organs in the cardiovascular and respiratory systems.

3. What roles do respiratory therapists and physiotherapists play in respiratory assessment and care?

4. What is included in a chest assessment, and what is the purpose of this assessment?

5. What is the principle by which pulse oximetry works?

6. Why are blood gases sometimes ordered along with or instead of oximetry?

7. What is unique about an order for sputum for cytology or AFB?

8. Describe the purpose and use of the spirometer on the patient-care unit.

9. What would you do if a patient had a respiratory or cardiac arrest?

APPLICATION EXERCISES

1. Summarize the physiology and function of the respiratory and cardiovascular systems. Use a detailed diagram to illustrate the structure of each.

2. With one or two other students, research three common respiratory conditions and three common cardiovascular conditions. For each, describe the following:

   a. Common assessments used to diagnose and monitor the condition

   b. The etiology of the condition

   c. How the condition interferes with oxygenation

3. Review the standard procedures for cardiopulmonary resuscitation (CPR) online. If your program does not require CPR certification, research available resources in your area where these courses can be taken (including the cost). Organize a group—maybe the class—to become certified.

4. Mr. Loton is in hospital with CHF and SOB. He is weak and semi-conscious.

   a. What is meant by the acronym SOB?

   b. What is meant by the acronym CHF?

   c. Why might Dr. Bobb have ordered suction after the patient had chest physio?

   d. Briefly describe the function and purpose of the Venturi mask.

   e. Why were ABGs ordered based on O_2 sats from oximetry?

   f. What is meant by PA and lateral in the order for the chest X-ray?

   g. Why is a portable X-ray ordered in this case?

   h. Transcribe the orders in Figure 20.7 according to the protocol outlined by your professor.

Date Sept 1/xx	Time	Physician's Name Printed Dr. R. Bobb	Physician's signature *Dr. R. Bobb*	Loton, Walter 477 Grange St. Acton, ON L7R 2R4 M 17 04 38 034902 2779453775 Dr. R. Bobb

V/S quid x 48 then bid
Chest physio quid suction after physio PRN
Sputum for cytology x 3
O_2 by Venturi mask @ 34%
Pulse ox quid. ABGs if sats drop below 92%
EKG in 2 days & chest X-ray PA and lateral stat portable

Figure 20.7 Doctor's orders for Walter Loton

WEBSITES OF INTEREST

Canadian Heart and Stroke Foundation

www.heartandstroke.com/site/c.ikIQLcMWJtE/b.3479403/k.BF78/Health_Information.htm

Chapter 21
Orders Related to Rest and Activity

Tyler Olson/Fotolia

LEARNING OBJECTIVES

On completing this chapter, you will be able to:

1. Summarize the criteria used to assess rest and activity orders.

2. Interpret the most common rest and activity orders.

3. Transcribe rest and activity orders correctly.

4. Discuss the rationale for the use of restraints in the hospital setting.

5. Identify the equipment used for rest and activity.

6. Understand the concept of activities of daily living.

The advantages of activity far outweigh inactivity for the hospitalized patient. After surgery, for example, patients are encouraged to get up and walking as soon as they can, usually the first postoperative day, even for most major procedures. Bed rest and limited activity have harmful effects on most body systems. The respiratory system is compromised because of ineffective breathing patterns, including decreased ability to cough and breathe deeply. Secretions can pool in the alveoli, harbouring bacteria and leading to **hypostatic pneumonia**. The circulatory system is compromised, and blood clots or thrombus can result. The muscular system loses tone and strength. The integumentary system is affected. Some people develop pressure sores, especially older

hypostatic pneumonia pneumonia developing as a result of decreased air exchange combined with an inability to drain pooled bronchial secretions.

591

patients or those with compromised skin integrity. Probably the greatest barrier to getting patients up and moving following surgery is the patient him or herself, because of the pain and discomfort that can result from moving; this can be reduced somewhat with proper pain management. Other things that impact the patient's ability to ambulate include physical and cognitive limitations.

However, as important as activity is for maintaining health, rest is also required to help the body heal from disease, trauma, or surgery. The goal is to find a balance that provides the optimal level of activity for each patient. Physiotherapy helps patients maintain and improve their ability to be active.

L01 CRITERIA USED IN ACTIVITY ORDERS

When a person is admitted to hospital, the physician will provide a specific order related to activity level. To determine the optimal activity level, physicians consider several factors.

Physical Energy

Activity orders must be realistic and take into account the patient's strength, endurance, and desire to be active. Disease and surgery can undermine a person's physical energy. Age also plays a role. Usually, a 21-year-old will have more energy than an 80-year-old, even in the face of illness. Requiring patients to do too much is as harmful as allowing them to do too little. It can be difficult to find the balance. Sometimes, after surgery, patients just do not want to move because of pain and weakness.

Physical Capabilities

Often, physical disabilities limit the extent and type of activity a patient is capable of, especially in the hospital. Space is limited and unfamiliar, and the patient may not have the same assistive devices he or she has at home. A patient may ambulate with assistance at home; however, with limited staff, the same kind of assistance may not be available in hospital. However, patients should be encouraged to be as independent as they can safely and comfortably be. The doctor may order an assessment by a physiotherapist, who will provide appropriate assistive devices and a modified activity routine. The physiotherapist may come two or three times a day to get the patient up and walking.

The Nature of the Illness

Some illnesses can best be treated with a period of rest; others require activity. For example, with an unstable heart condition, activity increases the heart's workload and this can lead to further problems, such as angina. A patient with such a condition may be required to rest initially and then gradually increase activity. In contrast, the sooner a stroke victim begins an active rehabilitation program, the better it will be for him or her.

Consciousness and Cognition

Altered consciousness can range from being unconscious to simply being confused or disoriented. It may result from a number of conditions, including a stroke, head injury, terminal illness, or sedation.

Patients who are unconscious or semi-conscious are obviously unable to ambulate. They will be on bed rest and dependent on staff to meet all of their needs.

Patients who have had narcotic analgesics may know where they are and where they want to go but lack the neuromuscular integrity to do so safely. Often, patients who have had sedation experience some altered cognition and, perhaps, confusion. For example, a postoperative patient may know where the bathroom is and think he or she can manage getting there unassisted but may misjudge his or her abilities and end up falling. Nurses may leave the side rails on the bed up for patients who have been sedated. Leaving side rails up is controversial. On the one hand, it may stop a patient from getting up; on the other hand, a patient who is determined to get up (often becoming increasingly agitated by barriers) may climb over the side rails and be at increased risk of injury.

Patients often ring a bell and ask for help going to the bathroom, getting out of bed, or getting back into bed. You may be tempted to help them if the nurses are busy. However, this is considered nursing care and is generally not within your scope of practice. Without the proper training and experience, your help may result in injury. Reassure the patient that you will find a nurse.

Any alteration in a person's ability to think clearly will affect the level of activity that can be safely allowed. Patients who have dementia or Alzheimer's disease may be able to walk and move independently but have little idea how to interact with the environment. People with severe cognitive impairment may be cared for in a "secure" or locked unit to prevent them from wandering off and getting lost or injured. A doctor's order might read "Not to leave the floor unless accompanied by a nurse or family member."

Surgery

Many patients recovering from major surgery will have their level of activity restricted initially. The seriousness and type of operation naturally affects how much and when the patient can ambulate. Most patients do get out of bed the first postoperative day. Even patients with numerous tubes, intravenous lines, and heart monitors can be helped to get up. Heart transplant recipients are often up and walking within a couple of days.

Many patients dread getting up the first couple of times after an operation. Getting a patient up, particularly for the first time, can be as difficult for the nurse as it is for the patient! Patients often do not appreciate the need to become active—or do not care—and view the nurse as not having any compassion. To deal with pain, nurses often give the patient an analgesic half an hour before getting them up or remind patients with a patient-controlled analgesia pump to self-medicate. Regardless, some patients flatly refuse to get out of bed. Nurses will often contract with the patient to work up to ambulation. For example, the patient agrees to sit on the side of the bed for the first time, the next time to move to the chair, the next time to walk to the door of the room, and so on.

Sometimes the doctor will intervene, telling the patient that remaining in bed is not an option. He may write an order, such as "encourage ambulation" or "patient must ambulate at least qid."

L02 L03 L04 ACTIVITY ORDERS

There are a variety of activity orders geared to the capabilities of the individual patient. These orders are usually transcribed onto the PI screen. They do not require a requisition unless someone other than the nurses—a physiotherapist, for example—is needed.

Any time a patient leaves the unit for a test or an appointment, notify anyone who will be working with the patient of any limitations in mobility or independence.

Requisitions for tests that involve moving the patient will ask for this information. On a computerized requisition, it may be a mandatory field.

Complete Bed Rest

Complete bed rest (CBR) means that the patient must stay in bed at all times. The patient must eat, eliminate, and wash in bed, and the bed must be changed with the patient in it (this is called making an occupied bed). Unconscious and semi-conscious patients are on CBR by necessity; otherwise, doctors order CBR for more than a brief period only when absolutely necessary because of the risks to the cardiovascular, respiratory, musculoskeletal, and integumentary systems.

Orders for complete bed rest might be written in one of the following ways:

CBR

Bed rest

Strict CBR

When the doctor orders CBR, nurses may sometimes decide that it is less stressful to allow the patient to get up to use the bathroom or commode than to struggle with a bedpan. When the doctor orders "strict CBR," it means that the patient must not get out of bed for anything. Transcribe this order as written to maintain this emphasis.

Patients on CBR require certain extra nursing care to minimize its harmful effects.

Bedpans   In some facilities, bedpans are labelled and assigned to patients for a limited time frame before being replaced. These bedpans are emptied in a disposal unit called a *hopper* that also sterilizes them. More recently, hospitals have supplied a sterile bedpan for each use as a step toward better infection control. Many facilities (especially acute-care hospitals) have disposable bedpans. You may have to order bedpans (and perhaps washing basins) for patients unable to use bathroom facilities.

hypoxia insufficient oxygen in blood or tissue.

Turning   Even the gentle pressure of a mattress, when applied to the same spot for a prolonged period, can cause tissue **hypoxia** and breakdown, especially on bony prominences, such as the hip bone, tail bone, and elbows. This pressure can cause decubitus ulcers (pressure sores or bedsores). The elderly, very thin people, and those with thin, dry skin are at increased risk. To alleviate pressure, patients unable to move about in bed themselves must be turned regularly. Realistically, nurses rarely have time to turn a patient more than once every two to four hours.

The physician may order "Turn q2–4h and PRN" or "turn q2h," or "turn q1h." Transcribe this order onto the PI screen under "Nursing Measures" or "Comfort Measures." If the doctor does not specify, nurses may make their own orders to turn a patient. The nurse will usually note the decision on the PI screen under "Nursing Care" or "Nursing Interventions."

range of motion (ROM) exercises a set of exercises that puts joints through their full range of positions.

Physiotherapy   Patients who are relatively or completely inactive must maintain mobility of all body parts to avoid muscle wasting, progressive muscle weakness, and contractures (permanent contraction). Physiotherapy is ordered to maintain muscle and joint functions or to regain lost mobility caused by disease, trauma, or surgery. Exercise may be classified as active (done by the patient independently), assisted (done by the patient with help), or passive (done by someone else, such as a physiotherapist, a nurse, or a trained family member). The physician may order **range of motion (ROM) exercises**: moving limbs through normal movements to take each joint through its complete range of positions.

Bed Rest with Bathroom Privileges

Bed rest with bathroom privileges (BR with BRP) means that the patient is allowed up only to go to the bathroom. Sometimes, even when getting up to go to the bathroom involves some discomfort or physical problems, it is less stressful for the patient than struggling with a bedpan or urinal; most people find using these devices unpleasant. Some may be unable to defecate, both because of the psychological barrier and the awkward position, which does not allow gravity to help with the bowel movement. Bed rest with bathroom privileges is often a helpful compromise.

> **TIP**
>
> A patient may ask you for assistance out of bed, back to bed, or to the washroom. Do not attempt to help any patient ambulate, ever. This is a nursing responsibility. You cannot determine a patient's ability to support him or herself. Assisting without the proper techniques and knowledge can result in injury to the patient or to yourself. What you can do is find a nurse to help the patient as quickly as possible.

Bed Rest with Commode Privileges

When the doctor wants to allow an anatomically sound position for elimination but does not want the patient to walk, he or she may write this order, allowing the patient to get up only to use a commode. A commode is like a small chair with arms (Figure 21.1). Part of the seat is cut out and a bedpan is fitted underneath. The commode can be brought right to the bedside.

Up in Chair

This order indicates that the patient may be out of bed and in a chair but may not ambulate freely around the room or out in the halls. The doctor may specify a frequency: "Up in chair bid" (or tid or qid). Sometimes a regular chair is used, and sometimes a special chair called a geri chair—a large reclining chair with a footrest—is used, especially for older patients and those with chronic medical problems. The

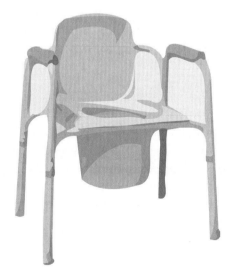

Figure 21.1 A commode

patient allowed up in the chair is usually also allowed bathroom privileges unless otherwise stated.

Up with Assist

"Up with assist" means the patient may get up with someone helping him. "Up with one assist" means one person must help; "Up with two assists" means two people must help, one taking each arm. This may be ordered as "assist × 1" or "assist × 2."

Activity as Tolerated/Up Ad Lib

"Activity as tolerated" (AAT) or "up ad lib" means that there are no formal limits on the patient's activity—he or she may be as active as the patient can manage. This does not necessarily mean that the patient will be fully active. It means that the nurses should help the patient to be as active as appropriate for his or her physical abilities and energy needs. A postoperative patient, for example, will likely start with bed rest and progress to sitting in a chair, taking a short walk with a nurse's help, and ultimately to ambulating independently. Most people do walk on their first postoperative day. Sometimes the doctor will order "Ambulate 1st postoperative day."

Occasionally, the surgeon will order that the patient "dangle" on the evening of the day of surgery. The nurses help the patient sit on the edge of the bed with his or her feet dangling over the side. Next, the patient may be able to sit in a chair briefly.

Restraints

The use of any type of restraint in a health care facility is controversial. They are, in most cases, used as a last resort—and most frequently on patients who are confused or suffer from dementia. Any interventions that can prevent the use of restraints are overwhelmingly preferable.

Restraints include any physical or chemical means to prevent a patient from causing harm to him or herself or others. In an acute-care hospital, restraints are sometimes used on patients who are recovering from surgery if they are temporally confused from medication they are receiving for pain or as a result of an anesthetic. In such cases, the patient may try to pull out an intravenous line, a catheter, or even an endotracheal tube. Wrist restraints might be applied until the patient refrains from such actions. They would not be needed if someone could remain with the patient, reminding him or her not to pull at various lines and tubes. Other physical restraints include ankle restraints, mitts, and an abdominal or chest belt.

The use of restraints can have serious legal implications for all involved. Their use must be ordered by a physician (and often require the family's permission), and even then ethical, moral, and legal issues may arise. While they may, on occasion, be deemed by some to be necessary, restraints usually make patients more restless and combative and are disturbing for family members. The patient may be struggling, crying, shouting, begging, pleading, or bargaining with anyone who will listen to have the restraints removed. Even confused people seem to recognize that they are being held captive and hate it. Family members and friends may not understand the need for restraints and resent their use:

"How could you do such a thing? Aunt Mary isn't dangerous. Take those off."

"Why have you got Dad tied into that chair? You are treating him like a criminal."

"What kind of people are you? This is unacceptable. Take those off now."

You cannot deal with such issues. Remain calm and be empathetic. Imagine how you would feel if your mother or brother were tied into a chair and struggling to get out. Tell the family member that you will get the nurse so that they can discuss the matter.

Chemical restraints involve the use of sedation to immobilize a patient or to keep him or her quiet and sedated. Patients who are continually aggressive and combative are often kept sedated. The use of chemical restraints is also controversial.

A restraint should not be used without serious consideration, and there must be a doctor's order. Orders for restraints may state "May use restraints PRN." Transcribe the order onto the PI screen.

L05 EQUIPMENT RELATED TO REST AND ACTIVITY

A number of devices related to rest and activity are used. Most of these are ordered from central supply. Some may be kept in the patient-care unit.

Special Mattresses

To alleviate the effects of constant pressure on a patient's body, a doctor or nurse may order an alternating-pressure mattress (also called a low-flow air mattress or ripple mattress). Usually a nurse can make the decision to use this type of mattress (and thus issue one with a nursing order). This mattress is electric; a device applies alternating air pressure to various parts of the mattress. The alternating pressure stimulates blood flow to the skin, relieving pressure points (i.e., elbows, heels, and other bony prominences). A small machine that controls the air flow to the mattress may be hooked onto the bottom of the patient's bed or set on the floor. It changes the air pressure in the mattress at preset intervals, often causing a fairly audible whirring or swishing noise that may startle the patient or visitors until they become used to the noise. If asked, assure them that the sound is normal and explain what it does.

Another option is an egg-crate mattress, named for the varied heights of the surface. As the patient shifts in bed, a spot on the body will rest sometimes on a bump and sometimes on a hollow, producing variable pressure. Although not as effective as a ripple mattress, an egg-crate mattress does help and can be purchased for home use.

Sometimes a sheepskin is also ordered—a pad made from the wool-pile of tanned and shorn sheepskin or lambskin. The high-density wool fibres provide a cushion that distributes the patient's weight and relieves pressure. The sheepskin also absorbs moisture. It must be changed and laundered frequently. Elbow and heel protectors made out of sheepskin are also available in most hospitals. They reduce reddening and chafing of the skin and help prevent skin breakdown.

Anti-Embolism Stockings

Blood clots in the legs, technically known as *venous thromboembolism* (VTE), is of significant concern and can cause deaths in hospitals—particularly for patients who are on prolonged bedrest (anyone with significantly reduced mobility), postsurgical patients, and those with pre-existing impaired circulation in the lower extremities. Deaths like these are often preventable. The risk of developing VTE is greatly reduced by requiring at-risk patients to wear anti-embolism stockings in designated situations while in hospital. An individual may be required to wear them at home as well.

Anti-embolism or pressure stockings (also called TED stockings for a common brand name) use elastic support to augment circulation in the legs, thus helping prevent venous **embolisms** and blood clots. They may be full length or calf length. They

embolism obstruction of a blood vessel by a blood clot, an air bubble, or foreign matter.

may be ordered for patients who are on bed rest, have poor circulation in the legs, or are at risk of developing clots. You may be responsible for ordering stockings from central supply by phone or computer. Although the stockings come only in small, medium, and large sizes, the patient must be carefully measured for the suitable size. When you call for the stockings (or submit an online requisition), central supply requires the patient's measurements. This consists of the diameters of the calf and thigh and the length of the leg from groin to ankle. The nurse takes these measurements before giving you the order. Some physicians routinely use stockings for postoperative patients. In this case, you would order them ahead of time and have them available for the patient when he or she returns to the floor postoperatively. Measurements can be done in the preadmit area. Some facilities have all patients wear the stockings preoperatively. The use of these stockings must be carefully monitored by the nurse. Contraindications to their use include individuals with overly large legs, individuals with fragile skin or skin conditions, and patients with impaired sensation in their legs.

Foot Boards

These are boards that fit at the bottom of the bed. They help the patient keep his or her feet in the proper position. The patient pushes his or her feet against them in exercising or to stay sitting up in bed. They also help keep the patient from sliding down in the hospital bed.

Bed Cradles

A bed cradle is a hoop that fits over the bottom part of the bed to keep the covers off the patient's legs. This may be ordered for a patient with sensitive skin or one who has had leg trauma or surgery, such as for varicose veins.

Trapeze Bar

The trapeze bar is ordered for patients who need something to grab onto to assist with exercising, positioning themselves in bed, and getting in and out of bed. This is often used for patients who have had orthopedic surgery.

Abduction Pillow

A long, wedge-shaped, firm pillow, called an abduction pillow or wedge pillow, is used primarily immediately after hip surgery to keep the legs apart.

Side Rails

All hospital beds should have side rails. Some beds have one long side rail and others have two on each side, one that starts at the top and goes to the midpoint in the bed and the second starting at the midpoint and going close to the bottom. Side rails are used to help patients position themselves. They are also kept up when a patient has been sedated or is confused or unconscious.

Sometimes, the doctor will order "Keep side rails up." Often, patients feel claustrophobic if both side rails are up. Keeping one side rail up may be adequate. Sometimes a physician will specify "Side rails up × 1." Usually, the nurses make that decision and decide on any other necessary safety measures. The nurses may write their own nursing orders and add them to the patient-care plan.

Hoyer Lift

A Hoyer lift is a device used to get patients who are too heavy to get up any other way out of the bed and perhaps into a chair. It operates with a series of supports and levers operated by a hydraulic pump. The Hoyer lift is found primarily in long-term care, rehab, and chronic care settings, but sometimes in acute-care settings as well.

Assistive Mobility Devices

A variety of assistive devices increase mobility. The most common assistive devices are canes, walkers, and wheelchairs. Some patients bring their assistive devices to the hospital with them, preferring to use the familiar devices they are comfortable with rather than rely on unfamiliar hospital supplies. Ensure that any devices that belong to patients are clearly labelled with their names. Keep them in a safe place—in the patients' rooms if there is space. Sometimes other patients—or even nurses—borrow privately owned devices, thinking "Mr. Bowman won't mind." Patients *do* mind. Never suggest that a nurse might be able to use someone's personal property.

Most hospitals have a few wheelchairs available for patients to use. They are usually standard ones that fold up in the middle for easy storage. Even fairly mobile patients are often transported to other units in a wheelchair for speed and safety. In some hospitals, it remains the policy to discharge patients in a wheelchair regardless of their level of mobility. Patients who normally use wheelchairs may bring their own to the hospital. Motorized wheelchairs are not usually brought into the hospital but may be seen in a rehabilitation unit if space allows.

Patients who use wheelchairs routinely do so for a variety of reasons, including loss of limbs, weak leg muscles, spinal or brain injury or disease (including paralysis), and arthritis. For some, the use of a wheelchair is temporary; for others it may be permanent. Some people use wheelchairs only for longer distances and are able to walk short distances independently or with the use of other devices. Wheelchairs can become a routine part of a person's lifestyle. Although people may think of someone as "confined" to a wheelchair, users often value the greater mobility and independence the wheelchair offers them. Do not assume that wheelchair users are necessarily particularly sick; certainly do not assume that they have mental limitations. Treat them with respect, as you would treat anyone, in and out of hospital. Wheelchairs should be kept in a designated place on the unit and never left out where they can be a fire hazard or impede traffic flow on the unit.

L06 ACTIVITIES OF DAILY LIVING

Think about the activities that you carry out as part of your daily routine. You probably take for granted most of the following:

- Getting up in the morning
- Going to the bathroom
- Brushing your teeth
- Washing your face, showering, or having a bath
- Eating your breakfast, lunch, and supper
- Getting ready for bed

Activities of daily living (ADL) are those activities performed every day as a routine part of self-care: eating, dressing, getting up, grooming, toileting, and bathing. Being able to complete ADL independently is important psychologically, affording the patient a sense of dignity and privacy. Nurses make every effort to help patients complete their own ADL or to do as much as possible on their own.

Following surgery, most patients rely on the nurses for much of this care but quickly progress to accomplishing much of their ADL independently. Patients with advanced disease states or conditions that interfere with muscle strength, coordination, or cognition need varying degrees of assistance. Some will need only a little help in reaching or need a steadying hand; others cannot participate at all. Quadriplegics may be reliant on health professionals but are fully aware of the tasks and their degree of dependence. They should be allowed to direct their own activities when possible.

Patients' ADL status may be classified as "independent" (or "self"), "self with assistance," or "by nurse." Doctors do not usually provide this information, but it must be noted on the health record. If you have the information, enter it on the PI screen in the ADL section. If not, the nurses will add it after they have assessed the patient.

SUMMARY

1. Each patient admitted to hospital must have an activity order written by a physician. It is important to find a balance between activity and rest. Activity levels are individualized to the patient's condition and capabilities. Usually, these orders are only noted on the PI screen. A requisition is needed only if staff other than nurses (e.g., physiotherapists) are involved.

2. Common rest and activity orders include complete bed rest (CBR), bed rest with bathroom privileges (BR with BRP), and activity as tolerated (AAT or "up ad lib"). An order may specify that a patient needs help getting up ("assist 1" or "assist 2").

3. All rest and activity orders should be transcribed accurately on the PI screen. A requisition is not required unless someone other than a nurse (e.g., a physiotherapist) is needed.

4. Restraints may be physical (e.g., wrist restraints) or chemical (sedatives). The use of restraints is controversial. They must be ordered by a physician. If family members are upset by restraints, be empathetic and refer them to the nurse.

5. Devices to support rest and activity include special mattresses to vary pressure, anti-embolic stockings, foot boards, bed cradles, trapeze bars, abduction pillows, side rails, and lifts.

6. Activities of daily living (ADL) include eating, dressing, getting up, performing hygiene, grooming, toileting, and bathing. Patients' ADL status may be "independent," "self with assist," or "by nurse." Patients should be helped to do as much as they can because taking care of their own basic needs preserves dignity and privacy.

KEY TERMS

embolism 597

hypostatic pneumonia 591

hypoxia 594

range of motion (ROM)
exercises 594

REVIEW QUESTIONS

1. What is the philosophy behind encouraging the patient to be as active as possible as soon as possible?

2. What criteria does the physician consider when ordering a patient's level of activity?

3. When is a requisition needed for activity orders?

4. Where are activity orders usually transcribed?

5. Why do nurses turn immobile patients?

6. Why is the use of restraints controversial?

7. Explain the purpose of anti-embolic stockings. Where would you order them from? What measurements would you need?

8. What is a geri chair?

9. What is a Hoyer lift used for?

10. What information must you note when requisitioning a test off the unit? Why?

APPLICATION EXERCISES

1. Define each of the following rest and activity orders, and explain when it would be given. Using a PI screen supplied by your professor, transcribe each order appropriately:

   a. AAT

   b. BR with BRP

   c. Up assist 1

   d. Commode privileges

   e. Strict bed rest

   f. Turn q2h

   g. Nurse in prone position

   h. Up with physio

   i. ROM qid by physio

   j. May be up in geri chair PRN

2. Fred, 72 years old, has been hospitalized and is new on your unit. You go down to discuss his menu choices with him. Fred looks desperate as you enter the room. He pleads with you to help him get up to the bathroom and to put his side rails down. He claims it has been over an hour since he called for the nurse and he can't wait any longer. He looks fit and appears oriented. With another student, discuss what you would do. List reasons why you might want to help him, and reasons why not. Discuss the risks involved both for yourself and for Fred. How can you maintain his dignity and show compassion, yet stay within your scope of practice? Are there extenuating circumstances under which assisting him to the bathroom would be acceptable?

3. Janice comes to the floor to find her elderly mother in a geri chair with a chest restraint and arm restraints on. She has an IV. Janice is furious and lashes out at you, asking how the staff could sanction such inhumane and cruel behaviour. She claims her mom is a little confused but does not deserve this. The patient is anxious and crying at this point, asking to be untied. There is no nurse in sight. The daughter moves to take off the restraints. With a classmate, review this situation and discuss how you would deal with it, and what you might say to the daughter.

4. Mrs. James arrives at the patient-care unit to find her mother, Mrs. Anderson, sitting in the hall in a geri chair. She is held in the chair with an abdominal restraint, and her wrists are tied to the arms of the chair. Her hair is messy. She has her hose rolled down to below her knees and no shoes on. She is crying and saying, "Get me out. Oh God, get me out! Look what they are doing to me. I want to go home. Please let me go." Mrs. James stands for a moment looking at her mother. She bursts into tears and turns to the nursing station where you are sitting. "How could you? How could you? Look at her! Do you people have no compassion?" Her voice is rising. You look around and see no nurses. How would you handle this situation?

WEBSITES OF INTEREST

Explanation of Decubitus Ulcers or Pressure Sores

www.apparelyzed.com/pressuresores.html

College of Nurses Ontario: Practice Standard for the Use of Restraints

www.cno.org/globalassets/docs/prac/41043_restraints.pdf

absorption the process by which a medication is taken into the body, broken down, and transformed into a form the body can use.

acid-fast bacilli (AFB) a "rapid" test done to isolate and identify microorganisms such as the one that causes tuberculosis.

active infection an infection in which signs and symptoms are present.

acute care care for a patient who is acutely ill, that is, very ill but with an illness expected to run a short course (as opposed to a chronic illness). Acute care is provided for patients with a variety of health problems.

acute infection an infection that is time limited.

administrative health professional (AHP) a graduate from an accredited health office administration program who assumes administrative, communication, and/or clinical responsibilities in a health-care setting.

aerobic bacteria bacteria that require oxygen to grow.

affinity, cluster, categorization, or analogous scheduling scheduling similar appointments together, for example, scheduling physical examinations on a certain day.

allied health care any duty or profession that supports primary health-care professionals, such as physicians, nurse practitioners, or midwives, in delivering health-care services.

alternative health care nontraditional methods and practices based on a natural approach, including chiropractic, acupuncture, massage, and aromatherapy. Also known as *complementary health care*.

AMA an acronym that means "against medical advice." This refers to a patient leaving the hospital without the physician's approval.

anaerobic bacteria bacteria that do not require oxygen to grow.

angiocatheter a plastic tube, usually attached to the puncturing needle, inserted into a blood vessel for infusion, injection, or pressure monitoring. Usually just called an *Angiocath*.

antenatal before birth.

antibody a protein specific to a certain antigen that weakens or destroys pathogens.

antigen a pathogen or any other substance that induces an antibody response.

antiseptic a cleansing agent that can be applied to living tissue to destroy pathogens.

archive removing a file from active status and storing it in a secondary location or on a secondary medium.

arrhythmia loss of normal rhythm of the heartbeat.

arteriosclerosis hardening of the arteries; reduces blood flow.

asepsis a state in which pathogens are absent or reduced. There are two principal types of asepsis: medical and surgical.

asthma a disease that affects the air passages in the lungs, causing wheezing and shortness of breath.

asymptomatic without clinical signs or symptoms.

atherosclerosis arteriosclerosis because of deposits of fat in arterial walls.

atrial fibrillation an abnormality of heart rhythm in which chambers of the heart no longer beat in synchrony, with the atrium beating much faster than the ventricles. The heart rate is fast and irregular.

attribute an inborn personal quality or characteristic.

autoclave a device using steam for sterilization.

autonomy a person's right to self-determination. In health care it refers to a patient's right to make his or her own decisions without coercion; for example, decisions for treatment based on fact and being fully informed of all treatment options.

autopsy the examination of a body to determine the cause of death or to identify disease processes.

bactericidal killing microorganisms.

bacteriostatic reducing or inhibiting the number of microorganisms.

Bard button (MIC device) a feeding device placed permanently in the stomach to facilitate supplemental feedings.

behaviour a person's discernible responses and actions.

beneficiary a person eligible to receive insurance benefits under specified conditions.

bolus the usually rapid infusion of additional IV fluids in addition to the base amount ordered for the patient.

bowel obstruction a blockage in the intestines that prevents their contents from moving forward.

bowel resection surgery where a section of bowel is removed, and the remaining bowel is reconnected.

bowel sounds present (BSP) the audible return of gastrointestinal movement or function, also called peristalsis, often charted as BS ×4, meaning it sounds audible in all four abdominal quadrants.

bradycardia extremely slow heartbeat.

bruit a sound, especially an abnormal one, heard on auscultation or by ultrasound.

capitation or population-based funding a funding system that pays a physician a given amount per patient enrolled, regardless of the number of services performed.

catastrophic drug plan a plan that would cover overriding drug costs causing impending financial hardship on individuals.

cc cubic centimetre; 1 cc equals 1 millilitre (mL). In hospitals, cc is used more often than mL.

cerebral vascular accident (CVA) (stroke) damage to the brain that occurs when the blood supply to an area of the brain is diminished or occluded completely.

chronic care care for someone with a chronic illness (one that typically progresses slowly but is often lifelong).

chronic infection an infection that is persistent over a long period, perhaps for life.

chronic obstructive pulmonary disease (COPD) any chronic lung condition in which the flow of expired air is slowed down.

coronary intensive care unit (CICU) an intensive care unit that specifically looks after patients who have had heart attacks and cardiac surgery, including heart transplants.

clapping or percussion using cupped hands to gently but firmly strike affected regions of the chest to move secretions.

clawback the amount, dollar for dollar, that the federal government cuts health transfer payments to a province or territory that permits extra-billing.

clinic a facility providing medical care on an outpatient basis. It may be freestanding or associated with a hospital. Many clinics have a specialty, such as ongoing care for diabetes, orthopedics, or cancer. The term is currently also applied to primary-care groups that offer out-of-office services where rostered patients can seek medical care when their physician is unavailable.

clinical secretary a health office professional working in a hospital who assumes responsibilities for the secretarial, clerical, communication, and other designated needs of a hospital unit or department.

code of ethics a set of guidelines for ethical conduct.

collaborative partnership the relationship among hospitals that have entered into an agreement to form a partnership, sharing clinical and administrative responsibilities.

colonoscopy a diagnostic procedure used both as a screening test and to investigate certain gastrointestinal complaints. Using an endoscope (equipped with a small camera), the physician can view the entire rectum and colon. The physician can also take a biopsy, if needed.

colostomy a surgical procedure that creates an artificial opening from the colon to the surface of the abdomen through which feces are excreted.

combination or blended scheduling a combination of affinity and random scheduling.

complementary health care nontraditional methods and practices, based on a natural approach, including chiropractic, acupuncture, massage, and aromatherapy. Also known as *alternative health care.*

computed tomography (CT) a type of X-ray that produces three-dimensional images of cross-sections of body parts.

computerized physician order entry (CPOE) an electronic, multifunctional software system used in health-care facilities that, among other functions, enables the physician (or other provider) to enter orders directly into the computer.

congestive heart failure (CHF) a condition in which a weakened heart is unable to pump all of the blood out of the lungs each time it beats. Blood pools at the bottom of the lungs, interfering with breathing.

contagious or communicable disease a disease that is spread from person to person.

contamination the presence of pathogens on an object.

controlled drugs drugs defined by federal law that special rules apply to because they are liable to be abused.

core competency the basic or essential skills that one needs to succeed in a particular profession.

crepitation or crackles sounds produced by air passing over airway secretions.

crash cart a cart carrying the supplies needed for immediate treatment of a heart attack.

credentialling a process whereby a peer group judges an individual's qualifications to perform certain services.

critical value a test result that indicates a life-threatening situation and requires immediate attention.

critically ill experiencing life-threatening problems; in medical crisis.

cross-coverage moving from one area to another, or covering two units.

cultural competence a set of behaviours, attitudes, and policies that work together to meet the needs of a cross-cultural population in a positive, culturally sensitive manner; individuals are culturally knowledgeable, informed, and act without personal bias.

culture any combination of the languages, beliefs, values, norms, behaviours, and even material objects that are passed from one generation to the next.

cystectomy surgical removal of the urinary bladder.

cystoscope a long, thin, flexible instrument with a light at the end used to examine the bladder. It is inserted through the urethra and threaded up into the bladder.

day surgery surgery conducted with a hospital stay of less than 24 hours.

deductible the portion of a benefit that a beneficiary must pay before receiving coverage.

deep suctioning introducing the suction catheter into the lower trachea and bronchi.

deregulated when a service is removed from a province's or territory's fee schedule so that it is no longer insured under that jurisdiction's health plan.

diastolic pressure the pressure on the vascular walls when the heart is relaxing.

discharge any release from a health care facility by doctor's orders.

disinfectant a chemical substance that destroys or eliminates specific species of infectious microorganisms. It is not usually effective against bacterial spores.

disinfection a more thorough removal of contaminants than sanitization but less thorough than sterilization.

distal the part farthest from the body.

distribution the process by which metabolites are transported to various parts of the body.

diversity differences and variety, including people from different ethnicities, sexual orientations, and social backgrounds.

diverticulitis inflammation of a sac-like bulge that may develop in the wall of the large intestine.

doctors' orders written or oral directions given by a physician to the nursing staff and other health professionals regarding the care, medications, treatment, and laboratory and diagnostic tests a patient is to receive while in hospital.

double scheduling or double-column booking scheduling two patient appointments at the same time, on the assumption that one of the appointments will involve little of the doctor's time.

dressing tray a specially prepared sterile tray containing the basic equipment to change a dressing on a wound or surgical incision. It contains a K-basin, 4 × 4 gauze dressings, a galley cup (a small metal or glass cup about the size of a shot glass used for cleansing solutions), and usually two sets of disposable forceps.

drops per minute (gtt/min) a measure of the rate of an IV infusion.

duty a moral obligation.

dysphagia difficulty swallowing.

dyspnea difficulty breathing.

elective surgery surgery that is necessary but not an emergency and can therefore be booked in advance. Examples of elective surgery include removal of a tumour, a hip replacement, or a hysterectomy.

electronic health record (EHR) an accumulation of essential information from an individual's electronic medical records that is accessed electronically at different points of service for purposes of patient care.

electronic medical record (EMR) a legal health record in digital format. It contains the patient's health information collected by one or a group of providers in one location. It is a subset of the electronic health record (EHR).

electronic medical records system a total medical office system, including both hardware and software, with the capability of replacing all components of a paper chart (health record) electronically.

electronic transfer (ET) a vehicle for the electronic transmission of medical claims from the source computer to the ministry's mainframe computer. ET is used generically to refer to various names for electronic transfer across Canada.

embolism obstruction of a blood vessel by a blood clot, an air bubble, or foreign matter.

emergentologist a physician specializing in emergency medicine.

emesis basin a small basin, usually kidney shaped, used for patients to vomit into or cough up sputum or phlegm. It is also used to hold solutions for a variety of purposes. It may be ordered sterile or just clean.

emphysema a disease characterized by the gradual destruction of the alveoli, which fuse to form large air spaces. Exchange of oxygen and carbon dioxide through these larger air sacs is inadequate.

endoscopic retrograde cholangiopancreatography (ERCP) a diagnostic test allowing visualization of the pancreas and bile ducts. A biopsy can be obtained, if necessary, during this test.

endoscopy examination of a canal, such as the colon, with an endoscope: a thin tube with lenses to allow visualization.

endotracheal suctioning suctioning through an artificial airway known as a tracheostomy.

enema the introduction of liquid into the rectum for cleansing the bowel and for stimulating evacuation of the bowels.

enteral feed feeding by tube directly into the gastrointestinal system.

enzyme a protein capable of initiating a chemical reaction that involves the formation or breakage of chemical bonds. When muscle damage or death occurs, enzymes within the muscle cell are released into the circulating blood.

esophagogastroduodenoscopy (EGD) a diagnostic procedure used to investigate complaints of the stomach and upper part of the small intestine. Using an endoscope (equipped with a small camera), the physician can view the throat, stomach, and part of the small intestine. A biopsy can be obtained, if needed.

ethics the philosophical study of standards accepted by society that determine what is right and wrong in human behaviour.

ethnic relating to groups of people with a common racial, religious, linguistic, or cultural heritage.

ethnocentrism the tendency to use one's own culture's standards as the yardstick to judge everyone; the belief in the superiority of one's own group or culture.

exacerbation a period in which a chronic infection shows symptoms.

externship a cooperative or workplace experience or period of training for a student that is provided by the student's educational facility.

extra-billing charging a patient more than the amount paid by the provincial or territorial health plan for a medically necessary service.

fee-for-service a system under which a provider is paid for each insured service rendered to an insured patient. These providers are considered "opted-in" to the public payment system.

fixed oils (also called base or carrier oils) oils, extracted primarily from plants, that do not evaporate.

flag (of a chart) to draw attention to a new entry by sticking a coloured marker in the chart, placing a coloured sticker on the back of the chart, or using some other device to visually draw attention.

fluid retention an accumulation of fluid in body tissues or body cavities.

fob a small security device that can be added to a computer for access purposes. It displays a randomly generated access code that changes every few seconds.

fundus the top of the uterus. Measuring how high the fundus is in the abdomen provides valuable information about the size of the uterus and the progression of fetal growth.

gastric suction also called Gomco suction, this is gentle suction applied to a tube placed in the stomach to remove excessive secretions, such as saliva and gastric juices, that tend to accumulate in the stomach after surgery or trauma because the intestine is sluggish. This can prevent or relieve nausea and vomiting.

gastritis inflammation of the stomach.

gastrostomy tube (G-tube) a feeding tube inserted through an incision in the abdomen into the stomach.

global budget any arrangement in which a facility or provider receives a fixed amount of money for medical services, regardless of patient volume, length of stay, or services rendered.

head injury routine a special assessment for a patient who has had head trauma or surgery, including checks on neurological functioning, such as verbal response and pupil dilation.

health according to one definition, "a relative state in which one is able to function well physically, mentally, socially, and spiritually in order to express the full range of one's unique potentialities within the environment in which one is living."

health information any information pertaining to someone's physical or mental health, condition, or infirmity, whether given orally or recorded in any manner, that is created or received directly or indirectly by a health professional or health organization.

health information custodian a person or organization who has the responsibility for safeguarding and controlling personal health information in connection with the powers and duties performed.

health record any documentation relating to a health care patient. The term *record* is used for a single document, such as a doctor's note on an assessment or a lab report; it also refers to a collection of documents, such as a patient's chart.

hemorrhage loss of a large amount of blood (greater than 500 cc for an average adult).

heparin an anticoagulant (blood thinner) given to people who are at risk for developing blood clots.

heparin (hep) lock (saline lock, PRN adapter) a device that provides intravenous access when needed, without continuous infusion. It sits in the vein and must be flushed at specific intervals with saline solution or heparin solution.

hiatus hernia a condition in which the upper part of the stomach, which is joined to the esophagus or feeding tube, moves up into the chest through a hole (called a hiatus) in the diaphragm.

homeostasis a balance between the body's internal conditions and the environment.

hospital number (also called a medical records number, or MRN) a unique number assigned to each patient admitted to hospital.

hypertension (high blood pressure) excessive force of the blood against the vessel walls as the heart pumps it through the body.

hypostatic pneumonia pneumonia developing as a result of decreased air exchange combined with an inability to drain pooled bronchial secretions.

hypoxia insufficient oxygen in blood or tissue.

identification (ID) band a plastic bracelet bearing the patient's name, hospital number, and a bar code that can be scanned to validate patient identification (e.g., for medication administration). The bracelet is removed upon discharge.

ileostomy a surgical procedure that creates an artificial opening from the ileum to the surface of abdomen through which feces are excreted.

immunity an individual's ability to fight off disease.

immunoglobulin a serum that contains antibodies that can help protect an exposed person from contracting the disease.

incontinence the inability to control urine elimination (urinary incontinence) or bowel function (referred to as *incontinent of bowel*).

indwelling left in place.

infection a disease process that results from the entry and spread of a microorganism.

insured health care services medically necessary hospital, physician, and surgical-dental services provided to insured individuals.

interstitial in between the body's cells.

intracellular within the cells of the body.

intravascular within blood vessels.

intravenous (IV) administered directly into the circulatory system via a vein.

ischemia a local lack of red blood cells because of mechanical obstruction of the blood supply, usually caused by arterial narrowing.

IV push (IVP) a medication given into the vein or an ongoing IV infusion using a syringe and a needle.

jejunostomy tube (J-tube) a feeding tube placed through the abdominal wall into the small bowel.

kidney stones or calculi hard objects built up from salts and minerals in the urinary tract.

laparoscope a type of endoscope (a visualizing instrument with a tube and lens) that allows surgeons to visualize internal structures. Using this tool, surgery can be done through incisions often 5 centimetres in length or smaller.

latent infection an infection in which the symptoms disappear and recur, but the disease-causing agent remains in the body.

licensure a legal document, obtained after passing written and clinical examinations, that is required for health-care practitioners in regulated fields.

loading dose a medication ordered as a single-order stat medication with a dose that is higher than the usual or routine dose.

local infection an infection that is confined to a specific region of the body, for example, a finger.

locum tenens (locum) a doctor temporarily taking over another doctor's practice.

machine-readable input/output (MRI/MRO) any information that can be read by a computer, whether it is sent or received.

magnetic resonance imaging (MRI) a diagnostic tool that uses a magnetic field to produce images of body structures and organs.

mammography a specialized X-ray of the breast.

managed care a set of strategies, procedures, and policies designed to control the use of health care services, sometimes by organizing doctors, hospitals, and other providers into groups to improve the quality and cost effectiveness of health care.

medical assistant (U.S.) a person who is trained to assist a physician with various clinical tests, examinations, and procedures.

medical office assistant (Canada) a person who handles primarily administrative but also some clinical duties in a health office. The title varies (e.g., medical secretary, medical office manager).

medically necessary referring to those services or supplies that are essential to the care and treatment of an illness or injury and that could not have been omitted without adversely affecting the patient's medical condition or the quality of the health care rendered under generally accepted professional standards of medical practice at the time and place incurred.

metabolic disorder a condition characterized by the body's inability to synthesize or process food into forms the body can use for energy, growth, and development.

metabolic rate the amount of energy expended in a given period, or the physical changes that occur in the body that result in heat production.

metabolism the physiological and biochemical processes that promote growth and sustain life. It is also the process of breaking down a drug or other substance into metabolites used by the body, or the altering of a substance so that it may be inactivated and excreted from the body.

microorganism an organism so small that it can only be seen under a microscope.

midstream urine specimen (MSU) also called a clean catch urine specimen; a urine specimen collected after cleansing oneself and discarding the first part of the urine stream to avoid contamination; used for culture and sensitivity tests.

morals what a person believes to be right and wrong pertaining to how to act, treat others, and get along in an organized society.

myocardial infarct (MI, heart attack, or coronary) damage to the heart caused by a blockage in one of the coronary arteries, cutting off blood supply to a part of the heart.

nasogastric tube (N/G tube or Levine tube) a feeding tube put through the nose into the stomach.

nasopharyngeal suctioning suctioning with a catheter through the nose to reach the mouth and throat (pharynx).

new admission a patient recently admitted to hospital.

nonpathogenic not causing disease.

nonretention or straight catheter one that is inserted to drain urine and then removed.

nosocomial infection a hospital-related infection; one that is not present or incubating when a patient is admitted to a hospital or health care facility.

ophthalmic relating to the eye.

ophthalmoscope a device used to examine the eyes.

opportunistic infection an infection that does not ordinarily cause disease but does so under certain circumstances, for example, in compromised immune systems; so called because it takes advantage of an "opportunity."

opted-in (of a physician) billing the provincial or territorial plan for health services rendered.

opted-out (of a physician) billing patients for services rendered; patients pay the fee to the doctor and submit a claim to the health plan. Very few physicians chose to opt out. This may change, however, if private health care becomes more prevalent and patients can buy private insurance for medically necessary services.

order entry the process of interpreting, recording, and generating the administrative steps required for doctors' orders to be implemented.

oropharyngeal suctioning suctioning with a catheter through the mouth to reach the mouth only or the mouth and the back of the throat.

orphan patient a patient who does not have a family physician and must get medical services from clinics and emergency departments.

otic via the ear.

otitis media infection of the middle ear.

otoscope a device used to examine the ears.

outguiding a system for keeping track of paper health records taken from their normal location.

palliative care care for a person with a terminal illness who is in hospital to die, to have the condition stabilized, or for pain control.

pandemic a global outbreak of a specific disease that does or has the potential go affect a large population.

parenteral by injection or intravenous administration.

partial claims payment a payment to a provider of a lesser amount than that claimed; an explanation of why the payment was reduced will be provided.

pathogen a microorganism that causes disease.

patient in the past, a person seeking or receiving health care; the term has evolved to represent an individual who is also actively involved in all aspects of his or her care, from diagnosis to treatment, and who assumes responsibility for his or her heath.

patient-controlled analgesia (PCA) a mechanism by which a patient can self-administer analgesic intravenously with the assistance of a computerized pump. It allows for the introduction of specific doses at preset intervals into the IV line.

patient flow the process of maximizing efficiency for moving patients through their health care experience; mainly associated with hospitals and other health care facilities. It is ensuring patient access to the *right care* in the *right place* at the *right time* in the most efficient way possible.

patient intervention (PI) screen a computer-based patient-care document listing a patient's information, including the code status, health education/teaching requirements, discharge planning, and patient assessments and interventions that have been ordered. It will identify the status of the order.

percutaneous endoscopic gastrostomy tube (PEG tube or PEG catheter) a feeding tube inserted via endoscopy into the stomach or jejunum.

peristalsis wavelike movements of the gastrointestinal tract that propel food and other contents along.

pharmacology a biological science and academic discipline that deals with the properties, uses, and actions of drugs and chemicals in living beings.

physician incentive when physicians are monetarily remunerated for maximizing services related to preventive medicine (e.g., immunizations, Pap smears, mammograms). This involves encouraging their patients to have screening tests.

physician registration number or billing number a unique number assigned by the Ministry of Health to every provider eligible to bill a provincial or territorial health plan; it is required for billing.

placebo effect an improvement in symptoms without active treatment that occurs for psychological reasons when a person thinks he or she is getting treatment.

pneumonia an acute infection of the tissues of the lung.

postpartum after delivery.

postural drainage positioning the patient with the head lower than the body so that gravity can help drain the mucus and secretions.

pre-admission a process wherein patients who are booked for surgery receive preoperative and postoperative teaching and fill in documents ahead of time.

preceptor a mentor who guides and supervises a student throughout a workplace experience.

primary care groups (PCGs) a variety of structurally similar groups of physicians or other health professionals working collaboratively under an organizational framework to deliver primary health services. The health professionals may or may not be in one physical location.

primary health care (1) integrated health care by a provider who addresses the majority of a patient's health concerns; (2) treatment administered during the first medical contact for a health concern.

prophylactic a measure taken to prevent a problem from developing.

provider any person or group of persons who delivers a health care service.

provincial or territorial billing the process whereby a health care provider submits a claim to a province or territory for insured health services rendered.

provisional diagnosis a diagnosis subject to change after an actual diagnosis has been established.

provisional diagnosis a tentative diagnosis made before a procedure is done, which may be confirmed or changed by findings.

pulmonary function test (PFT) a test done on a patient to measure the breathing capacity of his or her lungs.

purge (of file) review and reorganize to remove outdated information that is no longer actively needed to provide care to the patient.

quality assurance any systematic process that checks if a product or service is meeting specified requirements. In health care, it is a systematic assessment to ensure that services are of the highest possible quality using existing resources.

quarantine isolating or separating a patient, patient-care unit, or facility.

range of motion (ROM) exercises a set of exercises that puts joints through their full range of positions.

rationalization of services centralizing certain services, particularly those that require specialized care, to one hospital in a region.

reciprocal agreement an agreement among provinces and territories (with the exception of Quebec) that allows providers to bill their own ministries for services rendered to insured residents from other parts of Canada (e.g., a person from Manitoba visiting a doctor in Nova Scotia).

recurrent infection a distinct episode of an infection after recovery from the initial infection; may involve the same pathogens or different ones.

reference range the normal range; the values expected for a particular test.

regulated profession a field legally restricted to practitioners with a specific professional qualification or provincial or territorial registration.

relapse the reemergence of an initial infection after it appears to have subsided but has not been cured.

remission a period in which a chronic infection shows no symptoms.

remittance advice (RA) a monthly statement of approved claims from the ministry.

repatriation returning a patient who has been discharged to another facility back to the original hospital. For example, if a patient requires a higher level of care and is sent to another hospital, returning the patient to the original hospital is called repatriation.

rhonchi or wheezes musical-pitched sounds produced by air passing through narrowed bronchi, heard on auscultation of the lungs.

right a moral, legal, cultural, or traditional claim.

role a position in life that carries expectations of responsibilities and appropriate behaviour.

rostering establishing a list of patients who agree to participate in a primary health network according to the rules of the province or territory.

sanitization removal of gross contaminants and some microorganisms from instruments, skin, and so on; the lowest level of medical hygiene.

sanitizer a substance that significantly reduces the bacterial population in an inanimate environment but does not destroy all bacteria or other microorganisms.

scope of practice working within the parameters of duties and responsibilities outlined by one's professional training and skill set.

septicemia an infection in the blood stream that can worsen rapidly and is often life threatening.

serum the fluid portion of the blood. Often used in phrases describing levels of blood components, as in serum creatinine.

service code, billing code, fee code, or item code a number that identifies the service a provider has performed for an insured patient and determines the fee to be paid by a provincial or territorial health plan.

sharp any instrument with a sharp edge or point, such as a scalpel, scissors, or a needle.

shift report when essential patient information is passed on to the next shift of nurses.

sick role a particular social role that an ill person adopts, which involves giving up normal responsibilities and accepting care. May sometimes involve uncharacteristically passive behaviour.

specialist a physician who holds a certificate from the Royal College of Physicians and Surgeons and who has completed postgraduate studies in a particular specialty field.

sphygmomanometer a device used to take blood pressure.

Standard Precautions a set of internationally accepted infection control measures, policies, and procedures used in health care facilities to prevent the transmission of diseases that can be acquired by contact with blood, body fluids, nonintact skin (including rashes), and mucous membranes. These measures protect both health professionals and patients.

stat (short for Latin *statim*) immediately.

sterile completely free of pathogens.

sterile technique methods to avoid contamination of sterile materials.

sterilization the process of destroying all microorganisms, including bacterial endospores and viruses. This is the highest level of cleanliness.

stethoscope a device that amplifies sound and is used by doctors and other health care professionals to listen to the heart and to take blood pressure.

stoma an artificial opening; in this case, one from the bowel through the abdominal wall.

stream scheduling or fixed-interval scheduling allotting a specific, unique time slot for each patient appointment; the most common method of scheduling.

subacute, transitional, or step-down care medical and nursing care that is less intensive than traditional acute-care hospital treatment.

subculture the values and practices of a group that distinguish it from the larger culture.

subdural hematoma a blood clot under the dura mater, the fibrous membrane forming the outer envelope of the brain and spinal cord, usually resulting from trauma to the head.

suture removal tray a specially prepared sterile tray similar to the dressing tray, but containing suture removal scissors or clip removers. Some facilities use a dressing tray, and nurses simply add a disposable suture removal blade or prepackaged clip removers.

systemic circulating through the bloodstream to produce a general effect on the body.

systemic infection an infection that has spread to more than one region of the body.

systolic pressure the pressure on the vascular walls when the heart is contracting.

template a computerized file with a predesigned and customized format that can be used for specific functions (e.g., letterhead, formatted letters, or for scheduling purposes).

teratogenic causing abnormalities in the fetus.

terminal cleaning a thorough wash with a disinfectant solution of all equipment (bed, bedside unit, etc.) used by a patient upon his or her discharge.

third-party service a service carried out at the request of someone other than the patient or for the explicit use of someone other than the patient.

topical applied to the skin or affected area.

tracheostomy an artificial airway through an incision in the trachea.

transcription creating a written copy of a dictated or recorded message.

transfer the act of moving a patient from one place to another within the same health care facility.

triage assessing the seriousness of a patient's presenting problem to determine who needs to have medical help first. For example, someone coming to the emergency department with chest pain would be brought in to see the doctor immediately, whereas someone with a sore throat would be considered a nonurgent case and able to wait.

ulcerative colitis inflammation and ulceration of the innermost lining of the colon (the large intestine).

ultrasonographer a technician who operates an ultrasound machine.

ultrasonography a procedure that uses high-frequency sound waves directed at an organ or object to produce a visual image.

values the beliefs a person holds dear and that guide that person's decisions and behaviour or conduct.

vibrations rapid movements of flattened hands over the patient's chest to move secretions.

virulence the power of a microbe to produce disease in a particular host.

volatile oils oils, extracted primarily from plants, that evaporate.

ward clerk an individual who manages the administrative and communication needs of a patient-care unit. The title is being replaced with *clinical secretary* or *communications coordinator*.

wave scheduling scheduling several patients for the same block of time, typically an hour.

wellness a state of physical and emotional well-being, broadly considered.

A

abduction pillow, 598
ABG. *See* arterial blood gases
aboriginal peoples
    cross-cultural health care and, 68–69
    culture of, 64
    Inuit, 74
absorption, 183
Academic Ambulatory Care Centre at
    Vancouver General Hospital, 405
accounting number, 347
accreditation, 107, 408
acid- fast bacilli (AFB), 580
acknowledgment phase, of illness
    response, 50
Acquired Immune Deficiency Syndrome
    (AIDS), 111, 119, 133
acronyms, 219
action codes, 355
action phase, of illness response, 50
activated partial thromboplastin time
    (APTT/aPTT), 145
active infection, 112
active verbs, 218
activities of daily living, 493, 599–600
activity
    nutrition and, 542
    as tolerated, 596
activity orders, 593–597
    complete bed rest (CBR), 594
    consciousness and cognition,
        592–593
    criteria, 592–593
    nature of illness, 592
    physical capabilities, 592
    physical energy, 592
    physiotherapy, 594
    surgery, 593
acute blood loss, 537
acute care, 406
acute infection, 112
adaptive interpersonal skills, 13
address change, 299
administration, routes of, 179–183
administrative health professional
    (AHP), 3, 20–22, 205, 375
    attributes of, 10–17
    communication and, 205
    duties and responsibility, 20–22
    employment opportunities, 5–10
    ethics and, 17–20
    hospitalization and, 55–57
    illness behaviour and, 53
    implications for, 94
    medical secretary, 3–5

professional growth, 24–33
    skills of, 15–17
    telephone and, 225
    workplace, 22–24
administrative manager, 3
administrative nursing coordinator, 6
administrative responsibility, 20–21
admissions
    completing face sheet, 451–452
    date, inpatient, 348
    elective, 446
    emergency, 446–449
    insurance and type of
        accommodation, 450
    interview, 456
    obstetrical, 449
    outpatient, 449–450
    preparing ID band, 452–453
    procedures, 450–452
    sheet, 451–452, 454–456, 455f
    types, 446–453
admitting/client flow department,
    411–412
admitting diagnosis, 455, 492
adopted children, 297
adrenergic, 175–176
ADU. *See* automatic medication
    dispensing units
advanced access scheduling,
    264–265
adverse effects, 184
aerobic bacteria, 113
AF. *See* atrial fibrillation
AFB. *See* acid-fast bacilli
affinity scheduling, 262
African Canadians, 73
after-hours clinics, 91
against medical advice (AMA), 471
age, 185
    of client, 290
    nutrition and, 542
aggressive clients, 243–244
aging population, 45, 47
AHCIP. *See* Alberta Health Care
    Insurance Plan
AHP. *See* administrative health
    professional
AIDS. *See* Acquired Immune Deficiency
    Syndrome
airborne transmission, 115, 116
Alberta
    action codes, 355
    after-hours clinics, 91
    chiropractors, 99
    health numbers, 289

primary care reform, 90
    regional health authorities, 87
    serice code, 324
Alberta Health Care Insurance Plan
    (AHCIP), 311
alcohol, 126
    isopropyl, 125
alcoholic addiction treatment
    centres, 407
allergies
    to drugs, 184–185
    to foods, 185
    list of, 379
allied health care, 7, 9
allied health professionals, 140
alphabetical filing systems, 390–391
altered cognition, 133
alternative health care, 8
AMA. *See* against medical advice
ambulance services, 288
amyotrophic lateral sclerosis (ALS), 17
anaerobic bacteria, 113
analgesic, 176
    PCA, 528–529
analogous scheduling, 262
analytical thinking, 13
anastomosis, 561
Ancomycin-resistant Staphylococcus
    Aureaus (VRSA), 122
2/3 and 1/3, 532
anemia, 537
anesthetic, 176
anesthetic record, 460
angiocath, 523
angiocatheter, 523
angiogram, 159
animal sources of drugs, 171
annual health examination (AHE), 314
answering devices, 222–223
answering service, 222
antacid, 176
antenatal preventive health assessment,
    317
antenatal visit, 317
anti-anxiety, 176
anti-arrhythmic, 176
antibiotic, 176
antibiotic-resistant bacteria, 45–46
antibody, 117
anti-cholinergic, 176
anti-coagulant, 176
anti-coagulant orders, 512–514
anti-convulsant, 176
anti-depressant, 176
anti-diabetic/anti-hyperglycemic, 176–177

H

mobile devices
    and clients, 434
mobile phones, 427. *See also* cell phones
mobility impairment, 133
mode of transmission, 114–115
    for HIV, 119
modesty, 75
morals, 17
morbidity, leading causes of, 47
morning rush, 227–228
most responsible physician (MRP),
    446, 481
motor vehicle insurance, 302
MPI. *See* Master Patient Index
MRI. *See* machine-readable input;
    magnetic resonance imaging
MRP. *See* most responsible physician
MRSA. *See* methicillin-resistant
    Staphylococcus aureus
MSU. *See* midstream urine specimen
    (MSU)
multiculturalism, 66
    policy, 62
multidisciplinary note, 457–458
multi-drug resistant (MDR-TB), 118
multiple sclerosis (MS), 73
mumps, 118
mutual respect, 79
mydriatic, 178
myocardial infarct (MI), 148, 574–575

N

NAHUC. *See* national association of
    health unit coordinators
name change, 297
narcotics, 178
    control records, 196–197
nasal prongs, 583, 583*f*
nasal route of administration, 180
nasogastric suction, 562–564
nasogastric tube (N-G tube), 551–552
nasopharyngeal, 585
National Association of Pharmacy
    Regulatory Authorities
    (NAPRA), 173
National HIV and Retrovirology
    Laboratories, 138
nationality, 64
National Microbiology Laboratory,
    138–139
natural health products (NHPs), 186–187
Natural Health Products Regulations, 186
nephrology, 414
networking, 29
neurology, 414
new admission, 444
newborns, registering, 297
Newfoundland and Labrador Dental
    Association, 87
next of kin, 456
no added salt/Na diet, 545

noise level, 133
nonmaleficence, 18. *See also* beneficence
nonpathogenic, 113
nonretention catheter, 569
normal saline, 527, 533
Northern Health Travel Grant, 286
no-shows, 271–272
nosocomial infections, 113
NP. *See* nurse practitioners
NPLC. *See* nurse practitioner-led clinics
numeric component, of billing
    code, 323
numeric filing systems, 391
nurse practitioner-led clinics
    (NPLCs), 100
nurse practitioners (NPs), 100
nurses, 576
nursing assessments, 578–579, 586
    chest assessments, 578–579
    peripheral vascular assessment, 586
    vital signs, 578
nursing homes, 407
nursing procedure maunal, 476
nursing station, 427–438
    blood pressure cuffs, 427–428
    equipment and materials, 427
    flashlights, 428
    ophthalmoscope/otoscope kit, 428
    percussion hammer, 428
    sphygmomanometers, 427–428
    stationery supplies, 428
    stethoscopes, 427
    tongue depressors, 428
    tuning fork, 428
nursing unit assistant, 3
nursing unit coordinators, 3, 405
nutrition, 492–493
    activity and, 542
    age and, 542
    Canada's Food Guide, 543
    clinical secretary and, 543–544
    diets ordered, types of, 544–549
    factors influencing needs, 542
    gender and, 542
    genetics and, 542
    in hospital, 543–544
    hospital meals, 543
    illness and, 542
    pregnancy and, 542
    therapeutic diets, 544–549
    total parenteral, 538, 554–555
nutritional/dietary services, 413

O

OB. *See* occult blood
obstetrical admissions, 449
    admitting baby, 449
occult blood (OB), 152
Occupational Health and Safety, 110
occupational roles, 52
occupational settings, 7–10

ODAA. *See* Ontario Dental Assistants
    Association (ODAA)
ODB. *See* Ontario Drug Benefit
office forms, filing, 392
oil retention enemas, 560
oils, 171
ointments, 180
oncology therapy, 415
online job sites, 29
Ontario
    after-hours clinics, 91
    assessments, 290
    billing codes, 323
    diagnostic codes, 320, 321*t*–322*t*
    electronic transfer and, 342
    error codes, 355
    fee schedule, 291
    health cards, 292, 297
    health care financing and, 86
    health/physical examinations, 324
    immigrants and, 63
    interchangeability in, 173
    payment of premiums in, 291–292
    physician registration numbers,
        317–322
    primary health-care models, 92
    suffixes, 323–324
    universal emergency codes, 437*t*
    workers' compensation and, 303
Ontario Dental Assistants Association
    (ODAA), 26
Ontario Drug Benefit (ODB), 173, 287
Ontario Medical Association, 87
open scheduling, 261
open text, 376
operating room charts, 462
operative reports, 382
ophthalmic route of administration, 180
ophthalmoscope kit, 428
opportunistic infection, 112–113
opted-in, 96
opted-out, 96
optometrists, 99
optometry, 288–289
oral glucose tolerance test (OGTT), 148
oral route of administration, 181
order entry, 480, 496–500
    tools, 481–496
orderlies, 420
order requests, 232
order sets
    active, 486*f*
    electronic, 484, 484*f*
    postoperative, 486, 487*f*
    pre-admission, 486–488
    preoperative, 484, 485*f*
    requisitions, 488, 488*f*
organizational skills, 15
organizational structure
    of hospitals, 408–411
oropharyngeal suctioning, 585

sphygmomanometers, 427–428
spiritual wellness, 44
spirometry, 152–153, 580–581
sputum
    specimens, 581
    tests, 152
stable health status, 57
staff, 377–378
stand-alone devices, 309
standard orders for major surgery, 515
standard precautions, 127–131, 127*t*
    aprons, 129–130
    equipment used for client care, 130
    examinations and procedures, assisting
        with, 130–131
    face shield, 129
    gloves, 128–129
    gowns, 127, 129–130
    health environment, 130
    linen, 130
    masks, 129
standard terminology, 259
start date, 531–532
Statistics Canada, 47
stat medication orders, 502–503
status of appointment, 255*f*
steam autoclave, 126
step-down care, 410
stereotyping, 66
sterile, 124
sterile processing department (SPD), 413
sterile technique, 124
sterilization, 126–127
    chemical, 123
    dry heat, 124–125
    steam autoclave, 126
stethoscopes, 427
stigma, of mental illness, 74
stoma, 561
stool culture and analysis, 152
storage room, 430–431
stores/materials management, 413
straight catheter, 569
stream scheduling, 263–264
stress, 44, 51
    test, 158
stroke, 575
Student Services, 28–29
subacute care, 410
subcultures, 63
subcutaneous injection (s/c), 182
sublingual route of administration, 181
suctioning, 585
    deep, 585
    endotracheal, 585
    gastric, 550
    nasogastric, 562–564
suffix, of billing code, 323–324
Sunnybrook Health Sciences Centre, 75
superbugs, 110
suppositories, 181, 560–561

suprapubic catheters, 569
surgery, 593
    date, notification of, 233
    gastrointestinal, 561–563
    medication orders related to, 515–516
    request for approval of proposed, 334
    scheduling clients for, 276–277
    standard orders for major, 515
surgical asepsis, 123–124
surgical assist premium codes, 327–328
surgical charts, 459–462
    anesthetic record, 460
    consent form, 460
    fluid balance record, 461–462
    history and physical assessment, 460
    pre-anesthetic questionnaire, 460
    preop checklist, 460
surgical patient-care units, 415–416
surgical procedures, 455
surgical soft diet, 547
susceptible host, 115
suspension, 182–183
sustained release, 181
suture removal trays, 429
synthetic drugs, 171
Système Internationale (SI), 194
systemic effect, 179
systemic infections, 112
systemic therapy, 415
systolic pressure, 575

T

tape cartridge and disk, 342
tap water enema, 559
Tay-Sachs disease, 64
teaching
    health, 159, 160*f*
teaching/education and emotional
        support, 492
teaching material, 475
technical components, of billing codes,
    332
telehealth services, 315
telemetry, 414, 586
telephone
    AHP and, 225
    answering options, 226–227
    cellphones, 224
    confidentiality and, 233–234
    pagers, 224
telephone equipment, 220–221
    automated attendant, 221
    automated routing, 221
    automatic call distribution, 221
    call answer/voice mail, 220
    call display, 221
    call waiting, 221
    conference calling, 221
    EMR integration, 221
    indent-a-call, 221
    universal messaging, 221

telephones, 433
telephone skills and techniques, 225–226
    answering phone, 226–227
    appointment cancellations, 228
    appointments, calls to make, 229–230
    clarification of instructions,
        calls for, 228
    community agencies, 233
    controlling telephone time, 238
    dealing with volume, 227–228
    dental treatment cost, calls for, 230
    doctor, calls to speak with, 231
    ending a call, 237
    family members, calls for information
        about, 230–231
    greetings, 227
    hospital, calls from, 232–233
    incoming calls, handling, 227–228
    laboratories calling with test
        results, 232
    medical advice, calls for, 230
    more than one call, handling, 236
    morning rush, 227–228
    new clients, 231–232
    notification of surgery date, 232
    order requests, 232–233
    outgoing calls, handling, 237–238
    personal calls for doctor, 231
    prescriptions, calls relating to, 232
    promptness, 226–227
    taking messages, 234–235
    test results, calls for, 228
    typical calls, handling, 228–233
teleplan, 343
teletriage, 223
templates, scheduling, 259
temporary health cards, 292
teratogenic, 121
terminal cleaning, 413
terminal digit filing systems, 391
territorial billing, 282
territorial formula financing (TFF), 86
territorial health insurance coverage,
        294–297
    absence from territory of origin, 300
    adopted children, registering, 297
    newborns, registering, 297
    out-of-territory clients, billing for, 301
    temporary health cards, 292
    three-month waiting period, 300
    updating and correcting cards,
        297–299
territorial responsibility, 86
territorial websites, 29
tertiary care hospital, 407
testing facilities, 138–140
test results
    clients calling for, 228, 230–231
    laboratories calling with, 232
    receiving and ordering, 163–164
    recording, 164

W

wafers, 562
waiting room, 432
wait times, 47. *See also* care, access to
walk-in clinics, 91
ward clerks. *See* clinical secretary
wave scheduling, 261–262
WBC. *See* white blood cell count
WCB. *See* workers' compensation board
WCB/WSIB claims, 352
WCB/WSIB forms, 213–214
web-based claims submission, 342–343
web-based validation, 308
weekly schedule, 254f
well-baby assessments, 131
well-baby visits, 316
wellness
    concepts of, 43
    defined, 43
    emotional, 43–44
    intellectual, 44
    physical, 43
    social, 44
    spiritual, 44
West Nile virus, 115
wheezes, 578
white blood cell count (WBC), 143
WHMIS, 110. *See* Workplace Hazardous Materials Information System
WHO. *See* World Health Organization
whole blood, 537
Wi-Fi, 434
Winnipeg lab, 139
workers' compensation, 110, 303
Workers' Compensation Act, 303
workers' compensation board (WCB), 86, 110, 303
    claims, 352
    forms, 213–214
Workopolis, 28
workplace
    cooperative experience, 31–33
    environment, 22–23
    experience, 27–28
    job prospects, 23–24
    salaries and benefits, 24
Workplace Safety and Insurance Board (WSIB), 303
    claims, 352
    forms, 213–214
workstation on wheels (WOW), 430, 431f
World Health Organization (WHO), 111, 113
WOW. *See* workstation on wheels
written communication, 209–216
    incoming mail, 212–215
    signs, 211–212
WSIB. *See* Workplace Safety and Insurance Board

X

X-ray, chest, 153

Y

Y tubing set, 527

Z

Zika virus, 113
Z-Track, 182–183